編　　委/ 王國耀　但漢然　戴金象　蔡　驅
　　　　　戚永安　劉秀庭　張興定　李永暉
　　　　　施友義　黃福坤
主　　編/ 施友義
副主編/ 黃福坤
攝　　影/ （以姓氏筆劃爲序）
　　　　　王洪柳　王富弟　朱　浩　牟航遠
　　　　　汪傳樹　李顯榮　何懷強　武永發
　　　　　祝雲清　陳　錦　陳池春　陶懋元
　　　　　梁希毅　戚永安　張宏開　張問漁
　　　　　黃加法　黃尙建　黃福坤　葉建成
　　　　　費叢高　喬德炳　楊大武　解特利
　　　　　趙貴林　熊源美　嚴越培　蘇　揚
　　　　　蘇　琳
撰　　文/ 熊源美
英　　譯/ 李榮寶　王　晶
文字編輯/ 胡　強
責任編輯/ 黃福坤
裝幀設計/ 黃福坤
封面題字/ 吳廼光

Editorial Board:　　Wang Guoyao　　Dan Hanran　Dai Jinxiang
　　　　　　　　　Cai Qu　　Qi Yongan　Liu Xiuting
　　　　　　　　　Zhang Xingding　Li Yonghui　Shi Youyi
　　　　　　　　　Huang Fukun
Chief Editor:　　　Shi Youyi
Deputy Chief Editor:　Huang Fukun
Photographers:　　Wang Hongliu　Wang Fudi　Zhu Hao
　　　　　　　　　Mou Hangyuan　Wang Chuanshu　Li Xianrong
　　　　　　　　　He Huaiqiang　Wu Yongfa　Zhu Yunqing
　　　　　　　　　Chen Jin　Chen Chichun　Tao Maoyuan
　　　　　　　　　Liang Xiyi　Qi Yongan　Zhang Hongkai
　　　　　　　　　Zhang Wenyu　Huang Jiafa　Huang Shangjian
　　　　　　　　　Huang Fukun　Ye Jiancheng　Fei Conggao
　　　　　　　　　Qiao Debing　Yang Dawu　Xie Teli
　　　　　　　　　Zhao Guilin　Xiong Yuanmei　Yan Yuepei
　　　　　　　　　Su Yang　　Su Lin
Text by:　　　　　Xiong Yuanmei
Translators:　　　Li Ringbao　Wang Jing
Text Editor:　　　Hu Qiang
Responsible Editor:　Huang Fukun
Layout Designer:　Huang Fukun
Cover Inscription by:　Wu Naiguang

長江三峽

THE THREE
GORGES ON
THE YANGTZE RIVER

海風出版社
HAIFENG PUBLISHING HOUSE

前 言 FOREWORD

　　三峽，是萬里長江一段山水壯麗的大峽谷，為中國十大風景名勝之一。它西起四川省奉節縣的白帝城，東至湖北省宜昌市的南津關，由瞿塘峽、巫峽、西陵峽組成，全長192公里。它是長江風光的精華，神州山水中的瑰寶，古往今來，閃耀着迷人的光彩。

　　長江三峽，無限風光。瞿塘峽的雄偉，巫峽的秀麗，西陵峽的險峻，還有三段峽谷中的大寧河、香溪、神農溪的神奇與古樸，使這馳名世界的山水畫廊氣象萬千——這裏的羣峰，重岩叠嶂，峭壁對峙，烟籠霧鎖；這裏的江水，洶湧奔騰，驚濤裂岸，百折不回；這裏的奇石，嶙峋崢嶸，千姿百態，似人若物；這裏的溶洞，奇形怪狀，空曠深邃，神秘莫測……三峽的一山一水，一景一物，無不如詩如畫，並伴隨着許多美麗的神話和動人的傳說，令人心馳神往。

　　長江三峽，地靈人傑。這裏，是中國古文化的發源地之一，著名的大溪文化，在歷史的長河中閃爍着奇光異彩；這裏，孕育了中國偉大的愛國詩人屈原和千古才女王昭君；青山碧水，曾留下李白、杜甫、白居易、劉禹錫、范成大、歐陽修、蘇軾、陸游等詩聖文豪的足跡，留下了許多千古傳頌的詩章；大峽深谷，曾是三國古戰場，是無數英雄豪傑馳騁用武之地；這裏還有許多著名的名勝古跡，白帝城、黃陵廟、南津關……它們同旖旎的山水風光交相輝映，名揚四海。

　　長江三峽，風情絢麗。奉節的人日踏磧，如一幅優美的風俗畫；秭歸的龍舟賽，似一首磅礴的交響樂；沿着江邊一級級石階，可到巴東去欣賞那奇特的背簍世界，順着彎彎的山路，可到土家人家中參加那別有情趣的婚禮…

清澈碧透的香溪中，那隨桃花開而來，又伴桃花落而去的桃花魚，將使人眼界大開；奔湧不息的江流裏，那神熊威武的中華鱘，會令人讚嘆不已；兩岸那些青青的柑桔園，正飄出誘人的芬芳……

朋友，投進長江三峽熱情的懷抱吧，在這神奇而美妙的山水世界中，作一次風光之旅、文化之旅、風情之旅。這裏的一切，會令你終生難忘！

The Yangtze Gorges is a great valley with a most splendid landscape on the Yangtze (Changjiang) River and it is one of the ten most famous scenic sites of China. It extends from White King Town in Fengjie County, Sichuan Province to Nanjinguan Pass in Yichang, Hubei Province, consisting of Qutang Gorge, Wu Gorge and Xiling Gorge, with a full length of 192 km. It converges the essence of the scenery on the Yangtze River. As a rarity of landscape of China, it has been displaying its special charms for thousands of years.

The Yangtze Gorges presents a scene of boundless variety with the magnificence of Qutang Gorge, the elegance of Wu Gorge, the perilousness of Xiling Gorge as well as the primitive simplicity and the mysteriousness of the Daning River, Xiangxi River and Shennong River, which flow into the great valley. The whole landscape is so kaleidoscopic: the peaks tower into the sky, the steep cliffs facing one another with mists and clouds shrouding them all the year round; the river rolls forward with swashing waves beating on the shore; the jagged rocks are of grotesque shapes; the karst caves are unfathomably deep and fantastic in shape... It is picturesque everywhere, and what's more, each scene is related to a wonderful fairy tale or a moving legend which will kindle your meditation on the remote past.

The beautiful landscape of the gorge region has given birth to a splendid culture. It is one of the birthplaces of the civilizations of China. The famous Daxi Culture, which originated here, has shed brilliant light on the civilizations in the long history. It was here that Qu Yuan, the earliest Chinese patriotic poet, and Wang Zhaojun, an outstanding talented woman, were born and brought up. It was also here that Li Bai, Du Fu, Bai Juyi, Liu Yuxi, Fan Chengda, Ouyang Xiu, Su Shi, Lu You and other poets and men of letters travelled and left their immortal poems behind. The valleys were once the battlefields during the period of the Three Kingdoms, where countless heroes displayed their prowess and talent. Besides, a great many well-known historical sites, such as White King Town, Huangling Temple and Nanjinguan Pass, add charm to the landscape.

The folkways of the gorge region are colourful. The Commemoration of the Eight-Element Battle Formation on the seventh day of the first moon is like an exquisite painting depicting the folkways of the local people. The dragon boat race in Zigui sounds like a thundering symphony. The stone steps beside the river will lead you to Badong, where you will find yourself in a world of baskets carried on the back and the winding path will take you to a family of Tujia nationality where you may be invited to a wedding ceremony full of distinctive flavour...

The gorge region is also rich in natural resources. Minnows come to the Xiangxi River when the peach trees are in full bloom and leave when the blossoms are falling; Chinese sturgeons with a fierce bearing swim freely in the Yangtze River; green tangerine orchards deliver captivating fragrance...

You are welcome to the Yangtze Gorges to enjoy the charming landscape and splendid culture as well as the colourful folkways. You are sure to be intoxicated with everything here.

縱將萬管玲瓏筆
難寫瞿塘兩岸山

　　瞿塘峽西起白帝城，東到大溪鎮。峽長雖然祇有8公里，順流而下，瞬間即過，但却有"西控巴渝收萬壑，東連荊楚壓羣山"的雄偉氣勢。兩岸懸崖絕壁，羣峰對峙，赤甲山巍峨江北，白鹽山聳立南岸，山勢岌岌欲墜，峰巒幾乎相接。每當晴空麗日，遠眺赤甲、白鹽，一如仙桃凌空，一如鹽堆萬仞，兩山雲遊霧繞，時隱時現，乃為瞿塘一奇觀。峽中江面最寬處一二百米，最窄處不過幾十米。入峽處兩山陡峭，絕壁相對，猶如雄偉的兩扇大門，鎮一江怒水，控川鄂咽喉，形勢非常險要。正如唐代詩人杜甫所描寫的那樣："衆水會涪萬，瞿塘爭一門"，故有"夔門天下雄"之讚。

　　"若言風景異，三峽此為魁"。當你乘船經其間，仰望千丈峰巒，祇見雲天一綫，奇峰異石，千姿百態。俯視峽江，驚濤雷鳴，一瀉千里，猶如萬馬奔騰，勢不可擋。遊人至此，眞有"峰與天關接，舟從地窟行"之感。

　　瞿塘峽不僅雄偉壯觀，而且名勝古跡衆多。這裏有雲集各朝代書法精品的碑刻；有三峽第一古跡白帝城和孔明巧佈的八陣圖；有傳說奇特的孟良梯；有難解之謎風箱峽和充滿神話色彩的錯開峽。

QUTANG GORGE

　　Qutang Gorge extends eastward from White King Town to Daxi Town. Although the gorge is no more than eight kilometers long and a downstream voyage is only a wink, it has a momentum of controlling the waters from Sichuan on the west and dominating the mountains of Hubei on the east. The river is flanked with steep cliffs and towering peaks. Mt. Chijia on the north and Mt. Baiyan on the south penetrate into the sky, facing each other closely with the crags almost touching in the mid-air, dangerous and tottering. Looking from a distance in a fine day, one sees the former resemble a huge pink peach and the latter a huge heap of white salt glittering all the time. The two mountains disappear in the mist and cloud every now and then. That is the most spectacular scene of the Yangtze Gorges. The widest spot of the river is about two hundred metres and the most narrow spot is only tens of metres. At Kuimen, the entrance of the gorge, the steep cliffs on either side look like two gigantic door leaves closing in on the roaring river and holding the strategic pass between Sichuan and Hubei, perilous in every way. As is depicted in the lines of Du Fu, a poet of the Tang Dynasty: *"All the rivers converge at Fuwan, breaking a way through the rocks at Qutang"*, Kuimen has been marvelled at as "the most dangerous pass of the world".

　　If the landscape of the Yangtze Gorges is a wonder, Qutang Gorge is the wonder of wonders. When you travel through the gorge in a boat and look up at the towering peaks, you see thousands of grotesque crags darkening the daylight with only a narrow opening overhead and the thundering river rolling by vigorously, just like thousands of horses galloping ahead irresistibly. You can't help marvelling at the scene and wondering whether you are sailing to the hell.

　　Qutang Gorge boasts not only splendid sights but also places of historical interest. Concentrated here are the masterworks of calligraphy and stone engravings of different dynasties. There are in the region such historical or legendary sites as White King Town, which is the most ancient town in the Three Gorges, the former site of the Eight-Element Battle Formation designed by Zhuge Liang during the period of the Three Kingdoms, Meng Liang Ladder, which is legendary, and Fengxiang Crevices and Cuokai Gorge, which were wrapped in mystery for thousands of years.

夔門雄姿　The Magnificence of Kuimen.

晨曦
Morning glow.

夔峽出口處
Exit of Kui
Gorge.

瞿塘峡 Outang Gorge

夔門秋月　Autumn moon beyond Kuimen.

古城奉節

　　奉節，是三峽西端第一座城市，扼守瞿塘峽西口。奉節原名魚腹縣，爲春秋時期的夔國，是一座有着兩千多年歷史的古城。古城週長3公里，設有五座城門，每座城門都有題額，東門爲「瞿塘天險」，西門爲「全蜀咽喉」，大南門爲「縱目」，小南門爲「觀瀾」，北門爲「肅威」。這些題額都與城門內外的風光相關，由此可想象當年的壯麗景色。現在祇剩下大小城門兩座。

　　大南門是奉節的大門，名爲「依斗門」，取自杜甫的「夔府孤城落日斜，每依南斗望京華」詩句。依斗門高出江面數百級石階，下船後拾級而上，登高遠眺，夔峽風光盡收眼底。

　　昔日奉節「肩挑背馱行路難，三步一打杵，五步一長嘆」。今日奉節水陸交通發達，工農業發展飛快。這裏盛產黃花、夔柚、柑桔、香桃、枇杷。每臨秋末，柑黃桔紅遍佈街頭，把奉節古城裝點得分外妖嬈。

　　奉節古城內外還有許多名勝古跡，如唐代詩人杜甫住過的草堂寺，劉備托孤的永安宮遺址等。古人曾經把奉節風光歸納爲「十二景」，如「白帝層巒」、「白鹽曙色」、「峽門秋月」、「文峰瑞彩」等，山水日月渾然一體，引人入勝。其中尤爲出名的，是位於城東梅溪河入江處的諸葛亮八陣圖。這裏是一片沙灘，佈滿大大小小的石頭，可傳說它們能千變萬化，神鬼難測，諸葛亮用它擺下戰陣，曾幾乎困死東吳大將陸遜，嚇退了他帶領的百萬大軍。

FENGJIE, AN ANCIENT CITY

Fengjie, the first city at the western end of the Yangtze Gorges, is situated on the western entrance of Qutang Gorge. Fengjie was fomerly called Yufu County, which was the seat of Kui State during the Spring and Autumn Period. It is a city with a history of more than two thousand years. The ancient walled city has a circumference of three kilometres with five city gates, each with an inscription on it. The inscription on the eastern gate reads: "Natural Barrier of Qutang", the western gate "Throat of Sichuan", the larger southern gate: "Looking Far and Wide", the smaller southern gate: "Viewing Waves", and the northern gate: "Solemn and Mighty". All these inscriptions are related to the surrounding scenes. From the inscriptions we may imagine how spectacular the sights were in the past. At present, however, only two of the city gates are extant.

The larger southern gate is the entrance of Fengjie. It was named Yidou Gate after the lines of Du Fu: *The sun is setting behind the isolated city of Kui State, I am looking to the capital at Yidou by the southern gate*". Yidou Gate is several hundred steps up the river. From here the tourists may feast their eyes on the landscape of Kuimen.

In the past Fengjie's transportation was so poor that people had to carry things by shoulder or back faltering along the narrow paths. Both land and water communications have been greatly developed by now. The development of the communications has made it possible for the agriculture and industry to grow rapidly. Fengjie abounds in day lily, shaddock, tangerine, orange, peach and loquat. In the late autumn the ancient city is decorated with yellow tangerines and red oranges.

In and out of the walled city there are a number of historical sites. Among them are the Thatched Cottage Temple, where Du Fu, a poet of the Tang Dynasty, once lived, and the former site of Yongan Palace, where Liu Bei, the king of Shu Kingdom, entrusted his son to Zhuge Liang, the prime minister. The ancient people divided the landscape of Fengjie into twelve particular scenes such as "the Distant Peaks Around White King Town", "Mt. Baiyan in the Morning Sunlight", "Autumn Moon Beyond Kuimen", "Beautiful Colour of Wenfeng Peak", etc. The mountains and rivers and the sun and the moon come into an integral whole, changing in a fascinating way. Of the kaleidoscopic scenes, the most distinctive is the former site of the Eight-Element Battle Formation designed by Zhuge Liang. The site lies at the mouth of the Meixi River in the east of the city. It is a vast expanse of sandy beach with stones of different sizes scattered all over. The scene changes with the rising and falling of the river. It was said that Zhuge Liang took the topographical advantage and set his Eight-Element Battle Formation here on the beach, which almost bottled up Lu Xun, a general of Wu Kingdom, and thousands of his soldiers.

川東古城奉節　Fengjie, an ancient city in east Sichuan.

鎖江鐵柱，在夔門北岸草堂河口處的石盤上，有兩根鐵杜，各高6.4尺，爲宋代末年所置，當枯水時才露出水面，是古代攔江守關的鐵索柱。

River-Locking Iron Post: On the rock at the gorge entrance near The Thatched Temple at Kuimen north of the river stand two iron posts 2.13m tall, set in the late Song Dynasty for chaining defence boats. They emerge only when the river goes down.

"水八陣"
The site of Zhuge Liang's Battle Formation.

白帝城

　　白帝城，又名白帝廟，像一座孤山兀立於瞿塘峽口，面朝夔門，下臨大江，是三峽最負盛名的名勝古跡。

　　西漢末年公孫述據蜀，在山上築城，因城中一井冒白氣，宛如白龍，就自稱白帝，並命名此城為白帝城。

　　白帝城是劉備托孤的地方。蜀漢章武二年，蜀國皇帝劉備伐吳兵敗，退守白帝城。劉備臨死前，將幼子劉禪和國家大事托與丞相諸葛亮。白帝城與三國結下了不解之緣，那屋脊上和飛檐旁一幅幅彩色圖畫，每一幅都是一個生動的三國故事。白帝城內輝煌的古建築中，明良殿內有劉備、諸葛亮、關羽、張飛塑像；武侯祠內有諸葛亮祖孫三代像，個個神采奕奕，栩栩如生。

　　白帝城是三峽文物薈萃之地，這裏雲集了隋、元、明、清各朝代碑刻74塊，詩文、楹聯、繪畫和書法作品，琳瑯滿目。我國歷代許多大詩人如李白、杜甫、白居易、劉禹錫、蘇軾、黃庭堅、范成大、陸游等，都曾旅居此地，給白帝城留下了許多膾炙人口的詩文。白帝城內，還收藏了不同朝代數以千計的文物，其中有新石器時代的石斧、石箭；奴隸社會的巴式劍、銅斧；戰國時的銅編鐘；秦漢的銅鑒；蜀漢的青瓷虎子；唐代的白瓷畫盒；宋代的描金碗……等等，它們都可作為歷史的導遊，帶你走進三峽古文化的燦爛畫廊。

1 俯瞰白帝城
  Bird's-eye view of White King Town.

2 白帝廟
  White King Temple.

3 諸葛亮觀星亭
  Zhuge Liang's Astrology Pavilion.

4 劉備托孤羣像
  Statue group—Liu Bei entrusting his son.

WHITE KING TOWN

White King Town, also called White King Temple, is a walled town over the entrance of Qutang Gorge, facing Kuimen. It is the most famous historical site of the Three Gorges.

Towards the end of the Western Han Dynasty, Gongsun Shu built a walled town on the mountain before he occupied Shu, the present-day Sichuan Province. And as a well in the town often gave off white steam shaped like a white dragon, Gongsun Shu called himself White King and named the town White King Town so as to match the white dragon.

It was in White King Town that Liu Bei, the king of Shu, entrusted his son to his prime minister. In the second year of his reign, Liu Bei attacked Wu and was completely defeated. He retreated to White King Town in despair and bad health. Just before he died he entrusted his little son Liu Dan and the state affairs to the prime minister Zhuge Liang. White King Town has so much to do with the Three Kingdoms that it is full of memorial spots. Each of the paintings on the ridges or eaves of the buildings tells a vivid story about the Three Kingdoms. In the ancient buildings of the town, many statues of the Three Kingdoms heroes are erected lifelike. Among them are Liu Bei, Zhuge Liang, Guan Yu and Zhang Fei in Mingliang Palace and Zhuge Liang and his father and son in the Temple of Marquis Wu.

White King Town is a museum of cultural relics. Assembled here are seventy-four pieces of stone engravings of the Sui, Yuan, Ming, Qing Dynasties, as well as countless poems, couplets, paintings and works of calligraphy left behind by the ancient people. Many famous poets of different dynasties, such as Li Bai, Du Fu, Bai Juyi, Liu Yuxi, Su Shi, Huang Tingjian, Fan Chengda, Lu You and others once toured and produced their celebrated works here. What's more, thousands of tools, weapons, instruments and other articles of different times are collected in the town. Among them are stone axes and stone arrows of the New Stone Age, bronze swords and axes of the slavery society, the serial bells of the Warring States, bronze mirrors of the Qin and Han Dynasties, celadon tiger cubs of the Shu Han, white porcelain painting box of the Tang Dynasty and gold-traced china bowls of the Song Dynasty... They will all be the guides to show you to the splendid culture of the Yangtze Gorges.

鳳凰碑，碑上刻有號稱鳥中之王的鳳凰、花中之王的牡丹、樹中之王的梧桐，故又稱三王碑。

Phoenix Stele Engraved on the stele are phoenixes, king of birds, peony, king of flowers and Chinese parasol, king of trees, so it is also called "Three Kings Stele".

竹葉詩碑，由一叢竹葉組成一首詩文，融詩、畫、金石於一碑，構思別致。

Bamboo Blades Poem Stele A bamboo blades pictographic poem is engraved on the stele, the art of stone carving, poetry and painting ingeniously integrated.

粉 壁 牆

"舉目眺白鹽，碑刻銘千古"。夔門南岸的鹽山上，有一塊斑白的巨石，高數十米，寬千餘米，壁立江畔，如同一堵粉白的牆壁，上面滿是摩崖題刻，行、楷、隸、篆、草書，應有盡有，風格各異，琳瑯滿目。

粉壁牆石刻，自宋迄今，展示了我國歷代的書法藝術。字體最大的是近人孫元良將軍的"夔門天下雄，艦機輕輕過"，每字有一人多高。字體最小而文字最多的是南宋書法家趙公碩書寫的《宋中興聖德頌》，全文980多個字，大的五尺見方，小的如指頭大小，刻在高約4米、寬約7米範圍內，是一方罕見的巨型壁刻。清人張伯翔所書"瞿塘"，劉心源所書"夔門"，蒼勁有力，古樸凝重，與巍峨夔門交相輝映。

THE WHITEWASHED WALL

"Looking up at Whitewashed Wall of Mt. Baiyan one sees
The engravings by different people in different times."

As the lines describe, there is a huge white rock on Mt. Baiyan at Kuimen on the southern side of the gorge. The rock is dozens of metres high and more than a thousand metres broad, facing the river like a whitewashed wall, and it is covered with engraved inscriptions in running hand, cursive hand, regular script, official script, or seal character. Almost all styles of all schools of calligraphy can be found on the rock.

Ever since the Song Dynasty, the rock engraving on the Whitewashed Wall has been revealing the essence of the art of Chinese calligraphy. The largest characters on the rock are those by Sun Yuanliang, a contemporary general. The words read *"Kuimen stands in splendour and sails pass in silence."* Each of the characters is taller than a man. And the characters by Zhao Gongshuo, a calligrapher of the Song Dynasty, are the smallest in size and largest in number. The whole text of 980 words of *Ode to the Resurgence of the Song* was engraved on the rock. The largest characters are five inches square and the smallest as tiny as a finger. The engraving covers a surface of about four metres high and seven metres broad. It is a rare huge rock engraving. Among the other engravings are "Qutang" by Zhang Boxiang and "Kuimen" by Liu Xingyuan, of the Qing Dynasty. The characters appear bold and vigorous setting off the landscape of Kuimen beautifully.

粉壁牆 The Whitewashed Wall.

翹首望夔峰，何須再登山?

Raise your head and see the Kui Peak.
Do you have to scale the mountain?

倒吊和尚

Monk Hung Upside-Down.

孫元良將軍的題刻："夔門天下雄，艦機輕輕過。"

"Kuimen stands in splendour and sails pass in silence",
engraved inscription by General Sun Yuanliang.

孟良梯

Meng Liang Ladder.

古 棧 道

蜀道難，難於上青天！古代三峽的交通，全靠水路，每遇洪水，祇好停航，旅行斷絕。直至清光緒年間，棧道聯通，三峽交通才得以改善。

三峽棧道分為兩種，一種是在絕壁上開鑿的，途中有石橋連結溝壑的棧道，這種棧道貫穿三個峽段，高出江面數十米，寬二、三米，工程險要艱難，令人心悸目眩。《戰國策‧秦策》有 "棧道千里，通蜀漢" 之說。瞿塘峽北岸絕壁邊十公里長的棧道，就是古代勞動人民身依絕壁，下臨大江，在刺破青天的岩壁上鑿出的一條石路，路寬五六尺，能過八人大轎，鑲嵌在千仞峭壁之腰，"驚濤駭浪建瓴下，顛崖撲谷相吐吞。"

另一種是沿著絕壁鑿孔打樁，墊板攀援而上的棧道。這種棧道主要分佈在瞿塘峽和小三峽內。如瞿塘峽中的孟良梯就是殘留下來的棧道石孔。石孔深和口徑各一尺，四四方方，孔與孔相距三尺，自下而上直到半山腰。相傳，宋朝名將楊繼業被奸臣害死後，屍骨埋在白鹽山頂的望鄉台上。楊繼業的親信孟良懷念他，想把他的屍體悄悄搬走，就在一天深夜，在峭壁上鑿石穿孔，架木為梯，攀援而上，不料才至半山腰，被一個和尚發現，他佯裝雞叫，孟良以為天亮，前功盡棄。後來，孟良發現是和尚作祟，盛怒之下就將和尚倒懸在山岩上，讓世人唾罵。

ANCIENT PLANK ROADS

"The road to Shu is harder than to cilmb to the sky."

In ancient times, all communications in the Yangtze Gorges region depended on the waterway. Whenever the flood came, the sails had to come to a halt and the travel in the region became impossible. Not until the years of Guangxu's reign in the Qing Dynasty was the plank road of the gorge region opened and the communications improved.

There are two kinds of plank roads — the one cut out of the cliffs with ravines spanned by flagstones, and the one protruded from the cliffs with the planks supported by piles driven into the cliffs. The former runs through the region of the Yangtze Gorges. The road is two or three metres wide and dozens of metres above the river. The project was both difficult and dangerous. Some sections of the road were cut by people of the remote past. Recorded in *Strategies of the Warring States — the Strategy of Qin* is "long miles of plank roads lead to the Shu Han (the present-day Sichuan Province)". The ten kilometres cut out of the precipice on the north side of Qutang Gorge is a wonder created by the working people of ancient times. The road of this section is five to six feet wide and a sedan-chair carried by eight people can pass it easily. From the road one can overlook thousands of valleys connected with one another and the roaring river flowing by.

The other kind of plank road, however, is built along the precipices by cutting holes in the rock and setting piles in the holes to support the planks. Such plank roads are mostly distributed in Qutang Gorge and the Lesser Three Gorges. Meng Liang Ladder, for instance, is the remains of this kind of plank road. It is made up of a flight of holes reaching halfway up the cliff. The holes are one foot cubic and three feet between each other. As the legend has it, in the Song Dynasty a noted general named Yang Jiye was murdered by treacherous officials and was buried at Wangxiangtai on the top of Mt. Baiyan, which was guarded by soldiers. Meng Liang, one of Yang's followers, cherished so much the memory of Yang that he tried to bring back the body. One day late at night he began to cut holes in the cliff trying to set a ladder to reach the grave. He was, however, overheard by a monk, who mimicked the crow of a cock for a prank. On hearing the crow, Meng Liang had to give up his task, thinking that dawn was breaking. So the task was only half done. Meng Liang flew into a rage when he knew it was the monk who had played a prank upon him, and he hanged the monk upside-down on the cliff so that people would curse and spit at him.

遊客爭看古棧道 Tourists eager to see the ancient plank road.

絕壁凌空古棧道
Ancient plank road high up the precipice.

棧道縴痕　Tracking rope marks.

架設航標燈，夜 晚 的 三峽江面上，一盞盞航標燈宛如顆顆明珠鑲在懸崖上，撒在激流中。目前，由重慶到吳淞口的航標，共設置了4000多座，其中以天險三峽的航標最為重要。

Setting up beacons At night, beacon lights glimmer all along the Yangtze Gorges like bright pearls inlaid on the cliffs or scattered on the surging river. Of the more than 4,000 beacons along the line from Chongqing to Wusongkou, the ones in the Gorges are the most important.

峽棧道，全長約五、六十公里。 Plank roads in the gorge region, full length 50-60km.

風箱峽之謎

風箱峽，與孟良梯隔江相對，在一處黃褐色的懸岩絕壁上，有幾條豎立的岩穴裂縫，從中露出一些長方形的木匣，高約幾十米，可望不可及。有人說它是魯班幫大禹治水，疏通三峽時用過的風箱，故稱爲風箱峽。也有人說它是諸葛亮藏兵書寶劍的兵書匣。古往今來，它像謎一樣令人猜想。

1971年，幾個身懷攀岩絕技的人，終於解開了這個千年之謎。原來，木匣是戰國時期巴人的岩棺，內有巴式銅劍、紡輪、木梳、草鞋、錢幣等一批十分珍貴的文物。

The Mystery of Fengxiang Crevices

Fengxiang Crevices, as it is named, consists of some vertical crevices on the brown-coloured precipice facing Meng Liang Ladder across the river. Some rectangular wooden boxes can be seen set in the crevices. The boxes are dozens of metres high within sight but beyond reach. Some said they were blacksmith's bellows left there by Lu Ban, a legendary craftsman, who came to help Yu, the legendary emperor of the Xia Dynasty, dredge the river. So the place was named Fengxiang, meaning bellows. Others said that the boxes were the containers for Zhuge Liang to hold his tactics books and swords. Throughout the ages the boxes remained mysterious.

It was not until 1971 when some skilled climbers got up to the crevices that the age-old enigma was solved. The boxes turned out to be the coffins of the Ba people of an ancient tribe in the period of the Warring States. Inside the coffins were such precious cultural relics as bronze Ba swords, loom wheels, wooden combs, straw shoes and coins.

風箱峽
Fengxiang crevices.

大溪文化遺址

　　位於瞿塘峽下口的大溪西岸，曾於一九五九年在此進行了兩次大規模的發掘工作，發現了一處距今約6千年至4千年的新石器時代原始人社會後期的村落遺址，出土了大量的陶器、石器、骨器、玉器等。大溪文化，屬長江流域的重要古文化。

The Remains of Daxi Culture

In 1959, two archaeological excavations were made in Daxi, at the east mouth of Qutang Gorge west of the river. Ruins of villages of the New Stone Age and the late stage of the slave society, about 4,000-6,000 years ago, were unearthed together with a great many pottery, stone, bone, and jade wares. Daxi Culture is an important ancient culture of the Yangtze valley.

錯開峽
Cuokai Gorge.

巫 峽

巫山十二峰
皆在碧虛中

"瞿塘迤邐盡，巫峽崢嶸起"。當你乘巨輪穿過一段山舒水緩的寬谷地帶，便進入了奇峰綿延、峭壁夾岸、美如畫廊的巫峽。巫峽因巫山得名，西起巫山城東的大寧河口，東至湖北省巴東縣的關渡口，全長45公里，整個峽谷奇峰削壁，羣巒疊嶂。船行其間，忽而大山當前，似乎江流受阻；忽而峰迴路轉，又是一水相通。咆哮的江流，不斷變換着方向，忽左忽右，七彎八繞，令人目不暇接。

幽深秀麗的巫峽，處處有景，景景相連，最爲壯觀的則是著名的巫山十二峰。這些山峰神態各異，有的若龍騰霄漢，有的似鳳凰展翅，有的青翠如屏，有的彩雲繚繞，有的常有飛鳥棲息於蒼松之間。而其中神女峰則最令人神往。還有與巫峽相連的大寧河、香溪、神農溪，青山綠水，風景別致，充滿山野情趣。

巫峽中有巫山、巴東、秭歸等峽中名城，名勝古跡多而悠久，風土人情妙趣橫生，令人流連忘返。

巫峽
Wu Gorge.

"While the magnificence of Qutang Gorge is left behind, the splendour of Wu Gorge comes in sight." Coming out of Qutang Gorge and sailing through an open area where the hills are low and the river is gentle, you enter Wu Gorge, which is characterised by beautiful peaks and steep cliffs on either side.

Wu Gorge is named after Mt. Wushan. It extends eastward from the mouth of the Daning River in the east of Wushan Town, Sichuan Province, to Guandukou in Badong County, Hubei Province, with a length of forty-five kilometres. The gorge is flanked with towering peaks and steep cliffs. Downstream you have to go through countless twists and turns. The river now seems to be blocked by the huge mountains, now breaks through and changes its direction. The changing course of the roaring river makes it difficult for you to take your bearings.

The deep gorge is so kaleidoscopic that you may feast your eyes on the beautiful scenes everywhere all along. The twelve peaks of Mt. Wushan make up a most spectacular scene. The peaks are varied in shape and posture. Some look like dragons flying to the sky, some like phoenixes spreading their wings and others like green screens. Some are shrouded in the cloud and others covered with ancient pinetrees. Among them Shennu (Fairy) Peak is most enchanting. The landscapes of the Daning River, Xiangxi River and Shennong river provide a unique flavour of primitiveness with the green mountains and the blue water.

In addition, located in the region of Wu Gorge are such famous walled cities as Wushan, Badong and Zigui, where there are a number of noted historical sites and where the folkways are so unique and colourful that one can enjoy himself heartily.

銀裝素裹 Pure and spangling snow.

峡江初春
Early spring in the gorge.

1 霞光伴船歸
   Returning boats in sunset glow.

2 孔明碑
   Zhuge Liang Niche—engraving allegedly
    by Zhuge Liang.

3 楚蜀鴻溝
   Wide chasm between Chu and Shu.

4 峭壁長廊
   Long gallery of cliffs.

無奪橋　Wuduo Bridge.

峽險林更茂　Dangerous gorge and luxuriant trees.

輕舟過險灘
Skiff sailing down a dangerous shoal.

1　波光船影
  Boats on glittering water.

2　金光一道破霧來
  The sun radiating through mists.

3　曉嵐
  Morning Haze.

33

風景勝地巫山

巫山是四川省最東部的一座古城，位於長江北岸大寧河與長江交滙處，山環水繞，風景迷人，名勝古跡甚多，素有「風景勝地」之稱。

巫山古城建有12條大街小巷，分別以巫山十二峰命名，充滿詩情畫意。尤其是起雲街，古建築與現代建築並存，古建築古色古香，現代建築挺拔雄偉，相映生輝，吸引着大批遊人。

巫山的風光名勝集中體現在三台八景十二峰。三台即：斬龍台、楚陽台、授書台。八景即：寧河晚渡、青溪魚釣、陽台暮雨、南陵春曉、夕霞晚照、澄潭秋月、秀峰禪刹、女觀貞石。十二峰即：登龍、聖泉、朝雲、神女、松巒、集仙、聚鶴、翠屏、飛鳳、淨壇、起雲、上昇。這些名勝屹立巫峽兩岸，面臨滔滔大江，風光無限。

巫山物產豐富，土特產中以藥材、生漆和水果出名。大廟的黨參享有盛名，素稱廟黨。

WUSHAN, A FAMOUS SCENIC SPOT

Wushan is an ancient walled city in the eastern tip of Sichuan Province. Lying on the northern side of the gorge, where the Daning River and the Yangtze River converge, it is surrounded by mountains and rivers, famous for its scenic spots and historical sites.

The Wushan walled city consists of twelve streets named after the twelve peaks of Mt. Wushan and filled with poetic atmosphere. Qiyun Street, in particular, combines harmoniously the antiqueness of the ancient buildings with the magnificence of the modern ones, creating a great attraction to the tourists.

The landscape of Wushan is presented by " Three Terraces ", " Eight Scenes " and " Twelve Peaks ". The three terraces are "Dragon-Slaying Terrace", "Chu Terrace" and "Reading Terrace". The eight scenes are "Night of the Ninghe Ferry", "Angling by the Qingxi River", "Evening Rain at Yangtai", " Dawn in the Spring of Nanling ", "Sunset Glow", "Autumn Moon Mirrored in the Clear Pool", "Temple Among Beautiful Peaks" and "the Taoist Temple and the Stones". The twelve peaks are Denglong (Soaring Dragon), Shengquan (Holy Spring), Chaoyun (To-the-Cloud), Shennu (Fairy), Songluan (Pines), Jixian (Fairy-Gathering), Juhe (Flock-of-Cranes), Cuiping (Green Screen), Feifeng (Flying Phoenix), Jingtan (Purity Temple), Qiyun (Rising Cloud) and Shangsheng (Ascent). All these well-known scenic spots are located on either side of the gorge, facing the roaring river and offering ever-lasting charms.

Besides, Mt. Wushan is rich in natural resources. Among the most well known are medicinal herbs, raw lacquer and fruits. The *dangshen* produced in Damiao enjoys a world fame.

巫山峽口　Entrance of Wu Gorge.

巫山旅遊船碼頭
Wushan Cruise
Liner Harbour.

幽深秀麗的巫峰
Serene and beautiful
Wufeng Peak.

35

金盔銀甲峽

金盔銀甲峽雖是巫峽中的一段小峽，但風景名勝毫不遜色。這裏有橫石溪、老鼠洞、穿山箭、箭穿洞等奇特景觀。

橫石溪位於江北岸，平時溪水清澈見底，流水潺潺，暴雨時變成洪流飛瀑，奔騰而下，十分壯觀。

老鼠洞位於江南岸半山腰上，高、深約丈餘，洞口有一塊米黃色的岩石，遠遠望去，形如一隻老鼠，它前腿立起，後腿曲蹲，栩栩如生。

老鼠洞的東面有一石柱直指藍天，這就是穿山箭。傳說此箭是項羽留下的一支神箭，它射穿了北岸的一座山峰。

箭穿孔位於長江北岸朝雲峰下一座黑黝黝的山樑上。傳說當年楚霸王項羽與人比武，看誰能用箭射穿山樑。霸王拔弩張弓，祇用一箭就射穿了對面的山樑，留下了這個洞口。

JINKUIYINJIA GORGE

Jinkuiyinjia Gorge is a section of Wu Gorge, though short and small, the scenery of the area is as marvelous. The most fantastic is the Hengshi Brook, the Rat's Cave, the Mountain-Penetrating Arrow and the Arrow-Penetrated Hole.

The Hengxi Brook flows into the gorge from the north. The brook is usually clear and gentle but in the time of a heavy rain it becomes torrential offering a grand sight.

The Rat's Cave is situated halfway up in the cliff of the southern bank, about four metres deep. Just at the entrance of the cave stands a cream-coloured rock. From a distance the rock looks like a squatting rat with its four legs propping.

To the east of the Rat's Cave there is a column-shaped rock towering high into the sky. The rock is called Mountain-Penetrating Arrow. The legend has it that it was a magic arrow left there by Xiang Yu, a leader of the peasants' uprising army in the end of the Qin Dynasty. The arrow dropped there after piercing through a peak on the north side of the gorge.

The Arrow-Penetrated Hole is spotted on the black ridge of the mountain just at the foot of Chaoyun (To-the-Cloud) Peak. It is said that Xiang Yu once had a shooting contest with someone to see who could shoot through the ridge of the mountain with an arrow. Xiang Yu succeeded with the first arrow. The hole was thus left there.

1　金盔銀甲峽
　　Jinkuiyinjia Gorge.

2　龍脊石
　　Dragon Back Rock.

3　箭穿洞
　　Arrow Penetrated Hole.

4　箭石
　　Arrow Stone.

巫山十二峰

"放舟下巫峽，心在十二峰"。

巫山十二峰屹立長江兩岸，北岸六峰——登龍、聖泉、朝雲、神女、松巒、集仙。南岸三峰——聚鶴、翠屏、飛鳳。這九峰均在江邊，可一覽無餘。還有淨壇、起雲、上昇三峰，由於"隔山之表"，如欲遊覽，須從青石溪上行，方可領略其英姿。

為了便於遊人記憶，古代文人將十二峰名聯成一首七言詩：

神女朝雲千古談，

聚鶴過江飛集仙。

翠屏青葱松巒綠，

飛鳳授書瑤姬傳。

登龍騰空六峰攢，

獅子銀牌飲聖泉。

起雲上昇何處去，

小溪河畔訪淨壇。

巫山十二峰，峰峰雲纏霧繞，幽深秀麗。而最多情、最秀麗的則是神女峰。

神女峰位於長江北岸，與青石鎮隔江相望。這個高約十米、環圍六米左右的人形石柱，屹立在海拔1020米的山巔上。每當晨曦初照或黃昏時，神女峰白雲繚繞，彩霞輝映，遠遠望去，就像一位亭亭玉立的少女，含情脈脈地凝視着江面。神女峰不僅峰姿秀麗，而且傳說動人。相傳，神女是西天王母的幼女瑤姬的化身。她邀十二仙女下凡，幫助大禹開鑿三峽，疏通九水。她還為樵夫驅虎豹，為農人保豐收，為病人種靈芝，為船民指點航向，深受百姓愛戴。千百年來，神女美麗動人的故事廣為流傳。

THE TWELVE PEAKS OF MT WUSHAN

"Sailing downstream to Wu Gorge, I have my heart only in the twelve peaks of Mt. Wushan."

The twelve peaks of Mt. Wushan stand on both sides of the gorge. On the north there are six peaks — Denglong (Soaring Dragon), Shengquan (Holy Spring), Chaoyun (To-the-Cloud), Shennu (Fairy), Songluan (Pines), Jixian (Fairy-Gathering) — and on the south three — Juhe (Flock-of-Cranes), Cuiping (Green Screen) and Feifeng (Flying Phoenix). All the above nine peaks are so close to the river that you can take them in sight at a glance when sailing past. The sight of the other three peaks — Jingtan (Purity Temple), Qiyun (Rising Cloud) and Shangsheng (Ascent) — is blocked by the mountain. You can, anyhow, enjoy the view on shore walking upwards along the Qingshixi River.

In order to make it easy for tourists to remember the names of the twelve peaks, the names were composed into the following lines by some men of letters in the ancient times:

The Fairy is going up To-the-Cloud as the tale goes,
And a Flock-of-Cranes are flying to Fairy-Gathering peak.
The pines form a Green Screen for the fairy and the cranes,
To whom the Phoenix passes letters from Yao Ji in paradise.
The Soaring Dragon is now high over the six peaks watching
The lions drinking the Holy Spring and meanwhile wondering
Why does the Rising Cloud make such an Ascent and where to?
Oh, she's on a pilgrimage to Purity Temple by Xiaoxi River.

The twelve peaks which are often capped by mist and cloud appear both serene and elegant, and Shennu Peak stands most remarkable.

Shunnu Peak stands on the northern side of the gorge facing Qingshi Town across the river. The peak towers on the summit of the mountain 1, 020 metres above sea level and the tip of the peak is a rock about ten metres in height and six metres in circumference. In the first rays of the morning sun or in the sunset glow, the white clouds float round the peak, creating a charming view. From a distance the peak looks like a slim and graceful young lady gazing at the river with great affection. Not only does Shennu Peak have a beautiful appearance but also have a moving tale related to it. As the tale goes, Shennu Peak as well as the other eleven peaks of the mountain are the fairies incarnate. Shennu is the incarnate of the little daughter of the queen of Heaven, named Yao Ji, who descended to the world with other fairies to help Yu, the emperor of the Xia Dynasty, to cut open the Yangtze Gorges and dredge the rivers. She drove away fierce beasts for woodmen, looked after crops for farmers, grew medicine herbs for the sick and set the course for boatmen, and she was thus loved by the local people. The moving tale about Shennu has been getting round for thousands of years.

從青石看巫山　Viewing Mt. Wushan from Qingshi.

淨壇峰　Jingtan Peak.

神女峰　Shennu Peak.

集仙峰　Jixian Peak.

神女峰　Shennu Peak.

巫 山 雲 雨

"曾經滄海難爲水，除却巫山不是雲。"這是唐代詩人元稹對巫山雲彩的讚嘆。古往今來，無數人爲巫山雲雨所傾倒。獨特的峽谷氣候，使巫峽時而細雨濛濛，竟日難晴；時而雲纏霧繞，似若幻境；時而晨晴午雨，變化莫測；時而雨止天晴，白雲成帶。正如一首古詩所描繪的："巫山十二峰，皆在碧虛中。迴合雲藏日，霏微雨帶風"。巫山雲雨，令人叫絕！

巫山雲雨，因其綺麗多彩，虛幻莫測，給人以無限的情趣。那飄浮在十二峰上的白霧，似烟非烟，似雲非雲，似雨非雨，使巫山羣峰顯得絢麗多姿，恍如仙境；巫山的雨，來則濃雲滾滾，鋪天蓋地，像要覆蓋四野，淹沒大江，船行疑無路；雨止則縷縷淡雲在峽谷中悠悠飄蕩，忽聚忽散，變化萬千；雨後，則山川一碧如洗，峰青巒秀，彩霞萬朵。有時，還會出現東邊日出西邊雨，江南降雨江北晴，山上下雨山下晴的奇異景觀，令人大飽眼福。

THE RAIN AND CLOUDS OF MT WUSHAN

"Having been to a vast sea, one will never think much of the water in a river, and one will find no clouds appealing comparing them with those of the Wushan Mountain." That was how Yuan Zhen, a poet of the Tang Dynasty, marvelled at the clouds of Mt. Wushan, which, through the ages, have been admired by thousands of people, too. The unique climate of the gorge region produces varied scenes of different weathers in Wu Gorge. Mt. Wushan is sometimes shrouded in the fine drizzle all day long and sometimes twined by floating clouds and mists. Sometimes it rains in the morning and clears up in the afternoon, and sometimes the sunshine alternates with the rain, creating a sea of clouds after rain. In a word the change is unpredictable just as it is descibed in a poem:

On Wushan stand twelve peaks,
All in a visionary world one sees.
When the clouds hide the sun,
A rain will come with winds.

The rain and clouds of Mt. Wushan are so changeable and colourful that they are always appealing to the beholders. What is drifting around the peaks can not be exactly called cloud nor mist nor haze. It is something of the mixed feature that makes the peaks as fair as in a fairyland. The rain, on the other hand, usually comes with black clouds overcasting the mountains and the river, and the sails at the time seem to lose their courses. When the rain stops, the clusters of light clouds will linger in the valley, now converging and now dispersing, changing in various ways. After the rain the valley appears completely fresh, and rosy clouds set off green peaks and hills beautifully. Sometimes when the sun is shining in the east, it is raining in the west, or when it has cleared up in the north, the rain is still pouring in the south, or when it is drizzling on the top of the mountain, it is sunny at the foot. What wonderful views!

奇峰綿延，雲霧昇騰　Chains of peaks and seas of clouds.

峽谷幽深，雲雨繚繞
Deep serene valleys shroud
in clouds and mists.

峽口初晴
Misty gorge after rain.

巫峽雲雨
Clouds and mists
of Wu Gorge.

"五嶽歸來不看山，寧河歸來不看峽。"這是遊人對寧河小三峽的由衷讚美。大寧河發源於大巴山南麓，全長250公里，由北向南，在巫峽西口注入長江，是長江在三峽最大、最美的一條支流。小三峽位於大寧河下游，從巫山至大昌；由龍門峽、巴霧峽、滴翠峽組成，全長60公里。這裏"有山皆翠，有水皆綠，有峰皆奇，有瀑皆飛，"不是三峽，勝似三峽。

龍門峽古名雊門，因峽口有一巨石兀立，形似蘿卜，故素稱蘿門，峽長3公里，是小三峽中最短的一個峽。峽口兩岸峭壁高聳入雲，峰峰相對，宛若門戶，雄奇壯觀，其形勝宛如夔門，故又有夔門之稱。峽內有常年不涸、水花四濺的龍門泉；有高聳雲端、岩坎層叠的九龍柱；有浪濤洶湧的銀窩灘。

巴霧峽從東坪壩起至太平灘止，長10公里。峽內奇峰爭雄，怪石爭形，碧流爭湧。似人、似物、似獸的鐘乳石千姿百態："龍進虎出"、"馬歸山"、"猴子攬月"、"烏龜灘"……無不惟妙惟肖，並伴有許多美麗的傳說。

滴翠峽從雙龍的牛鼻洞至涂家壩，長20公里，是小三峽中最長最美麗多姿的一個峽。峽兩岸羣峰競秀，翠竹葱蘢。河面上，時而激流似箭，時而波平如鏡；在岩影波光中，常有成對鴛鴦戲水，羣猴攀枝。這裏有銀絲千縷的水簾洞；有栩栩如生的摩岩佛像；有終年烟雨濛濛、迷離恍惚的天泉飛雨；有高逾百丈、橫亘數里、金碧輝煌的"赤壁摩天"等風景名勝。

龍門峽　Longmen Gorge.

小三峽風光
Scenery of the Lesser
Three Gorges.

Back from the Five Mountains, ①
One wants not to tour other mountains.
Back from the Daning River,
One wants not to visit other gorges.

This is tourists' hearty praise of the Lesser Three Gorges along the Daning River. Daning is the biggest and loveliest tributary in the Yangtze Gorges region. It rises in the south foot of the Daba Mountain, flows 250km southward and joins the Yangtze at the west end of Wu Gorge. The Lesser Three Gorges, in turn, lie on the lower Daning, stretching from Mt. Wushan to Dachang for 60km. They are named Longmen, Bawu and Dicui. There is a saying about these gorges that "no mountain is not verdant; no water is not green; no peak is not peculiar, no fall is not swift". They are different from the Yangtze Gorges, and better.

The Longmen Gorge was named Luomen in ancient times. It is now often referred to as the "Radish Door", because at the entrance of the gorge there is a huge radish-shaped rock. This 3km -long gorge is the shortest of the three. At the entrance, precipitous cliffs tower into clouds and face each other closely across the river, thus forming a natural gate magnificent and spectacular. As it resembles Kuimen, the gorge entrance is also known as the "Small Kuimen". In the gorge, there are the never-drying, ever-splashing Dragon Door Spring, the sky-scraping, thousand-stepped Nine Dragon Pillar, and the torrent-washed Yinwo Shoal.

The 10km-long Bawu Gorge starts at Dongpingba and ends at the Taiping Shoal. Along the gorge, all fantastic peaks contend to gain supremacy, all grotesque rocks strive to show peculiarity, and all green waters race to surge forward. The stalactic structures of all descriptions resemble human beings, concrete things and animals, such as "Dragon In and Tiger Out", "Horse-Returning to Mountain", "Monkeys Reaching for the Moon", "Tortoise Shoal", etc. All are remarkably lifelike, and many have beautiful legends about them.

Dicui Gorge extends for 20km from the Bull Nose Cave at Shuanglong to Tujiaba. It is the longest and the most picturesque of the Lesser Three Gorges. On the banks, each peak seems more beautiful than the other, and the bamboo groves are luxuriantly verdant. The river dashes on like an arrow at one moment, and smooths down like a mirror the next. Mandarin ducks sail in pairs across the crags reflected in the river, and monkeys leap from branch to branch in the reflected sunlight. Other scenic spots include the Water Curtain Cave with thousands of silver threads hanging down, the lifelike rock statue of Buddha, the Dancing Rain from Heavenly Spring, drizzly and dreamy all the year round, as well as the 1000-foot-high splendid, magnificent "Sky-Scraping Red Wall", which stretches for a few miles.

---

① Five Mountains: Mt. Taishan in Shandong, Mt. Hengshan in Hunan, Mt. Huashan in Shaanxi, Mt. Hengshan in Shanxi and Mt. Songshan in Henan.

銀窩灘上飛舟激浪　Shooting the rapids down Yinwo Shoal .

懸棺
Coffins in precipice crevices.

馬歸山
Horse-Returning Mountain.

绵羊崖

1 滴翠峽
Dicui Gorge.

2 摩崖佛像
Stalactic Buddhas on cliff.

3 綿羊崖
Mianyang (cheep) Cliff

4 馬渡河
Madu River.

5 仿古棧道
Imitation plank road.

6 青翠欲滴
Green and fresh all over.

翠谷輕舟 Skiff passing green valley.

跨河索橋 Chain bridge across the river.

白龍過江. White dragon crossing the river.

50

巴 東 風 光

巴東位於長江南岸,地處巫峽與西陵峽之間,南依巴山,北臨大江,是川鄂兩省交通要衝和鄂西山區的門戶,有"鎖鑰港"之稱。

巴東歷史悠久,風光名勝眾多,有"巴山夜雨"、"烟寺曉鐘"、"鳳山夕照"、"鹿洞晴雲"、"古亭秋月"、"仙洞靈泉"、"瓖溪晚渡"、"千米石屏"等八大景觀。其中,以"瓖溪晚渡"和"千米石屏"最讓人流連。

"瓖溪晚渡"又名神農溪晚渡。神農溪發源於神農架南坡,沿途接納17條溪澗,由北向南穿行於深山峽谷之中,至西瓖口注入長江,全長60公里。神農溪有龍昌、鸚鵡、棉竹三峽,有"鄂西小三峽"之稱。龍昌峽裏,寶塔峰拔地而起,古戰場依稀可辨,兩岸絕壁,曲折迂迴,深若幽巷重門,雄偉壯觀,以"雄"見長。鸚鵡峽山巒聳立,灌木繁茂,碧流清泉,山花遍野,燕飛鳥鳴,以"秀"見長。棉竹峽兩岸山勢險峻,峭壁崢嶸,河體狹長,溪水洶湧,以"險"見長。

當你乘坐古式木船從棉竹峽漂流至龍昌峽時,你不僅會目睹巴船似箭離弦,溪水清澈見底,深潭碧綠可愛,泉眼飛瀑遍佈,以及巴人岩棺、原始扁舟、古老村落、土家風情,還會從中領略到大三峽所沒有的古樸、自然的野趣。

"千米石屏"又名格子河石林,位於巴東西南棗子坪鄉。這裏奇峰異石,千姿百態,青松挺拔,綠草如茵。30多座孤峰和7個洞穴,被三處草坪、四個一綫天、五座重門、六條巷道、八條幽巷相隔相通,縱橫交錯、宛如迷宮,與週圍穿心岩、九龍觀等景區相連,形成了方圓十多公里的格子河石林風景區。加之人們給奇石所取的那些饒有趣味的名字:天字碑、一綫天、蜂窩座、夫妻峰、雙峰駱駝、穿雲含石、觀音坐蓮台、猪八戒守門等,更爲石林增添了許多情趣。

淺灘行舟 Sailing down the shoal.

BADONG SCENES

Badong, situated on the south bank of the Yangtze between Wu Gorge and Xiling Gorge, with Mt. Bashan on the south and the Yangtze on the north, is known as the "key port" for its significant location on the communications hub between Sichuan and Hubei Provinces as well as the gateway to the western Hubei mountain areas.

With its long history, Badong boasts numerous scenic beauties to tourists. The eight main spots are "Night Rain of Mt. Bashan", "Dawn Bell of the Smoke Temple", "Sunset on Mt. Fengshan", "Cloudscape of the Deer Cave", "Autumn Moon Over the Ancient Pavilion", "Celestial Spring in the Immortals Cavern", "Dusk Ferry on the Rangxi Stream", and "Thousand-Meter Stone Screen", among which the last two are the top attractions.

Dusk Ferry on the Rangxi Stream is also known as Dusk Ferry on the Shennong River. Extending 60km from the south slope of Mt. Shennongjia to the Yangtze at Xirangkou, the Shennong River takes in 17 streams as it runs southward in the remote mountains and deep canyons. The river cuts its way through Longchang, Yingwu, and Mianzhu, known as the "Lesser Three Gorges of Western Hubei". Longchang Gorge is flanked by precipitous cliffs, where the Pagoda Peak towers over a dimly identifiable ancient battlefield. The twists and bends of the river reminds one of going into a house through endless doors or walking in a deep lane that keeps turning mystically. The magnificent and spectacular Longchang Gorge, therefore, is noted for its "grandeur"; Yingwu Gorge, among undulating mountains, where streams babble through lush bushes and birds chirp high and low across the flowering fields, is noted for its "beauty"; while Mian-zhu Gorge, with mountains soaring behind the stern cliffs and boisterous torrents surging through the narrow passage, is noted for its "danger".

Drifting downstream in an ancient-style boat from Mianzhu Gorge to Longchang Gorge one will see local boats shooting by like arrows, limpid water showing the riverbed, and dark green pools, gurgling springs, tumbling waterfalls, ancient coffins lodged in cliff crevices, primitive skiffs, age-old villages, the Tujia nationality customs, etc., thus enjoying the natural simplicity of the wilderness that the Yangtze Gorges are devoid of.

The Thousand-Meter Stone Screen, also known as Gezi River Stone Forest, lies in Nanzaoziping Town in the southwest of Badong. It is a spot where each of the many fantastic peaks and grotesque rocks presents its unique shape, and tall, straight pine trees rise sheer out of verdant carpets of lush grass. More than thirty single peaks and seven caves are linked up by three meadows, four spots of "thread of sky" (extremely narrow passage between huge rocks, where only a streak of the sky is seen), five gates, six tunnels and eight deep lanes, all crisscross to make a labyrinth of the whole place, which, together with the nearby Chuanxin Rock, Nine Dragons Scene, etc., has formed the famous scenic spot of Gezi River Stone Forest, covering a circumference of over 10km. Besides, the stone forest area gets more charm and appeal from the names people have given to the grotesque rocks, such as Tianzi Tablet (tablet shaped like the Chinese character 天, pronounced as "tian"), Thread of Sky, Honeycomb Rock, Man-and-Wife Peak, Two-Humped Camel, Through Clouds with Stones, Goddess Guanyin on Lotus Throne, Pigsy Keeping Door, etc.

春到巴東 Spring coming to Badong.

灘多水急，駕舟漂流 Drifting down shoals and rapids.

碧綠清透的神農溪 The green Shennongxi River, clear as crystal.

鐘乳——象鼻 Stalactite elephant's trunk.

齊心協力 United as one.

農溪
e Shennongxi River.

格子河夫妻峰
Man-and-Wife Peak by Gezihe River.

一綫天
A thread of sky.

三 峽 奇 石

三峽的石，如三峽的風光一樣瑰麗多姿，風采迷人。它們有
的雄偉挺拔，嶙峋崢嶸；有的小巧玲瓏，如花似玉。特別是在大
寧河和神農溪的河灘上，那些大大小小的鸞卵石，色彩斑斕，令
人愛不釋手。鸞卵石上，有不同的花紋，有的黑底白點，如雪花
飛舞；有的紅白相映，若白雲襯着彩霞；有的珠圓玉潤，似潔白
的珍珠。更吸引人的是那些象形石，如充滿詩情畫意的"南國之
夏"、"巴山夜雨"；惟妙惟肖的"姜太公釣魚"、"女媧補天"，
以及形形色色的"動物石"、"植物石"等，令人讚嘆，爭相收
藏。

GROTESQUE STONES OF
THE YANGTZE GORGES

The stones on the banks are as magnificent, charming, and varied as the riverscape
there. They range from lofty, steep and forbidding crags to dainty, graceful and exquisite
boulders. And variegated are the alluring cobbles of various sizes on the banks of the
Daning River and the Shennongxi River. These cobbles display all kinds of coloured patterns: some with white spots against a black background, a picture of snowflakes dancing
at night; some with mixed red and white patches, like the rosy dawn setting off white
clouds; others either round and white as pearls or glossy as jade. But the top attractions
are the multi-shaped cobbles, such as the idyllic and picturesque "Summer in the
South", "Night Rain of Mt. Bashan", the lifelike "Jiang Taigong Angling", "Nuwa
Mending the Sky", as well as a great variety of "animal cobbles" and "plant cobbles" —
all of these marvels of nature are tourists' favourite souvenirs.

三峽石
THE COBBLES OF
THE YANGTZE GORGES

"南國之夏"
" Summer in the South".

"踏花歸來"
" Returning from Spring Outing".

"姜太公釣魚"
" Jiangtaigong Angling".

"春江水暖鴨先知"
" Duck Reporting the Coming of Spring".

三峡石　Rocks of Yangtze Gorges.

十丈懸流萬堆雪
驚天如看廣陵濤

"十丈懸流萬堆雪"的西陵峽,西起秭歸縣的香溪河口,東至宜昌市的南津關,全長76公里。這裏峽中有峽,大峽套小峽;灘中有灘,大灘含小灘,灘多流急,以險著稱。

"西陵灘如竹節稠,灘灘都是鬼見愁。"昔日西陵有三大險灘,青灘、泄灘、崆嶺灘。灘險處,漩渦翻滾,水流如沸,驚險萬狀。由於航道狹窄,怪石橫陳,水亂流急,祇有空船才能過去。一首民謠中唱道:"腳踏石頭手扒沙,當牛做馬把船拉,一步一鞭一把淚,恨得要把天地砸。"解放後,航道上的險灘經過整治,如今航船已日夜暢通無阻了。

峽內從西向東依次有兵書寶劍峽、牛肝馬肺峽、燈影峽、黃牛峽等。燈影峽一帶,不僅有掩映的飛瀑,還有奇特的石灰岩洞,神奇的傳說故事,爲西陵峽增添了奇妙的色彩。

XILING GORGE

Xiling Gorge, described by an ancient poet as *"torrents from above falling upon ten thousand snow drifts"*, stretches 76km from the mouth of the Xiangxi River in Zigui County in the west to Nanjinguan Pass out of Yichang City in the east. All along Xiling there are gorges upon gorges and shoals upon shoals—small gorges hidden in bigger ones and small shoals set on bigger ones. With the great number of shoals and the swift torrents Xiling is well-known for its danger.

Like a bamboo full of joints is Xiling with its shoals,
And each one baffles even supernatural beings.

Xiling used to be more hazardous with the three most dangerous shoals: Qingtan Shoal, Xietan Shoal, and Kongling Shoal. Some places were extremely hazardous with turbulent whirls and boiling rapids. And in places where the channel got too narrow and where the boisterous torrent raced on like ponies among grotesque reefs, only empty boats were able to pass. An old folk rhyme goes:

Trampling upon rocks and clutching at sands,
Like oxen and horses we are hauling boats,
In tears we're whipped to crawl step by step,
And how we wish we could smash the evil world.

After liberation, however, the dangerous rocks and shoals were blasted away, and day-and-night navigation has since been made possible.

In Xiling Gorge lie a few small gorges from west to east in the following order: Tactics Books and Sword, Bull's Liver and Horse's Lung, Shadow Play, and the Ox Gorge. Along the Shadow Play Gorge, there are half-hidden waterfalls, peculiar karst caves and mystic legends, all adding greatly to the wonder of Xiling.

西陵烟雲 Mists and clouds in Xiling Gorge.

西陵峽　Xiling Gorge.

屈原故里秭歸城

　　秭歸位於長江北岸的臥牛山麓，因城垣形如"葫蘆"，故有"葫蘆城"之稱。又因城牆均由石頭疊砌而成，又叫"石頭城"。

　　秭歸是我國偉大的愛國詩人屈原的故里，他誕生在山青水秀的樂平里。屈原是一位具有遠見卓識的政治家，是中國文學史上第一位大詩人，是三峽裏的"第一流才子"。他憂國憂民，最後投汨羅江，以身殉國。屈原留下的《離騷》、《九章》、《九歌》等光輝詩篇，聲貫古今，名揚中外。

　　在樂平里，有關屈原的名勝古跡和傳說甚多，古人曾集為"八景"並以景名聯詩一首："降龍伏虎嘯天來，響鼓岩連擂鼓台。照面井寒奸佞膽，讀書洞出離騷才。坵生玉米合情操，濂滴珍珠蕩俗埃。鎖水回龍含澤畔，三閭八景勝蓬萊"。

　　秭歸還是歷史悠久的柑桔之鄉，屈原在他的名篇《桔頌》中，曾對桔樹的形象和性格作過深刻的描寫。今天，秭歸已成為我國七大柑桔生產基地之一。深秋時節，滿目都是柑桔林，青枝綠葉藏紅果，如詩如畫。

ZIGUI CITY, QU YUAN'S NATIVE PLACE

　　Zigui is located at the foot of Mt. Woniu on the north bank of the Yangtze. As the city wall is shaped like a gourd, it is also known as the "Gourd City", and, stone walled, it is sometimes called the "Stone City".

　　Zigui is the native place of Qu Yuan, the great poet and patriot born over 2,000 years ago to the green hills and clear waters of Lepingli. Besides being a statesman with foresight and sagacity, Qu Yuan has been established as the earliest great poet in the Chinese literature and is referred to as the "No. 1 Talent of the Yangtze Gorges". He was so deeply concerned over the fate of his nation that he ended up drowning himself in the Miluo River in despair when he failed to help save his kingdom, leaving behind brilliant poems such as *Li Sao*, *Jiu Zhang*, *Jiu Ge*, etc., which are famous throughout the times and all over the world.

　　Lepingli abounds with legends and sites concerning Qu Yuan. Among the eight major scenic spots are the Mirror Well, the Study Cave, the Pearl Curtain, etc.

　　Zigui also has a long history as a land of oranges. *Ode to Tangerine*, one of Qu Yuan's best poems, renders a detailed description of the shape and character of orange trees. Zigui has now developed into one of China's seven orange bases. The place is especially idyllic and picturesque in late autumn, when the orange and tangerine trees all over the hills become overloaded with golden fruits half-hidden among the green foliage.

屈原祠　Qu Yuan Temple.

秭歸縣遠眺　A long shot of Zigui County.

綠水悠悠話香溪

香溪鎮位於長江北岸香溪河與長江交滙處，鎮的東面，香溪清澈碧綠，像一條玉帶從遠方緩緩飄來，滙入長江。香溪河畔的寶坪村是漢代明妃王昭君的故鄉。「昭君自有千秋在，胡漢和親見識高。」「昭君出塞」的故事，流傳千古，家喩戶曉。人們把她看成是三峽裏的「第一流佳人」。

乘船至香溪昭君台後，西行6公里，越過香溪河橋，便可到風景秀美的寶坪村（明妃村）一遊。寶坪村有許多處紀念王昭君的名勝古跡，如昭君祠、昭君院、楠木井、梳妝台、繡鞋洞等，以及許許多多有關昭君的美麗故事和傳說。

"NO. 1 BEAUTY" ON THE GREEN XIANGXI RIVER

The town of Xiangxi sits on the north bank at the confluence of the Xiangxi River and the Yangtze. On the east of the town, the limpid, green Xiangxi River, like a jade belt, flows lazily from afar into the Yangtze. Baoping, a village on the Xiangxi River, is the birthplace of Wang Zhaojun, the celebrated imperial concubine of the Han Dynasty. The story of Wang Zhaojun married into a northern kingdom, handed down from ancient times, is known to every household in China. She is regarded as the "NO. 1 Beauty" of the Yangtze Gorges.

Take a boat to Zhaojun Terrace on the Xiangxi River, head westward for 6km, and cross the Xiangxi River Bridge, then you can go sightseeing in the picturesque Baoping Village (or Imperial Concubine Village), where you will see Zhaojun Temple, Zhaojun Courtyard, Nanmu Well, the Dressing Table, the Embroidered-Shoe Cave and various other Zhaojun memorial sites. You will also hear many beautiful stories and legends about Wang Zhaojun.

飛來廟　Feilai Temple.

香溪雲霧　Xiangxi River in mists.

相傳昭君汲水的楠木井
　　Nanmu Well, where Zhaojun is said to
have fetched water.

昭君村的昭君宅
　　Zhaojun's former residence in Zhaojun Village.

似人若物三名峽

西陵峽中的兵書寶劍峽、牛肝馬肺峽和燈影峽，似人若物，最富情趣。

"兵書寶劍"位於長江北岸，峭壁上有一叠層次分明的岩石，形似書卷堆放，人稱"兵書"。在兵書的側面，有一塊石頭，形如寶劍，插入江中，即所謂"寶劍"。相傳諸葛亮晚年時，將平生用兵之計寫成一部兵書，因蜀中無人可授，又恐落入亂臣手中，故將兵書寶劍藏於大峽之中，讓後世勇士取拿。天長日久，兵書和寶劍就化作了岩石。

牛肝馬肺峽位於長江北岸青灘下十餘里處。在半山腰石壁間，東邊懸掛一團赭黃色的頁岩，形似牛肝；兩邊垂下一堵黯褐色的岩石，酷象馬肺，形態逼真，故人稱之牛肝馬肺峽。歷經滄桑，怪石依然如故，為人們爭睹。

燈影峽位於西陵峽的東段，緊靠石牌鎮。山上有四塊奇石兀立，狀如《西遊記》中唐僧師徒四人的模樣。四塊奇石在落日餘輝的映照下，更是活靈活現：孫猴子手搭涼棚，豬八戒挺着圓肚，沙和尚昂首闊步，唐三藏指手於後，映於天幕之上，酷似燈影戲中的角色，故人稱燈影峽。

GORGES FAMOUS FOR LIFELIKE ROCKS

The rocks known as Tactics Books and Sword. Bull's Liver and Horse's Lung. and Shadow Play are true to life. hence a good fun.

Tactics Books and Sword on the top of a north bank cliff is a stack of rock slabs that resemble a pile of books, called "tactics books". and a sword-shaped rock on one side. which is thrust in the river. referred to as "sword". The legend goes that Zhuge Liang. in his remaining years. wrote books of tactics he had used in all of his military life. As there was no one in Shu (his native place. a kingdom then) so gifted as to be able to learn his tactics and as Zhuge wanted to keep the books out of the reach of the treacherous court officials. he ended up hiding the books and his sword in the gorge for valiant people of later ages to find. The books and the sword, however. have turned into stone with the passage of time.

Bull's Liver and Horse's Lung are rocks about 10 *li* down Qingtan Shoal on the north bank. From a cliff halfway up the mountain suspended a lump of reddish brown shale in the east. which is shaped like a bull's liver. and a dark brown rock in the west resembling a horse's lung. Both are strikingly true to life. hence the name "Bull's Liver and Horse's Lung". Thousands upon thousands of years have passed. these rocks are still there. jutting out in their old peculiar way. unravished. for tourists to marvel at.

Close to Shipai Town at Mt. Shibi on the south bank is the Shadow Play. where four grotesque rocks rise in the shapes of four legendary figures in *Journey to the West*. These rocks are most lifelike in the setting sun—Monkey Sun making an awning with his palm. Pigsy sticking out his pot-belly. Monk Shaseng striding vigorously ahead and Monk Xuanzang pointing forward in the rear—all silhouetted against the sky in the twilight so much similar to the figures in the shadow play that people named the rocks "Shadow Play".

1 **兵書寶劍峽**
Tactics Books and Sword.

2 **燈影峽**
Shadow Play Gorge.

3 **牛肝馬肺峽**
Bull's Liver and Horse's Lung.

峽 中 名 灘

三峽險灘中，以青灘和崆嶺灘最爲有名。

青灘位於兵書寶劍峽與牛肝馬肺峽之間。灘長1.5公里，從西至東依次分爲頭灘、二灘、三灘，灘中亂石如林，白浪翻滾，水流甚急，人稱入江「鐵門坎」。來往船隻下灘急如箭，上灘如登梯，祇有走「S」形航道才能通過，古人曾用「扁舟轉山曲，未舟已先驚」來形容此處的險情。

崆嶺灘位於廟河段大江中，向有「青灘泄灘不算灘，崆嶺才是鬼門關」之說。灘內礁石林立，犬牙交錯。由大珠、頭珠、二珠、三珠等24處礁石組成。其中大珠像一條大鯊魚縱臥江心，把江流分爲南北兩漕，南漕亂石密佈，泡漩無常；北漕彎曲狹窄，暗礁如林。灘中原有一個「對我來」礁石，令人望而生畏。凡船隻經此過灘，祇能左避右讓，穿縫航行。

解放後，經過多次炸礁疏浚，已化險爲夷。特別是葛洲壩工程興建後，水位昇高，昔日的險灘已變爲坦途。

PROMINENT SHOALS IN
THE YANGTZE GORGES

Of all the most dangerous shoals in the Gorges, Qingtan and Kongling are the best known.

Stretched between "Tactics Books and Sword" and "Bull's Liver and Horse's Lung", Qingtan — First Shoal, Second Shoal, and Third Shoal—runs 1.5km from west to east, teeming with reefs and convulsed with sweeping, boisterous rapids, an "Iron Threshold" to the river. Boats and skiffs used to shoot downstream like flying arrows and flounder upstream as if scaling a ladder, zigzagging their way either up or down. One ancient poet described these breathtaking journeys as follows:

So dangerous rapids the boat is to shoot.
And so fast your heart beats before you start.

Kongling Shoal lies in the Temple Reach of the river. The local people have always said, "Qingtan and Xietan are not real shoals compared with that hell gate of Kongling Shoal". Twenty-four reefs, named Great Pearl, First Pearl, Second Pearl, Third Pearl, etc., are crammed in the shoal, bulging into each other's way. The Great Pearl, for example, sprawls in the middle of the river, dividing it into two channels, the south channel full of jagged reefs and fickle eddies, the north narrow, twisted, and forbidding with submerged rocks. Besides, there was a hideous reef called "Coming-at-Me", which used to fill people with fear. This is a shoal where passing boats had to thread their way through the reefs, dodging from side to side all the time.

After liberation, however, rocks were blasted away and waterways were dredged to make these shoals less dangerous, and especially with the accomplishment of the Gezhouba Dam, the water level is higher now, and the earlier dreadful gorges have become easy of access.

晨光秀色 Charming landscape in the morning sun.

崆嶺峡
Kongling Gorge..

黃 陵 廟

　　黃陵廟位於長江南岸黃牛岩下九龍山麓正中，背依山岩，前臨大江，掩映在香柑金桔林中，是三峽中最大最古老的建築。

　　相傳黃陵廟始建於春秋時代，原叫黃牛廟。三國時諸葛亮率師入蜀，途經黃牛峽，看到此廟已破爛不堪，便親自主持重建，并寫下膾炙人口的《黃陵廟記》，後人把它刻碑珍藏於廟，尊為"武侯碑"。

　　黃陵廟內供奉大禹像，相傳遠古時候，大禹率眾來此治水，因高山阻擋，八年難以疏通，百姓深受水災之害。土星被感動，變成一頭勇猛的黃牛，觸開高山，犁出峽道，助禹治水成功，并深愛這裏的百姓和山水草木，化成了一座高入雲端的黃牛岩。

　　黃牛岩高千餘米，霞光之中，遠看好像一幅畫：一位粗黑的壯士牽着一頭牛，正昂首向前。

　　黃陵廟與黃牛岩吸引着歷代文人墨客，歐陽修、蘇東坡、陳子昂、李白、白居易、劉禹錫等都在這裏留下了足跡，寫下了許多千古流傳的詩篇。

HUANGLING TEMPLE

Huangling Temple, the biggest and the oldest building in the Yangtze Gorges, is located right at the foot of the Nine Dragons Hill in front of the Ox Rock on the south bank. Backed by the huge mountain rocks and facing the river, it sits in a garden of fragrant golden oranges.

The story has it that Huangling Temple was first built in the Spring and Autumn Period (770~476 B. C.) and named Huangniu Temple (the Ox Temple). In the Three Kingdoms Period (220~265), when Zhuge Liang passed the temple, leading his troops on their way to Shu (one of the kingdoms) and saw it on the verge of collapse, he stopped over and put himself in charge of the renovation. It was here that he wrote the admirable essay *Hungling Temple*, which was later inscribed on a stele, worshipped as the "Wuhou Stele".

Enshrined in the temple is the statue of Yu the Great. The legend goes that in ancient times, Yu was here leading the people in their fight against floods. But for eight long years they could not find an outlet for the floods, which were always blocked by the mountains. As a result, the local people were constantly harassed by floods. The god Tuxing was so much moved by Yu's unremitting efforts that he turned into a valiant ox, gored the mountain apart, and ploughed up a gorge, thus helping to fulfil Yu's task. Then, reluctant to leave the local people and the land that he had come to love so much, the god changed into the sky-high Ox Rock.

The Ox Rock is over 1,000m high. Seen from a distance in the sun rays, it looks like a dusky statue of a sturdy man heroically leading an ox forward.

Throughout the ages, Huangling Temple and the Ox Rock have attracted many literary men. Famous writers and poets such as Ouyang Xiu, Su Shi, Chen Zi'ang, Li Bai, and Liu Yuxi visited this place and bequeathed a number of excellent poems, which will be handed down forever.

1　三斗坪
Sandouping.

2　黃牛峽
Huangniu Gorge.

3　黃陵廟
Huangling Temple.

西陵晚霞
Xiling Gorge in sunset glow.

春雪
Spring snow.

西陵峡春色
Spring scene
in Xiling Gorge.

九龍過江
Nine dragons crossing river.

南沱 "三把刀"
Three Swords at Nantuo.

涉險 "天生橋" Venturing on Heavenly Bridge.

險奇的西陵峽
Dangerous and quaint Xiling Gorge.

馬鈴巖
Horse-Bell Rock.

石牌青獅
Mt. Qingshi in Shipai Town

南 津 關

南津關位於西陵峽東門，"三峽至此窮"，為三峽尾端的天然門戶。

南津關北岸的下牢溪，傳說劉備曾派兵在此駐守，至今尚有劉封城和張飛擂鼓台遺址。南津關兩岸地勢險要，陡壁直立，江面狹窄，猶如細頸瓜口，鎖住滔滔大江，"縱關蜀道，巍鎮荊門"，歷來為兵家必爭之地。

長江一出南津關，便急劇南折，兩岸山勢坦蕩，江面驟然變寬，江流由飛旋洶湧而漸趨平緩。關口內外，景色迥異。如果是出峽，便會使人有"送盡奇峰雙眼豁，江天空闊而夷陵"之感。

THE NANJINGUAN PASS

"The Yangtze Gorges ends at the Nanjinguan Pass." Situated at the eastern end of Xiling Gorge. the Nanjinguan Pass is the natural exit of the Gorges.

It is said that Liu Bei (king of Shu) once posted his troops there to garrison the pass. Today we can still see the relics of Liu Bei's fortress and the spot where Zhang Fei (a general under Liu) beat the drum. As sheer cliffs close in on the river, the Nanjinguan Pass banks are difficult of access. It is like the narrow neck of a flask curbing the mighty Yangtze waters. "Impregnable Shu pass. garrison of Jingmen Gate", the pass was a strategic point all through the ages.

Rushing out of the Nanjinguan Pass. the Yangtze bends sharply southward. Then the mountains stretch away and the river widens abruptly. the surging. whirling waters calmed down. The landscape varies drastically in and out of the pass.

Cruising out. one experiences the sensation described in a poem:

Sending off peaks so spectacular,
I am greeted by the open sky and water.
The river is so vast and the horizon so far.
That the mountains seem all razed.

南津關 Najinguan Pass.

變化奇妙的三峽水

　　三峽之險，不僅表現在陡岩峭壁、急流險灘上，而且還表現在令人望而生畏、變化奇妙的險水上。那由水底向水面翻湧、宛如沸騰的開水的泡水，那旋轉不止並集於一點的漩水，那翻騰着朵朵水花的花水，以及奇形怪狀的橫流水、眉毛水、跌水等，在江面上時隱時現，此起彼伏，變化無窮，使你眼花繚亂，情趣橫生。

FICKLE AND MIRACULOUS WATERS

　　The danger of the Yangtze Gorges is found not only in the precipitous cliffs and jagged crags, but also in the treacherous waters that daunt people at first glance with its miraculous changes. The bubbles welling up from the riverbed like boiling water, the eddies that whirl on and on at one spot, the sprays that splash and splatter about wildly, as well as the curious crossing current, the brow-shaped flow, and the tumbling torrent — all on and off, one after another, full of changes, always dazzle the spellbound tourists and have added greatly to the charm of the Yangtze Gorges.

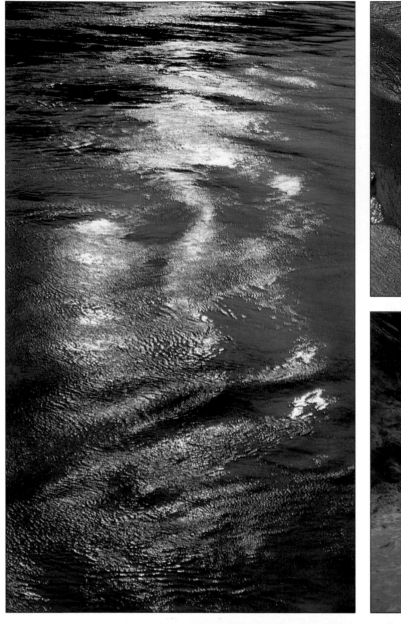
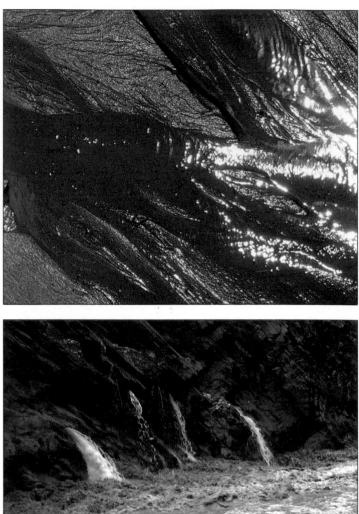

三峽溶洞奇觀

"怪怪與奇奇，萬狀不可名。"

三峽溶洞有200多個，其中絕大部分分佈在石灰岩特別多的西陵峽中。這些洞分佈在兩岸山崖上，有的臨近水旁，有的處於山腰，有的高踞山頂。洞內流水濛濛，迂迴曲折，乳石橫生，千奇百怪，萬千景象。

位於瞿塘峽北岸絕壁山腰上的七道門溶洞，洞深曲折，洞中有洞，景中有景，景色奇異。洞寬處大如廣場，洞窄處僅能容一人側身通過。洞中怪石嵯峨，各種石筍石乳千姿百態，琳瑯滿目。在二道門頂端，有一天窗面對大江，從這裏眺望夔峽江天，雲天一綫，妙不可言。

位於巫峽與大寧河交滙處北岸的陸游洞，因陸游曾在此夜宿而得名。由清水洞、金柱洞、玉林洞交錯組成，相連貫通，各具特色，融洞景峽景於一體。清水洞寬敞高大，四壁如刀削斧劈，洞頂石乳高低錯落，燈光中如繁星點點；金柱洞由一條長10米寬5米的長廊組成，洞內有20米高的乳白色石柱，由洞底直插洞頂，氣勢磅礴，柱身玲瓏剔透，名曰"金柱撐天"。

燕子阡溶洞位於神農溪鸚鵡峽西岸，洞高80米，寬30米，洞深5公里，呈長方形，好似張開大嘴的河馬。洞內棲息着成千上萬的珍禽——短嘴金絲燕，故名燕子阡。洞內上有燕子飛舞，下有流水濛濛，岩溶堆積，宛如層層梯田。

三遊洞位於宜昌市西北郊西陵山的峭壁上，面臨清澈的下牢溪。相傳唐元和十四年（公元819年），白居易與其弟白行簡和詩人元稹相約同遊此洞，各賦詩20韻刻於壁上，由白居易作《三遊洞序》："以吾三人始遊，故曰爲三遊洞。"到了宋代，著名文學家蘇洵、蘇軾、蘇轍，慕名同遊三遊洞，也各題詩一首，刻於壁上。後人稱白居易等三人之遊爲"前三遊"，蘇軾父子之遊爲"後三遊"。洞中鐘乳石、石筍和石柱比比皆是，千姿百態，妙狀難名。洞分前後兩室，前室明曠，題刻滿壁；後室幽暗，奧妙莫測。洞內頂部原有石鐘二處，以石擊之，其聲如鐘；石子落地，其響如鼓，故有"天鐘地鼓"之說。洞中還保存有各種題刻、壁畫等古文物。

金獅洞位於宜昌市郊的長江北岸，因入洞口處有一巨型乳石形如雄獅而得名。金獅洞是距今約100萬年的石灰岩溶洞，洞深1585米，洞內千奇百怪、瑩光明潤的鐘乳石及種種石灰質結構，造成了一個規模宏大的地下宮殿，展現出一個由具體的景觀與想象和幻覺交織而成的神話世界。

KARST GROTTO WONDERS IN THE YANGTZE GORGES

Ten thousand shapes beyond description,
Each more grotesque and bizarre than the other.

There are more than 200 karst grottoes in the Yangtze Gorges region, mainly distributed along Xiling Gorge, an area abundant in limestone. These grottoes are scattered on the cliffs on either bank—some close to the river, some halfway up, and some high up right on the top. In the grottoes, small streams murmur around the twists and turns. Stalactites and stalagmites are everywhere in multifarious shapes. A scene of wonders indeed.

Seven Gates, a karst grotto halfway up the cliff on the north bank at Qutang Gorge, is very deep, where a winding path leads into one grotto after another. There are grottoes inside grottoes and karst scenes over karst scenes, all unique and spectacular. The grottoes may be as spacious as a plaza and may be so small that one has to sidle through. The limestones are steep, sharp and peculiar, and the display of stalactites and stalagmites of all shapes is a feast for the eyes. On the top of the second gate, facing the river, there is a skylight, where one can look into the distance at Kui Gorge, a scene of the river, and the clouds too beautiful for words.

Lu You Grotto, so named because Lu You (great poet of the Song Dynasty) had once stayed in it overnight, is situated on the north bank where the Daning River runs into Wu Gorge. It consists of three small caves—Qingshui, Jinzhu, and Yulin—connected in a crisscross pattern, each with its own distinctive features. Here the landscape of the gorge and the grotto sights interplay in a harmonious whole. The spacious Qingshui Grotto has walls that seem to have been cut out with a sword. When the grotto is lit up, the stalactites hanging from overhead, high and low at random, look like many stars strewn across the night sky. Another cave, Jinzhu (Golden Pillar), is actually a passage 10m long and 5m wide. A 20m-high cream-coloured karst column, exquisitely sculptured by nature, rises sheer out of the ground and up to the roof with great momentum. This sight is known as "Golden Pillar Propping the Sky".

The Swallow Path, a rectangular karst grotto on the west bank of Parrot Gorge on the Shennong River, 80m high, 30m wide, and 5km deep, looks like a yawning hippopotamus. In it live thousands and thousands of short-billed collocalias, rare birds of the swallow kind. Hence the name Swallow Path. Here swallows flit high and low over a murmuring stream and the heaped karst, which resembles terraced fields.

Facing the limpid Xialao Stream, Three Tourists Grotto is in the cliff of Mt. Xiling in the northwest suburbs of Yichang City. The story goes that in the year of 819, the well-known poet Bai Juyi, his brother Bai Xingjian, and another famous poet Yuan Zhen visited this cave together. Each of them composed a 20-rhyme poem and inscribed it on the wall, and Bai Juyi wrote the *Preface to The Three Tourists*, in which he claimed, "as we are the first three tourists here, we hereby name the cave Three Tourists". Later on, the famous Song Dynasty literary men Su Xun (father), Su Shi and Su Zhe (sons) came to visit the cave out of admiration. They each wrote a poem, too, and inscribed them on the wall. Since then the first group have been referred to as "the earlier three tourists", and the Sus as "the later three tourists". In the grotto, the ubiquitous stalactites, stalagmites and karst columns present a variety of indescribably grotesque shapes. The grotto is divided into a front cave and a back cave—the front one bright and spacious, its walls full of inscriptions, and the back one dark and mysterious. There used to be two karst bells hanging from the roof. When hit by a stone, they sounded like bells; when the stone fell onto the ground, there was the thundering of a drum. Hence the name "Heaven Bells and Earth Drums". There are also valuable antiquities, such as various inscriptions and mural paintings, kept in the grotto.

The Golden Lion Grotto lies on the north bank in the suburbs of Yichang City, so named because of the huge lionlike stalactite at the entrance. The grotto is 1,585m deep and 1,000,000 years old. The gleaming, moist stalactites of all fantastic shapes and various stalactic structures make a grand subterranean palace of the cave, thus displaying a mythological world—a combination of real sights, imagination and visions.

巫峽陸游洞
Lu You Grotto in Wu Gorge.

1 溶洞
  Karst cave.

2 世界上最大的天坑——奉節小寨天坑
  Xiaozhai Natural Pit. world's largest.

3 神農溪燕子阡洞
  Swallow Path on Shennongxi River.

4 西陵峽溶洞景觀
  Karst cave scene in Xiling Gorge.

5 金獅洞
  Golden Lion Cave.

三遊洞石壁古代題刻
Ancient rock engravings
in Three Tourists Grotto.

三遊洞
Three Tourists Grotto.

萬里長江第一壩

萬里長江第一壩——葛洲壩水利樞紐工程，橫跨在南津關前３公里處寬闊的大江之上。

葛洲壩全長2561米，高達70米。葛洲壩水利樞紐主要建築有發電站、船閘、泄水閘、衝沙閘、防淤堤等。二座電站分別在大江、二江，總裝機容量271萬５千千瓦，年平均發電138億度。三座船閘，其中一、二號船閘閘室寬34米，長280米，可通過萬噸級客貨輪和大型船隊，是目前世界上最人的船閘之一。27孔泄水閘和12孔衝沙閘，每秒鐘可宣泄11萬立方米的洪水，即使遇到特大洪水，也能安全泄洪。

雄偉壯觀的葛洲壩水利樞紐工程具有發電、通航、泄洪等綜合功能，它像一顆燦爛的明珠，閃爍在萬里長江之上，為美麗雄偉的三峽增添了新的異彩。

與葛洲壩水利樞紐相連的宜昌市，"控楚蜀之交帶，當水陸之要衝"，素有川鄂咽喉之稱，是長江上、中游的中轉港。葛洲壩水利樞紐工程的興建，大大推動了宜昌的城市建設和工業的發展，使這座歷史古城面貌煥然一新，成為水電新城。宜昌山青水秀，風景優美，名勝古跡除享有盛名的葛洲壩和三遊洞外，還有清幽典雅的爾雅書院和巍峨壯觀、風鈴悅耳的天然塔等。

THE FIRST DAM ON THE YANGTZE RIVER

The first dam on the Yangtze — Gezhouba Key Water Control Project — runs across the broad section of the river 3km down the Nanjinguan Pass.

The dam is 2. 561m long and 70m high. The project is made up of three parts. Dajiang. Erjang and Sanjiang. consisting of hydro-power stations, ship locks, sluice gates, scouring sluices and anti-silt dykes. The two hydro-power stations are built on Dajiang with a total installed capacity of 2. 715. 000km and an annual electric energy production of 13. 8kwh. There are three ship locks. The passages of No. 1 and No. 2 locks are 34m in breadth and 280m in length, large enough for 10. 000-ton-class passengers and cargo ships or a large fleet to get by. It is one of the largest ship locks in the world. The 27-tunneled sluice gate and the 12-arched scouring sluice can drain off 110. 000 cubic metres of floodwater every second. They can let out a catastrophic flood without any danger.

The magnificent project has a comprehensive function of power generating. navigation. flood discharge and so on. Like a bright pearl. it gives off ever-lasting brilliance on the long river. adding a special charm to the Yangtze Gorges.

Yichang City. which is close to Gezhouba Key Water Control Project. is regarded as the throat of Sichuan and Hubei Provinces, being a hub of water and land communications and a transfer port in the upper and lower reaches of the Yangtze River. This project has greatly accelerated the urban construction and the development of the industry in Yichang City. and. consequently. the ancient city has taken on a completely new look and become a modern city of hydro-power. Besides the giant dam. Yichang boasts a lot of scenic and historical spots. Among them are Three Tourists Grotto. Erya Classical Learning Academy. which is antique and elegant. and Natural Pagoda. which is magnificent. with the aeolian bells pleasing to the ear.

葛洲壩水利樞紐鳥瞰
Bird's-eye view of Gezhouba Key Water Control Project.

泄洪闸
The sluice gate.

船闸
The ship lock.

三峽是川鄂兩省人民生活的地方，這裏主要居住着漢族和土家族，他們有着許多獨特的風俗和習慣。這裏還是國寶中華鱘的生息之地，龍舟競渡的聖地，萬紫千紅的水果生產基地。來到三峽，你能處處領略到濃郁而多彩的民族風情。

在奉節，你可看到熱鬧的人日踏磧活動，它是夔州百姓的傳統風俗。每年正月初七人日這天，男女老少懷着對諸葛亮的敬仰，穿紅著綠，成羣結隊出遊諸葛亮排八陣圖的磧上。人們在磧上鳴鼓奏樂，載歌載舞。婦女們在磧上挑揀些五彩斑斕的石子，用五彩絲綫穿幷在一起，繫於釵頭，或戴在小孩身上，用它來興吉避邪。

在巴東，你可看到一個背簍世界。因三峽城鎮大多依山臨江，街道陡斜，居民上下唯有步行。在街上，在山路邊，男女老少身後都揹着一個背簍或是一個木架了，或是揹着貨物，或是揹着一個小孩。行走時以木杖助力，休息時以木杖支撑竹簍。此情此景，別有情趣。

在土家族居住地，你可看到那獨特的婚俗、喪俗。新娘出嫁前要哭半月，由人揹送轎上。喪俗即跳喪舞，靈前置一大鼓，一人擊鼓，數人對舞，擊鼓者領唱，舞者邊舞邊唱，唱腔高亢粗獷。

在秭歸，你可看到那熱火朝天的龍舟賽。每年農曆五月初五龍舟賽，是楚鄉人民爲表達對屈原的崇敬而舉行的一種祭禮活動。屆時，龍舟競發，浪花飛濺，蕩槳聲、鑼鼓聲、號子聲，滙成一曲高亢激昂的交響樂。

此外，你還可到清澈碧透的香溪，去尋覓那形狀如傘、乳白透明的桃花魚；到古樸的巫山水口鎮，去品嘗那細如髮絲、味道鮮美的水口掛面；到波濤洶湧的江流中，觀賞那被稱作魚類之冠、神態威武的國寶——中華鱘；到沿岸那五彩繽紛的柑桔園中，品嘗芬芳，擷取詩情……

THE FOLKWAYS OF THE GORGE REGION

The region of the Yangtze Gorge is populated by a large number of Han and Tujia people of Sichuan and Hubei Provinces with various unique customs and folkways. It is also a place for the Chinese sturgeon, a national treasure of China, to propagate and the birthplace of the dragon boat race, which is so popular in China, as well as in the other countries and regions of Asia. What's more, it is a base of fruit production. Everywhere in the region you may enjoy yourself with the colourful folkways and customs characteristic of the ethnical flavour.

In Fengjie you may happen to see the exciting scene of the commemoration of the Eight-Element Battle Formation designed by Zhuge Liang during the period of the Three Kingdoms. The commemoration is a traditional folk-activity of Kuizhou. On the seventh day of the first moon every year men and women, old and young, all in their best, gather on the beach, which is the former site of Zhuge Liang's Eight-Element Battle Formation, beating gongs and drums, singing and dancing heartily. Women pick up colourful fine pebbles and string them up with coloured silk thread and then wear the string on their hairpins or around the necks of the children to ensure good luck.

In Badong you will see a world of baskets carried on the back. Since the towns and walled cities of the gorge region are mostly situated on riverside mountains, the streets are oblique or even steep. The citizens can only get about on foot. In a street or on a path you may come across men and women, old and young, who carry a basket or a wooden rack with goods or a little child in it. While walking they have a stick to support themselves and while resting they have the stick to support the baskets. The scene is really of exotic flavour.

In a Tujia dwelling place, you may get some idea of the unique wedding and funeral customs. As to the former the most unique is that before she is married off, a bride has to force a weep for half a month until she is carried on the back and put into a sedan-chair. The funeral custom, on the other hand, is characterised by the funeral dance: a big drum is set before the coffin and a man beats the drum while others dance. The man leads a chorus and the others sing loudly in an unconstrained manner.

In Zigui you see the rousing scene of the dragon boat race. On the fifth day of the fifth moon every year, the people of Chu Township hold a memorial ceremony to express their great reverence for Qu Yuan, a great poet of Chu State. At the time hundreds of boats compete with one another, water spraying, oars paddling and drums and gongs resounding to the skies, making a sonorous symphony.

Besides, you may go to the Xiangxi River to look for the minnows which are cream-coloured and transparent in the shape of an umbrella, to Shuikou Township in Wushan to taste the delicious noodles as thin as hair, to the surging Yangtze River to view and admire the powerful-looking Chinese sturgeons, a national treasure of China, and to orange and tangerine orchards by the river to enjoy the fragrance and refresh your poetic inspiration...

光與影　Light and shadow.

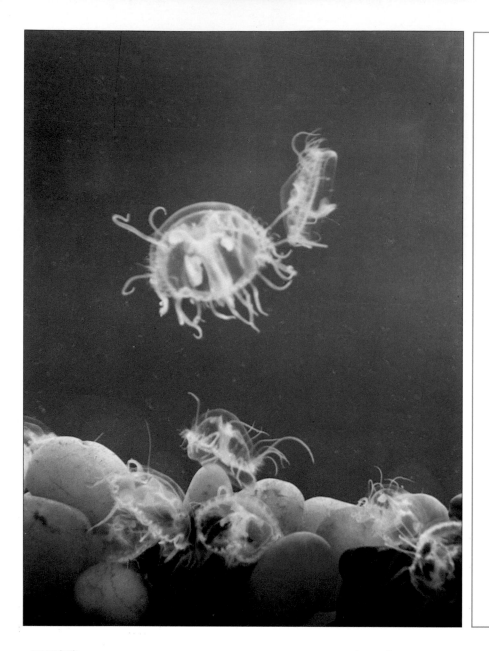

桃花魚，又名桃花水田，每至桃花盛開時節，一簇簇桃花魚，一閃一閃地蕩漾在碧波裏，仿佛在與岸上的桃花相媲美。當桃花凋謝時，它也隨花消逝，故名桃花魚。

Minnow.called " Peach fish" in Chinese, come in schools when peach trees are in blossom. They glisten in the limpid river, as if rivaling peach blossoms on the banks in beauty. They disappear with the withering of the peach blossoms. Hence the name.

巫峽夜泊　Night mooring at Wu Gorge.

峽岸牧羊　Tending sheep on the bank.

三峽猴　Monkeys of the Gorge region·

輕舟晚唱　Eventide skiff.

Chinese sturgeon·

The Chinese sturgeon is mainly distributed in the trunk tributaries of the Yangtze River and some coastal rivers. Between summer and autumn every year,they swim in schools upstream to the Jinsha River, where they spawn. After their young are bred, they all swim downstream to grow in the East Sea and the Yellow Sea. The Chinese sturgeon is large in size and imposing and dignified in bearing. A grown-up Chinese sturgeon can reach over 4m in length and over one thousand pounds in weight, ranking the biggest of all the 27 sturgeons in the world. It is among the government-protected aquatic animals.

中華鱘，主要分佈於長江干流和沿海水域，每年夏秋，成羣溯江而上，到金沙江一帶產卵；繁殖後順流而下，到東海、黃海育肥成長。它個體碩大，形態威武，成年中華鱘體長可達四米多，體重超過千斤，爲世界二十七種鱘魚之冠。是我國重點保護的水生動物。

峡江小渡　Gorge ferry.

待渡"小餐"　A snack before ferry.

缧夫　Boat trackers.

編織　Weaving.

寧河之晨　Morning of the Ninghe River.

龍昌渡口　Longchang Ferry.

高山小吊樓　Ever-Hanging house.

晚歸　Returning in the dusk.

三峽廣柑，三 峽 是 我 國 著 名 的柑桔產地之一。僅以屈原的《桔頌》爲據，三峽栽培柑桔的歷史就有兩千多年。如今峽江兩岸郁慾慾的柑桔樹上，金黃赤紅的菓實掛滿枝頭，給雄姿險峻的三峽，又添上了美麗富饒的色彩。

Yangtze Gorges tangerine The Gorges region tangerine is one of the well-known tangerine growing areas in China. Qu Yuan's Ode to Tangerines has borne out the fact that tangerines were grown in the area at least 2,000 years ago. Now, the luxuriant tangerine and orange trees on either bank, laden with golden and red fruits, add a touch of beautiful abundance to the scene of magnificence and peril in the gorges.

川寨人家
Mountain village household.

獼猴桃
Chinese gooseberry
(actinidia chinensis).

冬雪千坵
Drifts of winter snow.

2 巴東風情
Badong folkways.

3 長階小巷
Long flight in little lane

4 滿載而歸
Back from a fruitful journey.

巴人祭火
Local fire-worshipping ceremony.

包粽子　Making Zongzi.

土家族婚俗——交杯酒　Mutual toasting—a Tujia wedding custom.

龍舟競渡　Racing dragon boats.

映江光影
Shadow playing on the river

三峽是全國重點旅遊綫之一。爲了讓中外遊客飽覽三峽風光，以中國長江輪船總公司爲核心的中國長江航運集團，不僅開闢了客運兼旅遊的普通客輪航綫（乘坐此輪，旅客既可觀賞峽內風光，又可登岸參觀沿岸名勝古跡），還開闢了豪華型旅遊船航綫，成立了專業化的長江輪船海外旅遊總公司，擁有崑崙、神女、三峽、峨嵋、巴山、西陵、隆中、白帝、長江之星、長江明珠、長江公主等十多艘符合國際水準，又具中國特色的豪華、高級旅遊船。遊船集吃、住、行、遊、娛、購於一體，服務週到，生活舒適，堪稱水上樂園。

此外，長江上游段各地方航運公司也開闢了中小型客輪航綫。現在，武漢至重慶，宜昌至重慶，宜昌至奉節，每天都有大中小型客輪上下，是遊覽三峽的主要交通工具。

The Yangtze Gorges is one of the key tourist lines of the country. In order that tourists from home and abroad can enjoy the scenery of the Yangtze Gorges, Changjiang National Shipping Blocl, headed by Changjiang National Shipping Corporation, has opened up a shipping line for ordinary and luxury cruise liners as well as passenger ships. Aboard you can view all the gorge landscapes and ashore you can visit the scenic and historical sites along the river. Changjiang National Overseas Shipping Tourist Corporation possesses more than ten high-graded and luxury cruise liners such as *Kunlun*, *Shennu*, *Sanxia*, *Emei*, *Bashan*, *Xiling*, *Longzhong*, *Baidi*, *Star of the Yangtze*, *Bright Pearl of the Yangtze*, *and Princess of Yangtze*, which are all up to international standards and of the distinctive Chinese national features. The ships include the service of the basic necessities of life as well as shopping and recreation. They are regarded as paradise on water for their good service and comfortable accommodations.

In addition local shipping companies have opened up lines for the small and medium-sized tourist ships.

Every day ships of different sizes sail up and down the river from Wuhan to Chongqing, from Yichang to Chongqing and from Yichang to Fengjie. They are the main means of transportation for Yangtze Gorges tour.

三峽古詩選

● 瞿塘峽

早發白帝城

（唐）李白

朝辭白帝彩雲間，
千里江陵一日還。
兩岸猿聲啼不住，
輕舟已過萬重山。

長江

（唐）杜甫

眾水會涪萬，瞿塘爭一門。
朝宗人共挹，盜賊爾誰尊？
孤石隱如馬，高蘿垂飲猿。
歸心異波浪，何事即飛翻。

竹枝詞

（唐）白居易

瞿塘峽口冷烟低，
白帝城頭月向西。
唱到竹枝聲咽處，
寒猿闇鳥一時啼。

瞿塘峽

（清）張問陶

峽雨蒙蒙竟日間，
扁舟真落畫圖間。
縱將萬管玲瓏筆，
難寫瞿塘兩岸山。

白鹽赤甲

（清）張問陶

白鹽雲外落，赤甲雨中蟠。
峽坼天光細，山童石氣完。
關河夔府秀，疏鑿禹功難。
孤艇愁風雪，飄飄逼歲寒。

峽門秋月

（清）張宗世

燭龍不照古陰崖，
偏有明蟾度嶺來。
三峽憑將秋送人，
雙門似背月推開。
當關以望珠懸闕，
排洇而登鏡在台。
好景一年剛一見，
莫辭風露立蒼臺。

夔州歌十絕句（選二）

（唐）杜甫

中巴之東巴東山，
江水開闢流其間。
白帝高為三峽鎮，
瞿塘險過百牢關。

赤甲白鹽俱刺天，
閭閻繚繞接山巔。
楓林桔樹丹青合，
復道重樓錦繡懸。

峽中鐵柱

（元）何同男

白帝城邊春草生，
黃牛峽裏水波清。
追思昭烈千年事，
長使英雄氣不平。

夔州竹枝歌九首（選一）

（南宋）范成大

赤甲白鹽碧叢叢，
半山人家草木風。
榴花滿山紅似火，
荔子天凉未肯紅。

● 巫峽

三峽歌

（宋）陸游

十二巫山見九峰，
船頭彩翠滿秋空。
朝雲暮雨渾虛語，
一夜猿啼明月中。

巫峽

（清）張問陶

雲點巫山洞壑重，
參天亂插碧芙蓉。
可憐十二奇峰外，
更有零星百萬峰。

巫山高

（唐）李端

巫山十二峰，皆在碧虛中。
迴合雲藏日，霏微雨帶風。
猿聲寒度水，樹色暮連空。
愁向高唐去，清秋見楚宮。

巫山曲

（唐）孟郊

巴江上峽重復重，
陽台碧峭十二峰。
荊王獵時逢暮雨，
夜臥高丘夢神女。
輕紅流烟濕艷姿，
行雲飛去明星稀。
目極魂斷望不見，
猿啼三聲淚滴衣。

過巫峽

（唐）李頻

擁棹向驚湍，巫峰直上看。
削成從水底，聳出在雲端。
暮雨晴時少，啼猿渴下難。
一聞神女去，鳳竹掃空壇。

過楚宮

（唐）李商隱

巫峽迢迢舊楚宮，
至今雲雨暗丹楓。
微生盡戀人間樂，
祇有襄王憶夢中。

巫山道中

（明）黃輝

未曾五里巴三溪，
幾許寒崖掛斷霓。
亂石壘成春雪碓，
斷橋橫作上天梯。

神女廟

（唐）劉禹錫

巫山十二鬱蒼蒼，
片石亭亭號女郎。
曉霧乍開疑捲幔，
山花欲謝似殘妝。
星河好夜聞清風，
雲雨歸時帶異香。
何事神仙九天上，
人間來就楚襄王。

即事

（唐）杜甫

暮春三峽巫峽長，
晶晶行雲浮日光。
雷聲忽送千峰雨，
花氣渾如百和香。
黃鶯過水翻迴去，
燕子啣泥濕不妨。
飛閣捲簾圖畫裏，
虛無祇少對瀟湘。

夜雨寄北

（唐）李商隱

君問歸期未有期，
巴山夜雨漲秋池。
何當共翦西窗燭，
卻話巴山夜雨時。

● 西陵峽

上三峽

（唐）李白

巫山夾青天，巴水流若茲。
巴水忽可盡，青天無到時。
三朝上黃牛，三暮行太遲。
三朝又三暮，不覺鬢成絲。

黃牛峽

（清）張問陶

好奇須過古巴東，
千水千川貌不同。
看到黃牛三峽盡，
可憐丘壑滿胸中。

過東灘入馬肺峽

（宋）陸游

船卜急灘如浪鷁，
人緣絕壁似飛猱。
口誇遠嶺青千峰，
心憶平波綠一篙。

扇子峽

（宋）陸游

不肯爬沙桂樹邊，
來嘗丁古向岩前。
巴東峽裏最初峽，
天下泉中第四泉。
嚙雪飲冰疑換骨，
掬球弄月可忘年。
清遊自笑何曾足，
疊鼓咚咚又解船。

初入峽有感

（唐）白居易

上有萬仞山，
下有千丈水。
蒼蒼兩崖間，
闊峽容一葦。

入崆嶺峽

（清）劉肇紳

峽壁千尋並，
羣峰一綫開。
江聲呼岸走，
山影壓船來。

初入峽山效孟東野

（南宋）范成大

峽山偪而峻，峽泉湍似琦。
峽草如氀毛，峽樹多樛枝。
峽禽惟杜鵑，血吻日夜啼。
峽馬類黃狗，不能長鳴嘶。
峽曉虎跡多，峽暮人跡稀。
峽路如登天，猿鶴不敢梯。
僕夫負嵎哭，我亦呻吟悲。
悲吟不成章，聊廣峽哀詩。

過黃牛峽

（唐）張蠙

黃牛來勢瀉巴川，
疊日孤舟逐峽前。
雷電夜驚猿落樹，
波濤愁恐客離船。
盤渦逆入嵌空地，
斷壁高分繚繞天。
多少人經過此去，
一生魂夢泊瀟瀸。

新灘

（宋）蘇軾

扁舟轉山曲，未至已先驚。
白浪橫江起，槎牙似雪城。
番番從高來，一一投澗坑。
大魚不能上，暴腮灘下橫。
小魚散復合，瀺灂如遭烹。
鸕鶿不敢下，飛過兩翅輕。
白鷺誇瘦捷，插腳還欹傾。
區區舟上人，薄技安敢呈。
祇應灘頭廟，賴此牛酒盈。

竹枝歌

（明）揚升庵

無義灘頭風浪收，
黃牛開處見黃牛。
白波一道青峰裏，
聽盡猿聲是峽州。

長江沿綫風光名勝

　　遊覽完雄奇秀美的三峽，人們還可從此出發，飽覽大江上下的無限風光。從夔峽溯江而上，可目睹石寶寨、酆都鬼城、山城重慶的豐采。在西陵峽順江而下，可觀賞荊州古城，湖南的岳陽樓，武漢的黃鶴樓，九江的廬山，彭澤小孤山，安徽的九華山、黃山，南京的中山陵、鎮江塔，南通的狼山和上海市容、浦江風光。

SCENIC BEAUTIES
ALONG THE YANGTZE

　　Having cruised through the magnificent and beautiful Yangtze Gorges, you can start a new sightseeing tour to enjoy the beautiful landscape along the river. Sailing upstream from Kui Gorge, you will admire the Shibaozhai Village, the Fengdu Ghost City, and Chongqing, the mountainside city; floating downstream from Xiling Gorge, you will be able to see the ancient city of Jingzhou, the Yueyang Tower in Hunan, the Huanghe (Yellow Crane) Tower in Wuhan, Mt. Lushan in Jiujiang, the Xiaogushan Island in Pengze, Mt. Jiuhua in Anhui, the Sun Yetsen Mausoleum and the Zhenjiang Tower in Nanjing, Mt. Langshan in Nantong, etc., and to go sightseeing in Shanghai and on the Huangpu River.

瞿塘峽 Qutang Gorge

巫峽 Wu Gorge

西陵峽 Xiling Gorge

奉節 Fengjie

萬縣 Wanxian

巴東 Badong

宜昌 Yichang

酆都 Fengdu

重慶 Chongqing

洞庭湖 Lake Dongt

▲重庆之夜 Night Scene in Chongqing

▲鬼城 Ghost City　　　　　▲石宝寨 Shibaozhai　　　　　▲岳阳楼 Yueyang Tower

▲黄鹤楼 Yellow Crane Tower

南京
Nanjing

上海
Shanghai

蕪湖
Wuhu

太湖
Lake Taihu

安慶
Anqing

武漢
Wuhan

九江　鄱陽湖
Jiujiang　Lake Poyang

▲上海市　Shanghai

▲黄山　Mt. Huangshan

▲南京中山陵　Sun Yetsen Mausoleum in Nanjing

長 江 三 峽

THE THREE GORGES ON
THE YANGTZE RIVER

*

出版/海風出版社

Published by Haifeng Publishing House

製版印刷/福建彩色印刷有限公司

Printed by Fujian Colour Printing Co. Ltd.

開本/21×28.5 1/16

Format: 21X28.5 1/16

1994年5月第一版第一次印刷

The First Impression of the First Edition May. 1994

ISBN 7—80597—050—5/J·25

00050   00080

Contents

Acknowledgements   iv
Dedication   v
Guidance Web notes   vi

Core units

Unit 1 Introduction to business activity   **1**
1.1 Business activities   2
1.2 Classification of business activities   25
1.3 Resources, aims and objectives   41
1.4 Management processes   54

Unit 2 Introduction to exploring business pressures   **93**
2.1 Customer expectations   94
2.2 Competitive pressures   123
2.3 Stakeholder expectations   142
2.4 External influences   169

Unit 3 Investigating financial control   **199**
3.1 Profit and break even   200
3.2 Cash flow management   221
3.3 Budgets for planning and monitoring expenditure   236
3.4 Recording transactions   250

Specialist units

Unit 5 Employee contribution to working conditions   **269**
5.1 Terms of employment contracts   269
5.2 Recruitment and staff development   284
5.3 Industrial relations   293
5.4 Adaptability to change   302

Unit 7 Sales and customer service   **307**
7.1 Explore sales promotion techniques   307
7.2 Pre-sales preparation   322
7.3 Sales practice   341
7.4 After-sales service   348

Unit 8 Business online   **354**
8.1 Online business activity   354
8.2 The benefits of an online business presence   377
8.3 The potential disadvantages of an online business presence   391
8.4 Considering the business feasibility of going online   398

Index   **405**

> **Note to tutors**: The following additional specialist units can be found in the *BTEC First Business Tutor Resource File and CD-ROM* (ISBN 0435 40135 1):
>
> Unit 4 Business communication
>
> Unit 6 Business administration
>
> Unit 9 Starting up a new business

Acknowledgements

The authors would like to record their personal thanks and gratitude to all those friends, relatives and associates whose advice and expertise proved so invaluable in the writing of this book.

Particular mention must be made of the help given to us by Joanna McGowan, MA, BA (Hons), GIPD for – yet again – willingly sharing her expertise on human resources management and employment law; to Peter Nangle, MEd, for his guidance and good ideas on sales and sales promotions; to Susan Holden LLB for steering us safely through the complexities of consumer law; to Paul Carysforth, BA, for devoting considerable time and energy as our online business guru; to Matt Neild, B Eng, for his many useful suggestions and to Claire Mitchell, BA, for her email assistance just when it was needed! Thanks, too, to our indexing team – Matt, Paul and Caroline – who not only did the job accurately and quickly but also managed to give us a fun night at the same time!

Special thanks are also due to Richer Sounds management and colleagues for their ongoing support and for agreeing to an extension to the Richer Sounds StudentZone to link with the BTEC First Diploma scheme. Thanks are due to Julian Richer, the owner and founder of the business for his original vision and ideals; to David Robinson, MD, for his continued interest in and support for our work. Many Directors and colleagues in the company also deserve recognition and thanks for responding with cheerful good humour when we pester them for information and updates. They include: Jez Avens, Deputy MD and Store Operations Director, John Currier, Financial Director; John Clayton, Training Director; Tracey Armstrong, Colleague Support Manager; Claudia Vernon, Marketing Director; Dan Burnham, Marketing Manager; Darren Woodward, IT Manager; Perry Sillett, Repairs and Servicing Manager; Lee Lynane, Property Manager and Solomon Essah Essel, Distribution Director. Thanks are also due to Lee Nelson, Clive Lambert, Andrea Day, Lol Lecanu and James Donnan for their colleague profiles on the StudentZone. A special thanks are also due to Julie McCabe – David's PA – both for her colleague profile and for her help in coordinating all our requests.

As ever, thanks must go to all those at Heinemann without whom this book would still be a data file on our computer! In particular, thanks are due to Anna Fabrizio for her unenviable and valiant efforts to keep us simultaneously on track and problem free; to Camilla Thomas for her awe-inspiring efficiency and constant encouragement and to Gavin Fidler, for all his hard work in editing the book to very tight deadlines. Last, but by no means least, huge thanks also to Mick Watson, for putting the book into its final appley pie order with his usual panache, wit and skill!

The authors and publishers would also like to thank the following individuals and organisations for permission to reproduce photographs and other copyright material:

Amnesty International and CACI Ltd.

Amazon page 48; Apple page 6; Arnos Design pages 2, 12, 18, 109, 117, 124, 250, 334, 335, 350 and 384; Blockbusters page 51; CD Epos Systems page 65; Corbis cover and page 209; Cumulus/Eyewire page 57; Fairtrade page 106; Getty Images/Photodisc page 76, 103, 127, 154, 180 and 264; Getty page 359; Granada page 27; Harcourt Education page 309; Harcourt Education/Gareth Boden page 284; Hornby page 82; Photofusion pages 288 and 332; Renault (UK) pages 72 and 314; Renault/Antoine Bernier page 211; Rex Features pages 8, 28, 29, 31, 45, 46, 54, 134, 142, 148, 149, 156, 157, 163, 172, 178, 193, 272, 279, 307, 355, 363 and 370; Rex Features/Andrew Drysdale page 209; Sainsbury's page 338; Science Photo Library pages 32, 166 and 183; The Number page 131; The Royal National Institute for the Blind (RNID) page 67; Virgin page 43 and Wembley National Stadium page 241.

Every effort has been made to contact copyright holders of material reproduced in this book. Any omissions will be rectified in subsequent printings if notice is given to the publishers.

To the irrepressible Claire, and the love of her life, Jon.

May life together as Mr and Mrs Barnes include lots of love, luck and laughter and surpass even *your* wildest dreams!

Guidance web notes

Researching business organisations on the Internet and using the Richer Sounds StudentZone

Today the Internet is a major resource for all business studies students. You can use it to find out about specific aspects of businesses as you progress through the course. You will also find it invaluable if you decide to investigate a national business for one of your assessments.

There is, however, a skill to researching business organisations on the Internet, even for quite experienced Internet users. Given that you have a choice of about 4.8 billion sites (at Google's last count!) you may find it useful to read these notes to help you:

- Find the best sites for what you need.
- Find what you need within a site.

The sheer number of sites means that you are in danger of wasting time sifting through irrelevant information or getting despondent because you can't find what you need.

In addition, all students who use this book have access to The StudentZone on the Richer Sounds website. This has been specifically created to help you understand in more detail how the topics you learn apply to a real business. You will find out more about it on page viii.

Finding the sites you need on the Internet

There are two main ways in which you can research business organisations on the Internet.

1. You can go direct to the website of an organisation if you know its URL or web address, e.g. www.richersounds.com

   It will help you to recognise the correct website if you remember that the suffix varies depending upon the type of organisation and its location. The main ones are:

- .com is the suffix used by many large international or American businesses.
- .co.uk is the suffix used by many UK businesses. Some firms have *both* a .com *and* a .co.uk address – such as international car firms.
- .org.uk is the suffix used by charities and not-for-profit businesses.
- .gov.uk is used by many public sector organisations, such as government departments and local councils.
- .ac.uk is used by schools, colleges and universities in the UK.
- foreign businesses have different types of suffixes. Apart from America, which is an exception, these tell you the country, e.g. .au = Australia, .Za = South Africa.

Knowing these suffixes can help you because you can often guess the website address without using a search engine at all. For example, if you know charities use .org.uk then it is worth trying www.nspcc.org.uk if you want to find out about the NSPCC. In this case, your guess would be right!

2. You can use a good search engine, such as www.google.co.uk to help you to find the URL of a business or to suggest appropriate businesses. If you use Google, then you may find the following tips useful.

- You are usually better to use www.google.co.uk rather than www.google.com (the international site). On the UK site you have the option of searching the whole web or just UK sites. If you are trying to find a UK company, then you should choose 'pages from the UK'. If you are trying to find a European or international company then click 'the web' option.
- Search engines work by looking for key words in relevant sites. Therefore you need to enter these key words for the correct or best ones to be listed somewhere near the top.

- If the business is well known and you know the name (e.g. Oxfam) then type 'Oxfam website'. This should then be the top entry on the list you see.
- If you wanted to read articles about Oxfam as well, then just type 'Oxfam'. Then skim down the list you see and read each abbreviated entry before clicking on those which look useful. If you want to know about a specific issue then put this in too, as it will narrow down the choice you are offered, e.g. Oxfam and Ethiopia.
- If the company has a common name then try to give Google as much information as possible. For example, there is a Business matters about Pilkington Glass on page 7. Just entering 'Pilkington' would give many other hits. Entering 'Pilkington Glass' is better and putting in 'Pilkington Glass website' will narrow the search even further and should give you the company's site first.
- If you are searching for businesses that undertake a specific activity, again try to give as much information as possible. For example, if you wanted to find a list of charities which help the homeless then putting in 'homeless charity' is better than just 'charity'.

- On the list of sites suggested by a search engine you can click on the top line or you can click on the word (Cached) after the summary. The difference is that the top line takes you to the current site, the 'cached' link takes you to an older saved version of the site that contains the term you wanted. Use this if you click on a link and then can't work out the relationship between the page you get and the item you are seeking!
- Enter 'Search Help' into Google and spend a few minutes reading about how it looks for words and phrases. Then click Advanced Search to find out even more – such as the benefits of adding '+' or '-' to a search – or putting double quotes around an exact phrase or name you want, e.g. "First National Bank".
- If you are checking a recent event, don't forget that Google has a News tab in addition to its Web tab. Whichever search engine you use, it pays to know all the options available and how to find your way around it.
- If you would find further hints and tips useful, then turn to Unit 8, page 361, which explains about researching on the Internet and gives you additional links to sites that will help you.

Within a site – finding what you need

Business websites are designed in different ways, but the first, introductory page of any site is normally called the **home page**. You will then see options to access other pages, which may be across the top, down one side (or both) or along the bottom of the web page.

The first test is your reading skills! Scan through all the options. Generally, the information you require will *not* be located in the same place as customer information, particularly on retail sites – and may be hidden away right at the bottom of the page! Headings to look for are:

- About us.
- Investor relations.
- Corporate information.

In these sections you are likely to find out about the history of the company, its directors or managers, the way it is organised, its current plans and, if it is a public company or large charity, its accounts.

If you look through all the headings and can't find anything you recognise at all, see if there is a link to the **site map**. This will often be organised alphabetically, so you can see all the topics covered on the website and click on those which are relevant.

You may also find useful updates about the company in their press releases, if these are held on the site.

Two further points to be aware of:

- Information in booklets and in annual reports is likely to be stored in PDF format. To download this you need Adobe Acrobat installed on your computer. If the document is very long then printing it out may not be an option if you have to pay for every page you print. Instead, read it through on screen and then select the more relevant pages to print, which is cheaper. Another alternative is to save the file and then see if your tutor will print it out for you.

- With the exception of the Richer Sounds StudentZone (see opposite), the information on company websites is normally written for customers or investors – not for students! This means that there may be many references you do not understand or need. If you are interested in a page and read unfamiliar words, it is sensible to ask your tutor what they mean. That's how you learn! Another technique is to do what you did automatically when you were younger. Read the item to get the overall sense and meaning without worrying too much about the details. You can normally tell whether a business is reporting a successful or disastrous year without understanding every single word. And some businesses produce clearer reports and descriptions than others – just like students!

Finally, you do not need to worry whether any Internet link in this book is suitable or even still accessible. The Heinemann hotlinks service continually checks all the sites listed to ensure they are correct and still online – which is why you should use that link, when it is provided, rather than try to access the site direct.

The Richer Sounds StudentZone

Because you are using this book to help you achieve your BTEC First Diploma in Business qualification, you have special access to the Richer Sounds StudentZone. Richer Sounds is a national retailer selling hi-fi separates and related equipment, such as DVD and mini-disc players as well as plasma screens and home cinema equipment. Julian Richer started his first store at the age of 19 – because he wanted to run his own business. Today there are 48 Richer Sounds stores in the UK and 2 in Ireland and Julian is worth over £40 million! One of his aims is to 'keep the fun' as he runs his business. He has been very successful at doing this. In both 2002 and 2003 Richer Sounds was listed as the top British-owned company in the official list of the UK's 100 Best Companies to Work For.

You can find out how Julian's business operates today by entering the Richer Sounds website at www.richersounds.com and clicking on the StudentZone. Or you can go direct to the site at www.richerstudentzone.co.uk. You will then be prompted to enter the password. This is RICHERLEARNING (upper case, no spaces).

The site is divided into two parts, one for students taking the BTEC First Diploma in Business and one for students taking GCSE Applied Business. Click on the first option and you will see a series of menus which allow you to find out detailed information about Richer Sounds relevant to Units 1, 2 and 3 of this award, and many of the specialist units, too. You may find this invaluable as you prepare for many of your assessments, where you have to provide information relevant to a business organisation of your choice.

This information is updated every summer so, no matter when you are taking your award, you can find the details you need, as and when you need them.

Unit 1 Introduction to business activity

Every day, all over the world, millions of organisations are involved in business activities. Some are small firms or shops, such as those in your own neighbourhood. Others are large companies that may operate across a region, a country, or even trade all over the world.

These businesses may be involved in producing or selling goods – from ice creams to jumbo jets. Others provide a service to their customers, such as local cab drivers or travel agents. Some businesses do both – such as computer stores that also offer a maintenance and advice service to their customers.

As a customer yourself, you are already involved in the business world. Every time you send a text message, buy a CD or have your hair cut you are helping a business to achieve its goals, which normally involve tempting customers to buy their goods or services. All businesses have goals they aim to achieve. Most businesses must make a profit to survive. This means that they have to earn more than they spend. Some, however, don't do this. They may provide goods or services free of charge to users, such as your local hospital and voluntary organisations like the Samaritans.

All businesses carefully plan what they want to achieve and decide how they can best use their resources (such as people, equipment and finance) to be successful. They must check their progress regularly, so that they can take prompt action if there are any problems. This is one of the most important tasks of managers in all organisations. If you have a part-time job, you will know about the type of tasks managers want you and other staff to carry out. In this unit you will learn about the reasons for some of their requests.

All these aspects of business are the focus of this unit. The information you learn will help you to build on your existing knowledge of business, both as a customer and, if you work, as an employee. It also gives you a sound basis for moving on to the other units in which you will cover some of these topics in more depth.

This unit is assessed through an Integrated Vocational Assignment (IVA) set by Edexcel.

In summary

This unit is divided into four sections:

1.1 Business activities. Here you will learn about the different types of businesses which exist, their activities and main goals.

1.2 Classification of business activities. This section tells you how businesses in Britain are classified, or grouped, according to their main activity, and which types of activity are increasing and decreasing today.

1.3 Resources, aims and objectives. In this section you will find out about the type of resources required and how businesses use these to achieve their aims and objectives.

1.4 Management processes. The final section tells you how businesses are organised and managed to help achieve their planned aims and objectives.

This section covers

The activities of business

Key business goals

Different business sectors

The size and scale of business organisations

What are business activities?

All businesses exist for a purpose. In other words, they all *do* something – and have a reason for doing it. They may produce or supply goods or offer a service to their customers. For example, Ford produces cars and Walkers produces crisps. Retailers such as Debenhams, Matalan and Richer Sounds supply goods made by other organisations. Solicitors provide legal services both to businesses and individuals, and banks provide financial services.

Businesses are all around us everywhere we go

Many businesses produce or supply *both* goods and services.

- Heinemann produces books, such as this one, stocks them in its warehouse and supplies them to its customers. Its representatives and customer services staff also give information and advice to schools and colleges.
- Tesco supplies a wide range of goods and sells them both in its stores and online. It also offers financial services, such as its own credit card, personal loans and various types of insurance. It operates a loyalty scheme to reward its regular customers with vouchers and discounts and provides a home delivery service for online shoppers.
- Boots Healthcare International manufactures and distributes branded products such as Strepsils and Nurofen whilst its main division, Boots the Chemist, sells health, beauty and toiletry goods as well as services such as photo processing.
- Dell produces computers and sells them online. It also offers an after-sales service to its customers. Its website enables customers to track their purchases from dispatch to delivery. Customers are also regularly sent brochures on new products, to tempt them to buy again.
- Richer Sounds sells goods in its shops but also services and repairs equipment. You can find out more on the Richer Sounds StudentZone at www.richerstudentzone.co.uk

Small businesses, too, may undertake more than one activity. Your local garage may sell and service cars as well. Your local hairdresser may sell hair and beauty products as well as cutting and styling hair. Firms do this to encourage customer loyalty and to increase their profits.

Which activity is the most important?

Although businesses may undertake several activities, the **core business activity** is the one which is the most important for the business and usually generates the largest amount of income. As you will see in section 1.2, businesses are classified by their main activity. If demand is falling in one area, businesses may change or adjust their activities. They may choose to **diversify** or to do just the opposite, and **specialise** in what they are good at.

- Boots diversified to make its stores more interesting and different. It introduced its Wellbeing services (such as reflexology, aromatherapy, dentistry, chiropody and optician service), opened Pure Beauty stores, and started Boots for Men shops. Not all of these ideas proved successful and most are now closed. Only dentistry, chiropody, opticians and laser eye surgery clinics remain.
- EasyJet owner, Stelios Haji-Ioannou has expanded his empire with easyCar, to provide car rentals; easyInternetcafe; easyMoney, which provides loans and credit cards; and easy.com, a free email service. His latest ventures are easyCinema, a discount cinema chain, easyDorm, to provide cheap hotels, easyCruise, an easyBus minibus service and easyPizza. Whether all his ventures will be successful is not yet known!
- Tesco not only sells food, clothes and financial products in its stores and online but has diversified into selling DVDs, plasma televisions and mobile phones. In 2003, it announced plans to offer an online travel service and to provide a new retail telecommunication service.
- Many farmers who struggled to keep their

businesses going after the foot and mouth crisis in 2001 have changed direction altogether. Some have set up touring caravan parks on their land, diversified into offering quadbiking and paintballing, or converted their barns into self-catering holiday cottages.

Business terms

Diversification Extending the number and types of activities undertaken by the business. This can help to spread the risk because, if one area of the business is struggling, the other areas may still be profitable. This means the business, as a whole, is not at risk.

Specialisation Reducing the number and types of activities undertaken by the business, usually because some are making a loss or because the costs of a particular activity are too high.

What price to charge?

Most businesses charge us, as customers, for buying or using their products or services. This is because, to stay in business, the organisation must make a profit. You will learn more about profit on pages 5 and 6.

For various reasons, however, some businesses may offer their goods and services free, or for less than the normal selling price. In some cases, the whole organisation may focus upon undertaking activities which result in free, or below cost, services for users, as you will see on page 8. You will find out more about how businesses charge for their activities in the next section.

Business matters

Most people are familiar with sellers of *The Big Issue*. This magazine is produced by professional journalists and sold by homeless people to enable them to earn money legally. The price of the magazine is deliberately kept low, to encourage people to buy it and support the cause. Businesses who advertise in the magazine, however, pay commercial rates, although the exact charge varies depending upon the region and size/type of advert. Services provided by *The Big Issue* to the homeless are free, such as education, training and housing advice, because

this is the core work of the charity – and is funded by various means, including donations.

Broadly speaking, all charities have two main types of activities – they raise money and deliver a service. However, the range of activities they carry out must be linked to their main purpose. Therefore *The Big Issue* carries out activities related to producing and publishing its magazine, training its sellers and helping the homeless. You can find out more on *The Big Issue* website; a link to this site is available at www.heinemann.co.uk/hotlinks (express code 1386P).

Over to you!

Before you start the first question, make sure you have read, and understand, the Guidance notes for researching business organisations on the Internet on page vi. Check with your tutor if there are any terms in these notes that you do not understand. Links to the websites mentioned below are available at www.heinemann.co.uk/hotlinks (express code 1386P).

1 a Copy out the table below and tick the correct column according to whether the business is mainly involved in selling goods, providing a service or both.

   b Add the names of three businesses you know or use regularly and tick the correct column for these, too. Then compare your suggestions with those of other members in your class.

Business	Sells goods	Provides a service	Provides both goods and services
Argos			
easyJet			
BT			
Pizza Express			
Blockbuster			

2 Look back at the list of activities that Tesco undertakes on page 3.

   a Explain how each activity helps Tesco make a profit.

   b What might happen to Tesco's profits if *any* one of these activities was not carried out.

   c Investigate the Tesco website and see if you can find any more activities the business undertakes. Find out, too, about their Debut scheme for students who work with them. If any of your group works at Tesco, find out if they are members and what the benefits are.

3 Manchester United Football Club is unusual. Its core business activity does not bring in the most money. Investigate its website and answer the following questions. Note: you will find out more information if you also look under the Investor Relations, Financial Data section of the website.

   a What is the core business activity of Manchester United?

   b Which other activities earn revenue for the club?

   c How much profit (before tax) did it make last year?

   d What was the value of its sales last year? To find this, look for the word **turnover**.

   e Identify the **three** key activity areas into which Manchester United sub-divides its turnover.

      i Decide how the activities you have already identified fit into each of these key areas.

      ii Identify the percentage of income earned by each one and find out if Manchester United is still not earning the most money from its core activity.

> **View 1:** The Big Issue does a wonderful job for homeless people, and other charities provide essential services such as cancer research and helping when there are worldwide disasters.

> **View 2:** Charities shouldn't be necessary. It should be the government's job to sort out homelessness, pay for cancer research and help the starving in third world countries. Individuals should not have to donate to good causes.

With which viewpoint do you agree – and why?

What are business goals?

All businesses have goals or aims. The key goals are the main targets the business wants to achieve.

- All privately owned businesses will have a main goal of making a **profit**. This is very important because without a profit the business will not survive. Making a profit means that the money received from sales is greater than the costs of buying the stock (for resale) or the raw materials (for production) and running the business.
- Some organisations provide goods or services free of charge or at a very reduced price. This may be a free or special offer, to tempt customers to buy other items. Many companies produce free brochures that advertise their goods and services, such as product catalogues issued by Argos, Ikea and Richer Sounds or free magazines like those published by Boots, British Airways, Marks & Spencer and Virgin Trains.
- Alternatively, the services themselves may be free because the business does not operate to make a profit, such as charitable organisations and your local council – which provides many services for the community. The goals of these businesses will be linked to the services they provide.
- Many businesses set goals related to **improving their performance**. This helps

them to increase their profits if they are privately owned, or to increase the range of services they can offer to the needy or the local community.

You will find that successful businesses undertake activities that will help them to achieve their goals.

Business matters

If you went on holiday to Tenerife, Lanzarote or the Costa del Sol in summer 2003, you might have been treated to a free personal radio! The radios were being given away, many as part of competitions, to establish a base for Holiday FM. This is a new, English speaking radio station for Brits abroad which has been launched in conjunction with Capital Radio.

Holiday FM needs to demonstrate that many of the 36 million UK foreign holidaymakers are listening in to them to tempt advertisers, whose revenue is essential for the success of the station – hence the giveaways. You can find out more – and even listen to the station – at their website. A link to this site is available at www.heinemann.co.uk/hotlinks (express code 1386P).

Business terms

Profit Making a profit means that the revenue (money) received is greater than the costs of buying the stock and running the business. Profit is calculated by deducting all the costs from the sales revenue.

Costs The money spent on buying stock and/or producing goods and running the business, e.g. paying wages, rent, electricity etc.

Revenue Income received by the business. This is usually from sales to customers or from donations in the case of a charity. Sometimes, as in the case of Holiday FM, it may come from other sources, too.

Turnover The value of sales each year. You will sometimes see it written as 'sales turnover'. Don't confuse turnover and profit! Turnover may be very high, but profits could still be low or non-existent if the costs are too high.

More about goals and profit

All privately owned businesses have the goal of making a profit. This means that they have to provide goods or services which customers want, and sell these at a price that customers are willing to pay. They must also receive more money from their total sales than it costs to provide the goods and run the business.

Profit is the owner's reward for taking the risks of running the business. If you owned a business then the profit is the amount you can keep, or reinvest in the business each year. This is essential if both you and your business are going to survive.

Privately owned businesses often set goals linked to increasing profit such as:

- **Maximising sales**, which means to sell as much as possible. One way to do this could be to sell goods over the Internet as well as in stores, or the business could focus on improving the design or quality of their products to beat their competitors. Another method is to reduce the prices of some goods. Supermarkets often have 'price wars' to win customers from their competitors. However, lower prices *must* result in overall increased sales or the profits will actually fall!
- **Reducing costs**, so that the costs of supplying the goods and running the business are lower. This means there are fewer deductions from the sales revenue when the profit is calculated. Costs are lower if fewer

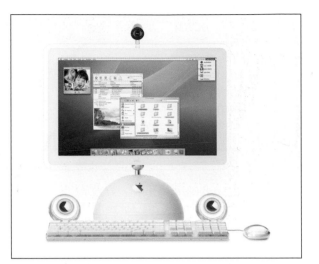

The launch of the iMac was a great success for Apple

staff are employed or the business moves to cheaper premises.

- **Increasing productivity**, so that more goods are produced or sold by the same people in the same time. If packer A works twice as quickly as packer B, then packer A is more productive and makes more money for the company. Ideally, everyone will work as fast as packer A so that the goods can be produced as efficiently as possible. Businesses may introduce a bonus system to reward staff who work quickly or automate some processes so that the work is carried out by machines, rather than people. They will also replace machines with new ones which operate more quickly, for the same reason.

Business brief

Calculating profit

Profit is calculated as:

Revenue from sales minus the cost of production and supply

This rule applies to all businesses, no matter what their size. A market trader, for example, will sell goods at a price to cover the purchase price *plus* the other costs associated with the business; such as the stall rental, the costs of a vehicle to transport the goods and the income they need to earn. The trader must, however, be aware of the prices charged by local competitors. If they are greedy, and try to charge too much for the same product, sales will fall. So deciding the right price

to charge is never easy. It can be even harder for a large business which has many other costs to cover – particularly if there is strong competition or if the demand from customers is difficult to forecast.

A drop in sales or a rise in costs will reduce profit. Computers help managers to forecast profit by summarising current sales and costs, often on a daily basis. This means that immediate action can be taken if there is likely to be a problem.

Business matters

Pilkington is the world's second largest glass maker. In 1957, it invented the float glass process, which boosted its profits because it could sell licenses to manufacturers all over the world to use this new process. Critics say the business then became complacent. It failed to notice its competitors or take any other actions to keep the business profitable. It employed too many people, operated too many factories and its costs were too high. By the 1990s, sales had halved and profits had fallen dramatically.

Pilkington supplies glass for cars, buildings and aeroplanes but it could do little to boost the demand for glass worldwide and it couldn't increase its prices because this would mean it couldn't compete against other glass manufacturers. Instead, therefore, it changed the way it operated. In 1997 it introduced its Step Change restructuring programme. Since then it has cut about 14,000 jobs, improved productivity, and closed loss-making factories. It has also introduced Pilkington Activ – the world's first self-cleaning glass.

These actions have resulted in five consecutive years of improved profits. You can find out more by going on the Pilkington website – a link to this site is available at www.heinemann.co.uk/hotlinks (express code 1386P).

Over to you!

1 People set goals as well as businesses! They often do this at the start of a New Year – and call them 'resolutions'.
  a Suggest **three** goals you could set for yourself related to improving your own performance.
  b Identify **two** activities you would carry out, for each goal, to help to achieve it.

2 a Kate owns a florist shop. She buys her flowers fresh each day from the wholesale market early in the morning. She displays the flowers attractively just outside the shop to attract passing trade. She also advertises her business locally, so that everyone knows she can do displays for special events, such as weddings. She delivers flowers and will set up displays at special venues. In the shop she also sells greeting cards, dried displays and a small range of vases and flower holders. She will gift wrap any items free of charge.
    i Does Kate need to make a profit? Give a reason for your answer.
    ii State the main activity of Kate's business.
    iii Identify at least **five** further activities she undertakes to help her achieve her business goals.
    iv As a group, suggest **one** further business goal that Kate might have.
  b Identify **one** business in your own locality or neighbourhood which must make a profit to survive. Suggest **three** activities it carries out to achieve this goal.

    Compare your ideas with those of other students in your group.

3 Your friend's parents own a sandwich shop near the college.
  a State how they will calculate their profits each year.
  b Explain why making a profit is so important to them.
  c If their profits are too low, suggest two ways in which they could improve this.
  d If they increased the price of their sandwiches to increase their overall sales revenue, suggest one disadvantage this could have.
  e If their sales revenue was £20,000 last year and their costs were £12,000, what would be their profit?
  f If their sales revenue stayed the same but they reduced their costs to £10,000, how would this affect their profit?

View 1: *If a business wants to maximise sales this is good thing for consumers because the prices are low and the service is good.*

View 2: *Maximising sales causes problems because consumers may be persuaded to buy things they don't want or can't really afford.*

With which viewpoint do you agree with – and why?

Emergency services are provided free of charge

Other goals linked to supplying services

The government and your local authority provide a range of essential services to the whole population. These include health care, education, crime prevention and detection, social services and refuse collection. These are considered necessary for everyone, regardless of income or wealth.

Voluntary or charitable organisations operate to promote a particular cause or meet a special need. They will target their services at this area. For example, the NSPCC helps children in need whereas the RSPCA helps animals.

Both these types of organisations may therefore set goals to:

- Supply certain goods or services **free of charge**. Examples include museums and art galleries which don't charge an entrance fee and the police, ambulance and fire service which provide essential services in the cases of accidents and emergencies. Your local council will provide refuse collection, social services and education for young people without charge, because these are also essential. If there is a major crisis in the world, such as an earthquake or famine, voluntary organisations like Oxfam and Save the Children will provide medical assistance and essential supplies immediately. These will always be free of charge to the users, regardless of the actual cost.

- Supply certain goods or services **to a certain level**. This restricts the number or type of people who can use them. For example, government benefits, such as child credit and job seeker's allowance are only given to people who qualify against strict criteria. Otherwise the cost of providing them would be too high.
- Charge a price which is **below the cost price**. Examples are NHS prescriptions for expensive drugs, bus passes for school children and extra refuse bins. Here the difference between the amount charged and the true cost is **subsidised** by the government or local council.
- Charge a price which is **the same as the cost price**. In this case the organisation decides to recover the cost without making a profit. A local drama club, for example, may set a ticket price which just covers the cost of a production. The price will be low to attract customers and this is possible because all the members in a drama group are volunteers and don't receive a salary. This is different from a commercial theatre or cinema group which has to pay wages and also aims to make a profit.

Goals to improve business performance

Many organisations set goals linked to their business performance. They set targets for performance and then check regularly if they have achieved these.

- Privately owned businesses will measure their performance by checking their sales, costs and final profit figure. They will obviously want sales to increase to boost their profits. This may mean developing new products or services, selling them to new groups of consumers, or adapting their activities to help them achieve these goals. For example, a retailer such as Next or Matalan may have a goal to sell more goods. To achieve this, it may open more stores, introduce a delivery service, sell goods from its website or change its stock lines to make sure it always stocks what customers want. It will also aim to give customers an excellent service, so that they return again and again.
- Schools, colleges and universities want to improve their position in league tables, which depends upon examination results. Your college will aim to improve its performance by offering a wide range of courses, attracting more students, retaining them and helping them to succeed.
- Charities often set goals to increase the amount of money raised through donations. This gives them more money to spend and helps them to achieve other goals related to increasing the number or type of services they offer.

Business brief

Who pays for free services?

Many services are available to everyone either free, or at a reduced charge. You can borrow books from your local library, report lost or stolen property to the police and visit many museums and art galleries – without paying a penny. If you have a serious personal problem you can ring the Samaritans for advice; if you knew someone who was homeless you could tell them to contact several organisations for help, such as Shelter or Crisis.

So where does the money come from to provide these services?

- All public services are funded through **tax**. The most well-known is income tax, which is paid by everyone who works and earns more than a basic, tax-free amount. Businesses pay tax, called corporation tax, on their profits. VAT is another type of tax, which we all pay when we buy many goods and services. All these taxes are collected by the government and used to pay for national services such as education, social services and health care. Locally, all householders pay council tax and all businesses pay business rates. This money contributes towards paying for local services such as libraries and refuse collection.
- Voluntary services are funded through **donations**. All charitable organisations work hard at fund-raising, trying to raise as much money as possible each year. All the surplus money, after administration charges have been paid, must be spent on the purpose for which the charity was formed.

This means that these organisations can set goals which are not related to making a profit. Overall, though, they must balance their income and expenditure and must not spend money they do not possess!

Talking point

View 1: *If people want good public services, such as health and education, they must be prepared to pay more tax.*

View 2: *If tax rates increase, this puts people off working harder or longer, because they will simply pay more. Instead, those who have money should have to pay for their own health care and education.*

With which viewpoint do you agree – and why?

Business matters

Many business organisations have a mission statement. This is useful because it tells you the main purpose of the business and, sometimes, the main goals it aims to achieve. For example, the mission statement for Greenpeace states that:

'Greenpeace is an independent non-profit global campaigning organisation that uses non-violent creative confrontation to expose global environmental problems and their causes. We research the solutions and alternatives to help provide a path for a green and peaceful future.

Greenpeace's goal is to ensure the ability of the earth to nurture life in all its diversity.'

From this, you should be able to tell that Greenpeace doesn't aim to make a profit and operates all over the world.

In contrast, the mission statement of a privately owned business will usually mention customers, employees and, sometimes, costs or profit. For example, the Sainsbury's mission statement says that:

Our mission is to be the consumer's first choice for food, delivering products of outstanding quality and great service at a competitive cost through working 'faster, simpler and together'.

Over to you!

1 As a group, decide whether each of the following goods or services is likely to be provided:
- Free of charge.
- For sale below cost.
- For sale at cost price.
- At a profit.

In each case, give a reason for your answer and then discuss your ideas with your tutor.
a A new computer from a retail store.
b Meals on wheels for the elderly.
c A passport.
d Tourist information leaflets.
e A driving test (theory and practical).
f An evening foreign language course at your college.
g Membership of your local community sports centre.
h Membership of a private gym.
i Planning applications for householders to change or extend their homes.

2 Working in a small group, investigate **one** of the following organisations. Identify its main goal and then identify the activities that it carries out to help it to achieve these goals. Links to websites are available at www.heinemann.co.uk/hotlinks (express code 1386P).

Compare your answers with those of other groups to compile a list of the type of goals and activities you are likely to find in these kinds of organisations.
a Your local council. You can find out its website address by using a good search engine such as Google and then entering the title of your council.
b Your local NHS trust or primary care trust. The trust is the organisation that oversees all the hospitals in your area. You can find this through going to the NHS website and then clicking on 'local services search' and then 'NHS organisations.'
c The Advertising Standards Authority.
d The Samaritans.
e The Environment Agency.
f Trading Standards.

3 Decide **one** goal that each of the following businesses may have in relation to improving its performance, then suggest how each could measure its success. Compare your ideas with other members of the class.
a A doctor's surgery.
b A bus company.
c A superstore.

d A restaurant.

e The Royal Mail.

f The fire service.

4 Obtain a copy of your college's mission statement and use this to answer the following questions.

a What is the main purpose of the organisation?

b From your knowledge of the activities it carries out, and through discussions with your tutor, suggest how its activities help it to achieve its main goal.

5 Compare the mission statements of the following organisations by finding each one on their website. Links to the websites are available at www.heinemann.co.uk/hotlinks (express code 1386P). From your investigations, identify the main activity of each business and at least **one** of its goals.

a Lancashire Labels and Print.

b Easy Internet Café.

c iVillage UK.

d Red Carnation Hotels.

e HTS Malvern Ltd.

f Cancer Research UK.

g Interactive Office Systems.

h Queen's Park Rangers Football Club.

What are business sectors?

Every type of business belongs to a business sector. There are **three** main business sectors and you will find that the goals of businesses vary according to the sector they are in.

Knowing about business sectors will help you to realise why there may be considerable differences between the activities carried out by different organisations, even within the same sector. It will also help you to understand more about the differences in size and scale of many businesses when you reach the next section on page 17.

	Private sector	Public sector	Voluntary/not-for-profit sector
Types of businesses	Businesses owned and controlled by private individuals	Businesses owned or controlled by the government	Mainly charitable and voluntary organisations
Examples	Shops and stores of all sizes, builders, manufacturers and suppliers, such as Barratt Homes, Toyota and Fedex	All government departments Local authorities The BBC The Royal Mail Group	Oxfam Friends of the Earth Canal Preservation Society Amnesty International
Key goal	To make a profit	To provide a range of services either free or below cost	To raise money to provide free goods and services for the needy
Additional goal To improve the overall performance of the business			

Figure 1.1 *Business sectors*

The private sector

The private sector includes very small businesses, such as your local greengrocer or corner shop, and very large ones, such as PC World or BP, which operate on a national or global basis.

- **A sole trader** is the name for the smallest type of business. It is owned by one person, even though there may be several employees. A sole trader is personally responsible for every aspect of the business, from keeping the premises clean to doing the accounts and paying the tax due on the profits. Examples include plumbers, decorators, hairdressers and some local retailers. The sole trader can keep all the profit each year, after paying tax.
- **A partnership** is owned and run by two or more people. The partners are then jointly responsible for running the business. Most partnerships are small, such as local accountants, solicitors and doctors. However, a few larger organisations are run on the basis that the employees become partners when they join the company. The largest partnership in Britain is the John Lewis Partnership, where all 59,000 staff who work for John Lewis and Waitrose supermarkets are classed as partners and receive a share of the profits as a bonus each year.

- **A private limited company** is easily identified because its name always ends with the abbreviation 'Ltd'. The owners each own a share of the business and are therefore known as shareholders. If the company is successful the shareholders will receive a financial reward in the form of **dividends**. Many private companies are family businesses where the owners have two roles. As well as being shareholders they are also directors and run the company.

- **A public limited company** is the largest type of business. These companies end their name with the letters 'plc.' The shares are usually traded on the Stock Exchange and can be owned by members of the public and institutional investors, such as large banks or insurance companies. The directors are paid a salary to run the company and may, or may not, own shares. Selling shares to the public means that this type of company can raise large amounts of money to expand or develop the enterprise.

Two variations on these types of businesses are:
- **Franchises**, where a small business is started using the name of a larger organisation. The owner of the small business (the franchisee) pays the larger company (the franchisor) a share of the profit and a fee to use the name. In return, he or she is given help and support to run the business. Examples of franchise businesses include Prontoprint, Kentucky Fried Chicken, The Body Shop and Benetton.
- **Workers' cooperatives**, where the business is jointly owned and run by the workers. All the profits are shared and the owners make joint decisions about how the business should be run. Workers' cooperatives in Britain are normally quite small, unlike the CRS – the Cooperative Retail Society – which is owned by its customers and operates all over the country.

John Lewis is the largest partnership in Britain

Why form a company?

A company is a business organisation which is registered at Companies House. A private company may still be very small and be set up by one person, who chooses to do this rather than operate as a sole trader because of the benefits of operating in this way.

- Banks and other financial institutions are normally more willing to lend money to companies than to individuals or partners who run a business, and large suppliers prefer to deal with companies rather than private individuals.
- If the business fails, then the owners only lose the amount they invested in the business. This is known as **limited liability**. A sole trader or partnership, however, normally has **unlimited liability**. This means they have to repay all their debts, even if they have to sell their personal possessions to do so. If they cannot do this, they are declared **bankrupt**. A business which buys expensive stock, such as a jeweller, or one which could have serious problems if a key customer fails to make a payment, is therefore far more likely to operate as a company.
- There are fewer problems if one of the owners leaves the business. This is because the company has a separate legal identity and would still continue until it was officially 'wound up'.

You will find out more about the differences between sole traders, partnerships and companies if you study specialist Unit 9.

Private companies can convert to being a public limited company. The correct term for this is **floating** the company. Yell, the telephone directories business, floated on the London Stock Exchange in 2003. A total of £1.3 billion was raised and the company was valued at more than £2 billion.

Yell's owner, John Condron, who built up the business after it was sold by BT in 2001, made more than £5 million on the deal by cashing in some – but not all – of his shares. The two businesses that had backed him financially made a profit of £800 million on their investment in less than three years.

You can see how much Yell shares are worth today by looking in the financial pages of most newspapers, and can find out more about the business by reading About Yell on their website. A link to this site is available at www.heinemann.co.uk/hotlinks (express code 1386P).

The public sector

The public sector relates to all the departments and enterprises owned or controlled by the state. The state, of course, is basically the same as the government, so all government departments and organisations funded by the government (such as Jobcentres, most schools and colleges, and the army) are also classed as being in the public sector.

Organisations in the public sector can be divided into four groups.

- **Government departments** which deal with different matters at national level. These include education, the NHS, social security benefits, defence, the police and prison service, environmental issues and concerns, major road building programmes and the collection of taxes.
- **Local authorities** which provide services for the local community. These will vary, depending upon the area, and the services in a rural community will be very different from those offered in a large city. In most of England, **county councils** offer services over a wide area and **district**, or **parish councils**, run those for smaller communities. A variation is authorities with **unitary status**, which provide all of the services for their area. The range of services offered by local authorities is shown in Figure 1.2.

Figure 1.2 *Council services*

Many of these services are provided free of charge, but not all of them. You will find that your local authority has separate departments to deal with each main area of work, or activity, such as housing, highways, waste disposal, environmental health and so on.

- **Health trusts** which are set up to receive money from the government and to deliver health care without making a profit.
- **Public corporations** which are businesses owned by the government, such as the BBC and the Royal Mail service. The government oversees the way the business operates by appointing a Minister to be responsible and to report on its activities to Parliament. This is usually the relevant Secretary of State, so, for example, the Secretary of State for Culture, Media and Sport reports on developments at the BBC.

On a day-to-day basis, the business is run along normal lines by executives who are paid a salary. Today the state owns very few business organisations and expects each business to break even or operate profitably, like organisations in the private sector.

Business matters

At first sight, you may think that the BBC, ITV and Sky operate almost identical businesses and undertake the same activities because they all produce, or buy, television programmes and transmit these on a daily basis. However, there are some key differences between them, which are linked to their ownership.

The BBC is in the public sector. It is a public corporation and responsible to the government for its television programmes. It obtains most of the money to make these through the TV licence fee. In 2003 the BBC received £2.5 billion in income from the £116 licence fee paid by each household.

In contrast, ITV and Sky are both in the private sector. They raise the money to make programmes by advertising and, in the case of Sky, also by subscriptions. This puts pressure on these businesses to raise enough revenue each year to operate profitably.

Some argue that this is unfair. They claim that even if viewers rarely watch the BBC they still have to pay a licence fee. They also say that the BBC has an easier life because it doesn't have to work hard to raise its money and knows every year how much it will get.

The BBC disagrees. It argues that it cannot just please itself which programmes to make or screen. It has to produce programmes 'in the public interest' – such as the news – and has to buy 25 per cent of its programmes from independent production companies. ITV and Sky both have more flexibility and Sky can screen soaps virtually all day if it wants to. In addition, many people think that MPs will tighten the regulations under which the BBC is allowed to operate when its royal charter next comes up for renewal in 2006.

The voluntary or 'not-for-profit' sector

Voluntary organisations are so called because staff may work there without being paid, such as those who work in charity shops. They are also called 'not-for-profit' because they use their income to provide a service to those in need. They aim to make a **surplus** every year, after necessary expenses, which is used to support and promote their own particular cause.

In 2004, the annual survey of the National Council of Voluntary Organisations (NCVO) showed that in the previous ten years, the number of UK charities had increased from 98,000 to 153,000 and was still increasing by about 7,000 a year. They employed more than 570,000 paid staff – one in 50 of the UK workforce – and over 3 million volunteers. Although most are very small, others are very large indeed. In 2001/2, over 153 UK charities had a total income of around £20 billion.

Some charities receive subsidies from the government and also special relief from tax and business rates. Because of this they must abide by a number of regulations overseen by the Charity Commission. They have to show that they are operating for the benefit of the public and are undertaking one of the approved activities that are allowed.

Charities are overseen by trustees who are responsible for ensuring that the money raised by the charity is managed carefully, as if it was their own. Being a trustee is a voluntary position. The trustee must not receive a salary, although some expenses, such as travel, can be repaid.

Today large charities are run on a professional and business-like basis. They are divided into departments and employ professional fund-raisers and administrators. They spend money on advertising and promoting the charity.

All charities and voluntary organisations have to be properly run and keep accurate records. If a charity went bankrupt because of incompetence, or if the funds were used for non-charitable purposes, the trustees may be both legally and financially liable.

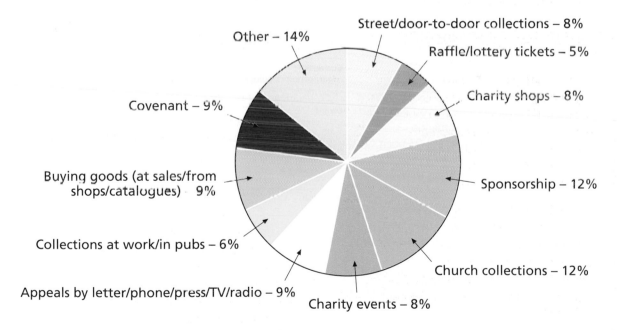

Figure 1.3 *How charities raise their money (Adapted from CA/NCVO Research report August 2003)*

Business terms

Bankrupt An individual who cannot pay his or her debts, even after possessions have been sold. Only private individuals can go bankrupt. A company which fails is said to 'go into liquidation' when its belongings are sold to pay off debts.

Surplus In the voluntary sector, the amount remaining from donations and fund-raising activities after essential expenses have been paid.

Talking point

View 1: *Workers' cooperatives are a great idea because everyone is equal and all the profit is shared between the workers.*

View 2: *Workers' cooperatives will never work because there is no overall leader in charge and some workers will always work harder than others, thus deserving more money.*

With which viewpoint do you agree – and why?

Business matters

A key goal of most banks is to make a profit. Indeed, banks are often criticised for making too much profit at the expense of their customers. They can do this if they charge high interest rates to borrowers and pay very poor interest rates to savers.

One bank, however, is different. Street is a not-for-profit bank which lends money to unemployed people who want to start their own business as well as providing loans and advice to people who already run very small firms, such as newsagents, market traders and window cleaners. Normally the large banks aren't interested in helping these types of traders.

Street can operate in this way because it obtains the loans from other banks, such as Barclays and the Bank of Scotland but its day-to-day running costs are paid by charitable organisations. One of Street's goals is to operate about 40 branches across the UK by 2007.

Over to you!

1 a Identify **six** activities you did last weekend which meant you were involved with a business organisation. For example, you may have worked in a part-time job, visited the cinema, watched TV, been shopping, visited someone in hospital or even helped take rubbish to the local tip. Now add your own examples and then, for each one, name the business organisation with which you were involved and identify the sector it is in.

  b Compare your suggestions with those of other members of your class and check if there are examples of organisations from every sector.

2 a Working in a small group, copy out and complete the table below. Then discuss your ideas with other groups and with your tutor.

  b Extend the table by adding **four** organisations in your own area that you know about. These

Business organisation	Sector it belongs to	One main goal it may have	Two activities it undertakes to help achieve this goal
Dixons			
A vet			
NSPCC			
The ambulance service			
Your local chemist			

could be local businesses, a business where you have worked either part-time or on work experience, or a business you know because a member of your family works there. Compare the ideas of your group with the suggestions made by other groups to build up a picture of business activities in your own area.

3 a Although the average monthly donation to charities has gone up every year from 1997, men are less generous than women and 16–24

year olds give lower amounts than any other. Can you suggest any reason for these differences? If you ran a charity, what would you do to appeal to these groups? Use the pie chart on page 15 to help you.

b In 2002 the most popular charities were medical research, children or young people, animals, other medical/health care, religious organisations and overseas relief. Those for the blind, disabled, elderly, deaf and rescue services raised far less. Investigate a charity of your choice online to find out how successful it is, how much money it raised last year and how it did this. Refer to the guidance notes about researching online on page vi to help you.

c Martin has agreed to help out in a charity shop each Saturday for a few weeks. Previously he worked at Sainsbury's. As a group, suggest four differences he may find in the way the shop operates and say why you think these differences are likely to occur – then decide two aspects of working in the shop that are likely to be the same.

4 The Government and the BBC want your views on what changes should occur when the BBC charter is next reviewed in 2006. You can investigate the issues and decide what you agree by holding a debate and then sending in the views of your group on behalf of your school or college. You can find the information on how to do this at the BBC website – a link is available at www.heinemann.co.uk/hotlinks (express code 1386P). Or you can complete the questionnaire which is posted on the site yourself. All the information is given on the site, including a leaflet summarising the key issues which you can read or download. Everyone is being asked for his or her views in the widest public consultation ever undertaken. If you are studying for your award after 2006 then check what has happened – and see if you agree with it!

5 The Citizen's Advice Bureau (CAB) is a national network of advice centres operated on a not-for-profit basis. It is run by salaried staff helped by dozens of volunteers. Some of these are specialists who give their advice without charge or at a much lower fee than they would normally charge. Prepare a group facts sheet on CAB that includes details of its activities, its goals, the sector in which it operates and how it is funded. To do this:

a Find out about the services offered by CAB on their website – a link is available at www.heinemann.co.uk/hotlinks (express code 1386P).

b If possible, select two students to visit your local CAB and talk to one of the staff there to find out more about CAB work in your area.

What is size and scale?

The **size** of an organisation is easy to understand. Some businesses are very small and may only consist of one person, or a few staff – such as a taxi driver or your local greengrocer. Others are very large and may employ thousands of people. However, this isn't the only method used to judge size and you may also need to consider other factors, such as the profit made or the sales turnover to get a more accurate picture, as you will see later in this unit.

The **scale** of an organisation relates to the scope of its operations. Some firms supply only a small area, such as a newsagent who serves a local community. Others trade on much wider basis, perhaps across a region, all over the country, throughout Europe or even on a global basis.

There is usually a link between size and scale. Whereas your local newsagent will be a small business and will operate on a small scale, a business, which trades all over the world, such as Microsoft or Coca-Cola, will be much larger. Today, however, the Internet has meant that even small businesses can advertise and sell their goods to customers across the country or even in different countries through their websites.

Changes in size and scale

Some businesses start small and stay that way. They are normally only known by and used by people in a local area. Others are much larger and may operate all over the country or even all over the world. They become household names. Between these two extremes are many other businesses of varying size, which may operate in one region, or several.

A question of size

Many small businesses are those which offer a personal service to their customers, such as hairdressers. Although it is possible to grow much larger – Toni & Guy is a good example – this is unusual. You are therefore likely to find ice cream sellers, taxi drivers, window cleaners, plumbers and decorators in your area who only work for themselves, or perhaps employ one or two other people to help them.

Small to medium sized businesses are often found when a business owner is quite ambitious and wants to increase sales or operate over a wider area. He or she may open a chain of shops in an

In the last 30 years, Toni&Guy has grown from one central London salon to 250 salons worldwide

business is more likely to expand successfully if it sells a specialist product or can offer a specialised service, such as shops like Long Tall Sally which cater for the needs of a particular type of customer – in this case, tall women. Others specialise in making or selling particular products such as Tie Rack, Sock Shop and Knickerbox. Specialist manufacturers include Patak's, which produces Indian sauces, and TVR, the specialist sports car firm in Blackpool. Specialist services are offered by businesses such as software or games developers, or firms specialising in 3D graphics. Equally, many customers prefer to do business with smaller companies where they are known and will obtain good service coupled with specialist knowledge. This is why a company like Richer Sounds can compete against much larger businesses, such as Dixons.

Large organisations include national retailers, such as Boots, Marks & Spencer and manufacturers, such as Heinz and Toyota. There are several benefits to being large, known as the **economies of scale**. Tesco and Sainsbury's, for example, can buy stocks more cheaply than your local grocer because suppliers are eager for large supermarkets to stock their goods, so will sell them at larger discounts. They can also afford to advertise on national television, so that everyone knows their name. You will find out more about this when you read about market share in Unit 2.

Finding out about the size of a business

You can assess the size of a business if you know:

- **The number of employees**. It is sensible to think that a business employing 1000 people is larger than one with only 100 employees. Remember, though, that the total number of staff may not be a good guide, particularly if one company has many part-time staff and another does not. Normally, businesses with fewer than 50 employees are classed as 'small' and those with fewer than 250 are described as 'medium'. The Department of Trade and Industry calls all firms with fewer than 9 employees 'micro' businesses.

- **Sales turnover**. You may remember, from page 5, that this relates to the value of the goods sold or the income from services which have been provided. Quite obviously, a large company like Next will sell more goods than a local clothes shop each year. A small company can be expected to have a turnover of about £1 million whilst a medium sized company would probably sell around £11 million of goods a year.
- **The scale of its operations**. Generally, the larger the scale the larger the size – but not always. Martins Seafresh is the website of a Cornish fishermongers and Jack Scaife is a butcher. Both are small businesses but both sell nationally and even internationally over the Internet. You can find out more by visiting their websites – links are available at www.heinemann.co.uk/hotlinks (express code 1386P).

Business brief

Mary, Mary, how does your business grow?

There are five main ways in which businesses grow bigger.

- **Ploughing back profits**. The owner can keep back as much of the profit as possible as **reserves** and use this to finance growth. The problem is that it can take a long time to grow large using this method.
- **Borrowing to expand**. The owner can borrow money from a bank or a specialist company which invests in developing businesses. Many new technology companies have used this method. The disadvantages are that banks may not want to lend very much to small businesses and specialist companies may take a share of the profits (or shares) in return. Borrowers must also pay interest on their loans.
- **Mergers**. The business may **merge** (join) with another, similar, business. This reduces the overall costs of running the business. Many

solicitors and accountants have grown bigger by merging together – which is why you may find so many partners listed on their nameplates! Mergers can take place between any similar businesses – schools, universities and even very large companies. In 2002 Hewlett-Packard merged with PC maker Compaq and cut over 12,500 jobs.

- **Takeovers**. One business may **takeover** another by buying it. This has the advantage of getting rid of a competitor at the same time. Ryanair bought out Buzz for 20.1 million in 2003 and easyJet bought out Go for £374 million in 2002. This dramatically reduced the number of no-frills airlines in operation and increased the size of Ryanair and easyJet at the same time.
- **Franchising**. A business may become a franchisor and start up branches run by franchisees (see page 12). Because the franchisee has to pay money to use the name and has to pay the costs of running the business, this is a relatively cheap way of growing big quickly.

A question of scale

You may hear people say that the world is getting smaller. One reason is that you can travel from one country to another easily and quickly and, if you are away, you can email, text or ring a friend in a matter of seconds. Another is because many products are now sold on a global basis – from television programmes to canned drinks. If you have ever watched the TV programme Friends while sipping from a can of Coca-Cola you will know this! These types of products and services are provided by **multinational organisations**, such as McDonalds, Shell and Microsoft.

Other businesses may be less ambitious. They may produce or sell goods and/or services only within an area, within a particular region, or throughout the UK; or they may expand, but only to cover European countries. Decisions on scale will depend on several factors, as shown in Figure 1.5

- **Existing size of the business**. Small businesses are less likely to have the money, staff or expertise to operate on a large scale. Therefore a 'one man business' – such as your local DJ – could only work in a small area. A small business that tries to expand too quickly is likely to let down customers because it cannot meet its commitments.
- **Type of product or service**
  - Some services are specific to a region or country. Most local football teams, for example, do not offer a 'service' which would be appreciated elsewhere (Manchester United excepted!). Local solicitors and accountants concentrate on UK laws and regulations and only the largest firms employ international specialists. Other services are required worldwide, such as those provided by banks, cinemas and hotels. This is why

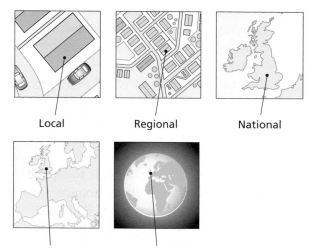

Local   Regional   National

European   Global

Figure 1.4 *The different scale of business operations*

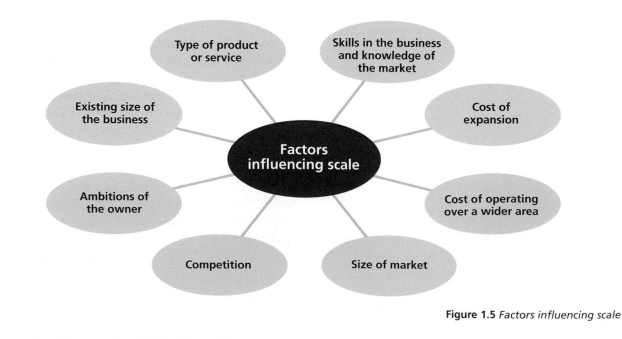

Figure 1.5 *Factors influencing scale*

you will find many of these businesses operating on an international basis.

- Products with international or global appeal have the potential to be sold in many countries, such as computers, clothes, chocolate and cameras. However, ethnic and cultural differences must be taken into consideration (you wouldn't try to sell wine, for instance, in Saudi Arabia).
- If a product is highly perishable, like bread or cakes, it would not pay to transport it a long distance – so most bakeries operate on a local or regional basis. If it is very heavy, like stone or concrete, this also limits the distance over which it could be carried without adding greatly to the cost.

- **Skills in the business and knowledge of the market**. It is not wise to expand – especially abroad – without researching the market first. There may be many key differences which can cause problems. JJB Sports closed its Spanish shops in the mid-1990s because, although the Spanish are keen sports fans, they were less eager to buy sportswear because of the climate and the different types of sports played there. The company still has European outlets in Holland, France and Belgium because there are fewer differences between the needs of sportswear customers there and those of English sportswear customers.

- **Cost of expansion**. Increasing the scale of a business costs money. Selfridges aims to expand its department stores in England and first opened outside London within Manchester's Trafford Centre in 1998. In 2003 it spent £40 million on its new store in Birmingham's Bullring and it is now looking at new stores in Glasgow, Leeds, Newcastle and Bristol. It needs all its new stores to be profitable to make the investment worthwhile but it has the advantage of a famous name to attract customers. It can also raise money for expansion from selling shares and can borrow money based on its financial track record to date. Small or medium sized businesses often have problems raising money and unsuccessful expansion can threaten the whole business.

- **Cost of operating over a wider area**. These costs can include:
  - Production costs in another region or country. In some cases these may be cheaper than in the UK. Dyson moved the production of its vacuum cleaners to Malaysia to save money and BT is using call centres in India for the same reason.
  - The costs of opening branch offices and/or extra retail outlets.
  - The costs of adapting a product for a foreign market – such as changing a car from right- to left-hand drive.
  - Advertising to attract new customers and printing leaflets and instructions in different languages.
  - Transport/distribution costs if goods are made in the UK and sold abroad. JJB said that high transport costs to Spain were another reason why it decided to close its operations there.

- **Size of market**. It is only sensible to expand if there are enough potential customers. On page 18 you saw the value of the Wal-Mart market. This is large enough to tempt many grocery firms to expand to try to meet customers' needs. If the market is much smaller, or is decreasing, then expanding the scale of operations is less sensible. This is why you don't find large stores in rural areas – there simply aren't enough customers nearby to make it worthwhile.

- **Competition**. Competitors will feature heavily in a firm's decision to expand – even to a nearby town. That is why firms like Richer Sounds carefully investigate potential new locations to check the number of people in the area *and* the existing suppliers of hi-fi goods in that area.

- **Ambitions of the owner**. Some entrepreneurs are very ambitious and want their business to grow as large as possible. Richard Branson (Virgin) and Stelios Haji-Ioannou (easyJet) are two examples. Others may be happier with a quiet life, providing that their business is earning enough profit to meet their needs.

Business matters

There are four large supermarket chains in the UK. All are large businesses but each operates on a slightly different scale. William Morrison was a regional supermarket chain operating mainly in the north of England, until it spent £3 billion buying Safeway so that it could expand to the south of England. ASDA, too, is based in the north but operates throughout the UK. It is owned by Wal-Mart, the largest retailer in the world. Sainsbury's operates all over the UK and also has a wine store in Calais. It also owns stores in the US under the name Shaw's Supermarkets Inc. Tesco has stores in the UK and Ireland, and in nine other countries. It has over 150 stores in Europe and over 160 in

Asia, with nearly half of these in Japan. The business is successful because it tailors its stores to local consumers wherever it operates, but admits that it took it a long time to understand the Japanese market and Japanese customers. The one important market where Tesco does not operate is America. The reason given is because it is such a big and competitive market that the effort is unlikely to be worthwhile – but Tesco reserves the right to change its mind! You can find out more by visiting individual supermarket websites – links are available at www.heinemann.co.uk/hotlinks (express code 1386P).

Over to you!

1 a Divide into small groups, with each group investigating **one** of the private sector organisations below by looking on its website. Then answer the following questions. Links to the sites below are available at www.heinemann.co.uk/hotlinks (express code 1386P).
   - Carphone Warehouse.
   - Cadbury's.
   - Amazon.
   - Whitbread.
   - Innocent drinks.
   i Suggest **one** key goal of the business related to money.
   ii Suggest **one** key goal the organisation may set to improve its performance.
   iii Identify at *least* **three** activities the business carries out to help to achieve these goals.
   b Compare all your answers as a group, and identify the type of goals and activities which are common to these private sector organisations and those which are different. Try to suggest reasons for any differences you find. Finally, compare your answers with other teams and together answer the questions that follow.
   i Identify which two companies operate on a global basis.
   ii Identify which two companies operate on a national basis.
   iii Identify the company that currently operates in the UK but aims to make an impact in Europe.

   iv Decide which company is the smallest.
2 a Copy out the tables below then, as a group, suggest the names of businesses in your area, or the names of businesses which you know from advertising or researching on the Internet, to complete each one. Try to think of different businesses for each table.

Size of business	Name of business
Micro business (under 10 employees)	
Small business (10 to 50 employees)	
Medium sized business (50 to 250 employees)	
Large sized business (250+ employees)	

Scale of business	Name of business
Local area only	
Regional area covered	
National business	
European business	
Global business/ multinational	

   b Divide into groups, to investigate **one** of the businesses you have named. You may have to investigate more than one business if you are in a small class – or your tutor may decide which businesses you should investigate. List the activities and goals of these different businesses, and check which sectors they are in. Share the information you have found with other groups in your class.

c Assess your information as a whole to see what patterns you have found. For example, what type of activities are undertaken by very large businesses or global businesses? How do these compare with the activities carried out by much smaller or local firms? Are their goals different? See what conclusions you can draw in relation to the way size and scale can affect both the activities and goals of business.

3 The publishers of OK! magazine are thinking of launching the title in America because they think that an American edition could sell more than one million copies, whereas sales in the UK are 70,000.

a What changes would need to be made, in your opinion, for OK magazine to be successful in the US?

b What could be the extra costs involved in launching the magazine in the US? Try to think of at least **two**.

c Do you think the idea is a good one? Give a reason for your opinion.

4 In 1987 one business had 11 stores and 100 employees. At the start of 2004 it had 7,225 stores in 32 countries and over 70,000 employees worldwide. The name of the business is Starbucks. It argues that its success has been due to being totally focused on its main activity, that of being a coffee company.

Investigate the Starbucks website – a link is available at www.heinemann.co.uk/hotlinks (express code 1386P). Look at its timeline, history and its mission statement and suggest **three** reasons why Starbucks has managed to develop successfully from a small coffee shop to a global name. Then compare your ideas with other members of your group.

5 Tilly owns a successful nail bar in her home town. She is thinking of expanding and opening nail bars in two nearby towns in her area.

a Suggest **three** factors she would need to consider before she does this.

b Suggest **two** advantages and **two** disadvantages of expanding her operation.

c An alternative would be for Tilly to extend her existing nail bar by opening a beauty salon. This would involve diversifying, as she will be undertaking another activity. Suggest **one** advantage and **one** disadvantage of this.

Talking point

View 1: Large scale organisations, like Microsoft, bring immense benefits because they can invest a lot of money in developing new products. This helps us to move forwards.

View 2: Large scale organisations have too much power because smaller businesses can't compete. This actually restricts the choices for customers.

With which viewpoint do you agree – and why?

Now you have completed this section, you should understand what is meant by business activities and goals, business sectors and the size and scale of organisations. You should also understand how and why the main activities of a successful business support the achievement of its key goals. Test your skills now by doing the following activities.

Check your understanding of this section by answering the following questions. Check all your answers with your tutor before moving on.

1 **a** Identify **two** types of business activity carried out by organisations.
   b Explain what is meant by the term 'key business goal'.
   c Briefly explain why all private businesses need to make a profit.
   d Explain why many businesses set a goal related to improving their performance.
   e Who owns businesses in the private sector?
   f Who owns or controls businesses in the public sector?
   g Identify the key difference between organisations in the private sector and those in the voluntary sector.
   h Explain the difference between 'profit' and 'turnover'.
   i Identify **one** way in which you could compare the size of two organisations.
   j What is meant by the 'scale' of business organisations?

2 On page 7 you read about Pilkington, the glass manufacturer. Turn back to that page now and refresh your memory. Then investigate their website – a link is available at www.heinemann.co.uk/hotlinks (express code 1386P). Answer the following questions.
   a What activities does the company carry out?
   b Is which sector does the business operate, i.e. private, public or not-for-profit?
   c What are its future goals?
   d What is the scale of the business?

This section covers

The reasons why business activities are classified

Primary, secondary and tertiary sectors

The growth and decline of sectors

Classifying business activities

All businesses are classified, or put into different groups, depending upon their main activity. You already know that businesses may undertake activities such as producing or making goods and/or providing a service. These are the main groupings, or sectors, used to classify different types of businesses:

- **The primary sector** comprises all the businesses that are involved in producing raw goods, from farming to mining.
- **The secondary sector** is made up of businesses that manufacture or construct goods, such as ICI, Heinz, and Barratts, the house builders.
- **The tertiary sector** includes all the businesses that provide a service, either to businesses or to individuals. This sector includes retailers and banks as well as many other types of business.

The naming of the sectors is not random, or accidental! This is because the sectors are linked as a sequence of production. Primary is therefore the first stage, secondary is the second and tertiary is the third. (The word 'tertiary' actually means 'third'.) This sequence is often referred to as the **chain of production**.

You can see how this works in Figure 1.6 (on page 26).

Why classify business activities?

Grouping businesses into different sectors means that it is much easier to see what is happening to each sector in the UK. In addition, industries are put into sub-groups within each sector, so that it is easier to check which types of activities are increasing and which are decreasing. Business activities are constantly changing, for various reasons:

- **Businesses are attracted towards profitable activities and away from unprofitable ones.** This is why some farmers have changed from running traditional farms to holiday homes – as you saw on page 3 – or to opening farm shops or even, in one case, brewing real ale!
- **Consumers will normally want to buy good value products at a reasonable price.** If foreign goods are cheaper this may mean that British companies go out of business because they can't compete. At one time there were dozens of shoe manufacturers in Britain but today there are very few, because shoes are produced far more cheaply abroad.
- **Technological developments change the demand for goods.** An obvious example was the explosion in mobile phone ownership in the late 1990s which benefited many businesses. The growth in computer ownership has meant an increase in businesses that provide related services – from selling accessories or offering an Internet service to producing software to eliminate viruses.
- **Fashion, trends and lifestyles affect the type of goods and services people want to buy.** In recent years there has been a huge increase in the number of fast food outlets in Britain, and the fast food industry now

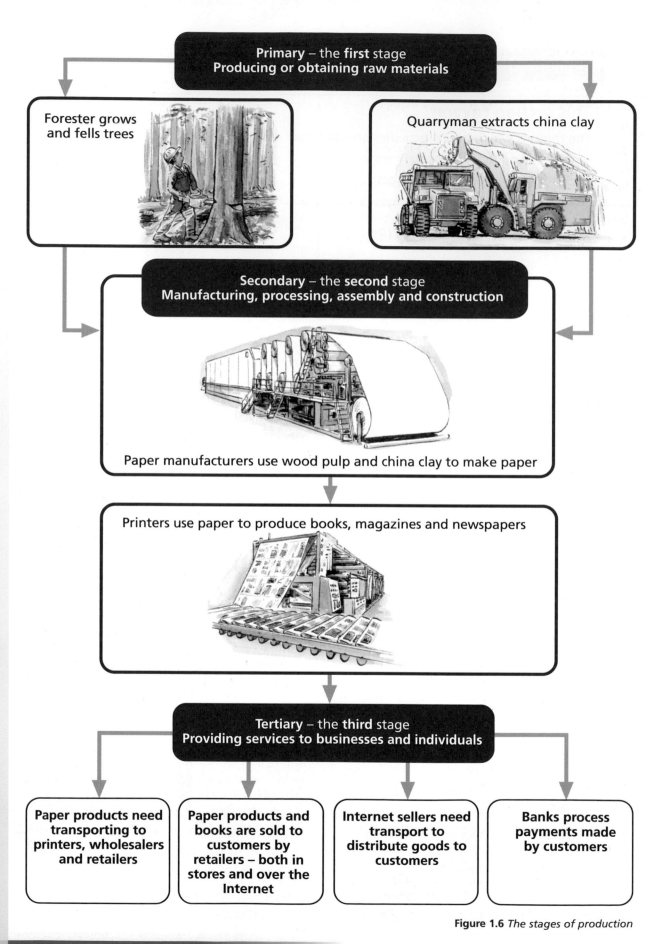

Primary – the first stage
Producing or obtaining raw materials

Forester grows and fells trees

Quarryman extracts china clay

Secondary – the second stage
Manufacturing, processing, assembly and construction

Paper manufacturers use wood pulp and china clay to make paper

Printers use paper to produce books, magazines and newspapers

Tertiary – the third stage
Providing services to businesses and individuals

Paper products need transporting to printers, wholesalers and retailers

Paper products and books are sold to customers by retailers – both in stores and over the Internet

Internet sellers need transport to distribute goods to customers

Banks process payments made by customers

Figure 1.6 *The stages of production*

employs more people than all the traditional manufacturing firms put together. There has also been a growth in the sale of chilled ready-meals which help families to cope when parents work long hours.

You will find that changes in business activities are shown by the growth or decline in each sector and the sub-groups within each sector. This means you can distinguish what is happening in the retailing industry, for example, from changes in the hotel industry. For that reason, the next stage is to learn more about each different sector and the businesses that are in it.

Business terms

Consumer demand The degree to which consumers want to buy certain products or services.

An industry A group of businesses undertaking the same activity and offering the same or very similar products, e.g. the retailing or banking industries.

Sector of production The primary, secondary and tertiary sectors which, together, include all the business activities in the UK.

Over to you!

1 Draw a diagram showing the sequence, or chain, of production (i.e. primary, secondary and tertiary) for each of the following items.
   a Wool.
   b Petrol.
   c Frozen chips.
   d A wooden desk.
   e Cement (which is made from limestone and clay).
2 a Working in a small group, copy out the table below. Then complete it by identifying **three** products for which demand has increased in recent years, and **three** for which it has declined.

Demand has increased	Demand has fallen
Bottled water	Video recorders

   b In each case suggest one reason for the change.
   c Decide which types of business activities would be affected in each case – both positively and negatively.
   d Compare your ideas with other groups, to find out the range of products and activities you have identified between you.

Business matters

Ground Force, Changing Rooms and television programmes like them can have a dramatic effect on what we buy. Garden centres and DIY suppliers saw a surge in sales when homeowners tried to copy the ideas put forward by Alan Titchmarsh and Charlie Dimmock, such as wooden decking. Carpet and wallpaper manufacturers have seen the opposite occur. The trend for 'minimalist' decorating, with white painted walls and wood-effect floors is hitting home. In 2003, Sanderson wallpapers ceased trading after the firm ran up over £4 million in debts because of the fall in sales for wall coverings.

Sales of carpets have also plummeted. In 2003, Carpets International, which employed 1,200 people across Britain, also ceased trading In 1990, the trade sold about 212 million square metres of carpet. This fell to 197 million square metres in 2001, and the numbers employed by the industry have fallen, over the last 30 years, from 45000 to 7,500 This is partly because we now import 65 per cent of our carpets every year but also because it is more fashionable to have wooden floors.

The news isn't all doom and gloom for British firms. The producers of wood and laminate flooring are celebrating, with sales more than tripling between 1990 and 2001.

New trends affect consumer demand

View 1: Britain needs farmers – even if this means that the price of meat and vegetables increases. They must be paid enough to make a living.

View 2: It is silly to pay high prices for homegrown food when it can be bought more cheaply from abroad. This helps to keep prices down in the shops.

With which viewpoint do you agree – and why?

The primary sector

Deep sea fishing is in the primary sector

The primary sector includes all those businesses that produce raw goods, from the land or the sea. There are four main categories of activities in this sector.

Agriculture, hunting and forestry
What's in this group

This category covers the production of crops, such as vegetables, cereals and flowers, and the farming of animals, such as cattle, sheep, pigs and chickens. Some farmers specialise in one type of activity, such as dairy farming, whilst others run mixed farms. On mixed farms they grow crops and rear farm animals. You can find out more on the Defra website – a link is

available at www.heinemann.co.uk/hotlinks (express code 1386P). In this category you will also find landscape gardeners and horticultural businesses as well as those concerned with animal husbandry, such as herd testers who check that cows are free from disease. Also included are those connected with hunting and game breeding, such as gamekeepers.

What's not

Vets and pet boarding catteries and kennels – these belong to the tertiary sector.

Forestry and logging
What's in this group

This category includes all businesses involved with planting, conserving and felling timber as well as Christmas tree growers such as Festive Forestry. You can find out more about Festive Forestry on their website – a link is available at www.heinemann.co.uk/hotlinks (express code 1386P). Both the overall woodland area and the amount of softwood grown in Britain has increased in the past ten years, although Britain still doesn't grow enough to meet its needs and both softwood and hardwood are imported from abroad.

What's not

Sawmills, which process logs, as these belong to the secondary sector.

Fishing
What's in this group

This group includes fishing fleets – which in 2002 landed 686,000 tonnes of fish in the UK and abroad, with a total value of £546 million – as well as fish farms, such as trout hatcheries, salmon farms and freshwater mussel growers. Scotland has the largest number of fish farms in the UK – but not all of them. If you want to find out more, check out the links to Suffolk Fish Farms Ltd and Defra available at www.heinemann.co.uk/hotlinks (express code 1386P).

What's not

The 14,000 fishmongers in the country, who belong to the tertiary sector.

Mining and quarrying

What's in this group

Coal mines, oil and natural gas extraction, quarrying of all types of stone, slate, gravel, sand and clay as well as salt production. Today the largest coal producer in Britain is UK Coal which produces nearly 20 million tonnes a year. Large quarrying companies, such as the Tarmac Group and Blue Circle specialise in materials required by building and construction companies. There are very few salt producers in Britain, as their location depends entirely on where natural salt deposits are found. The main producer in the UK is British Salt Ltd at Middlewich in Cheshire. Links to industry websites are available at www.heinemann.co.uk/hotlinks (express code 1386P).

What's not

Stone masons (who cut, shape and finish ornamental stone) and firms which manufacture cement or make bricks or tiles from clay. These are in the secondary sector. Builder's merchants or garden centres, which sell stone and other building materials, are found in the tertiary sector.

The secondary sector

Manufacturing sweets is in the secondary sector

The secondary sector includes all those businesses which manufacture, process or assemble products. In addition, this sector also covers energy production and the construction industry. There are three main categories of activities in this sector.

Business matters

Growing watercress may not seem very important, but if you are one of the 1,000 people who are employed in doing it, then you might feel very differently. You may know all about watercress farms if you live in Hampshire or Dorset, where watercress has been grown for more than 300 years. In fact, in the 19th century, watercress growers built a railway called 'the watercress line' from Hampshire to London, to transport their wares to Covent Garden.

Watercress has been staging a comeback in recent years, mainly through supermarkets including it in mixed bags of leaves in their ready-made salad ranges. The trend towards vegetarianism has also helped.

Watercress growers in the UK are currently protesting to the Government over plans to make them use purified water to irrigate their fields, rather than river water. Growers argue that the river water contains essential nutrients which add to the flavour. For that reason, all watercress farms are located next to rivers fed by natural springs. In addition, using purified water would add millions of pounds to the process in extra costs.

At present watercress growing is a £40 million industry and Britain supplies most of Europe with the watercress it needs. The growers have recruited Antony Worrall Thompson, the TV chef, plus the page three girl, Jo Guest, to fight their corner. You can find out more about this on the Internet – a link is available at www.heinemann.co.uk/hotlinks (express code 1386P).

Manufacturing

What's in this group

All businesses which make or produce the goods that you see around you every day – regardless of their size or what they make. Quite simply, every product you see, hear, touch or buy has been made somewhere – and often contains components which were made somewhere else before the final item was assembled. This even applies to the cheapest biro you own! The plastic case is made separately from the ink tube inside it – and then the two are put together.

The table below shows the divisions used by the Office for National Statistics to separate different types of manufacturers. This is helpful because they enable you to see which types of manufacturing businesses are thriving – and which are not (see page 35).

What's not

Film and television production companies – they are in the tertiary sector.

Product groups

Food products, beverages and tobacco, e.g. meat and poultry, fish freezing, fruit and vegetable processing, dairy products and ice cream, breakfast cereals, pet food, bread, sweets, chocolates, wines, mineral water, soft drinks, beer and tobacco.

Textiles and textile products, e.g. cotton and woollen goods, soft furnishings, carpets, knitted and leather clothes.

Leather and leather goods, e.g. handbags, luggage and footwear.

Wood and wood products (excluding furniture), e.g. sawmilling, wood containers, plywood and veneers.

Pulp, paper products, publishing and printing, e.g. paper, cartons and boxes, wallpaper, book and newspaper publishing, reproducing sound or video recordings or computer media.

Coke, refined petroleum products and nuclear fuel processing

Chemicals, chemical products and man-made fibres, e.g. chemicals, industrial gases, dyes, plastic, synthetic rubber, paint, printing ink, pharmaceuticals, soap, detergents, perfume, glue, man-made fibres, manufacturing unrecorded media (e.g. blank CDs).

Rubber and plastic products, e.g. rubber tyres, plastic tubes and packaging, plastic floor coverings.

Non-metallic mineral products, e.g. glass, ceramic goods (such as sinks, baths and tiles), bricks and cement manufacture, finishing of ornamental and building stone.

Basic metals and fabricated metal products, e.g. iron, steel, aluminium, lead, zinc, tin and copper goods, central heating radiators and boilers, cutlery, tools, locks, wire, screws.

Other machinery and equipment*, e.g. pumps, compressors, furnaces, ventilation equipment, agricultural machinery, power tools, earth-moving machinery, domestic appliances.

Electrical and optical equipment*, e.g. office machinery, computers, electric motors, batteries, electric lamps, televisions and radios, medical and surgical equipment, cameras, watches and clocks.

Transport equipment, e.g. motor vehicles, trailers, caravans, motor vehicle parts and accessories, ships, boats, trains, aircraft and spacecrafts, motorcycles and bicycles.

Other manufacturing not listed above, e.g. furniture, mattresses, jewellery, musical instruments, sports goods, games and toys, brooms and brushes, recycling of scrap metal.

* Engineering industries

Figure 1.7 *Manufacturing groups*

Business matters

Kodak is having to rethink its business activities after 120 years in business. Once famous for its traditional cameras and distinctive yellow boxes of films, Kodak had been watching sales and profits start to slump for some time. In 2003 the fall in tourism through the SARS virus and continued growth of digital photography had a dramatic effect. As a result Kodak announced a further 15,000 job cuts – to add to the 22,000 it had made since 1998. By 2007, Kodak's 1998 workforce of 86,000 will number fewer than 50,000. The firm is now reducing its range of films and photographic products and moving rapidly into digital commercial markets, where it will compete against famous names such as Xerox, Canon, Hewlett-Packard and Seiko, who are already well established in this market. Kodak also wants to expand its health imaging business and transform this into a digital operation.

Digital photography has already seen one major victim – Polaroid – which mistimed its move into digital cameras and went bankrupt. Normally only those businesses which accurately forecast technological change and make appropriate changes at the right time are successful. Many think that the heat is now on for recording companies as UK sales of CD singles fell by 33 per cent between 2003 and 2004 – although album sales rose by 6 per cent. They also argue that the explosion in music download sites, such as Apple iTunes and My Coke Music could threaten sales from traditional outlets in the future. You can find out more about these sites on the Internet – links are available at www.heinemann.co.uk/hotlinks (express code 1386P).

Business brief

What do engineers do?

Engineers are employed in manufacturing industries throughout Britain, but mainly where machinery and equipment are concerned. They help to design hundreds of products and ensure they work efficiently – from cars and aeroplanes to light bulbs and mobile phones. You can also sub-divide engineering businesses into two categories. The first are involved in 'light engineering' such as making microscopes, machine tools and scientific equipment, where precision is important. The second are involved in 'heavy engineering' – such as building ships or cranes. The common factor is that these are all made of very large sections of metal.

The Office for National Statistics classifies two groups of manufacturers as engineering businesses – as you can see in the table on page 30. This term is also used in the financial papers which give the share prices of businesses, to distinguish engineering firms from other 'industrial' businesses or those which produce a specific product, such as pharmaceuticals.

If you are puzzled about engineering and are still unsure what it means, check out the websites of Today's Engineer and Enginuity – links are available at www.heinemann.co.uk/hotlinks (express code 1386P). Or you can search in Google for examples of light and heavy engineering companies.

An engineer at work

Energy production

What's in this group

In addition to products, we all need electricity, gas and water. This group includes all the organisations which produce and distribute gas and electricity, such as Powergen and London Energy, and those which collect and distribute water. This includes regional water companies, such as Anglian Water Services and water collection and bottling companies. Although the world's largest water suppliers are the French (think of Perrier and Evian), there are UK firms too, such as Highland Spring in Scotland and Buxton Water. You can find out more about this on the Internet – links are available at www.heinemann.co.uk/hotlinks (express code 1386P).

In the future Britain is looking at obtaining more energy from alternative sources, such as wind farming and tidal energy. These businesses, too, will come into this group.

What's not

Any business which sells or maintains gas or electricity appliances, or any business which provides or maintains water coolers. These are in the tertiary sector because they are all services.

Construction

What's in this group

Basically, house builders and civil engineering companies. Between them they construct all types of buildings as well as motorways, bridges, roads and railways. Also included are electricians who work on building sites and plumbers, plasterers, joiners, painters and glaziers (who put in windows).

What's not

Estate agents who sell houses – they are in the tertiary sector.

The tertiary sector

The tertiary, or services, sector is by far the largest sector and includes many types of businesses. Because it includes every type of business that offers a service, you can sub-divide this sector to link to the business sectors you learned about earlier.

- **Private services** are offered by privately owned businesses and can be purchased by businesses and individuals. These services include retailers, accountants, banks, consultants, private clinics and hospitals,

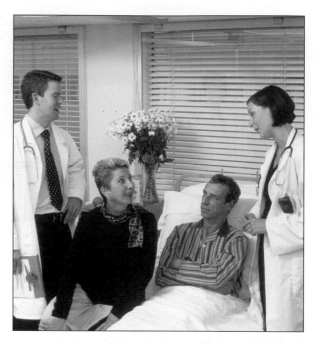

Health care in the tertiary sector

publishers, transport and distribution firms, travel agencies and many others.

- **Public services** are provided locally and nationally by the government and local authorities, e.g. education, emergency services, housing, law and order, defence and military activity, social services and so on.
- **Voluntary and not-for-profit services** are provided by charitable and voluntary organisations in areas such as social care, community health care, environmental and wildlife protection.

The Office for National Statistics groups services slightly differently, because different types of business may offer the same service. Education, for example, is provided both by state schools and by private (independent) schools. Health care is similar, and voluntary organisations such as MIND or Help the Aged may also be involved. Several voluntary organisations are involved in environmental protection, such as Greenpeace and the RSPB – but the government is involved in this area and the Department for the Environment provides advice to businesses and individuals.

The official categories are shown in Figure 1.8.

Main groupings

Wholesale and retail trade, e.g. all wholesalers and retailers, including market stalls and dispensing chemists, plus repair/maintenance businesses such as garages, watch repairers, cobblers.

Hotels and restaurants including camping sites, youth hostels, holiday centres, takeaway food shops and stands, pubs and bars.

Transport, storage and communication, e.g. taxis, furniture removals, freight transport by road, rail, sea, canals and air, all passenger transport, pipelines, cargo handling and storage, travel agencies and tour operators, post and courier services, telecommunications.

Financial services, e.g. banks, building societies, finance houses, insurance companies and pension funds.

Real estate, renting and business activities, e.g. estate agents, car hire firms, all rental firms, computer consultants, software developers, office equipment repairers, solicitors, accountants, market research companies, quantity surveyors, architects, advertising agencies, recruitment companies, security firms, industrial cleaners, photographers, secretarial agencies, call centres, debt collectors, exhibition organisers.

Public administration and defence, e.g. government agencies which oversee health care, education and other services, defence activities, the justice system, the police and fire service.

Education, e.g. all schools, colleges and universities, driving schools, private training firms.

Health and social work, e.g. hospitals and nursing homes, doctors, dentists, vets, social workers.

Other community, social and personal service activities, e.g. sewage and refuse disposal, professional organisations and trade unions, religious and political organisations, film and video production and distribution, radio and television, theatres, fair and amusement parks, news agencies, libraries, museums, sports centres, dry cleaners, funeral directors, hairdressers, beauty therapists, gyms and fitness centres, nature reserves.

Figure 1.8 *Tertiary sector groupings*

What's in this group

Virtually every kind of service you can think of, plus – surprisingly – film making. This is because making films, videos, radio and television programmes and theatre productions are all classed as 'creative', as is the writing of newspapers or books and the design of computer games and programs. All are therefore 'services', rather than 'manufacturing' activities.

What's not

The printing and publishing of newspapers and books. This is found in the secondary sector. So is the production of blank video and recording material and its reproduction.

Business terms

Distribution Moving goods around the country to where they are required. You will often see large distribution centres near motorways, where goods are held before being taken to local shops and stores.

Wholesalers Wholesalers supply all types of goods. They buy large quantities of items and sell these in smaller quantities to retailers.

Freight Industrial goods and products being transported, often by large distribution companies which operate fleets of customised vehicles, such as those which carry frozen or perishable items.

Business matters

Services are affected by consumer trends just as much as products. The National Lottery, for example, has seen sales fall dramatically over the last few years as people have realised that the chances of 'It could be you' happening are much smaller than they first thought! At their height, in 1997/8, sales were worth £100 million a week, but by 2003 these had fallen to £88 million. To try to revive interest, various new versions are now being offered, such as a six day Lotto draw and games on the Internet.

Another service industry where sales have fallen is traditional mail order retailing. Profits have dropped from £126 million in 1998 to £33 million in 2002. These catalogue firms, such as Littlewoods and Kays recruited 'agents' – often housewives – who earned commission for obtaining sales amongst friends and relatives. Today, the growing popularity of credit cards, the increase of bargain clothing retailers such as Matalan and George at ASDA and the growth of Internet shopping has meant people no longer need to flick through catalogues and then wait weeks for delivery. Other firms have approached customers direct, such as Next, which sells goods through its stores and its catalogue. Kays was owned by GUS – Great Universal Stores – which has tried to solve the problem by diversifying (see page 3). GUS bought Argos in 1998 and Homebase, the DIY chain, in 2002 and has sold off its home shopping business altogether to cut its losses.

Over to you!

1 a Draw a table with the headings of Primary, Secondary and Tertiary production. Enter each of the following people in the correct category, according to the job they do.

Carpenter	Bank clerk	Teacher
Estate agent	Engineer	Journalist
Website designer	Fisherman	Musician
Charity worker	Taxi driver	Oil driller
Retailer	Lorry driver	Printer

  b Now identify at least **12** more occupations and categorise these. Try to make them as varied as you can (from a confetti maker to an acrobat!). Make sure that you add at least **two** under each heading on your table.

2 a List **ten** types of services which, as an individual, you use regularly. Use the table on page 33 to help you.

  b Imagine you have started out in business on your own producing your own version of delicious curry sauces. Identify **six** business services you would be likely to use.

3 a On your own, identify the main purpose of **two** voluntary or not-for-profit organisations which are listed in the 100 top charities by funding. You can find out more by visiting the BUBL UK website – a link is available at www.heinemann.co.uk/hotlinks (express code 1386P).

  b List at least **three** services which are provided by the organisations you have identified.

  c Compare your answers with other members of your group and compile a list of the main types of services provided by voluntary and not-for-profit organisations.

4 There are many different people – and business activities – involved in many of the products you buy, such as a CD of your favourite band. This has involved all the activities in the box below.

Transporting CDs to warehouses
Devising advertising campaign to promote CD
Printing of insert sleeves
Manufacture of blank CDs
Recording of band by technicians onto master disc
Felling trees for converting into wood pulp
Reproduction of master recording to produce multiple CDs
Assembling of boxes, CDs and insert sleeve
Producing card for insert sleeve
Selling CDs in shops
Making card from wood pulp and other materials
Creation of graphics and information for sleeve
Manufacture of plastic box to hold CDs
Converting logs into wood pulp

  a As a group, decide a sensible order in which you think these activities would take place.

  b Then, against each, decide the type of business and the sector of production that is involved.

View 1: *The National Lottery is a good idea as it gives people the chance of winning a lot of money and it donates money to good causes. Increasing the number of games each week will help it to do better.*

View 2: *The National Lottery is a waste of time because the chances of winning are so low. It encourages gambling when people should spend their money more wisely and on essentials like food and clothing.*

With which viewpoint do you agree – and why?

The relative growth and decline of sectors

You have already seen that the demand for different products and services changes over time, for several reasons. This has two effects:

- Whole sectors can grow or decline, over a period of years.
- Within different sectors, certain types of businesses may flourish whilst others do not.

General sector changes

One hundred years ago, the UK led the world in manufacturing. Today, most manufactured goods are imported from abroad. Far more people are employed in the tertiary sector. Indeed, there are now 40,000 people working in call centres alone – more than in the coal, steel and car-making industries combined.

How do we know this? Because we can measure sector changes by looking at different types of figures – and one way is to look at the numbers of people employed in each sector.

Employment by sector

All businesses need people. Therefore, one way is to identify the number of people employed in each sector to see whether employment is rising or falling. Generally, if the number of jobs is increasing, this is because this type of activity is increasing.

If you look at the chart of employment by sector below, you will see that between 1993 and 2003, employment:

- Fell in the primary and secondary sector.
- Increased in the tertiary sector.

Year	Primary	Secondary	Tertiary
1993	2.2%	24.0%	73.8%
1998	2.0%	23.0%	75.0%
2000	1.7%	21.8%	76.5%
2003	1.4%	19.9%	78.7%

Figure 1.9 *Share of UK employment by sector*

There is, however, a danger with relying totally on employment figures. Sometimes employment may increase but a large number of employees are part-time workers. This can give a false impression, especially if you are comparing two types of industries. In retailing and catering, for example, there are more part-time workers than there are in manufacturing.

Sector output

All businesses produce output. A fisherman's output relates to the number of fish caught, a manufacturer's is measured by the number of goods made and a retailer's by the number sold, and so on. If output is increasing, then you can expect the activity to be growing.

This is often a more reliable measure, because increased output *usually* results in higher profits. Quite obviously, a farmer who grows 500 tonnes of potatoes is more likely to make more profit than one who only grows 250 tonnes – unless prices fall dramatically. If profits are good, then more businesses will be attracted to that activity, which means that it is expanding.

Output is normally shown as a value. This, then, takes account of price differences. If the value of the farmer's output has increased from £60,000 to £80,000 then we know he or she is making more money. However, we can only count the amount of value the farmer 'adds' to each product. If he or she buys a calf for £50, fattens it and sells it for £80, the value of their output is £30 – the difference they made through their own efforts.

You may think that the trends shown by employment and output figures would match. This is often the case, but not always. Sometimes output can increase because more modern machinery or technology is used so fewer people are needed. Banks, for example, now need to employ fewer staff in their branches because of cash machines, call centres and Internet banking. However, whilst overall employment by banks has fallen, output has risen because technology means that transactions can be processed more quickly and easily.

The following table shows the share of UK output by sector from 1993 to 2003. Check this to see if it shows the same trends as the table for employment, and make a note of any differences.

Year	Primary	Secondary	Tertiary
1993	4.1%	28.9%	67.0%
1998	4.0%	28.7%	67.3%
2000	3.5%	26.5%	70%
2003	3.1%	22.5%	74.4%

Figure 1.10 *Share of UK output by sector*

Rises and falls in output

Experts are usually more interested in whether output for each sector is increasing or decreasing, month by month. This is why you often see sector output as a line graph, as this makes it easier to see what is happening. A line graph to show the changes in manufacturing output over the last six years is shown in Figure 1.11.

Manufacturing output
Three months on the previous three months, %

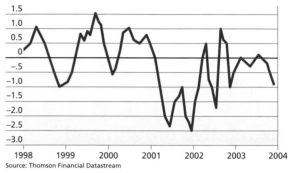

Source: Thomson Financial Datastream

Figure 1.11 *Graph of manufacturing output*

Experts also want to see what is happening to total national output – known as Gross Domestic Product (GDP). If this is growing then it shows that Britain should be doing well. It is producing more and so it is earning more money.

Comparing these figures helps to determine whether a sector is in absolute decline – when it would eventually disappear – or in relative decline.

Business brief

Types of decline

There are two ways in which a sector can decline.

- **Absolute decline** means it will one day disappear.
- **Relative decline** means that it is just not doing as well as the other sectors – but may be doing quite well on its own.

In Britain, there has been much concern about the decline in manufacturing. But is this in absolute or relative decline? That is the important question.

A sector is declining if:

a The *share* of people it employs is falling.
b Its *share* of UK output is falling.

but if its overall output is increasing or the total

number of people it employs are increasing, then this is likely to be *relative* decline.

It will be in *absolute decline* if it is employing fewer people every year and if the output of the sector is falling.

In 2001, British manufacturing was having a terrible time. Employment, output, investment and profits were all falling. This is often known as a **recession.** Between 2002 and 2003, certain industries performed rather better and in some months there was an increase in output. Overall, though, experts would describe manufacturing output performance now as 'flat' or 'stagnant'. In other words, for every month there is an increase, this is cancelled out by a bad month. In contrast, the tertiary sector is often described as 'buoyant'.

Changes within sectors

Just because a sector is growing or declining, this doesn't mean that all the different types of business activities within it are doing the same thing. As you have already seen, manufacturing in Britain is declining, but some industries in the secondary sector are doing much better than others. The same applies to the other sectors.

The table in Figure 1.12 shows how different industries were performing in Britain in 2003.

Business terms

Employment The number of people employed in a sector or industry.

Share of employment The percentage of working people involved in a sector or industry.

Output The amount of goods produced and their value.

UK output The total amount of goods produced in the UK.

Gross Domestic Product (GDP) The total output and value of all the goods produced by a country in a year.

Investment The amount of money put into a business to enable it to grow and develop.

Recession When output, employment, profits and investment are all falling. This is the same as absolute decline.

Business matters

In 2003, at the Labour party conference, the government was lobbied by the trade unions and the Confederation of British Industry (CBI) about the problems faced by manufacturers in Britain. They gave examples of British manufacturers, such as Dyson, who have moved production to Malaysia because of the costs of running a business in the UK. They stressed how manufacturing in Britain accounted for nearly 40 per cent of the economy in 1950 and is now nearer 17 per cent. They emphasised the importance of manufacturing – it provides work for thousands of people and exports of products are worth more than exports of services. They pointed to a report by the Institute for Public Policy Research that by 2050, less than 5 per cent of the working population in Britain would be employed in manufacturing. Quite simply, they wanted the government to take action to remedy this situation.

Various ideas have been put forward. Cut taxes on business, give grants and loans to new businesses, encourage more young people to obtain the skills they need to work in manufacturing, help people to appreciate the varied jobs and careers in this sector and make it easier for businesses to sell goods abroad.

It is not all doom and gloom, however. Some experts argue that Britain's manufacturing industries are changing, not disappearing. They say that hi-tech, specialist equipment should be our aim rather than traditional products. This is often called 'knowledge-based industry'.

You can find out more by going to the TUC and CBI websites and searching under 'manufacturing' – links are available at www.heinemann.co.uk/hotlinks (express code 1386P). The TUC represents employee interests and the CBI represents employer interests. They often don't agree – but saving manufacturing businesses and jobs is in everyone's interest.

Doing well		Having problems	
Primary	Oil and natural gas extraction	Primary	Agriculture, hunting, forestry and fishing Coal mining
Secondary	Energy supplies, e.g. electricity, gas and water Construction Electrical and optical equipment Paper and publishing Chemicals and man-made fibres Rubber and plastic products Transport equipment Food, drink and tobacco	Secondary	Wood products Non-metallic mineral products Textiles, leather and clothing Basic metals and metal products Machinery and equipment
Tertiary	Wholesale and retail Transport, storage and communication Financial services Real estate, renting and business activities Education Health and social work Personal services	Tertiary	Hotels and restaurants Public administration and defence

Figure 1.12 *The state of play in 2003*

Business brief

Statistics and damn lies!

The word 'statistics' worries many people, but all it really means is 'numbers', collected for a reason. The problem is that some numbers can give a false impression and tempt you to jump to the wrong conclusion. Although you won't have to interpret numbers in your assessment, it's useful to know what to watch for, especially if you are investigating a business or researching on the Internet.

Try this as an experiment. For each item below, rank the three types of business in order of merit, with the one that seems to be the most successful first.

1 In 2001, there were 7,706 food producers, 32,493 firms involved in the paper and publishing industry and 5,665 firms making transport equipment.
2 In the same year, these industries employed 511,000 people (food), 482,000 people (paper and publishing) and 395,000 people (transport).
3 The value of sales for each industry for that year was £74,804 million (food), £44,903

million (paper and publishing) and £61,018 million (transport).

At this point, you should have three different rankings! So which one is right?

Let's add one more line:

4 The value of output for each industry in 2001 was £20.3 million (food), £19.4 million (paper and publishing) and £17.4 million (transport).

This is probably the most reliable line, simply because some industries have a few large firms, which produce high value goods and use lots of machinery (so employ fewer people). Others have lots of small firms who do many jobs by hand, but the sales price on these items may be low. Output, however, shows the amount of value which has been added by each industry – so you can compare them more easily. If output is falling, then fewer goods are being made and sold. If output is increasing, then the industry is doing well – regardless of the fact there may be fewer firms or fewer people employed – or that reduced prices might mean that the total value of sales has fallen.

Over to you!

1 The tables on pages 35 and 36 show that the primary sector as a whole is declining and one part of this sector are farmers.

a In 2001, when farming output fell by 11 per cent, many farmers lost money and went out of business. As a group, can you remember the event that caused this problem?

b Many people are hoping that customer preferences for organic food will help British farmers. In what way could this affect employment and output in the primary sector?

c Find out more about the help the government gives to British farmers at the websites of Defra (click on Farming), Organic Farmers and The Soil Association – links are available at www.heinemann.co.uk/hotlinks (express code 1386P).

2 The change in output of several industries in the secondary sector between January and June 2003 is shown below.

Business activity	Percentage change in output
Chemicals and man-made fibres	+0.3%
Electrical valves and tubes	+4%
Pulp, paper, publishing and printing	+0.2%
Rubber and plastic products	+0.7%
Textiles, leather and clothing	+1.1%
Weapons and ammunitions	+11%
Wood and wood products	+2.5%

a This list is shown in alphabetical order. Rearrange it so that the table shows the best performing industry at the top and the worst at the bottom.

b All the changes in this table start with a '+' sign. Is this good or bad? Give reasons for your answer.

c Give **one** reason why output figures are usually a more reliable guide to sector trends than employment figures, number of firms or sales figures.

d Study the industry at the top of your table. Can you suggest any reason for the performance of this industry in the first six months of 2003?

e As a group, can you suggest any other events, or changes in consumer demand, that could have affected any of the industries in your list?

f Overall output in manufacturing for this period was described as 'flat'. What does this mean and how could this occur?

3 In the first six months of 2003, the services sector was doing well and retailing, hotels and restaurants, post, telecommunications and education were reported to have strong growth. Business services had moderate growth. Output fell in land and air transport, banking and insurance, health and social work. Wholesaling and recreation, sport and culture were both described as 'flat'.

a How many industries were listed as doing very well?

b In which industries was there no change?

c Which industries were experiencing problems?

d Select **two** industries from the list above and, for each one, suggest **one** factor which can influence demand for its services. Compare ideas with those of other members of group.

💬 Talking point

View 1: It doesn't matter if manufacturing disappears in Britain as we have plenty of service industries here.

View 2: All countries need a manufacturing base otherwise they are totally dependent on imports from abroad.

With which viewpoint do you agree – and why?

Now that you have completed this section you should understand how business activities are classified and which industries are growing and declining. Test your skills now by doing the following activities.

Check your understanding of this section by answering the following questions. Check all your answers with your tutor before moving on.

1 **a** Identify **two** business activities in the primary sector of production.

    b Explain what is meant by the term 'output'.

    c Both manufacturing and engineering businesses are in the secondary sector. Briefly explain the type of work engineering businesses are involved with.

    d Identify **four** business activities in the services sector.

    e Bovis Homes and Bryant are house-building firms. Which sectors are they in?

    f Which sector(s) are declining in Britain?

    g Which sector(s) are growing in Britain?

    h Briefly explain how employment figures can help you to identify which sectors are growing and declining.

    i Briefly describe **one** danger in using employment figures on their own to decide what is happening in an industry.

    j What is meant by the term 'relative decline' of a sector?

2 **a** Working in small groups, list **ten** businesses in your own town or region. Then decide the business activity of each one.

    b Identify the sector each business is in.

    c Compare your ideas with those from other groups and identify which sectors have generated the most and the fewest names.

    d If any sectors are empty, can you suggest reasons why? For example, do you think your location could have anything to do with this,

and to what extent? Discuss your ideas with your tutor and then see if you can find at least **two** businesses in your own area which would fit into any remaining blank sectors.

3 It is always difficult to forecast the future for different business activities, but one website can help you to do this. You can find out what the industry was like originally, what is happening today and what is predicted to happen in the future.

To do this, work in pairs or groups of three and choose **one** of the industries listed below:

Construction	Manufacturing	IT
Environmental	Food and drink	Retail
Broadcasting, film and video	Advertising	Health
	Hospitality	Tourism
Oil, gas, and petroleum	Sport and leisure	Legal
	Financial services	Science
Voluntary sector	Fashion and textile	

Then go to the Prospects website and select 'explore job sectors' under the jobs and work section – a link is available at www.heinemann.co.uk/hotlinks (express code 1386P). Although this website is aimed at graduates looking for jobs, it will give you an excellent overview of any industry and a forecast for the future. Click on the sector you are investigating and find out what has happened to that industry in the past, what is happening now and what is predicted for the future. You can also find examples of the 'big players' in each industry.

Prepare a short presentation on the key points for the industry you have chosen and include the sector it is in. In addition, prepare an information sheet which summarises these points for each member of your class to keep.

This section covers

The resources used by businesses

The aims and objectives of organisations

Using resources to achieve aims and objectives

What are resources?

We all use resources every day. We need the natural resources of air and water to live. You need some financial resources to go out at weekend! Quite simply, a resource is something you need to enable you to do something else. This book is a resource to help you to achieve the goal of obtaining your BTEC First award. Your ability to read and concentrate are personal skills and resources that you need to be able to use it.

Businesses also need resources to function and to achieve their goals, which you read about in section 1.1. You might think that the more resources businesses have, the more successful they will be. This isn't always true. If you had to research a topic, then being given a library full of books might be confusing. You would be better with a few good books that you liked and which focused on that subject. For that reason, businesses aren't just concerned with obtaining resources, but on choosing the best and using them wisely.

What resources do businesses need?

Even the smallest business, such as your local newsagent, needs some basic resources:

- **Premises**, such as a shop.
- **Equipment**, such as a cash register.
- **Money** to buy stock, such as sweets and newspapers.
- **Staff**, such as someone to serve customers and delivery boys and girls.

All these are essential for the business to function. If our newsagent wants to be very successful, a few other resources would be helpful as well.

- **Business skills** to be able to run the business efficiently and solve problems as they arise. Buying a computer to do the accounts and to forecast future profits (or losses) is helpful, providing the owner has IT skills. Previous experience of retailing or working in a newsagents would be a huge advantage.
- **Personal skills**, such as the energy and drive to get up early and work hard, seven days a week, plus the ability to get on well with people – to keep both customers and staff happy.
- A **good location**, so that the business benefits from passing trade as well as being in a relatively large community where people buy newspapers and related products. If it's easy to park a car outside the shop, this is another benefit.
- A **good name and reputation** in the district, built up by being honest, reliable and giving a good service, so that customers recommend the business to their friends and stay loyal over many years.

Classifying business resources

In the previous section, you learned how business activities are classified. Business resources can also be grouped into categories, as you can see in Figure 1.13 (on page 42).

Resource type	Examples
Land, buildings and location	Land is needed by businesses such as farmers, horticulturalists and the Forestry Commission. Most businesses need buildings, such as a shop, factory, warehouse or office. The location of the business can often be a very important factor in its success (see page 44).
People	The owner and all the staff – who may include managers, specialists, office workers and general assistants/operators. Some businesses consider these the most valuable resource because staff who are highly skilled and keen to work hard can mean the difference between success and failure.
Plant/equipment or access to facilities	'Plant' is heavy equipment, such as earth-moving machines used by construction firms. Specialist equipment includes machinery for making a product or machinery used in research work and office equipment, such as computers, telephones and fax machines, which are needed by most businesses. Some specialist equipment can be hired as needed and/or specialist facilities and services used, e.g. those found in an office bureau.
Financial	Money invested by the owner and/or the ability to borrow additional finance from a bank or other institution. Cash held by the business to pay immediate debts.
Business skills	The owner's professional and business skills/abilities, such as industrial experience, IT and financial skills, problem-solving, decision making and the vision to develop the business. Energy is needed to work hard and drive the business forward.

Figure 1.13 *Types of business resource*

This seems quite straightforward, but there are four other aspects of resources that are often forgotten.

- **Quality**. There is a huge difference between owning a building that is modern and exactly fits your needs, and owning one which is too small and needs urgent repairs. Machines and IT systems can be evaluated in the same way. So the age, condition, capability and even the location of each resource is very important.
- **Fit**. Do the type of resources match what the business is doing now? Resource needs change all the time. This is why banks have sold many of their branches and turned, instead, to telephone and Internet banking. They have exchanged one type of resource for another. Businesses need to do this to stay up to date.
- **Intangibility**. If you asked someone to list 'resources' they would probably automatically tell you about machines, vehicles, staff and money. What is often forgotten, however, are the intangible resources that can make all the difference. These include good customer relations, having a well known brand or a superb reputation, having loyal and productive staff, owning an extensive customer database, having many contacts in the industry which help the managers to keep up to date or ahead of their rivals. Another important asset is a good **supply chain** – which means that stocks of goods can be delivered promptly, whenever they are needed.
- **Uniqueness**. The best resources a business can own are those which are unique, so that it becomes famous and associated with that resource. J K Rowling owns the rights to Harry Potter. This is a unique resource because no one else has it. Every time someone uses the name to promote a product, she receives payment, because she has protected the name, legally, to stop anyone using it without her permission. This is one reason why some companies invest heavily in innovation – to develop new products or ideas

(see page 76). They then protect these, by taking out a **patent**, to prevent anyone copying them. Being 'the first to market' always gives a business a competitive advantage (think of Sony and the Walkman and Playstation). Employing staff with brilliant technical skills or who are well known in their field is another asset. So innovation, developing good ideas and employing brilliant staff can all be considered as other types of resources.

Business terms

Asset Something the business owns which is worth money. A tangible asset is something you can touch and easily measure or value, such as equipment. An intangible asset is something you cannot touch and is less easy to measure or value, such as a brand name.

Brand name The name of a specific and distinctive product or service which distinguishes it from similar products or services and promotes a particular image, e.g. Innocent Drinks, which are free from additives. Most brand names are protected by their owners, under copyright law, to prevent other people from using them.

Capital The money invested in a business and used to buy business resources.

Intellectual capital Specialist knowledge that can be used to make money.

Human resources The name often used to describe the staff who work in a business.

Market presence To be well-known in a particular market for goods or services. Factors which help this include: being a long-established firm, having a good reputation for honesty and reliability, promoting the business to customers.

Patent The legal right to make exclusive use of an invention or process for a specific period of time.

Supply chain The suppliers, storage facilities, distributors and transporters that are involved in providing every product purchased from an organisation.

Business matters

Many people have criticised Richard Branson for his publicity stunts – such as dressing up in drag to launch Virgin Bride, appearing on Friends and Baywatch, being photographed in the nude (for his autobiography) and travelling around in a hot air balloon. Branson is a sharp, clever and successful entrepreneur who left school at 15 and is now estimated to be worth £1 billion, so why do this?

One answer could be his love of adventure, his restless spirit or his unconventional approach to life. However, Branson hasn't become wealthy without being very astute about money. He owns very little that he doesn't consider a business asset and which he doesn't use to make more money – and that includes his Caribbean island, Necker – which he rents to people who have enough money to pay for it. So it is more likely that he gets involved in publicity stunts for a reason – and what better one than to promote his own businesses?

Today we are all familiar with the Virgin brand, which is just what Richard Branson wants. Choosing a distinctive name and putting it under

Limobikes provide a service and promote the Virgin brand

our noses at every opportunity means that he owns another asset – worth money because of its familiarity. Think air travel, think Virgin Atlantic; think DVDs, think Virgin Megastores; think phones, think Virgin Mobile. That is Branson's aim. The brand name also helps him to have an immediate market presence in any new ventures – from credit cards to Limobikes!

You can find out more about the Virgin brand on the Internet – links are available at www.heinemann.co.uk/hotlinks (express code 1386P).

Business brief

Location as a resource

Location is a very important resource for some businesses – but not for all of them. It is important if:

- Highly skilled workers are needed who are mainly found in certain areas of the country (e.g. motor engineers in the East Midlands).
- The business needs heavy raw materials, which are best obtained nearby (e.g. cement companies who need limestone or chalk).
- Certain natural resources are essential (e.g. the spring water for watercress farms that you read about on page 29).
- Good transport links are needed to take goods to warehouses or customers (e.g. supermarket distribution centres).
- Attracting passing trade is an important aspect

of the business (e.g. many retail shops, petrol stations and garden centres).
- Nearness to other similar businesses is important (e.g. solicitors and barristers located near to each other and near to law courts; pizza restaurants near to cinemas).

Other businesses may have more choice about their location, such as call centres and firms that sell their goods over the Internet, but they will still need skilled staff and will want good transport links.

All businesses have to match their need for a good location with the cost of premises, which are much more expensive in popular areas, such as on main roads in towns and cities. This is particularly important if the building must be large or spacious and could therefore be very expensive. This is why you find large factories on industrial estates and large hypermarkets and trade centres out of town.

Over to you!

1 Working in small groups, select **one** of the small businesses below. Then carry out the following activities.

A mobile hairdresser   A restaurant
A DJ who works for himself   A photographer
A landscape gardener   A taxi firm

   a List the resources you think would be needed by your chosen entrepreneur when he or she is just starting out in business. Include examples under the headings of 'land/buildings/location', 'people' 'plant/equipment' and 'financial'.

   b For your chosen entrepreneur, list the skills and experience which he or she would need.

   c Decide all the intangible resources which would help this entrepreneur to succeed. If you can think of any unique resources (i.e. a resource that local competitors don't have), even better.

   d Decide on a distinctive brand name for the business, which would help new customers to distinguish it from other, similar, businesses in the area. Remember that the name you choose should promote the image you want customers to associate with the business and

allow enough scope for the way the business might want to grow in the future. Risky Rides, for example, would hardly be suitable for a taxi firm!

   e Suggest **two** ways in which your entrepreneur could aim to have a market presence in the area as soon as possible.

   f Put your proposals and ideas for your entrepreneur to the rest of your class and then see if anyone has any other suggestions to offer.

2 Test your knowledge of brand names to find out which businesses have a market presence according to your group.

   a On your own, write down the name of the first brand that you think of, for each of the following items.

   i A pair of jeans.
   ii A computer games machine.
   iii A pair of trainers.
   iv A computer software package.
   v A box of cornflakes.
   vi A jar of coffee.
   vii A tin of beans.

b Now list the name of the first business that comes to mind when you think of:

   i A bank.

   ii A nightclub.

   iii A clothing retailer.

   iv A record/CD store.

c List the answers from everyone in your group and find out which name is the most popular for each item listed in **a** and **b** above.

d As a group, suggest reasons why each name has become so well known.

3 In the summer of 2003, when David Beckham visited America, he signed a management deal with Simon Fuller – well known in the music world for managing the Spice Girls – to promote the 'Beckham brand name' in the US. Fuller argued that David Beckham's image meant they could create a $1 billion brand.

a As a group, what do you think the 'Beckham image' represents?

b Why do you think many businesses – from Marks & Spencer to Vodafone – are willing to pay to have Beckham promote their goods?

c In 2003, Madonna published a children's book which had immediate market presence. Can you suggest why this occurred?

d Suggest **one** other famous name yourself, which could be considered a 'brand', and say the image that this brand brings to mind.

4 As a group, suggest **two** important factors that each of the following businesses would need to consider when choosing their location:

a A hotel.

b An estate agent.

c A hospital.

d A video/DVD rental shop.

e A drive-thru fast food outlet.

f A large superstore.

5 If you want to find out more about managing your own financial resources as a student then you can find out more at the MSN website and at the NUS website. Links are available at www.heinemann.co.uk/hotlinks (express code 1386P). You might also find this useful if you intend to continue your studies.

David Beckham has his own brand logo

💬 Talking point

View 1: *The Beckham brand is so powerful that allegations or scandals won't have any effect.*

View 2: *The Beckham brand has been built on his family image. Anything which destroys that image will ruin the brand.*

With which viewpoint do you agree – and why?

The aims of businesses

All businesses have aims, or goals they want to achieve, as you saw in Section 1.1.

- In the private sector, businesses aim to make a profit, as you saw on page 5. Most will also want to increase this each year. Many, however, will aim for **profit maximisation** – which means making as much profit as possible.

- If trading is difficult, for some reason, then profit maximisation may be unrealistic. In this situation, the business may aim just to **survive**, until things improve.

- One method of surviving is to aim to **break even** over a certain period. This means making enough money to cover the total costs involved in producing and selling the goods or services and running the business. There is no profit, but there is no money lost, either. You will learn more about break even in Unit 3.
- The business may aim for **growth**, so that it sells more goods or services. This may mean expanding by opening other branches or buying out a competitor (see section 1.1, page 19).

- Another aim may be **service provision**. This may mean offering a new service or improving current services to attract more customers, such as businesses which extend their websites to allow customers to order and pay for goods online and track deliveries.
- Many businesses have a constant aim of expanding their **market share**. This normally means taking business away from their competitors.

Although a business may have more than one aim, it is sensible not to have too many. Most focus on two or three and concentrate their resources on achieving these.

Business brief

What is market share?

The 'market' for a particular product or service is the total number of consumers who buy it. Each business that offers that item then has a 'share' of that market.

Market share can be increased in two ways. It is easy to achieve if the whole market is growing. When a new product is launched, from Apple i-Pods to Skinny Cow ice cream, demand often increases at the start. Later, it slows down and suppliers have to think of other ways to tempt people to buy – such as introducing variations or reducing prices. This is because the only way they can increase their market share is to take business away from their competitors. You will learn more about this in Unit 2.

Sales of Magnum contribute to Wall's market share

Market share is always shown as a percentage of the total market. If you like ice cream, you may be interested in the table opposite.

Wall's brand ice cream is made by Unilever and, even if you've never heard of Richmond Foods then this doesn't mean you haven't bought their ice cream! The company makes branded ice cream for Nestle, Weightwatchers and other firms as well as its own products.

Note that the figures don't add up to 100 per cent because of other manufacturers whose market share is very small indeed.

Manufacturer	Annual sales	Market share
Wall's/Unilever	£386 million	42%
Richmond Foods	£230 million	25%
Mars	£87.8 million	9%
Fredericks	£46.6 million	5%
De Roma	£31.2 million	3%

When websites and web pages were in their infancy, businesses saw these as an additional method of reaching out to customers. This applied just as much to service providers as to firms wanting to sell online. Now the mood is changing, with many service providers starting to expect their information websites to pay for themselves or, even better, to make a profit.

A good example is FT.com – the online site for the Financial Times. Like all newspaper sites, this carries online news and information – but mainly about businesses. The site cost an estimated £200 million to design and develop and offers a high level online service for users. The problem was that the site was losing money – until the FT introduced a subscription charge for users who wanted access to specialist content and archived (older) material.

By December 2002 the site was breaking even and in March, 2003, the website showed a profit for the first time – partly through cutting the costs of running the site and partly because of increased revenue. Although only a small number of users have taken out a subscription, revenue is also earned by advertising and by syndicating stories (i.e. letting other newspapers and sites use them). The fact that the site has nearly 4 million users means it is attractive to advertisers who are willing to pay for space.

Other newspapers are watching developments with interest – as many of them would like their sites to break even or make a profit, too. It is estimated that within the next two years the UK is likely to follow the USA, with most information sites charging for specialist content.

If you want to find out what is free and what you would have to pay for, check out the FT website – a link is available at www.heinemann.co.uk/hotlinks (express code 1386P).

Business objectives

Objectives are more specific than aims. They are targets which must be achieved for an aim to be met. For example, you may have several personal aims you want to achieve – to get fitter, lose weight, save for a holiday next year, achieve your BTEC First Diploma. The danger of any aim is that it is very broad and may seem overwhelming. It is easier to achieve if it is broken down into smaller steps.

For example, to get fitter you may decide to join a gym, walk more and eat more fruit and vegetables. These are your objectives. Identifying these isn't particularly difficult – doing them over and over again is a lot harder! But if you do, then you will achieve your aim.

In the Business Matters article above, the management at FT.com decided to change their aim with the website, from providing a free service, to firstly breaking even and then making a profit. They did this by first identifying the steps needed, then divided their site into both free and chargeable content, setting a price that would attract subscribers.

You will always find aims and objectives linked in this way. It is no use having a personal aim of saving money and setting the objective of eating fruit and vegetables! The two have to match up – both for personal and business aims and objectives.

SMART objectives

The problem with many objectives is that they aren't precise. They don't pin you down enough. Look back at the three personal objectives for getting fitter. Can you see anything wrong with them? Try this. You join a gym – but only go once a month; you only walk once a week – for 5 minutes; you eat a banana once a week, too, but previously you only had one a fortnight, so you are achieving your objective of 'more' fruit. Would that be good enough? The answer is obviously 'no'! So what has gone wrong?

Quite simply, the objectives weren't precise enough to enable you to meet your aim. SMART objectives do this because they have the following characteristics. They are:

Specific This means writing a clear definition, usually including a number, such as the government target that everyone should eat 5 portions of fruit and vegetables each day.

Measurable This means you can easily check if you have achieved your objective. You could do this, for example, by keeping your 5 portions separate each day and checking there are none left before you go to bed!

Achievable An objective must be sensible so that you can attain it if you stretch yourself a little. Setting an objective to live on fruit and vegetables for a fortnight isn't sensible and, because you would probably feel ill, wouldn't be easy to achieve.

Realistic The objective must be achievable with the resources you have available. If all items of fruit and vegetables cost £10 each, then you would be setting yourself an unrealistic objective to eat 5 items a day.

Time-related Every objective should have a date for achievement or review. Therefore you could say 'for the three months from 1 May to 31 July.'

It should be fairly obvious from this list that it is very difficult to wriggle out of an objective that is SMART. You either achieve it or you don't!

More about business objectives

If businesses talk about getting 'fitter' or 'leaner' they usually mean in terms of their financial shape rather than their physical shape. Their objectives will usually be linked to targets which relate to financial success. These normally include:

- **Outputs** – e.g. how many goods must be produced or how many sales must be made over a certain period.
- **Profit** – i.e. the difference between revenue and costs (see page 5). Remember they may want to make a profit, increase a previous profit, or maximise their profit. To be SMART, however, they have to include a number, e.g. 'increase profits by 5 per cent in the current year'.
- **Service delivery** – e.g. the speed at which orders are processed, enquiries are handled or patients are treated and the overall quality of the service. This links to improving business performance, which you read about in Section 1.1 on page 8.

Processing orders involves targets for speed and accuracy

Milestones are set when a target is over a long period. These are 'staging posts', which break down the target into shorter intervals. This makes it easier to track progress.

Business brief

How do you maximise profits?

In section 1.1 you learned how to calculate profits and you also learned about maximising sales (see page 6). You might think that maximising sales and maximising profits are the same thing, but you would be wrong.

Maximising profits isn't as easy as it sounds. It means selling as many items as possible and keeping costs as low as possible at the same time. It is difficult because there are several problems in doing this:

- Selling more often means more advertising or promotions (or additional sales staff or more branches) all of which increase costs.
- Sales will be lost if there aren't the right (or enough) products in stock. But buying and storing more stock also adds to costs.
- Increasing the selling price to increase revenue can lose sales if the items are then uncompetitive.

- Trying to improve business performance to process sales more quickly may require more staff or better equipment, which also adds to costs.

True profit maximisation would mean running the business for nothing, producing (or buying) and storing the goods at no cost and selling them for a small fortune – which is obviously impossible. So businesses have to decide the best possible profit they can achieve. Unless you are selling designer goods like Armani or Ferrari, where people are more interested in the brand name than the price, this means selling at the highest competitive price. It also means offering the best service you can and keeping costs as low as is reasonably possible. You will learn more about this when you study unit 3.

Over to you!

1 Decide on **one** personal aim you have this year. Then write **two** SMART targets to help you to achieve this.

2 Greggs, Britain's largest bakery chain, announced that it intended to expand abroad. It said it would be opening three or four stores in Belgium within three months and would sell Belgian delicacies alongside traditional British fare. Greggs also wants to open another 500 stores in the next five years and mainly grow in the south east and the midlands.

   a What is the main aim of Greggs at the moment?

   b Identify **two** objectives it has announced which will help it to achieve this.

   c Are Greggs' objectives SMART or not? Give a reason for your answer.

   d How will Greggs' objectives help it to meet its aim?

3 Your local Chinese takeaway is struggling and profits are poor. During most weekday evenings trade is slack and sometimes food is wasted. On Friday and Saturday nights, they are very busy – but this means people are kept waiting whilst orders are completed. The owners are wondering how to improve the business and have decided to start a free delivery service to see if this will help.

   a Working in a small group, suggest **two** aims the business should have over the next twelve months.

   b For each aim, choose and write a SMART objective which will help them to achieve it.

   c Identify **one** milestone which would help the owners to check they are on target in three months' time.

   d Compare your ideas with those of other groups in your class.

> **View 1:** *Profit maximisation is just greedy and means the business is either overpricing its products or underpaying its staff. A fair profit should be enough for anyone.*

> **View 2:** *Profit maximisation is a good thing. The more profit a company makes the more it can invest back into the business, and the more it can pay its staff and its shareholders. As businesses pay tax on their profits, this also helps the country.*

With which viewpoint do you agree – and why?

Using resources to achieve aims and objectives

It is very difficult to achieve any aim or objective without using any resources. If you want to get fitter, then you need to spend time exercising. Time is a resource. Another is money. You would need to spend money to join a gym or to buy fitness equipment to use at home. You would also have to be committed to what you wanted to achieve and have the energy to keep going.

In business, these resources translate into:

- **Staff time** to carry out additional tasks or staff expertise to do specialised jobs.
- **Capital** for investing in new projects or expansion.
- **Equipment or additional technology** for new developments.
- **Business or personal skills** to see the task through.

These relate to almost all the categories you first saw in business resources! If you have forgotten about them, look back to the chart on page 42.

At the start of this section you learned that businesses not only need the right resources, but they need to use them wisely to be successful. Increasing resources just adds to costs, so this means that any aim related to profit maximisation is likely to be unachievable. Therefore, businesses will often redeploy their existing resources to help them achieve any new aims.

Using resources wisely

Blockbuster, the UK's largest home entertainment retail chain, aims to increase its sales and profits each year by making it more convenient for customers to use their services. The two are connected because more customers will increase sales and also increase profits, if costs are kept down. Blockbuster has a few problems, however. It is facing threats from developing technology which could result in video-on-demand services. It also faces competition from supermarkets like ASDA and Tesco who now sell DVDs at low prices.

To help to continue to achieve its aims in the UK Blockbuster has:

- Bought the UK-based games retailer, Gamestation – a computer console and games retailer.
- Introduced a DVD by post service through their website.
- Extended the range of products it sells 'for a great night in' to include beer and wine as well as snacks, ice cream and confectionery.
- Linked with Sainsbury's so that customers can collect a movie with their shopping, and introduced rental vending machines in some Tesco supermarkets.
- Installed vending machines at petrol stations, universities, food stores and railway stations.
- Launched 'new look' stores with colour-coded categories.
- Increased its back catalogue of movie titles and called it the Gold Collection. This will include classic films and popular films people may have missed the first time around.
- Launched a trial video on demand service in Hull, in conjunction with Kingston Communications. This means that about 6,000 homes in Hull can receive films and programs from Blockbuster over broadband.

Blockbuster's website is only one of its many resources

How has this affected the way Blockbuster uses its resources?

- **Buildings**. Blockbuster is selling and/or renting a wider variety of products in the same area, which is why revamping its stores was seen to be important. The aim is that customers can find what they want easily and quickly because there are discreet, colour-coded areas for each category. Revamping a store is much cheaper than moving to larger premises, which would increase costs considerably.
- **Location**. Blockbuster is well aware that research has shown that people will not travel more than a mile or two to rent a DVD. Whilst their stores are situated on main roads and in easily accessed small retail centres, they are now catering for people who don't live near a store with their postal and vending machine systems.
- **People**. Blockbuster isn't employing any additional staff in the stores just because it is selling a wider variety of goods, although existing staff must be trained to be able to sell all new products. Specialist staff are employed in 'new media' developments, such as delivering videos by broadband in Hull and developing the website.
- **Equipment**. Vending machines for DVDs are new, and would need to be designed, made and installed by a specialist supplier. They will also need to be serviced. The aim will be for

the increased revenue from these to more than pay for these costs. Developments in the stores will not have led to any new equipment, except for – perhaps – some additional cash tills.

- **Stock**. Blockbuster ensures current stock includes all new releases and popular items but boosting its back catalogue and promoting this is a good way of renewing interest in existing stock which may have been lying idle.
- **Capital**. Finance would be needed to buy the Gamestation stores and to develop new technology. Other developments, such as investments in the back catalogue, could be financed out of profits.
- **Technology**. Blockbuster is keeping abreast of technological developments and is using the Internet to help to develop its services to customers. It took advantage of the slimmer DVD format to start up its postal service, which wouldn't have been suitable for videos.
- **Industry experience**. The company employs experienced Directors with a special responsibility for key areas of the business. They also have branch managers for each store and district managers who oversee stores in a region.
- **Market presence**. Blockbuster enforces its market presence through advertising campaigns and slogans such as 'Bringing Entertainment Home'.
- **Brand name**. The choice of name is clever as the word 'blockbuster' is associated with highly successful films. It is punchy and easy to remember.

Business terms

Deploy To use a resource in a particular way.
Efficiency Providing the best service or product at the lowest reasonable cost. If efficiency is improved, this means delivering more or better products or services for the same cost.
Redeploy To use the same resource in a different way.

Business matters

Running a police force is not very different from running any type of business organisation. There are still aims to achieve, objectives to meet and a limited number of resources.

The police force in the UK has three main aims:

- To promote safety and reduce disorder.
- To reduce crime and the fear of crime.
- To contribute to delivering justice in a way which secures and maintains public confidence in the rule of law.

There are eleven objectives. Four of these are: to prevent terrorism; improve public safety; keep order and reduce anti-social behaviour; contribute to improving road safety and reducing casualties. Specific targets are set for each force, for example to reduce burglaries in their area by a stated per cent by a fixed date; to reduce vehicle crime by a stated per cent by a fixed date.

The police service hasn't got unlimited resources. It is financed by public money and spending is monitored by the Home Office. The aim is to get the 'Best Value' out of every penny spent by operating efficiently. Therefore, if more 'front line'

policing is required to achieve an objective, the money to pay for this has to come from savings in other areas. Another method is to redeploy police officers. When they sign up, police officers normally agree to be deployed anywhere within their District, unless travelling distance from home would be excessive. They can also be redirected to change their work patterns, e.g. from traffic policing to community policing. The Gloucestershire Constabulary has undertaken a programme of resource mapping, so that it can show how it is using its resources to focus on priority areas.

You can find out about the aims, objectives and targets of your own regional police force – and how it is achieving Best Value by going to the Google website and typing in the name of the county you live in and the word 'police', e.g. 'Gloucestershire police'. Then search the police site for the information you need. A link to this website is available at www.heinemann.co.uk/hotlinks (express code 1386P).

Over to you!

1 Jack has met a Spanish nurse who works at his local hospital. He wants to impress her by learning the language. He finds out that an easy way to do this is to join an evening class at his local College.
   a List the resources Jack will have to use to achieve his objective.
   b What suggestions could you give Jack on using these wisely?
   c Learning Spanish is an objective. What is Jack's aim?
   d How well are you using your resources to achieve your BTEC First Diploma? Suggest one way in which you could use these more wisely!

2 Alex has decided to open a snack bar selling drinks, sandwiches and snacks. Her aim is to make a profit and provide an excellent service to her customers. To make a profit, she needs to attract as many customers as possible.

She has already identified the shop to buy. It is near the town's business district and also close to

the college, however, the floor area is not large.
   a From the following list of resources decide which are important to Alex's aims and which are not. Give a reason for any item you reject.
      i   A skilled and efficient staff.
      ii A computer.
      iii A good location.
      iv Catering experience.
      v   Toilet facilities for customers.
      vi A good brand name.
      vii A reputation for cleanliness, efficiency and good service.
      viii A freezer.
      ix Finance for expansion.
   b Alex has the choice between having a large serving area and small counters and stools for customers or having a smaller serving area with plenty of tables and comfy chairs. Which should she choose and why?

3 Many businesses have seasonal variations in trade. Alton Towers and Blackpool Pleasure Beach are busier in summer, large department stores are busier in winter – particularly near Christmas.

If you owned a greetings card shop, which was particularly busy in November and December, then it would be sensible to reorganise your resources at this time to ensure you didn't lose any sales.

In groups of two or three, suggest **three** ways to do this. Compare your ideas with other groups.

4 Find out about more recent developments at Blockbuster by reading through the information and press releases on its website – a link is available at www.heinemann.co.uk/hotlinks (express code 1386P).

Then decide whether you think Blockbuster will continue to be successful or whether it will struggle in the future.

Give a reason for your opinion and compare your views with other members of your group.

Talking point

View 1: *It isn't normally a good idea to redeploy staff, especially if they don't want to do a different job. At the end of the day, if more jobs need doing, more people need to be hired even if this increases costs.*

View 2: *Redeploying staff is better than spending too much and then having to get rid of people. Many people enjoy the challenge to learn new skills and do something different.*

With which viewpoint do you agree – and why?

1.3 Section review

You have now reached the end of this section, and should know what is meant by business resources, aims and objectives. You should also understand how businesses use their resources to try to achieve their aims and objectives. Test your knowledge and skills now by doing the following activities.

Check your understanding of this section by answering the following questions. Check all your answers with your tutor before moving on.

1 a Identify three tangible business resources used by organisations.
  b Explain what is meant by the term 'human resources'.
  c Give two reasons why it benefits a business to have a well-known brand name.
  d Give three examples of businesses for which location is important and state the most suitable location in each case.
  e What is a business aim?
  f List three aims a business may have.
  g What are the key characteristics of a SMART objective?
  h What is meant by the term 'profit maximisation'?

  i If you read that the Sun newspaper has the largest market share in the UK, what does this tell you?
  j Explain why businesses must use their resources wisely to achieve their aims and objectives.

2 B&Q, the large DIY chain, prides itself on responding quickly to seasonal demand, which can be heavily influenced by the weather. It used to land its goods at Southampton docks and other southern ports, but traffic congestion and a shortage of HGV drivers in the area was causing up to three days' delay moving the goods to the warehouse. To solve the problem it now lands its containers on Humberside, more than 200 miles to the north.
  a What is a major aim of B&Q?
  b Why does B&Q have to react quickly to demand for goods such as barbecues and garden furniture?
  c What resources does B&Q need to move its goods to its stores?
  d Explain how it is now using the same resources more efficiently.

What is the specialisation of labour?

In Section 1.1, you learned that businesses often choose to specialise in one activity. This means that they concentrate on what they are good at. People can specialise too – in fact, the word 'specialist' is often used in job titles, especially in the medical and IT professions.

In business, people specialise when they concentrate on one particular type of task. Even the smallest organisation has a number of key tasks, or functions, that must be done regularly – stock must be bought, bills must be paid, customers must be served and customer enquiries must be answered. In a very small firm, such as a local shop, all these jobs may be done by one person. In a larger organisation, people would specialise in different tasks. Tesco and

Specialist buyers attend fashion shows to select their stock

Sainsbury's, for example, have buyers to purchase the stock, accounts staff to pay the bills, checkout staff to serve customers and customer service staff to answer queries.

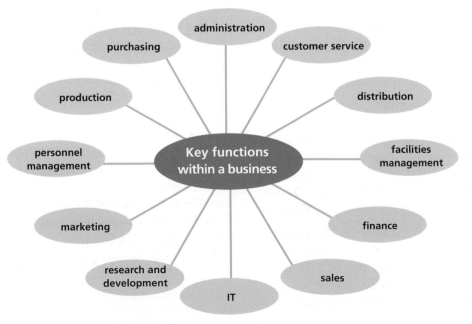

Figure 1.14 *Key business functions*

Functional departments

In a large organisation, people work together in functional areas or departments. Each department is responsible for carrying out the tasks that relate to its particular area. The main ones you are likely to meet in business are shown in Figure 1.14.

Some businesses won't have all these functions – and not all businesses use the same titles for their departments. It will usually depend upon the business activity. For example, a retail organisation would not need a production department, because this is where goods are manufactured. Other differences you might find include:

- The term 'human resources' being used for personnel management.
- Administration being carried out within other departments, rather than being a separate department on its own.
- Sales and marketing being grouped together in one department.

- No separate department for facilities management – the function which looks after buildings and maintenance (see page 60). Instead this may be an extra responsibility of a senior manager who runs a different department, such as Office Services or Administration.
- Purchasing being part of the production department – or a separate department on its own.
- The term 'operations' being used instead of 'production'. This often applies when organisations offer a service, such as an airport. In this case, the main 'operation' is getting outgoing flights in the air and making sure that incoming flights land safely.

You therefore need to be flexible when you are investigating any organisation yourself. However, if you know the main work that is usually carried out by each functional area, this helps you to make sense of any differences you find.

Business matters

Amnesty International (AI) is a worldwide movement of people campaigning to improve human rights with around 2 million members all over the world. Amnesty International's supporters come from many different backgrounds and different political and religious beliefs. The work of AI is directed by an International Secretariat based in London with a staff of nearly 400 researchers, campaigners and legal and other experts.

The head office of Amnesty International UK is also in London. There are also offices in Edinburgh, Cardiff and Belfast. AIUK has more than 195,000 members, and hundreds of affiliated groups and organisations across the United Kingdom. There are about 120 paid staff and 70 volunteers working in four departments.

- **The Campaigns department** plans and develops AI's campaigns, lobbies politicians, keeps the media informed about current events and concerns, and educates people about human rights. The department is made

up of six teams: Media Unit, Activism, Policy and Government Affairs, Campaigns Coordination, Human Rights Education, and Nations and Regions.

- **The Marketing department** raises funds to pay for AI's work, raises AI's public profile, holds high profile events, and keeps the membership informed through its magazine and other materials. The department is made up of three teams: Supporter Care and Development; Brand, Events and Fundraising; and Major Donor Development.
- **The Human Resources department** which recruits and looks after staff and volunteers has two teams: Human Resources and Office Management.
- **The Finance department** is made up of two teams: Finance and IT.

You can find out more about the work of Amnesty International at their website – a link is available at www.heinemann.co.uk/hotlinks (express code 1386P).

1 Ask your tutor to describe the main functional areas in your college. You will probably find these are quite different to those illustrated on page 54. As a group, identify the title of the department(s) which:

  a Deals with the finance and accounts of the college.

  b Looks after the buildings and arranges maintenance.

  c Gives information to potential new students.

  d Deals with staff queries about their employment.

  e Installs and repairs computer equipment.

  f Pays the bills received by the College.

  g Prepares the College prospectus and brochures

  h Maintains the website.

  i 'Produces' successful students, i.e. educates and helps them to achieve their qualifications.

2 Look back at the information on Amnesty International on page 55, and answer the following questions.

  a What is Amnesty's main aim or goal?

  b What experts, or specialists, does Amnesty employ at its International Secretariat – and why do you think these are needed?

  c Why do you think Amnesty needs a Campaigns department?

  d In which departments would you find IT staff and administration staff at Amnesty?

  e Amnesty staff can specialise at two levels. They can specialise by working in a particular department and they can specialise by belonging to a particular team. If you worked for Amnesty, which team would you most like to work with, and why?

Talking point

View 1: It's better to work in a small firm, and do a variety of different jobs, than specialise in one area.

View 2: It's better to work in a large firm, in one department, learning as much as possible about one particular type of work.

With which viewpoint do you agree – and why?

Business terms

Centralisation When one department carries out a particular type of work for the whole organisation, e.g. an Administration department. Some businesses have a centralised Head Office, where virtually all the major decisions are made and the key functions of finance, marketing and purchasing are carried out for all the branches.

Decentralisation When a function is carried out within departments, such as administrators working in each department. The term can also be used when a business gives more freedom and responsibility to branch managers to make most of their own decisions – even though some key functions will be carried out centrally for a consistent approach.

Functional departments in business

In each of the following sections, the main functions – or tasks – that you can expect to find carried out by different departments are identified. Don't try to remember all this information as you read it. It is more sensible to get a broad overview first, and then return to it to find any information you need.

The Administration department

Administration is a main support activity required by all businesses. If you have any pre-conceived ideas that this just involves keyboarding or filing then forget them now! Senior administrators today have very responsible jobs and carry out a wide range of tasks, from monitoring budgets to interviewing staff for their departments.

Some administrative tasks are, of course, routine – such as opening the mail, preparing and filing documents, sending emails and faxes. Others require more creativity and flexibility, such as arranging travel or important events, from staff meetings to visits by foreign customers. Dealing with external customers is part of the job for most administrators – and customers will judge the business on the way their enquiry is handled.

Poor or sloppy administration can be disastrous for a company's image and reputation. A lost order, a badly typed letter, an important message that is not passed on or the wrong date scheduled for a meeting can cause endless problems and, in some cases, lose customers. Senior managers also depend on the efficiency of their administrators to ensure everything runs smoothly. This allows the manager to concentrate on the task of running the department or business, without having to worry about other aspects as well.

The range of tasks carried out by administrators will depend upon whether they work in a centralised department, or work within a particular department – in which case their work will be slightly different. An administrator in a sales department may be involved in making regular overseas travel arrangements whereas an administrator in personnel would be involved with arranging job interviews. In a small organisation, an administrator is often expected to be a 'jack-of-all-trades', and expected to turn a hand to anything – from checking and paying invoices to keeping the firm's website up to date.

A summary of the range of tasks which is carried out by administrators is listed below. You will learn more about this type of work if you study specialist Unit 6 as part of your BTEC First Diploma.

The Customer Service department

This department is responsible for looking after existing customers who have an enquiry, concern or complaint. Today, customer expectations are high. When customers contact a business they expect a prompt and polite response. They also expect to speak to someone who knows about the products and services, can answer their queries and give advice and information. Unless they get a high level of service they are likely to take their business elsewhere in the future.

Customer service is now recognised as one of the most important aspects involved in running a business

Administration – key tasks

- Collecting, distributing and dispatching the mail.
- Storing records safely and securely, both on paper and on computer, and retrieving these when required.
- Organising meetings, taking notes at meetings and distributing these to participants.
- Responding promptly to enquiries from other members of staff and from external customers.
- Preparing documents using word processing, spreadsheet and presentation packages, such as PowerPoint.
- Sending and receiving messages by telephone, fax and email.
- Making arrangements for visitors to the organisation.
- Making travel arrangements for members of staff who travel on business.
- Purchasing routine supplies, such as stationery and small items of office equipment.
- Making arrangements for events, such as interviews or sales conferences.
- Researching information required by a manager.
- Keeping company and/or departmental records up to date.

Customer Service – key tasks

- Answering customer enquiries about products and services and other related matters.
- Providing specialist advice, tailored to the needs of the user and that particular product or service.
- Giving information and advice about payment options.
- Solving customer problems – from late deliveries to damaged goods.
- Providing after-sales service, including dealing with returned goods, replacing damaged goods, arranging for repairs to be carried out or for spare parts to be obtained and fitted.
- Dealing with customer complaints, both minor and serious, according to company procedures.
- Keeping records of customer complaints and analysing these to resolve problem areas.
- Recording and analysing customer feedback to improve customer service generally and to advise on improvements that could be made in other areas of the business to improve customer satisfaction.

For this reason, most businesses have customer service staff – or a customer service department – where staff are specially trained to handle enquiries and complaints positively and professionally. This does not mean, of course, that other staff can ignore customers and their needs. It simply means that a group of staff specialise in assisting customers.

Organisations that deal mainly with industry, and which manufacture and sell complex products on a large scale, often include technical specialists or engineers in their customer service teams who can give detailed advice and information to users of their product. An example is BAE Systems, which sells planes like the Eurofighter and Hawk jets. Answering queries related to these obviously needs in-depth and specialist knowledge. Similarly, computer suppliers like Dell or PC World, and Internet service providers like BT, have trained IT specialists to handle customer problems – whether from other businesses or from individuals.

Business matters

If you were buying an airplane, you wouldn't expect to pay in cash, obtain a receipt and simply fly it away. At least, not if you were sensible. Instead, you would expect a huge amount of information and advice, negotiated payment terms and customer service and support for as long as you owned it. You might even want your pilots to be specially trained or for the plane to be customised for your own requirements.

All these are part of the 'package' of customer support and service offered by companies such as BAE Systems. BAE Systems has manufacturing sites and support facilities all over England. It is part of a multinational organisation which is involved in designing, manufacturing and supporting civil and military aircraft, ships, submarines and space systems – to name but a few. It is little wonder that working for Customer Solutions and Support (CS&S) at BAE is a highly skilled job. In addition to maintenance and technical advice, BAE also offers an aircraft repair service, a spares service, training for aircrew, flight operations support, and will specially customise planes. An example was a unique BAE 146 Atmospheric Research Aircraft, designed to undertake atmospheric research related to climate change and atmospheric pollution. This aircraft has to fly higher than normal and needs to carry extra fuel tanks for long missions. In addition, special sensors and instruments have been designed and installed.

Although this is an extreme example of highly technical support for the life of a purchase, a similar system is used by many companies which provide expensive or complex products or services – from lifts or cranes to IT systems and security.

If you want to find out more about BAE Systems or BAE customer service, you can visit their website – links are available at www.heinemann.co.uk/hotlinks (express code 1386P).

In addition to dealing with enquiries and providing information and advice, customer service staff also have to deal with complaints and problems. Most businesses have a special procedure for dealing with customer complaints, to make sure that these are dealt with quickly and in a consistent way. In some cases, steps must be taken to make sure that the problem doesn't occur again. Customer service staff have to be aware of the legal rights of customers – and this means a knowledge of consumer law. You will learn more about this if you study specialist Unit 7 for your BTEC First Diploma.

The Distribution department

The main task in distribution is ensuring that all the goods produced or stocked are delivered to the right place on time and in the right condition. Some companies deliver direct to the customer, particularly when goods are bought online. Examples include Amazon and Debenhams. Other businesses hold stocks in giant regional warehouses, such as B&Q, Tesco and Sainsbury's, for delivery to stores around the area. Superstores may use special vehicles which can also carry chilled or frozen items. Other businesses have to move more difficult loads or hazardous substances, such as large engineering parts, cars or chemicals.

It may seem a simple matter just to arrange for goods to be collected. However, distribution involves more than this. A key requirement is that it must be cost-effective – in other words, the cost of distribution must be kept as low as possible. This means obeying a few simple rules:

- Vehicle routes must be planned carefully, preferably so that each vehicle only travels in one direction. This keeps fuel costs down and saves time.
- Making sure, so far as is possible, that vehicles never return empty. This is only possible, of course, if goods are both delivered and collected. If vehicles are only delivering goods, it is cheaper to make sure they operate from a regional or local base, to minimise 'empty journey' time.

Working out the routes of many vehicles, with many different loads – some of which are urgent and some not – can be very complicated. Computer programs help to do this, and it is the specialist job of staff skilled in **logistics** to work out the best routes.

Distribution – key tasks

- Ensuring that goods are properly stored before dispatch.
- Ensuring that all goods for dispatch are properly packed, secure and labelled correctly.
- Checking that vehicles are loaded correctly and safely and that the weight doesn't exceed legal requirements for the vehicle.
- Ensuring that perishable items are stored and distributed in the proper conditions and at the right time.
- Checking that all deliveries match orders in terms of quantity and type of goods – or notifying sales if there is a discrepancy.
- Completing the documentation to accompany each delivery.
- Planning and scheduling the routes of vehicles.
- Notifying sales staff of delivery schedules so that customers (or stores) can be informed.
- Dealing with distribution problems, e.g. through bad weather or vehicle breakdown.

Outsourcing business functions

Outsourcing means employing an external specialist to do a key function required by the business.

A variety of different functions can be outsourced. Warehousing and distribution is one example. IT security services are another – as you will see on page 66. Some service organisations outsource the ordering of office stationery to stationery suppliers who will monitor the stocks and provide goods as needed. Marketing may be outsourced to a specialist agency that will carry out market research and analyse the responses and/or create advertisements and other promotional materials. Catering, cleaning and security are also often outsourced to specialist firms – this may be the case in your college – and standard customer service enquiries may be outsourced to a call centre.

Outsourcing is preferred if:

- The function requires specialist skills which no-one in the business possesses.
- The function requires specialist equipment or facilities which would be expensive to provide and maintain.
- The cost of recruiting specialist staff and providing the required facilities would be more expensive than outsourcing the function.

Small businesses may outsource some of their finance tasks, such as the preparation of their statutory accounts. They will employ a firm of accountants to do this on an annual basis because this is cheaper than employing a specialist accountant themselves.

Many organisations outsource both storage and distribution to external contractors. This is sensible for retailers who buy from many suppliers and have several branches, such as Richer Sounds. A famous distributor in the UK is Eddie Stobart, with its distinctive vehicles – each lorry cab has a female name. Although the company was sold to WA Developments (International) in October 2003 it is still trading under the same name – to keep brand loyalty. Find out more by visiting the Eddie Stobart website – a link is available at www.heinemann.co.uk/hotlinks (express code 1386P). In particular find out how technology is used by the business to help with logistics – including the computers and communication systems on board each vehicle.

The Facilities Management department

If you think about the NHS, you probably think about health. If you think about colleges and universities, you probably think about education. What do they have in common? The answer is large buildings – which need to be kept clean, safe and attractive. For this reason, in all businesses with a large building or campus to look after, you are likely to find a Facilities Management department. Smaller businesses are more likely to outsource this task to a specialist organisation – or rent space in a building where facilities management is part of the agreement.

What do facilities management staff do? The mission statement from the Facilities Management Directorate (another word for Department) at Reading University should give you a good idea:

> Our mission is to deliver services and provide facilities which fully meet the University's present and future needs. In achieving this goal, a safer and secure environment will be maintained in which effective teaching, research, working, residential and recreational activities can take place.

Business terms

Logistics Originally a military term meaning to move people or goods where they are most needed. Now used in business to describe the storage, transportation and delivery of goods.

Risk assessment Checking an area to decide whether each risk or potential danger is high, medium or low and then deciding whether action needs to be taken to reduce the level of risk so that fewer accidents will occur.

Your College will have a similar department, although it may go under a different name, such as Estates Management. This department will be involved in planning any building alterations or refurbishments and arranging for maintenance to be carried out – such as replacing a broken window or making sure that potholes in the car park are filled in. The staff will be responsible for costing and buying buy new furniture and equipment, when needed, and arranging for it to be installed. Even more importantly, they will ensure that you work in a safe environment by regularly carrying out **risk assessments** related to fire or other hazards. They will also test and check all electrical equipment at routine intervals and be responsible for ensuring any

hazardous substances are stored safely. This is very important where there are laboratories or research facilities – as is the case in educational buildings, hospitals and many manufacturing businesses. They will also be responsible for the cleaning and security of the site. In some cases, IT support may also be part of this department.

If you want to find out more, you can see the range of services carried out by the Facilities Management Directorate at Reading University by going to their website – or you can check the services provided to smaller companies by experts in this field, such as Facilities Management Services Ltd. Links are available at www.heinemann.co.uk/hotlinks (express code 1386P).

Facilities Management – key tasks

- Ensuring all buildings are kept well maintained.
- Ensuring any external areas – such as gardens, car parks or recreational facilities are well maintained.
- Carrying out routine maintenance and making or arranging repairs.
- Supplying catering and vending services and, if appropriate, residential accommodation.
- Ensuring the security of all premises owned by the business.
- Ensuring that all buildings and furnishings meet legal health and safety requirements in relation to space, ventilation, heating, cleanliness etc.
- Carrying out risk assessments to ensure all buildings are safe.
- Checking new buildings and advising on adaptation and refurbishment (including the cost of carrying these out).
- Planning and arranging refurbishments, such as interior design, new flooring, new lighting, painting and decorating.
- Costing new projects – including the replacement or addition of furniture items – to ensure these are best value for the price paid.
- Providing advice to other managers relating to facilities management issues.

Talking point

View 1: *Outsourcing is a good idea because specialist skills can be hired – such as security guards and IT experts. This saves money for the business in the long run and gives work to smaller firms and individuals so everyone benefits.*

View 2: *Outsourcing isn't as good as doing it yourself because the people you hire aren't as committed to the success of your business, because they will simply work somewhere else if the business fails.*

With which viewpoint do you agree – and why?

Over to you!

1 The most popular website for administrators and PAs (personal assistants) is PA Assist – a link to this site is available at www.heinemann.co.uk/hotlinks (express code 1386P). It was launched in May 2000 to offer essential information, products and services to senior support staff. In 2003, the site was voted the number 1 online resource in the OfficeTeam annual survey. Use the site to find out more about the work of senior administrators and PAs. List **five** facts about this work that you didn't know before and compare your list with those made by other members of your group.

2 Many businesses now use technology to improve their customer service, such as companies that trade online. They often include frequently asked questions (FAQs) on their websites or enable customers to click on a link to write an email. Alternatively, you may see a 'contact us' option or PhoneMe button, which the customer clicks to make free telephone contact.

  a Suggest **two** reasons why FAQs pages on websites are useful for both the customer *and* the organisation.

  b Many organisations enable customers to track their orders online. Again, suggest **two** reasons why this is useful.

  c Check out the following websites that operate customer service sections online and compare them – links are available at www.heinemann.co.uk/hotlinks (express code 1386P).
In each case, say why you think this particular company has taken this approach. Then decide which one you would find the best if you were a customer, and why.
    • Amazon (look at the foot of the page and click Help for more questions).
    • Dell (select Support at the top of the page).
    • Fedex (select your country first, then click on Customer Service).

3 Facilities managers have to make some decisions which would never occur to you at home, such as how often to replace a light bulb. At home, you would replace one as soon as it failed (assuming you had a spare in the cupboard!). This wouldn't be practical, however, if you had a huge building to maintain, such as a large hospital or airport terminal.

  a As a group, identify *why* light bulbs aren't replaced immediately in this situation.

  b Then suggest the best way to deal with this, bearing in mind your resources and your customers' needs.

4 Try and solve some distribution problems! Work in small groups and then compare your ideas.

Your retail business sells cut flowers in all its stores. Stores send in their orders overnight, based on sales the previous day and their predicted sales for the day of the week to follow. The flowers are transported in special vans to keep them cool. For your area, you only have two vans and these must be loaded and on the road by 6 am to deliver to all the stores by noon. The two routes involve a circular path through towns in your area. Route 1 covers 12 stores to the west and route B covers 14 stores in the east, each starting at the nearest store to the depot.

Your job is to ensure that all orders are fulfilled promptly and that, if this is not possible, action is taken to maximise sales wherever possible.

  a You discover that there aren't red roses to meet the orders. Every store has ordered roses and the total required is 1300. You only have 1092.

  b The store at the furthest point of route 1 has a large order which the customer wants to collect at 9.30 am.

  c At 11am, the driver on route 1 tells you that he has no flowers for the next store – they are missing from the van. You find that, by mistake, they have been loaded on the wrong vehicle.

  d At 11.30am, the van on route 2 breaks down with a serious mechanical problem which will take several hours to fix.

The Finance department

This department is the 'engine room' of all businesses. This is because no business can function without a regular stream of income to pay the bills. It is the job of finance staff to keep track of all the money being earned and spent so that the senior managers always know exactly how much profit (or loss) is being made by each product or by each part of the business and how much money is currently held by the business. This enables critical decisions to be made rapidly, based on accurate information. In some cases, this can mean the difference between success or failure of the business as a whole.

In many large businesses, different types of financial experts are employed.

- **Management accountants** monitor departmental **budgets** and current income from sales, prepare forecasts and specialise in analysing day-to-day financial information and keeping senior managers informed.
- **Financial accountants** are concerned with the preparation of the **statutory accounts**. All companies must provide a Balance Sheet and Profit and Loss Account each year, and most produce a **cash flow statement** as well. You will learn about cash flow in unit 3.
- **A credit controller** monitors overdue payments and takes action to recover any **bad debts**. You will find out more about credit control in Unit 3 (page 230).

They are supported by finance staff who undertake the activities of recording and banking receipts, chasing up late payments, making payments for items purchased and making sure that all these amounts are recorded in the accounts system. Today virtually all businesses use computer accounting packages to record financial transactions and prepare accounts. They also use spreadsheets to analyse financial data. Some finance departments are also responsible for preparing and paying staff salaries and preparing payroll documents, but other businesses outsource this to a specialist agency or bureau.

Finally, all businesses need to spend money. They may plan to expand and want to buy new premises. They may need new machinery and equipment to keep up to date with technology and remain competitive. Capital expenditure on these items may be financed from **reserves**, but additional money may need to be raised. If the business needs to borrow money then it will want to do so at the cheapest rates possible and also want good repayment terms. Deciding the best place to obtain these funds is a specialist job and normally the task of a senior financial manager, who will be responsible for advising the **board of directors** (see page 81).

Finance – key tasks

- Producing invoices, checking payments are received and chasing up overdue payments.
- Recording all money received.
- Checking invoices received and paying these.
- Preparing the payroll and paying staff salaries.
- Checking departmental budgets to ensure managers are not overspending.
- Issuing regular budget reports to all departmental managers.
- Producing cash flow forecasts and regular financial reports for senior managers.
- Advising senior managers on sources of finance for capital expenditure.
- Producing the statutory accounts each year.

Statutory accounts Financial accounts required by law, e.g. Balance Sheet and Profit and Loss Account.

Reserves Money kept back from previous profits for future use.

Capital investment Money spent on major permanent items, e.g. new buildings or machinery.

Cash flow The amount of money flowing into the business and from which expenses are paid.

Cash flow forecast A forecast of the expected income over the next few months and expenses due. This shows if there will be sufficient funds to pay all the bills.

Budget A plan which shows agreed amounts of expenditure over a period, usually for each department.

Bad debts Debts which have not been paid.

The IT department

This department may also be known as IT services or IT support – because as well as being responsible for obtaining and installing IT systems in the business, a key role is supporting users and maintaining the system. This is vital, given the number of crucial business tasks that are now carried out on computers and the importance of the data stored in the system. A failure of the IT system can be catastrophic.

Most businesses today operate a computer **network** system with all the computers linked through servers, which are themselves interlinked. Maintaining the **servers**, installing new (communal) software and additional hardware, such as printers and scanners, is all part of the job for the IT staff. In addition, they will often give advice on – or purchase and issue – computer supplies, such as cabling and network cards as well as **consumables** such as CDs and printer cartridges – to ensure that those used are compatible with the system.

IT specialists are also involved with potential new developments. Technology is changing all the time and senior managers will be expected to be kept up to date with those aspects which would benefit the company. In addition, current equipment will need replacing and software upgrading at regular intervals.

Above all, however, the IT team is responsible for system security. Making sure that only authorised users have access to the system, protecting the system against viruses and hackers and ensuring there is a full back-up system to restore critical data in an emergency is vitally important.

Finally, IT staff will help and assist users themselves – from repairing problems and glitches to advising on the best way to use the software installed or updating the company Intranet. The website of the company is likely to be technically maintained by the IT staff, but the content will normally be devised by marketing staff – as you will see on page 66.

Server A computer which allows access to files and programs stored as shared resources on a computer network.

Network A system of linked computers which can communicate and share information.

Consumables Items which are used regularly and need to be routinely replaced.

Intranet A private area on a network on which information is stored that can only be accessed by authorised users.

Firewall A program, or set of programs, that protects a computer system from unauthorised access.

Downtime The time when a computer system or production machine is not functioning and sales and profits are affected.

- Recommending the purchase of new computers and/or software to keep up to date with technological developments and matching these to the needs of the business.
- Buying and installing new computers and connecting these to the network.
- Installing software on servers.
- Operating a helpdesk to advise users experiencing computer problems.
- Providing assistance and guidance on new equipment or software.
- Repairing the computer system when required.
- Advising on and/or obtaining/issuing computer supplies and consumables.
- Connecting new or additional equipment to the system.
- Devising a security system which allows access only to authorised users by means of passwords and computer IDs.
- Technical maintenance of the website to ensure it is constantly operational and runs smoothly.
- Monitoring computer use by staff to ensure this complies with the published company IT policy.
- Installing security devices to protect against hackers, such as a **firewall**, which prevents external users from accessing company data.
- Installing virus protection and monitoring systems and installing automated protection systems to reduce the risk of viruses being downloaded.
- Operating a full back-up system for critical data so that this can be recovered quickly in an emergency.

Business matters

The abbreviation POS stands for **point of sale** and EPOS stands for **electronic point of sale**. POS is a critical area for businesses, especially in the retail trade. Marketing, for example, will create special POS materials to attract you at the checkout. EPOS refers to computerised cashpoints – sometimes also called POS tills or POS systems, which automatically capture and process data and link to the company financial system. Additional software means that debit and credit cards – and cashback – is also available through these tills.

Quite simply, every customer purchase is recorded as a sale. Multiple purchases are broken down into each separate product. Each night a report analyses the sales made at each till, and the total sales from all the tills. Products which are selling well are highlighted, and so are those that are not. The report can be on every manager's desk within hours. This enables rapid decisions to be made about stock lines and stock to be moved, when necessary, from one branch to another.

Data can also be analysed in other ways. Customer accounts can be analysed to see which products they are buying and how often. This is how Tesco targets its loyalty card customers with voucher offers. Staff codes can be analysed to check sales levels and to calculate any bonuses or commission. Most EPOS systems also include

Modern EPOS systems do a lot more than just add and subtract

stock control software, so that as each sale is made the stock level is automatically updated. A report then shows the amount of replacement stock then required.

You can find out more by searching under EPOS or POS tills in Google – a link is available at www.heinemann.co.uk/hotlinks (express code 1386P). You will also learn more about them in Unit 3.

Increasing attacks on computer systems by hackers and viruses such as Blaster and Sasser, both of which affected Microsoft programs, have created a surge of interest in computer security. The sales of security software are now expected to rise to more than £7 billion by 2006.

Whereas you might buy an off-the-shelf firewall and virus protection package to install at home, large business networks need a lot more. But there is a problem. Employing IT specialists who can forecast security problems, choose, install and maintain the best software and monitor the system 24 hours a day is both difficult and expensive. In many cases it is more sensible – and cheaper – to outsource the job to a specialist security provider.

This has resulted in a sharp increase in the number of companies which make security appliances and businesses which specialise in managing firewalls, intrusion detection systems, antivirus systems and web filtering. They regularly test their clients' network and keep up to date on the latest threats. Additional protection is given to companies who are involved in e-business, including advice on data encryption and authentication for protecting customer payments. One research company, IDC, predicts that the market for computer security appliances alone will be worth over £2 billion by 2005.

Protecting the system from electronic attack isn't the only security aspect to concern businesses – particularly since 9/11. For that reason, some companies, including Richer Sounds, have gone underground – keeping their computer systems in The Bunker. The Bunker isn't a disused bomb shelter but a former NATO station which is 30 metres deep. It not only provides computer security but guarantees to keep systems operating through a 40-hour physical or man-made disaster. You can find out more on the Internet – a link is available at www.heinemann.co.uk/hotlinks (express code 1386P). You will find this information useful when you go on to study Unit 2 (page 193) and if you are interested in e-business you will learn more if you study specialist Unit 8.

The Marketing department

The best definition of marketing was given by an American called Peter Drucker. He described marketing as 'looking at the business through the customer's eyes'. This sums up marketing. It is all about identifying and meeting customer needs.

Many businesses consider this so important that they are described as being **marketing-led**. This means that every single person in the organisation is trained to put the customer first – from the production worker who has to produce high quality goods to the accounts clerk who must respond to a customer enquiry promptly and accurately.

Another easy way to understand marketing is through the **marketing mix** which consists of four Ps.

- **Product**. Who are our customers? What do they want to buy? Are our customer needs changing? Which products are we offering and how many are we selling? What new products are about to be launched? In which areas are sales growing – and how can we sustain this? Which products are 'mature' so that sales are static – and how can we renew interest? Which sales are falling and what, if anything, can we do?

- **Price**. How much should we charge? Should we reduce the price at the start to attract the most customers – or charge as much as we can because the product only has a short shelf life? Can we charge different prices to different types of customers? What discounts can we give? What services or products should we give away or sell very cheaply – and what benefits would this bring?

- **Promotion**. How can we tell people about our products? Should we have specialist sales staff? Where can we advertise? Where should we advertise to attract the attention of our key customers? How else can we promote the product – should we give free samples or run a competition? Where and how can we obtain free publicity? Should we send **direct mailshots** and, if so, what product information should we include?

- **Place**. How can we distribute our product(s)? Should we sell direct to the customer or through retailers? Do we need specialist wholesalers or overseas agents to sell for us? What can we sell over the telephone? How can the Internet help us to sell more?

These aspects are all the questions that marketing staff need to ask themselves – and answer. They start by aiming to identify their target customer and future customer needs through **market research**. You will learn more about this in unit 2. Products are then developed (or adapted) or services offered which will meet these needs. If this is done well, it gives the company an edge over its competitors. James Dyson proved this when he invented the bag-less vacuum cleaner. Although traditional cleaner manufacturers have copied his lead, his name is still associated with radical change in the type of cleaners on sale. He has now invented a cleaner which 'talks' to the service department when it is faulty, to reduce service time, again in response to feedback from customers.

Of course, it is no use developing new products or offering new services if no-one knows about them. Marketing is therefore responsible for all the promotional activities which tell the customer what is now available. This can include advertising, sales promotions and publicity campaigns.

The **company website** is, of course, a key way of communicating with customers. For this reason, the image and the content of the company website is usually the responsibility of the marketing department who will regularly update this and send update newsletters to registered users of their site by email. Monitoring the use of the website and obtaining information on the customers who use it may be undertaken by the company or outsourced to a specialist agency.

A relatively new area is **e-marketing**. No doubt you know that every time you go on the Internet you see adverts. Sometimes these are helpful,

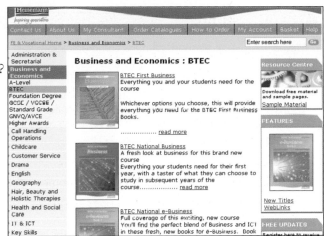

Figure 1.15 *The Heinemann website*

other times they are just annoying! E-marketing includes more than just pop-up ads, however. Kelloggs launched a TV advert asking viewers to describe the taste of Crunchy Nut on their website to win a trip to New York. This links the traditional media with a marketing opportunities. You can expect to see this area developing further and faster over the next few years – with many businesses outsourcing their e-marketing requirements to specialist agencies.

You can find out more about the role of marketing on the Internet – links are available at www.heinemann.co.uk/hotlinks (express code 1386P).

One **microsite** is part of the Royal National Institute for the Deaf (RNID) web campaign and targets telling young people about the dangers of loud music as part of the 'Don't Lose the Music' campaign. If you like going to clubs or chilling out to loud CDs in your room, you might want to read it – a link is available at www.heinemann.co.uk/hotlinks (express code 1386P).

Figure 1.16 *'Don't lose the music' logo*

Business terms

Media Traditional methods of mass communication, e.g. newspapers, magazines, TV and radio.

New media Digital and electronic methods of communication, e.g. websites and SMS messaging.

Sponsorship Giving financial or other support in return for recognition.

Endorsement Promotion of a product or service, usually by a celebrity, which implies that they use it or approve of it, e.g. David Beckham and Vodafone; Jamie Oliver and Sainsbury's.

Direct mail Mailshots promoting a product or service (or, in the case of charities, asking for a donation) direct to people's homes.

Publicity campaign A linked combination of marketing activities, often used for a product launch.

e-marketing Marketing using new media or electronic methods of communication, especially via the Internet.

Press release A short article summarising a new development and sent to the press. If published, these provide free publicity.

Marketing – key tasks

- Carrying out market research to obtain feedback on potential and existing products and/or services.
- Analysing market research responses and advising senior managers of the results and their implications.
- Promoting a new product launch through appropriate advertising and promotional methods.
- Obtaining information on the profile of existing customers and applying this to advertising and promotional campaigns.
- Producing press advertisements for newspapers, magazines, television, radio, billboards etc.
- Preparing direct mailshots to send to the homes of existing customers and potential customers who fit the right profile.
- Organising publicity campaigns, such as through press releases about business activities and developments.
- Obtaining **sponsorship** or **endorsement** for company products.
- Arranging company stands at trade shows and exhibitions.
- Producing and distributing publicity materials, such as catalogues or brochures.
- Ensuring that the company website reflects the image of the company, that the content is up to date and that customer enquiries via the website are handled promptly.
- Ensuring that the company website comes out at the top (or very high) on search engine lists. The correct term for this is **search engine optimisation (SEO)**.
- Arranging online promotions and advertisements, including **microsites**. These are 'mini' websites created for a special campaign.
- Identifying other **e-marketing** and **SMS marketing** opportunities, such as online competitions and text messages. This also includes **viral marketing** – where customers spread the message by forwarding the email or SMS to their friend.

Talking point

View 1: Pop-up ads and other adverts on the Internet are a waste of time and very irritating. They should be banned.

View 2: Adverts on the Internet can be a useful source of extra information when you are looking for something. More firms should do it.

With which viewpoint do you agree – and why?

The Personnel department

The Personnel department is concerned with the welfare of the staff, or human resources, of the business. It is also involved with prospective employees because it is responsible for recruitment. Making sure that each job vacancy is filled by the best person is time-consuming but very important. The recruitment process, from advertising to interviewing, is expensive. Hiring the wrong person can be very costly and cause serious problems both for the individual and the business.

Once each new member of staff has been appointed, it is usual for them to attend an **induction programme** which tells them about the business, their rights and responsibilities as employees, the company rules and the requirements of their new job. All internal training courses are organised by personnel, which also monitors attendance, popularity and suitability of the different types of training available. Requests and arrangements to attend external courses are also handled by this department.

Personnel has a key role in helping to ensure that, so far as is possible, the company retains good, experienced staff. As a first step, it will analyse **staff turnover figures**, which show the rate at which people leave the organisation. It will study the reasons for this, to see if there are any problem areas which can be remedied. People may leave for justifiable reasons, such as moving to another area or for promotion elsewhere, but dissatisfaction with the job or the company should be investigated. In some companies, exit interviews are held with staff to find out their views on the business when they leave.

Personnel – key tasks

- Advertising job vacancies at the Jobcentre, in newspapers or magazines or at an employment agency – whichever is the most appropriate for the job.
- Notifying internal staff of promotion opportunities.
- Receiving and recording all job applications, arranging interviews for short-listed candidates and notifying candidates of the interview result.
- Ensuring all new staff receive a contract of employment and other essential information, such as details of the company's grievance and disciplinary procedures.
- Arranging staff training, e.g. induction training for new employees, internal training and courses linked to the job and company developments and external courses to help personal and career development.
- Overseeing and monitoring the working conditions of staff.
- Ensuring the company complies with health and safety requirements and keeping accident records.
- Recording sick leave and reasons for absence.
- Carrying out company welfare policies. These may include long-service awards, help for families during times of serious illness, a company loan scheme, etc.
- Providing employees with appropriate information which affects them, such as details of the company pension scheme, security policies and procedures, holiday entitlement, staff benefit schemes etc.
- Advising managers on employment law and the **legal rights and responsibilities** of the company and its employees.
- Keeping records of any grievances and disciplinary actions and their outcome.
- Monitoring the terms and conditions of employment, and wage rates, to make sure that these are fair and reasonable and similar to those offered by other employers.
- Maintaining staff records and keeping these up to date.
- Liaising with any staff associations or trade unions which represent the workforce.

All human beings normally have certain key expectations or requirements from their employer. They expect to be treated and paid fairly, to have appropriate working conditions, to have training opportunities which will improve their promotion prospects and support if they are ill or have serious personal problems. They also want a varied and interesting job and appreciation when they have done well or put in an extra effort. All these factors help **motivation**, which means people are keen to work hard – and this benefits both the staff and the business. Personnel has an important role to play in this process by monitoring working conditions, offering a range of welfare policies to help and support staff with problems and ensuring that the pay rates of the company are both fair between types and grades of staff but also similar (or better) than those of other businesses employing the same types of workers.

Many organisations have **staff associations** which monitor the views and conditions of staff and make these known. Other businesses are involved with one, or more, trade unions which represent the workers, especially on pay and conditions. A senior personnel manager will liaise with these organisations, keep them informed of changes and developments and be involved in any negotiations with senior management.

Today all employees and employers have a number of legal rights and responsibilities. These relate to health and safety at work, to data protection (which restricts the type of information that can be held on employees and customers and how it is used) and to employment issues. It is the task of personnel to make sure that the business complies with the current laws and stays up to date with legal changes and developments. This is particularly important if there is a dispute of any type. All employees must receive the written terms and conditions of their employment in a document within one month of starting work and must know how to report a serious problem at work through the grievance procedure. They must also be clearly aware of any actions they could take which would result in disciplinary action or dismissal – and exactly what would happen. This information is contained in the disciplinary procedures.

You will learn more about this area in Unit 2 (pages 149–155) and find out more about employment law and trade unions if you study specialist unit 5 for your BTEC First Diploma.

Over to you!

1 Understanding financial management isn't just important in business, it's vital for people in their private lives too. No matter what you do, or how much money you have, if you regularly spend more than you earn then you will sooner or later have serious problems. Yet living within a budget isn't easy and Imran, a student on a two-year course, really struggles. How would you advise him to solve each of his problems?

  a Imran earns £40 per week in his part-time job, yet is always broke by the middle of the week. When you ask him how much he spends, and what he buys, he hasn't a clue.

  b Imran likes to impress his friends by having the latest CDs, DVDs and computer games and by wearing fashionable clothes. He also doesn't like turning down invitations to go out. He estimates that he spends about £60 a week on these activities alone but doesn't like the idea of cutting back.

  c You find out that Imran has been paying for these with his credit card – and now has over £1,000 in debts. Which of the following would you advise him to do, and why?

    i Pay off his credit card when he can, even though they are charging him high interest.

    ii Transfer the debt to a credit card offering an 'interest free' period for 6 months.

    iii Borrow the money from a bank.

    iv Pay off the debt with an interest free student overdraft and try to pay this back whilst he's still a student.

    v Ask his father for the money.

  Compare your ideas as a group.

2 Find out about the IT policy at your college and how this affects both staff and students. Then find out how IT staff monitor the way computers are used in college and the security measures that are in place to prevent hacking and viruses being introduced into the network. Make a short summary list of your findings. If you have a home computer, then compare the systems at your college with the security you need at home. If you have broadband access, or are online for long periods of time, you are more vulnerable. Find out if any IT experts in your class know why!

3 a Find out the customer profile of your course. This means listing all the key facts about each member of your group – gender, age, address, previous school, previous qualifications, interests etc. and then seeing which are the most common features.

b Use this information to decide **three** ways in which you could advertise or promote the course to make sure most people who would be interested would know about it .

c Finally, decide **six** places where it would be a waste to advertise or promote it, because none of your group would see it or hear it.

4 Are you motivated as a student or in a part-time job? If so, then you want to work hard and do your best. However, the factors that motivate people are many and varied. As a group, score each of the following factors by giving 12 marks to the one which is most important to you and 1 to the one which is least important. Then see which are most important to your group as a whole. An important lesson here is to realise that everyone is different!

- A good rate of pay.
- Praise for doing well.
- Plenty of up-to-date equipment.
- Interesting work.
- A sympathetic and understanding boss/tutor.
- Having responsibility.
- Colleagues you like and enjoy being with.
- Good facilities, e.g. refectory or staff restaurant, rest rooms etc.
- Being kept informed and consulted on changes that affect you.
- Long holidays.
- Hours that fit in with your family commitments or social life.
- The opportunity to move 'upwards and onwards' if you work hard and do well.

The Production department

Production is responsible for all the aspects relating to the manufacture or assembly of goods. Production staff are responsible for ensuring that the goods are produced on time and are of the right quality. Quality requirements can vary considerably. If a filing cabinet is 0.01 mm too wide, this is unlikely to be a problem. For businesses which produce silicon chips or DVDs, or many types of scientific equipment, this tiny difference could make the item unfit for use.

Quality no longer involves just checking goods after they have been produced. By then it is too late! Instead quality is 'built-in' at every stage of the production process, starting with the raw materials. Marks & Spencer, for example, sets down precise standards for all its producers, starting with the type of raw materials used. In clothing, for example, this includes not just the type and weight of material, but the thread and fastenings too.

Raw materials will be stored near to the production area in a separate 'stores area' or stores department. If a manufacturer uses a large number of parts – such as a car producer – this can be very expensive, in terms of the space required and the manpower to oversee the stock. For this reason, many manufacturers today operate a **just-in-time** (JIT) system. This involves having an agreement with specific suppliers to provide small quantities, quickly, when they are needed. There are benefits for both parties. The suppliers know that they have a regular buyer. The manufacturer no longer needs to store large quantities of goods or worry about having sufficient stocks on the premises all the time.

Today most production departments use automation as much as possible. This means that

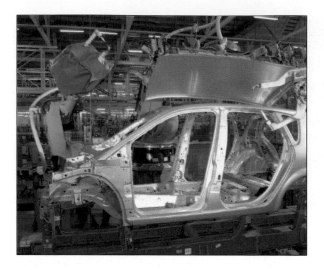
Most production departments are automated

machines or robots do all the routine or dangerous jobs. If you went to watch a bottling plant, for example, you would find that the cleaning, filling and labelling of the bottles is all done as a continuous process by machines. The task of the operators is to check that the production 'line' is functioning as it should – often by checking consoles and computer screens as much as by watching the work as it progresses. Some industries use CIM, where the control of the process is also done by computer.

Another change has been away from standard production lines where each worker only does one small part of a process that cannot be automated. Instead, teams of operators work together and are responsible for a sequence of operations. This makes the job more interesting and makes it easier to ensure high quality, as the team is also responsible for each one of their tasks being done correctly. This system is also more flexible because changes can easily be introduced at any stage by giving instructions to the teams affected. For that reason, it is used by many car manufacturers who often want to vary certain models.

Production staff are responsible for all the following aspects of production:

- **Production planning** – which involves deciding what will be made, when, and which machines and operators will be used. They must prevent bottlenecks or other operational problems and calculate a realistic timescale for completing a job, bearing in mind other jobs that are in progress.

- **Production control** – which means constantly checking progress to make sure that production plans are met – and taking remedial action if problems occur. This could be because of machinery breakdown, substandard raw materials or labour shortages.

- **Machine utilisation control** – which is concerned with minimising problems by keeping all the equipment and machinery in good working order. This involves checking to ensure none is overloaded or overused without being routinely checked and maintained. This is important because if a machine malfunctions it may produce damaged goods. If it breaks down altogether then production of that product will cease. Because this aspect is so important, many organisations have a maintenance plan which shows the dates on which machines will be out of operation for inspection and servicing. These dates are then taken into consideration when production plans are made.

- **Staff utilisation control** – which concentrates on making sure all the staff are working effectively and efficiently and concentrating their efforts on key production areas and targets. This is very important in industries which are labour-intensive and use more people than machines, such as assembling circuit boards or sewing jeans.

- **Final quality checks** – to make certain that the product is of the correct standard. This can be done in a variety of ways – and may even be done by machine. Each item may be examined by hand – or passed through a machine which checks that the size and tolerance is correct or items may be selected for inspection on a random sampling basis. This would be the case if a large number of identical items is being produced, such as cups or biros.

Production – key tasks

- Storing and checking the stocks of raw materials.
- Planning production schedules to maximise machine capacity and staff levels.
- Producing or assembling the finished product.
- Checking the quality of the product at all stages of the production process.
- Checking that production is on schedule and taking action if there are any delays or problems.
- Undertaking any finishing processes required.
- Packing and storing the final products, ready for distribution.
- Scheduling routine machinery inspections and maintenance.
- Carrying out repairs to machinery and equipment as required.

Finally, production will also be involved in preparing items for dispatch. This may involve simply packing the finished items – such as household equipment or clothing – and transporting them to the dispatch department. In other cases, it may involve various finishing processes. For example, paper is produced in huge rolls. These may be transported intact but,

in many cases, the paper is cut to different sizes and boxed or packaged. It then looks like the type of product you would see on the shelves of a stationery store.

The Purchasing department

All businesses need to buy a wide variety of items on a routine basis. You have already seen that manufacturers need to buy raw materials. Retailers need to buy stocks of goods to sell. Service providers such as hotels and hospitals will need to buy food, bed linen and towels and, in the case of the hospital, medical supplies and drugs. Even the smallest office will need some basic supplies, such as paper, and small items of equipment.

Buying consumable items such as these is normally the job of specialist buyers in an organisation. This is usually cheaper than each department buying its own goods, because standard items can be bought more cheaply in bulk. Purchasing staff will take out contracts with regular suppliers and make sure that the terms of the contract are met, in relation to delivery, cost, quantity and quality. They will also ensure that all items are checked on delivery and refer any problems back to the supplier.

Purchasing staff must ensure that the items required are purchased at a competitive price. This is not necessarily the cheapest price, but takes account of other factors, such as the reliability of the supplier, the quality required and the delivery date. Retail buyers must also take account of customer needs, alternative sources of supply, current fashions and trends and the price the

Business terms

Job production The production method used for 'one-off' items or when only a small number of similar items is made – such as designer clothes 'originals', ships, satellites, bridges.

Batch production The method of producing different quantities of a number of similar goods – such as in a bakery, cosmetics producer and frozen food processing firm.

Mass production The method of producing large quantities of identical products on a continuous production line. This is the case with many household appliances, cars and consumer electronics.

Flow production Where the product is produced continuously using a technological process – such as gas, oil or paper.

Line The term used for the main production line. Keeping this moving as planned is crucial to meeting production targets.

Bottleneck When one stage of the process disrupts the rest because it cannot operate at the correct speed.

Computer Integrated Manufacturing (CIM) Where the design and manufacturing process is controlled by computer.

Quality assurance Ensuring quality is built-in at each stage – from purchasing raw materials to final checks.

Purchasing – key tasks

- Ordering raw materials, stock and/or consumables from authorised suppliers.
- Solving problems when there are supply issues. This may mean chasing up or changing the supplier.
- Evaluating alternative sources of supply in relation to price, reliability, quality, payment terms, terms of delivery etc.
- Liaising with managers and stock controllers over levels of supplies and reordering as necessary.
- Finding sources of supply to satisfy new requirements or changes in demand.
- Monitoring alternative supplies or sources of supply which could result in a cost saving or other benefits.
- Ensuring that all items are checked on delivery and referring problems relating to quality or quantity back to the supplier.
- Maintaining good relations with the suppliers.
- (In a retail business) deciding and advising on the best lines to stock for the next season, bearing in mind current sales levels and future trends.

customer will be expected to pay. The difference between the total sales and the cost of goods sold is known as the gross margin. All retail businesses aim to operate at a certain margin, e.g. 10 per cent, and will source their supplies to try to achieve this. In some cases this will mean buying products from abroad, in which case the purchasing staff must be aware of import restrictions and regulations and understand how currency rates may change and how this would affect the price paid. The main aim is not to pay more, which would reduce the **gross margin**.

Computers have revolutionised buying methods in many firms, as goods can be purchased and paid for online. These are known as **B2B (business to business) transactions**. This speeds up the buying process and means there is less need to keep large stocks on the premises.

The Research and Development department

The title of this department is usually shortened to R&D and, in many industries, it also involves product design as well. Staff working in R&D are concerned with new product developments as well as improvements to existing products or product lines.

Improvements to existing products are often ongoing as a result of market research or

customer feedback (see page 67). You can see these improvements around you all the time – ring-pull cans, microwaveable containers for ready meals, transparent jug kettles and memory sticks for computers to name but a few!

New products may be developed because of scientific or technological scientific advances, such as mobile phones, new drugs, Wi-Fi (wire free computers which link to each other, related equipment and the Internet by radio waves) and satellite direction systems in cars. Or they may occur because someone has a good idea – such as James Dyson and his bag-less vacuum cleaner or Trevor Bayliss, who invented the wind-up radio.

The word 'research' may conjure up ideas of scientists peering into microscopes and, in some cases, this may be appropriate – but not in all of them. You can divide research into two types. **Pure research** aims to help us to learn and understand more about anything – from outer space to DNA. It is mainly carried out by universities and scientific establishments. **Applied research** is focused investigation into how new discoveries can be used to improve products – such as non-stick pans which were developed from space research. This is the type of research done in business organisations.

The aim of R&D is to work with designers to develop a usable product that can be manufactured at a reasonable cost, sold at a competitive price and is safe to use. The type of activities undertaken, however, can vary considerably, depending upon the type of industry. Trying to discover new, safe drugs is a very different matter to improving car performance! For that reason, this area attracts staff who are not only very experienced in their own industry, but also in their own field – from software developers to food technologists.

Many organisations aim to continually improve *both* product design and performance. **Industrial design** relates to the appearance of a product – from a computer to a car, or even the packaging of a standard product – from perfume to soap. Designers want their product to stand out from its competitors and to look attractive. The iMac is an excellent example of a successful industrial design project. Today most products are designed using Computer Aided Design (CAD) packages, which enable a designer to sketch a basic shape and then vary the dimensions, angles and sizes of certain parts. The product can even undergo stress testing by computer. **Engineering design** relates to product performance. In the case of a computer,

this means more memory and greater operating speed.

Organisations are often very secretive about R&D because of the costs involved in developing a new product. Car manufacturers, for example, will keep their new designs or the results of performance tests on a new car 'under wraps' and swear all the staff working on the project to secrecy, to ensure their competitors don't find out about it.

Technological advances through R&D not only affect our lives but also the ways in which businesses operate. New developments in computer software and hardware change the way all departments create, store and share data and communicate with their customers. New types of machinery and equipment can revolutionise a production process. Developments and inventions can also change promotional techniques. Blackburn Rovers football club used new technology to get local people to support the team by installing talking posters in bus shelters. Whether Graham Souness's pleas proved annoying or fascinating to local people waiting in the wind and rain is another matter!

Research and Development – key tasks

Note that the exact activities will depend upon the industry.
- In the pharmaceutical industry, scientists are employed to research and develop new medicines and drugs.
- In the food industry, technologists work with chefs to prepare new products such as ready meals (and low-calorie versions) and new sauces or flavourings.
- Electronic companies concentrate on new technology products, such as plasma screens and WAP phones.
- In the aerospace and car industries, R&D specialists concentrate on the performance of the product and on its design. Engineers will focus on improving performance and safety whilst reducing emissions or noise. Designers will concentrate on the shape and look, both internally and externally.
- In software and IT, specialists will concentrate on improving existing programs or games and developing new ones, or improving/developing computer hardware – normally smaller, faster or with a greater range of functions.

The Government is keen to increase innovation in the UK, especially as this has been proved to increase profits and enable firms to be more competitive. It provides advice and information to businesses and tax incentives for R&D spending.

However, R&D is only one type of innovation. Businesses may choose instead to use different types of equipment and make things in a different, more efficient way; train their workforce to have higher (or more) skills or introduce new ways of working.

You can find out more by reading case studies about innovations on the Innovations website. In the past these have been introduced at companies from Dolland & Aitchison (the opticians), to an oyster farm on the Innovation website – a link is available at www.heinemann.co.uk/hotlinks (express code

1386P). This proves that innovation doesn't just bring advantages to manufacturing businesses but to primary producers and those providing a service as well.

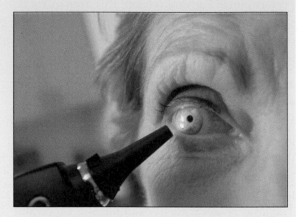

Teamwork innovations improved optical services at Dolland & Aitchison

Business terms

FMCGs Fast moving consumer goods, such as toiletries and groceries.

Merchandisers Sales people employed by household product firms. They visit supermarkets to persuade them to stock the brand, display it prominently and carry out in-store promotions.

Telesales Selling goods over the telephone.

Cold calling Calling on people at random to sell them a product or service. Householders can prevent telesales cold calling by registering their telephone number with the Telephone Preference Service.

Sales lead Information that a particular person is interested in making a purchase.

The Sales department

Sales is a crucial function for all businesses. There is no point making superb products (or stocking them), or offering a wide range of services, and then not being able to sell very much. For that reason, most businesses have sales targets, which you will read about on page 83–4. Meeting these targets is the responsibility of the sales staff or sales team.

Sales staff must be in constant touch with their customers, although their job varies, depending upon the industry. In a supermarket, for example, there is no need to do much actual selling in a store. Customers only visit if they want to buy something, they choose the goods themselves and take them to a checkout to be processed. The same applies to many standard products bought from a retailer, such as books, toiletries and CDs, all known as **FMCGs**. The only time you may need assistance is to find what you are looking for, check what's in stock or ask for basic information on a specific product. This is why producers of FMCGs employ **merchandisers** rather than traditional sales staff.

You would expect rather more than this though, if you wanted to buy a technical product, such as a digital camera, home cinema system, or an expensive item, such as a car or a special holiday. You would need expert information and advice and expect the sales staff to know their products in detail. Stores which sell these type of items therefore need trained sales staff who are friendly, easy to talk to and can both describe or demonstrate their products and link these to the customer's specific needs.

Business buyers also expect a high quality service and in-depth advice and information. They may be buying highly complex and expensive industrial or scientific equipment and need to negotiate special finance arrangements – particularly if they are overseas buyers. Business buyers will also want to negotiate discounts for bulk purchases. Sales representatives are employed who travel to potential customers and regularly visit existing companies to ensure their current needs are met.

Some of the most involved business negotiations are between engineering consultants who bid for complex projects all over the world – from building bridges or tunnels to sports arenas. They have to specify what they will do, how they will do it and what it will cost – and then 'sell' their project to the buyer against strong competition. As you can imagine, this type of 'selling' is very skilled indeed. You can find out more about these type of projects if you look at the ARUP engineering website – a link is available at www.heinemann.co.uk/hotlinks (express code 1386P).

At a more basic level, many organisations train all their staff to try to recognise customer situations when a sale may be made or additional items may be sold which would fit a customer's requirements. This is why you are nearly always offered shoe cleaner when you buy a pair of shoes and why bank staff may recommend one of their accounts or cards when you are visiting about something else. Telesales staff may also be employed to follow up customer enquiries made online or in response to press advertisements. Because cold calling often annoys people, ethical businesses are more likely to restrict their activities to contacting existing customers or to following up sales leads.

Employing a skilled sales force is expensive, especially if they are paid bonuses or commission. However, the benefits are considerable as an effective sales person can convert most enquiries into a firm sale and build strong links with customers to encourage repeat business.

There are strong links between marketing and sales – and in many businesses these are part of a 'joint' department. They will work on sales promotions together, both devising them and organising them. Sales staff are in an ideal position to pass on useful customer feedback. They will ensure that marketing have access to customer records and information so that promotional materials can be sent at regular intervals. Sales staff will also be responsible for ensuring that customer enquiries by email or online are answered correctly and sales opportunities pursued. This is just one of the many links between functional areas that you will read about on page 79.

All sales staff have to be aware that there are a number of laws which protect customers and must know which type of sales activities are legal and which are not. You will find out more about this area if you study specialist Unit 7 for your BTEC First Diploma.

Sales – key tasks

- Organising sales promotions (unless this task is undertaken by the marketing department).
- Contacting or dealing with customers either by telephone or face-to-face to sell the product or service.
- Preparing quotations or estimates for customers and following these up if a response isn't received.
- Negotiating discounts for bulk sales to special customers.
- Negotiating financial terms for the payment of large items with business customers.
- Providing technical advice to customers.
- Answering customer queries and enquiries.
- Identifying the best item to meet the customer's needs.
- Ensuring that customer enquiries are handled promptly.
- Keeping customer records up-to-date.

Over to you!

1 a All production facilities are set out so that the work is undertaken in sequence. Following this basic principle, copy out the plan alongside and decide in which section (A–E) you would locate the following areas of production in a factory producing denim jeans. Give a reason for each of your choices.

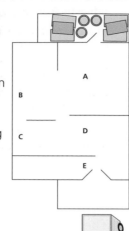

   i   Packing.
   ii Finishing.
   iii Cutting fabric.
   iv Dispatch area.
   v   Sewing fabric.

b Could you prevent a bottleneck if you worked in production control? Work in groups of two or three to find the answer! Your task is to produce Easter Eggs. To do this you need to use four types of machines. Your problem is that each machine works at a different speed.

   - A mixes enough chocolate for 400 eggs every hour.
   - B cooks enough chocolate for 1200 eggs every hour.
   - C moulds the eggs at the rate of 800 eggs an hour.
   - D wraps the eggs at the rate of 600 eggs an hour.

You have been told that you can have as many of each machine as you want, but you must avoid idle capacity, spare capacity or bottlenecks. You have to tell your boss:

   i How many of each machine you need.
   ii How many Easter Eggs you will be making every hour.

c Find out about the benefits of just-in-time by investigating the Toyota Production System. You can also find out how Toyota uses **kaizen** – a Japanese word – to ensure best quality, improved efficiency and to eliminate waste at the Toyota website – a link is available at www.heinemann.co.uk/hotlinks (express code 1386P). Look under About Toyota and then under their Production System.

2 a Every year, the Office for National Statistics (ONS) publishes a report on Family Spending. This shows how our buying habits change over time. The ONS also updates the typical shopping basket of UK consumers so that it reflects current spending. The list below shows products which were included for the first time during each of the last seven decades. Your task is to decide which decade applies to which group of products from the following options: 1940s, 1950s, 1960s, 1970s 1980s, 1990s, 2000s.

A	Satellite dishes, camcorders, mobile phones
B	Crisps, jeans, sliced bread
C	Canned fruit, camera film, televisions
D	Condensed milk, sewing machines, wireless sets
E	Electric hairdryers, yoghurt, wine, duvets
F	DVD players, disposable cameras, designer spectacles
G	Frozen ready-meals, low-alcohol lager, microwave ovens, CDs

b Obtain a copy of the latest report on Family Spending either from your college library or online at The Government's statistics website – a link is available at www.heinemann.co.uk/hotlinks (express code 1386P). Then suggest **four** types of information a marketing department would be interested in and how they could use it.

💬 Talking point

View 1: *Concorde was the most advanced passenger aircraft in the world. No other commercial plane can fly faster than the speed of sound. Getting rid of it was silly and a backward step, given that it cost over £11 billion (in today's money) to develop it.*

View 2: *Concorde had to go. Its sonic booms meant it couldn't fly over land and only the rich could afford it. It's better to concentrate on bigger planes that everyone can afford.*

With which viewpoint do you agree – and why?

Linking functional activities and departments

No department in a business organisation can work in isolation. Each needs information and support from other departments for the organisation to operate effectively. Constant communication and cooperation between departments is absolutely essential for the business to achieve its aims and objectives. This often means that joint decisions have to be made between departmental managers, or their staff, to take account of everyone's needs.

Some of the reasons why departmental links are essential are shown in the table below, which identifies some of the issues over which departments communicate. There are many others which are not listed, quite simply because the list of reasons is almost endless.

Managers cannot just cross their fingers and hope that departments will work together productively and cooperatively. Neither can they make plans and just trust to luck that these are translated into positive action. A key role of all managers is to make sure this happens by coordinating the work done by each department so that they work together to achieve the aims and objectives. How they do this is the subject of this section.

Departments	Link
Sales and Production	Sales must know production schedules and agree delivery dates of orders with Production so customers aren't promised dates which cannot be met. Production must tell Sales about production problems which will affect customers
Sales and Finance	Finance must know about customer enquiries to check their credit rating before sales are made. Finance will be involved when discounts are agreed or when there are problems with customer payments
Distribution and Finance	Finance must know when goods have been dispatched so that invoices can be sent out
Sales and Marketing	Must liaise over sales promotions and adverts so that sales staff can expect/handle enquiries
Purchasing and production, sales and marketing	Purchasing must liaise with production about raw material stocks and requirements. In a retail organisation, they will liaise with sales and marketing about the promotion and selling of new product lines or special offers obtained at discount prices
Finance and all other departments	Finance monitors departmental spending and achievement of financial targets
Finance and personnel	Finance will liaise with Personnel over wage and salary matters
Customer service, sales and marketing	Customer service must pass on customer feedback that could affect future product developments or future sales
R&D and production	Liaise over new product developments and methods of production
Personnel and all departments	Personnel handles job vacancies, promotion opportunities and training courses for every department
IT and Facilities Management	Any changes or maintenance issues which will affect staff must be negotiated with and communicated to all departments
Administration and all departments	Administrators are contacted whenever information or data is required, in any area, and to organise meetings between departments

The hierarchy of managerial authority

In all but the smallest businesses, there are managers at different levels in an organisation. The way they are organised is often called a **hierarchy**. The number of levels will vary – it can be as great as nine or as small as two or three.

A hierarchy is normally illustrated as a pyramid, because at the top level there is only one person, whilst at the bottom there will be several.

The important facts about hierarchies are listed below.

- The person at the top of the hierarchy has the most power and authority.
- At each level, (apart from the very top), managers are directly responsible for those who are below them and accountable to the level above. Therefore a supervisor, whilst being responsible for his/her own staff, also reports to the manager immediately above.
- It is important that managers aren't responsible for more people than they can sensibly control. This is known as the **span of control**. In most situations, a manageable

Figure 1.18 *An example of retail hierarchy*

group consists of about 12 people, but it does depend upon the type of work being done. It is easier to manage a large number of people who are highly skilled professionals (such as in an R&D department) or who are doing exactly the same task (such as in some production departments) than it is to manage a large number of people all doing different types of work. This means that as a business expands, and staff numbers increase, more managers are needed. This can result in a new layer being introduced, to keep the span of control of each manager to a realistic limit.

- At each level, managers will be responsible for different functions or areas of the business. You will therefore find a Finance Manager, a Sales Manager, a Production Manager and so on. However, the job titles used for different types of managers can differ quite considerably (see below) and may also depend upon the type of organisation and departments. A hierarchy for a retail organisation, for example, is likely to show managers with increasing scopes of responsibility, as you can see in Figure 1.18.
- The responsibilities of managers at each level are different, particularly in relation to planning. Their roles in this process are linked together, as everyone must work together to achieve the agreed plans. How this works is explained next.

Figure 1.17 *An example of a management hierarchy*

Job titles in business can be confusing. Some people are managers, others are directors and in other cases you will find officers or presidents! Who is who – and how do you tell the difference?

Directors have a seat on the Board of Directors. They are therefore senior to managers, who do not. The 'chief' director is often called the Managing Director (MD) and is assisted by a Chairman. The MD is responsible for running the business, not the Chairman. His/her role is to 'chair' (run) the meetings of the Board of Directors and advise the MD.

Not all organisations call their top executive the MD. Local authorities and some companies prefer the title Chief Executive or Chief Executive Officer (CEO). The BBC uses the term Director General and American companies prefer the terms President and Vice President. The government, of course, is headed by the Prime Minister and Cabinet Ministers have a similar role to company directors.

In a specialist organisation, you may find different terms. The term Managing Editor is often used in publishing and scientific companies often have Scientific Officers. Schools have a Headteacher, colleges have a Principal and a Vice-Chancellor heads universities. The civil service has Permanent Secretaries and Under-Secretaries – who have nothing to do with administration!

You can see the job titles of managers in a business if you look on its organisation chart, which shows who is who at each level. This shows the hierarchy as it really is. On the StudentZone at www.richerstudentzone.co.uk for example, you can see an organisation chart for the whole of Richer Sounds and one for the Finance Department – which shows each level of the business.

The planning process

Senior managers have to think about the organisation as a whole. They have to decide where the organisation is at the moment, where they want it to be in the future – and how to get there. This is known as deciding the future **business strategy**. The aim is to ensure the organisation moves forward and does the right thing in the future, bearing in mind aspects of the business such as customer expectations, the actions of competitors and other external influences on the business – all of which you will learn about in Unit 2. Discussions about future business strategy result in decisions about:

- The strategic aims of the business.
- The resources that would be required.
- The outcomes by which success will be measured.

Once this has been agreed, the next task is to convert this into an overall plan for the business, called the **strategic plan**.

To achieve the overall plan, each department must play its part. The role of each department is stated in the **operational plan**. This concentrates on working efficiently to achieve the objectives. It identifies the tasks which must be carried out, how these must be done, and sets targets for achievement.

Each department receives a departmental plan which identifies their own contribution to achieving the overall plan and the targets they must achieve. Their tasks obviously depend upon the objectives set and the work they do. If the business wants to improve an existing product, this would involve R&D, whereas an improvement in customer service would not. Increasing sales would affect mainly sales and marketing whereas aims and objectives to reduce costs would involve every department.

At this point, the resources are allocated (shared out) between departments to reflect their involvement in achieving aims and objectives which will require additional resources.

Decide future business strategy

↓

Agree mission, aims and objective

↓

Decide strategic plan

↓

Identify resources required

↓

Decide departmental plans

↓

Allocate resources between departments

↓

Carry out plans

↓

Monitor results

↓

Take corrective actions if required

Figure 1.19 *The planning process*

Business terms

Coordination Bringing together separate elements of the business so that they operate together in the most effective way.

Strategic plan A long term plan which covers the whole business and focuses on where the enterprise wants to be in the future and how it can get there.

Operational plan A plan which identifies what must be done to achieve the strategic plan. This is normally sub-divided into departmental plans.

Cascading Passing down information or tasks from one layer to the next.

Targets Short-term, measurable objectives at departmental or even individual level, which must be met to achieve the overall plan.

Performance Indicators (PIs) A type of target, often shown as a percentage, e.g. 80 per cent of customers report being satisfied.

Business matters

A good example of strategy in action helps to show how the process works. Hornby Trains is famous for its model trains and railway sets and also makes Scalextric – but demand for its traditional products declined. Hornby had to develop a new strategy to survive. This it did successfully – with sales turnover increasing 20 per cent in the year to 31 March 2003. What was this strategy and how was it implemented?

The company decided to 'grow the business' – this was their main aim and their strategic plan focused on how to do this. The way forward was to develop a range of new products aimed at their two main groups of customers – collectors and children. They launched a Scalextric 'Sport' range plus 'My First Hornby' and 'My First Scalextric' for younger children and introduced new models for their collectors, too, with improved detailing. Their departmental plans would have set out the role of each department – marketing to identify what customers want and to promote the new products, R&D to develop them, production to produce them. Target dates for each product launch would be agreed and advance publicity obtained. For example, in November 2003, the company was announcing the launch of its new Scalextric motorbike racing range in spring 2004.

You can find out more at the Hornby and Scalextric websites – links are available at www.heinemann.co.uk/hotlinks (express code 1386P).

The cascade of management direction

Responsibility for achieving the plans falls upon everyone in the business but is a key task for all managers. However, the level of management will affect the scope of the plans for which each manager is responsible.

- **The most senior manager** will be responsible for the overall strategic plan and for ensuring that progress in achieving this is monitored. At Hornby, for example, this is the task of Frank Martin, the Chief Executive.
- **Senior managers** are responsible for a wide area and will have the task of achieving all the objectives relating to this. For example, the Sales and Marketing Director in a business like Hornby will be responsible for coordinating market research and for all promotional activities relating to the new lines. This is obviously not a job for one person, so the next stage is to involve the managers directly below.
- **Middle managers** such as a sales manager and a marketing manager, will be informed of all the aspects which relate to their own specific areas – and the resources they have been allocated. They will work with the senior manager to decide how they should organise departmental activities to achieve their departmental targets. For example, one

departmental target may be to increase sales over the Internet and to ensure that all new lines are promoted on the site. At this stage, they need the assistance of the next group of managers.

- **Supervisors** or **team leaders** are responsible for a group of staff. They will be told what their group must achieve and discuss how this will be done. They then work with their group to do the required tasks. For example, one group of staff may be responsible for the content and display of products, and information on the website. If they have problems, they can refer these upwards for advice and help.

You can see how this works in Figure 1.20 below.

What do plans say?

The plans for an organisation are rather like a jigsaw. If you put all the departmental plans together then they should give the same picture as the organisational, or strategic, plan.

Most managers, however, are particularly concerned with the plans for their own department. The production manager wants to know how many items must be produced, whereas the sales manager wants to know how many must be sold. All departments are involved in achieving plans related to profits – which can include selling more and/or reducing costs.

Level of management	Key responsibilities	Example	Time horizon
Senior managers	Responsible for making strategic plans, achieving business aims and objectives and obtaining key resources	To increase sales of new product by 15% over the next 2 years. Budget for this agreed at £450,000	Often 1–5 years, but may be as great as 10
Middle managers	Responsible for carrying out operational plans which relate to their own area, allocating resources and achieving targets	Marketing Manager responsible for new promotional campaign – budget £250,000	Six months to 2 years
Supervisors	Responsible for ensuring tasks contributing to departmental objectives are carried out and using resources appropriately	Marketing Supervisor to ensure online campaign launches in 2 months – budget £30,000	From a few hours to up to a year

Figure 1.20 *The cascade of management direction*

However, selling more to increase profits won't just concern the sales department. Marketing may be involved in more promotional activities and customer services may be involved in improving customer satisfaction so that consumers are more likely to buy from this business than a competitor. Quality is also important, so this will include the production and even the R&D department. For these reasons, all the plans are inter-related and this is shown in the way the plan is set out.

The information on a plan normally includes:

- **A link to the strategic plan** – so that people can see how their plan links to the main mission and aims of the business.
- **A link to the other departmental plans** – for example, if sales are being increased, this will involve purchasing (more raw materials are required), production (more goods have to be made), sales (more goods must be sold) and marketing (advertising and promotional activities may be increased).
- **The key issues or objectives** – that must be achieved by each department.

- **The actions** – which must be taken to achieve each particular objective.
- **The timescale** – over which these tasks will be carried out.
- **The targets** – which help to measure and assess progress.
- **The final outcome** – which should be achieved.

There is also likely to be some reference to resources. This may be a general note – because the allocation of resources within the department is at the manager's discretion. Or it may break down the resources to show fixed amounts against each target. The danger with this is that it doesn't allow for flexibility. If a marketing campaign is very successful and achieves its target quickly, it may be sensible to redirect any remaining resources to areas that aren't doing as well.

You can see how a departmental plan comes together by studying the example below. Remember, however, that organisations have different ways of devising their plans, so if you look at one for a particular business, you can expect it to be slightly different.

Departmental plan for customer services

Links to other departmental plans	**Link to strategic plan aim** – to improve market share by providing best customer service in the industry.
Finance	
Sales	
Marketing	Share of budget for current year: 5%
Personnel	
IT Services	**Departmental objectives:**
	Identify priority areas for improvement
	Improve quality of advice by customer service staff
	Increase contact opportunities for customers
	Increase customer satisfaction levels
	Promote the image of our customer services to consumers

Objective 1 – Identify priority areas for improvement

Action point	Action	Target/PI	Planned outcome in next 6 months
1	Issue and analyse questionnaires to obtain customer feedback on current service	Feedback from minimum 5,000 customers	Accurately assess key areas of concern and devise plan to address these
2	Monitor speed of response to telephone enquiries	Maximum of 2 minutes wait	Awareness by staff of importance of rapid response/improved response times
3	Monitor and analyse telephone calls and responses by staff	Monitoring of 100 calls a week	Improved responses by staff/ identification of staff training needs
4	Analyse customer complaints over last year	Identification of top 20 complaints issues	Identify key complaints issues and devise plan to address these

Business brief

Top down or bottom up planning?

Top down planning is the term used when plans are set by the most senior manager(s) and then communicated down through the organisation. This is commonly used by small businesses that are run by one or two people. It is also used by very large international concerns like McDonalds – who cannot possibly involve everyone in the planning process and have operations all over the world that they want to manage and control in the same way.

Other businesses, between these two extremes, may also use **bottom up planning**. This involves allowing organisational staff at all levels to contribute to the process. This can be invaluable because senior managers cannot know everything and may be out of touch with the customers themselves and what they want. The danger is that staff will mainly be concerned with their own areas and are unlikely to consider strategies that would help the whole company, such as long-term investment in new equipment or buildings.

Many businesses, therefore, use a combination of both approaches so that the eventual plan takes account of staff views but also covers the long-term needs of the business as a whole. When you access the StudentZone at www.richerstudentzone.co.uk, you can find out how this is done at Richer Sounds!

Over to you!

1 Identify the levels of managers, and their titles, *either* in your college or in any business where you work part-time.
   a Draw a pyramid which shows the hierarchy.
   b Suggest **three** decisions the top manager will have to make which a manager lower down your pyramid would not. Compare your ideas with those of other members of your group.

2 All Colleges have a strategic plan and then produce plans for each department. Your tutor may be able to show you these documents, or extracts from them. Try to find:
   a An objective or target which will affect several departments.
   b An objective which needs additional resources.
   c An objective or target which affects your tutor's department – and what action is being taken.
   d An objective or target which affects your tutor personally – and what he/she is doing to achieve it.

3 Make out your own operational plan, using the illustration opposite as a guide. Your tutor will give you your personal strategic aim – which may be related to achieving your BTEC First award, your attendance or your contribution to class activities.
   a Start by identifying any other people you need to help you to achieve your plan. These are your 'links to other plans'.
   b Decide on the resources you need. These may be tangible (e.g. an alarm clock or Internet access at home) or intangible (e.g. more effort or more energy)!
   c Decide on your main objectives, e.g. go to bed earlier, watch TV less, improve your IT skills etc.
   d Identify at least **two** action points for **two** of your objectives and set yourself a target in each case. Remember, you need to include a number in each of your targets so that they are measurable.
   e Decide your planned outcomes and decide the timescale over which you aim to achieve them.

To do this properly, you then have to monitor your progress. The importance of this is the topic of the next section. Keep your plan safely – you will need it again when you reach page 90.

> **View 1:** *Most members of staff want to work hard and do well. They care about their employer's business. It is the manager's job to recognise this, encourage, help and support them.*

> **View 2:** *Most staff only work for the money and have little interest in the business, providing they have a job and are paid well. They will often get away with doing as little as possible. It is the manager's job to make sure this doesn't happen.*

With which viewpoint do you agree – and why?

Monitoring performance

We all know that if we aim to do something, it is all too easy to forget about it after a few weeks – particularly if it requires an effort. You only have to think about the number of people who vow to keep fit at the start of a year, join a gym and then stop going by March!

At home, if you have promised to do something, then you may find your family nags you to remind you! At college, your tutor will do the same thing.

Whilst this may be irritating, it does have an effect. It stops you forgetting or just letting things slide. At the end of the day, if your target was important, you might even be grateful!

In business, managers can't afford to let people forget targets or let things slide. The success of the business is dependent upon achievement. They can, of course, go around talking to individual members of staff to encourage them and, if they are good managers, they do this regularly. They check how things are going and ask if there are any problems. They resolve these, whenever possible, so that staff can concentrate on the task in hand.

This is one way of monitoring performance. The problem is that many staff may say things are 'fine' when they are not, just for a peaceful life. (You might identify with this yourself!) Therefore managers need another method that leaves out staff opinions. For this reason, they monitor the achievement of targets.

Deciding targets

You can set a target or PI for anything. Commercial businesses will set them for product quality, sales, prices and profit. Your college will have targets for recruitment, retention and exam success. Voluntary organisations will set them

---

Business brief

Inputs deserve outputs

If you put extra effort into your work then you would expect some improvement in return. If you invested money in something, you would expect a financial reward. Your efforts and your money are both resources, as you saw in section 1.2. Resources can also be classed as **inputs** – things you put into something else to get a result, from gas to heat radiators or low-fat food to lose weight.

Outputs are things you get out. If you were paying for a central heating system and the radiators were cold you would be annoyed. If you were on a strict diet and not losing weight you would be peeved. Quite simply, you expect the right output for your inputs!

So, too, do businesses. They aren't prepared to commit their resources (inputs) without a result. They therefore set targets. These are the outputs they want to achieve. Another term for these is **performance indicators (PIs)**. Your performance indicator for dieting could be to lose 2 lbs a week. You can check this by standing on the scales and take action if things aren't going right.

This is whole point of targets or PIs. They give you an exact standard to measure output against and allow you to take action if things aren't as expected. In business they may be set for a whole department or even for individuals. Sales staff, for example, may have their own targets they have to achieve.

for charity donations and consumer awareness. Virtually all businesses set them in relation to customer satisfaction. For that reason, if you are asked to take part in a student survey giving feedback of your views, you are actively contributing towards one of the targets of your organisation!

Targets should be:
- Specific.
- Measurable (they include numbers).
- Achievable.
- Realistic.
- Time-constrained – in the short-term (e.g. a month or two).

You should recognise this list! These are the SMART criteria which also apply to objectives (see page 48).

In the private and voluntary sectors, targets are often agreed with the staff involved. There is a good reason for this. People generally don't like imposed targets and are more enthusiastic about trying to achieve a target over which they have been consulted. They also get annoyed if they achieve a target, only to see it increase, time after time. Obviously, this can eventually become silly – and completely unachievable. You couldn't keep asking production to increase by 5 per cent each month without considerable extra resources, neither could you ask customer services to reduce the number of complaints until eventually there are none at all.

To prevent this, the targets normally follow from the overall annual objectives, for example:

- Senior managers decide the **overall profit** they want to achieve and then the sales income they need and how much money can be spent to achieve this.
- **Sales income** is defined by deciding how much must be produced and sold. Production figures are broken down into monthly targets, bearing in mind key factors such as seasonal

sales. Sales targets are done in the same way.
- **Expenditure targets** are studied carefully and each department is told how much it is allowed to spend every month, again allowing for any seasonal factors.

The results are then checked. This is the task of the finance department, assisted by technology. If you turn back to page 63 you will see that this is often done by the management accountant, who monitors all the data on a daily basis and produces regular reports for senior managers. These show which financial targets are being met and which are not. Departmental managers will be expected to comment – and react – to the results from their own area.

The government has set targets to reduce truancies by ten per cent between 2002 and 2004

Corrective action

There are many reasons why targets may not be met. Some of these will be valid reasons and some will not. A valid reason is an external event which no-one in the business could do anything about. An obvious example is the decline in demand for air travel after 9/11 which not only affected airlines but many of their suppliers – from travel agents to catering companies.

Invalid reasons are those which should have been prevented, but were not, such as machine breakdowns or stock shortages.

Managers are expected to identify the reasons for any problems meeting a target, provide an explanation and then suggest what should be done to put things right. They may argue that:

- **The target itself is unrealistic or an external event has prevented achievement**. This will be debated by senior management and can result in a change to the overall organisational plan. For example, after 9/11, British Airways had to reduce staff numbers dramatically because of the fall in demand by customers. This wasn't part of their original plan!
- **There is a genuine reason for the problem**, such as staff problems, lack of training, equipment difficulties or supplier issues. In this case there will be discussions to identify what can be done. The answer, of course, will depend upon the type of problem and the effect it has had.

Solving some important problems

Key targets which the business will want to meet relate to production, sales and costs – because all of these have a direct impact on the overall profit figure. If you've forgotten why, look back to page 6 for a reminder!

Production figures

Production figures will be studied closely. If too little has been produced then the company is losing sales. If the number of sales lost is significant then action must be taken. If the problem has been caused by a shortage or problems with raw materials, then alternative suppliers will be found. If the problem is because the demand is too great for the current level of resources then these may be increased, for example:

- **Temporary staff** may be employed.
- **Additional machinery** may be purchased if this would be cost-effective because demand is likely to continue.
- Some production **work may be outsourced** to another manufacturer.

If too much has been produced, then this is because customer demand has fallen or sales haven't done their job. Any business will be keen to identify this as quickly as possible to prevent a long-term build up of unsold stocks. These may be sold at a discount price, to cover the basic cost of production, and production targets revised for that particular product. Marketing may then be given the job of finding out *why* customer demand has fallen and, if this relates to the basic design or performance of the product, R&D may be given the task of improving it.

Sales figures

Sales figures are critical because they have a direct impact on production in a manufacturing company. In most businesses, particularly retail, they are the most important target to be achieved. Both the number of sales and the revenue from sales will be analysed – together with the overall gross margin. It is no use selling more but making a loss on every item!

Very few businesses will complain if sales are higher than expected – they will either try to produce more or buy more stock from their suppliers. The problem is when sales are lower than expected or if prices have had to be reduced substantially. The sales director is expected to be aware of the 'market' for the product and actions being taken by competitors. If competitors are doing well, then the spotlight will be onto the sales team to improve. This may involve improved training for staff and a review of the marketing mix (see page 66) for that product, for example:

- **A new promotional campaign** by the marketing department to renew customer interest.
- **A review of the price charged** for the product or special discounts offered (but remember that selling more cheaply means more must be sold, at the same overall cost, for the same level of profit to be achieved).
- **A review of the ways in which customers can buy the product**.
- **A review of the product itself** (or range of products) – to see what improvements can be made. In some cases this may be impossible if sales are declining overall because of technological development (think of video

recorders) – in this case there may be a strategic decision to drop this product in future.

Expenditure figures

Expenditure figures are often the most difficult to control. As you will see in unit 3, keeping costs down in business is very important – and has more impact on profits than increasing the price (which can also lose sales). All departments are allocated a **budget** which states how much they are allowed to spend each year – and, like other targets, this is usually broken down by month. A close watch is kept on spending and managers need some good explanations if they have over-spent for any reason.

Valid reasons may include suppliers increasing their prices – from raw material suppliers to utility (gas and electricity) companies. Unless the business can switch to an alternative, cheaper, supplier then there is little they can do in this situation. However, in the cases of other external price rises, this usually results in cutbacks. When advertising prices rise, for example, marketing will look at alternative promotion methods, reducing the length of a campaign or choosing smaller/ shorter adverts. If staff costs increase beyond agreed levels, then there may be a halt to recruitment for a while, or even redundancies.

On some occasions, overspending may be just that. In some departments, either greater quantities or more expensive goods have been purchased than originally planned. No matter what the reason for this, it obviously can't go on indefinitely. The only exception might be if sales are increasing dramatically and the two are related, such as an expensive marketing campaign which has resulted in a huge increase in sales. In this case, the business may decide the extra expenditure is justified. Otherwise the usual two stage approach will apply:

- Find an alternative and cheaper supplier in future.
- If this is impossible, reduce the amount purchased or used.

You will learn much more about targets for profits, sales and expenditure, and budgets, in Unit 3.

Business matters

When Ben Gordon took over a well-known business, in September 2002, his main resources were its brand name, 247 stores in the UK, 166 stores abroad, just over 3,000 staff – and a company which was losing sales and money. That business was Mothercare.

Ten months later, Ben Gordon announced increased sales of 6.6 per cent, increased gross margins of 5.8 per cent and profits of £13.4 million for the half year to 11 October (compared to losses of £10 million the previous year) He credited these improvements on the 3-year turn around programme he put in place on his arrival.

The new strategy included improving distribution – there had been problems with the supply chain (see page 43) and stock deliveries had been too slow – revamping the fashion ranges and better buying from manufacturers. Ben Gordon is also testing three new types of store design, before refitting the stores, and introducing new IT systems and buying techniques. He is also testing two new formats for town centre stores – 'Lite' which focuses on clothing and M & B (Mother and Baby) which focuses on newborn to 2 year olds.

On his arrival Ben Gordon set targets. The first was to improve the amount of cash in the business, which had fallen from £30 million to £10 million. Gordon set up a committee to focus on this and gave them three months to do the job. The target was achieved.

There are still changes in the pipeline. Distribution – which is outsourced – is still a concern as Gordon thinks the Daventry location is rather expensive and not set out as he would prefer. Whatever changes he makes, you can check his progress on the Mothercare website – a link for this is available at www.heinemann.co.uk/hotlinks (express code 1386P).

Over to you!

1 Go back to the operational plan you created for yourself when you did the activity on page 85. It may be a week or two since you made it, so now would be a good time to assess your progress.

   a Decide which targets you are meeting and which you are not.

   b For any targets you are not meeting, identify the reason. If you are meeting all your targets, or if it is only a day or so since you wrote them out, identify things that *could* go wrong.

   c Suggest **one** action you could take for each problem identified to correct the matter.

2 Overspending is always difficult to avoid, even if you are careful with your money.

   As a group, suggest as many reasons as you can why this can occur in your private life – and what actions you can take to rescue the situation. Then decide why monitoring expenditure is so important!

3 All local authorities set performance targets. Obtain a copy of the summary of the Performance Plan published by your local authority which identifies its performance in meeting targets over the last 12 months. You may be interested in seeing the full plan (which will be published on their website). If you can't see it immediately then words to search for include 'performance' and best value'. Don't print this without permission, as it's likely to be a very long document. In this case, your tutor will be able to obtain a copy for you.

   a Look through the plan or the summary to find the explanation of how the Council sets and monitors its targets.

   b Then check how it has performed against **three or four** of these targets, such as recycling, library loans and swimming facilities. If you have members of the class who live in different areas covered by different authorities, then you can compare these to see which is performing the best and in which areas. Note that this will also increase your knowledge of the range of services provided by local

Talking point

View 1: *It is silly to work hard to beat targets as it only means you get a harder one next time. It is better to just do enough.*

View 2: *Beating targets is great because it gives you a 'buzz' and shows you just what can be achieved.*

With which viewpoint do you agree – and why?

The company's 2004 sales targets

Company targets – a challenge or a nuisance? What is your view?

You have now reached the end of this section, and should understand that management processes cover the way the business is organised into departments so that each can specialise in a key area of the business. It also includes the way these are linked and how the managers make plans and set targets, monitor these and take corrective action when there are problems. Test your knowledge and skills now by doing the following activities.

Check your understanding of this section by answering the following questions. Check all your answers with your tutor before moving on.

1 **a** What is the name of the department which is responsible for developing new products?

b Identify **three** activities undertaken by the personnel department.

c A customer phones customer services to query a bill for some goods she has bought. Which **two** departments could the customer service assistant contact to obtain more information?

d Production has problems because of inferior raw materials which mean this week's production targets won't be met. Which **two** departments would it contact about the problem – and why?

e You are investigating a business which says it outsources its distribution function. What does this mean?

f Identify **two** reasons why departments need to work together.

g Explain what is meant by a hierarchy.

h Senior managers decide on an overall organisational or strategic plan. How do they make sure each department knows what to do to achieve this?

i Explain why it is important that managers constantly monitor performance and the achievement of targets.

j Identify **two** key targets that most businesses normally need to meet to achieve their overall aims and objectives.

2 You can find out more about the work undertaken in some of the departments in your college and the management processes that exist by talking to some of the specialist staff who work there. It may be possible for you to arrange for people to visit your group to talk about their job. If so, prepare a short list of questions to send to them first, so that they know what you want to find out. Alternatively, see if you can interview a person from each area in groups of 2 or 3 and then present your findings to the class.

Prepare questions on the work that is carried out, the management processes that control the use of resources and how performance against targets is monitored. You could also ask each person to give you an example of corrective action they have taken to solve a problem. Ideally, speak to **one** person from each of the following areas:

i   Administration.

ii   Customer (or student) services.

iii Facilities management.

iv   Finance.

v   IT.

vi   Marketing.

vii Personnel.

3 The problem is yours! The profits of Thorntons, the chocolate retailer, were down by 9.6 per cent in 2003. Sales were hit by the good weather that year. Normally Thorntons achieves 10 per cent of its annual sales at Easter with 3 million chocolate eggs sold. But in 2003 fewer Easter Eggs were bought, and far less chocolate was bought in the summer. Thorntons is also having problems competing with large out-of-town supermarkets which are continually improving the range of chocolates they sell.

Its resources include a £50 million manufacturing site in Derbyshire, its brand name and reputation, its supply chain and its contracts to sell branded chocolates to retailers such as Marks & Spencer. It has 600 high street outlets. Its busiest time is Christmas when it achieves 35 per cent of its sales. Its main raw materials are chocolate, cream, alcohol and nuts.

If you, as a group, were running Thorntons, how would you try to improve sales and profits? Start by thinking about how the business could perhaps improve the use of its resources. Ideally, before you do this, check the Thornton's website to get more information about the business – a link is available at www.heinemann.co.uk/hotlinks (express code 1386P). Use some of the successful examples of business turnarounds in this section to give you some ideas – but remember, chocolate is different from clothes! Then decide the following:

a   The aims and objectives you would set for the business.
b   The key factors you would include in the organisational plan.
c   The main targets you would set.
d   The corrective action you would take if:
  i   The purchasing or marketing departments were over-spending.
  ii Sales were not as planned.
  iii You had production problems.

Finally, compare your ideas for improving Thorntons with those which have been decided by the Chief Executive. Your tutor will be able to download and print out his statement, as part of the Annual Report and Accounts for 2003.

Businesses are constantly under pressure because they operate in a dynamic environment. This simply means that the world in which they operate is always changing. You know this yourself. As a consumer, you will often make different decisions about what you want to buy – and where you want to buy it. Trends come and go, and these influence the clothes you wear and the CDs that you play. Technological developments bring new products and updated versions of older ones, such as faster computers, and mobile phones with more features. Yesterday you might have visited a local store to buy a book or DVD – today you may prefer to buy it online.

All businesses have to respond to changes in customer demand. They also want to respond more quickly than their competitors. The Internet has extended the range of available sources for many goods and services. If you want to buy a camera, you can search online for dozens of suppliers and obtain 'best buy' reports. Local shops and stores can no longer depend upon your business and have to decide how to meet this challenge.

Businesses are also under pressure from other groups of people, besides customers and competitors. Employees have legal rights and need to be motivated to work hard. They may belong to a trade union that will represent their interests to management – who may have different views about what is best for the business. Suppliers may want to negotiate higher prices, bankers will want to check the accounts each year if there is a loan outstanding, local communities may be unhappy about business plans to extend the premises or work longer hours. All these different groups are often referred to as stakeholders – because they have a 'stake', or an interest in the business. They can often have an impact on the way the business operates and the decisions that are made.

Finally, businesses are under pressure from external forces they can do little, if anything, to control. It is common knowledge that the events of 9/11 had a dramatic effect on many organisations – especially airlines and travel businesses. Another external force is the British Government – which can pass new laws, increase taxes or take other actions which affect the economy. Foreign businesses and governments, too, can take independent actions which have a direct affect on the share price, or overall value, of a British business.

All managers must consider the possible effects of all these factors and decide how to respond. This may sound an impossible job – but successful businesses rise to the challenge. How they do this is the subject of this unit.

In summary

This unit is divided into four sections:

2.1 Customer expectations. Here you will learn about the different types of customers that businesses deal with and how they differ, as well as what businesses do to respond to customers.

2.2 Competitive pressures. In this section you learn how businesses identify their main competitors, how they try to find out about their activities and future plans and what they do to try to maintain or increase their own sales.

2.3 Stakeholder expectations. This section looks at all the other types of groups that can put pressure on businesses and how businesses respond to them.

2.4 Political, economic, social, technological, legal and other external influences. This final section looks at all the additional pressures on business from external factors. You will find out how these affect different types of business and what actions businesses can take in response.

This section covers

Key customer expectations

Different types of markets

Different types of customers and their attributes

How products can be matched with market demand

What are customer expectations?

As a customer, you have a wide range of expectations. Whether you are buying a magazine, going on holiday or visiting your doctor, in each case you will 'want' something from the experience. Exactly what you want, however, is likely to depend upon four factors:

- What you are buying or experiencing.
- How much you are paying.
- The type of person you are.
- Whether you are buying for yourself or someone else.

You also have certain **key expectations**. Unless these are met you will be dissatisfied and disappointed. Any business which regularly fails to meet its customer's key expectations will struggle to survive for very long.

The product or experience

The law gives all customers certain legal rights as a consumer. The aim is to ensure that nobody is cheated or misled by being sold a faulty product or one that doesn't match its description. Nor must consumers receive poor or shoddy service, regardless of whether they are having their car serviced or their central heating repaired. You will find out more about these laws if you study specialist unit 6 of your BTEC First award.

So a key expectation of all customers is that the products they buy will be of satisfactory quality, will do what they claim to do, and that there won't be any hidden charges they don't know about. If a product doesn't work, then you have the right to expect a prompt replacement or your money back. These are minimum expectations,

Level	Expectation	Airline example
Basic	The minimum required - product will work, service will meet your basic needs	'No frills' airline takes you safely from A to B
Expected	Other basic conditions are met – availability of product, safety, cleanliness, friendly and knowledgeable staff, care and consideration of your needs, returns policy	Pilot is highly qualified, airplane is regularly serviced, cabin staff are friendly and well-trained, baggage arrives when you do
Augmented	Specific benefits associated with a particular product above what you may have expected	Good food, free newspapers, additional legroom, up-to-date film to watch, sociable departure and arrival times, convenient destinations
Potential	Additional benefits which give customers extra value	Rapid check-in, special lounges, free drinks, frequent flyer programmes, discounts

Figure 2.1 *Levels of expectations*

but normally people want far more than this – especially if they are buying a service or spending a lot of money on an expensive item. In fact, up to four levels of expectations have been identified as you can see in Figure 2.1.

Businesses have to decide which level of expectations to meet, and this will depend upon the needs of the customers that they want to attract. 'No frills' airlines only offer an expected level of service – but are very successful because many people will 'trade off' higher level expectations for a cheap flight. However, even at a low price, key aspects such as safety and reliability have to be met by every airline.

Key customer expectations vary, depending upon what we are buying or doing. If you are visiting the dentist your key expectations are that he/she will be competent, kind and will give you a painless experience. You would be prepared to wait for half an hour to obtain this because 'speedy service' isn't one of your key expectations in this situation. You would take a different view, however, if you were rushing to buy a sandwich in your lunch hour, because your key expectations are now different.

The price you pay

For most products, customers expect value for money. You would be very surprised if a DVD cost twice as much as normal but had only one disc and no special features or booklet to make it worth the extra cost.

Generally, the more we pay, the higher the quality we expect. Therefore, for example, airline passengers who pay to travel first class expect many more features and benefits. Their expectations are higher on the scale. In the same way, you wouldn't expect the same type of food in an expensive restaurant as at your local take-away, or the same type of service in a luxury hotel as a much cheaper one.

In some cases, however, 'value for money' is not top of the list. A collector of vintage Star Wars figures will be prepared to pay for rarity value. People will also do this if they rank 'image' higher than 'value for money' – which is one reason why designer label goods cost more than others.

Porsche proved the importance of image many years ago. It dropped its cheapest model because its other customers were complaining that almost anyone could afford it! Sales fell until Porsche ensured that only wealthy customers could afford to buy one of their cars – they did this in order to protect the image.

The type of person you are

Your personality and attitude to life affects your expectations, what you buy and how you buy it, regardless of how much money you have. You might be a millionaire, but you can also be tight-fisted! Some people are very careful with their money. They obtain lots of information before they buy anything and shop around to compare prices. Even then, they will be likely to stick to known suppliers and known brands. Other people take more risks and enjoy trying anything new – something unusual and different will appeal to them more.

Your personality will also influence what you do, what you spend your money on and where. An introvert might like a quiet night in with a rented DVD whereas an extrovert would prefer to go out with friends to the cinema. Your friends will influence you too – if someone says something is 'naff' it will often put you off, especially if you normally respect their opinion. Even where you live has an influence. If you go abroad then you don't expect to see exactly the same products in the shops because tastes and buying habits differ by locality.

You can see how many factors in your life affect your personal expectations and preferences by looking at Figure 2.2.

Whether you are buying for yourself or someone else

Most people struggle when they are buying for other people – it's one thing to buy yourself a treat, but quite another to choose a present for someone else unless you know exactly what they want.

In business, many staff may buy items on behalf of their employer. If your boss asked you to buy something simple like a biro, then you may hesitate, wondering what colour, what thickness and how much to spend. Now think of the problem for industrial buyers who buy very expensive items which will be used by, or sold to, other people – and whose career and reputation may depend upon their decisions about what to buy and when!

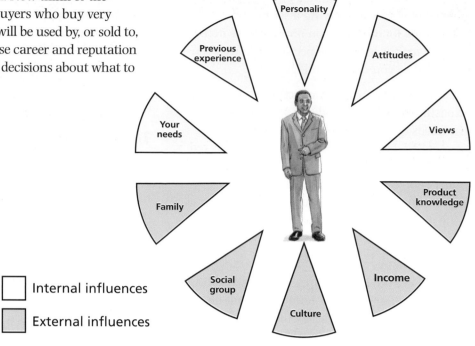

Figure 2.2 *Where do your personal preferences come from?*

Business matters

Products flop if they don't meet customer expectations. In some cases this can result in the failure of the whole business. Product disasters can result if a firm offers goods or services without understanding what their customers really want or how they think. There are numerous examples. Probably the most famous is the Millennium Dome, which never attracted enough visitors to make a profit. Another, less well known product failure, was the Thirsty Cat! and Thirsty Dog! bottled water drinks for pets. Famous brands and large businesses aren't immune from product disasters either – such as 'New Coke' which resulted when Coca-Cola changed the formula of its drink – for no apparent reason. Customers hated it, sales fell and – very hastily – the company resurrected 'Classic Coke'. A key expectation of Coke drinkers is the taste, so tampering with this was a risk that didn't pay off.

In the media, there are many examples of big name disasters. Movie flops include Disney's Treasure Planet, which cost £94 million to make and only grossed £11 million at the box office, and Madonna's Swept Away, which was only shown in a few cinemas. Album flops include Victoria

Beckham's first solo album which cost £5 million to produce and only sold about 50,000 copies. Nova magazine came out once, failed and was then relaunched but only lasted twelve months because of poor sales.

Sometimes things go wrong when products for the UK market are sold abroad. Many bands and artists have struggled to succeed in the US – including Robbie Williams with his Escapology album. Translations, too, can put the kiss of death on a product. Electrolux (a Swedish company) advertised its vacuum cleaners in America with the campaign 'Nothing sucks like an Electrolux' and wondered where it had gone wrong. (The word 'sucks' means 'is rubbish' in American slang!)

Two UK businesses took a gamble in 2003. ASDA started a trial selling diamond rings in four of its northern stores and Cosmopolitan magazine considered shrinking its size to match its arch-rival Glamour – a move which many predicted to be a big mistake. Whether both firms have accurately assessed their customer expectations – or not – is still to be decided.

1 All customers have needs, wants and preferences. For example, you may need a drink (because you're hot and thirsty), want something cold and non-alcoholic but really prefer a can of diet Coke. If a vending machine only sells coffee or tea, this meets your needs, but not your wants or preferences. If it sells lemonade you are still a bit disappointed because the product range in the machine still hasn't met your expectations.

a Compare your own needs, wants and preferences, as a group. For each of the needs below, list your own personal 'want' and 'preference'. Remember that what you 'want' is a general description, what you 'prefer' is more personal. To help, the first is done for you.

Need	Want	Preference
Car	Reliable car, cheap to run	Fast red sports car
A pair of jeans		
A pair of trainers		
A new jacket		
A night out		
To go on holiday		
To go to the dentist		
Your hair cut		
Driving lessons		

b Compare your lists with other members of your group. Identify where there are differences between the responses from males and females in your group.

c Ask your tutor to tell you what his or her list would be. Then decide how needs, wants and preferences change according to customer age groups. If you were deciding to group customer needs into different age ranges, which groupings would you use – and why?

2 Your key expectations vary depending upon what you are buying or doing. As a group, identify **three** key expectations which apply in each of the following situations. Then suggest **three** expectations people may have which are not as critical. If you are stuck, use the chart opposite as a guide.

a Buying this book.

b Going into hospital as a patient.

c Buying a computer game.

d Buying a television.

e Using an Internet banking service.

f Buying an expensive photocopier for a firm.

Range of customer expectations	
The product or service purchased	Good quality High quality Reasonable, competitive price Free of charge Functional (i.e. will do the job) Clean Comfortable Attractive or decorative Interesting Informative Challenging Exciting Meets personal needs Standardised so compatible with other items Additional items as optional extras
Information/ communications	Accurate, easy to understand, information Regular updates Security of personal information Not to be asked inappropriate personal questions
The buying experience	Rapid order processing Skilled, highly trained staff Range of payment options Good availability at local outlet Prompt and efficient service Friendly service Flexibility to meet individual needs Prompt delivery
After-sales service	Tracking and tracing of order Reliable performance Guarantee or warranty Expert installation Routine follow-up service Regular, efficient servicing Repair service Speedy/effective problem solving

3 The list of customer expectations in the chart above isn't exhaustive. Start by identifying how many applied to you when you first started at your college or on this course. Then see how many you can add that aren't on the list. Compare these with other students in your class to see how many you can identify.

4 a For each of the following failures why do you think things went wrong?

i Clairol's Touch of Yoghurt shampoo.

ii Harley Davidson's attempt to launch perfume.

iii Pets.com – which tried to sell pets online.

iv The band Hear'Say (or any other band or album of your choice!).

v Polaroid cameras (page 31 for clues!).

b As a group, identify **one** business in your own area which has closed down or **one** product you know about which has flopped and suggest reasons.

View 1: *ASDA's idea to sell diamond rings is great. Their top ring sells for £200 less than it would in a jeweller's shop. Everyone loves a bargain.*

View 2: *ASDA's idea won't work. No woman would admit her diamond ring came from ASDA and any man who wanted to buy it there would be called a cheapskate!*

With which viewpoint do you agree – and why?

What is a market?

All businesses have to identify the type of customers they have and their main expectations. They do this because they want to meet – or preferably exceed – customer expectations. The starting point is to identify the market for their product or service.

Size of the market

A 'market' represents all the possible consumers for a product or service. You have probably heard the term **mass market**. This means the whole market, so products aimed at the mass market, such as washing powder, are aimed at everyone, rather than a particular group of people.

Generally, however, markets are defined more precisely to relate to specific groups who buy certain products or services. You will normally find them described in terms of their size, the product or service and the amount of sales and/or value of sales over a period of time.

- At the top of the scale are **global markets**. These are the worldwide markets for certain goods, such as the global market for cars. In 2002, over 47 billion cars were sold worldwide with sales valued at more than £500 billion.
- Because the global market is so large, it is then broken down into markets which cover a particular area of the world, such as the European or South American car markets.
- Producers, like Ford, BMW and Honda will also want to look at the size of **national markets,** such as the UK, French or Japanese markets. All national markets relate just to one country. They will study forecasts about whether each market is expanding or contracting to help them to decide where to focus their efforts in the future.
- UK car dealers will be more concerned with **regional markets**, such as sales in Scotland or in the south-east of England.
- Other suppliers, such as small second-hand garages, may only be interested in **local markets**, such as in your town or in one part of a city, for example North London.

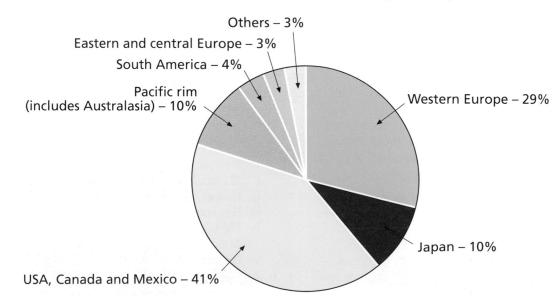

Others – 3%
Eastern and central Europe – 3%
South America – 4%
Pacific rim (includes Australasia) – 10%
Western Europe – 29%
Japan – 10%
USA, Canada and Mexico – 41%

Figure 2.3 *Share of world car market 2003 – by region*

Sub-markets, market segments and niche markets

In the UK, in 2002, over 10 million cars were sold – but 8 million of these were used cars. This information is of more interest to local car dealers than the global figures used by the large companies. For that reason, markets are often sub-divided into different types, called **market segments**. TVR, for instance, would only be interested in the market for sports cars and Jaguar would study the market for luxury cars. A small sub-market for a specialist product, such as that for kit cars, is often known as a **niche market**. Small businesses often do well in niche markets, because large organisations are more likely to stick to standardised products that sell in large quantities.

Related markets

No industry works in isolation. Therefore other businesses, with related interests, are also keen to study trends in the main market to see how this will affect them. In the motor industry, related markets range from car insurance companies to suppliers of car parts.

You can see how this works in Figure 2.4, which shows you some of the sub-divisions of the car market. Each of these shows you the market for buyers of a particular product or service.

Internal and external markets

Most markets are external. This means that buyers are individuals or businesses from another industry or even another country. Car manufacturers will sell fleets of company cars to a wide range of businesses and will also sell family cars to individuals. It therefore targets its products at an external market.

An **internal market** exists when buyers and sellers are located in the same industry or business. In Britain, the main example is the National Health Service (NHS), although many types of education can be seen as internal markets, such as

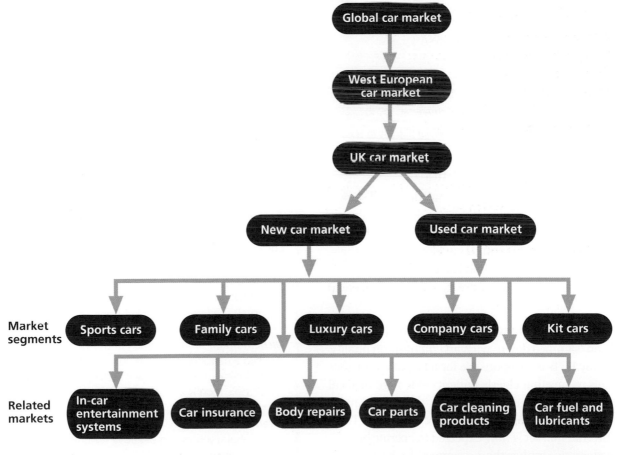

Figure 2.4 *Examples of car markets*

further education colleges, who may share out courses – or students – between them or compete with each other by specialising in different subjects.

In the NHS, different groups are divided into purchasers and providers. The main purchasing group are Primary Care Trusts (PCTs). These are NHS organisations responsible for improving the health of local people. They are led by a team of GPs and community nurses and hold a budget (see section 3.3) to improve the quality of care in an area. They buy health care for patients in the area from hospitals and other providers, and work with other agencies responsible for health care.

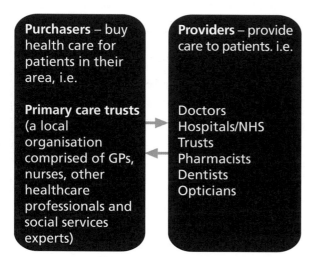

Purchasers – buy health care for patients in their area, i.e.	Providers – provide care to patients. i.e.
Primary care trusts (a local organisation comprised of GPs, nurses, other healthcare professionals and social services experts)	Doctors Hospitals/NHS Trusts Pharmacists Dentists Opticians

Figure 2.5 *The internal market in the NHS*

Cooperation or competition?

Some internal markets are competitive and some are cooperative. The NHS system described above is relatively new. Before 1998, some GPs had their own budgets. They could buy health care for their patients and so, too, could Local Health Authorities. Providers were expected to compete to offer value for money.

This system didn't work very well and has now been 'slimmed down' with an emphasis on quality. Today PCTs are responsible for all a patient's needs. This means that elderly patients who need medical and social care, as well as help with housing and benefits, can be assisted by one organisation. This internal market is now expected to operate on a cooperative, rather than a competitive basis.

Business terms

Market The term for a set of consumers or customers who buy a certain product or service.

Mass market The market as a whole, not divided into specific groups.

Global market The worldwide market. For example, the total global food retail market is estimated to be worth $2.8 trillion (about £1.7 trillion).

National market The market for an area or country. For example, the UK market for grocery stores, food retailers and supermarkets was worth £80.4 billion in 2002.

Regional market The market for an area or county, e.g. South Yorkshire.

Local market The market for a town or city area, e.g. South Manchester.

Market segment A smaller chunk of a larger market (see page 99). In 2002 the UK market for frozen food was worth £5.4 billion. Frozen food is a smaller segment of the whole food market.

Niche market A small portion of a large market with a narrowly defined group of customers who are often ignored by large volume producers. Organic food is a niche market and, in the UK, is now worth over £1 billion a year.

Internal market A market that exists – either collaboratively or competitively – within a particular industry.

Over to you!

1 Test your numeracy skills! A million has 6 noughts. A billion is a thousand million and a trillion is a million million. Now write out the figures for the (sterling) value of the **four** different food markets listed on the previous page!

2 Your father's friend runs an MOT garage – testing cars that are over three years old to make sure they are safe to drive. He is thinking of taking on another mechanic, but this decision is only sensible if demand for his services will increase.

You have told him that he can obtain this information by studying the right markets. Now he wants to know which ones. What would you tell him? Use the chart on page 99 to help.

3 Working in small groups, study the tables on car markets opposite (Figure 2.6) and then answer the following questions.
   a Identify **three** *types* of business organisations which would be interested in these tables. Think of different examples from those shown in the chart on page 99!
   b Explain the difference between 'projected' figures and 'actual' figures.
   c In which area of the world are there the most cars? Suggest **two** reasons for this.
   d Suggest **one** country which is included in the 'others' row and suggest why so few cars are sold there.
   e You work for a car producer who currently sells in the USA and Western Europe. In 2003, you could choose **two** new global markets – which would you have selected and why?
   f Which country in Europe would worry you most – and why?

Global (projected):

Volume sold (thousands)	2002	2003	2004
Western Europe	14,392	13,727	13,816
Japan	4,441	4,605	4,645
USA, Canada and Mexico	19,532	18,993	19,648
Pacific rim	4,612	4,829	5,102
South America	1,728	1,890	2,057
Eastern and central Europe	1,456	1,497	1,773
Others	1,237	1,318	1,444
Total	47,399	46,859	48,485
Annual growth/decline	0.5%	–1.1%	3.5%

(Source: adapted from just-auto; industry sources)

European (actual): January to June 2003

Market	Volume sold (thousands)	Growth/decline
Germany	1,668	–1.5%
UK	1,347	0.0%
France	1,069	–7.7%
Italy	1,233	–2.3%
Spain	688	–1.7%
Others	1,519	–4.8%
Total	7,525	–3.0%

(Source: Global Insight – provisional data June 2003)

Figure 2.6 *Trends in car markets – 2002–4*

4 Find out more about the work of the Primary Care Trust in your own area by entering the name of your local authority area followed by 'primary care trust' into Google and clicking on Search – a link is available at www.heinemann.co.uk/hotlinks (express code 1386P). List **two** of the priorities for healthcare in your own area – and then see if your own doctor is listed as being a member!

Talking point

View 1: *Pop Idol went global when it successfully sold its format all over the world – eventually resulting in World Idol. This was a great idea and will be a huge success.*

View 2: *Pop Idol may work in different countries, with national audiences, but World Idol is a disaster because people's musical tastes vary so much in different countries.*

With which viewpoint do you agree – and why?

Types of customers and their expectations

There is another way in which markets can be divided. They can be split into two main types:

- The **consumer market** relates to private individuals and households who buy goods and services for their own use.
- The **industrial** or **organisational market** consists of all the individuals, groups and organisations that buy goods for resale, raw materials for use in making other products or goods and services for using in their day-to-day operations.

Some businesses concentrate on selling products and services to the consumer market – such as retailers and hairdressers. Far more, however, are involved in supplying the organisational market. Every item of stock you see on the shelves in a store has been made and supplied by another business – which, itself, needs to buy equipment, raw materials and other consumables. Some businesses, of course, operate in both markets – such as banks which provide both private and business banking services, and solicitors who deal with both private individuals and companies over legal matters.

Some organisations supply specific items or services to other businesses, others are involved in managing large projects – such as building and equipping airport terminals and shopping malls. Some of these are done for private organisations but others are undertaken for the public sector, such as building new schools or motorways. The voluntary sector, too, is a customer for a wide variety of goods and services – from uniforms to financial services.

All these different types of organisational customers have different needs. Therefore, the first step for any business is to identify which groups of customers it wants to supply and then decide how it can best meet their expectations. This means knowing three things:

- Who makes the buying decision.
- What process is followed.
- The factors that are important to buyers when they decide what to buy.

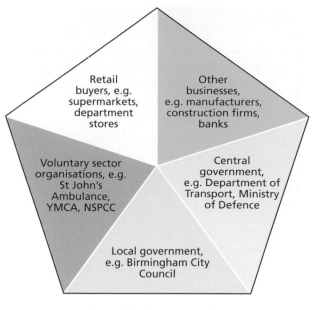

Figure 2.7 *Organisational customer groups*

Business brief

What is a product?

This may seem a silly question, until you think about what customers want from a product.

They all want a package of benefits or features that meet their needs

In other words, a product may be superb but unless customers are clear about the benefits and features offered by this particular product – as opposed to others on the market – then they will not buy it.

Benefits can include:

- **A brand name** everyone knows and trusts, e.g. Vodafone or Nike.
- **Great quality at a reasonable price**, so the overall 'value' is better.
- **Convenience and accessibility** because the product is available locally or over the Internet.
- **Reliability**, e.g. a name you can trust and a service that always delivers on time.
- **Other benefits** which particularly attract the type of customers who buy the product.

When you learn about how products (or services) can be adapted later in this section, remember that changing any of the benefits or features is one way of adapting the product.

Retail buyers

There are thousands of people in the UK who buy for the retail trade – from small shopkeepers to large store buyers. They all make decisions about the best product lines to stock and sell to their customers.

In a large business, buyers will specialise in specific lines of merchandise. For example, Tesco will have different buyers for clothing, vegetables, meat and so on. In a small shop, one person – often the owner or manager – will be responsible for buying all the stock. Some small shops, such as grocers and florists may buy most stock from a local wholesale market or cash-and-carry. Others, such as jewellers or toy shops, will rely more on visits from representatives or buy from trade catalogues. Large stores rarely have to seek out their suppliers – they will be constantly approached by businesses hoping to persuade them to stock their products, although their specialist buyers will also attend trade shows and exhibitions to find out about new trends and developments. Large stores often buy direct from manufacturers and some retail buyers are also responsible for obtaining 'own label' items, such as Bhs pyjamas or Tesco Value cheese. This means working with manufacturers to develop and obtain the right product for the customer.

Fish fingers are produced in large quantities for retail buyers

What do retail buyers want?

Retail buyers have the following main aims:

- **Achieve target sales on all lines**. If goods fail to sell, the buyer will be criticised for stocking it in the first place. For that reason, retail buyers would only stock a small quantity of an unknown product on a trial basis. They generally prefer well-known brand names or products that they know will fulfil their customers' current needs. To tempt them, some suppliers will offer goods on a 'sale or return' basis. This means that any unsold goods can be returned to the supplier, without charge, after a certain period.
- **Maximise stock turnover**. This means selling stock as quickly as possible and is especially important for fashion items that will go out of date rapidly. Buyers also take into consideration seasonal changes when deciding what to stock and any factors that may influence the life of a product when deciding how many to buy. For example, they wouldn't buy large quantities of equipment that could soon be out of date because of technological advances.
- **Achieve target sales margins on each product**. This means buying quality products at the best price possible and selling them at the best competitive price. Some businesses, such as Argos or Matalan, deliberately opt for a low margin to achieve high volume sales. Despite this, all retail buyers try to negotiate the best buying price possible. This is where large stores have more power than small shops – especially with small suppliers. They can simply refuse to stock the goods if they can't buy them at the right price.

Retail buyers also expect the following:

- **Quality and reliability**. No store wants to be faced with hundreds of customer complaints because of product faults or delivery problems. Suppliers will be judged by the quality of their product and whether they can supply the quantities of goods that are needed on time.

- **Complementary products that link with their reputation, image and ethics**. A retail store will not normally stock products outside its usual range, unless it has made a deliberate decision to expand into a new area – such as when Blockbuster decided to stock wine as part of their 'Everything you need for a good night in' experience. Retailers are also concerned about their reputation and image. Therefore a jeweller known for high quality, expensive items would not stock cheap costume jewellery. All reputable toy shops are concerned that their stocks conform to current safety standards – and so on. Business ethics also relate to the source of the product and the materials that are used. Well-known retailers would not want to be accused of selling products produced using cheap labour or linked to an endangered species, for example, no matter how cheap they were. You will find out more about this in Section 2.3.
- **Additional features and benefits**. Buyers will be tempted to buy if there are additional benefits for themselves or their customers. This can include superb packaging, a famous brand name or products that are the subject of special marketing promotions, as these will help to increase sales.

Other businesses

All types of businesses need to buy goods and services – from farmers and manufacturers to construction companies and banks. In this case they are not buying stock for resale but equipment, raw materials or consumables to operate their own business. Selling to industry is often known as **B2B (business to business) marketing**.

There are several reasons why this is different from selling to retailers or to the consumer market.

- The product may be very complex, custom-built or very large and bulky and impossible to describe easily or demonstrate on the customer's own premises.
- A product or service may be highly technical and only understandable to specialists in a particular area.
- There may be several people involved in making the buying decision, besides the actual purchasing manager or buyer. This is because there will be the users' needs to consider, the views of specialists to take into account and the main decision for a major purchase will be made by a separate group altogether – such as the Board of Directors. Suppliers often refer to this group as the **Decision Making Unit** or **DMU**.

Therefore, whereas photocopier supplies or paper towels may be relatively simple to sell to businesses, it is a different matter if you are dealing with industrial machinery or equipment, commodities like steel or wheat, or sophisticated software for large computer installations.

What do business buyers want?

This depends upon the item they are buying, the cost and their location. As a general rule, for expensive or complex products, they will expect demonstrations and presentations of the product, to negotiate over discounts and/or payment terms, to discuss delivery, installation and contract terms and to have a guarantee of ongoing support and/or spare parts whenever they are needed.

This is why many businesses that sell to industry employ representatives with a high level of technical knowledge about their products and/or services. They will spend many years developing a network of contacts to include the key 'decision makers' in an organisation and will be willing to spend a considerable amount of money, time and energy to finalise a sale.

What is a contract?

A contract is a legal agreement between two individuals or organisations. A **sales contract** is formed between a buyer and a seller. You are involved in a contract of sale every time you buy something – as you will see if you study specialist unit 7. However, this is unlikely to be a written contract unless you are making a major purchase, such as a house or car.

In business, small purchases must be recorded on an official order form, so that there is a written record. All major purchases are also agreed in writing, this time in a **written contract**. This states all the terms of the sale. It will include the price, any delivery terms and conditions, give details of the exact product or service being bought (often known as a **specification**) plus any other details which the buyer thinks are important.

For example, many contracts include a **penalty clause**. This means that money is deducted from the supplier if the goods or service are delivered at a later date to that specified in the contract. Both the buyer and the seller sign the contract and the terms must be kept by both of them. If one of them does not keep to the terms, this is known as **breaching the contract**, and the other party can take legal action.

The contract may last for several years. These types of contracts are prized because they guarantee work for the supplier – from supplying tins of tomatoes to Sainsbury's to providing cleaning services for a hospital or government office building. In some cases contracts are signed before a product is made or built. This would be the case for construction companies and suppliers of customised equipment and machinery.

Central and local government departments

The Government is the largest buyer in the country, purchasing over £13 billion in goods and services every year.

Central government departments are responsible for buying all the items they need themselves and also all those supplies which are required to fulfil government plans or targets. Some of these are routine items – such as police cars and uniforms. Others are for specific reasons – such as bridges or buildings, hospital equipment, new aircraft or IT systems.

Local government departments undertake a similar role at local level. Your local authority may be responsible for buying its own equipment and materials and many of those required by schools in the area. It must also be able to supply a range of services for the community – from refuse collection to the provision of libraries. This means entering into contracts with suppliers to provide the goods and/or services that are required.

Purchasing decisions by central and local government are only made by approved groups of officials and must conform to many laws and regulations to prevent any allegations of favouritism or over-spending. One reason for this is because each decision can be reported in the press and is open to public scrutiny and criticism if something goes wrong. Each government (and local government) department is allocated a budget and spending decisions are often made at specific times of the year. For example, decisions about school supplies are likely to be made at the start of the budget year, in April or May, so that the items are available at the start of the new term in September. You will learn more about budgets when you reach Section 3.3.

What do government buyers want?

Budget holders in public sector businesses normally buy routine, consumable items themselves – so headteachers will buy textbooks and hospital managers will buy medical supplies. They will want to receive information on the latest products available, linked to their budget year. By arrangement, they may agree for representatives to call and talk to themselves or their staff.

More expensive goods and services are purchased using a different system and buyers will expect businesses to know how this operates. All

Government contracts are often very complex – and can be worth millions of pounds to the successful supplier. In August 2003, a company in Cornwall was awarded a contract by the government's Warship Support Agency to refit a Royal Fleet Auxiliary ship. The contract was worth up to £10m and guaranteed employment for employees in the yard for quite some time.

The public sector is often under pressure to give as many contracts as possible to British suppliers –

especially if this will help to save jobs. This is why there was a row in October 2003, when a contract to build three new ferries to run between Plymouth, Devon and Torpoint, in Cornwall, went to a Scottish firm of shipbuilders. The decision, made by the committee of councillors from Cornwall and Plymouth, angered unions because a local firm, Appledore, in north Devon, had also put in a very close bid and needed the contract to survive. All 550 workers at Appledore had to be made redundant after the decision.

interested suppliers have to **tender** for the work. This means that all the suppliers obtain details of what is required and submit an offer, or bid. These are often sealed, for security. On a specific date, all the offers are compared and the buying group decides which supplier to use. The choice will be made using a variety of factors – not just cost. Reliability, quality and the supplier's reputation will also be taken into account to achieve the 'best value' possible. The successful supplier is then contracted to carry out the work – from supplying aeroplanes to the RAF to emptying rubbish bins for your local council.

Voluntary sector organisations

All voluntary sector organisations are very aware that they are spending other people's money when they buy anything, as all expenditure reduces the amount of money from donations that can be spent on charitable activities. In addition, charity trustees are legally accountable for the way money is spent.

What do voluntary sector buyers want?

They often want a discount, because of their special status. Many suppliers offer these to the voluntary sector – from insurance companies to web design agencies. They also need to take into account ethical considerations. Oxfam, for example, promotes Fairtrade products which give a fair deal, such as living wages, to small scale producers of basic commodities like coffee, tea,

chocolate and bananas in third world countries. Because of this it cannot afford to buy from sources that don't subscribe to this idea. Equally, Friends of the Earth would immediately be criticised if it didn't buy 'green', environmentally friendly goods itself.

Fairtrade products give a fair deal

Two organisations help buyers in this sector. The National Council for Voluntary Organisations (NCVO) is the 'umbrella' body for the voluntary sector and most voluntary organisations are members. One of the things that they gain is to benefit from bulk purchasing by NCVO to obtain products and services. They also receive a quarterly newsletter with updates about discounts and a directory of suppliers. Charitybuyer.com Ltd is an independent company that provides an online resource to save not-for-profit buyers time and money by giving up to date information about suppliers of goods and services to the voluntary sector. You can find out more on the NCVO and Charitybuyer websites – links are available at www.heinemann.co.uk/hotlinks (express code 1386P).

Merchandise The products sold by retail stores.
Tender A written bid or offer to do specific work at a stated price.
Penalty clause A clause in a contract that states the fine which the supplier must pay for delayed completion or delivery.

Specification Details of an item, identifying each component and stating type or quality required.
Best value The criteria on which tenders are judged in the public sector.
Decision making unit (DMU) The people in an organisation who decide what to buy.

Over to you!

1 Working in a small group, summarise the key needs or expectations of different types of customers by copying out and completing the table below. To help, the first line has been done for you. Aim to find at least **two** more expectations for each type of customer. When you have finished, compare your ideas with the suggestions made by other groups.

Retail buyers	Other business buyers	Government buyers (central and local)	Voluntary sector buyers
Buy popular goods which sell quickly to meet sales targets	Technical support and assistance	Obtain best value	Buy cheaply to minimise running costs

2 Many businesses sell both to private individuals and to other businesses – but differentiate their goods in some way. For example, food producers supply large catering packs and estate agents issue leaflets featuring commercial property. In a small group, investigate **one** of the following businesses and find **two** examples of the products or services they offer *only* to businesses rather than to private individuals. In some cases you will also find specific information for buyers in the public sector. Remember to look for 'business services' or 'business to business' information on each website

– links are available at www.heinemann.co.uk/hotlinks (express code 1386P).

  a A well-known bank, e.g. NatWest or Barclays.
  b British Telecom.
  c Office World.
  d Dell Computers.
  e Microsoft.
  f An insurance company, e.g. Norwich Union.
  g A car hire firm, e.g. Avis or Hertz.

3 John Whitley is a photographer. Until now he has specialised in doing portraits for family groups and weddings. He now wants to expand his operations by offering a commercial service to businesses too.

  a Identify **five** key expectations you think his private customers have when they make a booking with John.
  b As a commercial photographer, what type of businesses do you think he will work for – and what type of work will he do? Investigate some of the websites listed at UK 250 to get a few ideas – a link is available at www.heinemann.co.uk/hotlinks (express code 1386P).
  c Suggest **four** expectations that his business customers will have that will be different from his private customers.
  d Suggest **three** ways in which you think John can be responsive to these expectations to launch his new operations successfully.

Talking point

View 1: *UK Fairtrade product sales have increased by 90 per cent since 2000 and there are now over 180 retail products which carry the Fairtrade mark. This shows that people are prepared to spend on ethical goods, even when they cost more. This will teach the multinational producers a lesson.*

View 2: *Fairtrade will only ever work on a small scale because big companies are too powerful and will reduce prices, if necessary, to regain the advantage. You need only look in an average shopping basket – how many people really bother to buy Fairtrade goods?*

With which viewpoint do you agree – and why? To find out more before you start debating, check out the Fairtrade, Oxfam, Cafedirect and Coop websites – links to these sites are available at www.heinemann.co.uk/hotlinks (express code 1386P).

Customer attributes and market segmentation

Because different types of customers have different needs, wants and expectations it would be very difficult – if not impossible – to cater for everyone. This is one reason why small businesses specialise in supplying goods or services to a certain group. Larger businesses can only be successful if they have some way of reducing the number of expectations they need to meet. One way of doing this is through market segmentation. Quite simply, the market is divided into different chunks, or segments, based on customer attributes. These are often different for consumer markets and organisational markets, as you can see from the table below.

	Consumer markets	**Organisational markets**
Personal/organisational factors	Age Gender Culture Socio-economic group Family size Status in family Lifestyle	Type of industry Industry sector Size Number/type of buyers Profitability
Geographic factors	Location Language Culture	Location Language Culture
Buyer behaviour	Perceived needs/wants/preferences Buying patterns Size of purchase	Purchasing procedure Use of purchase Volume Special requirements (e.g. 24/7 back-up service)

Figure 2.8 *Customer attributes in consumer and organisational markets*

Business brief

More about market segments

Many marketing specialists believe that there is no such thing as a 'market' – only market segments. This is because a 'market' consists of such a disparate group of people it is impossible to meet all their different needs.

You have already seen that the car market can be divided into different sub-markets or segments, such as sports cars, family cars and luxury cars. Another way of looking at this is to say that each market segment represents a group of customers who think in the same way.

- They are attracted by the same type of products and benefits.
- They value the product in the same way.
- They use the product in the same way.
- They behave in a similar way when they are buying.

Identifying the market segments means that businesses can decide which needs and whose needs they must meet. They can then target their products or services at market segments and not at the whole market.

Segmentation in the consumer market

Personal factors

In the consumer market, many factors are demographic. Demography relates to a study of the population – which can be sub-divided into different age groups as well as by gender, income and family size. All of these factors are crucial for many different products and services:

- **Age** is critical for producers of disposable nappies, toy makers, clothes for teenagers and, at the opposite extreme, products for the elderly.
- **Gender** segmentation is used in many industries, such as those involved in producing toiletries, cosmetics, clothing and magazines.
- **Culture** relates to people's religion, language, customs, ethnicity and dietary habits. In many areas of England you will find newspapers and leaflets in different languages. In different communities you will find kosher or halal butchers to serve Jewish or Muslim customers.
- **Socio-economic** groups divide the population into different groups based on their occupation. It assumes that the higher you are on the scale,

This shop targets budget shoppers by providing reasonably priced products

the more you will earn and therefore the more **disposable income** you have to spend. Stores like Harvey Nichols and Selfridges target themselves at affluent customers – so do producers of luxury goods like Gucci. At the other end of the scale stores like Aldi, Netto and IKEA target those on a tight budget.

- **Family size** is often relevant because larger families are presumed to have slightly different needs and – most likely – less time and less money to spend. Food producers target this market with giant pizzas and 'value' products. In the US there are even magazines and websites targeted at large families.
- **Status in family** is relevant to the type of products/services bought and the power to make the decision to buy. The 'head' of the family will make key decisions about fundamental purchases – from electricity to groceries and can 'over rule' junior members – as you may know if you tried to influence what went into your family's weekly shopping trolley when you were young! This doesn't stop businesses targeting adverts at junior family members, because 'pester power' can sometimes be very effective.
- **Lifestyle** relates to the way we live. Businesses develop and target products and services at different lifestyle groups – such as Amazon, which includes 'Lifestyle and Hobbies' as one of the search criteria on its website. Many leading marketing companies have devised their own

Group	Profession
1	Large employers and higher managerial occupations
	Higher professional occupations
	Lower managerial and professional occupations
2	Intermediate occupations
	Small employers and own account workers
	Lower supervisory and technical occupations
3	Semi-routine occupations Routine occupations
4	Never worked or long-term unemployed
Other categories	Full-time students Not classifiable for other reasons (e.g. occupation not coded)

Figure 2.9 *Socio-economic classifications 2001*

lifestyle categories, such as the ACORN system, devised by CACI, (see below). This is based on census data and includes factors such as age, education, type of house and car ownership. Super Profile, devised by CDMS, Experian's Mosaic and Equifax's Micromatch are other databases that segment customers according to lifestyle labels. This enables them to assist businesses to target prospective customers more effectively.

Category	Lifestyle group
Wealthy achievers	Wealthy executives Affluent greys Flourishing families Prosperous professionals
Urban prosperity	Educated urbanites Aspiring singles Starting out Secure families
Comfortably off	Settled suburbia Prudent pensioners Asian communities
Moderate means	Post industrial families Blue-collar roots Struggling families
Hard pressed	Burdened singles High rise hardship Inner city adversity

(Courtesy of CACI Limited)

Figure 2.10 *ACORN lifestyle classifications*

Geographic factors

These identify where customers are based and are of particular interest to businesses that want to increase the scale of their operations.

- **Location** may focus on a town, city or region of England or the UK, or cover a range of countries. Businesses can obtain data on prospective customers in any area. This can help them to make decisions from where to open offices or stores overseas to which countries would be interested in importing their products or services.

- **Language skills** are often overlooked, but are very important in selling products abroad. Advertisements, information leaflets and instructions all need translating. A foreign language version of the website is a bonus, as are sales staff who can speak the language of the country where major customers are based.

- **Culture** varies from one country to another. Laws, regulations, business practices and even holidays may be very different. Understanding how business is carried out in different countries is often crucial to success.

Buyer behaviour in consumer markets

There are literally hundreds of research studies on how buyers behave. Some buyers are logical and methodical, others are impulse shoppers. Some stay loyal to businesses for many years, others prefer to shop around – and so on. Three ways of segmenting customers in this area are by:

- **Perceived needs, wants and preferences**. This often links to lifestyle and socio-economic groupings but, as you saw at the start of this section, people are often different! Other key variables that can be analysed are sales figures and stock movements to see which products and services are currently preferred by different groups.

- **Buying patterns**. How and where do people buy? How much do they spend each time? Which products do they buy – and which do they ignore? One way of finding this out is to analyse the behaviour of existing customers, which is the aim of large stores like Tesco when they issue loyalty cards. The details of every transaction can be analysed to target money-off vouchers and promotions to try to influence future behaviour. Special sales, discount events and promotional advertising are just some of the other methods used to persuade customers to change their buying patterns.

- **Size of purchase**. All consumers can be defined by a 'usage profile' which includes frequency and purpose of use. This is why hotel questionnaires normally ask customers how often they stay in hotels and whether the visit is for leisure or on business. Businesses can then target or offer special incentives to heavy users or frequent visitors – such as preferred guest and frequent flier programmes offered by hotels and airlines.

Segmentation in organisational markets

Organisational factors

Some of the main factors to be considered are listed below.

- **Sector and industry**. These will be decided using the categories you read about in section 1.2. These are the primary, secondary or tertiary sectors and the specific industries within each sector.
- **Size** of the business will give an indication of its purchasing needs, and the likely volume of its orders. For example, a firm that employs 5 people would normally need a lower quantity of consumable items than one employing 500.
- **The number and type of buyers** will affect the buying process which is likely to be undertaken, as you saw on page 104, both in terms of the main decision makers and the length of the process.
- **Profitability** is the organisational equivalent

of wealth. Businesses with high or regular profits are far more likely to be buying more equipment or expanding than those that are suffering heavy losses.

Geographic factors

In this case there is little difference between the type of factors considered for consumers and for organisations. All can be segmented by location, language and culture.

Buyer behaviour in organisational markets

Segmenting buyer behaviour in organisations helps to identify the best way to approach the customer to meet his or her needs. Some of the main factors to consider are given below.

- **Purchasing procedure** – this will vary depending upon the product and the type of organisation. You already know that selling office stationery is less complex than selling expensive technical equipment and that the purchasing procedure is different in a small shop and a large store group. Businesses which sell to government departments need to be familiar with the procedures used there – and so on.

Business matters

Most businesses store customer data on their computer databases but a new technique called **data mining** is now used by many companies to extract more detailed information on individual customers. This is often part of an overall strategy of **customer relationship management (CRM)** used by businesses to find out more about their customers.

All companies want to persuade existing customers to spend more money with them, so they need to know as much as possible about individual buying habits, tastes and spending levels. They want to analyse existing information as thoroughly as possible, too, to help them attract new business.

To do this, a variety of CRM computer packages are available which record the details of all customer transactions. This information is then available to

anyone who deals with a customer's call, whether in a call centre or marketing department. It can also be used to predict the future buying behaviour of both that customer and others with similar characteristics.

Although customer information can be obtained from phone calls and personal visits, it is the Internet which can often provide the greatest insight. This is because a company can record the buttons a customer clicks, the pages viewed and responses to different aspects of the site.

Website monitoring may lead to a business making changes. For example, Victoria's Secret, a lingerie retailer, believed most of its customers were women in their 20s and 30s. Website monitoring showed that most visitors to its site were men aged 40 – 55. As a result the company redesigned its website to make it more appealing to this group.

- **Volume** relates to the amount purchased – and is similar to 'size of purchase' in the consumer market. It is used to differentiate important institutional buyers which, because of the size of their orders, are usually crucial to the supplier's profits and may be given preferential treatment or discounts.
- **Special requirements** can be many and various – from special financial arrangements to on-site maintenance, 24 hour back-up and spare parts availability. These needs will vary depending upon the type of product, size of order and location.

Market analysis – segmentation in action

Businesses use segmentation to help them to meet customer expectations more accurately. This is normally a two-stage process:

- They analyse the market – by identifying the main segments.
- They carry out market research to find out more about their existing and potential customers.

Market research

Businesses can carry out market research themselves, or employ a specialist company to do it for them. Or they can buy market research reports which contain the statistics they need from a market research company like Mintel or Keynote.

There are two main types of market research. Dealing with customers direct to obtain new information is known as **primary research**. You will read about this on page 116. Using reports produced by agencies and other statistics is called **secondary research**. Some businesses will use both methods to obtain a broader picture – or, the most expensive option, they will pay a specialist to carry out both types and analyse the market for them. Whilst this may be an option for large businesses, it is usually too expensive for small firms.

The aim of the exercise is for each business to identify its **target market** and its **key customers**.

Market analysis

This means using market research and the most important segments of a particular market to identify the best products to offer, the price to charge, how to promote them and where to sell them. If you have studied unit 1, you should see that this links to the four main components of the **marketing mix** – Product, Price, Promotion and Place (page 66). For example:

- A different range of products can be offered to suit the needs (and pockets) of different customers. This is why supermarkets not only stock a wide range of brands and products but also have a top range (e.g. Tesco Finest or Sainsbury's Taste the Difference), a standard range and a value range; and also why many car producers make luxury, family and sports models available with a range of different features.
- Prices often link to particular products and ranges but special discounts may be offered to frequent customers or higher prices may be charged to customers who can afford to pay more. This is known as **price differentiation**. Business visitors to city hotels during midweek periods are charged more than weekend visitors, who are tempted with discounts at a time when the hotel may otherwise be empty. Train tickets are more expensive during peak business travelling times than other times and bargain air tickets will be available during off-peak times and days – but not during school or college holidays!
- Many products are promoted to specific market segments. Toys are advertised on television when children will be watching; products aimed at youth markets will be promoted during programmes like Friends or Home and Away. If you check the type of adverts in the press, you will see these are far different in *The Financial Times* and *The Sun* – or between magazines like *Marie Claire* and *FHM*. Marketing will often devise a memorable **strapline** – or short slogan – to appeal to a particular segment of the

market, such as L'Oreal's 'Because you're worth it.'

- Understanding about location – linked to demographic data – helps major stores to decide where to locate certain products. This is why only a few stores in a chain will stock some top ranges, such as Marks & Spencer Autograph or Per Una ranges. A large superstore will stock product lines in each store, based on its particular customers, their lifestyle and socio-economic grouping.

Business matters

Market research and advertising companies have recently identified a new group of customers and labelled them **kidults**, adultescents or the rejuvenile generation. These are successful and independent semi-adults with free time, money to spend, good jobs and busy lifestyles. What makes them unique is that they reject adult choices in favour of younger options – such as theme parks, rock concerts, children's films, cartoons, teenage clothes and video games. Marketing experts have now assessed that the average age of video game players is now 29 whereas in 1990 it was 18 and one American authority now estimates that adolescence can last from age 10 to 34!

Businesses have been quick to cash in on this trend. The Harry Potter books, for example, were so popular with kidults that the publishers, Bloomsbury, designed two book jackets for each title – one for young kids – and one for older ones! At the same time, the trade magazine *Booklist* used the term **crossover** for books that span a range of age groups.

So if you know people in their 20s or 30s who like to read comics, go to an adventure park or watch a fantasy film in their leisure time, you can tell them that they're not alone. You can even find out more about their profile at the Kidult Games website on the Internet and download some free games yourself – a link is available at www.heinemann.co.uk/hotlinks (express code 1386P).

Talking point

View 1: *Teenagers are the most difficult market segment to analyse because they are contradictory. They want to impress their friends but also want to be unique. They don't like anything their parents like and hate being targeted in an obvious way.*

View 2: *Teenagers are easy to analyse as a market because they all want to follow the latest trends. You only have to look around you to see how similar their preferences are.*

Kidadults prefer young activities

With which viewpoint do you agree – and why?

Over to you!

1 Find out how the **ACORN** system would classify you and your family on the Internet – a link is available at www.heinemann.co.uk/hotlinks (express code 1386P). On the site, read through some of ACORN's case studies and identify **three** ways in which this type of segmentation information is used by businesses.

2 Although car manufacturers produce different models, their brand name alone is often associated with a particular segment of the market (such as Rolls Royce and luxury cars). They will therefore target most of their press advertising at this segment by promoting their cars in newspapers or magazines that also target the same market.

   a In the table below four magazines are listed, each with their strapline or title. Copy out the table and decide the profile of the key customer for each of the publications listed. If you need to find out more, then check out each one in your local newsagent or on the Internet.

   b You work for an advertising agency. You are advising the following manufacturers which of the four magazines to advertise in. As a group, discuss which you would select in each case. If your group doesn't contain any car 'buffs', then check each one out on the Internet before you complete your table!

   Cars/models: Fiat Siecento, Jaguar, Land Rover, VW Beetle, BMW 5 Series, Subaru Impreza, Audi TT, Suzuki Baleno.

3 Several segments of the clothing market are given below. As a group, suggest a profile for the type of customers who would be attracted to buy each type of clothing, by deciding the main customer attributes in each case. Then suggest **one** way in which knowing this would help the manufacturers or retailers to increase their total sales.

   a Natural fabrics, e.g. pure wool, cashmere and leather.
   b Artificial fabrics, e.g. plastics and nylon.
   c Leisure wear, e.g. leggings and fleece tops.
   d Formal clothing, e.g. suits, overcoats, tailored skirts.
   e Casual clothing, e.g. jeans, T-shirts

Publication	Key customer profile	Car manufacturer/model
Company magazine ('For your freedom years')		
Esquire magazine ('The sharper read for men')		
Country magazine ('When your heart is in the country')		
Financial Times monthly supplement ('How to spend it')		

Matching products with market demand and customer expectations

It is pointless analysing a market unless the information will be used to the advantage of the business. Organisations that are good at spotting new opportunities to fulfil or exceed customer expectations are normally one step ahead of their competitors. They increase their sales, increase their profits and avoid unsold or unsaleable stocks.

Exploiting market potential

To make the most of new opportunities, the first step is to identify areas where demand is increasing. This can be done by studying market research reports on the industry or statistics that show current consumer trends, such as the Office of National Statistics (ONS) report on Family Spending (see page 78).

The process to follow is shown below.

Figure 2.11 *Applying market analysis*

New trends and opportunities

The business has to decide which new trends apply to the market segments that it already supplies. It also has to decide which opportunities fit the current business profile and activities. For example, food manufacturers can take advantage of increasing demand for more vegetarian ready-meals, more organic produce and more low fat goods – but these trends wouldn't be of interest to a computer supplier. In this case, one area of interest could be the growth of broadband and online shopping in the UK which has increased demand for security software (see page 66).

Some trends are very short-lived. Unless the business can respond very quickly it cannot take advantage of them. Computer game designers Eidos, raced to finish the game of The Italian Job to coincide with the movie release in 2003 but had problems with its new Tomb Raider game, which should have been released to coincide with the film The Cradle of Life. The impact of the delay on their annual profits resulted in a fall in the value of company shares.

For that reason, businesses must assess if they can respond in time and if any investment they make, in terms of time and money, will pay off. In most cases this means that the new trend must be relatively long-term and affect a considerable number of customers.

The only exceptions are businesses which are small and operate in a niche market. They may be able to take advantage of trends which will attract fewer new customers. For example, skiing clothes and accessories are sold by a large number of suppliers but the more recent interest in snowboarding has only been exploited by small suppliers and specialist shops so far. This is why you won't find snowboarding gear in many regional stores yet or many snowboarding DVDs for sale!

Adapting products

Products (and their features) can be adapted or changed in several ways – and so can services and service arrangements.

- Existing products can be adapted in response to new technology and trends (e.g. computer printers that print digital photographs as well as text or graphics).
- Product features or benefits can be enhanced (e.g. longer guarantee period whereby free repairs are offered, faster operation – such as washing machines with a 'speed wash' facility, cheaper operation – such as fuel efficient cars).
- New services can be introduced or existing services extended (e.g. chemists who offer a home delivery service, 24 hour opening by supermarkets and phone and Internet banking).
- Products and services can be improved following customer feedback (e.g. ring pull tins, microwaveable packaging, faster appointment times in hospitals, a recorded message for customers reporting a fault with a service to give them a status update).

Avoiding unsold/unsaleable stocks

Stock which is unsold is normally reduced in price to tempt customers to buy. This means the business is reducing its own margins to get rid of it, on the basis that it is better to break even than to lose money.

If you are an astute buyer, you may know that sale discounts often increase if goods remain unsold. Goods that start off being marked down by 10 per cent eventually end up being reduced by 50 per cent or even more. The business just wants to get its money back – or even some money back – to recoup its losses on the stock.

If the goods won't sell at any price, then they are unsaleable and the business has lost money. It may give them away as part of its community or social policies. Marks & Spencer, for example, gives to charity all unsold sandwiches and other food products that have reached their 'sell by date' at the end of each day. It would not, however, like the idea of giving away its unsaleable clothing as well! In this case, the buyer(s) would be criticised for over-stocking an item or misreading the 'trend' signs at the start of the season. However, the main message is that this item has been unsuccessful and should not be stocked in future. At this point, the business should start to work out what went wrong. One reason could be that it did not fit with current customer expectations or market trends.

Monitoring market trends

Market trends are constantly changing, for a variety of reasons (see page 129). However, no business can assume that because it has spotted a trend it can now become complacent. Constant monitoring is essential. Trends can change rapidly – rather like the weather forecast. Just because you listened to it three days ago doesn't mean that you can depend upon it this morning!

Information can be obtained by using primary or secondary market research techniques – or both.

Business brief

The importance of validity

Designing and analysing questionnaires is not easy – which is why many businesses pay experts to do this for them. For one thing the questions must be easy to understand, asked in a logical order and should give specific options to choose. Otherwise analysing the responses is very difficult.

All the hard work is ruined, however, unless the right people are asked. Unless the results really do reflect the views of the key customer then the research will not be **valid**. For example, it is no use asking pensioners about Club 18–30 holidays or women about shaving products. Equally, enough people must be asked to obtain a **representative** opinion or **sample**. If only a few people are asked, some may have unusual views, which could 'skew' the research results. If enough people are questioned, then any outlandish opinions by a minority are usually cancelled out.

Primary market research

This involves collecting and analysing information from customers. The advantage is that the information is original and up-to-date. The most widely used methods are given below.

- **Postal surveys** involve sending customers a questionnaire through the post, together with a Freepost envelope for the reply. This method is commonly used because a large number of people can be contacted quite quickly and cheaply. The problem is that unless customers are offered an incentive or prize for taking part, many people can't be bothered so the number of responses received may be quite small.
- **Personal surveys** involve face-to-face interviews, often using a questionnaire. These may be carried out by researchers in shopping centres. The problem with this method is that people may not be prepared to stop and may not be truthful with their answers, particularly if they are accompanied by someone else!
- **Telephone questionnaires** are the cheapest method and quite effective if people will agree to talk.
- **Online questionnaires** are becoming more popular. After using a website or buying products online a customer may be asked to complete a short pop-up questionnaire to summarise their views and preferences. Alternatively, questionnaires may be emailed to customers who have registered on a site.
- **Focus groups** or **consumer panels** are a representative group of customers or people who are recruited to give their views on a range of issues. They meet regularly to discuss important issues which concern the business and to give their opinions and suggestions.

Secondary market research

This involves looking at information that already exists or has been obtained by another organisation. All businesses store information on their own database systems about their existing customers and their buying habits. Businesses can also buy information other company databases and obtain government statistics about consumer expenditure and details of their competitors. They can also use a variety of press and online sources to keep up to date with trends in their industry.

- **The trade press** carries updates for members of a particular industry, such as *The Grocer, Travel Trade Gazette* or *The Bookseller*.
- **Local newspapers** and business supplements contain information on activities in their own area or region.
- **National newspapers** all have business sections. These are more detailed in what are traditionally called the broadsheet papers, such as *The Financial Times, The Times* or *The Guardian*.
- **International publications** provide a broader

Business matters

If you are broke as a student you may be tempted to earn extra money by doing online surveys and questionnaires or joining a focus group for a reward. Whilst this is a possibility, it can become tedious and you may soon be either swamped with surveys or dejected because none are sent to you! Several US websites such as Paidsurveys.com offer

these opportunities but mainly for residents in the US or Canada.

To find out if you are eligible for many of them, you first have to provide your personal details. As well as contact details, most also ask for educational qualifications and your occupation, as well as your age and gender. These details are required to obtain your socio-economic and demographic profile. This then enables the research company to match you against surveys or focus groups where your views would be relevant.

Companies are willing to offer rewards because this tempts the right people to give their views. Otherwise it can be difficult persuading consumers to do this. If you are interested in finding out more, links to the Paid Surveys and Survey Spot websites are available at www.heinemann.co.uk/hotlinks (express code 1386P).

Good market research plays a vital part in the running of any business

view, e.g. *The Economist*, *Business Central Europe*, *Business Week* (American) and *Company Digest*.

- **Online sources** – from news sites such as the BBC and Ananova to specialist research sites where users pay a subscription to access information. Most newspapers and magazines also have an online information service, e.g. *The Financial Times* – a link is available at www.heinemann.co.uk/hotlinks (express code 1386P). Businesses may also pay a subscription to a market research company such as Mintel, Datamonitor, Keynote and Gobi International to be able to access specific reports or search for current information on their own markets.

Action planning

Once businesses obtain customer feedback and identify trends the first step is to decide how to respond. You will read about the range of responses and the factors that affect these in the next section.

Assuming they wish to take action, they have to decide what to do. This will obviously depend upon the trend they have identified, but normally it will involve adapting the product or service in some way (see page 115). Bear in mind that this could mean:

- Changing the range, type or features of a product or service.
- Adjusting the price.
- Changing or increasing the source(s) of supply to improve availability.
- Improving the benefits, e.g. better back-up or after-sales services.

They must then communicate this change to their customers. How they do this will depend upon the action taken and the type of customers.

In the consumer market a large company can ensure that customers are kept aware of changes and improvements through adverts and mailshots to customers. A small local business would probably push a leaflet through your door.

In the business market, advertisements would be placed in the trade press or large buyers notified individually by sales representatives during a visit. New or adapted products may be launched at trade fairs or exhibitions, such as the British Toy Fair, held each January, and Engineering Lasers, held in March.

The process of action planning is summarised in Figure 2.12.

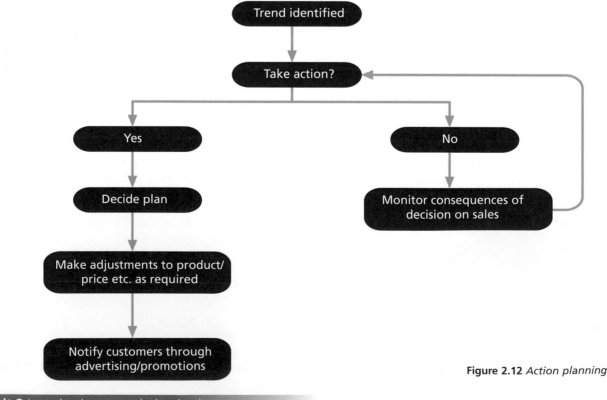

Figure 2.12 *Action planning*

Sir Terry Leahy is the Chief Executive at Tesco. In his time at the top he has turned Tesco into the UK's leading supermarket with an appeal to many sectors of the market – from millionaires to those struggling to manage on a tight budget. In 2003, he was awarded CSC Business Leader of the Year.

What is his secret? In the early 1990s Tesco's sales were flagging. As marketing director he asked for lots of customer research to find out why there was a problem. He discovered that customers felt let down because they thought Tesco was just trying to copy its arch-rival Sainsbury's, rather than trying to find out what they really wanted. At that point, Tesco changed its approach and started listening to its customers.

As a result it introduced its Value line and its Clubcard. It developed new store formats, such as its Express and Metro outlets. It started selling petrol, clothing, music and financial services. It introduced a revolutionary online retailing site – and all because it listened to its customers.

Leahy talks about the moment when he realised that Tesco wasn't listening properly as his 'crikey moment'. He still thinks that improvements can be made and in every store you can complete a suggestions form to give feedback yourself. If you want a hand in Tesco's next developments, you know what to do!

Range of responses

There are three possible responses to customer feedback and information about new trends:

- Respond quickly and make the necessary changes to products or services.

- Wait and see. Only respond if absolutely necessary.
- Disregard it and do nothing.

Responding to customer feedback

As you can see from the story on Tesco, responding to customer feedback promptly and positively pays dividends. Indeed, some of the critics writing about Sainsbury's said it has focused too much on what it wanted to do (improve quality) and too little on what customers wanted it to do (lower prices). So a business which operates in its own interests, rather than those of its customers, will normally be less successful than one which responds quickly to market trends.

Some businesses may be more apt to drag their heels. Whether this matters will depend upon whether the changes relate to customer's key expectations or not – and the service that is provided. You may therefore put up with your favourite hairdresser refusing to accept a debit card because they haven't installed the technology, but rapidly change your evening shopping habits if your local store closes its doors promptly at 6pm but another starts staying open until 8pm.

Businesses that disregard customer feedback and do nothing are taking a huge risk. There are very few types of business that can totally ignore the views of their customers. Businesses have more power when customers have little choice – as you will see in the next section. For example, there are too few dentists to go around these days, so you could argue that patients can't be too fussy. However, any dentist who continually ignored the key expectations of patients would still be in

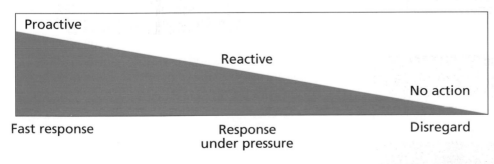

Figure 2.13 *Range of responses to market trends*

danger of losing many of them. If there were serious problems, customers might complain to the press or even to the General Dental Council, which would then have to investigate. This could seriously affect the dentist's livelihood and/or future ability to practice.

Business brief

You can please some of the people some of the time...

It is easy to say that businesses must always take action to meet customer expectations. But what does a business do if customers don't agree – or suggest 'impossible' actions, like opening a small shop every hour of every day?

Many businesses divide customer suggestions and comments into two groups. Those they can – and should – do something about and those that they can't. Richer Sounds does this, as you will see on the StudentZone at www.richerstudentzone.co.uk. As another example, a city centre hotel could take action about complaints of constant queues at reception, but may be unable to do anything about limited parking spaces.

It is also impossible to please all of the people all of the time. Sometimes, an idea that pleases one person would annoy other customers. As a student, you might wish that all your classes started at midday, but other members of your class may disagree.

Businesses therefore have to find a balance. They can do this by looking at the key expectations of their key customers. If they also gain a reputation for being responsive, flexible and trying to do their best, this helps to attract and retain customers too.

Responding to new trends

Again the business has the choice whether to respond immediately, take its time or not bother. However, in some cases there may be sound reasons for not doing anything immediately. Businesses need to think about:

- The importance of the trend to their core business.
- The possible actions of their competitors. (See section 2.2.)
- Their power or influence in the market.
- The 'style' of the organisation and the way it is run – which may also link to its size. These combined factors are often known as the **organisational culture**.
- The cost of making an immediate response against the potential benefits.
- The consequences of waiting or doing nothing.

Many experts divide businesses into different types:

- **Type A firms** will want to act quickly. They will constantly be looking for new opportunities and may be keen to experiment to try new things. This is important if the business operates in a fast-moving industry, such as IT or fashion. It is normally easier, too, for a small business to put new plans into operation quickly.
- **Type B firms** will let others make the changes first and then follow. In many cases this may mean missing out on new opportunities but can be a safer option, especially if there is no guarantee that the trend will be permanent or if it would cost a lot of money to react quickly.
- **Type C firms** adopt *both* strategies – adapting them for the different types of products and services they supply.

Businesses which refuse to make any changes are likely to be the least successful. They may get away with it for a short time if they are very powerful and are very efficient at what they do but eventually they will fail. You only have to think how many businesses today could operate without computers or Internet access and still provide the same products and services as they did twenty years ago to realise that *all* businesses must keep up with the times and new customer demands to survive.

Over to you!

1 All Colleges ask for student feedback, so your group may have completed forms about your course and the facilities from time to time.

   a As a group, suggest **two** student concerns that you think your college could address – and **two** which it couldn't.

   b For each concern you raise that it could address, say what you think it could do.

   c For each one, decide the consequences of the college taking action *and* ignoring your suggestions.

2 Each of the following is a new or adapted product or service, developed in response to trends or customer feedback. As a group, in each case state whether you think it will be successful or not – and give your reasons.

   a A device the size of a computer mouse that finds missing golf balls. It costs about £45. In competitions, it would mean fewer golfers accrue penalties because they can't find a ball.

   b Detox kits to help people lose weight and become clean inside as well as outside.

   c Robot shop vending machines that stock over 180 everyday essentials, such as milk, tea and coffee. They are protected by bulletproof glass and open around the clock.

3 The traditional high street banks, such as Barclays, Lloyds TSB, HBS and NatWest have been criticised for two main reasons. First, for paying very low interest rates on their savings accounts. Second, for diverting incoming calls to call centres, so that it is almost impossible for a customer to speak to a local branch. Recently, some banks have taken action about the last issue – and NatWest based a television advertising campaign on the fact that customers can now speak to a 'personal banker'. None of them, however, has done much about their interest rates!

   a As a group, which of the two issues do you think is more important to customers – why?

   b Why do you think banks chose to concentrate on the second issue – and not on the first?

   c Obviously, customers who are unhappy can change banks – but most can't be bothered.

      i Why do you think so many customers stay with the same bank, even when they dislike the service?

      ii To what extent do you think banks can take advantage of this when it comes to being unresponsive to customers?

💬 Talking point

View 1: *Most customers have to take what they're given. They haven't time to keep shopping around, even if the service is poor.*

View 2: *Today's customers are more demanding than ever before. Any business that ignores this won't last for long.*

With which viewpoint do you agree – and why?

Now that you have completed this section you should understand how customer expectations affect businesses and what businesses can do to take account of these. Test your skills now by doing the following activities.

Check your understanding of this section by answering the following questions. Check all your answers with your tutor before moving on.

1 **a** What is meant by the term 'market'?
  b Explain the difference between an internal market and an external market.
  c Identify **two** key expectations of retail buyers.
  d Give **two** reasons why salespeople are employed to sell goods to business customers.
  e What is meant by the term 'market segment'?
  f Identify **four** personal attributes of customers which are taken into consideration when markets are segmented.
  g Explain the difference between primary and secondary market research.
  h Identify **two** information sources businesses can use to monitor market trends.
  i Explain **three** ways in which products or services can be adapted in response to customer feedback.
  j Identify **three** ways in which businesses may respond to new trends or customer feedback.

2 Saga was the first business in Britain to specifically target older people. It started by offering 'off-season', affordable holidays for pensioners. This was so successful that the company soon developed into a full-service travel company for customers over 50. Today the company offers a wide range of services, particularly for this age group – including insurance, credit card facilities and investment services. You can find out more on the Saga website – a link is available at www.heinemann.co.uk/hotlinks (express code 1386P). In 2003 Saga was put up for sale by its family owners – with a price tag of £1 billion.

In Germany, a supermarket chain called Activ Markt has opened stores specially designed for customers over 50 in Vienna and Salzburg. There are non-slip floors, special shopping trolleys have holders for walking sticks and all shelves and cabinets above floor level to save bending down. All the staff, too, are aged between 50 and 60. The stores have been a huge success with takings over 20 per cent higher than other stores in the area.

  a How would you describe the market that Saga operates in?
  b How would you describe Saga's 'key customers' in terms of main attributes?
  c What demographic trends do you think have helped Saga's growth and prompted the launch of Activ Markt's new stores? Compare your ideas as a group.
  d To what extent do you think Saga has been responsive to new trends and customer expectations? Give a reason for your answer.
  e Do you think there is scope for one of Britain's supermarket groups to open specialist stores in England? Compare your ideas as a group.
  f If Saga and Activ Markt have identified a successful new trend, can you suggest any opportunities for other businesses that could be linked to this?

This section covers

Competition in business
Identifying the competitive market
Knowing and understanding the market place
Evaluating market position
Action planning to strengthen the market position

Competition in business

Most businesses operate in a **competitive market**. This means that there are several suppliers offering similar goods or services to the same or similar markets. Consumers can choose where to shop and which products to buy. In some markets, such as those for clothes, toiletries and magazines, customers can choose from a huge variety of products, so suppliers have to work hard to tempt people into buying their goods. In other markets the choice may be more limited, particularly if there are only a few suppliers.

- Businesses that produce or sell the same type of products or services to the same market are in **direct competition** with each other, e.g. Next and River Island, *The Sun* and *Daily Star* newspapers, Cadbury's Dairy Milk and Rowntree's Yorkie bars, BBC and ITV.

- Businesses that produce similar types of goods for comparable markets are in **indirect competition** with each other, e.g. train companies and bus companies both want to take you from A to B, cinemas offer an alternative to watching television – and so do DVD/video rental stores. In these cases consumers have a choice of products or activities to meet the same need.

Businesses must not only be aware of the market they are in, but the actions of their existing *and* potential competitors. They need to look carefully

Business matters

Competition is usually good for consumers. If many suppliers offer a similar product, then prices will usually be lower than if one supplier controls the market. This is because a very powerful supplier can try to restrict other firms from entering the market. This is one reason why Microsoft, which sells over 85 per cent of computer operating systems, was investigated first by the US government and then by the European Commission. It was accused of abusing its near monopoly position by deliberately designing its Windows software to be incompatible with competitors' products, so that fewer of these will sell and was fined 497 million in March 2004, although it is appealing against this decision.

In Britain, no business is allowed to control 85 per cent of the market. **The Competition Act 1998** allows the Office of Fair Trading (OFT) to investigate a company which has a dominant position in the market (usually more than 40 per cent of the total) to check that it is not abusing its position by keeping prices artificially high or dealing with customers unfairly.

The Competition Act also prevents suppliers deliberately limiting production or taking other actions to prevent open competition, such as agreeing between themselves to control prices. In 2003, JJB Sports, Umbro, Manchester United Football Club and seven other firms were fined nearly £19 million by the OFT for their uncompetitive behaviour when they were found guilty of price-fixing replica soccer kits.

Sometimes consumers can choose from a huge selection of products

at ways in which they can make their product or service more attractive or different to customers, preferably in ways that their competitors would find difficult to copy. This is known as gaining **competitive advantage**. How businesses go about this and what they do when competitive pressure intensifies is the subject of this section.

Identifying the competitive market

The competitive market in which a business operates will depend upon the goods or services it provides and the scale of its operations.

Local competitors

A local market refers to a town or a specific area in a large city, e.g. Telford or Wimbledon. A business will have local competitors if it provides a personal service or convenience goods to a local community. This is because customers are unlikely to travel far to visit a doctor, buy a sandwich, have their hair cut or go to the gym. The situation may be different for goods that can be delivered by mail – so some customers prefer to take out a magazine subscription rather than visit the local newsagent's

shop. A local florist may be in competition with national firms that will deliver standard flower arrangements all over the country but retain customers when a personal service is preferred, such as flowers for weddings and funerals.

The same applies to organisations that provide goods or services to industry. If there is a 'personal service' element – such as cleaning, catering or maintenance, then a local supplier is often preferred. Therefore locksmiths, plumbers and caterers are likely to be hired locally and will compete with other suppliers in the same area. Some of these may, however, be national firms with a network of local outlets or rapid response systems – such as security companies or industrial cleaning firms. Local businesses that provide products such as computer supplies or stationery, both of which can be purchased locally or nationally by telephone or over the Internet will have a wider range of competitors.

Regional competitors

A regional market refers to a county or an area within a large county, e.g. Teeside or north west Lancashire. Businesses will compete within a region when they offer goods and services that customers will be prepared to buy over a wider area. Multiplex cinemas and theatres, shopping centres like Bluewater and large car dealers are three examples. Generally, customers will be prepared to travel further if they are making a more expensive purchase or want to make the most of their leisure time. Some businesses use this knowledge to reduce the numbers of branches they need to operate within a region. Richer Sounds knows that customers will be prepared to travel several miles to obtain high value, competitively priced goods, therefore it doesn't need to open a branch in every town in the country.

Business services such as security, industrial cleaning or specialist equipment hire (e.g. scaffolding) will compete on a regional basis. These firms will be prepared to travel to customers within a specific area but may not find it cost effective to offer their services on a national basis.

National competitors

Many large businesses operate on a national basis and sell goods in a variety of ways – by telephone, mail order or over the Internet. Therefore Hamleys, the London toy shop, can now compete with local toy shops as well as large national suppliers like Toys R Us. In many industries, supplying to customers across the country enables the business to buy in bulk and sell goods more cheaply which, in turn, makes them more competitive. This is why you will find the same well-known high street chain stores, such as Boots and Next, in virtually every town in Britain.

Most organisations which offer a specialist service or supply specific goods to industry compete on a national basis – from marketing or graphic design agencies to construction companies. This is because they need to operate in a larger market to survive. In most cases there wouldn't be sufficient work for them if they operated over a smaller area.

European competitors

One of the fundamental reasons for the formation of the EU was to enable all businesses to compete equally in the European market. Therefore, in many industries, British businesses are competing with European firms, such as in the food, drink and clothing markets. You can buy British cheese, British lager or British clothes – but you can also buy cheese from France or Holland or lager from Germany or Denmark. On the clothes scene, European firms such as Hugo Boss, Calvin Klein, Lacoste and Dolce and Gabbana are household names all over Europe.

International competitors

Oil companies, car producers and pharmaceutical (drug) companies are just three examples of businesses that compete on an international basis. (To read more, look back at multinational companies on page 20.)

Many businesses that sell to industry or governments across the world compete on an international basis – from computer businesses such as IBM to civil engineering companies, such as Ove Arup, which builds sports stadiums and bridges.

The effect of the Internet

The scale of the competitive market is often determined by the type of industry and/or product or service supplied. However, the growth of the Internet has broadened the market for many businesses – and their competitors. Today many traditional local suppliers can supply customers all over the UK and even abroad. In the north of Scotland, one small enterprise making wedding garters uses the Internet to sell all over the world and competes with large department stores!

There is, however, a limit to this type of competitiveness. You may be able to buy a mountain bike at a store around the corner or over the Internet, but which one would you choose? The danger with buying over the Internet – and especially from abroad – is that you can't try the product first, you can't have a 'trial run' and the price may not include all the extra items such as import duties or delivery charges. You may have problems with customs regulations or if the product later develops a fault. This means that most customers still prefer to buy expensive products from a source they know – even if the products have been imported from abroad in the first place!

Business terms

Monopoly When one large supplier dominates a market, e.g. Microsoft. The danger is that they can use their power to stop new businesses from competing.

Oligopoly A specialist term for when a few large suppliers dominate a market, e.g. oil companies or the traditional high street banks. This may mean they can work together in their own interests, rather than those of their customers.

Cartel When several suppliers join together to fix prices. This is illegal in the UK.

Competitive advantage The advantage gained by offering superior products or services than competitors.

1 Identify which of the following firms, products or services are:
- Examples of direct competition.
- Examples of indirect competition.
- Not in competition.
  - **a** Macleans and Ultrabrite toothpaste.
  - **b** Adidas and Nike.
  - **c** Multiplex cinema and bowling alley.
  - **d** Capital radio and ITV.
  - **e** FreeView and BSkyB.
  - **f** Garden centre and clothes store.
  - **g** Microsoft X-box and Sony PS2.
  - **h** Club 18–30 holidays and P&O cruises.
  - **i** Sophie Ellis Bextor and Victoria Beckham.
  - **j** Eurostar and easyJet.

2 a As a group, identify whether each of the following businesses would be most likely to have mainly local, regional, national, European or international competitors. In each case, give a reason for your choice.
  - **i** A slimming club.
  - **ii** A designer shoe business, e.g. Jimmy Choo.
  - **iii** A large shopping centre, e.g. Bluewater.
  - **iv** A company that specialises in demolition work.
  - **v** A mobile phone handset manufacturer, e.g. Nokia.
  - **vi** A multiplex cinema.
  - **vii** A major film maker/distributor, e.g. Universal.

  b Theme parks may compete at almost any level. You may, for example, be prepared to travel to Florida or Paris to visit Disneyland, but if you live near to Alton Towers, you would be unlikely to drive to Blackpool Pleasure Beach!
  - **i** As a group, try to think of **one** theme park (small or large) which you would class only as a local attraction. Then move upwards to select a regional, national, European and international example.
  - **ii** Now decide the factors that differentiate the parks you have chosen which determine the size of their competitive market.

3 Your college is in competition with several other organisations – not just for students on full-time courses but also for those who attend in their spare time. As a group, identify **two** direct competitors and **two** indirect competitors. Then decide whether your college competes for other students locally or on a wider basis – and whether this is the same for all the different types of courses it offers. Ask your tutor for help if you get stuck!

4 In February 2003, Argos and Littlewoods were fined £22 million for illegally fixing the prices of many popular games and toys. Hasbro, the toymaker which was also involved in the secret discussions, was let off a possible £15 million fine for disclosing information on the case. Argos and Littlewoods are still appealing the decision. You can find out more, and see what cases the OFT is investigating now on their website – a link is available at www.heinemann.co.uk/hotlinks (express code 1386P).

Knowing the market place

Understanding the market place is crucial for all businesses, because it means knowing who the customers are, what they want, who the competitors are and what they are doing. If your college offers both further education and higher education courses, you will find that whereas it competes locally for 16–19 year old students, the situation would be different for full-time degree level courses. This is because the college would have to compete against universities all over the country, for a different type of student who may have particular needs, such as to gain a recognised degree and to live away from home. Quite simply, it

◯ Talking point

View 1: *The spread of high street chains has killed many small shops that just can't compete on price. This is boring and gives little choice for customers. It was better when town centres had lots of local, individual shops selling different items.*

View 2: *No matter where you go, you can find the same national outlets like Boots, Next, JJB Sports, HMV etc. This is great because you can always find the goods you need at the best prices – no matter where you are.*

With which viewpoint do you agree – and why?

would be in a different market and so would have to act and respond differently.

All businesses need to identify the market they are in, not just in general terms, but for the different products or services they offer. As you have seen, some businesses operate in more than one market. Sony, for example, operates in a different market with its Playstation than its digital cameras. It is appealing to a different group of customers with different needs.

The importance of market share

Even a simple product like your mobile phone can relate to more than one market. For example, there is your handset, where you bought it and which network you use. Statistically, you are more likely to have a Nokia handset, which you bought from Carphone Warehouse and use a Vodafone network! Why? Because these three businesses have the largest **market share** in each case. If you have studied Unit 1, you will already know that this relates to that business's share of all the product sales in a particular market. In other words, these companies are the **market leaders**.

Using a mobile phone involves several markets – no matter where you are!

Global handset market – worth $42 billion a year – Handsets (June 2003)

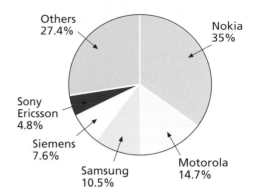
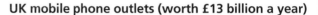

UK mobile phone outlets (worth £13 billion a year)

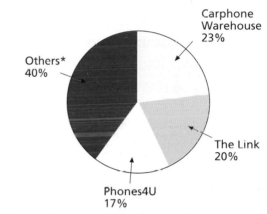

*Includes Asda, Tesco and other outlets

Mobile phone networks (No. of customers in UK Dec 2003 = 54.5 million)

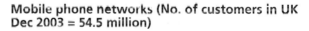
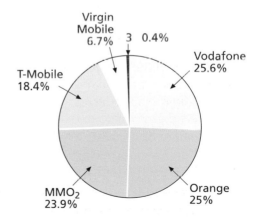

(Note: Virgin Mobile is a 'virtual' operator and uses T-mobile's network)

Figure 2.14 *Mobile phone markets 2003: the market leaders*
(Source: company websites)

Business matters

Businesses will always try to improve their market share, because losing ground can have disastrous consequences. In 2003, Golden Wonder, the crisp manufacturer, had to lay off 375 workers because sales had fallen. Golden Wonder has 14 per cent of the crisp market but has lost market share to Walkers, which has more than 53 per cent market share. Largely thanks to Gary Lineker, this seems to be increasing every year.

In the mobile market, Phones4U has launched an aggressive campaign to topple Carphone Warehouse. It has pledged to match the price of any handset bought from another retailer or pay the difference plus 20 per cent. This campaign is costing the firm over £20 million but their MD, Anthony Catterson, sees this as crucial to its survival. Phones4U wants to boost its market share to 20 per cent by 2004 and become the market leader. The Chief Executive of Carphone Warehouse, Charles Dunstone, argues that mobiles are about more than just price – customers want the whole deal, which is what his company can offer best. You can find out who wins by checking out their websites – links are available at www.heinemann.co.uk/hotlinks (express code 1386P).

Degree of competition

Competition is more intense in some markets than others. Let's take two extreme examples to find out why.

Jack and Alistair are friends. Ten years ago they both went to College. Jack studied IT and computer graphics; Alistair went on a catering course. Jack is now Technical Director in a special effects computer graphics firm. Alistair runs his own sandwich shop in the town centre. One of them works in a very competitive market, the other does not. Can you work out which is which – and why there is a difference?

Alistair is the one who works in a highly competitive market. Many outlets in the town sell sandwiches – Boots, Marks and Spencer, all the supermarkets, various bakery shops and specialist shops like Pret a Manger. There are also lots of lunchtime eating places in the area – pubs, wine bars, pizza places and burger bars. These provide alternatives – often called **substitutes** – for Alistair's customers. New small shops are opening all the time – and some close just as rapidly. Alistair tries to make his sandwiches special, but this just adds to the price. Large stores often sell their sandwiches more cheaply.

Although Jack works hard, his company has less pressure from competitors. All the technical staff have highly specialist skills and the hardware and software they use is very expensive to buy. This means it is more difficult for new firms to enter the market. There is increasing demand for their services from film companies, television companies and advertisers – yet very few know enough to argue with the quotes or costs they are given for a

Very competitive	Less competitive
Large number of suppliers	Few suppliers
Little difference between products on offer	Existing suppliers are well established, have sound reputations or known brands
Buyers have good information and can pick and choose easily	Buyers know little and find comparisons difficult
Suppliers willing and able to offer discounts or reduce prices to gain advantage	Suppliers have technical expertise or specialism and can dictate price more
Easy for new suppliers to enter the market	Difficult for new, unknown firms to enter the market
Many alternative or substitute products available	Few, if any, product alternatives for buyers

Figure 2.15 *Factors that influence the degree of competition*

When the big boys win

It is often difficult for small businesses to compete with large ones for two reasons. Firstly it may be hard to match them on price, because their costs will be higher per unit of production. Large businesses often benefit from **economies of scale**. This means that by producing goods on a large scale it actually costs less to make each one.

This occurs because the large producer can buy raw materials in bulk, can afford expensive or specialist equipment to mass produce goods very quickly – and can even take advantage of lower resource and labour costs in other countries. This was why James Dyson moved production of his vacuum cleaners and washing machines to

Malaysia – and saw an immediate increase in his profits. All these options are impossible for a small business with much more limited financial resources and fewer overall sales.

Small businesses can also find it difficult to challenge powerful organisations with known brands, loyal customers and a well-established distribution network. If the type of equipment they need is very expensive or they need to pay for specialised skills, this can make the problem even worse. All these factors are known as **barriers to entry**. If they are high for an industry, existing firms will be more protected from competition than if they are low.

---

job. They just know what they want to achieve to impress the viewers – and how much they can afford to spend. Often, using computer graphics is the only way to achieve an effect – or is cheaper than the alternative, which may involve casting hundreds of extra actors (e.g. to replace the digital Orcs in Lord of the Rings!) Although Jack's company has to compete with one or two other specialist firms, there is enough business for all of them.

The table in Figure 2.15 summarises the factors which influence the degree of competition experienced by businesses.

Past market history and likely future developments

All markets are different. Some markets are relatively stable whilst others are changing rapidly. Some are growing and others are declining. In other cases, unexpected customer trends can suddenly make a difference – such as the fad for the Atkins diet, which emphasised low carbohydrates as the way to lose weight. Whilst this caused Unilever problems when their Slimfast range stopped selling and gave the British Potato Council a headache – it boosted the fortunes of the British Egg Council!

Businesses try to predict likely future developments when they can, and one way to do this is to look at past market history on the basis that usually – but not always – it will give a good indication of what might happen next.

Stability versus dynamism

- **Stability** assumes that the product, the needs of buyers and the level of competition will stay roughly the same over time. Examples of relatively stable markets include biscuits, garden plants and funeral services. In all these cases, what you buy today – and how you buy them – hasn't changed very much since your grandparents were young.
- **Dynamic markets** are constantly changing. This may be because the product is a 'fad' and demand is likely to be short-lived or because new competitors are entering the market with product variations. The market for pop music is an obvious example – which is why some of the singers and bands you hear about today are gone tomorrow! Other relevant factors are new technology – which results in constant product changes or new innovations, threats from overseas competitors or new laws or regulations that affect what can be provided and how.

Growth versus decline

All markets and all products have a life cycle. This means that there is a starting point and, at some stage, an end point. In some markets, such as bread, the life cycle may be hundreds of years – but in most cases it is much shorter than this. In the case of a pop record it may be a matter of weeks.

The main point for the business is to locate the life cycle position of each of its products or services. This helps them to decide what action to take.

Successful businesses maximise sales during the growth phase by **differentiating** their product in some way. This means making it different from those offered by competitors, preferably so it is unique. IAMS pet food launched into a stable market promoting 'healthy choices' for cats and dogs – and a wide range of products for different ages and weights. It was an immediate success as it linked the need for customers to buy food for their pet with a modern desire for health, fitness and low weight. This has triggered other pet food firms to copy them, but IAMS has retained the advantage by being 'first to market'.

At the saturation or decline stage, businesses may concentrate on new developments to renew interest in the product. When sales of traditional mobile phone handsets declined – basically because everyone who wanted one already had one – the industry concentrated on developing WAP phones and promoting MMS messaging to stimulate demand again. In other cases, businesses may concentrate on 'retro' appeal or new marketing campaigns – or selling in emerging markets where the product will still be a novelty.

If the decline cannot be halted, because a product is likely to become obsolete, most businesses will leave the market.

Forecasting the future

It is always difficult for businesses to forecast exactly what will happen next but specific trends they note include:

- **The arrival of new competitors.** This signals that the market is growing, that there are opportunities for other businesses to make a profit and that barriers to entry are relatively

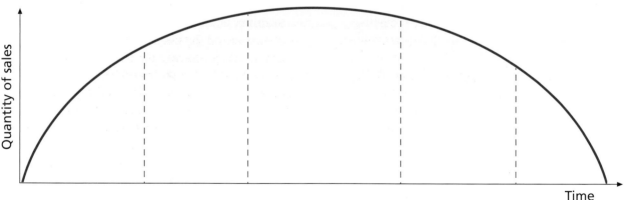

Development stage	Growth stage	Maturity	Saturation	Decline
Few buyers	Increased sales	Sales at maximum	Sales falling	Sales fall
Product at 'trial' stage	Product accepted	Buyers can 'pick and choose'	Buyers satisfied	Few buyers
Profits low	Profit rising	Profits have levelled	Reduced profits	Profits very low
Few competitors	More competition	Maximum competition	Difficult to maintain market share	Some competitors leave market
Actions	**Actions**	**Actions**	**Actions**	**Actions**
Enter market	Fight for market share	Build on strengths, reduce prices	Minimise costs, Increase efficiency	Relaunch product
	Differentiate product in some way		Improve or adapt product	End production and leave market
			Launch in new markets (e.g. overseas)	

Figure 2.16 *Product life cycle*

low. In some cases, new competitors may offer a slightly different product, a better service or similar products at a reduced price – or copy what a successful company has done, like IAMS.

- **The arrival of peripheral competition**. This is often overlooked by businesses because, initially, the competition is not thought to be important. Often it is a small firm which has identified the needs of a niche market, unfulfilled by larger organisations. The danger is that when the market changes, the peripheral competitor becomes a huge threat. When easyJet first entered the airline market, British Airways never saw it as a direct threat because BA was confident of its superior service and strong customer base. But the market changed and European travellers demonstrated that they were prepared to sacrifice all the 'extras' for a cheap, no frills service. BA then realised that it had misjudged the threat. It then had to take action to lower its prices to compete. In 2004, easyJet hopes to overtake BA on passenger numbers – a far cry from its more modest beginnings.

- **Implications of technological development**. Technology is changing the way we live and work. It influences the products we buy and the way we use them. No business can ignore this – although powerful firms may try to halt progress if it threatens them. An example was the reaction of the music industry to falling CD sales. It tried to prevent the free downloading of music over the Internet – first by taking Napster to court and then by prosecuting several US citizens – including one twelve year old girl. Despite this, millions of people continue to fileshare and to burn CDs every day with music downloads! The music industry has now had to accept the fact that the main way ahead is likely to be through paid-for download services, such as Apple's

Business matters

Deregulation occurs when a previous regulation is abandoned – often allowing more competition in a market. This happened in 2003 when the market for directory services was opened up by Oftel, the former telecoms regulator. (The current regulator is called Ofcom.) Oftel hoped that this would lead to cut prices and improved services. Until then, BT had a monopoly on providing a directory enquiry service.

Advertising gave 118 a valuable headstart in the directory enquiry market

As a result, about 16 new companies entered the market. One spent huge sums advertising their new 118 number in advance, on the basis that customers would first dial the one they remembered! Newspapers printed complicated charts comparing their pricing structures – from a straight fee to far more complicated charges for time to find the number and additional, optional connection fees. Customers were simply confused – but many realised that there was no need to pay for any service if they had access to the Internet, where free information is available on several sites.

Within a few weeks, three firms had left the market and several others were making a loss. Why? Because customers were fed up with poor service and reported up to 40 per cent wrong numbers by some providers. Many went back to BT as the firm they knew and trusted. Oftel was accused of overestimating the size of the market. There were simply too many competing firms for them all to survive. Experts predict that by the end of 2004 only a few firms will remain, and these will be the ones that offer customers accurate information quickly and cheaply.

iTunes download shop and the revamped (legal) Napster, and cooperate with these services, rather than compete with them.

- **Trends towards market concentration/ consolidation**. A new or emerging market often tempts new firms to enter, because they spot the opportunity to make a profit. This is why many firms have copied Apple, such as Coke and Sony, and others plan to start music download services. These include a Cable & Wireless/Tesco joint deal. Over time, as the market reaches saturation point, those businesses that cannot lower their prices or do not improve the product will fall by the wayside. The market then becomes more 'concentrated' because there are fewer players.

Business terms

Market share The percentage share of one market held by a particular business.

Market leader The business with the largest market share in a market.

Substitutes Alternative products a customer can select if the original choice is unavailable/too expensive (e.g. apples or bananas, sweets or chocolate.)

Product differentiation Producing a product that is unique, different or better than competitor's products in terms of performance or price.

Deregulation Removing restrictions from a market.

Market concentration Some firms leave the market so there are fewer competitors overall.

Over to you!

1 As a group, decide whether each of the following markets is very competitive or not very competitive. In each case give a reason for your answer. (You may find it useful to look back at the chart on page 128 and also to consider your own experiences as a consumer.)
   a Train services in your area.
   b Personal computers.
   c Watches.
   d Postal services (for private individuals, not businesses).
   e Greetings cards.
   f Plumbers.

2 Identify which of the following markets are dynamic and which are relatively stable. In each case support your decision with a reason.
   a Paper.

   b Hairdryers and related equipment/accessories.
   c Photograph frames.
   d Photograph processing.
   e Recording media.
   f Dog food.

3 At what point of the life cycle would you position each of the following products? For any that are at saturation point or declining, what actions – if any – do you think a producer could take?
   a Plasma screen televisions.
   b Floppy disks.
   c WAP phones.
   d Blackboards.
   e Broadband connections.
   f Home computers.
   g Apple iPod.
   h Washing machines.

Talking point

View 1: *In ten years' time, music CDs will be a thing of the past. No matter what the music industry tries to do, no-one will buy music if they can get it for free.*

View 2: *People will always buy some CDs to build up a collection or give as presents. They will also be prepared to pay for legal downloads, providing these are competitively priced.*

With which viewpoint do you agree – and why?

Evaluating market position

Once a business has established the market it is in, identified its competitors and predicted likely future developments, it now needs to turn the spotlight on itself. It has to look at its own position in the market and how it could be affected by future trends. This will help it to focus on the key areas for improvement or development in the future.

The method used to do this is known as a **SWOT analysis**. SWOT stands for

- **S**trengths
- **W**eaknesses
- **O**pportunities
- **T**hreats

Strengths and weaknesses relate to internal factors; opportunities and threats relate to external factors – such as actions by competitors. The aim is to match the strengths and weaknesses within the business to the external factors that are affecting it.

Product quality

Good quality products are a strength, especially if they are sold at a competitive price. This is because customers obtain extra value from their purchase. Top quality may be a requirement if the business is competing in certain markets, e.g. designer clothes or luxury cars. All businesses have to balance quality with price – and getting this right is important.

The business also has to consider the product quality of its main competitors – and how this is changing. If competitors' products are improving faster, then this is a threat – and the business must decide what to do to challenge it. Equally, if technological advances can be used to improve quality, this is an opportunity.

Consistency

This can be measured in terms of goods rejected during the production process, goods returned by customers or complaints received. Many businesses set a **benchmark** for both quality and consistency. This is a target they aim to meet. For example, your college will have a benchmark, or target, for the percentage of students who are successful on each course each year. Constantly achieving or beating the benchmark demonstrates consistency. A high level of consistency is an obvious strength – a low one is a weakness which must be addressed.

In many industries there are standard benchmarks that businesses can use to compare themselves with their competitors. This helps them to monitor their own performance and identify opportunities and threats in relation to their competitors.

Customer service

Many businesses compete on customer service. If a business gains a reputation for excellent customer service then this gives it an obvious 'edge' over its competitors. It is important to evaluate customer service objectively, by obtaining feedback over time. You can see how Richer Sounds does this on the StudentZone at www.richerstudentzone.co.uk.

The actions of competitors are important, too. If they are offering a better service, or enhancing their range of services, then this is a threat. Equally, if a key competitor has just been criticised in the press for offering a poor service, this provides an opportunity for the business to benefit by attracting new customers.

Image/branding

A major strength is a memorable name or a strong brand which customers associate with positive benefits. This is so important that when the Royal Mail Group changed its name to Consignia it was forced to change it back again when customers said they disliked the new name, regularly forgot it and the press constantly criticised it. The image of the company is also important – which is why most businesses do their utmost to avoid bad publicity.

A brand name can save millions of pounds in advertising. For example, Heinz, the market leader in baked beans, sells more than 500 million cans in the UK every year, despite being more expensive than many rivals and using the same slogan 'Beans Meanz Heinz' for over 30 years. Most shoppers automatically reach for Heinz because they know and trust the brand – and all these sales add substantially to Heinz's profits. Therefore, the brand name alone is very valuable.

It is far harder to compete in a market where one supplier has built up a strong brand through promotions where customers associate the brand with good value. You only have to think about the number of times you see a new computer with the sticker 'Intel inside'. Intel has used this approach to associate its name with leading edge computer chip technology. The aim is that over time, customers will reject products which don't carry the slogan, because they consider them inferior.

Reputation

The reputation of a business and its products takes a long time to establish – but can be lost very quickly if there are serious problems or a scandal. There is absolutely no point spending money on marketing a product if customers are spreading the word that it is a waste of money – or that the business is dreadful to deal with. According to the experts, it costs five times as much to gain a new customer as it does to keep an existing one, and a satisfied customer will recommend a product or

service to at least four other people, whilst an unhappy one will tell at least seven others about the experience. For that reason, getting customers to 'spread the word' is the best and cheapest way to gain a good reputation – and the quickest way to get a bad one.

Unique selling points (USPs)

Unique selling points are the key factors that differentiate one product or service from another. They help to build up a brand by telling the customer exactly what is different about buying this product than any other. The more differences there are, the more likely it is that customers will buy it. For example, Harley Davidson bikes are different to other bikes, to the extent that their USPs have resulted in a cult following. In the catering industry, Jamie Oliver's USP with his restaurant called 15 is the fact that it is staffed by catering trainees. This, together with his own reputation, differentiates his restaurant from all the others in the area.

The distinctiveness of Harley Davidson bikes is a key USP

Business matters

The soft drinks market in the UK is worth £10 billion. In 1998, Proctor and Gamble launched the drink Sunny Delight to gain a share of this market. The name was appropriate, the marketing campaign emphasised the health benefits and sales soared. Then disaster struck. The drink was found to contain only 5 per cent fruit and lots of sugar. Even worse, a young girl in Wales went yellow after she drank too much. Although this was simply a harmless reaction to beta carotene (a constituent of oranges and carrots), sales fell dramatically after her picture appeared in all the newspapers.

Proctor and Gamble relaunched the drink and launched adverts starring bands like S Club 7 to promote its new formula, with 5 per cent fruit and four sugarless varieties. It spent £15 million on advertising to rescue the brand – now changed to Sunny D – and its reputation. Sales have still never recovered to their earlier levels, proving that once a brand is distrusted, it is almost impossible to rescue it.

You will often find USPs featured in advertisements – both nationally and locally. One removal firm, for example, has the slogan on its vans: 'Large enough to cope, small enough to care'. It has therefore focused on these USPs to make itself different from its competitors. USPs can include any aspect of the business that is relevant, for example:

- Product specialities or features.
- The range of products or services.

- Better value at that price than competitors.
- Superior or very friendly service.
- Superior quality.
- Pure/organic ingredients.
- Environmentally friendly policies.
- Talented or well-qualified staff and/or a famous name.
- Availability to areas or regions not covered by other organisations.

To be effective, USPs must be specific and mustn't be something that is average or can't be proved – like 'good service' – which everyone expects anyway.

Competitive pressures

Competitive pressures will be greater if there are several threats which can be identified. These can include:

- Market trends which affect any product.
- A product which is just at the start or near the end of its life cycle.
- A fall in the number of potential buyers or customers.
- An increase in the number of competitors in the same market.
- An increase in the speed at which technological change is affecting the product and/or consumer demand.

- Innovative actions by competitors which could increase their market share.

Competitor resources/strengths

As you can see from Gillette's reaction in the Business matters section below, a strong competitor with many resources can react very sharply to challenges from smaller businesses. A lengthy legal battle took place between Hoover, the original market leader for vacuum cleaner sales in the UK, and Dyson – the inventor of the bag-less cleaner. Hoover was ultimately forced to pay out £4 million for copying Dyson's idea. Originally Dyson had offered to settle the claim out of court for £1 million but Hoover had refused. Dyson was determined to fight for its rights, but had it lost, the cost would have been considerable. It can therefore be a hazardous undertaking to go into business against a well-established firm with a strong financial base.

Not all businesses, of course, resort to legal action. Large businesses, however, can try other tricks like reducing prices until a small competitor goes out of business – and then raising them again. Or they may spend enormous sums of money on a major marketing campaign. It is therefore fairer if competitors are roughly the same size, with the same type of resources. In this case, the strengths that count will include flexibility, innovation and

Business matters

Technological developments don't just affect the computer world. In the shaving industry, a major row broke out between Gillette, the market leader, and its arch-rival Schick, which sells under the Wilkinson Sword brand in the UK. In 1998, Schick launched the Quattro – its response to Gillette's Mach 3. Gillette claimed Schick had copied its design, which cost over £600 million to develop, and started legal action in the US. Some experts argue that Gillette is behaving badly because it is unused to competitive pressure – it has had control of the world's £3.75 billion razor market for so long that it has become used to charging what it likes. Lack of competition has meant prices are high – with Gillette averaging a 38 per cent margin on everything it sells.

Who will win? No one knows – and the battle could go on for years. If Schick loses it will have to pay Gillette millions of dollars earned from sales of the Quattro. If Gillette loses, Schick could win billions of dollars in damages because its commercial reputation has been attacked. Perhaps that could signal a change in the shaving market. Gillette is using its power and resources to try to remove troublesome competitors. Schick only has 15 per cent of the UK market (Bic is next with 6 per cent) – but the situation is different in Asia, Japan and Latin America where Gillette is steadily losing ground. For the first time, its future is uncertain.

speed. This will often favour the smaller business as it can usually respond more quickly when necessary and also benefit consumers, who have a wider choice of rapidly improving products.

Evaluating the market position of a product

Businesses that concentrate on one main product or service, such as an accountant or an estate agent – or a retail store that only offers one type of goods – can carry out a SWOT analysis on their business as a whole to establish their market position.

Businesses that offer several products or services cannot do this, because the market position for each one may be different. ASDA and Tesco, for example, will have different market positions in food and in clothing and Ford has to evaluate the market position of each model of car it makes. Similarly, the market position of the courses offered by your college will be different. Some may be thriving, with many strengths, few weaknesses and no immediate threats from competitors. Others may be declining or having problems. In this case, knowing the market position of the business as a whole would not help to identify which products are strong and which are weak.

To evaluate the market position, the first stage is to carry out a SWOT analysis and compile a list of strengths, weaknesses, opportunities and threats. The next is to evaluate it. This means assessing the importance of these factors in relation to other aspects – such as the type of market, the life cycle of the product, likely future developments and the possible actions of competitors.

Business terms

Unique selling point (USP) A feature which sets a product or business apart from its competitors. For 3 (see Business matters below), this was video calls, which could not be made from other networks, and faster online services.

Benchmark An industry standard of quality and consistency in a particular area.

Business matters

When the government awarded licences to run third generation (3G) mobile phone services, it issued five. One went to each of the established operators (see page 127) and one was for a new entrant, so that competition in the market would be increased. This new company is called 3 – and in March 2003 it was open for business, specialising in 3G services, which allow users to download data quickly, make two-way video calls and browse the Internet from their handsets.

To offer a competitive service from the start, 3 introduced low price tariffs on its basic voice service and discounted video calls for the first three months of a contract plus, in some cases, free handsets. It announced a special package for football fans and developed partnerships with games development companies. It took out agreements with companies such as ITN, Emap, the Ordnance Survey and MyMovies for news, location and movie information. It set itself the target of one million UK customers by the end of 2003.

Then problems hit. 3 had aimed to launch a 'pay as you go' pre-pay service by December 2003 but had to delay this when its Japanese manufacturer could not deliver the new handsets in time because of technical problems. These are important because lightweight 3G phones with a good battery life are in short supply – and holding up progress. 3 had already abandoned its target of one million UK customers and, at the end of December had only 200,000 customers. Missing out pre-pay services at Christmas was disastrous, because 70 per cent of new phones are pre-pay and one third of all phones are sold between October and December each year. Therefore 3 lost out on its temporary advantage over its more established competitors.

Over to you!

1 Identify the main USP of each of the following businesses or products

  a Pringles.

  b eBay.

  c IKEA.

  d Argos.

  e Lego.

2 a A SWOT analysis for 3, the new mobile phone company described on the previous page, is given below. Check that you understand the reason for each entry. Then copy out the analysis and complete the 'Opportunities' and 'Threats' sections from your reading of this book and/or from information you have obtained on the Internet – links are available at www.heinemann.co.uk/hotlinks (express code 1386P). You can also get information from 3G promotions at major mobile phone stores, e.g. Carphone Warehouse or The Link.

Internal factors	
Strengths	**Weaknesses**
Specialises in 3G services	Newcomer to mobile phone market
First to offer video calls	Initial problems signing up people
Discount tariffs	Name/reputation not widely known
Football tie-in for fans	Still developing promotional services
Links to major partners in news and media for updated content	Pre-pay handsets not available for Christmas market 2003

External factors	
Opportunities	**Threats**

b In December 2003 the market share of 3 was negligible, but 3 obviously does not see this as its long term market position. As a group, from your research, discuss what you think is 3's market position at the moment, bearing in mind the type of market, the life cycle of 3's product, the needs and expectations of customers, likely future developments and the probable actions of 3's competitors.

3 As you saw on page 128, the visual effects market is fast-moving in terms of technology but less intensely competitive than the mobile phone market. In Britain, the main players are Framestore CFC, Jim Henson's Creature Shop, The Moving Picture Company and, to a lesser extent, Red Vision.

  a Divide into four groups and access **one** of the following websites each: Framestore CFC, The Moving Picture Company, Jim Henson's Creature Shop and Red Vision. Links for these sites are available at www.heinemann.co.uk/hotlinks (express code 1386P). If you look at Framestore or The Moving Picture Company, try to do this on broadband so that you can download and view some of the video clips. For the company you are investigating, identify two USPs.

  b To what degree do you think quality, consistency and reputation will be important in this market – and why?

  c Suggest **four** important resources for a company in this industry. (Refer to page 47 if you are unsure what is meant by the term 'resources'.).

  d Suggest **two** ways in which a company in this market could try to improve its market position.

💬 Talking point

View 1: The reputation of businesses isn't of much interest to consumers, providing they get good service themselves. Very few people read the papers anyway.

View 2: Reputation is very important and critical articles in the press can destroy a business very quickly, especially in a very competitive industry where customers have a lot of choice.

With which viewpoint do you agree – and why?

Action planning

The purpose of evaluating the market position is to identify what action to take next. Even if a business launches a very successful product, it is not enough to sit back and sip champagne! The business world – and consumer tastes – changes far too rapidly for that.

There are three main options. A business may decide to concentrate on one of these, or even attempt all three. It must be careful, however, not to try too much too quickly.

Consolidate and strengthen the market position

This is usually done when demand for a product is still growing. The main aim is to maintain or, better still, increase market share. This can be done in one of four ways:

- Build the reputation of the brand through marketing and promotions and favourable press reports.
- Promote the 'added value' for customers through product or price differentiation, such as Tesco's Finest and Value ranges.
- Extend the product line to include different varieties to reach a broader market. Crisp firms do this when they add new flavours and Coca-Cola did this when it introduced Cherry Coke and Diet Coke. Today Diet Coke is the best selling brand in the UK. In other words the business tries to offer enough alternatives that it can appeal to as many potential customers as possible.
- Introduce product variations, e.g. computers with different processing speeds/peripherals, televisions in different sizes and with plasma or flat screens.
- Respond rapidly and positively to customer expectations and feedback.

Address key competitive threats

In this case, the main aim is to retain market share despite new developments by competitors. The best response will depend upon the type of threat and the actions of competitors but can include the following:

- Offer discounts, incentives or start special promotions to attract customers away from competitors.
- Copy a good idea brought out by a competitor, but try to differentiate the product slightly.
- Continually improve the product to stay 'one jump ahead'.
- Increase the product benefits so that these are greater than those offered by competitors.
- Reduce the price to undercut competitors' products.
- Regularly review the whole product range and adapt where necessary to stay ahead of the competition and give customers what they want.
- Buy in additional expertise, if possible from successful competitor.

Identifying opportunities for expansion

Businesses may choose to expand if they have a successful product, especially if growth is falling in one particular market. In this case, they may want to increase the type of products or services they offer or explore other markets. Their options are listed below.

- Offer related products and services to provide a better or more complete customer experience, e.g. superstores selling food, clothing, mobiles, operating a restaurant, providing home shopping etc.
- Sell existing products in new markets, e.g. overseas.
- Adapt products for new markets, e.g. software companies developing versions for private consumers as well as businesses.
- Identify new product markets where customer demand is rising and offer quality goods at competitive prices. Reckitt, the household products company owes much of its success to this strategy. For example, it chose to concentrate on dishwasher detergent (a growth market) rather than washing machine detergent.
- Diversify by expanding into other product areas. In response to sluggish PC sales in 2003, Dell diversified by also selling printers, data storage systems and cash registers.

Over to you!

1 Below are some of the actions which well-known businesses have taken to improve their market position. In each case, decide whether the business was mainly:

   a Consolidating and strengthening its market position.

   b Addressing key competitive threats.

   c Expanding.

   Then, as a group, decide how successful the strategy is likely to be and what subsequent actions by competitors might affect it.

   i Levi's decided to sell its owns jeans in the cut-price market eight months after Tesco lost a legal battle to sell Levi's jeans at discount prices.

   ii P&O, struggling on its ferry routes with a downturn in passengers, announced plans to start an additional service between Portsmouth and Caen in 2004.

   iii Kwik Save altered its product ranges to reflect the current buying habits of customers, following customer feedback.

   iv Tesco extended its Finest range to clothes – to appeal to customers prepared to pay a bit more.

   v Sainsbury's started creating a new in-house fashion brand to rival Tesco's Cherokee and ASDA's George ranges and hired a new chief executive – from Marks & Spencer.

   vi *The Independent* newspaper was launched in tabloid (compact) format as well as broadsheet for customers who want to read easily when they are travelling.

   vii *The Times* copied *The Independent* a week later but only in the London area.

   viii Argos extended its product range by moving into furniture.

   ix DFS Furniture hired celebrity designer Linda Barker to promote its furniture to try to win more customers.

   x On Demand Distribution (OD2) announced it had sold three million songs since March 2002 and had signed deals with five major record companies.

2 Boots appointed a new chief executive, Richard Baker, in 2003, to try to improve the company. Feedback had shown that customers were unhappy with the opening hours, were annoyed when products were often out of stock disliked the signage in the stores which they often couldn't understand, thought the promotions were confusing and said they didn't like queuing. Boots has lost market share in pharmacy sales to supermarkets and Superdrug, and its market share in beauty and toiletries was reported as 'flat'. Experts say Richard Baker should do a good job as he knows the world of competitive retail well.

   a Recommend **four** ways in which Richard Baker could make Boots more competitive, bearing in mind his customers' expectations.

   b Suggest **two** ways in which Boots could respond to its key competitors for pharmacy products

   Compare your ideas with suggestions from other members of your class.

3 Debenhams wants to target more high spenders in the 15–25 year age group, especially girls, initially through revitalising its own fashion labels, such as Red Herring and Designers. It wants to improve its market position in relation to its major competitors.

   a As a group, suggest **three** competitors to Debenhams for this market.

   b Then suggest **two** actions that Debenhams could take to appeal more to this market.

Talking point

View 1: *Intense competition is a good thing. It keeps businesses on their toes, forces them to update their products and keep their prices low.*

View 2: *Intense competition distracts businesses. They are too busy copying each other to concentrate on the customer and spend far too much on advertising, just to try to beat each other.*

With which viewpoint do you agree – and why?

Now that you have completed this section you should understand how customer expectations affect businesses and what businesses can do to take account of these. Test your skills now by doing the following activities.

Check your understanding of this section by answering the following questions. Check all your answers with your tutor before moving on.

1 **a** What is meant by the term 'direct competition'?

   b The National Lottery has to compete against other forms of gambling, such as the football pools, bingo and horseracing. Is this an example of direct or indirect competition? Give a reason for your answer.

   c Identify **two** well-known businesses that operate in a competitive market:

   i   At national level.

   ii At global level.

   d Briefly explain how the Internet has extended the competitive market for many small businesses.

   e What is meant by the term 'market leader'?

   f State **three** factors which contribute to the intensity of competition in a market.

   g What is meant by the saturation point of a product's life cycle?

   h Explain why market consolidation is likely to occur when demand for a product starts to fall.

   i What do the letters 'SWOT' stand for in SWOT analysis?

   j Explain what is meant by the letters USP and why it is important.

   k Suggest **two** ways in which a business can address key competitive threats.

2 In May 2001, BMW relaunched the 1960s icon, the Mini. Was this a success and what is the market position of the new Mini now? This task will help you to find out.

   a In the table on the next page there are 16 facts about the new Mini and the 'supermini' market. Working in small groups, use these facts to compile a SWOT analysis on the car. Remember that strengths and weaknesses refer to the car itself (think about factors like product quality, consistency, customer service, image/branding, reputation and USPs) and opportunities and threats refer to the market or external factors.

   b Find out more about the Mini today and its competitors by accessing any of the following company websites: Mini, Toyota, Honda, Ford and Top Gear (where you can compare prices). Links are available at www.heinemann.co.uk/hotlinks (express code 1386P). Try to extend your SWOT analysis with **two** new facts of your own in any category. Then compare your ideas with other groups in your class.

   c In the United States, the Mini has been a huge success. It is virtually the only sporty compact car on the market. Traditionally, Americans have always been associated with buying large, gas-guzzling cars, but the Mini has captured their imagination. Now BMW is looking at capitalising on this by launching a convertible and a pick-up version in the future.

   i   Can you suggest **two** reasons why the Mini was such a hit in the US?

   ii Why do you think BMW now want to launch new versions?

   iii How successful do you think *each* of these versions would be in Britain – and why?

   iv If you were competing against the Mini, would its success in the States inspire or depress you? Give a reason for your answer.

   d To what extent do you think the Mini is under competitive pressure? Give a reason for your answer.

   e From the work you have carried out, evaluate the market position of the Mini today:

   i   In the UK market.

   ii In the US market.

Facts about the new Mini, the supermini and related car markets

- Superminis were one of the big car success stories of 2002 and 2003. In twelve months, superminis improved their UK market share by 7.3% to 34.1%*.
- Another big success story were diesel cars.
- In 2002, 144,000 Minis were sold worldwide. Estimated sales for 2003 were 165,000.
- In January 2003, the Mini won the award for best new car in North America at the Detroit motor show.
- The Mini Cooper was voted number one small car by American drivers and replaced the VW Beetle as the most appealing compact car.
- In the first twelve months after its launch, 24,000 British-made Minis were sold in North America
- Demand for the Mini is also high in Japan, Germany and Italy.
- The new Mini featured in the Austin Powers films.
- BMW have launched a diesel model of the Mini.
- The average mini driver is under 40 and loves the Mini's cult status.
- The Mini is available in four models, with a wide range of standard fittings and many optional 'extras'.
- Test drivers were ecstatic about its looks and performance – particularly the Mini Cooper and Cooper S – and said it was great fun to drive.
- Critics disliked the lack of space for backseat passengers, lack of luggage space and weren't too keen on the instrument layout.
- The supermini market is highly competitive – virtually all large manufacturers include at least one model in their range – often more.
- In 2001, the top five selling superminis were the Ford Fiesta, Peugeot 204, Vauxhall Corsa, Renault Clio and Fiat Punto.
- The Toyota Yaris was European car of the year and a 'best buy' in the 2003 *Which?* report – as was the Honda Jazz. In this report, Honda, Toyota and Ford all came ahead of BMW (who make the mini) for product reliability.
- Top Gear adored the new Mini, particularly its performance, thought the new diesel was the 'coolest small car around' but disliked the lack of space in the back. In its owner's survey, the Mini came out at number 4 – owners said it was fun to drive, cheap to run, but quality was variable, with gearbox and electrical problems.

* Source: Society of Motor Manufacturers and Traders (SMMT)

Do this by studying your SWOT analysis, checking on the success of the Mini's closest competitors and finding out about new developments on the Mini. You can also get updates from news sites like the BBC website, or by using a good search engine like Google – links are available at www.heinemann.co.uk/hotlinks (express code 1386P). Remember that because this is an evaluation, you should say whether you think the market position is strong or weak and whether the Mini is gaining or losing market share – and give facts to support your opinion.

f Suggest **one** future development BMW could consider under each of the following headings:

   i To consolidate the market position of the Mini still further.

   ii To respond to future competitive threats.

   iii To expand in the future.

This section covers

Stakeholders and their expectations

Customers and suppliers as stakeholders

Financial stakeholders

Staff, trade unions and staff associations

Sponsors as stakeholders

Local communities and environmental concerns

Pressure groups and ethical concerns

Responding to stakeholder concerns

Who, or what, are stakeholders?

A **stakeholder** is any person or organisation that has an interest in a business. You are a stakeholder in several businesses. As a student, you are a stakeholder in your college. If you work part-time, you are a stakeholder in your employer's business. You are also a stakeholder, as a customer, in all the shops you buy from and anywhere you go in your leisure time – from visits to the cinema to supporting your local football team. Why are you a stakeholder? Because many of the actions these businesses take will affect you in some way – from cancelling a class at College to a business you use regularly moving to another part of town or closing down altogether.

Football clubs have many different types of stakeholders

Stakeholder groups and their expectations

All stakeholders have expectations, although what they expect is often different. At College you expect to be taught in class, to cover the scheme for your course, to be given advice and help when you need it. In a shop, you expect to be given courteous service, to be sold quality goods at a reasonable price, to be able to take them back if they are faulty. If you are a football supporter, you no doubt expect your team to do well and to score a few goals now and then!

So expectations vary depending upon:

* The type of stakeholder.
* The relationship between the stakeholder and the business.
* The way the stakeholder perceives the business and its responsibilities.

Key stakeholders

These are important groups of stakeholders that the business dare not ignore. These, too, will not be the same for all businesses. In a college, the students are a **key stakeholder** group because if a large number of students were unhappy, or left, then this would damage the reputation of the college in the future. This is why the views of students are often sought on issues that affect them and why you are asked to complete questionnaires or give your opinions to a student panel or committee.

Most businesses consider their customers to be a key stakeholder group. However, the size of organisation can affect this. If you and your fellow students buy stationery from a local store on a regular basis and then find somewhere cheaper, the local store will suffer. So you are a key stakeholder here. If, though, you suddenly stopped buying Coca-Cola and bought Pepsi instead, or went to Pizza Hut instead of McDonalds, it is unlikely such a large business would notice unless lots of people did the same thing. Therefore your personal ability to influence the actions of these organisations is much less.

Bear in mind that the actual names used for stakeholders can vary – for example, 'supporters' are key stakeholders in football clubs, 'viewers' are stakeholders in television productions and 'pupils' are stakeholders in their school.

Business terms

Stakeholder A person or group with a particular interest in a business.

Key stakeholder An important stakeholder or a stakeholder group that can seriously affect the business by its collective actions.

Over to you!

1 A list of the stakeholders you will learn about in this section is given in Figure 2.17, together with a brief explanation of each one. As a group, suggest **one** expectation of each. Keep your answers safely and check that you are right as you progress through this section.

2 Suggest **three** types of stakeholders involved with each of the following types of organisations. Bear in mind some of the names used may be different from those in Figure 2.17.
   a A large charity.
   b A hospital.
   c An airline.
   d Your local library.
   e A famous band, such as Coldplay.

3 **Three** members of your group dislike the fact that you have had a timetable change at college. Five members prefer it and the rest are not bothered. How powerful are you as a stakeholder group to argue for the change to be reversed? What difference, if any, do you think there might be if all the members of the group agreed?

Groups	Relationship with business
Customers	Buy the product or service
Suppliers	Rely on the business for orders
Employees	Rely on the business for employment
Owner(s)	Have invested money in the business
Bankers	Have lent money to the business
Trade unions	Represent the employees on key issues and promote fair play and employee rights
Employer associations	Represent the employer and promote employer rights on key issues
Sponsors	Pay money to associate the name of their product or business with an event or person
Local and national communities	Directly affected by the actions and operations of the business in a particular area
Pressure groups	Represent specific interest groups e.g. on the environment (Greenpeace) or human rights (Amnesty International)
Tax collection authorities	Government bodies that collect taxes owed by law

Figure 2.17 *Stakeholder groups*

Customers as stakeholders

If you have already studied section 2.1, you will already know a lot about consumers and their expectations when they are making a purchase. Are these expectations any different when customers are considered as stakeholders?

In many ways, the answer is 'yes'. This is because stakeholders are existing customers. This group therefore includes loyal customers who regularly deal with a business and would be very affected by any changes.

In addition, the range of stakeholder customers in a business can include different groups of people. For example:

- You are a stakeholder, as a customer, in your college – but so are your parents and several business organisations who send their employees on courses.
- You are a stakeholder if you buy a magazine, but, in a different way, so are all the advertisers who buy advertising space.
- You are a stakeholder if you are a patient in your local hospital – but so is your GP who probably arranged the bed or appointment for you in the first place.

The expectations of each of these groups of customers will vary, because they each have a slightly different relationship with the business. Your parents, for example, may be more concerned about overall examination results, student facilities and – dare we say it – discipline at the College than you are. If you think back to your first day, you were probably more worried about your timetable and who else would be in your class!

Similarly, if you buy a magazine you want it to be interesting to read and worth the money. The advertiser is concerned about circulation figures, which say how many readers there are, and positive responses to the advert. As an in-patient in hospital you will be concerned about your treatment but also about the food, the length of your stay, whether there will be other people to talk to. Your GP is only concerned with the first of these.

Therefore, all customer stakeholders are apt to look at the business from a personal point of view. This includes private customers and 'trade' customers, such as builders who buy supplies from a builder's merchant or your college, when it buys stationery, furniture or computers.

In general, customer expectations cover:

- Opening hours and availability of goods.
- Good quality, value for money and – for trade customers – discounts on large orders.
- The range of goods or services, additional facilities and services (such as technical advice and free delivery).
- The attitude of staff and personal service.
- The efficiency and reputation of the organisation including speed of response and staff expertise.
- The overall success or performance of the business.

Customers may also be concerned about the ethics of the business – such as how it treats its staff and suppliers, whether its executives are overpaid, where it sources its supplies or complies with its environmental responsibilities. You will learn more about business ethics and stakeholders on page 159.

Suppliers as stakeholders

All businesses need supplies – raw materials, general consumables or stock for resale. As trade customers they buy these from other business organisations, as you learned in Section 2.1. In this case all these suppliers are also stakeholders because they depend upon their business customers for their livelihood. To be successful, each supplier needs to keep receiving orders.

The danger for a supplier is that it relies too heavily on a few business customers. In this case, if it loses orders, it may have serious difficulties. Another problem is when a small supplier has to meet the demands of a powerful buyer, who can dictate terms on price, quantity and quality because there are so many other suppliers to choose from. Therefore, whether a supplier is a key stakeholder or not will depend upon the

Weak	Strong
Few buyers for product or service Many suppliers of product or service Market highly competitive Buyer places large orders on which supplier depends	Many buyers want product or service Few alternative suppliers Few/no substitute products Buyer only places small orders that won't be missed

Figure 2.18 *The power of suppliers*

relative size of both organisations and the market in which they operate.

Supermarkets are an obvious example of a powerful buyer – and have been criticised frequently for making life difficult for small suppliers such as farmers and growers. Safeway was criticised for over reliance on **supplier funding** – where it charges suppliers for giving products prominence on its shelves and for running discount promotions to promote a product line. Suppliers don't dare complain about price cuts because they are too scared of losing their contract. Another worry for small suppliers is late payments, which can severely affect their **cash flow** (see Unit 3, page 221.)

Some businesses dislike an imbalanced relationship so much that they may change their business activities to avoid this. Some suppliers will extend their activities to sell direct to the customer, such as farmers who prefer to sell in farmers' or local markets than sell to wholesalers or supermarkets. Equally, some business buyers prefer to produce their own goods than depend upon an external supplier – such as cider producers who operate their own apple orchards.

Business matters

How often do you eat apples and, more importantly for Britain, where do they come from? Why? Because British apple growers are warning their industry that their livelihoods are in danger now because 70 per cent of the apples we eat come from abroad. It may seem stupid to import apples from as far as Chile and China when we have bumper harvests at home, but supermarkets aren't prepared for the variation in size, colour and quantities that naturally occur in British orchards. They are prepared to swap flavour for the economies of scale that come with buying huge quantities of the same types, week after week.

Supermarkets defend themselves by arguing that they promote British apples quite aggressively, but according to Friends of the Earth, only 38 per cent of the apples sold in Tesco and ASDA are British and in convenience stores the figure falls to 27 per cent. The trade group British Apples and Pears says that this has resulted in a steady decline in apple growers and orchards in Britain – from 1,500 in 1987 to 500 today. Several groups are campaigning for change, including environmental groups like Sustain and Common Ground.

The supermarkets argue that their main role is to meet customer demand – and customers don't want apples that are too small, too big or the wrong colour. The main worry, however, voiced by the British Independent Fruit Growers Association is that unless farmers can count on new orders, they cannot afford to renew the trees in their orchards which they must do every 10 or 15 years. Some are selling off their land or turning to other kinds of farming. A few are specialising in producing traditional craft ciders or selling rare apples in farmer's markets. Whilst this might help smaller producers, it is no answer for those with larger orchards. So if you want them to continue in Britain, make sure that the next apple you eat is English!

Financial stakeholders

These stakeholders all have a financial interest in the business. They either give money, lend money or are otherwise involved in the financial aspects of a business. The main groups are shown in the chart in Figure 2.19.

As you may realise, very few people or organisations are prepared to put money into an enterprise without wanting something in return! They will study the performance of the firm and the accounts carefully to check that their money is being used wisely and the business is thriving. They will want reassurances that prompt and appropriate action is being taken if it is not.

Owners, shareholders and investors

The founder of the business needs to provide **capital** to start the business. This is needed to buy basic items, such as equipment, furnishings and stock or raw materials. Many small firms are started with the owner's savings, perhaps supplemented by a loan or grant from a financial institution (see below). In a partnership, each of the owners would be expected to contribute financially towards the start-up capital.

If a business registers as a company, then investors in the business receive shares – literally 'a share' in the business. The number of shares owned will depend upon the size of each person's investment. In a private company, there may be only a few shareholders, as shares can only be issued to the owner(s), family members, employees or other people as agreed by the existing shareholders. In a public company, there may be several hundred thousand shareholders because shares are sold on the Stock Exchange to large **institutional investors** and to the general public. Institutional investors are businesses that buy shares in large

companies – such as investment banks, pension companies and insurance companies. Employees may also own shares through a share option scheme. Legally, the shareholders are the owners of the business.

Owners, shareholders and other investors expect to make money out of their investment. They have three main expectations:

- **They want the business to make profits**. The reward for the owners is a share of the profits and the knowledge that the value of the business is increasing.
- **They want a return on their investment** – just like you expect to receive interest if you save your money in a bank or building society account. Investors who lend money to businesses also receive interest, but the return paid to shareholders is called a **dividend** and is usually paid twice a year. The amount of dividend will vary each time, depending upon the company's profits and financial commitments. The directors of a company may decide to pay only a small dividend (or none at all) if profits are low. They may also reduce dividend payments if they want to use more of the profits to expand the business. In this case the interests of the shareholders and the company's directors will conflict.
- **They want their investment to increase in value**. This is because investors can sell their investment to someone else and will want to make a profit on the transaction. This only happens if the business is doing well.

If investors' expectations are not met, they may protest at the firm's Annual General Meeting or just sell their shares. This can reduce the value of everyone's shares, and the business as a whole, and make it vulnerable to a hostile takeover bid (see page 193).

Who they are	What they do
The owner(s)	Invest their own money (capital) to start up the business
The shareholders	Invest money in the business in exchange for shares
Investors	Supply or lend money to a business
Banks	Provide financial services to business including lending money
Financial service providers	Provide finance, give financial advice or help to manage debts

Figure 2.19 *Financial stakeholders*

Banks and financial service providers

All businesses need a bank account into which they can pay money received and use to make payments themselves. Most businesses have more than one account. There will also be an account for reserves they hold, which pays interest; another for any loans they have, and foreign currency accounts if they trade overseas. There are several other differences between the facilities and services a business expects from a bank and those which private individuals want. In addition to bank accounts and banking online, businesses may also want advice on finance, merchant services (so that they can accept credit and debit cards in payment), insurance, credit reports on new customers or suppliers and payroll handling – for paying employees direct into their personal bank accounts.

Even more importantly, most businesses want overdraft and loan facilities.

- **An overdraft** means that the business can spend more than it has in the bank. Overdrafts must always be negotiated, or the charges are very high indeed and the bank can 'freeze' the account at any time.
- **A loan** is money that is borrowed for a specific length of time. The borrower pays interest and bank administration charges. The interest rates may be fixed or variable.

In return the bank will have the following expectations and requirements:

- To approve the firm's business plan at the start of trading and to inspect the firm's accounts at least once a year together with the updated business plan if further funds are required.
- To meet regularly with the business owner and to be notified immediately if the firm is experiencing any problems.
- To receive **service payments** on time. This includes all interest payments and any other administration or handling charges.
- For the business to be well managed financially. This includes:

- Profitable trading – so that selling prices more than cover the costs of making or providing the product.
- Proper credit checks on all new customers or suppliers.
- Realistic credit limits set for each customer, based on the credit check, and for these limits to be kept to.
- Debts owed to the firm to be collected as quickly as possible.
- Spending by the firm to be monitored and kept within budget levels.
- Debts owed by the firm to be paid on time.

Other financial service providers will have similar expectations, although these may differ depending upon their exact involvements. You will learn more about this aspect of business if you study specialist Unit 9.

Banks and other financial service providers have the ability to withdraw their financial help and can even force a business to close down if it is defaulting on its loan repayments. This makes them very powerful stakeholders whose expectations and concerns must be met if the business is to flourish.

Business terms

Supplier funding Making suppliers pay for in-store promotions, discount deals and shelf-space.

Capital The finance, or money, needed to buy business assets.

Cash flow The amount of money flowing into and out of a business. If money coming in is delayed, whilst bills and salaries still have to paid, this causes severe problems for a business.

Assets Items the business owns, such as furniture, equipment, premises, vehicles and stock.

Dividend Payments made to shareholders as their financial reward for buying shares.

Interest Payments made to lenders as their financial reward for making the loan.

Service payment Payments made by anyone who borrows money to the lender, such as interest or dividends. This is the 'fee' for borrowing which is the lender's reward.

Business brief

Prices, demand and supply

The prices of shares, vegetables, fish and almost anything else you care to name fluctuate because of demand and supply. When many people want something, then the value increases. When no-one wants it, the value falls.

You can see this quite easily if you think of a market trader selling tomatoes. On a summer day, with a limited supply, the trader can raise the price because everyone wants to buy some. They may still run out before they close. On a Saturday in winter, when it's cold and raining, they may have surplus stock – so will reduce the price to get rid of them.

The same thing happens with shares. If a business is doing well and lots of people want to buy the shares, the value increases. Conversely, if many shareholders sell at the same time and few people want to buy, the price falls. It will keep falling to a level where someone thinks it's a bargain – and buying starts again.

Prices of vegetables fall when there is a glut, but rise when there is a shortage

Talking point

Banks may be reluctant to lend money to a new business but they have been criticised in the press for lending too much to private individuals – to the extent that people get into financial difficulties and can't repay.

View 1: *Banks that do this are irresponsible and only do it to meet sales targets and make more money. There should be laws to make this illegal so that no-one can borrow more than they can afford to repay.*

View 2: *Banks are in business to make a profit like anyone else. If people ask to borrow more than they can afford it's their own fault if they get into trouble. It's not up to the banks or the government to control people.*

With which viewpoint do you agree – and why?

Over to you!

1 Identify one business or organisation in which you think your concerns will be taken seriously as a stakeholder, and two businesses or organisations where you think it will not. Then suggest why this difference occurs. Compare your ideas with other members of your group.

2 Dairy farmers are arguing with milk processors and large supermarkets about the price they are paid for milk. They claim they don't even earn enough to break even as they only receive about 18p a litre from the processor, even though milk sells for around 43p in supermarkets. The supermarkets blame the processors, such as Dairy Crest, which has the largest market share. Dairy Crest charges the supermarkets 36p a litre. The supermarkets say they must please their customers who want cheap milk. Dairy Crest says it now pays farmers 19p a litre which is more than its competitors pay.

   a The supermarkets are involved with two groups of stakeholders – suppliers and customers.
      i Which concerns do they appear to care about the most?
      ii Can you suggest a reason for this?

   b Revise some of the terms you met earlier in this unit or in unit 1. Explain what is meant by **break even** and **market share**. (If you're stuck, turn to pages 46 and 127.)

   c According to many people in the food industry, the main problem is that people drink less milk these days so Britain has too much. Read the Business Brief opposite and explain how this will affect prices.

   d Suggest why the farmers, as a supplier group, struggle to have their concerns recognised by milk processors and supermarkets.

   e As a group, suggest what could be done to solve the problem. Try to be as imaginative as possible!

3 As a group, find out more about financial stakeholders, especially what they do and what they want in return. Do this by dividing into small groups and investigating finance and help for small businesses at the websites for each of the following organisations. Check with your tutor if there are any specialist terms you do not understand. Then, for the organisation you have investigated, prepare a brief presentation and facts sheet for the rest of your class. Links to the websites mentioned below are available at www.heinemann.co.uk/hotlinks (express code 1386P).

   a The services offered to small business by any two of the large banks, i.e. NatWest, Barclays, Royal Bank of Scotland or HSBC.

   b Finance and grants on the Business Link website.

   c Finance for young entrepreneurs by The Prince's Youth Business Trust website.

   d Help to young entrepreneurs website by Shell LiveWIRE.

Staff, trade unions and staff associations

All staff have a vested interest in the activities of their employer and are therefore an important stakeholder group. At one extreme, actions by their employer can affect their livelihood, such as a decision to relocate, reduce staff or close down altogether. On a day-to-day basis, other decisions affect the quality of life for staff – from pay awards (or lack of them) to working conditions. In many organisations, staff can also expect support on key issues from their trade union representative or their staff association.

Employees are stakeholders and may protest against changes they dislike

- **Trade unions** are associations of employees formed to represent the workers in a particular industry, mainly on pay and conditions. In 2003, there were 71 unions in Britain representing nearly 7 million workers. These unions are affiliated to the Trades Union Congress (TUC) which represents all unions on a national basis. Because it lobbies the government on issues relating to workers – from health and safety to working hours – the TUC, and the unions themselves, can also be classed as pressure groups (see page 159).

  Joining a union is voluntary and involves paying a membership fee or subscription. The union to join depends upon where a person works and the type of work they do. The largest union in Britain is UNISON, which represents public sector employees, with almost 1.3 million members. An employee with a problem can consult his or her union representative for help and advice. Management will also consult union representatives about future proposed changes that may affect the workforce.

- **Staff associations** operate in many non-unionised workplaces. Other names for these associations include staff forum, professional association or works association. They consist of experienced staff, normally doing a range of different jobs in the organisation. In some cases, the staff representatives are nominated and elected by staff themselves. The association will usually be consulted about major issues and proposed future changes that may affect staff and representatives will help staff who have a problem and cannot solve it quickly through their own manager.

It is relatively easy to understand the main concerns of staff, trade unions and staff associations. All you have to do is to think about your own major concerns as an employee! What would you want? Your list is likely to include all the items listed below, if not a few more! These are therefore the main areas on which all these stakeholders concentrate.

Staff expectations are likely to include:

- To be paid a competitive wage for the job, based on their qualifications and experience.
- To be paid a fair wage in relation to their colleagues.
- To receive appropriate benefits, relevant to their job.
- To have good working conditions.
- To do an interesting job in which they can progress and develop their skills.
- To have job security.
- To be fairly treated and have the same opportunities as everyone else.
- To work in a safe environment.
- To receive further training and to be able to develop their skills.

Figure 2.20 *Staff expectations*

Wages and benefits

Most people need some financial rewards for working so that they can pay their own bills and, unless a business relies mainly on help from volunteers, it will find that wages and benefits are a constant issue for discussion. Staff not only expect to be paid a fair and competitive wage but also regularly want a pay rise. They may also expect bonuses, commission or other benefits – depending upon the job they do and the industry they work in. Managers are aware that unless they are competitive in this respect they will lose good staff and may struggle to replace them. This is especially true for talented or highly skilled staff, or in places where unemployment is very low.

For these reasons, most businesses monitor pay rates both for their own industry and within the firm. They need to ensure that:

- The wages are at the same rate, for the same type of jobs, as those offered by similar businesses in the same area.
- All wages are above the National Minimum Wage rate set by the government.

- Different levels of jobs are paid appropriately, according to responsibility, difficulty and expertise.
- Any differences between starting pay rates for the same job are based on factors such as qualifications and experience, and differences between pay rates of current employees are based on factors such as competence and performance.
- Additional payments, such as overtime, bonuses and commission are fair and no members of staff are unfairly excluded.

Many businesses also offer a range of **staff benefits**; these may vary from one industry to another. Retail staff, for example, usually receive discounts on goods they buy from their employer – from 10 per cent to 20 per cent – and free uniforms. Representatives or anyone else who regularly travels for business will either have a company car or, more commonly these days, will receive a car allowance. Many people have a company mobile phone or a phone allowance – and so on.

A modern trend is to offer a package of benefits up to a certain value. This may increase with years of service, so it also acts as a reward for loyalty. Each member of staff chooses benefits up to a certain value. Many employees prefer this because they can tailor the package to their own needs – so a single person may want gym membership whereas a family person may prefer childcare vouchers or an extra day's holiday.

Working conditions

The terms and conditions of employment are explained at a job interview and must also be contained in a formal written document or contract of employment. These relate to the location of the organisation and where the person will be employed, the hours of work, pay, holiday entitlement, sick pay arrangements, pension rights and how much notice must be given if the employee wants to leave.

If you mention working conditions to a member of staff, however, they may list the holidays and sick pay arrangements, but would also include their physical environment, the attitude of their

manager, overtime arrangements and welfare policies – such as loans to employees, stress counselling and medical checks. In other words, the whole 'package' that either makes the firm 'good to work for' – or not!

In many cases, people value working conditions more highly than an extra pound or two in their pay packet each week. If you work somewhere which is light, airy, has modern furnishings and equipment, good heating and ventilation, plenty of space and modern facilities *plus* a friendly staff, job security and a fair boss then you, too, may think twice about leaving to go somewhere else, even if the pay is higher.

Job development

Not all jobs are interesting. Anyone who works as a packer in a factory would tell you that – and if you've ever taken on a boring job to earn some holiday money, such as washing up, then you will know this yourself! However, most people need some variation in their life and want to feel they are developing and progressing at work. For this reason, most businesses aim to make jobs as interesting as possible by extending the range of tasks that a person undertakes as he or she becomes more experienced or increasing their responsibilities. This benefits both the employee, who is more motivated, and the business, which has a more highly skilled staff and can also see which members of staff may be more suitable for promotion.

In most organisations, staff discuss their personal views with a manager at regular intervals in a staff development or appraisal interview. They can discuss their strengths and weaknesses and ways in which they want to progress. Good managers use this information to provide additional opportunities for staff to develop their skills and experience in ways which link to future business plans. This may mean additional training (see page 154) but can also involve adapting a job. For example, a member of staff who wants to become involved with the company website may be made responsible for updating relevant pages for his or her department.

Job security

Many people prize job security more than job development – especially when they have family responsibilities and a mortgage to pay. The thought of being made redundant terrifies many people – particularly if they work in a trade or an area where it would be difficult to get another job quickly.

No members of staff, trade unions or staff association can stop a business from closing down if it is losing money. Neither can they prevent businesses from outsourcing operations or moving them abroad to save money, even if this will mean that some staff lose their jobs. They can, however, put pressure on to make sure that the business operates within the law in relation to making any staff redundant.

Redundancy is a situation where a person is dismissed because there is no work for them to do. In law, redundancy must be fair – an employer cannot pick and choose which employees to make redundant and must consult fully over the criteria for selection with the trade union and follow an agreed process. If there is a staff association, it must be consulted when more than 20 jobs will be affected.

Redundancy is normally a last resort. If a business is contracting, it will first try to cut staff through **natural wastage**. In this case staff who leave are not replaced. Alternatively, it may relocate staff to a different department. If this is not enough, it will ask for any volunteers who would like to opt for voluntary redundancy and will normally offer a financial package to tempt them. If this fails, then it may have to resort to compulsory redundancy. In this case, staff who have worked for more than two years must receive redundancy pay at, or above, a minimum legal level and must be offered free counselling or retraining and given time off to attend or to go for interviews for a new job.

Equal opportunities and treatment of staff

Many organisations today have equal opportunities policies. They may include a statement in their job advertisements which says that they do not discriminate against anyone 'on grounds of colour, race, nationality, ethnic or national origin, religious belief, sex or sexual orientation, being married or disability.' If this seems a long list, then after 2006 it will be even longer – because a new law will be introduced to outlaw discrimination on the grounds of age, too.

What is discrimination and why does it matter? Quite simply, discrimination means treating someone differently and unfairly because of a reason totally unrelated to their job. In Britain it is illegal to discriminate against employees just because they are a certain sex, a particular race, have a disability, have certain beliefs or belong to a particular religion, or because they are gay or bisexual. You will learn more about these laws if you study specialist unit 5. Discrimination matters because employers should only be concerned with people's abilities to do the job. It also matters because discrimination can make anyone's life a misery, as well as denying very capable people the opportunities they deserve. Wise businesses recognise this and have policies in place to prevent it. They also take action against any individuals in the organisation who disregard them.

Discrimination can occur at any stage of the employment process – such as during an interview, when selecting people for promotion or offering training opportunities. It also occurs if someone is treated differently on a day-to-day basis, for example if they are harassed or victimised.

- **Harassment** is unwelcome behaviour that offends, frightens or upsets someone.
- **Victimisation** is when one person is singled out for unfair treatment by another person, particularly for complaining about a discrimination issue.

Most businesses not only have policies in place to try to prevent this happening – and fully investigate any staff concerns in these areas – they also promote the fair and **positive** treatment of staff. This means expecting good behaviour by managers, having welfare policies and being understanding and helpful if people are having personal problems or difficulties. It also means having a workplace where all staff are treated with respect and courtesy, by everyone else, on a day-to-day basis. This doesn't mean to say people never get fraught or angry. It does mean that personal insults are firmly discouraged and any staff who indulge in inappropriate behaviour are disciplined.

Health and safety observance

There is one main law – the Health and Safety at Work Act – that governs health and safety in the workplace. However, there are also many regulations. These cover areas from workplace conditions and display screen equipment (i.e. your computer) to manual handling (i.e. lifting, fire precautions, noise, first aid, safety signs and many others). Both employers *and employees* must comply with these laws and regulations.

The reason employees must obey them is because the Health and Safety at Work etc. Act puts the responsibility for health and safety on both employers and employees – as you can see from the extract below. Any person who is negligent under the Act can face criminal prosecution. The agency which enforces the Act is the Health and Safety Executive (HSE). A HSE inspector can visit any industrial premises without warning to investigate an accident or complaint or to visit the premises. Offices and shops are inspected by an environmental health officer employed by the local authority.

To comply with the law, all businesses with more than five people must draw up a safety policy and have safety procedures that employees must follow in an emergency, if an accident occurs or if they are doing certain types of work. Businesses must monitor the risks in the workplace and take action to eliminate or reduce these as much as possible. They must also follow up employee concerns and investigate any accidents. You will find out more about health and safety if you study specialist Unit 6.

Staff turnover

Staff turnover relates to the rate at which staff start and leave an organisation. You are right to be suspicious if you find out that no-one stays longer than three months at an organisation that is offering to employ you. Businesses with separate personnel or human resources

The Health and Safety at Work etc. Act 1974

1   Applies to all work premises. Anyone on the premises is covered by and has responsibilities under the Act, whether employees, supervisors, directors or visitors.
2   Requires all employers to
   - 'As far as is reasonably practicable' ensure the health, safety and welfare at work of their employees. This particularly relates to aspects such as
     - Safe entry and exit routes.
     - Safe working environment.
     - Well-maintained, safe equipment.
     - Safe storage of articles and substances.
     - Provision of protective clothing.
     - Information on safety.
     - Appropriate training and supervision.
   - Prepare and continually update a written statement on the health and safety policy of the company and circulate this to all employees (where there are five or more of them).
   - Allow for the appointment of safety representatives selected by a recognised trade union. Safety representatives must be allowed to investigate accidents or potential hazards, follow up employee complaints and have paid time off to carry out their duties.
3   Requires all employees to
   - Take reasonable care of their own health and safety and that of others who may be affected by their activities.
   - Cooperate with their employer and anyone acting on his or her behalf to meet health and safety requirements.

departments monitor this figure carefully and investigate the reasons why staff are leaving. Acceptable reasons include moving house or obtaining a better paid job elsewhere. The situation is different if the reasons relate to staff dissatisfaction or unhappiness.

It is in everyone's interest for staff turnover to be low, because continually hiring and training new staff is expensive and time-consuming. For that reason businesses normally want to take action if there is some underlying reason why good staff are leaving, such as uncompetitive pay rates or a 'long hours' culture.

Staff training and development

Most people want to continue to develop their skills and abilities after they have started work. Becoming multi-skilled helps to make an existing job more enjoyable, having higher level skills means staff can apply for more responsible jobs with better pay. Usually staff are only eligible for promotion if they can prove they have done well in their current job, kept up to date with technology and continued to develop themselves.

- **Staff training** relates to specific opportunities to learn new skills or extend previous skills or knowledge – either in the workplace or at a college or training centre.
- **Staff development** relates to the personal development of the person, such as team

working, time management, how to give a presentation. In some businesses, virtually any development activities are encouraged as they are considered important for personal growth and achievement.

From April 2003, every member of staff in a workplace where a union is recognised is entitled to have a Union Learning Rep, who is entitled to attend training courses and have paid time off work to give advice and guidance, organising training or learning activities or work out what training is needed. This provides a more informal route for any workers who are worried about asking their manager or employer.

Staff training benefits individuals and the business

Business matters

For over 30 years the law has stated that women and men should receive equal pay if they are doing the same job. Despite this, a report by the Equal Pay Task Force called 'Just Pay' found that women still only earn 82 per cent of the male wage. Part-time workers are even worse off, taking home only 59 pence for every £1 earned by male full-time workers.

In 2001 the Equal Pay Task Force looked at the reasons for this and identified three main reasons. The first is the fact that women and men often do different jobs – with many female jobs being paid less; the second is the unequal impact of family responsibilities, which generally fall more on the

woman than the man. The third reason was discrimination in pay at work – where women simply weren't being paid fairly.

To help to remedy this, the Government has funded a TUC training programme for union representatives to become Equal Pay Reps. These reps work with employers to undertake pay reviews and find out where pay discrimination exists, and identify ways to eliminate it. Organisations that have been involved so far are from both the private and public sector, such as BMW at Oxford, BAE Systems, British Telecom and the Alliance and Leicester as well as the Public Records Office and several local councils, colleges and universities.

Most businesses recognise the value to both themselves and their employees of supporting training and development requests whenever possible. However, they have to consider the cost and their overall training budget as an organisation, whether the request is relevant to the work being done and how any time away from the job would affect the business. Young people under the age of 19 have the legal right to be provided with free training and time off work to gain an NVQ level 2 qualification but this is an exception. Adult employees are often expected to have enough commitment and interest in their own career to attend some courses out of working hours, even if they don't have to contribute towards the cost.

Over to you!

1 You can find out more about unions and what they do through the TUC website – a link is available at www.heinemann.co.uk/hotlinks (express code 1386P) which has a 'mainly students' section and a link to the student BizEd site. Access these sites to find out the answers to the following:
   a What is the role of the TUC?
   b Why do unions belong to the TUC?
   c Why do people join trade unions?
   d What is the relationship between the government and the TUC?
   e What impact do trade unions have on business?

2 Investigate the work of one of the following trade unions by visiting their website – links are available at www.heinemann.co.uk/hotlinks (express code 1386P). Alternatively, divide into small groups, investigate one union each and compare your answers. Find out specifically the type of workers the unions represents and the main services it offers to its members.
   a The Broadcasting, Entertainment, Cinematograph and Theatre Union (BECTU).
   b The Communication Workers Union (CWU).
   c GMB.
   d UNISON.
   e The Transport and General Workers' Union.
   f AMICAS-AEEU.

Benefits for staff

Shares in the business
Profit sharing or bonus scheme
Company goods at discount prices
Health insurance
Extra holidays (e.g. whole day or half day)
Childcare/nursery vouchers
Gym membership (free or subsidised)
Company car, car allowance or cash alternative
Dental and/or optical care
Vouchers for use with retail or holiday firms
Season ticket loans and other loans at cheap rates

3 a The following table shows a list of benefits which may be offered to staff. If you could choose any three, which would they be? Compare your answers with those of other members in your group and then rank them to find the most popular four benefits overall.
   b Richer Sounds offers a wide range of benefits to its staff – including stays in holiday homes abroad. Find out about these on the Richer Sounds StudentZone at www.richerstudentzone.co.uk. Why do you think these are slightly different for long-service and relatively new employees?

Talking point

View 1: The most important aspect of any job is the pay. You can put up with anything if you are paid good money.

View 2: Pay is only one aspect of a job. It's better to be happy and paid less, then to be miserable and earn a lot.

With which viewpoint do you agree – and why?

Sponsors as stakeholders

In December 2003, Coca-Cola paid £2 million to sponsor the pop charts, compiled by the Official UK Charts Company up to 2005. This was small change, however, when compared with the £36 million paid by Vodafone to renew its sponsorship contract with Manchester United Football Club until 2007. Sponsorship is so common, it almost goes unnoticed these days, particularly in sports – where we are used to hearing Barclaycard's name linked to the FA Premiership, seeing Kingfisher's name on Ellen MacArthur's yachts and watching cricket teams compete for the Cheltenham and Gloucester trophy. In 2003, Nike even paid $90 million to sponsor a rising 18 year old American basketball star!

Kingfisher sponsors Ellen MacArthur's yachts

Today there are sponsors of everything from television programmes such as Big Brother and Sex and the City to computers for schools; concert tours by bands and singers such as Sting, Kylie Minogue and Justin Timberlake to cheap theatre tickets. You may have sought sponsorship yourself, although in a far more minor way, when you have been trying to raise money for charity. But why was Vodafone prepared to pay so much to have its name on player's shirts? What's in it for these companies?

Sponsorship is a two-way process and both parties have to benefit for the deal to be a success. It is obvious what the recipient gains – normally additional money to spend. But what does the giver obtain? There are five main reasons why large companies spend money on sponsorship.

- **To gain a better return on their investment than standard advertisements**. Vodafone, in fact, expects a threefold return – so their deal with Manchester United Football Club has to be worth more than £100 million by 2007. This is not just through additional sales but also in money saved by cutting advertising costs in other areas. In marketing terms £100 million isn't excessive for the four years of worldwide advertising that Vodafone attains through Manchester United.
- **For greater brand recognition amongst their target market**. This is why banks, insurance and accountancy firms sponsor events like Monet in the 20th Century at the Royal Academy as well as the English National Opera, while T-Mobile prefers the Rolling Stones European Licks Tour. Coca-Cola is sponsoring the charts because it wants to promote the brand to young people, but this wouldn't be of interest to a business like Saga or Mothercare.
- **To promote their business in their own region**. Many Scottish firms sponsor the Edinburgh International Festival, such as Scottish Life, Scottish & Newcastle and Scottish Widows; the Royal Liver Assurance group sponsors prizes at John Moore's University in Liverpool and the CIS and Manchester Evening News sponsors events at the Manchester Art Gallery.
- **To improve or adjust their image**. Bailey's sponsored Sex and the City so that it would be associated with a young, adventurous image rather than be associated with older people. Sportswear manufacturers like Nike, Adidas and Reebok want to be associated with successful players and teams.
- **To demonstrate social and community responsibility**. Many businesses sponsor hospices, charities and charitable appeals, young people, community projects and many other small events or projects which often go unnoticed. You will learn more about responsible business practices in the next section (see page 159).

For these reasons it is not surprising that sponsors have a key interest in the people or events they have sponsored – and don't want to risk anything going wrong. At the 1998 Olympic games, Coca-Cola – a major sponsor – said 'anything that affects the positive image of the Olympics affects us.' The type of issues sponsors are concerned with include the following:

- **Problems between reputation and association**. Sponsor deals and controversy or scandal don't mix. In 1989 Pepsi dropped Madonna because of her unsuitable image at that time. Pepsi also paid a record $15 million to sponsor Michael Jackson in 1986 – but would be far more hesitant now. The type of products made by the sponsor can also create problems – the BBC pulled out of its deal to mention Coca-Cola on Top of the Pops and on its Radio 1 chart show following criticisms from health campaigners.

- **Prospects**. Poor prospects can lose sponsors – as any struggling athlete will tell you, but excellent prospects have the opposite effect. In 2003 the England rugby team and players were being courted by dozens of companies after winning the World Cup. Jason Robinson was immortalised as *The Beano's* Billy Whizz whilst Lucozade Sport and Adidas were rubbing their hands at their current links with Jonny Wilkinson. Meanwhile, O_2 was expecting to be asked to contribute more to continue its sponsorship of the team.

- **Performance**. Superb performance attracts more sponsors, but poor performance can lose them. When Leeds United was bottom of the Premiership in 2003, sponsors Strongbow, Harp, Sky and Nike were concerned at the team's dismal performance both on the field and financially.

Interestingly, research has shown that whilst people often remember the sponsors of different football clubs and athletes, very few associate the brand with the behaviour of a celebrity. Business sponsors, however, normally don't take that view and often try to dictate their own terms in respect of their sponsorship relationship. This can lead to problems as you will see in the Business Matters feature on page 158.

Local communities and environmental concerns

If you live near an airport, motorway, industrial complex or even in a rural area which is scheduled for a nearby wind farm, then you may already have experience of local community actions by campaigners who want change. This is often the case if residents feel that their way of life is threatened or the value of their houses may be reduced by local plans.

Key environmental concerns of local communities include:

- **Airborne pollution** – from factories, chemical sites and nuclear processing plants – and fears about long-term health and safety
- **Litter and waste disposal** – litter left lying around is a health hazard, and no-one wants discarded fridges or abandoned cars in their street. Residents will expect their local authority to have a clear policy for keeping all areas clean and tidy.
- **Noise** – either through building work nearby or as a result of new ring roads and motorways that increase traffic in urban areas. Near

When England won the Rugby Union World Cup their sponsors won too!

Business matters

Sponsorship relations often run into difficulties. In some cases the sponsors can be accused of being too dictatorial. When the Cricket World Cup was held in South Africa, fans who took cans of Coca-Cola to the ground had them confiscated, because Pepsi was one of the major sponsors. They were only allowed mineral water – with the label removed from the bottle. Nearer to home, T-Mobile would only allow mobile phone cameras in the stadium when the Stones were on tour.

But things don't always go in the sponsors' favour. From 2005 at the latest, Formula One must live without its tobacco sponsors – worth £250 million a year – because tobacco manufacturers are no longer allowed to advertise at sporting events. The problem is finding alternative global brands that can afford to take their place. Budweiser has sponsored the Williams team for a reported sum of £50 million but there are obvious problems with associating drink and driving. Protestors were out in force when Fosters sponsored the Grand Prix in Melbourne and in France no visible alcohol brands are allowed on television. So when Jaguar cars, sponsored by Becks, race in France, they only carry the colours and logo but not the name.

A newer area of disagreement is sponsorship by food manufacturers whose products are considered to contribute to child obesity. Cadbury's was criticised heavily for a schools promotion which entailed collecting chocolate wrappers, Coca-Cola was dropped by the BBC (see previous page) and McDonald's £15 million sponsorship of Euro 2004 came under attack. Whether food producers will eventually be as unacceptable as tobacco firms as sponsors is not yet known, but many sports would struggle without the large budgets of Coca-Cola, Pepsi and McDonalds.

- **Traffic** – the number and type of vehicles is often an issue, with campaigners arguing for bypasses and ring roads to reduce traffic through villages and residential areas. The speed of vehicles is also important for safety reasons and locals may argue for speed cameras or speed bumps to be installed to restrict this.
- **Crime** – local communities may argue for more visible policing if crime is rising, particularly on housing estates, in shopping centres and in town centres when pubs and nightclubs are closing. The government is keen for residents to work with local organisations to tackle these types of problem and has awarded grants totally £36 million to cover 15 areas of the country.
- **Environmental health** – this covers a wide range of issues such as pest control, the quality of drinking water, clean beaches and food safety. Local environmental health officers check hygiene standards in local restaurants and takeaways to ensure these are within the law and to prevent any outbreaks of food poisoning in an area. Even more serious is Legionnaire's Disease, which is caused by faulty air conditioning systems. Five people died and 140 were infected at Barrow-in-Furness in 2002 as a result of the old air conditioning system in the arts complex.

Most issues which concern communities are highlighted on a regular basis in the local newspaper – which will often 'champion' causes that it considers worthwhile. In this case the local media can support residents and put effective pressure on councils and large businesses by publishing their responses.

In other cases, residents may decide to take more direct action. Some chain themselves to trees and form barricades to stop developers building new motorways, ring roads or airport extensions which would turn vast swathes of the countryside into concrete. Such dramatic actions are usually well publicised in the national press.

airports proposals to increase night flights or add an additional runway usually cause serious local concerns.

Most people don't take such direct action but may form a community group to argue with a government, council or business decision. They may boycott a local business; lobby the media, local councillors and MP or even lodge a formal appeal. This is the most likely course of action if a community objects to a proposed business plan. If the appeal is complex then a special hearing or inquiry will take place. At the end of the investigation the inspector in charge submits the decision to the Secretary of State for the Environment who can, in exceptional cases, overrule it.

Pressure groups and ethical concerns

A pressure group is an organised group of people that aims to influence more powerful bodies such as the government, local authorities or large businesses. Some pressure groups, like Amnesty International and Greenpeace, are very large, operate internationally on a permanent basis, have millions of supporters and champion a particular cause. Others are much smaller and may be formed for a particular purpose and then disbanded.

The trade unions and the TUC, which you read about on page 149, are an example of pressure groups, as they lobby the government about the causes of workers – not just in the United Kingdom but in other parts of the world, too. The International Confederation of Free Trade Unions (ICFTU) lobbies on many issues including child labour, equality, health and safety, and labour rights worldwide.

Some pressure groups are particularly focused on ethical business practices – such as those identified by the United Nations. For example, the World Development Movement is sceptical of many of the motives and claims made by big businesses. It argues that many western government and business policies simply keep poor people poor. Friends of the Earth has a similar stance. Local groups such as the South Lakeland World Development Movement are keen for local people

to support Fairtrade goods (see page 106) and to support the rights of the poor.

The main concerns of pressure groups in relation to business practices are described in more detail below.

Buying goods from suppliers who exploit child or female labour in developing countries

The UN Convention on the Rights of the Child was passed in 1989 and the International Labour Organisation (ILO) passed a convention to outlaw the worst forms of child labour in 1999. Since then the ILO has since identified other types of work that are hazardous to children but still estimates that about 250 million children between 5 and 14 have to work on a full-time basis in developing countries. Save the Children and Human Rights Watch are just two of the many pressure groups actively involved in trying to change this situation – although they caution against naive responses (such as boycotting goods made by child labour in areas of extreme poverty) and other actions which can actually make things worse, rather than better.

Women are also exploited in many countries where they have little or no rights and are used as cheap labour. UNICEF, Oxfam and the ICFTU are just three of the pressure groups active in this area. Another group is Labour behind the Label which you can investigate on the Internet – a link is available at www.heinemann.co.uk/hotlinks (express code 1386P).

Environmental damage

On a worldwide basis, issues like global warming are frequently in the news. This can be caused through pollution by industrialised countries or by actions which threaten the environment. The 1997 Kyoto Protocol, designed to reduce emissions, continually runs into political difficulties – as did the more recent United Nations Climate Change Conference. Some pressure groups, such as the New Economics Foundation now suggest that the EU should tax imports from countries like the US, which refuse to comply. The foundation believes that business can work successfully in harmony with the environment to improve the quality of life for everyone. You can find out more on the New Economics website – a link is available at www.heinemann.co.uk/hotlinks (express code 1386P).

Many pressure groups campaign against the destruction of the rain forests

Other pressure groups are concerned with more specific issues. In Brazil and Central America, the destruction of the rainforests to clear land for cattle ranchers and sugar cane threatens local tribes as well as indigenous plant and animal species and may have a huge impact on global warming. Pressure groups such as The Rainforest Action Network, the Rainforest Alliance and Survival International are three that try to prevent this, and you can even click to help save a forest yourself at the Rainforest website – a link is available at www.heinemann.co.uk/hotlinks (express code 1386P). Closer to home, reports in the press may include local businesses fly tipping, farmers tipping slurry into a stream or a factory ignoring the law and dumping toxic waste into a river.

New European legislation, to come into effect by 2005 in the UK, makes businesses totally liable for any environmental damage they cause. The Confederation of British Industry (CBI) – a business pressure group – argues that this will cost British business a further £1.8 billion a year and will be unfair to those firms that are already environmentally responsible. Despite this, European MPs want individuals to be able to bring an environmental pollution case against any business. At the moment, firms can only be sued by local authorities for the damage they cause.

Dangerous working conditions

According to ILO, there are over 2 million people worldwide killed by work-related diseases and occupational accidents each year. Cancer, caused by asbestos, carcinogenic dust, chemicals and radiation causes the most diseases; followed by circulatory diseases, accidents and the communicable diseases. It would be good to think that in the UK, we have responsible employers who never ask staff to do dangerous jobs without training and the proper equipment, never ask them to handle asbestos or hazardous materials without proper safeguards, only have well-maintained equipment and proper safety procedures, never cause them stress or put them in a situation where they may be subjected to violence. Unfortunately, this isn't true, despite health and safety laws, the role of the Health and Safety Commission and pressure by the TUC and trade unions. A minority of unscrupulous employers continue to put profits before safety. In Britain, 226 people were killed at work in 2002/3 and over 28,000 seriously injured. Not all of these were due to easily preventable accidents but some were.

In 1998, one well-publicised case was that of Simon Jones, who died at the age of 24 on his first day working as a casual labourer for the Dutch-based firm Euromin at Shoreham Dockyard. He was a student, taking a year out from university. Without any training he was told to attach bags of stones to chains hanging inside a grab (a large mechanical device which grips an object). He died when the grab accidentally closed around his head. He had been at work for only two hours.

His family and friends formed a pressure group. They were concerned about several aspects of the existing legal system where only 30 per cent of workplace deaths end in a prosecution. You can read more on the Simon Jones website – a link is available at www.heinemann.co.uk/hotlinks (express code 1386P).

Hazards magazine argues that in the 21st century the top occupational diseases will be heart attacks, suicide and strokes, because people can't cope with ludicrously long working hours and never-ending stress. They cite the case of the 44 year old hospital doctor, Sid Watkins, who committed suicide because he couldn't cope with his 100 hour weeks. European law means the working hours of doctors must now fall to a maximum of 58 for junior doctors and 48 hours for consultants. Fines will be levied and posts taken away from any hospital which disregards this. Some hospitals now argue they now don't have enough 'doctor-hours' to cope with emergencies. For more information, visit the Hazards website – a link is available at www.heinemann.co.uk/hotlinks (express code 1386P).

Payment of unacceptable low wages

Companies like Gap and Nike have been under fire for paying sweatshop wages to their workers in third world countries. In 2002, the textile union Africa Forum and Unite asked shoppers to boycott Gap stores in the UK, arguing that its employees in many third world countries worked long hours for low pay and faced health hazards and brutal working conditions at factories making Gap products. Gap, which acknowledges the problem, says it tries to influence factory owners wherever it can; protestors say this isn't good enough. Oxfam Community Aid Abroad launched its NikeWatch Campaign, arguing that Nike workers live in severe poverty and suffer constantly from overwork. Oxfam Community Aid Abroad is a pressure group which exists to persuade **transnational businesses** to respect workers' basic rights. If you want to know more about the NikeWatch Campaign a link is available at www.heinemann.co.uk/hotlinks (express code 1386P).

All is not rosy in Britain however. Sweatshops still exist in backstreets which exploit child labour and don't pay a living wage; cleaners and those working in the catering trade – especially in London – often earn too little to live on, despite the minimum wage. In 2004 the government extended the minimum wage to include workers aged 16 and 17, although at a lower rate. It promised to get tougher on businesses that don't pay the minimum rate – and announced an amnesty for existing migrant workers to try to take them out of the 'black' economy. According to the Citizen's Advice Bureau, one Lincolnshire migrant agricultural worker only had £6 left from his wage after deductions by his 'gang master'. The Trades Union Congress (TUC) have argued that the problem affects a large number of people – not just those in agriculture. Their report 'Overworked, underpaid and over here' lists a range of employer abuse in several trades. A pressure group formed to fight for living wages for every worker is called No Sweat. You can read more at the No Sweat, Low Pay and DTI websites – links are available at www.heinemann.co.uk/hotlinks (express code 1386P).

Tax avoidance and evasion

No one likes paying tax, so planning and taking advantage of schemes which can help to reduce your tax bill is sensible. If you started to pay part of your wage into a stakeholder pension you would pay less tax, similarly you wouldn't pay tax on your interest if you saved in a cash ISA account. Other people, however, go to greater lengths.

- **Tax avoidance** is technically legal and used to be applied to any method used to reduce tax. But there is a snag. The Inland Revenue is suspicious of schemes which help people to avoid tax by finding loopholes in the law. It therefore has 'anti-avoidance' measures in place, to help to prevent these. It can investigate anyone if it suspects significant tax losses through involved avoidance schemes. The Government also regularly announces new laws to 'tighten up' or remove loopholes.
- **Tax evasion** is illegal. This is deliberately defrauding the tax authorities by not declaring earnings for tax or falsifying documents, or by not declaring sales on which VAT would be levied. Anyone doing this can be investigated

and may be charged with a criminal offence, as well as being fined and having to pay all the back tax owing.

At one end of the scale, people who claim benefits and then **moonlight** are evading tax. So are those who do jobs 'for cash', so that they can avoid paying National Insurance and income tax. People who work in this way are known as operating in the **black economy** – worth up to £15 billion in lost taxes every year. Other methods of evading tax include not paying for a tax disc on a car or motorbike (up to £200 million lost each year) and smuggling goods from abroad on which excise duty is payable. The problem with these activities is that it means genuine taxpayers have to pay more tax to make up the difference needed by the Government.

Some authorities and pressure groups claim that the tax authorities often go for 'soft targets' such as small businesses or individuals who have perhaps made a genuine mistake. The real villains, they say, are the very wealthy individuals and transnational businesses that pay huge sums of money to accountants to advise them on sophisticated ways to avoid tax, such as moving valuable assets to offshore tax havens or declaring profits in countries which have less onerous tax regimes. The British Chambers of Commerce and the Confederation for British Industry (CBI) both put pressure on the government over tax issues which they think will penalise British businesses or – in particular – small business owners. This is important, because Inland Revenue or VAT investigations can be stressful and frightening. The media and large City firms can also put pressure on the government if they feel a tax campaign is unjust or unfair.

Supply of socially harmful products

How many things that you buy do you good – and how many don't? If your weekly shopping basket contains fruit, vegetables and yoghurt then you are unlikely to have any problems. If you would rather live on chocolate, chips, beer and cigarettes then the law won't stop you, providing you are over 18, although other factors might. It could be argued that if you are old enough and intelligent enough

to know the difference it isn't up to big business or the government to make your shopping decisions for you.

This isn't the case, however, if you are poorly educated, live in a third word country and don't know enough to be able to withstand marketing pressure from big businesses. Neither is this the case if you are 12 years old, handed a gun and told to fight for your village. In other words, there is a difference between when people have a choice of what to buy or use, and when they don't. See what you think when you have read more about the products featured below.

Powdered baby milk substitutes

In 1998 manufacturers of powdered baby milk substitutes promoted the use of their products in Bangladesh, Thailand, Poland and South Africa by giving out free gifts to mothers and health workers. This was in direct violation of an international code to promote breast feeding to try and prevent the one and a half million unnecessary infant deaths each year through poor sterilisation of feeding bottles in the third world. The Nestlé Baby Milk Scam, as it became known, led to moves to boycott Nestlé products and the cause is still being championed by a number of charities. Reports against Nestlé (and Danone) were still being published at the Global Policy website in 2003 – a link to this site is available at www.heinemann.co.uk/hotlinks (express code 1386P).

IBFAN (the International Baby Food Action Network) is a non-profit organisation working globally to try to tighten controls on the marketing tactics of the baby feeding industry. If you are concerned about the issue, find out more at the Baby Milk Action website – a link is available at www.heinemann.co.uk/hotlinks (express code 1386P).

The arms trade

The arms trade is often the subject of debate and controversy. Some people believe that all arms production and sales should be banned, others consider that only illicit dealing is wrong – when guns and other weapons are sold to arms traffickers, guerrilla groups or to regimes which intend to crush resistance among the local people. Others believe that the type of weapons matters most – so land mines and cluster bombs are unacceptable but Scorpion tanks are allowable.

The British arms trade – officially known as the British defence industry – sells about £17 billion in arms a year, mainly to the British government for the defence of Britain and for use by British armed forces. About £4 billion in arms are exported each year – and some of these exports have caused controversy especially when they have been sold to trouble spots around the world, such as Columbia, Sri Lanka and Zimbabwe. Sales of Hawk jets to India were also criticised as it was felt these could add to tensions in the area.

If you, or your family, work for one of the large defence companies in Britain, such as BAE Systems, Rolls Royce, GKN or Vosper Thorneycroft then you might feel strongly that regulation is important, but wiping out the livelihoods of about 300,000 workers is not an option. Especially as the British armed forces would then have to buy from abroad. However, pressure groups like the Campaign Against the Arms Trade (CAAT) would disagree. They want the reduction and ultimate abolition of the international arms trade. You can find out more about this group on the Internet – links to the CAAT and The Defence Manufacturers Association (DMA) websites are available at www.heinemann.co.uk/hotlinks (express code 1386P).

The tobacco industry

Social attitudes towards smoking have changed dramatically over the last twenty years. Smoking was once accepted in cinemas, on trains, in shops and even hospitals, but today it is banned in all those places. Because of the health risks attached to passive smoking, many workplaces are also no smoking zones – and there are calls for bans to be extended to restaurants and pubs to protect workers in the catering industry. *The Lancet*, a leading medical journal, has even called for smoking to be criminalised – although it stops short of saying how the police could monitor this.

In several places, there are bans on smoking in all pubs and restaurants, including Toronto, Vancouver, California, Norway, New York and Ireland. It is likely that, over the next few years, more countries and cities will follow.

Smoking will soon be outlawed in UK pubs if the health lobby gets its way

In Britain, the main pressure group which would like this change is ASH – Action on Smoking and Health. On the ASH website you can find out about the size of the tobacco industry, how it advertises and promotes cigarettes and the cost of the additional health care required because of smoking. After reading this, you may wonder why the UK government isn't eager to ban smoking in every public place in England. A link to the website is available at www.heinemann.co.uk/hotlinks (express code 1386P).

The Government's dilemma is that it receives over £9 billion a year in tax from smokers, as well as tax on tobacco company profits. So if everyone stopped smoking, other taxes would have to be increased to compensate. Therefore, the Government goes for a softer approach, such as increasing taxes each year (which motivates more smokers to give up) and providing money for smoking cessation clinics and nicotine replacement products through the NHS. See the Giving up Smoking website for more details – a link is available at www.heinemann.co.uk/hotlinks (express code 1386P).

Forest is a pressure group which argues against a complete ban, on the basis that adults should have the right to choose whether they smoke or not. It argues, for example, that 45,000 restaurant jobs could be lost if non-smoking in public places is enforced. You can find out more at the Forest and tobacco manufacturers websites – links are available at www.heinemann.co.uk/hotlinks (express code 1386P).

Other examples – and what to do next

Once you start to identify socially harmful products, it is often harder knowing where to stop than it is to decide what to do. If you ran the government what would you outlaw? Pornography, alcohol and computer game 'nasties' which include sex and violence? Would you consider cannabis socially harmful or no worse (or perhaps better) than tobacco? And where would you stand on junk food with a high salt, sugar or fat content?

The state has the task of trying to monitor what is 'good' for the nation with its need to raise taxes and its dislike of being labelled a 'nanny state'. It is also caught between pressure groups arguing about consumer protection or fair trade and those which represent large businesses. Obvious unethical issues like the baby milk scandal, or spam emails linked to porn sites being sent to children are often easier to deal with than more complex debates.

The benefits, however, depend upon who you believe. According to research undertaken by Cooperative Financial Services, consumer spending on products marketed as ethically sound has increased by 13 per cent to 6.9 billion in 2003. The survey suggests that traditional manufacturers are now losing sales worth £2.5 billion a year if they are seen as being ethically unsound.

But when Research International polled 1,500 young shoppers in 41 countries it found consumers preferred to turn a blind eye to ethical malpractices when their favourite brands were involved. This was supported by the food industry's Institute of Grocery Distribution survey which also found most people never thought about ethical issues when they were shopping.

You will read more about social issues in Section 2.4 (see pages 182–7).

Business matters

Many people turn vegetarian or vegan because they are concerned about additives or cruelty to animals. In that case, it may come as a shock to find that the RSPCA found that many leading high-street supermarkets were using eggs from battery hens in their vegetarian ready-meals. The charity claims this will incense many vegetarians, who would only normally buy free range or barn eggs. In addition, few of the products were correctly labelled so customers couldn't make an informed choice.

The worst offenders were Morrisons, Iceland, Sainsbury's, Somerfield and Spar UK. ASDA didn't come out well either. Tesco, Safeway, Waitrose and Quorn were slightly better and the Coop a little better still. Top of the bill were Marks & Spencer, Cauldron Foods, Dalepak, Heinz and Realeat who all only use free range eggs and clearly label all products.

Supermarkets and food are two issues constantly raised by many pressure groups. Friends of the Earth is critical of the fact that supermarkets don't source food locally and is anti-GM crops (see also page 183). The leading UK watchdog is the Food Commission, which campaigns on all food issues. Their 'Parents Jury' constantly lobbies on issues which affect children – such as sweets at checkouts and vending machines in schools. Find out more at the Food Commission website – a link is available at www.heinemann.co.uk/hotlinks (express code 1386P). Then decide whether you think junk food for children is the next justifiable area for making businesses put health and safety before profits.

Responding to stakeholder concerns

Businesses that are faced with stakeholder concerns have two basic options. They can do nothing (and hope the problem goes away) – or they can take action. The decision will usually depend upon:

- The power of the stakeholder group.
- The issue that the group has raised.
- The effect of any action taken upon *other* stakeholder groups.

No business can please all its stakeholders all of the time. For example, many people are anti-smoking, but tobacco companies still have their shareholders to please, their existing customers and employees. It is therefore too simplistic to argue that they should just close down and make all their workers redundant because of the health problems caused by smoking. As long as smoking is legal, tobacco companies can still operate.

In most businesses, the issues are slightly less contentious, but problems still arise. A local business may wish to expand. This will result in job security for the current employees, more job opportunities, better services for customers – but may alienate the local community who fight against its plans. In another case, a business may be caught in between supplier interests (for a high price) and customer interests (for a low price, as you saw in the supermarket dispute on page 145).

In these cases, businesses have to juggle to reconcile the interests of different stakeholder groups. They may do this by adapting or modifying their previous plans or current activities. An example would be an airport which banned night flights or restricted these because of concerns of noise for local residents – or a business which built a larger distribution depot on an industrial estate, away from residential areas.

If a **key stakeholder** group is involved, then the business has no choice but to take note. You have already seen that this can be any group which has the power to dramatically affect the business by its actions. If a bank threatened to foreclose on a business unless it cut its costs by reducing staff, then the manager would have to make redundancies, or go out of business altogether. In this case it has put the needs of its key stakeholder before the needs of its employees. This is sensible. Even though the employees who have lost their jobs and their unions may object, it may have been the only option for the business to survive.

Stakeholders can increase their power by acting together. This is why pressure groups often try to organise consumer boycotts – such as the boycott on Nestlé because of the baby milk scandal. In 1995, Shell announced that it planned to dump its Brent Spar oil platform into the Atlantic. Greenpeace called for a boycott of Shell petrol and sales fell by about 50 per cent. As a result, Shell had to rethink its environmental policies. In 2003 Greenpeace, Friends of the Earth and People & Planet united with their Stop Esso campaign, again because of environmental concerns, and as a result claimed that 5 per cent of motorists have stopped buying from Esso petrol stations. However, this may not be enough to make Esso take action.

In any situation, therefore, where you are expected to evaluate the way in which a business has responded to key stakeholder concerns, you must therefore take into account:

- The consequences of doing nothing or too little.
- The consequences of trying to please other stakeholder groups instead.
- The scope for finding a possible compromise which would please everyone.

You can test your own skills in this respect when you reach the Section review on page 167!

Business terms

Lobbying Trying to influence political decisions and future laws by putting pressure on decision makers.

Transnational businesses Businesses which operate on a global basis.

Moonlighting Working in a job where income is not declared to the tax authorities.

Black economy The part of the economy where cash transactions aren't reported.

Over to you!

Links to the websites mentioned below are available at www.heinemann.co.uk/hotlinks (express code 1386P).

1 a T-Mobile sponsored the Euro 2004 football championship and, as part of the deal, obtained the rights to show highlights on mobile phones. As a group, suggest **three** other benefits for T-Mobile of this sponsorship deal.

 b For any sport you like, or team you support, find out the names of its main sponsors. Then, for any **one** sponsor, suggest **one** benefit to the sport or team and **one** benefit to the sponsor. Then identify **two** concerns the sponsor will have and **two** events which should threaten the relationship. Compare your ideas with those made by other members of your group.

2 The Country Land & Business Association is a pressure group which campaigns on several issues on behalf of rural residents and businesses. You can find out more at the Country Land & Business Association website.

 a Identify **three** main concerns of the Association by reading about its campaigns.

 b Suggest **two** benefits of pressure groups like the Association.

3 The Confederation for British Industry (CBI) represents employers in Britain whilst the Trades Union Congress (TUC) represents employees. They often go 'head-to-head' on issues relating to employment. For example, the CBI argued that restricting working hours takes away people's rights to work overtime if they want. The TUC argued that many people have to work too long hours and if these must be regulated to prevent employers putting pressure on staff.

 a If you ran a small business and were struggling to make a profit, what would be your view?

 b Would your view be the same as an employee? And do you think this would be different if you had a varied and exciting job or a boring one with no career prospects?

 c Both the CBI and TUC agree that businesses should be socially responsible. However, the CBI thinks this should be voluntary. The TUC thinks regulations are often needed. Investigate both their websites to find out more. Then decide which view you support – preferably by thinking through the advantages and disadvantages of both approaches. Now take a class vote. Be prepared to back up your argument if your tutor decides to challenge you!

4 The survey by the Cooperative Bank showed that consumer boycotts can be very successful – and can cost big brands £2.6 billion a year. This may sound a lot but actually only accounts for 4p out of every £10 we spend. Boycotts persuaded Barclays to pull out of South Africa in 1986 and Triumph, the lingerie manufacturer, to move out of Burma. But boycotts against BAT, the tobacco company have been less successful and Nestlé is thriving despite a long-term boycott linked to Baby Milk Action. You can find out about current boycotts relating to UK consumers by visiting the Ethical Consumer website.

 a As a group, suggest reasons why some boycotts are successful and some are not. Start by identifying the factors involved (some of the examples above might give you ideas) and then add your own suggestions. Aim for at least **five** or **six** reasons.

 b Working in a small group, choose **one** current boycott where you sympathise with the cause and list the main issues involved. Note that this may mean researching other sites or campaigns through the links on Ethical Consumer. Then present your findings to the rest of the class.

 c As a class, decide which of the boycotts identified is likely to be the most successful – and why.

View 1: *A Government proposal to introduce a fat tax for junk food is a really good idea because it will put people off buying unhealthy food and help them to live longer. Treating obesity costs the NHS a fortune so it's only right that those who eat fatty food should pay more tax.*

View 2: *What we choose to eat has nothing to do with the government. Taxing fatty food will only penalise low income families who haven't the money to buy expensive meals or the time to start cooking from scratch every night. It would be far better to teach people more about healthy eating and to force manufacturers to reduce fat and salt in ready meals.*

With which viewpoint do you agree – and why?

2.3 Section review

Now that you have completed this section you should understand how stakeholder concerns can affect businesses and what businesses may do to take account of these. Test your skills now by doing the following activities.

Check your understanding of this section by answering the following questions. Check all your answers with your tutor before moving on.

1 **a** Explain what is meant by the term 'stakeholder'.
   b Explain why the concerns of a key stakeholder are so important.
   c Identify **three** concerns that customers may have as a stakeholder group.
   d Identify **two** factors which mean that a supplier would have little influence as a stakeholder.
   e Explain **two** concerns you would have as an investor in a business.
   f Identify **four** concerns most employees have as stakeholders.
   g Give **three** reasons why businesses are prepared to sponsor sports or entertainment events.
   h Give the most likely reason why a sponsor may withdraw from supporting a football club or pop star's concert.
   i Explain **two** concerns which local communities may have in relation to their environment.

j Identify **three** ethical issues which often concern pressure groups.

2 In 2003, four contaminated ships sailed from the United States to Hartlepool. These were former US Navy ships which the Environment Agency had agreed could be dismantled by Able UK Ltd. Each contained more than 100 tonnes of hazardous chemical waste.

Residents living close to the dockyard were concerned about the environmental risks and won a legal injunction on safety grounds to stop any work taking place. In December, a High Court judge backed the campaign by Friends of the Earth to overturn the Environment Agency's decision. The conservation group was worried about the danger to nearby feeding and breeding sites for many species of wild birds.

Able UK blamed the Environment Agency for the situation. The Managing Director argued that the company had the experience and facilities to carry out the work in an environmentally friendly and safe way. He argued that further recruitment of local people was now on hold.

The company then had to reapply for a licence and submit to an environmental assessment before any work can continue. Friends of the Earth just wanted the ships made safe and returned to the US.

a There are at least six stakeholder groups involved in this controversy. Can you identify them?

b Do you think Friends of the Earth was pleased with the judge's decision or not? Give a reason for your answer.

c Do you think Able UK has acted responsibly or not? Before you answer this, check out its website – a link is available at www.heinemann.co.uk/hotlinks (express code 1386P).

d Find out what happened next by checking the Friends of the Earth website – a link is available at www.heinemann.co.uk/hotlinks (express code 1386P).

This section covers

External influences and their effects
The value of a PESTEL analysis
Political issues and their impact
Macroeconomic variables and their impact
Social issues and their impact
Environmental issues

The impact of changing technology
Changing legislation and its impact
Other external influences and crisis
    management
Business responses to external influences

External influences and their effects

If you have already studied unit 1, you will know that all businesses make plans for the future. In section 2.2, you also learned that businesses try to take account of key factors relating to their business when they carry out a SWOT analysis and identify their strengths, weaknesses, opportunities and threats. This helps them to prepare future plans more realistically and accurately.

All these can be disrupted, however, if an unexpected or disastrous external event occurs. In the UK in 2001, the closure of many footpaths due to the foot-and-mouth epidemic in sheep and cattle severely affected rural businesses – from farms to pubs and hotels. The terrorist attacks in the USA on 9/11 had even more devastating effects, not just on transatlantic travel but on other associated businesses – as you will see on page 00.

Fortunately, not all external influences on business are so sudden or unpredictable. Many are more foreseeable and are identified by a business when it undertakes a PESTEL analysis.

The value of a PESTEL analysis

This type of analysis is done when managers want to look at the type of external influence that may affect the business in the future. Each of the letters stands for a key area the organisation will consider.

- **Political** issues – such as a change of government or new policies relating to business.
- **Economic** influences – such as interest rates or tax changes.
- **Social** factors – such as changing attitudes, lifestyles and issues which concern the public, such as GM foods and the safety of the railways.
- **Technological** developments – such as high-speed broadband and third generation mobile phones.
- **Environmental** factors – such as new laws regulating waste disposal and packaging and environmental issues that concern people, such as the disposal of nuclear waste.
- **Legal** factors – such as new employment or safety laws.

Carrying out a PESTEL analysis is basically a five-stage process as shown in Figure 2.21.

Crisis management

Managers also need to plan for the unexpected – such as external events that could seriously affect stock market prices or erode future confidence in the business. Although this may seem impossible, this isn't the case – as you will see on page 193. Having contingency plans in place to cope with a major crisis or disaster means that action can be taken very rapidly if

Identify external influences most relevant to business (both the thinkable and the unthinkable)

↓

Monitor trends and changes in these areas

↓

Identify likely impact on business and severity

↓

Prepare action plan to minimise threat or maximise opportunities

↓

Take immediate action if event occurs

Figure 2.21 *Stages in a PESTEL analysis*

Business brief

The link between PESTEL and SWOT

On page 133 you saw how businesses undertake a SWOT analysis to identify their own strengths and weaknesses as well as the opportunities and threats in the market in which they operate.

Most businesses actually start off by doing a PESTEL analysis. This gives them more information about the outside forces that may have an effect and makes it easier to identify opportunities and threats.

For example, technological improvements such as high-speed broadband and social factors, such as more people owning a personal computer, can provide opportunities for many businesses to improve their websites and sell more goods over the Internet.

Business matters

The weather might not seem an unexpected influence – but many businesses blame it when things aren't going right. Fashion retailers struggle if autumn and early winter is warm and sunny – because no-one thinks about buying thick sweaters, coats and boots. They have to decide whether to start their sales in December – and take advantage of the Christmas trade – or keep their fingers crossed that it will be colder in January and February. Otherwise they have unsold stock left on their shelves when they want to be displaying spring and summer clothes.

MyTravel, the tour operator, also blamed the weather when it announced losses of £910.9 million in 2003. It said that fewer people had travelled abroad that summer because the weather was good in the UK. It also blamed the SARS virus and the Iraq War for the downturn in bookings.

Interestingly, the previous day, First Choice Holidays had announced a 20 per cent jump in profits to £87.1 million. The Chief Executive, Peter Long, said its success was due to common sense management and a flexible approach so that it could respond quickly to changing consumer trends. After the Iraq War people were making bookings much later and therefore it was bad business to sell off holidays cheaply too soon – which MyTravel had done and First Choice had not.

Other experts argued that although travel firms had been hit hard by external events – such as 9/11, the increased cost of aircraft fuel, a doubling of airport tax and terrorism attacks in Bali and Turkey – another factor they must take into account is changing customer behaviour. Through the Internet, people can create their own holiday, choosing the best flight and the hotel they like, often more cheaply. First Choice has picked up on this trend, allowing more customers to design their own holidays rather than buy 'off-the-shelf' packages.

In this case you might want to consider the validity of some of MyTravel's reasons for their poor performance in 2003!

necessary – and this can save the business. Following the IRA bombings in Docklands (London) and Manchester in 1996, many firms realised the wisdom of locating their computer facilities and back-up systems in secure sites (see page 66). In 1990, Perrier the bottled water giant had a major crisis when its bottles were contaminated with benzene. Because it responded very quickly and positively to the problem it kept its reputation as a seller of pure, high quality water. Although confidence in the company faltered, Perrier managed to restore its image and sales levels relatively quickly. Today the incident is virtually forgotten. If Perrier had taken months to take action or been perceived as dishonest or trying to avoid blame the situation would have been much worse and could have destroyed the company.

You can find out more about how businesses respond to emergencies and crises on page 193.

Business terms

External influences External factors, normally outside the control or influence of the business, which can affect it.

Crisis management Making plans to try to minimise the effects of serious problems on the business.

Over to you!

1 a Many businesses love hot weather – but some loathe it. As a group, decide which of the following businesses would celebrate, and which would not, during a long, hot summer.

   i   Ice cream manufacturer.
   ii   Bakery making bread, meat pies and sausage rolls.
   iii Town or city restaurant.
   iv Country pub.
   v   A dry cleaner.
   vi Indoor leisure centres.
   vii Theme parks.
   viii Cinema.
   ix Cat food manufacturer.
   x   Soft drink manufacturer.

b Many businesses buy long-range forecasts from the Met Office. This helps them to plan which goods to put on their shelves. Some, like B&Q, invest in high-speed distribution and delivery networks, so that they can move seasonal goods like garden chairs and sun loungers quickly to stores. In a small group, assume you have received a heatwave warning. You own a small, licensed general store. Identify the 10 top products you think you should stock. These should be your own ideas and not linked to the list in **a** above! Then compare your ideas with other groups to select the most appropriate ones.

2 a Re-read the Business matters feature opposite. Then list all the external influences which have affected airlines and travel companies – besides the weather. You should find eight or nine in total.

b As a group, suggest how each of the following newspaper headlines would affect the travel industry. Then compare your ideas.

   i   Government announces new runways for Stansted, Birmingham and Heathrow.
   ii   Three pilots sacked for drinking alcohol on duty.
   iii Government tax cuts = more money in your pocket.
   iv First Airbus A380 now in service, with 850 passengers.
   v   The Foreign Office travel warning – avoid Saudi Arabia because of terrorist threats.
   vi 60 per cent of households now have high-speed Internet access.
   vii Greenpeace insists air taxes must rise to cover pollution costs.
   viii Workers now have legal right to ask for flexible hours.
   ix 1 in 4 families now headed by lone parent.
   x   Strong Euro doubles cost of your holiday ice cream.

c If you worked for a travel firm, and had read the headlines in **b** above, how would you sub-divide them for a PESTEL analysis? As a group, decide which statements would fit best under which categories.

Political issues and their effect

If the idea of politics normally makes you yawn, be warned that businesses dare not be so dismissive! The actions and decisions of the government frequently affect businesses, either directly or indirectly – particularly in relation to its national priorities and its relationships with foreign countries and governments.

Elections and national/local priorities

In Britain, a General Election is held every five years – or sooner if the government wishes. If there is a change of government this can have a major impact on businesses because the priorities of the Labour, Conservative and Liberal

Voters' decisions in a General Election can affect business

Democrat parties are different; so this is a key event that businesses watch carefully. They also study the manifesto of each party to see how their policies would affect business. For example, businesses would be pleased if a government wanted to build more roads, because this would speed up the distribution of goods – even if environmentalists held other views.

Local governments also have priorities that affect businesses. In 2002, the Mayor of London, Ken Livingstone introduced congestion charging in the city centre. Most businesses have reported a positive effect, but not all. Shops that rely on passing trade, West End restaurants and the owners of small firms who have to pay to make regular deliveries in the centre have experienced a negative effect. Businesses in other large cities will be watching to see if their council introduces congestion charging and in regions all over the country businesses watch to see if their local council plans to build new roads, restrict parking or take other actions that could affect trade – either positively or negatively.

Business matters

The UK music industry employs more than 130,000 people, contributes more than £3 billion to the British economy and earns around £1.3 billion in exports. In January 2004, the Government supported the industry at the Midem festival in Cannes. Government ministers met music industry executives to promote British talent and sponsored British bands to play at the event. In 2003, it sponsored The Darkness to perform at an industry fair in Texas when the group was relatively unknown. You can find out more about the ways in which the government supports industry on its Trade Partners website – a link is available at www.heinemann.co.uk/hotlinks (express code 1386P).

International relations

International relations have a major impact because it is much easier for British companies to trade in countries with which we have good relations. The government is keen to promote foreign trade, because exporting goods earns money for Britain, and gives help and advice to exporters through its support agency, UK Trade & Investment. It also promotes British goods and services abroad. Some businesses are also heavily reliant on supplies from abroad – and so are consumers. Without imports, many of the everyday items you take for granted would disappear, such as coffee, oranges and bananas – not to mention foreign cars, electrical goods and clothes.

Businesses that trade overseas keep an eagle eye on the political situation in each of the countries in which they operate. They know that they may have serious problems if a situation develops or worsens. In the past, British businesses have pulled out of Iran (when the Ayatollahs took power), from the Lebanon (during the war in Beirut) and from Kuwait at the time of the Gulf War. Pressure by campaign groups about human rights abuses in Burma has resulted in Pepsico Inc, Amoco, BHS, Heineken, Apple, Levi Strauss, Reebok and Coca-Cola all ceasing operations there and many tour operators suspending travel to the country. In Yemen, Columbia and Nigeria, British workers have been killed or kidnapped in recent years. Although these events are relatively rare, businesses must be prepared to take action immediately if there is a risk to their employees. This normally occurs when there is political instability or when any of the following events occurs.

- **A regime change** through a 'coup' by a new government or dictator or the overthrow of a regime by a foreign power. In the past 12 years, the United States alone has been involved in promoting regime changes in Somalia, Haiti, Yugoslavia, Afghanistan and Iraq by military means.
- **Reports of guerrilla groups or terrorist activities**, such as drug gangs in Columbia, the Tamil Tigers in Sri Lanka and the bombings in Saudi Arabia and Turkey.
- **Border disputes**, such as in Eritrea, Ethiopia and parts of the Russian Federation.
- **Wars**, such as in Kosovo, Afghanistan and Iraq.
- **The threat of war** because of actions by a perceived unfriendly state and the response of other nations, e.g. in Cuba, Libya and North Korea.

The problems faced by UK firms in this situation will depend upon whether it sells goods, buys goods or operates in that particular country.

- **Businesses that supply goods** may find that their contracts are cancelled immediately and they are not paid for goods already supplied. Sales representatives, technical or maintenance staff working in the area may be in danger.
- **Businesses that buy supplies** may find that their supplies do not arrive and they lose any deposits they have paid.

National issues

- Government stability
- General and council elections
- Government priorities, e.g. public transport, roads, health care, benefits, nursery places for the children of working mothers
- Local government issues, e.g. designated industrial areas, road layouts and changes, car parking for shoppers, planning regulations
- Government support for business, e.g. grants or subsidies, assistance for small businesses

International issues

- Government support for importers and exporters
- Foreign trade regulations
- International relations
- Possible terrorist attacks and security measures
- Fears of war plus actions by other governments and United Nations
- Changing regimes in foreign countries where customers or suppliers are based
- Business and travel warnings by the Department of Trade and Industry and the Foreign Office

Figure 2.22 *Political issues which concern business*

- **Businesses that operate in the country** may have their assets seized, foreign workers may flee and UK staff may have to leave the country at a moment's notice.

Although businesses can reduce some of the risks of trading by taking out insurance, this will normally only cover monetary losses. The business still has to cope with risks to staff, the loss of customers or finding new sources of supply.

A summary of all the main political aspects that businesses consider is given in Figure 2.22. Remember that a business will focus on the key issues that could affect it – and these will depend upon its main activity and scope of operations.

Macroeconomic variables and their impact

In Britain, the Chancellor of the Exchequer, aided by the Treasury and the Bank of England, is responsible for managing the economy. But what is 'the economy' and how does it affect businesses?

- The **economy** refers to all the goods and services that are produced in the country and how these are distributed.
- The **macroeconomy** refers to the resources of a particular country. This contrasts with a

microeconomy, i.e. a small scale economy, such as exists in one business or even in your own household!

Therefore, whereas your family is concerned with financial resources such as how much money is earned, how much is saved and how much is spent, linked to your household priorities; the Chancellor the Exchequer is concerned about all these aspects for the country as a whole.

The problem is that all these factors are affected by the behaviour of millions of people and businesses, all of whom act independently. So forecasting what is going to happen in the future can be very difficult. If people or businesses act in a way that might create economic problems, the Chancellor will try to change this behaviour. This is because businesses need a stable economic environment in which to operate successfully – and Britain needs businesses to be productive in order to earn money for the country.

Economic variables that affect business and industry

An **economic variable** is any factor that can have an effect on the economy. These include tax and interest rates. If people pay more tax, they have less money to spend, so they buy fewer goods.

Business matters

The British Government and the European Union can invoke embargoes or sanctions on imports or exports to restrict the type of goods bought or sold from foreign countries where there is a perceived problem.

In 2003, the Commonwealth expelled Zimbabwe because of human rights abuses and the fact that Robert Mugabe, the President, was not fairly elected because he had rigged the elections and tried to repress political opponents. Even before this, in 2002, the European Union had forbidden the export to Zimbabwe, by any member state, of military equipment, weapons, surveillance equipment or any other items that could assist repression or human rights abuses. In addition, no business was allowed to provide military advice,

training in weapons use or software applications that could assist this type of activity. Normal business exports could continue, as could humanitarian aid and equipment.

The British Government has the right to impose restrictions on several grounds, including: threats to British national security, international legal obligations, concerns about terrorism or human rights violations. Businesses can check current regulations at the Trade Partners and DTI websites to ensure that they do not become involved in negotiations to buy or supply any prohibited goods or services. Links to these websites are available at www.heinemann.co.uk/hotlinks (express code 1386P).

Businesses sell less and have unsold stocks and so produce less. You will see how other variables affect the economy later in this section.

All governments want the economy to grow. In other words, they want more goods and services to be produced. This is called **economic growth**. Normally this is good because it means more income and wealth that everyone can share. There may be problems if the economy grows too quickly, as you will see below.

The size of the economy

The size of the economy is measured in three ways – all of which give the same result.

- **Output** – the number of goods and services produced and sold each year (see also page 35).
- **Income** – the value of the goods and services produced and sold each year.
- **Expenditure** – the amount of money that is spent in the economy each year.

At a basic level this is easy to understand if you think of a farmer. His income will depend upon the

output from his farm – and this will determine how much money he can spend. If he wants to spend more, then he has to produce more so that his income increases.

The UK economy falters, however, if demand for our goods and services falls. This can happen because:

- People buy more imported goods.
- People have less money to spend.
- Businesses stop investing and don't buy new equipment.
- The government spends less on public services.

The business cycle

Although the government would like steady, continuous economic growth, this is difficult to achieve. Instead, over time, the economy normally grows, slows down, then dips before it recovers again.

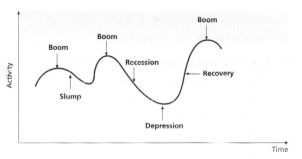

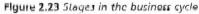

Figure 2.23 *Stages in the business cycle*

Economic boom

A rapid period of growth is known as a **boom**. You may also see reports of the economy 'overheating' when this is happening. During this stage:

- Consumers are spending more.
- Firms are producing as much as they can.
- Businesses are optimistic, profits are good, so they are investing more, too.
- The government is receiving more in tax revenue, paying less in benefits, so can spend more on public services.

Eventually businesses can produce no more without employing more staff – which might not be possible – or investing in far more expensive equipment. They will therefore probably increase the prices of their goods instead. They can do this because demand is higher than supply (see page 148).

There are many benefits in an economic boom. There are plenty of jobs, people are earning money and are prosperous. Businesses are doing well and the government is benefiting, too. So what can go wrong?

One problem is rising prices – because when demand is higher than supply, prices go up. This may not be a problem for people in work, who receive regular pay rises, but can be a disaster for pensioners and anyone else on a fixed income. But workers will object if their pay rises don't keep pace – and demand more – so they can enjoy the same standard of living. This can result in prices going up again – because the firm has to earn even more to afford the increased pay rise.

When price levels go up in an economy, this is known as **inflation**. All governments have a target for inflation. At the start of 2004 in Britain, the target was 2 per cent. If it rises above that, action is taken in one of two ways:

- The Chancellor increases taxes so that people have less money to spend.
- The Bank of England's Monetary Policy Committee (MPC) increases interest rates. This stops people borrowing as much because loans are more expensive. The problem is that businesses also stop borrowing as much – so may cut back on their investments.

Both these methods are often used to slow down the economy. The danger is that they may go too far. People may stop spending and businesses stop investing.

Economic slump

If the economy stops growing and starts to fall, this is known as a **slump**. Spending has slowed down and businesses start to become worried. They are concerned that they have stocks no-one will buy – so start to lower prices. If this works, the economy may pick up again on its own. If it doesn't, the economy may slide into recession.

Recession

A **recession** is a longer period of economic decline. Businesses start to cut back on production

and lay off workers. Consumers have even less money and will reduce their spending still further. Profits are low or non-existent and some businesses may fail. Other businesses will stop investing completely and spend as little as possible. The government finds its tax revenues have fallen and more people are claiming benefits. If the situation continues to worsen, this is known as a **depression**.

Now the government wants to encourage people to spend more, it may therefore:

- Reduce taxes. This gives people more money to spend at a time when prices are low.
- Lower interest rates. This encourages people to borrow because loans are cheap. It also encourages businesses to borrow for expansion too. The government may also borrow money so that it can increase its own spending.

The government will continue taking action until there is an economic **recovery**. It will then monitor this carefully because it is likely to be heading for another boom, when it may have to take action again.

The effect of time lags and confidence

How does the government know what the economy is doing – and how easy is it to 'fine-tune' any problems? Two factors that cause a problem are time lags and confidence.

Time lags

The government knows what the economy is doing because it looks at economic indicators. Unfortunately, many of these are only produced several months after the government has taken action.

- The Office of National Statistics produces quarterly statistics showing whether the economy has grown or not – and by how much. However, these are often adjusted at a later date. So the exact figures may not be known for about six months or more.
- Many business and professional bodies produce figures showing output for their industries – such as the Chartered Institute of

Purchasing and Supply (CIPS) which produces monthly economic reports on manufacturing, construction and service industries. These are often used by the Bank of England's MPC when it is considering interest rate changes.

- Consumer demand and spending can be analysed in several ways – by looking at spending on new cars, in retail shops and stores, the demand for loans, mortgages or new houses. All these figures are collected and analysed regularly and printed in the national press.

- Indicators such as unemployment statistics and inflation figures, collected by government departments and financial institutions and analysed by the Office of National Statistics also give information about other relevant aspects of the economy.

The government has to analyse all this information before it decides to take action. It also has to take account of consumer and business confidence.

Consumer and business confidence

People often behave according to their expectations, rather than reality. For example, if employment is high and there are dozens of good jobs in your area, then you may be very confident that you will have a well-paid job within the next year. This may affect your spending behaviour. If loans are cheap, jobs are plentiful and prices are low then consumers can easily convince themselves that now would be an ideal time to move to a larger house, buy a new car or simply shop till they drop! Similarly, if businesses are confident about the future, they will take on more staff and/or borrow money to expand.

Conversely, if unemployment is rising and people are worried about their job security or if businesses are concerned about future trade then they may cut back on spending – as a precaution rather than just because there is a slump or recession.

For these reasons, confidence has a key role to play in creating an economic boom or slump. Therefore, if the government wants to kick-start the economy or to fuel economic growth it will often 'talk up' the economy and prospects for Britain. If it is worried about the economy overheating, it may threaten to take action and issue a few warnings to reduce confidence.

Many employer organisations – such as the Confederation of British Industry (CBI) – regularly canvass their members to assess levels of business optimism. The government will monitor these surveys closely. It is aware that falling business confidence, whether justified or not, can have a serious effect on the economy.

Indications from the housing market

The housing market is important because it often reflects economic booms and slumps. During a boom, demand for houses increases. In a slump or a recession, demand falls. The housing market can also be affected by government interference in the economy – as the previous Conservative Government discovered to their cost. To understand this, it is important to know what happened.

In the early 1980s, the economy was booming. House prices rose every year. A house bought for £100,000 in 1983 would have been worth nearly £225,000 by the end of 1989! In 1988 and 1989 alone, prices rose by over 20 per cent each year. House owners were very confident because they could see their wealth increasing each year, so they started to borrow money against the value of their house. In May 1988, interest rates were only 7.5 per cent so this made financial sense. Some borrowed money to move to more expensive houses.

The government was concerned at the rising prices and took action to 'cool down' the economy by raising interest rates several times. At first there was no response, so it increased interest rates again – and again. Unfortunately, the government didn't wait for the early increases to have an effect. Between May 1988 and September 1990 interest rates were increased six times – to a high of 15 per cent. This had a dramatic, but delayed effect. House prices started to fall rapidly and by 1992 were falling at 6 per cent a year.

House prices rise when demand for houses is high

Homeowners now had to make huge mortgage payments on houses which were falling in value. In some cases, they owed more than their house was worth – a situation known as **negative equity**. Many people couldn't meet their mortgage payments and had to sell up. Even then, because their house was worth less, they still owed money.

The Government then reduced interest rates – bit by bit. It moved them down from 14 per cent at the end of 1990 to a low of 5.25 per cent in 1994. Because it did this very slowly, there was no immediate effect. In fact, it wasn't until 1996 that the housing market started to recover.

Since then housing prices have increased again. In 2003, the increase was about 17 per cent and interest rates remained low at under 4 per cent. This fuelled another boom in consumer spending. The government, however, didn't want to repeat the mistakes of the 1980s. It wanted to cool the housing market down – but not cause another slump.

Experts also said that there is another key factor to consider about housing prices in the UK. The main problem, they argued, was supply and demand. Quite simply, there aren't enough houses to go around. The government is therefore trying to make it easier to build new, affordable housing. As you know, if supply increases this will help to reduce prices, or slow down price rises, in a much more controlled way than changing interest rates. If you have forgotten why, look back at page 148!

The impact of interest rate changes on business

Businesses want interest rates to be as low as possible for two reasons:

- **Consumers will spend more**. They will be more prepared to borrow money in order to finance large purchases and, because mortgage payments will be lower, they will have more disposable income to spend. This means they will buy more goods and services – so businesses will increase their profits.
- **Business borrowing will be cheaper**. This means that banks will charge less for business loans and overdraft charges will also fall. This makes it cheaper for businesses to borrow money to expand.

If interest rates rise, businesses have to work out how much this will cost them on increased loan repayments and overdraft charges. It will also make them think twice about future loans – especially if they think consumer spending will also slow down.

The impact of interest rates on consumers

Between 1999 and 2003, consumer borrowing on credit cards rose from £29.7 billion to £52.7 billion – an all time high of over 120 per cent of disposable income. Many consumers borrowed because the value of their house had risen. They were confident that they could always use this increased wealth to pay off their debts if necessary. This fuelled a consumer spending boom which benefited businesses.

There is a problem. Borrowed money has to be repaid at some point and, if interest rates increase, many households could be in serious trouble. Their service payments (the amount paid in interest and debt repayments) would rise to an unacceptable proportion of their income.

The Bank of England's MPC can increase interest rates to stop customers borrowing as much, but this stops them spending. Yet, if interest rates stay the same, consumers may continue to borrow even more. If you were on the MPC, what would you do?

The impact of changing tax rates on business

Businesses want tax rates to be low. They want corporation tax to be low, so that they pay less tax on their profits. They also don't want VAT rates to rise above their current level of 17.5 per cent

---

Business brief

The budget – government spending, tax and borrowing

Twice a year the Chancellor of the Exchequer announces his budget. The main budget statement is in March, with a 'mini' budget statement each December. The budget states how much the Chancellor intends to spend each year and the government's priorities. It also states how the Chancellor intends to raise money. He can do this in two ways – by tax or by borrowing.

The most well known taxes are **income tax**, paid by employees and **National Insurance** (NI) paid by employees and employers. Businesses also pay **corporation tax** on their profits and **VAT** on their sales – although they can reclaim VAT they have paid on their own purchases. Other taxes include inheritance tax (payable when people die); stamp duty (paid when buying a house or shares) and excise duty, (the extra tax paid on petrol, cigarettes and alcohol). Council tax is paid to local councils, not to the government. Businesses don't pay council tax, but **business rates**. This is similar, but is a tax on business property in a local area.

No-one likes paying tax. In addition, tax reduces the amount people can spend, so governments have to be careful. Too many increases could result in them losing the next election – and trigger a slump in the economy.

If the Chancellor therefore needs more money, but dare not raise taxes again, he has to borrow money instead. In November 2003, he announced higher borrowing plans for the next five years. This was because government spending had increased, tax revenues had fallen (because people's income and business's profits were lower than he had estimated) yet he didn't want to increase taxes any further.

because this would result in a general increase in the prices they charge to customers – which may lower sales.

National Insurance is often called a 'tax on employment'. It is paid by both the employee and employer. In March 2003, National Insurance increased by 1 per cent (1p in the £). Most employees now have to pay 11 per cent of their weekly income in National Insurance and most employers have to pay 12.8 per cent. The increase was needed to fund increased spending on the National Health Service. Companies objected because it cost more to employ staff. Self-employed people objected because they pay NI out of their profits.

Businesses also don't want income tax rates to increase because this will mean consumers have less disposable income and will then spend less.

Finally, businesses are concerned if business rates increase, because this means they will pay more money to the local council in tax.

Central and local government spending

In the budget year 2003/4, the Government estimated it would spend £427.3 billion. By time we reach 2007/8, the Government thinks it will spend approximately £528 billion. Where does this money go to – and how do government spending plans affect businesses?

Broadly, the government has to allocate money for:

- Each department and departmental priorities, e.g. Education and Health.
- Its own spending on rent, goods and services.
- The grant it gives to local authorities each year.
- Benefit payments, grants and subsidies.

In the Budget – and in the Queen's Speech each November – the government's priorities and plans are announced. Similarly, every spring, each local council will fix its budget and announce its spending plans. Businesses watch these closely to identify any announcements that will affect their own industry or region.

For example, in 2002, the government announced that spending on the National Health Service would rise by 43 per cent over the next 5 years – an equivalent of £40 billion. Everyone employed in the health service was interested in this announcement – as was the general public, being potential patients. But there are also a large number of businesses that depend upon the NHS as a customer. You only have to think for one moment about all the resources needed by a hospital! Drugs and medical equipment are two obvious examples – but then you can add surgical supplies, dressings, catering supplies, linen – the list is almost endless! All these businesses were interested in the government's announcement because it affected their future prospects.

A summary of the main macroeconomic aspects that businesses consider is given in the table opposite. Most of these affect businesses in one way or another, so changes in the economy and the Chancellor's statements are continually monitored by all business organisations.

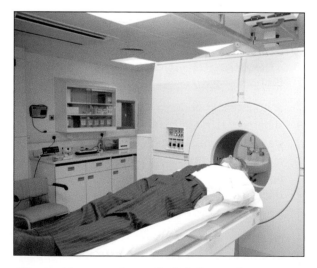

The need for expensive medical equipment has increased overall spending on the NHS

Macroeconomic variables that affect businesses

- Business cycles – booms, recessions, slumps, depressions and economic recovery
- Interest rates
- Inflation
- Tax rates and changes in taxation
- Central government spending plans
- Local government spending plans
- Reports on consumer spending (linked to employment, confidence, housing prices, size of disposable income)
- Reports on business confidence
- Exchange rates (particularly relevant for firms importing/exporting)

Business terms

Economic growth An increase in the production of a nation's goods and services.

Disposable income The amount of income individuals can spend after essential bills have been paid.

Economic boom A period during which the economy grows and expands.

Economic slump A short downturn in the economy.

Recession A period during which the economy contracts and declines.

Depression A serious and lengthy economic recession.

Economic recovery A period when the economy starts to expand.

Inflation A general increase in prices within the economy.

Base rate The interest rate set by the Bank of England's Monetary Policy Committee

Interest rates The cost of borrowing money from a financial institution.

Exchange rates The price at which one currency is exchanged for another.

Business brief

The impact of exchange rates on business

Your local newsagent is unlikely to be interested in the value of the pound – until the holiday season. A large business that regularly imports goods from abroad – or sells goods abroad – will have a different view.

Exchange rates relate to the value of the pound, i.e. how much you get when you change your pounds into another currency, such as Euros or American dollars. You need to change pounds when you are going on holiday. If the pound is strong, then you will do well. This means your holiday is cheaper. If the pound is weak then you won't get as many Euros or dollars – so your holiday is much dearer.

Businesses that import goods – like Richer Sounds – prefer a strong pound, too. This is because imports like DVD players are cheaper. So they benefit, and so do you, if you are buying from them.

Businesses which export goods prefer a weak pound. This is because their customers abroad need to spend less, in their own currencies, to buy from them. Because goods are cheaper abroad it is likely that they will sell more.

Talking point

View 1: Taxes should be kept as low as possible because this rewards people for working hard and gives them more money to spend, which in turn helps businesses.

View 2: Taxes are important because without them we wouldn't have essential public services like the NHS, education, defence and social services. Paying more tax means these services can be better for everyone.

With which viewpoint do you agree – and why?

1 A shopkeeper wants to expand and needs to borrow £20,000 to do this. He has the choice of a fixed rate loan of 8 per cent over 6 years or a variable interest rate loan over 5 years, starting at 6 per cent. Only with the second loan are there no penalties if he repays the money earlier.

  a Which factors should the shopkeeper consider when making his decision about the best loan to choose?

  b As a group, suggest one advantage and one disadvantage of choosing a fixed rate loan.

  c How will business confidence – or lack of it – affect the shopkeeper's decision?

2 The Bank of England has just announced an increase in base rates of 0.5 per cent and the Chancellor has said that VAT will go up by 1.5 per cent from next April.

  a At which point of the business cycle are these announcements likely to be made – and why?

  b Interest rates normally only increase by 0.25 per cent or 0.5 per cent at a time. Suggest why this is the case.

  c What do you think would be the reaction by each of the following – and why?

   i A manufacturer who has just borrowed money to build a new warehouse.

   ii A large retail firm.

   iii A retired couple who own their own home and have saved carefully for the past few years.

   iv A young working couple who want to buy a house.

3 Suggest two types of businesses that would be affected by each of the following government announcements.

  a Increased spending on defence and military equipment.

  b A complete embargo on travel and trade with an African country.

  c A smoking ban in all public places where workers could be affected by passive smoke.

  d Three new prisons to be built.

  e More money to be spent on the railways and less on road building for environmental reasons.

  f Increased security checks at all public buildings.

4 Look back at the summary tables of political and macroeconomic issues that concern businesses on pages 173 and 181. Check with your tutor if there are any terms or issues that you don't understand. Then select two from each table that you think would be important for each of the following businesses and give a reason for each of your choices.

  a An entrepreneur just starting a retail business in your town.

  b A large manufacturing company selling equipment worldwide.

  c A large chain of superstores buying supplies from many countries.

  d A national haulage company.

  e An estate agent.

Compare your ideas with other members of your group.

Social issues and their impact

You have already seen that businesses are concerned about social trends and how these affect the buying habits of consumers. Current trends include more working women, people getting married later and people living longer. Our attitudes to work and leisure all affect the way we spend money. So, too, do lifestyle changes – such as people taking more exercise, preferring organic food and giving up smoking – and fashions or fads, like the popularity of the Atkins Diet.

Businesses are also concerned about social issues that will affect them, especially if the tide of social opinion will affect their future prospects or customer relations. Examples of issues include:

- **The quality of products** – from safety to their content or ingredients.
- **Social injustice** – from poor treatment of workers to excessive rises in directors' pay.
- **Other areas of concern** – such as unfair pricing, health scares, product testing on animals and the transportation of live animals.

The GM debate

Genetically modified (GM) foods are those that have been genetically changed by scientists. At present, GM crops are grown in 16 countries of the world, including the USA, Canada, China, India and South Africa. The main GM crops are soya beans, maize, cotton and oilseed rape. Field trials of GM oilseed rape started in the UK in 1989 but were discontinued after public protests, until more was known about the crops. Imported GM crops are soya and maize – found in processed food and used in animal feeds. GM food sold in the UK must be labelled but foods from animals fed on GM foods need not be labelled.

In 2003 the Government tried to test the views of the public with a national GM debate. It concluded that 4 out of 5 people were against GM crops – although this figure was disputed by the University of East Anglia which had carried out its own research. Its findings were that 36 per cent opposed GM food, 13 per cent supported it and 39 per cent had no strong feelings either way.

Like many social/business issues, some people argue that people are always more important than profits; others claim that it is possible to make profits responsibly and without endangering anyone. In the meantime, many supermarkets have removed all GM products from their shelves and announced a 'non-GM' food policy. According to Greenpeace, the best of these is Marks & Spencer. Many supermarkets fail the test because they cannot guarantee that animal and dairy products are not GM free, because the animals may be fed on GM crops.

In 2004, the Government announced that it had decided to agree to the growth of the first crop of GM maize in Britain given that there was no scientific case for an outright ban on cultivation. You can read more at the GM Nation, Greenpeace, Monsanto and GM Jury websites – links to these sites are available at www.heinemann.co.uk/hotlinks (express code 1386P). A summary of the opposing views is given below. As you read it, try to identify the social versus profit argument.

The argument for	The argument against
GM crops can be developed which can grow in harsh conditions and provide greater yields.	GM crops are untried and untested, no-one knows their eventual affects.
GM crops are more resistant to pests so therefore less harmful spraying is required.	GM crops adversely affect natural plants and wildlife.
GM crops are a way of providing more food, more profitably to millions of people, and can feed the third world.	Cross-pollination can contaminate non-GM crops nearby.
GM foods are carefully and thoroughly tested and regulated and current GM foods are at least as safe as non-GM foods, if not more so.	In the third world, poor subsistence farmers do not grow GM crops. They need more resources to grow other crops.
	The growth of GM is mainly in the interests of large companies, like Monsanto, which is responsible for over 90% of current GM crops.

Figure 2.24 *GM foods – the debate*

Product quality

By law, every product you buy must be safe to use. If you bought a jug kettle which exploded or a hairdryer which overheated then you would have a case, in law, against the manufacturer. If you bought a toy as a present and it was later found to be capable of causing injury, then the product may be withdrawn from sale. This happened when retailers were prevented from selling Yo Balls by the Department of Trade and Industry after a strangulation hazard was identified. On other occasions, retailers themselves recall the products when they find that safety standards have not been met. For example Next recalled its baby girl diamante trainers when it discovered that the diamantes could come off and pose a choking hazard.

Many products we buy, however, may not be safe for other reasons. If you are on a low fat or low salt diet – or have a gluten or nut allergy – you need to be able to trust the labels on the food you buy. Consumers are alarmed when they read that many claims such as 'reduced fat' or 'low sugar' are relatively meaningless. They are also worried when they read that some food additives can cause health problems, or about meat products which are confiscated by inspectors as being unfit to be sold. Concern following BSE and variant CJD seriously affected the red meat trade in Britain and many shoppers will now only buy organic meat or meat products which have the source clearly stated.

Social issues normally result when consumers have assumed products will be safe but later find out there are serious concerns. One of the key areas relating to product quality in recent years has involved GM foods (see page 183). This highlights many concerns that consumers worry about – and the type of responses these provoke.

Social injustice

Social injustice occurs when a group of people are treated unfairly – such as when many of the 2,500 employees at The Accident Group found out by text message that the business was insolvent and that they had lost their jobs. Most didn't receive their final pay and were told that their benefits may not be paid because their National Insurance

Business matters

You may have been concerned about safety when you are buying food but how many times have you thought about safety when you were buying other items – like shampoo, shower gel, washing up liquid or even pyjamas?

In November 2003, Greenpeace publicised the fact that certain Disney children's pyjamas contained toxic chemicals including phthalates, which can cause damage to human organs. As a result, Disney stores, Debenhams and Mothercare withdrew the pyjamas from sale.

The EU is proposing to introduce new legislation to regulate the use of chemicals, called REACH. Under this law, if a company uses a hazardous chemical when a safer alternative exists, then it must stop using it. The aim is to remove all unnecessary toxic products from supermarket shelves, but campaigners are concerned that the chemical industry may try to weaken the regulations because they will be expensive to implement.

If you want to find out more about the chemicals currently in the products you buy – and which products are the safest, go to The Chemical Home page on the Greenpeace website – a link is available at www.heinemann.co.uk/hotlinks (express code 1386P).

contributions hadn't been made properly. The employees were further incensed by newspaper pictures of their former boss sunning himself on his luxury yacht in Spain. Since then the TUC and the administrators, Pricewaterhouse Coopers, who have the job of winding up the company, have obtained redundancy payments for the staff and the law has been changed to prevent employees being sacked unexpectedly by text message. In addition, legal action may be taken against the directors in this situation.

Fortunately, this is a relatively rare example, which is why it made the headlines. Most businesses have a far more responsible attitude towards their employees and policies in place to make sure that all staff are treated fairly. However, they are well aware that the actions of an irresponsible few can affect public opinion – such as the label of 'fat cats' to greedy directors or those who decide to pay themselves massive bonuses whilst paying low wages.

Other social issues

It is important to remember that while there are many social issues that concern people, the types of issues that will affect one business will have no relevance to another. Food producers may be criticised for product labelling and banks for their ethical investments (or lack of them) but both these areas wouldn't be an issue for your local hospital – which will be more concerned about health scares and reports relating to the MRSA superbug.

Therefore, as you look through some of the recent social trends or issues listed in Figure 2.25, think about the industries to which they would relate – in preparation for the Over to You! section on page 188.

Environmental issues

Environmental issues often overlap with social issues when they relate to public opinion. Many pressure groups, such as Greenpeace and Friends of the Earth frequently run campaigns which cover both areas.

In recent years there has been an increase in the number of environmental laws and regulations with which businesses must comply, related to:

- **Emissions** from manufacturing processes that can cause air pollution.
- **Noise pollution** from machinery and equipment.
- **Water pollution** through the uncontrolled discharge of toxic or hazardous substances.
- The **disposal of waste**, particularly toxic or hazardous materials, such as chemicals, and the type of waste which can be put in landfill sites.
- The use of **packaging and packing waste**.

Business brief

The 'fat cat' issue

Salaries for top directors often make the headlines, but it is important to realise that being paid a high salary is not socially unjust on its own. Otherwise there should be similar press headlines about the salaries paid to professional footballers and pop stars! In fact, it is easy to argue that a responsible and hardworking leader of a successful business, such as Richard Branson, who has created thousands of jobs for his employees, deserves his financial rewards more than stars like David Beckham or Robbie Williams.

The issue becomes contentious when directors appear to be greedy or cheating the workforce or, even worse, doing both at the same time. Therefore, a senior director's pay rise at a time when business is booming, jobs are safe and staff are receiving pay rises is fine – particularly if the success is largely due to the efforts of that director. Taking the same action when business is struggling is quite different. This is why the five directors at the parent company of MG Rover were criticised in the press when they gave

themselves a 300 per cent pay rise at a time when the company had lost £95 million and the pay rise to the workforce was only 2.2 per cent.

The TUC and other unions are keen to highlight social injustices in pay between directors and staff, the government, too, has vowed to take action about executives of failing companies getting huge pay-offs or golden handshakes. The Department of Trade and Industry (DTI) have said that in future, bosses' pay-offs should reflect their performance in the company. How successful it will be in enforcing this is another story.

Social trends

- Size of population and population changes (e.g. people living longer)
- Standard of living linked to average wages and distribution of income linked to tax and benefits
- Education – including university tuition fees and more graduates
- Increasing ethnic mix in Britain
- Changing patterns of work including more home and flexible hours of working
- Increased standards of living
- Changing lifestyles including Sunday shopping, more vegetarians/vegans, fitness culture, drinking and driving no longer legal/acceptable etc.
- Increase in Internet use and online shopping

Social issues

- Product quality including safety, chemical content, food labelling etc
- Directors' pay issues, workers' rights and unethical practices (see section 2.3, pages 159–164)
- Garden products and weedkillers which contain dangerous chemicals or are not environmentally friendly
- Fish farming – criticism of the conditions, the methods of killing and the safety of farmed fish for consumers
- Testing on live animals for cosmetics and other non-medical reasons
- Testing of potentially life-saving drugs on live animals
- Animal welfare, e.g. the transport of live animals in cramped conditions
- Health scares, such as DVT on long haul flights, superbugs (MRSA) in hospitals, Legionnaire's disease through substandard air conditioning systems, food poisoning etc.
- The safety of public transport, e.g. the railways and the London underground
- Crime and safety of individuals.
- Smoking and the effects of passive smoking on employees
- High levels of saturated fats or salt in food

Figure 2.25 *Social trends and social issues that affect business*

- The **scrapping and recycling of items** such as refrigerators (because of CFCs) and other items.

Responsible businesses undertake an **environmental audit** to check their sources of supply and how they are storing and using resources, including energy. Many publish **green policies**, confirming that they use biodegradable packaging, recycle where possible, source their goods from 'green' suppliers and use energy responsibly.

Despite all these actions many people are concerned that too little is being done. In a report to the United Nations, the Intergovernmental Panel on Climate Change forecast that the average surface temperature on earth would rise by about 6.5 degrees by 2100 and sea levels would also rise. It believed that the only way to protect the environment is to change the current system of mass production, mass consumption and mass waste to one that focuses on preserving natural resources. In addition, industry should aim at zero emissions of global warming gases, such as carbon dioxide, and zero discharge of wastes. This needs every government's involvement and the cooperation of industry. It also needs consumers to change their current 'use and throw away' behaviour.

Carbon dioxide is released into the atmosphere when fossil fuels are burned to produce energy. To reduce these emissions, by 2020 the Government wants all electricity supply companies in Britain to obtain 20 per cent of their energy from renewable sources. It also wants to cut carbon dioxide emissions by 20 per cent by 2010, which spells the end for coal-fired power stations that still account for 35 per cent of British power. This means obtaining far more energy from wind power, solar power, from the earth (called geothermal power) or from water – either hydroelectric power or by

Business brief

Britain's energy dilemma

The way energy is produced today is shown in the pie chart below.

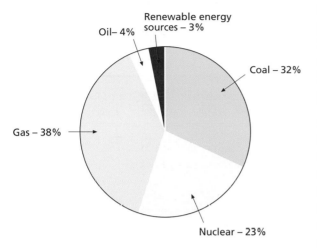

UK energy sources in 2003

Gas and oil resources are becoming more scarce, coal creates carbon dioxide emissions which contribute to environmental problems. Many people think nuclear energy is too dangerous and are very concerned about nuclear waste (see below). In 2003, the Government announced that no new British nuclear power stations would be built *at the moment* – but it has a problem. By 2023 all but one nuclear power station will be closed because

they will be too old. The final one will close in 2035. This means that by 2023, Britain may have to buy much of its energy from abroad. If this happens prices are likely to rise. The Institute of Civil Engineers also warns that there could be supply problems if there were political upheavals or terrorist attacks and forecast that unless immediate action is taken, power cuts could be common in Britain in 20 years' time. This could force the government to rethink its nuclear power policies.

An associated problem is the issue of reprocessing nuclear waste, which is an undesirable by-product of nuclear fuel. Environmentalists are also concerned about wider issues – such as how nuclear weapons and submarines are decommissioned – particularly in areas of the world without the technical expertise or money to do this properly, and how nuclear waste is treated in these regions. This is important because many other countries are expanding their nuclear energy programmes.

If you want to know more, a summary of the main pros and cons of nuclear power is given in Figure 2.26. You can also find out more about the UK nuclear industry at the DTI Energy, UKAEA, Greenpeace and Friends of the Earth websites – links are available at www.heinemann.co.uk/hotlinks (express code 1386P).

The argument for	The argument against
Nuclear power is cheap and efficient	There is no safe way of permanently disposing of or storing nuclear waste
Britain may have power shortages in the future unless nuclear power is an option	Nuclear waste remains toxic for centuries
Britain is unlikely to meet its target on reducing greenhouse gas emissions without nuclear power	Transporting nuclear waste is hazardous and risky
Well built power plants are clean and safe	Badly built or maintained plants have caused major disasters at Chernobyl and Three Mile Island
Less radioactivity is released into the atmosphere from nuclear plants than by burning fossil fuels in coal-fired power plants	There have been health scares in areas near to nuclear plants, such as at Sellafield
	Dismantling or decommissioning nuclear sites is expensive and dangerous

Figure 2.26 *The nuclear debate*

harnessing the energy from the tide or waves. All these methods are safe, environmentally friendly and do not use up scarce resources. The problem is one of size and investment. It takes a hundred 24-turbine wind farms to generate the same amount of power as a nuclear power station – and this is when the wind is blowing. In addition, there are concerns that the low frequency noise they produce could be harmful to people who live nearby. Tide or wave power is more reliable, and has fewer critics, but it costs a lot of money to build these power stations.

A summary of some of the main environmental aspects that businesses consider is given in Figure 2.27. Remember that, again, a business will focus on the key issues that could affect it – and these will depend upon its main activity and its scope of operations.

Environmental issues that affect businesses

- Regulations to limit pollution by air, noise or water
- Packaging regulations
- Waste disposal regulations (e.g. restrictions on landfill sites)
- Recycling initiatives and use of recyclable materials
- Resource use to save energy and scarce resources
- Protection of threatened species, e.g. certain hardwoods, fish quotas etc.
- Sourcing products responsibly, e.g. only buying tuna that has been caught using dolphin friendly nets, not using paper made from pulped Indonesian rainforests, not using hardwoods for furniture etc.

Figure 2.27 *Environmental issues affecting businesses*

Over to you!

1 The government has told businesses that they must not invent meaningless 'green' slogans when they have done nothing to improve the way a product is made or sourced. Defra (the Department for the Environment, Food and Rural Affairs) has issued a shopper's guide to explain the green symbols you now see in shops. As a group, decide which of the following claims it said are meaningless and which are real – then check your answers with your tutor.

a Made with care for the environment.

b Made from 100 per cent recycled paper.

c Made from recycled renewable resources.

d Environmentally friendly.

e Kind to the environment.

f Sustainable timber produced from a well-managed forest.

g Biodegradable.

h After use the ingredients used in this product rapidly biodegrade to water, CO_2 and mineral salts.

i This wood comes from well-managed forests independently certified in accordance with the rules of the Forest Stewardship Council.

j Tissues that don't cost the earth.

2 a Look back at the table listing social trends and social issues on page 186. Identify **one** trend and **one** type of issue which would concern each of the following types of businesses. Then compare your ideas with other members of your group.

  i A taxi firm.

  ii A travel agent.

  iii A garden centre.

  iv A cosmetics manufacturer.

b A large hotel wants to ensure that it takes account of current social trends and concerns about social issues. As a group, suggest **five** social trends which could affect it and suggest how it might want to adjust its operations.

3 Product safety is so important that several websites give updates of current problems, such as the BBC Watchdog, UK Recall Notice and Recall Announcements websites – links to these sites are available at www.heinemann.co.uk/hotlinks (express code 1386P).

a Use **one** of these websites to find **three** examples of products which have recently been recalled – with reasons.

b Suggest **two** reasons why companies need to act quickly if a product is found to be faulty.

Talking point

View 1: It's up to businesses to kick-start environmental improvements by making repairable products and reducing packaging. They should also stop making throwaway items like disposable nappies and paper tissues.

View 2: Businesses will always put profits before the environment so it's up to consumers to refuse to buy throwaway items and to insist that faulty goods are repaired.

With which viewpoint do you agree – and why?

The impact of changing technology

Technology affects the way we work and live – and the way in which business is carried out. In addition, it also presents opportunities for businesses to make new products and to do business in new ways – from creating and storing documents to buying and selling their products and receiving payments.

Generally businesses – like schools and colleges – take advantage of new technology as much as possible but can only do that within current budgets. Therefore they might not be as 'leading edge' as they would like. As a quick guide, you can check out how near your college is to the 'tomorrow' scenario in Figure 2.28 – and any business where you work part-time!

Today you are used to living in a world where you can communicate with people immediately by mobile phone or instant messaging, send a photo to a friend in Australia in a second, research information quickly on the Internet, buy a

	Classroom	Business
Yesterday	Blackboard, pens and paper	Typewriters, filing cabinets, sending documents by post, manual purchasing, selling face-to-face or by mail order, receiving/issuing cheques. Advertising in press/on TV. Face to face meetings. Manual diaries. Finger-dialled telephones
Today	Interactive whiteboards, separate IT suites. Text messages to absent students	Computers/laptops, electronic data storage, email, electronic purchasing over Internet (e-procurement), website, selling online, receiving e-payments, banking online, new media advertising (see page 68). Some video conferencing. Use of PDAs (electronic organisers) and electronic diaries. 'Smart' telephones
Tomorrow	Wi-Fi in classrooms and whiteboards and laptops = flexible Internet access. Digital tracking of absent students by means of tracking chips and satellite navigation technology!	Wi-Fi environment (no cables), interconnectivity of all systems/devices, integrated electronic filing and data storage, videophones, video conferencing from all PCs. Light projected keyboards, paper thin monitors, ultra-fast broadband, intelligent voice recognition software, intelligent PCs that learn by doing. 3G mobiles

Figure 2.28 *Technological changes*

birthday present online, download music files and burn CDs. How do these developments translate to the business world?

Design developments

Computers play a major role in the design and development of many products and systems. Computer Aided Design (CAD) packages aid engineers to design, simulate and test products such as cars, boats and planes, which reduces the need to produce physical models to test. For example, aerodynamics forms a major part of the design of a Formula 1 racing car. Optimising the car's aerodynamics allows it to travel faster around a circuit. The aerodynamics of the car can be studied and refined using specialist software packages so there is less need to produce costly models for testing in a wind tunnel.

Software can also be used to plan new road and building layouts. In 2003, researchers at the University of Greenwich won a European prize for their new program Exodus which helps design engineers to improve safety in buildings, on planes and anywhere else where there may be an emergency. It simulates how people react in these situations – including some of the irrational decisions they make, such as returning to collect personal belongings in a fire.

Production developments

Production systems today are frequently controlled and monitored by Computer Aided Manufacturing (CAM) or Computer Integrated Manufacturing (CIM) software which integrates the design and manufacturing process (see Unit 1, page 75). Today many CAD packages (see above) are both CAD/CAM – as the data generated when the item is designed is then be used to inform and control the manufacturing process.

Developments in robotics means that many dirty, dangerous or purely repetitive production operations are no longer carried out by humans. In the medical world, robots can be programmed to help to carry out complex operations. Honda has been working on the production of humanoid robots since 1986. In 2004, Asimo, the latest version, arrived in Britain for a short stay at the

Science Museum. Asimo is different because it can respond to changes in its environment, such as trying to keep its balance if it is pushed. It is also being developed to recognise people, calculate distance, identify sounds and respond to instructions. Robotic assistance in the home for the elderly or infirm is then a firm possibility within the next ten years, according to Honda.

Scientific and technological developments are also revolutionising the diagnosis and treatment of illnesses and diseases – from MRI (magnetic resonance imaging) scanners to genetic research and nanotechnology.

Communication developments

Communications have changed out of all recognition thanks to mobile phones, email and high-speed broadband access which means data, voice and graphics files can be sent and downloaded quickly and easily from one person to another. This has enabled far more people to work from home, and for collaborative working to take place between people all over the world.

Today, more computer systems and hardware devices are compatible with each other. This means that data, graphics and sound can be transferred to and from computers and between other devices either locally or over the Internet. For example, you can capture photos on a digital camera, download them to your PC and then email them to your friends around the world. These developments have affected many businesses. Journalists can take photos and transmit their reports from a laptop computer almost regardless of where they are working. The same technology enables engineers to send pictures of technical problems to specialists for advice, and property companies to include 'virtual tours' on their websites. Businesses can put film clips of promotions and important meetings on their websites for customers and shareholders. 'Virtual teams' can be formed that work together on a business project, sharing files and information even though they may be thousands of miles apart. In all these cases, the systems used must be able to communicate with each other in terms of their hardware, software, communications systems and methods of transferring data. This integration of systems, sometimes referred to as **digital interconnectivity** or interoperability, is an important consideration for technical computer staff and a key area of development amongst computer designers.

In addition to revolutionising communications, the Internet has also changed other commercial activities, from buying and selling goods to banking. Goods can be purchased and paid for online (called **e-procurement**) and sold online. A company website can be linked to the stock database so that customers can view products in stock and pay for their goods online using a credit or debit card. Online banking means that, apart from physically paying in cash or withdrawing it, all business transactions can be done online and money can be transferred around the world at the touch of a few keys. You will learn more about this if you study specialist Unit 8.

Business matters

The era when computers and monitors are ugly boxes, linked by unsightly cables, is rapidly coming to an end. New wafer thin screens add the designer edge and create more desk space. Bluetooth devices that communicate by radio chips, through doors and walls, mean that information can be transmitted between computers and other devices, like remote printers, without a wire in sight.

Wi-Fi (short for Wireless Fidelity) does even more. It enables you to communicate with the Internet without cables. Experts predict that 90 per cent of laptops will have Wi-Fi by 2006 so that their owners can use them in pubs, clubs, restaurants, coffee houses, hotels, airports, on the train – almost anywhere you can imagine.

Wi-Fi works by connecting devices using wireless networks. **Wi-Fi hotspots** are areas which are served by a network. Anyone using a laptop or a 3G mobile in a hot spot is instantly online – with very high speed access. The first place to offer this facility was a Starbucks café in San Francisco – but by December 2003 Wi-Fi was operational at over 3,000 sites in the UK.

Changing legislation and its impact

The Government is constantly introducing new laws or revising current laws. In addition, it must take account of certain decisions made by the European Union and introduce EU regulations and directives on specific issues, including equal pay, employee rights, human rights and health and safety.

Probably the most dynamic area is employment law, with frequent changes and amendments. Many employees benefited when the National Minimum Wage Act was introduced. The Working Time Directive then limited the number of hours most employees could work and specified a minimum paid holiday entitlement of four weeks for full-time employees. Since then, further laws have been passed to ensure that part-time workers are treated equally fairly.

Discrimination on grounds of gender, race or disability has been illegal for some time, although these laws have been amended since they were first introduced. In 2003 new laws made discrimination unlawful in relation to religious beliefs and sexual orientation. From 2006 it will also be unlawful on grounds of age. The employment of young workers is now regulated – so that you cannot do night work if you are under 18 and must not work more than 8 hours a day or 40 hours a week.

Constant legal changes can make life very difficult for businesses – particularly those which are only small and do not employ legal specialists to advise them. As one example, in December 2003, the Privacy and Electronic Communications Regulations came into force in the UK. These stated that businesses could now only send emails to people who had given their active consent, such as their own customers. They could no longer contact potential customers by 'buying in' a database of contacts and sending out emails. The aim was to prevent **spam emails**. In addition, customers must be informed if any websites use **cookies** to collect information from them and be allowed to 'opt out' if they wish. Any business which didn't know about the Regulations and

The constantly changing face of employment law

At a glance, employment law changes so quickly and so often, it is almost impossible for businesses to keep pace. You will learn more about this area if you study specialist Unit 5. However, a 'birds eye' view of some recent changes is given below.

- **1996 The Employment Rights Act** – gave all employees the right to a written contract within two months of starting work, covered maternity leave, the right to 'opt out' of Sunday working, the right to a minimum period of notice depending upon length of employment and the right to redundancy pay after two years' continuous employment. Many of these rights were extended later through the Maternity and Parental Leave Regulations and amendments.
- **1999 The Employment Relations Act** – improved maternity leave, introduced parental leave and gave workers the right to take time off in a family emergency. Further changes are

being made to include a 'no surprises culture' so that employees must be consulted about key decisions that affect them, such as redundancies. This will stop any repeats of employees being sacked by text message (see page 184). Further changes, probably to parental leave, are expected in 2006.

- **2002 The Employment Act** – introduced 'family friendly policies' and the right to request flexible hours, outlawed discrimination against temporary workers and also covered the ways in which disputes should be resolved at work. All businesses must now have formal grievance and disciplinary procedures. Employers and employees must follow these before any ongoing disputes are referred to an Employment Tribunal. This protects employers from unreasonable claims and gives more protection to employees when the correct procedures aren't followed – or none exist.

carried on as normal could be sued for compensation.

Many employer organisations, such as the Federation of Small Businesses and the Confederation of British Industry, complain that the burden of all these changes on many businesses is too much – as it is their responsibility to take note of any new laws which affect them and alter their business practices accordingly.

This is just one area where legislation is constantly changing. Others are listed in Figure 2.29.

Other external influences and crisis management

During 2003, many large banks with online services found themselves under attack through an email scam. Some of their customers received emails, asking for confirmation of their account details. The emails were designed to look as if they came from the banks themselves. A few customers were fooled into giving their details – which

- Laws relating to the formation of partnerships and companies and how they operate.
- Health and safety law and regulations.
- Employment law.
- Consumer protection laws and product safety.
- Laws to prevent money laundering, which require financial institutions to check the identity of their customers.
- The role of the Competition Commission to prevent monopolies.
- Data protection legislation – which limits the type of information a business can hold on its customers or employees and how it is used.
- Laws relating to computer use/misuse and sending 'spam' emails.
- Laws which affect methods of work, e.g. the prohibition on using handheld mobile phones when driving. Employers could be prosecuted if they ask employees to disregard the law.

Figure 2.29 *Legal changes that affect businesses*

enabled fraudsters to access their accounts. At the time, many of the large banks – Barclays, Nationwide, Halifax, NatWest and Lloyds TSB – were criticised for not reacting quickly enough and not posting warnings up on their sites. Although all have since done so, and tightened up their security procedures, there was concern that this type of activity could seriously undermine confidence in online banking. This is a key reason why businesses have to respond promptly if there are external events that could threaten their reputation – so that customer confidence won't be eroded resulting in a fall in sales.

Disasters and crises may strike any business. They can include:

- **Natural disasters** – such as floods or earthquakes.
- **Man-made disasters** – such as plane crashes or terrorist attacks.
- **Internal crises** – such as serious product defects, website failure or other technology problems (e.g. hackers or viruses), allegations of fraud or unfair customer practices.
- **Major stock market fluctuations** or a stock market crash – which affects the value of their business.
- **Major business failures** and corporate scandals – such as Enron and WorldCom.

Wise businesses normally prepare for these events by taking precautions and having a plan of action to follow in these types of situations. This includes having 'disaster recovery' and 'business continuity' plans as well as training their

managers and staff on action to take, and how to handle customers and talk to reporters. You will learn more about this if you study specialist Unit 6.

Dealing with disasters and internal crises

The best response will obviously depend upon the type of disaster or crisis and the type of organisation, but contingency plans for a major disaster are likely to include:

- The **rapid evacuation** of personnel in an emergency.
- **First aid** and health care if anyone is injured.
- **Counselling** for those traumatised by the experience.
- **Relocation** of the business, if necessary, and how this will be done.
- **Keeping copies of important data (both manual and electronic) offsite** so that this can be recovered promptly and the business can operate again as quickly as possible.
- **Locating computer servers in a secure site** (see page 66).

Internal crises normally involve a two-stage response:
- Repair the damage or solve the problem as fast as possible.
- Deal with customers and the media openly and honestly so that customer confidence is restored quickly.

Stock market variations

Businesses are very aware of the factors that can affect the value of their shares and any reserves they may have invested on the stock market. When the dotcom bubble burst in March 2000, the crash affected a great number of businesses – not just those involved in dotcom trading. Investors were nervous of any business linked to new technology so share values in many companies fell.

When share prices fall, a company is worth less. This is because it is valued at the price of its shares multiplied by the number of shares issued. So a business with 15 million shares worth £2 each will halve in value – from £30 million to £15 million – if its shares fall to £1 each. At this price shareholders are unlikely to be pleased because

Disasters can be costly and upsetting

they are likely to have lost money. Institutional shareholders may even try to get rid of the directors. In addition, the business may be considered cheap enough to buy.

Large businesses often look for opportunities to buy smaller firms if they are 'undervalued' because their share prices are low. To take control, they need to buy a minimum of 51 per cent of the shares. So in the example above, the larger business needs to pay only about £7.5 million to take control. If share prices then rise it has got a bargain!

Acquiring a business, against the wishes of the existing directors, is known as a **hostile takeover**. Afterwards, the new owners may sack the existing directors and managers and replace them. So a hostile takeover can result in many executives losing their jobs. This is a very important reason why executives in public limited companies watch their share price carefully and try to take action if it is falling. One method is to issue positive statements about the business to try to improve demand for shares, so that the price will rise again.

Key business failures and corporate scandals

When important businesses fail investor confidence is affected. The same is true if corporate scandals are reported, where senior executives are accused of mismanagement or fraud.

In 2002 a number of large American companies admitted to accounting 'irregularities'. In other words, they had been adjusting the figures to hide any problems. This is fraud and the situation led to a number of companies being investigated by the US Securities and Exchange Commission.

- **Enron** dealt in energy and was America's seventh largest company. It employed over 20,000 staff in over 40 countries. It was found to have inflated its profits by over $1 billion and to have concealed its debts. In addition, money was taken out of the company, illegally, by means of secret partnerships.

  Several executives were charged with fraud and conspiracy – although the Chief

Business brief

Understanding why share prices change

The shares in public limited companies are listed every day in most newspapers, together with their value. Shareholders can tell whether individual shares are rising or falling. An overall value of shares traded on the London Stock Exchange is given by the FTSE 100 index, which gives the daily rate based on the performance of the 100 leading companies in Britain.

Individual share prices are influenced by financial information about the company's performance. If the business is doing well, more people want to buy shares so the price goes up. If the business is having problems, many shareholders will sell, so the price will fall. Shares in a business are also affected by events in that sector. For example, if several retailers announced poor results, the shares of other stores could fall, because investors decide their money is safer elsewhere.

The overall stock market index can also rise or fall because of external events. Bad news – such as

the outbreak of the SARS virus, the threat of war or terrorist attacks – seriously affects all stock markets. After the bomb attacks in Turkey in November 2003, Istanbul suspended all trading after the index fell by 7 per cent to prevent panic selling. Other European stock markets fell but later recovered when the US stock markets hardly reacted. This is typical, because stock markets watch each other closely and if one important market is 'jittery' or falls, the others often follow.

Executive, Ken Lay, argued that he didn't know what was going on (even though he had just cashed in millions of dollars worth of his own shares!).

When the scandal broke, investors and creditors, to whom the company owed money, forced Enron into bankruptcy. Thousands of people lost money, including the employees who lost their jobs and their pension savings because these were invested in Enron's own shares.

Other businesses were implicated in helping Enron to cover up the problem – including several large investment banks that have since been fined. The largest casualty was **Arthur Andersen**, the firm which audited (checked) Enron's accounts. It was found guilty of obstructing justice by shredding important documents. As well as a hefty fine, Anderson – once one of the world's top accountancy firms – is facing compensation claims by Enron investors which could bankrupt it too. In addition, Anderson has lost most of its business as a result of the scandal.

- **WorldCom** was a technology firm. It too, filed for bankruptcy in June 2002 with the largest case of insolvency ever. WorldCom had reported profits in both 2001 and 2002 when it had really had losses, by falsifying its accounts. When it went bankrupt it had over $41 billion of debts and two of its financial staff are likely to face prison terms of up to 65 years.

WorldCom has since changed its name to MCI and aims to settle its debts and start trading again.

These cases were not the only ones – although they were two of the biggest. In America, a wave of scandals rocked the stock market, and seriously affected consumer/investor confidence throughout 2002 and into 2003. To counteract this, action was taken to make senior directors personally responsible for accountancy fraud and in Britain the Department of Trade and Industry announced tighter rules to try to prevent an Enron-type disaster happening in the UK.

Many people felt that corporate scandals in America and elsewhere have been caused through director share-option schemes – where directors' pay is linked to share prices. This has encouraged unscrupulous executives to 'fiddle the figures' so that profits appear good, to boost share prices and their own pay as well.

Business responses to external influences

Businesses will consider the main predictable events that could affect them when they are planning for the future. For example, when Blackpool College knew that the gaming laws in England were going to be relaxed, enabling large casino hotels to open in the resort, they launched a new course for croupiers. This is a positive response to an external event that will benefit the college, its students and local employers.

Business matters

Parmalat, an Italian food, drinks and dairy company, was labelled the 'European Enron' in December 2003 when £2.7 billion was found to be missing from its accounts. Investigators later revealed that missing money could amount to £7 billion.

Parmalat had expanded rapidly since the late 1980s – and borrowed money to do so. It had also advertised widely all around the world. Its founder and former chief executive, Calisto Tanzi, sponsored the opera and bought the local Parma football team. By the end of 2003, Parmalat was bankrupt and its stakeholders all over the world were feeling

the effects. Its suppliers were owed money, its 35,000 employees in 30 countries were likely to lose their jobs and its investors their savings. Several institutional investors in the UK held Parmalat shares, which were now worthless.

Parmalat isn't the first European business to have problems. A Dutch retailer, Ahold, was found to have accounting problems. Shares in Vivendi, the French media firm, crashed after its chief executive ran up a 13.6 billion loss. The company is now operating under new management, on a much smaller scale and struggling to recover.

Businesses react to unpredictable events by putting into place their crisis management plans. When Norwich Union, the UK's largest life insurance company, discovered that it had lost money it had invested in Parmalat, it immediately issued a statement to reassure its customers by saying that the money only represented a small fraction of its overall investments.

Business terms

Spam email Unwanted and uninvited emails.
Cookie Information sent by a web server and stored on the user's browser which can collect and send data back to the server every time the user accesses the website, e.g. login information or user preferences.

Creditor A person owed money by a business.
Investor A person or institution that has bought shares in a business.
Bankruptcy An official declaration that debts are greater than assets, so that debts cannot be paid. An official receiver is then in charge of selling the assets to repay as many creditors as possible.

Over to you!

1 a Working in a small group, suggest **two** ways in which technology has affected each of the following businesses. Then suggest **one** change that may occur because of future technological developments. Finally, compare your ideas with other groups in your class.

  i Interactive television programmes, such as Pop Idol.
  ii A record company.
  iii A video hire shop.
  iv Your family doctor.
  v A superstore.
  vi A bank.
  vii A newspaper.

b Each year European Information Society Technologies (IST) prizes are awarded for groundbreaking developments in information technology. Find out the current prizewinners by going to the IST website and discuss the implications of some of these developments with your business or IT tutors. A link to this site is available at www.heinemann.co.uk/hotlinks (express code 1386P).

2 Suggest **two** changes your college has had to make over the past few years because of the following changes to legislation.

  a The Disability Discrimination Act which covers access to public buildings and facilities for anyone with a disability.
  b The Equal Pay Act, which broadly means that men and women must be paid the same if they do the same job.

c The Health and Safety at Work Act, which includes passive smoking as a health hazard for employees.
d The Working Time Directive (see page 192).
e The Employment Act 2002 (see page 192).
f The law which prevents hand-held mobiles being used by drivers.

3 a Suggest **three** types of crises or disasters which could affect your college.
b As a group, suggest the action the college should take for each crisis or disaster you have identified to minimise the damage and retain customer confidence.
c Some people think that crises, scandals and disasters significantly change customer behaviour. Others disagree. As a group, decide which of the following would affect you, personally, and which would not – and give your reasons. Then compare your ideas.

  i The manager of your bank is prosecuted for fraud.
  ii A tutor at a local school is accused of falsifying assessment results.
  iii A local takeaway is prosecuted for selling food which is unfit for human consumption.
  iv Your local garage is featured in the newspaper, accused of charging for repairs to non-existent faults.
  v You find that your favourite shower gel is produced by a company which develops products using animal testing.

View 1: *The TUC believes that far too many people are working overlong hours without being paid. It wants hours to be restricted and everyone paid for overtime. This is sensible, otherwise bosses just expect something for nothing.*

View 2: *All jobs need flexibility and if you want to get on, you need to work hard. Counting up every hour and insisting on payment is silly. Working unpaid overtime usually pays off in terms of better career prospects and eventually a higher paid job.*

With which viewpoint do you agree – and why?

2.4 Section review

Now that you have completed this section you should understand how external influences affect businesses and the type of responses that are likely. Test your skills now by doing the following activities.

Check your understanding of this section by answering the following questions. Check all answers with your tutor before moving on.

1 **a** What are the six areas covered by a PESTEL analysis?
   b Suggest **two** ways in which international relations can affect businesses.
   c Identify **two** political issues that can impact on businesses.
   d Explain the difference between a boom and a slump.
   e Identify **two** effects on businesses if interest rates increase.
   f Identify **two** current social or environmental issues which impact on businesses.
   g Explain **two** ways in which technological developments have changed business communications.
   h Identify **two** types of legislation where changes would affect businesses.
   i Explain how a general rise in the stock market would affect a business.
   j Identify **two** impacts of the failure of a major business.

2 Figure 2.30 (on page 198) suggests some future changes in each of the areas covered by a PESTEL analysis. Working in small groups and in agreement with your tutor, select **one** of the businesses listed below and identify at least **four** external influences that would be relevant. Then suggest **three** ways in which the business could adapt its activities in response.
   a A children's nursery.
   b A local pub.
   c A manufacturer of 'smoothie' makers.
   d A privately operated town centre car park.
   e Your college.
   f A town centre foodstore.

Area	Forecast events
Political issues	Control over content of vending machines in schools/colleges
	Tightening of regulations for advertising/promoting food to children and type of food served to children
	Nightclubs and pubs may have to contribute to costs of late-night policing
	General Election 2005/6 could mean change of Government
	Congestion charging
	Tighter regulations over no smoking zones in pubs and restaurants
	Introduction of university top-up fees
Macroeconomic	Interest rates likely to increase
	Unemployment low
	Economy forecast to grow by 3% in next year
	Business rates likely to increase in 2005
	House prices rising
Social trends/ issues	Increasing health consciousness among customers
	Fast paced lifestyle
	Dislike of GM foods/additives and greater demand for organic foods
	Growing demand for vegetarian/vegan/low salt/gluten free options
	Most students now have part-time jobs
	Greater car use/ownership
Technology	Supplies can be ordered electronically
	Goods can be sold online via website
	Growth in Internet/broadband use
	Third generation phones = instant video/picture transfer
	Portable jukeboxes which store 5,000 songs on a hard drive
	Machines which accept payments by credit or debit cards as well as cash
	Better quality CCTV security systems
Environment	Minimising of packaging materials
	Greater use of recyclable/biodegradable packaging materials
	More emphasis on recycling
Legislation	Mobile phones cannot be used when driving
	Employment – age discrimination outlawed by 2006
	Government plans to expand parental leave
	Vetting of all those who apply to work with children
	Spam emails now illegal

Figure 2.30 *PESTEL list of future changes*

Unit 3 Investigating financial control

This unit looks at the financial aspects of running a business. It starts by looking at what is meant by **profit** and then looks at the steps businesses take to try to ensure that they will continue to be profitable in the future. This includes investigating the point at which income equals expenditure, known as the **break even point**. Businesses use break even calculations to work out what would happen if they change the selling price or if the cost of materials changes.

Businesses also carefully watch their **cash flow** forecasts. Cash flow is concerned with predicting the amount of money entering and leaving their bank account each day. When this is done, the actual amount of money in the bank – the balance – can be calculated. You need to learn how to calculate cash flow and explain what the resulting balance means. You will also find out how businesses aim to improve cash flow, such as by monitoring their **debtors** – the people and businesses which owe money.

Another way in which businesses control their financial situation is by using **budgets**. Budgets are used to help managers of individual departments to control their income and expenditure. In a sense, budgets are profit and loss calculations on a small scale.

This unit also looks at the ways in which businesses **record transactions**. The business has to keep a record of the transaction so that, amongst other things, it can carry out profitability and cash flow calculations. Records are also kept to help to prevent fraud. Businesses can lose hundreds, thousands or even millions of pounds through theft and they are very keen to keep this figure as low as possible.

For your assessment, you will need to show that you understand all of the financial control methods mentioned in this unit. This will include calculations based on figures in a typical business situation to demonstrate that you can apply these techniques. When you are investigating the use of cash flow analysis and budgets you will need to use a computer spreadsheet to carry out the calculations. You will also need graph paper to draw break even charts.

Because you are dealing with financial information you will have to use numbers and carry out calculations. When you are doing this it is important that you think about what the numbers really mean, rather than just 'do the arithmetic'. Only then can you understand how financial information is used in business to make important decisions.

In summary

In this unit you will learn about:

3.1 Profit and break even. Here you will learn how businesses subtract their total expenditure from total income to discover whether they have made a profit, a loss or broken even.

3.2 Cash flow management. This section shows how businesses examine the money flowing into and out of their bank account to find out if they have enough to meet their debts.

3.3 Budgets. In this section you will find out how budgets are used in financial planning and monitoring expenditure for departments in a business.

3.4 Recording transactions. This final section covers the various ways in which sales transactions are recorded and how fraud can be kept to a minimum.

This section covers

The calculation of profit
Calculating total revenue
Calculating total costs
Profitable operation of a business
Calculating break even

Which is your financial style?

Matt, Ruksana and Claire are all attending the same business studies course at college. They all have similar part time jobs which earn them £50 per week each. It is Friday afternoon and Claire suggests that they go to the cinema that evening followed by a meal at an Indian restaurant. She has just enough money left from last Saturday's pay packet to afford both.

Matt says that he can't afford to go out. His money ran out on Tuesday and he has had to borrow £5 from his mother to see him through until payday. Ruksana says that she is not short of money but is saving for a holiday and would enjoy a trip to the cinema – but doesn't want to spend money on a meal.

The financial circumstances of these three people can be compared to what happens in business organisations.

- Claire spends everything that she earns but gets by. When businesses do this they are said to be **breaking even**. In other words, they are not making a profit or a loss.
- Matt is spending more than he earns. If he was in business we would say that he is making a **loss**.
- Ruksana is spending less than she earns on a day-to-day basis. When this happens in business, the firm is said to be making a **profit.** When businesses make a profit they have money to pay a salary to their owners and to do other things, such as expand the business.

In this section you will learn about profit, loss and break even. You will also learn how the total income and expenditure figures are calculated. Then you will see what happens when these figures are changed – for example when income falls and costs increase. Finally, all of this information will be examined in more detail using break even analysis. This will help you to understand how managers use this technique to make decisions based on the options open to them.

Calculating profit

All businesses receive money from outside sources. This is called **income** or **revenue**. A particular business could receive income from several sources, such as charities which receive money from door-to-door collections, their own shops, appeals by letter and many more (see page 15). The government also has many sources of income such as VAT, income tax and excise duty on petrol. For businesses in the private sector the most common source of income is from customers paying for goods or services. A pizza takeaway shop would receive all of its income from customers. Income or revenue is the total amount of money received over a particular time span, such as a week, a month or a year.

Businesses also spend money. This can either be called **costs** or **expenditure**. For even quite small businesses, there will be many types of expenditure. The takeaway pizza shop would probably pay rent and business rates for the premises, staff wages, buy flour, milk and other ingredients for the pizzas and so on. For a charity like Guide Dogs for the Blind, the expenditure would include staff wages, training facilities for the dogs, dog food, vets bills etc. Again the total amount for all of these over a particular time span is called costs or expenditure.

In later sections you will learn more about how total income and expenditure figures are calculated.

Adam's pizza shop

In the first week of November, Adam looks at all the financial information he has and produces the following figures:

Income from sales of pizzas = £2,000

Total expenditure (ingredients, staff wages etc.) = £1,500

Adam then subtracts the second figure from the first.

£2000
− £1500
£500 profit

Because the income (£2,000) is higher than the expenditure (£1,500) the difference (£500) is a profit. This means that, at least for this week, Adam has money to pay himself a wage and will probably put the rest in a bank savings account.

Three weeks later, things don't look so good. The main oven breaks down and it takes three days to get it repaired. Most of the expenditure items, such as staff wages and rent still have to be paid. When Adam does his calculations he produces the following result:

Income = £1,000

Expenditure = £1,200

£1000
− £1200
− £200 loss

This time the expenditure is higher than the income, so the result of the final calculation is a negative figure (− £200). This means that Adam

lost money that week. He has no money to pay himself a wage and will have to draw some money from his savings account to contribute to paying staff wages and other expenses.

A few weeks later there is a bad snowfall. For a few days the number of customers falls dramatically. Fortunately, one of his staff has left so that the wages bill is reduced. The figures at the end of the week are:

Income = £1,400

Expenditure = £1,400

£1400
− £1400
£0 break even

In this case Adam has not made a profit or a loss because the income and expenditure figures are the same, so the business broke even. This is unusual in private sector businesses where the aim is usually to make as much profit as possible. On the other hand, in the public sector (local and national government) the overall aim is often to break even. In the not-for-profit/voluntary sector, break even is very important. The business should not spend more overall, including on supporting and promoting a special cause, than it receives in income.

Business brief

Calculating profit or loss

In a profit or loss calculation the expenditure figure is **always** subtracted from the income figure. If the expenditure figure is greater than the income figure this means that the business has made a loss. In other words the answer to the calculation is a negative figure. If the reverse is true, and the result of the calculation is a positive figure, then the business is profitable.

If the figures are identical then the result is break even.

Business terms

Income/revenue These mean the same thing. They are the total amount of money a business receives from outside, for example, from customers.

Sales turnover This term is sometimes used for sales income/revenue.

Expenditure/costs These mean the same thing. They are the total amount of money spent – e.g. to suppliers, on staff (wages) and for other requirements.

Profit Businesses make a profit when income is higher than expenditure

Loss Businesses make a loss when revenue is less than costs.

Profit and loss account Large businesses produce annual summaries of their performance. These reports include a profit and loss account which summarises the income and expenditure for a year and gives the overall profit – or loss.

Break even This occurs when the income and expenditure figures for a business are the same. Public sector and charitable organisations try to achieve this all the time.

Business matters

You might think that a company that is in the business of 'making' money could not go wrong! Unfortunately this isn't so. The Royal Mint makes bank notes and coins for the UK and also for foreign countries. When several countries in the EU began to use the Euro instead of the old national currencies, the Royal Mint spent millions of pounds on the new machines needed to produce the new currency. Unfortunately, it struggled to meet the high standards required – such as size tolerances. This meant that it was only able to capture 5 per cent of the market instead of the 20 per cent it expected. The end result was that the business made a loss of £6.5 million in 2002.

Producing Euros was not profitable for the Royal Mint

Business brief

Number crunching (1)

When you are using numbers in business, it is important to make sure that any calculations you have carried out are correct. For example, when calculating profit/break even/loss you should do two things after completing your calculation.

- **Rule 1** – always double check. Check your calculation by adding the expenditure figure to the final figure (profit or loss) to make sure that you get back to the income figure. For example, if your first calculation is:

Income	£4000
Expenditure	– £3600
Profit	£400

  Then add £400 to £3600 to give £4000

- **Rule 2** – always test that your answer is sensible! Do this by carrying out an estimate to check whether your calculation is approximately correct. For example, if you subtract 310 from 680 (answer 370) you should think that 300 from 700 gives approximately 400, so if the result of your actual calculation is 40, something is wrong. The trick is to look at the numbers you are using and round them to the nearest main number.

Income £	Expenditure £	Difference £	Result (profit, loss or break even)
25	20		
37	40		
1,500	1,200		
1,725	1,725		
2,735	2,294		
5,710	6,123		
100,445	97,003		
47,653	47,653		

1 Put the following words into two groups which mean the same. Income, costs, expenditure, revenue.

2 Copy out the table above. The first two columns give the income and expenditure for some businesses. In the third column work out the result and in the fourth column state whether the result is a profit, a loss or break even.

3 For each of the following organisations, decide whether their aim is more likely to be to make a profit or to break even.
- A County Council.

- ASDA.
- The BBC.
- Oxfam.
- Sky Digital.
- Help the Aged.
- Marks & Spencer.
- Your own school or college.
- The British Government.

4 In a group, brainstorm answers to the following question. Try to think of as many ideas as possible.

'What reasons might there be for a business making a loss?'

Talking point

View 1: Charities should pay high wages to talented people as they will be more likely to raise more money overall.

View 2: People working for charities should expect to be poorly paid so that more money can be spent on the cause for which that charity exists.

With which viewpoint do you agree – and why?

Calculating total revenue

So far in this unit we have examined ways in which businesses look at their past performance to decide whether or not they have been profitable. If they have made a loss the owners or managers will have to make decisions about how to improve things, such as cutting costs by reducing the number of staff or finding cheaper materials. However, businesses do not like to discover that they have already lost money. They would prefer to see possible problems coming up in advance so that they can try to stop them happening.

For that reason businesses make plans for the future of their finances. The starting point is to calculate the income that they may receive. This is followed by methods used to estimate total costs so that a profit forecast can be produced. Finally, as you will see on page 213, break even calculations can help businesses to look at the different options open to them and make decisions about items such as prices, costs and so on.

Businesses can obtain income from many sources, depending on the type of activity. For example, local authorities receive most of their money from residents who pay council tax, from business rates and from the government. Charities exist because people donate money. In the private sector, income comes from customers.

Samina's hat business

Samina is studying full time at college. She has no classes on Fridays and had been working for her uncle on his market stall selling clothing accessories. Unfortunately, her uncle has just retired and the new stallholder wanted to employ her own relatives. This happened in November and Samina knew that one of her uncle's suppliers could supply her with novelty Christmas hats. She has decided that she will try to make some money by selling the hats in the shopping centre. She asks for permission to do this from the local council. She then needs to work out how much she could earn – her income or revenue.

She decides that people would be willing to pay £2 for a hat, so she writes down how much income she could receive. She uses the following formula:

Income = unit sales price × number of units sold

She decides that, during December, she could sell 100 hats and puts the figures she has into the formula:

Income = £2 × 100 = £200

Most businesses sell more than one product or supply more than one service. For example, a hairdresser would offer anything from a simple dry cut to shampooing, styling and colouring. The price charged would depend on the type of service the customer wants. So, when forecasting income, the calculation can be complicated. The questions to be asked are:

- How many of each product or service will we sell?
- What price can we charge for each product or service?

The answers to these two questions are often linked. Normally, when prices are lower, more products or services are sold. This is why businesses reduce prices when they want to sell off surplus stock. If you have studied unit 2 you should know about this already! You will learn more about this in this unit, too.

An example is shown in the table below:

Product	Selling price	Number sold	Revenue
A	£100	10	£1,000
B	£50	100	£5,000
C	£75	20	£1,500
		Total revenue (£)	£7,500

Figure 3.1 *Examples of prices and revenue*

Business brief

What is income?

Income is the total amount of money that a business receives from *all* sources.

Businesses such as Currys receive most of their income from the sale of electrical goods, such as washing machines, dishwashers and TVs. However, they also receive income by offering extended warranties on the goods they sell. So Currys has two main sources of income.

Some people say that the warranties are often expensive because modern electrical goods are very reliable. Because they very rarely break down, the warranties on the equipment are often not needed. However, if electrical goods retailers reduced the price of the warranties or did not sell them at all, their income would fall by a significant amount – and this would affect their profits.

What if?

All businesses look to the future and try to plan activities so that they can maintain or improve their profits. They can test out ideas, sometimes called "What if?" calculations, and make decisions on the outcomes. For example, 'What if we increased the price of our products by 10 per cent? Our sales might drop but, overall, our income could rise'.

Careful planning helps to reduce mistakes

 Talking point

> **View 1:** A sensible business will aim to sell top quality goods for the highest price possible because the profit made on each unit sold is greater.

> **View 2:** It is easier to make lots of money by charging a low price and selling as many as possible, especially as people will always want cheap products and don't worry about quality too much.

With which viewpoint do you agree – and why?

Over to you!

1 Using the information given in the case described above – Samina's hat business, calculate her income if she sold:
   a 200 hats.
   b 57 hats.
   c 233 hats.

2 Joanne is a florist. What would her income be if, on one day she sold:
   a 10 roses at £1.50.
   b 50 irises at £2.00.
   c 120 carnations at 50p.
   Calculate the income for each type of flower individually and then work out her total income.

3 A large car dealer based in a major city decides to offer a promotion on a new model, the Familycarrier. The sales manager thinks that if the car is offered for sale at £15,000, then 50 would be sold. If the price was reduced to £14,000, 100 would be sold. Calculate the business's income in each case.

Calculating total costs

The last section explained how total income or revenue is calculated. For a business, this is vitally important, but it is only half of the story. As you learned earlier, businesses try to make a profit and to do this they have to subtract expenditure from income:

Profit (or loss) = income – expenditure

So the other important piece of information needed is the total expenditure or cost figure. Remember that now we are *forecasting* figures to *plan* what should happen in the future. These calculations can be more complicated than the total income figure since most businesses spend money in several ways. Expenditure items can include materials, wages, heating, stationery, business tax, insurance and many more.

Normally, items of expenditure fall into one of two categories:

- **Variable costs** – sometimes called direct costs.
- **Fixed costs** – sometimes called indirect costs.

Variable costs are the most obvious items of expenditure. They depend on the number of products sold or the amount of service provided. In the case of Samina and the hats, her main variable cost would be the price she pays the wholesaler for them. If Samina paid the wholesaler £1.20 for each hat she bought, the variable cost is this figure. If she bought and sold ten hats, her total variable costs would be £1.20 × 10 = £12.00.

Fixed costs are those which a business has to pay no matter how many products it sells or how many customers it has. If Samina has to pay the local authority £10 a week for a licence to sell in the street then this is a fixed cost because she has to pay this no matter how many hats she sells.

Variable (direct) costs	Fixed (indirect) costs
Are *directly* affected by the amount produced or sold e.g.	Have to be paid no matter how much is produced e.g.
Raw materials Stock for resale Staff commission on sales Overtime payments	Rent Rates Heating Most staff wages

Figure 3.2 *Examples of variable and fixed costs*

Business terms

Variable costs These change when the number of products sold changes. They are also called direct costs because they are *directly* affected by the sales level.

Total variable costs These are calculated by using the following formula: variable (or direct) cost per unit × number of units sold.

Fixed costs These are given this name because they are fixed no matter how many products are sold. They are also called indirect costs since the number of products sold does not *directly* affect them.

Overheads This is a term sometimes used for fixed costs.

Over to you!

1 Write out the following sentences and complete them by adding in the correct type of cost.
   a Costs which have to be met no matter how many products are sold are called _____ or_____ costs.
   b Costs which change in proportion to the amount of service provided are called _____ or _____ costs.

2 Tom runs a small garage which repairs and services customers' cars. He employs one mechanic, Bill, on a permanent basis and another, Fred, who is semi-retired and only helps out at busy times, as and when needed. The list below gives some of Tom's costs. Rewrite the list under two headings – fixed costs and variable costs.

   Bill's wages
   Heating
   Spare parts for the cars
   Business rates
   Oil for filling engines during servicing
   Fred's wages
   Insurance for the premises
   Coffee for waiting customers

3 Feroz runs a sandwich shop. Under two headings list **direct** and **indirect** costs that you think that his business might have. Some of the direct costs will be the same as those in the last exercise, so try to think of some different ones as well. Aim to have at least **five** items under each heading.

Talking point

View 1: *All costs should be kept as low as possible so that more profits can be made.*

View 2: *If costs can't be kept low it doesn't matter too much as prices can always be increased to keep profit levels the same.*

With which viewpoint do you agree – and why?

Calculating fixed costs

This calculation is fairly straightforward but time consuming. All a business has to do is to list all of the types of fixed costs, put an estimated figure against each and add them together to give the total. Unless a business is starting from scratch, records of past expenses will help when compiling the list. The records will also show how much has been spent on each item in the past. The forecast figures will have to be adjusted to allow for inflation and any changes which are planned. For example, if a business is planning to expand by building an extension to its factory, the amounts for items such as heating, lighting and business rates will have to be increased.

Over to you!

1 **a** The following list gives some of the fixed costs for a small business. Add the amounts together to calculate the total.

Business rates	£1,500
Heating	£800
Telephone	£500
Insurance	£1,000
Car hire	£2,000
Staff wages	£20,000

b An extra telephone line is to be installed which would double this cost. At the same time, a more efficient heating system is to be installed which will halve the heating bill. Finally, an extra member of staff is to be employed at a salary of £10,000. Recalculate the new total fixed costs after these changes.

2 In 2004, the total fixed costs of a business were £80,000. The manager thinks that for 2005, the amount will increase by 5 per cent because of inflation. She also knows that an additional £5,000 needs to be added after the inflation calculation, because of other planned changes.

Calculate the new total fixed cost figure by first working out the effect of inflation and then adding the extra amount.

Business matters

Richer Sounds sells home entertainment products from shops located in most major towns of the UK. It is very profitable because one of its aims is to keep its fixed costs to a minimum. It looks for premises which have a low rent or which are cheap to buy. It relies on giving customers excellent value for money and customer service. The customers are not concerned that the shops are small and not lavishly furnished. You can read more about this on the Richer Sounds' StudentZone at www.richerstudentzone.co.uk

Talking point

View 1: *Fixed costs such as restrooms, heating and staff parking facilities should be kept to a minimum. So long as the pay is good, staff will not mind.*

View 2: *Staff would not mind being paid less if they are warm and have good facilities.*

With which viewpoint do you agree – and why?

Business brief

Number crunching (2)

If you have a calculator, the first part of question 2, opposite, can be carried out by keying in 80000, then +, then 5, then %.

If you have dropped your calculator and it doesn't work, it is useful to remember that the percentage (%) of a figure means so many hundredths of that figure. Therefore 5 per cent means '5 divided by 100' and 20 per cent means '20 divided by 100'. You can therefore calculate the answer to 20 per cent of 500 as follows:

$$500 \times \frac{20}{100} = 5 \times 20 = 100$$

Calculating variable costs

As you have already learned, variable costs are directly affected by the number of products sold or the amount of service provided. So, the formula used to work out the total variable cost for a product is:

Variable cost of each product × number produced

The variable cost of a product is mainly the amount of materials which goes into the final unit. For example, in a sandwich shop, a cheese and pickle sandwich is made from bread, margarine, cheese and pickle. The variable cost of the final sandwich is the total cost of these four ingredients. The value of each item would depend on the amount and quality of the types of food used, but the figures could be:

Bread	5p
Margarine	1p
Cheese	18p
Pickle	6p
Total	30p

The 'total' figure is the variable cost for the sandwich. If the producer made and sold 1,000 of these sandwiches in a day, then the total variable cost would be:

$$30p \times 1,000 = 30,000p = £300$$

If you buy a cheese and pickle sandwich, you would probably pay in the region of £1. If you knew that the ingredients only cost 30p, you might feel that the business you bought it from is making 70p profit – but this is not true. The business has also got to cover all of its fixed costs – including the wage of the person who made and sold you the sandwich.

Over to you!

1 Copy out the table below and complete the end column by calculating the total variable costs.

No. of units produced	Variable cost per unit	Total variable cost
100	50p	
250	£1.00	
375	25p	
500	£1.30	
623	£2.00	
57	£50.00	
1374	£15.23	

2 In the last exercise, assume that all of the products are made by the same business. What is its total variable cost figure? What would this figure be if all of the direct costs were to increase by 10 per cent?

3 A manufacturing business produces small model vehicles which it sells separately. In addition it sells them in boxed sets containing two or more of the toys. The table below gives the types of vehicles produced together with the variable cost of each.

Product	Direct/variable cost
A Sports car	80p
B Train engine	90p
C MPV	85p
D Truck	60p
E Airliner	£1.20
F Cruise liner	£1.00
G Bulldozer	£1.50

The boxed sets are made up as follows:

a Set 1 – All vehicles
b Set 2 – Vehicles A, B and C
c Set 3 – Vehicles C, D, A and F
d Set 4 – Vehicles G, A, C and E

For each of these sets, calculate the total variable cost.

With which viewpoint do you agree – and why?

Profitable operation of a business

On page 201 you learned that:

Profit/loss = income – expenditure

and that if income and expenditure are equal, this is called break even.

Since then you have learned that businesses do not like to look back to find that they have made a loss. Instead they prefer to look forward by forecasting income and expenditure. This allows them to make decisions which help ensure that a profit is made. You have also learned that income is predicted by multiplying the selling price by the number of units sold. It is also important to remember that expenditure is made up of fixed and variable costs.

The overall conclusion from this is that all profit making businesses aim to *obtain as much income as possible and keep expenditure as low as possible.* More specifically, they try to make sure that their forecast income is greater than forecast expenditure.

Maximising income/revenue

Income is the selling price multiplied by number of units sold. Looking at this simple formula, it is obvious that the two main ways to increase revenue are to either increase the price or sell more units – or both.

Business matters

Over a number of years, a market has developed for economy air travel. Businesses such as easyJet and Ryanair have been successful by providing 'no frills' air travel. They have done this profitably by watching all their costs very carefully indeed.

Most of their costs are indirect (fixed) costs such as the price of planes themselves, insurance, airport charges and maintenance. All of these have to be paid whether the planes are nearly full or half empty. However, these costs are kept to a minimum by, for example, using only one type of plane. This reduces the cost of maintenance since fewer spares need to be held. Cheaper regional airports in Europe are also often chosen, rather than expensive city airports.

Variable costs, such as providing food during flights are also kept to a minimum. On some flights, food is not served at all, on others snack items such as sandwiches must be bought by passengers. All bookings must be made direct by passengers by phone or over the Internet so that no commission needs to be paid to travel agents.

Sales revenue is maximised by filling as many seats on every flight wherever possible – even if this means selling spare seats at discount prices. The strategy is very successful. Ryanair has grown remarkably quickly in the last 19 years and is described by industry analysts as the most profitable airline in the world. easyJet has also grown, buying up a rival airline 'Go' in 2002 and continually adding new routes ever since. You can check current profit figures at the easyJet and Ryanair websites – links to these sites are available at www.heinemann.co.uk/hotlinks (express code 1386P).

Empty seats cost money

If you like canned drinks and have a favourite, such as Coca-Cola or Pepsi, you probably know what prices different shops charge. Unless you are in a hurry, you will buy from the shop which charges the lowest price. So shops which charge higher prices will sell fewer cans, but make more profit on each can that they do sell. The message from this situation is that increasing the price of a product does not guarantee more overall income, as you will see on page 213 when you learn about break even analysis. The general rule is that higher prices result in fewer sales and vice versa. Therefore, a business might be able to increase its overall revenue by actually reducing the price – and selling more!

Businesses can also increase sales by marketing (see also Unit 1, page 66). This involves many types of activities including advertising, promotional displays in stores, sending out mail shots and direct selling by sales staff – who may be paid a commission or bonus for achieving target sales.

Marketing also involves liaising with customers to discover their preferences and then trying to make sure that the business can satisfy these requirements. This may include identifying additional ways to make money. All businesses aim to do this, both small and large. Your local hairdresser may increase income by selling a variety of hair products, or operating a nail bar, as well as by charging for the main hairdressing services.

Reducing fixed costs

In an earlier section, you learned that there are two types of costs which businesses have – fixed and variable. All businesses should try to keep both types of cost to a minimum.

Fixed costs are those which have to be met no matter many units are sold. All but the smallest types of business will have many types of fixed costs such as business rates, heating, telephone and insurance. Some of the costs are difficult to reduce. Business rates are set by the local authority and are calculated using a fixed formula. They can only be reduced by cutting down the size of the building occupied or moving to a cheaper location.

With some types of fixed costs, such as insurance, electricity and telephone, 'shopping around' between different companies or suppliers can save money.

Other fixed costs may be reduced more easily, such as by restricting telephone calls, turning off

Business matters

Organisations in the public sector also try to increase their income so that they have more money to spend. Local authorities receive most of their income from council tax and business rates. In 2003 many councils sharply increased their council tax charges to gain more income but found themselves strongly criticised by both council tax payers and by the government, which threatened to take action if these rises were repeated in 2004.

The government raises money mainly though taxes, such as income tax, VAT and corporation tax. On the surface, since governments set the tax rates, you may think they can decide what income they need without any problem. The snag is that governments which ask for too much tax can be voted out of office at an election or even face a revolt by consumers!

In 2000, lorry drivers blockaded fuel depots around the country in protest at the high level of tax on petrol. This created severe petrol shortages and the government was forced to lower the amount of duty paid. However, in Britain it is still very high compared to other European countries, at about 80p in every pound. For that reason, tourists and lorry drivers always fill their tanks up in Europe, before crossing the channel.

The government would argue that the high tax level helps them to fund road building and other services. At the same time, high petrol prices discourage unnecessary journeys and this helps to keep down air pollution.

non-essential lights or heaters, making photocopies on both sides of sheets of paper and reducing postal charges by sending emails and using electronic ordering systems.

Most staff are a fixed cost – because they have to be paid their basic wage regardless of sales levels. Cutting staff levels will reduce costs, but can cause problems (see page 212) if staff have to be made redundant. One option, if profits are low, is simply not to replace staff who leave. This is known as **natural wastage**. Business activity levels can remain the same if automated systems are introduced. An example was when the banks introduced ATM (cash) machines – and then didn't need to employ as many bank clerks.

Business matters

A survey carried out by the communications company OneTel listed some of the most common ways in which small businesses cut costs.

- Buying second hand furniture.
- Restricting Internet access.
- Banning personal telephone calls.
- Getting rid of the office cleaner altogether.
- Reducing the heating/air conditioning.
- Outsourcing specialised services such as cleaning and security.

However, the survey also suggested that some of these measures upset employees, such as banning personal telephone calls. It suggested that, in the end, this did more harm than good because if people cannot use the phone, they leave their desks to go outside and use their mobile.

The survey recommended that businesses would find better cost reductions if they tried to find the best deal for each of their utility bills – gas, water, electricity and telephone – because none of these measures would upset their staff. On the StudentZone website at www.richerstudentzone.co.uk you can find out how Richer Sounds tries to keep its costs down – and how it enlists the help of its staff to do this!

Reducing variable costs

Remember that these are the costs which change depending on the number of units or products sold. For example, each customer visiting a hairdresser, the business has to buy more shampoo, heat more water and use more electricity for the hairdryers.

The main ways in which variable costs can be reduced are:

- **Try to get a better deal from a supplier**. Large businesses can often negotiate lower prices for large value orders. Even small businesses may be able to reduce purchase prices by ordering larger quantities or negotiating a long-term contract.
- **Use a cheaper supplier**. Businesses sometimes use the same supplier over and over again out of habit. Forming a good relationship with a supplier is important but prices can change considerably over time. This is particularly true when a new supplier sets up in business and needs a lot of new customers quickly.

The plastic interior panels of this car are cheaper to manufacture than metal panels

- **Use less material**. This can be achieved by reducing the amount of material in the product or reducing scrap/waste.
- **Use cheaper materials**. 'Cheaper' does not necessarily mean inferior. New materials are being invented all the time. Many car

components which used to be made of metal are now made of plastic. Not only are plastic components easier to produce, they also reduce the weight of the car.

- **Cut labour costs by automation/ computerisation**. In a factory, the use of automation can reduce the need for overtime payments.
- **Increase productivity**. This means getting machines to run faster or for more of the time. It can also mean making staff work harder or more efficiently.

Business matters

Private sector businesses can come under fire just as much as the public sector when they want to reduce costs. Amicus, a major union, emailed over a million UK students asking them to support a boycott of all companies that sack UK workers to set up cheaper call centre operations in India. In 2003 several UK businesses including BT, British Airways, Tesco and Norwich Union reduced their costs in this way. When customers telephone the call centre, they have no way of knowing that their call is being handled in India, rather than in the UK. India has many well trained people and the average wage is a fraction of that in the UK – so huge savings can be made.

Amicus claims that 200,000 UK finance jobs could be lost to India by 2008 and the Communication Workers Union (CWU), says that the same number of telecommunications jobs could also go.

The CWU was also involved when the Royal Mail tried to cut costs in 2003 by reducing the number of mail deliveries from twice daily to once per day. This would reduce the number of journeys and so improve the productivity of staff and transport – but the union claimed there were no benefits in the package for staff and threatened strike action. In Wales, local residents campaigned against the planned closure of seven post offices, which the Royal Mail claimed were losing money because of lack of custom.

Reducing costs, therefore, is not always a simple matter when different groups of stakeholders become involved!

Over to you!

1 Write the letters **a** to **h** on separate lines on a piece of paper. Now against each letter write true or false for each of the statements below.
  a Businesses make a profit when expenditure is higher than income.
  b When a business is planning to increase its profit, it reduces costs or maximises income – or both.
  c Increasing the price of a product always increases total income.
  d Business rates is an indirect cost.
  e Buying second hand furniture will reduce the direct cost figure.
  f Reducing variable costs without affecting quality will improve profitability.
  g The more units sold at a fixed price, the greater the profit.
  h Staff would not be concerned if the heating was turned down.

2 Write the formula a manufacturing business would use to calculate its revenue.

3 Give three examples of ways in which a manufacturing business could reduce variable costs.

4 a You are involved in a small local charity which raises money for good causes. It now wants to run a campaign to obtain income for a local children's hospice. Working in a small group, think of as many ways in which you could do this as possible. Then compare your ideas with those of other groups in your class.
  b Identify **three** fixed costs the charity is likely to have and explain why it is important to keep these as low as possible.

Talking point

View 1: *Reducing costs means that customers get a better deal. If this reduces the number of jobs available and puts people out of work then this can't be helped. They can always find another job.*

View 2: *Businesses should not be allowed to cut costs if this means putting people out of work. Their first loyalty should be to their staff.*

With which viewpoint do you agree – and why?

Calculating break even

Break even occurs when income is equal to expenditure. Some types of business aim to achieve this all the time, such as public sector organisations, not-for-profit businesses and charities. In the private sector, businesses can also break even. However, this is relatively rare and most make a profit, some larger than others. In this case we say that their sales are above the break even point. As you have already learned, businesses can also make a loss and in rare cases this figure can be very large. This occurs when sales are below the break even point.

There are two ways of finding a break even point. You can construct a break even chart or use a formula. In this section you will learn to do both, using the following case study.

Len's lawnmowers

Len runs a successful garden centre. He sells all kinds of plants, shrubs and small trees. In addition, he sells fertilisers, compost and many types of garden tools and accessories. He is considering developing his business by selling lawnmowers. Having researched the market, he decides to sell one of the most popular models of mower to see if he can make a profit. If he is successful, he will expand his range of mowers and start to sell other mechanical garden aids, such as strimmers and hedge cutters. For safety and space requirements he needs to build an extension to his existing building and would have to take out a bank loan to pay for this.

Len does some calculations and produces the following figures based on his forecasts for the first year of selling mowers:

- Cost of each mower from the distributor (the variable cost) = £50.
- Fixed costs (including loan repayment, additional insurance, business rates, heating etc.) = £2,000.

Len decides to draw a break even chart to see if he could make a profit selling the mowers for £80 each. He thinks that the most he would sell in the

year is 100 mowers. A break even chart is a form of graph. The following sections take you through the five stages of drawing the chart.

Stage one – drawing and labelling scales for the graph

The first step is to draw and label the axes of the graph. The horizontal axis shows the number of mowers sold. Len has already decided that he will probably sell 100 at most so the scale goes from 0 to 100. The vertical axis represents both costs and revenue. The easiest way to work the maximum on this scale is to multiply the selling price by the maximum forecast sales. In Len's case this is

$$£80 \times 100 = £8,000$$

So the vertical scale goes from zero to over £8,000.

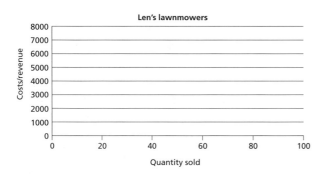

Stage two – plotting the fixed cost line

In Len's case, the fixed costs add up to £2,000. If you look at the next diagram you can see that this has been added to the graph by drawing a horizontal line starting at £2,000 on the vertical scale. The reason that it is horizontal and not sloping is that *fixed costs do not change with level of sales*. In this case, if Len hardly sells any lawnmowers, he will still have to pay the loan repayments, business rates etc. Perhaps looking at this graph helps you to understand why drawing a break even chart is so useful, because you can *see* that the fixed costs do not change with the level of sales.

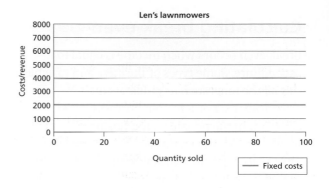

Stage three – including the total cost line

The variable cost line is now added to the chart. The first step is to calculate the total revenue if 100 mowers were to be sold. The variable cost for each mower is £50 since this is what Len pays for them, so if he sells 100 the total variable cost would be £5,000.

Since the fixed cost line has already been included, the variable cost line begins where the fixed cost line meets the vertical axis and ends at £7,000 for the 100 sales level (£2,000 + £5,000). In other words, if 100 mowers are sold, the total cost is the sum of the variable *and* the fixed costs – £7,000.

This time the line slopes upwards from left to right, showing that the variable cost amount increases in direct proportion to the number of mowers sold. This line can be used to find the total cost for any level of sales. For instance, if 80 mowers were sold, the total cost would be £6,000. Check this to see if you get the same answer. Ask your tutor for help if you are not sure how to do this.

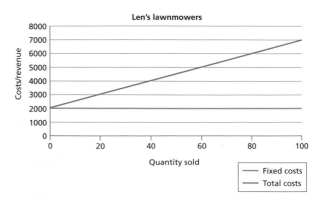

Stage four – adding the sales revenue line

The next diagram shows the final line added to the break even chart. The two points used are the bottom left zero point – if there are no sales there is no income! At the other end of the chart when 100 mowers are sold, the revenue would be $100 \times £80 = £8,000$. Again the slope is upwards from left to right showing that as sales increase so does the income. The line allows the revenue to be read off for any number of mowers sold. So, for example, if sales were 80, income would be £6,400.

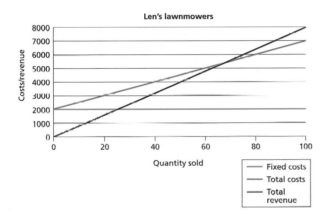

Len's lawnmowers

Stage five – analysing the chart

The final version of the chart has one additional line and some extra information. First, a line has been drawn from the point where the total cost line and the revenue line intersect. This meets the sales level scale at 67 mowers. This is the **break even point**. In other words, if Len sells 67 mowers he covers all of his costs (fixed + variable) but does not make a profit or a loss.

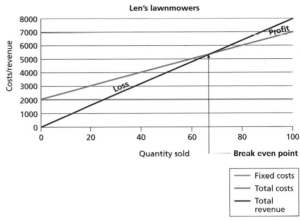

Len's lawnmowers

You should note that when you are reading figures from a break even chart, the answer is only approximate. If complete accuracy is needed, any required figure can be calculated. For example, you will learn later that there is a mathematical formula to calculate the break even point. This would show that Len would have to sell 66.666666 (recurring) lawnmowers to break even! He might struggle to sell 0.6666 of a machine to any customer. In this case 67 is quite accurate enough.

Above the break even point, the gap between the total cost line and the sales revenue line shows that Len would make a profit if he sells more than 67 mowers. The gap between these two lines for sales

Business terms

Break even point This is the level of sales where the total cost and revenue lines cross on a break even chart. Because the lines cross, the total income and expenditure figures are the same.

Margin of safety Sometimes called the safety margin. This can be measured when the level of sales is above the break even point – in other words, when the business is profitable. The margin of safety is the number by which sales would have to fall before the break even point is reached. For example, in the case of Len's lawnmower business, if sales were 85 then the margin of safety would be $85 - 67 = 18$.

Profit margin per unit This is found by subtracting the variable cost per unit from the unit selling price. Len buys his lawnmowers for £50 and sells them for £80 so his profit margin per unit is £80 – £50 = £30. Profit margin is sometimes called 'mark up' or 'margin'. The term is used in retail businesses because it is the difference between the amount of money a business pays for goods and the amount it sells them for. This amount of money is often given as a percentage. It is used to pay fixed costs and what is left is profit.

below 67 shows the amount of loss he would make.

Look carefully at the cost and revenue lines if 80 mowers were sold. The cost line intersects at £6,000 and the revenue at £6,400. Hence the amount of profit Len would make is £400. If you read off the figures for sales of 40 mowers you find that the total cost figure is £4,000 and the sales revenue is £3,200 so Len would make a loss of £800.

💬 Talking point

View 1: *Businesses such as charities, which aim to break even, should 'play safe' and keep some money as reserves in the bank – just in case.*

View 2: *Charities should spend all of their income, if not more, and put more effort into fundraising if they make a loss.*

With which viewpoint do you agree – and why?

Business brief

Number crunching (3)

When you have done a division calculation, check your result by multiplying your answer by the number on the bottom line. It should give you the figure on the top line.

For example, if you divide 600 by 12 the answer is 50. This would be written as

$$\frac{600}{12} = 50$$

You can check the answer by multiplying 12 x 50. This gives you the number on the top line, i.e. 600.

Over to you!

1 Using the completed break even chart for Len's lawnmower business, find the following:
   a The sales revenue for sales of 30 and 90 mowers.
   b The total cost for sales of 30 and 90 mowers.
   c The profit/loss for 40 and 80 mowers.
   d The margin of safety if 80 mowers are sold.

2 a Using the information given below, construct a break even chart for Super Smoothie Maker by following the five stages described earlier.

   Fixed costs £10,000
   Variable cost per unit £20
   Selling price £50 per unit
   Maximum sales 500 units

   Hints and tips: The horizontal axis should go up to the maximum possible sales – 500. The vertical axis (costs and revenue) should go up to £25,000 (500 × £50). Be very careful when plotting lines on your chart since, if they are not accurate, the figures you obtain from reading the chart will also be inaccurate.

   b When you have completed the chart, label each of the following items:
      i The fixed cost line.
      ii The total cost line.
      iii The variable cost for maximum sales.
      iv The profit area.
      v The loss area and the break even point.
      Now ask your tutor to check your completed chart.

   c Using the chart, find the following information:
      i The break even point.
      ii The income and expenditure at the break even point (they should be the same!).
      iii The income and total expenditure when the sales are 450 units.
      iv The profit or loss (say which) when sales are 400 and then 200.
      v For **ii** to **iv** above now calculate the figures to check your results.

Using a formula to calculate the break even point

The formula for finding the break even point is as follows:

$$\text{Sales for break even} = \frac{\text{fixed costs}}{\text{selling price} - \text{variable cost}}$$

The figures used for both selling price and variable cost are both per unit. Think back to the example of Len's lawnmower business. Len buys them for £50 (the variable cost) and sells them for £80 each. His fixed costs are £2,000. So these figures would go into the formula as follows:

$$\text{Sales for break even} = \frac{£2000}{£50 - £20} = \frac{£2000}{£30} = 66.666$$

The answer would be rounded to the nearest whole number, 67.

Over to you!

1 Copy out the following chart and complete the last column by calculating the break even point in each case using the formula. Remember to round your answers to the nearest whole number if necessary.

Business	Total fixed costs £	Variable cost per unit £	Selling price per unit £	Break even point
A	20	2	4	
B	1000	50	100	
C	500	21	31	
D	270	18	33	
E	1050	7	11	
F	2714	53	107	

2 The table below gives information about 6 businesses. This time the sales figures have been added. Copy it out and complete the last four columns. In the last column make the figure negative if there is a loss.

Business	Total fixed costs £	Variable cost per unit £	Selling price per unit £	Total sales	Total sales revenue £	Total variable cost £	Total cost £	Profit or Loss £
A	20	2	4	100				
B	1000	50	100	75				
C	500	21	31	700				
D	270	18	33	10				
E	1050	7	11	30				
F	2714	53	107	200				

Management decisions and action

Managers of businesses use break even charts and calculations to help them plan what they would like to happen in the future. They ask questions like:

- Could we increase our prices by 5 per cent and still make a profit if sales fall?
- If we reduce prices by 10 per cent will we increase sales by enough to survive?
- We are very dependent on one supplier, what would happen if they went out of business and we had to use an alternative source which charges higher prices?
- If we moved to cheaper premises, how would this affect our profits?

Break even analysis can help businesses to answer these types of questions.

Talking point

View 1: *Managers should not take break even calculations too seriously. They should go with their 'gut feeling'.*

View 2: *Managers should base all their decisions on the precise information given by a break even calculation.*

With which viewpoint do you agree – and why?

Over to you!

Think back to Len's lawnmowers. The figures used for the break even chart were as follows: fixed costs £2,000, variable cost £50 per unit and a selling price of £80. This information was used to produce the chart on page 215.

Len's lawnmower business has now been running for a year and he has sold 80 machines, making a profit of £400.

1 Len wonders what would happen if he spent money on advertising his lawnmower business for the next year. He thinks that he could spend £1,000 on 10 weekly advertisements in the local paper during the summer months. This amount would have to be added to his fixed costs since it would be spent even if his sales were not affected.

   Re-draw the break even chart with fixed costs of £3,000. In addition, since Len hopes that sales will increase you need to increase the maximum sales on the horizontal scale to 200 units. Compare your result with the original chart on page 215 and answer the following questions.

   a How many mowers would Len now have to sell to break even?

   b Use the formula to check this result.

   c How many more mowers must he now sell to break even?

   d Why is the break even point higher than it was originally?

   e How much revenue would Len receive if he sold 150 mowers? Read this from the chart and then check by calculation.

   f What profit/loss would Len make if he sold 150 mowers?

   g From the chart, find what Len's profit/loss would be if he still only sold 80 mowers, even after advertising.

   h Use the figures you have been given at the start of this section to check your answers to **f** and **g**.

2 Len looks at the two break even charts and tries to decide what to do. Should he spend the money on advertising or leave things as they are? Working in a small group discuss Len's problem and decide what advice you would give him. Compare your decision with that of other groups. Be honest and carry out this exercise before reading the next section!

Recommendations for management action

The decision Len has to make, which you have just discussed, is typical of the situation in which business managers often find themselves. A key point is that there is always an element of risk involved. Whenever you are making recommendations, the risks need to be pointed out. You will learn more about this if you study specialist Unit 9.

For the assessment of this unit, you do not have to make decisions. Your task is to make recommendations that include an assessment of the possible consequences of decisions. For example:

- If a business decides to reduce the variable costs by using cheaper materials, the quality of the product could suffer and sales could fall.
- If prices are increased, sales could fall to a point where overall profits are reduced.
- A retail shop is moved from a prime town centre location to cheaper premises on the edge of the centre. The fixed costs will be reduced but the number of customers could also fall.

The key issues you need to think about when making recommendations are:

- Increase/reduce selling price.
- Increase/reduce fixed costs.
- Increase/reduce variable costs.
- The best and worst possible outcomes.

Over to you!

Discuss the following situations in a group. Decide what advice you would give to the business, giving reasons for your answer which include comments on the risks involved. Include in your answer any effects on fixed and variable costs, sales revenue, break even point and profit.

1 A mail order company is thinking about transferring its customer call centre to a country where the labour is far cheaper.

2 A double glazing window manufacturer has found a cheaper source of the plastic raw material.

3 A school is considering building a new IT block to provide courses for adults.

4 A taxi firm is deciding whether to buy second-hand cars which would require repairing from time to time or new cars which would have warranties but which would cost more to buy.

Talking point

View 1: *Managers have no right to take risks. People's jobs may be at stake.*

View 2: *All business decisions have an element of risk. Businesses have to gamble to survive.*

With which viewpoint do you agree – and why?

Now you have completed this section, you should understand what is meant by profit and break even and how these are calculated. You should also understand why these calculations are so important and why they are used. Test your skills now by doing the following activities.

Check your understanding of this section by answering the following questions. Check all your answers with your tutor before moving on.

1 a Explain what is meant by the term 'total cost'.

b A business has a total revenue of £215,000 and expenditure of £175,000. Calculate the difference and say whether it has made a profit or loss for the year.

c Give **three** examples of variable costs and give another term which is sometimes used instead of 'variable' costs.

d Explain what is meant by the term 'break even'.

e Write the formula you would use to calculate profit or loss.

f Give **three** examples of fixed costs and state the term which sometimes used instead of 'fixed' costs.

g When would you use the following formula?

$$\frac{\text{fixed costs}}{\text{selling price} - \text{variable cost}}$$

h A business wants to increase its total revenue. Suggest **two** ways in which it could do this.

i Explain what is meant by the term 'margin of safety'.

j Suggest **two** ways in which a business could reduce its variable costs.

2 Rainyday is a small factory that makes collapsible umbrellas which people can carry in

> Waterproof cloth £5,000
> Heating £500
> Business rates £1,000
> Catch mechanisms to hold the umbrellas open and closed £1,500
> Insurance £300
> Telephone £150
> Metal struts to hold the umbrella open £3,000
> Wages for full time staff £20,000
> Telescopic shafts – the central umbrella support £2,000
> Water and electricity £1,200

their pocket. The following are its main costs in a typical month:

a List the above items under two headings, fixed and variable costs. Calculate the total of each.

b The managers want to give the staff a pay rise, but profits were low last year. This year, total costs are forecast to reach £420,000 and total revenue is estimated to be £460,000.

   i What is the forecast profit for the year?

   ii Suggest **four** ways in which the company could reduce its costs without damaging the business.

   iii The finance manager thinks the selling price of the umbrellas should be increased. Suggest **one** benefit and **one** risk associated with taking this action.

   iv The annual wage bill for the staff is £240,000. Calculate the new wage bill if the managers agreed on a 4 per cent pay increase and then calculate how this increase would affect the forecast profits.

   v The MD asks if there is any way in which the staff could be rewarded, but only if sales increased too. What would you recommend?

This section covers

Using spreadsheets to forecast cash flow
Monitoring actual cash flow
Improving cash flow by credit control

What is cash flow?

If you have a vivid imagination, the term cash flow could make you dream about a river filled with crates of money flowing past you! This idea is not a million miles from the way the term is used in business. Cash flow is a way of measuring the amount of money 'flowing' into and out of a business's bank account every day. This is rather like money in a pool in the river. If the pool is full, there is plenty to spend. If the pool is drying up – there is a problem!

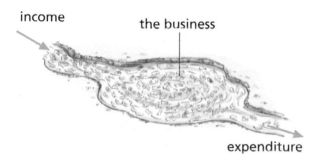

Figure 3.3 *Representation of cash flow*

In the last section you learned that businesses receive money as income and also need to spend money, called expenditure. The most important factor is that cash flow takes account of these two types of event only when they actually happen. The result of a cash flow analysis is the amount of money the business has in its bank account each day. The following two examples illustrate the principle involved.

- Ben is a plumber. He has only recently started his own business after working for a large

company. He specialises in quite small jobs such as mending leaks and installing washing machines or dishwashers at short notice. When Ben agrees to carry out work for a customer, he asks for a cash deposit to pay for the materials he will need. He pays the trade centre cash when he collects the materials. He also asks for cash when he has completed the work. When he finishes work for the day, he calls into the bank and pays in all of the cash he has earned, and this amount appears on his bank statement almost immediately – no later than the following day.

- Lauren runs a business growing house plants and bedding plants for garden centres. Seeds are planted early in the year and the plants develop in heated greenhouses before delivery to garden centres in May and June. She pays for the seeds soon after delivery and pays her staff weekly. In addition, greenhouse heating and maintenance are ongoing costs. The result of this situation is that her bank balance falls during the early part of the year but increases dramatically in May and June when she sells her plants.

These two different situations illustrate the importance of monitoring cash flow. Ben does not have a problem since he is paid almost immediately for materials and his work. Lauren has to spend money over several months before her business receives income for her plants.

The 'cash' in cash flow

The use of the word 'cash' in cash flow analysis is a little misleading. Businesses can receive and pay money in many ways. The most common of these are credit card, debit card, electronic transfer and cheque – as well as cash. When calculating cash flow, all of these payment methods are counted. The main point is the day when any sort of payment is paid into or paid out of a business's bank account.

This isn't always straightforward. For example, if someone gives you a cheque and you take it to your bank, it will take about five days to 'clear'. This means that the money will not actually go into your account until about five days later. You will learn more about this in section 3.4.

Calculating cash flow

Decorblock is a small business owned by Simon. It specialises in laying block paving for pathways and drives. At the end of October, Simon reviews his bank statement for the month. He notes that several cheques have been paid in to his account and that his income for the month amounted to £10,000. He also notes that various amounts of money have left the account for items such as materials from suppliers (like the blocks which he uses) and staff wages. He adds these expenses up and the total is £9,000.

Simon then uses the figures he has calculated to draw up a simple cash flow statement.

Summary cash flow statement – October

Income from sales	£10,000
Expenditure	£9,000
Net cash flow	£1,000

The figure he has calculated, net cash flow, is found by deducting income from expenditure. In this instance Simon has received £1,000 more than he has paid out and this is called a **positive cash flow**.

Simon then checks the amount of money in his account on the first day of the month. On that day he had £3,000 in this account. This is called the **opening balance**. Simon then checks the balance on the last day, called the **closing balance**, and sees that it is £4,000. Finally, he completes the cash flow statement to make sure that all the figures agree.

Completed summary cash flow statement – October

Income from sales	£10,000
Expenditure	£9,000
Net cash flow	£1,000

Monthly summary

Opening bank balance	£3,000
Net cash flow	£1,000
Closing bank balance	£4,000

Simon is pleased with this since he has more money in the bank at the end of the month than at the beginning. This is because his cash flow figure is positive.

Cash flow The actual amounts of money entering and leaving a business's bank account over a particular period of time, usually a month.

Net cash flow The difference between the total incoming cash flow and total outgoing cash flow.

Opening balance The amount of money in a business's bank account on the first day of a month.

Closing balance The amount of money in a business's bank account on the last day of a month.

Use the following information to produce cash flow statements for four businesses. Use the layout and headings given in the example of Simon's completed summary cash flow statement.

1 XYZ Trading. Opening balance £8,000, income £40,000, expenditure £37,000.
2 Widgets Unlimited. Opening balance £50,000, income £200,000, expenditure £180,000.
3 First Features. Opening balance £22,500, income £164,300, expenditure £158,360.
4 Creative Projects. Opening balance £16,429, income £287,987, expenditure £285,783.

View 1: *Owners haven't time to constantly monitor their cash flow. They should spend their time maintaining and improving the business.*

View 2: *So long as the owner monitors cash flow, the business will always be healthy.*

With which viewpoint do you agree – and why?

Negative cash flow

Simon looks at his bank statement at the end of November and receives a shock. The summary of his cash flow analysis is

Completed summary cash flow statement – November

Income from sales	£6,000
Expenditure	£10,000
Net cash flow	– £4,000

Monthly summary

Opening bank balance	£4,000
Net cash flow	– £4,000
Closing bank balance	£0

Simon notices immediately that his cash flow figure is negative. Because he only had £4,000 in the bank at the start of the month, the result is that his final bank balance is zero. When he investigates further he realises the problem is that some customers have not paid their bill even though the work was completed over two months ago.

Simon's problem is not unusual. Many businesses struggle to maintain a positive cash flow even though they are selling plenty of products and/or supplying services to many customers. This issue will be discussed in more depth later in this section.

Full cash flow statements

The two cash flow statements Simon produced are summaries. Normally they are produced in a little more detail. This is shown in Figure 3.4.

Small businesses have more problems with negative cash flow than larger organisations. This is because they have fewer customers and have not got the power to demand payment from large organisations. However, organisations at the other end of the scale can also have problems. In October 2003 the Government was forecast to have a negative cash flow of billions of pounds. It was said that the Chancellor, Gordon Brown – the Government's head of finance – may have to consider reducing public expenditure on education, health care and other public services. On the other hand he could consider raising taxes. Both of these options would be unpopular with the voters.

Gordon Brown solved the problem by borrowing money. Businesses, too, may have to do this either by taking out a **bank loan** or having an **overdraft**. In this case the bank gives the business permission to have a negative balance in their bank account, normally on a temporary basis. The problem then, of course, is that the business has to pay service charges to the bank for either the bank loan or the overdraft – which increases their expenditure.

	October £
Income from sales	10,000
Expenditure	
Blocks	4,000
Wages	3,000
Sand	1,000
Diesel fuel	500
Miscellaneous	500
Subtotal of expenditure	9,000
Net cash flow	1,000
Monthly summary	
Opening bank balance	3,000
Net cash flow	1,000
Closing bank balance	4,000

Figure 3.4 *Simon's cash flow statement for October*

If you study this carefully, you will see that all of the main headings are identical to his summaries. The only difference is that the total expenditure figure has been broken down into the various items. For example, during the month Simon spent £4,000 on the blocks he uses for his business. This expanded version of the statement is useful since Simon has more information to help him understand what is happening. As you will see later, this type of chart can be used to **forecast** cash flow.

Now study the cash flow statement in Figure 3.5. The figures for the next month have been added. You will see that Simon had a negative cash flow. This was mainly due to a drop in income. However, Simon can now see that he has bought more blocks and spent more on wages. He knows that these two increases were due to some extra work which he undertook. Finally, you should notice that the closing bank balance for October has become the opening balance for November.

	October £	November £
Income from sales	10,000	6,000
Expenditure		
Blocks	4,000	4,500
Wages	3,000	3,500
Sand	1,000	1,000
Diesel fuel	500	500
Miscellaneous	500	500
Subtotal of expenditure	9,000	10,000
Net cash flow	1,000	−4,000
Monthly summary		
Opening bank balance	3,000	4,000
Net cash flow	1,000	−4,000
Closing bank balance	4,000	0

Figure 3.5 *Simon's cash flow statement for two months*

Over to you!

Use the following information to produce a cash flow forecast for three months from January to March, using the layout you have seen for Simon's forecast above. The figures are for Garden Features, a small business making garden ornaments.

When you have completed the table, identify the month where the cash flow is negative. Then examine the table and say which figures have caused the problem by comparing them with those for January.

Item/month	January (£)	February (£)	March (£)
Sales income	20,000	18,000	22,000
Cement	2,000	3,000	2,500
Sand	1,000	1,000	900
Wages	14,000	15,000	14,000
Paint	500	500	500
Misc	300	200	200
Opening bank balance	3,000		

Garden features cash flow forecast

Talking point

View 1: *If a plumber insists on customers paying only in cash and pays for materials in cash, he/she has no problems with cash flow.*

View 2: *If the plumber does this he/she will lose customers who don't want to go to the bank and carry large amounts of cash. The tax authorities may be a bit suspicious of the plumber, too!*

With which viewpoint do you agree – and why?

Using spreadsheets to construct cash flow charts

Spreadsheets are an ideal way of constructing cash flow charts. As you will see later, they are particularly useful for forecasting cash flow since figures can be changed to explore the effects of possible changes in cost and revenue figures.

Study the cash flow chart in Figure 3.6. The figures are the same as those used in the exercise you have just completed but all of the numbers which you calculated have been replaced by formulae. If you have studied spreadsheets in your IT class, these will look familiar.

	A	B	C	D
1	Garden features cash flow			
2				
3		January	February	March
4		£	£	£
5	Income from sales	20000	18000	22000
6				
7	Expenditure			
8				
9	Cement	2000	3000	2500
10	Sand	1000	1000	900
11	Wages	14000	15000	14000
12	Paint	500	500	500
13	Misc	300	200	200
14				
15	Subtotal of expenditure	=SUM(B9:B13)	=SUM(C9:C13)	=SUM(D9:D13)
16				
17	Net cash flow	=SUM(B5-B15)	=SUM(C5-C15)	=SUM(D5-D15)
18				
19	Monthly summary			
20				
21	Opening bank balance	3000	=SUM(B24)	=SUM(C24)
22	Net cash flow	=SUM(B17)	=SUM(C17)	=SUM(D17)
23				
24	Closing bank balance	=SUM(B21:B22)	=SUM(C21:C22)	=SUM(D21:D22)
25				

Figure 3.6 *A cash flow spreadsheet*

Business brief

Spreadsheets and formulas

If you have created spreadsheets in your IT classes you will know that formulas are entered whenever you want a calculation to be carried out. If you feel like a refresher course would be useful, use this guide as you work through the cash flow forecast above.

- The expenditure sub-total is found by doing the 'sum' of all the items bought and, for the first month, entered in cells B9 to B13.
- The net cash flow in cell B17 is found by deducting the expenditure total in cell B15 from the income from sales in cell B5.
- The first opening bank balance in cell B21 is not a formula, because this must be entered.
- You can repeat the net cash flow figure in the monthly summary by entering a formula to repeat the cell number (i.e. B17).
- The closing bank balance is found by adding the opening bank balance in cell B21 to the net cash flow in cell B22. This formula will always be a *plus* – even when you are dealing with negative amounts – providing you precede the negative amount with a minus sign. This is because the spreadsheet will understand that a plus formula with a negative number equals minus. A useful check, if you are unsure, is to work out this number on your calculator to see you get the same total!
- You can enter the opening bank balance for the second and third months by entering the cell number of the *previous* bank balance.
- For second and subsequent months, you can save time by replicating formulas across columns. If you are not sure how and when to do this, talk to your tutor.
- Finally, whether you prepare forecasts on paper or on a spreadsheet, you may find it useful to enter a zero if there is no entry, rather than to leave a cell blank. This way, you are less likely to enter the wrong information.

Over to you!

1 Set up the spreadsheet shown on page 225 on a computer by keying in the headings on the left hand side, adding the income and expenditure figures, the opening bank balance and the formulas. Check that the calculations give the same result as those you worked out earlier.

2 Nikita runs a business selling shoes and trainers. In December, she decides to forecast her cash flow for the first six months of the next year. The Christmas period was good for sales and she plans to restock the store room ready for the busy summer period.

Nikita's opening bank balance on 1 January was 20,000. She sits down with a pen and paper and produces the income and expenditure figures given below. Set up a spreadsheet using the figures in the table below. Insert the formulas required to carry out the calculations needed.

3 Examine Nikita's forecast spreadsheet and identify the months when she has a negative cash flow. Also identify the months where her forecast bank balance is negative. Looking at the figures, can you suggest the main reasons for the negative figures?

Save your spreadsheet, as you will need to refer to it again later.

	January £	February £	March £	April £	May £	June £
Income from sales	50,000	48,000	50,000	55,000	58,000	60,000
Expenditure						
Shoes	45,000	30,000	25,000	20,000	22,000	20,00
Trainers	22,000	20,000	15,000	14,000	14,000	13,00
Wages	5,000	5,000	5,000	5,000	5,000	5,000
Rent	1,000	1,000	1,000	1,000	1,000	1,000
Miscellaneous items	500	500	500	500	500	500

Nikita's cash flow forecast

Business brief

Banks and overdrafts

Banks often offer overdraft facilities to their current account customers, particularly businesses. This enables the customer to draw out more money than is in their account. Banks are usually happy to provide this facility providing the customer arranges it in advance. They know that businesses normally sell goods on credit, which means that there is often a gap between goods being delivered and the payment being made (see page 229.)

The main features of these **arranged overdrafts** are:

- There is an agreed maximum amount which can be borrowed, known as the **overdraft limit**.
- The customer pays interest on the amount borrowed only for the period when the account is overdrawn.

- Interest is charged on a daily basis.
- Using an overdraft facility is also known as **going into the red**.
- An overdraft is a kind of "safety net". Although a business may plan to keep a positive bank balance, something unexpected may happen which means that it has to spend extra money quickly. If it has an overdraft facility, it knows that there is not a problem.

Banks do not like customers exceeding their overdraft limit or going into the red without permission. In these situations, they may refuse to allow any withdrawals or payments from the account. Alternatively, they may allow it, but charge a far higher interest rate. This situation is known as an **unauthorised overdraft**.

View 1: *Bill runs a small business. He has never taken the trouble to learn about spreadsheets and prefers to use a pen and paper for his calculations. He says that this is more straightforward and pens never break down!*

View 2: *Bill's friend enjoys using spreadsheets and uses them for all his cash flow forecasts. He believes there are many advantages of doing this.*

With which viewpoint do you agree – and why?

Monitoring cash flow

Nikita has a problem. She has negative figures for her closing bank balance for the first three months. In this case she must arrange finance to cover this amount. She knows it is cheaper to arrange an overdraft, because she will only pay bank charges on the actual amount owing on any day. She also knows that she must contact her bank immediately to ask for an authorised overdraft.

Nikita's cash flow forecast shows that she will go into the red by £12,000 in February, the worst month. If she is happy to pay the interest on this she should ensure that her overdraft limit is over this amount – say £15,000 or even £20,000.

This example illustrates a general point about cash flow forecasting. The most important figures on the chart are those on the last line – often referred to as the **bottom line** in company accounts. This shows how much money the business has or should have in the bank at the end of the month. If the figure is negative for one or two months, the business may not be too concerned if there is a good reason. If it is negative and getting worse month by month then the business could be in serious trouble.

You should now understand why bank managers and accountants often refer to the 'bottom line' when they are talking about company finances – and why they look at that line first!

Planning and monitoring cash flow

In the exercise involving Nikita's shoe shop you have an example of a business using a cash flow chart to plan what is likely to happen over a future period. There are two further aspects of this which are important.

- A plan can be adjusted to see what would happen if certain figures are altered. For example, Nikita may not be happy with the high negative cash flow figures in her forecast and decide not to buy as much stock in the early months. She can also check to see what would happen if sales were higher or lower than her first forecast.
- Once a cash flow forecast has been set up, it can be used to monitor what actually happens. Monitoring involves checking what actually happens to a businesses cash flow. In other words, forecast figures are replaced with actual amounts of money which enter or leave the bank account.

Nikita is not happy with her first cash flow forecast. She does not want to pay a lot of interest on her overdraft, in fact she would prefer not to let her account balance to fall below zero. She decides to reduce her stock purchases of shoes by £10,000 in January and her purchases of trainers by £2,000 in February.

Look at Nikita's changed spreadsheet on page 228 and compare it with the one you produced on page 226. The amounts of money for shoe purchases in January and trainers in February have been reduced. The result of this is that the closing bank balance in January is now positive and in February is zero. Nikita is happy with this since she does not now have to use an overdraft facility.

	January £	February £	March £	April £	May £	June £
Income from sales	50,000	48,000	50,000	55,000	58,000	60,000
Expenditure						
Shoes	35,000	30,000	25,000	20,000	22,000	20,000
Trainers	22,000	18,000	15,000	14,000	14,000	13,000
Wages	5,000	5,000	5,000	5,000	5,000	5,000
Rent	1,000	1,000	1,000	1,000	1,000	1,000
Miscellaneous items	500	500	500	500	500	500
Subtotal of expenditure	63,500	54,500	46,500	40,500	42,500	39,500
Net cash flow	−13,500	−6,500	3,500	14,500	15,500	20,500
Monthly summary						
Opening bank balance	20,000	6,500	0	3,500	18,000	33,500
Net cash flow	−13,500	−6,500	3,500	14,500	15,500	20,500
Closing bank balance	6,500	0	3,500	18,000	33,500	54,000

Figure 3.7 *Nikita's revised cash flow forecast*

Over to you!

Nikita is thinking about changes she could make to her business during the next six months.

1 Recall the original spreadsheet that you produced for Nikita's business on page 226. Then reduce the shoe purchases in January by £10,000 and the trainer purchases in February by £2,000. Check that your spreadsheet now exactly matches the one above.

2 For each of Nikita's ideas below, change the relevant figures on the spreadsheet and each time note the change in the closing bank balance. Do this by going back to the original spreadsheet you produced for question 1 each time, apart from the second section of part **d** below. Remember that you can save your changes if you select 'save as' and give the spreadsheet a different name (e.g. Nikita 1, Nikita 2 etc.). In business this makes it easier to examine each proposed change separately.

Finally, study the effect on the 'bottom line' in each case and suggest what Nikita's reaction would be.

a Spend £1,000 on advertising in March. Enter this as a new expenditure line. Nikita thinks this should increase sales by £2,000 in both April and May.

b Sell a cheaper range of trainers which would reduce purchase costs by £3,000 per month from April to June. In this case sales revenue would fall by £2,000 in April and £4,000 in May and June.

c Have a clearance sale of old stock in January. This would increase sales by £5,000. Since the stock has already been bought, this would not affect any other figures.

d i Employ an extra member of sales staff at the beginning of February at a cost of £1,000 per month.

   ii Assume that the new member of sales staff would increase sales by £3,000 per month from March onwards.

Check your figures, and your suggestions, with your tutor.

View 1: *Overdrafts give a business flexibility and often pay for themselves. This is because a business can buy new stock to sell even when it is short of money. Without an overdraft, it would be unable to do this.*

View 2: *Having an overdraft increases costs because of interest payments. Businesses should avoid borrowing money, because they are simply lining the banks' pockets and spending unnecessarily.*

With which viewpoint do you agree – and why?

The effect of making payments on cash flow

In the main part of this section we will look at ways in which businesses can improve their cash flow. This helps them reduce the need to have an overdraft, or even not need one at all. Before you learn about this, you need to understand how payments are made for goods and services.

If you buy a magazine from a shop and pay cash, the shopkeeper deposits the cash into his/her bank account on the same day, or shortly after. In this case the effect on cash flow is almost instantaneous. However, as you learned earlier, when businesses deal with other businesses, they do so mostly on a credit basis.

Credit payments

When businesses sell products to other businesses, they deliver the goods and then send an **invoice** asking for payment, often by post. The invoice has a date on it saying when payment is required. Typically, this is about thirty days after the goods are received. Even so, some customers take a lot longer to pay their debts.

This system is known as **credit sales**. The main point is that businesses receive money a lot later than they deliver the goods or provide a service. This obviously affects the cash flow of both customer and supplier as customers want to hold on to their money for as long as possible.

When a supplier deals regularly with a customer, there could be several deliveries of goods each month. In this case, an invoice is sent after each delivery but, in addition, a statement is sent by the supplier each month which lists all the invoices and any payments made that month and states the final amount owed.

Figure 3.8 *A credit sale transaction*

Timing of payments – and the effect of late or non-payment

You already know that a negative cash flow can lead to a business needing an overdraft. If a progressively higher overdraft is requested then the bank will be concerned that the business is not being managed properly and will eventually refuse to lend any more money. This, in turn, leads to a business not being able to pay its own bills or even, in some cases, the staff wages.

In this situation, the firm's suppliers will then refuse to provide any more goods and may eventually go to court in an attempt to recover the money they are owed. When the situation reaches this stage the business normally has to cease trading. If there is insufficient money to pay the creditors, to whom the debts are owed, the owner is declared bankrupt – or the company is declared insolvent. Any remaining assets are sold to go towards repaying the money owed. Any outstanding taxes must be paid first. After that, it is highly unlikely that all those who are owed money will receive very much.

Poor cash flow is usually the result of:

- **Insufficient orders** for the goods or services. In this case there is not enough income from sales to pay the bills.
- **Late payments** by customers. If a number of customers do this, or one customer who owes a very large sum of money fails to pay, then the situation can be critical.

Minimising bad debt problems

Suppliers can take action to try to minimise problems of bad debts and late payment in two ways.

- First, taking **precautionary action** before supplying any goods by:
  - Carrying out **credit checks** on the customer.
  - Drawing up a **sales contract** which states the terms and conditions of the sale and when payments must be made.
- Second, by taking action to receive payments promptly through **credit control**.

Taking precautionary action

Wonderwash plc manufactures and supplies industrial washing machines. These are similar to domestic washing machines, but much larger. They are used by businesses such as hotels and hospitals which wash large amounts of towels, bed and table linen every day. The sales manager, Tom, has been contacted by a large hotel chain, Countrywide, to re-equip several of their hotels with the latest energy saving machine.

Tom is delighted. The factory has the capacity to make the machines and the deal would increase

---

Business brief

Why do businesses fail?

It has been estimated that 60 per cent of new businesses fail within the first three years. The main cause is often poor cash flow because customers haven't paid their bills by the required date or in some cases, not at all. When debts are not paid, this is known as a **bad debt**.

The main point is that businesses can have good products and plenty of sales. The problem arises when customers do not pay bills on time, or don't pay at all. There are two main types of problem.

- Large, powerful, companies not paying small suppliers quickly and then threatening to withdraw further orders if the small business pushes too hard for payment.
- Customers going bankrupt. In this situation, the supplier will receive little or no money. If the supplier is a small firm and the customer

owes a lot of money, this can cause the supplier to go bankrupt too.

Several years ago, the government was concerned about the problem of large businesses making late or very late payments to small companies. It introduced the Late Payment Act to give the businesses the option of charging interest on late payments. It was hoped that this would result in more payments being made by the due date.

The Credit Management Research Centre at Leeds University found that the Act is largely failing. It discovered that from 1996 to 2002, the number of late payments rose from 52 per cent to 56 per cent. Small businesses were still reluctant to challenge large customers for fear of losing the business. In practice, the law was being used mainly by large businesses against small suppliers – the exact opposite of what was intended!

sales by 20 per cent in the next six months. This would increase profits by the same amount. However, he is also worried that he has hardly heard of Countrywide. Are they in a healthy financial situation so that they could afford to pay their bills? Do they pay their bills promptly or do they always pay late? How can he reassure himself over these concerns? The market is very competitive and he does not want a good deal to slip through his fingers because he upsets the potential customer.

The table below gives some of the actions that Tom can take. It also shows possible problems in each case.

Action	Reason	Advantages	Possible problems
Look at the published company accounts	Will show if the business is profitable and how quickly they pay their bills	The accounts of a public limited company are available to anyone, so Countrywide will not know about the investigation	At best the accounts will be a few months out of date. The accounts are not publicly available in the case of private companies
Ask for a reference from Countrywide's bank	The bank will give its view as to whether the business can meet a specific commitment	Information will be more accurate and up to date than published accounts	Countrywide will have to give permission. The Bank will charge a fee and the information may be very general
Use a commercial credit reference agency (CRA)	The agency will give an up to date assessment of Countrywide's financial status	Should be accurate and informative	A fee is charged for supplying the information
Ask for references from other suppliers	They will know how promptly the business pays its bills	No fee charged	The supplier may be hesitant to criticise Countrywide in case it loses business or may even be too busy to reply
Get Countrywide to sign a sales contract which guarantees payment by a certain date	A legal document exists which could be used in court if problems arise	Better than a verbal agreement for valuable orders	Normally only used for valuable orders. In practice, the contract could be difficult or expensive to enforce
Offer a discount for prompt payment	Improves cash flow	Gives Countrywide an incentive to pay quickly	Costs money as the discount reduces the amount received

Figure 3.9 *Checking out the customer*

Company accounts

All private and public limited companies have to produce annual accounts by law. Public companies must publish these. This is why you can find the accounts of many large companies on their website.

The accounts provide financial information about the business such as the profit and loss account. This gives several kinds of useful information, such as profitability and how quickly a business pays its creditors. The accounts also contain a balance sheet which shows how much money the business has in the bank.

The accounts are published some months after the end of the financial year so some people may argue that the information can be up to eighteen months out of date. However, obtaining and studying a company's accounts over a period of time provides useful information for anyone who is considering supplying goods to them. Businesses know this and many who wish to develop good relationships with new suppliers make their accounts available to them as a matter of course. Richer Sounds does this – as you will see on the StudentZone at www.richerstudentzone.co.uk

Business matters

Businesses are not the only ones on which credit checks are made. If you want to open a bank account or buy a new computer or television on credit then the supplier will carry out a credit check on you, too. The main **credit reference agencies** (CRAs) that provide this service in the UK are Experian, Equifax and Callcredit. You have the legal right to check your own credit file from each agency to ensure that the information they hold on you is accurate. At the time of writing, this costs £2 each time. At the same time you receive a leaflet which tells you how to interpret the file and what to do if you find something that is incorrect.

Business organisations use CRAs to check out private individuals, but there are other private firms which provide checks on other business organisations – such as Checksure, INFOprompt Ltd and Debt Warning Ltd.

Another organisation, known as the Better Payment Practice Campaign, points out that there are strong arguments for businesses paying their bills on time. It says that the benefits are:

- Improving a business's reputation and its public image in general.
- Avoiding the risk of suppliers refusing to supply goods or demanding tighter terms such as payment on delivery.
- The economy as a whole improves.

The campaign gives help and advice to businesses on credit control and managing debts. It also encourages good payers to sign up to the campaign.

Credit control

Once a business has sent goods to a customer or delivered a service, it then has to wait for the payment. The invoice will normally state a time by which the money should be paid. Probably the most common term is 30 days. By this time the customer will usually have used the goods or resold them.

In the case of Wonderwash and Countrywide hotels, the finance department at Wonderwash will carry out the task of checking up whether payments are being received on time. This process is known as credit control.

The main stages in credit control are:

- Make sure that invoices are sent out as soon as goods are received by a customer.
- Log invoices and payments on a computerised accounting system which highlights late payment situations.
- Identify customers who consistently pay late and consider refusing to take further orders.

- When a payment is overdue, have a procedure for dealing with the situation. The procedure should allow for the fact that there may have been an innocent mistake.

The procedure could include:

- A friendly telephone call "We have noticed that..."
- A first letter/fax which is friendly but firm, asking for payment within seven days.
- Follow up letters which mention sanctions including interest charges and legal proceedings.
- Taking legal action to recover the debt if payment is still not made.

It is usually the task of the **credit controller** in a company to monitor the overall level of debts and ensure that action is taken if payments are late. The credit controller is also responsible for agreeing to allow credit to new customers and setting the maximum level for each one. Once this level is reached, no further goods will be supplied until payment is made.

Staff are trained to contact customers who owe money, often by telephone. They have to be able to deal with those who have made a genuine mistake, those who have a serious financial problem

Sorry Tom, the cheque is in the post now, once again our accounts department seem to have mislaid your invoice

A polite phone call can get results

themselves and those who are just good at making excuses! According to one survey, some of the more common ones they hear include:

- The director who signs the cheques is on holiday.
- The computer has crashed.
- The cheque is in the post.
- We are waiting for a large payment from a customer. When they pay us, we can pay you.
- We can't find your invoice.

Business brief

The benefits of factoring

Factoring has nothing to do with factories! It is the term used when a business 'sells' its debts to another company that specialises in debt collection. Another term used for this is invoice discounting.

One finance company that offers this service is GE Commercial Finance. In this case the supplier would produce the invoices and then receive up to 90 per cent of the payment due immediately.

GE Commercial Finance would then recover the debt – in return for the remaining 10 per cent.

Many finance providers claim that the customer is not aware of this arrangement. Other experts are less sure whether this is true and think it could jeopardise some business-to-business relationships.

The aim, however, is to enable businesses to receive immediate funding for outstanding money to improve their cash flow.

Business terms

Debtor A person or business that owes money to someone else.

Creditor A person or business who is owed money.

Credit sales Providing goods and allowing payment to be made some time later.

Invoice Often known as a bill! The document which gives details of a transaction and states the money owing.

Statement Sometimes called 'statement of account'. It summarises all the transactions during a month and states the final sum owing.

Bad debts Debts which have not been paid at all.

Credit reference agencies Businesses which provide details of the credit history and credit rating of an individual or business for a fee.

Talking point

View 1: *All businesses should hold on to their money for as long as possible before paying suppliers so that they can gain interest from their bank.*

View 2: *Delaying payment to suppliers until the very last minute causes unnecessary administration costs and bad feelings. It is irresponsible and unethical as it can put small firms out of business.*

With which viewpoint do you agree – and why?

Over to you!

1 Jason has had the following ideas for checking out new customers before agreeing to supply goods. Decide which **three** are the best and give a reason for each of those you reject.

   • Ring the supplier's accountant and ask for a current bank statement.
   • Look at published accounts.
   • Ask for bank references.
   • Drive past the supplier's building to see if it is well maintained.
   • Use a commercial credit agency.
   • Ask for references from other suppliers.

2 Working in small groups, select **one** of the following for investigation through the website links at www.heinemann.co.uk/hotlinks (express code 1386P). Summarise its main services or benefits and then present your findings to the rest of your class.

   a A major credit reference agency, e.g. Experian, Equifax or Callcredit.

   b A business credit reference agency, e.g. Checksure, Infoprompt and Debtwarning.
   c Computer packages for collecting outstanding debts more quickly from CCS.
   d Invoice discounting and credit control at GE Commercial Finance.
   e The Better Payment Practice Campaign.

3 Your friend Karen, who runs her own business, is struggling to obtain payment from some of her debtors. Working in a small group:

   a Suggest **three** actions she can take to minimise the problem of bad debts when she has already supplied the goods.

   b Suggest how she should respond to the 'excuses' made for late payment on page 233 See how many ideas you can think of – and then compare these with the responses suggested by other groups in your class! Finally, decide which ones would work – and which ones would not.

Now you have completed this section, you should understand that cash flow forecasting looks at the difference between money flowing into and out of a business's bank account. You should also be able to use a spreadsheet to compile a cash flow statement. Finally you should be able to suggest ways in which businesses can minimise late payment of debts and avoid bad debts as much as possible. Test your skills now by doing the following activities.

Check your understanding of this section by answering the following questions. Check all your answers with your tutor before moving on.

1 a What is meant by the term 'cash flow'?
   b Explain two benefits of using spreadsheets to create cash flow forecasts.
   c Explain the difference between monitoring actual cash flow and forecasting cash flow.
   d What is a bank overdraft?
   e Give one reason why a bank overdraft may be needed.
   f Identify two tasks of a credit controller.
   g What does the term 'credit sale' mean?
   h Briefly explain how the timing of payments can affect cash flow.
   i Explain the term 'bad debt'.

2 a Jenny has decided to start working out her cash flow. She has never done this before and hasn't much idea of how to do it – or why she is doing it! You have offered to help her.
      i She has noted down the following items. Put these into the correct order and carry out the required calculations for the first month.

      Closing bank balance, Income from sales £10,000, Opening bank balance £2,500; Expenditure £6,000; Net cash flow (appears twice), Monthly summary.
      ii Identify for Jenny the main benefits of subdividing expenditure into separate items in a cash flow forecast.
      iii Jenny seems to think all she needs to do is to record her income and payments and work out her actual cash flow at the end of each month. Is this true? Give a reason for your answer.

   b Jenny wants to minimise late payments problems and has jotted down the following ideas. Divide her list into two columns, those actions she should take before she supplies any goods and those which she should take afterwards.

Ideas

1   *Send invoices promptly*
2   *Check published accounts*
3   *Pay for a credit check from a commerical agency*
4   *Have a computer system which flags up late payments*
5   *Send a polite but firm letter*
6   *Ask for bank references*

What is a budget?

In the previous two sections of this unit, you have learned about break even and cash flow. Both of these are concerned with looking at the business as a whole. The techniques help businesses to plan what they expect – or would like – to happen and are then used to monitor actual performance. The examples used to illustrate the principles have been relatively small businesses. In large businesses, the techniques are just as useful and are used by senior managers. However, they are not so useful for managers running departments within the business who have no direct responsibility for income and expenditure.

For example, Alex runs the transport department of a local newspaper. He is responsible for delivering the printed papers to newsagents and other businesses that sell the papers to the public. By attending management meetings, he has learned that the business must sell a certain amount of papers to break even, or better still make a profit. He also knows that there is constant pressure to keep costs down and get money back from newsagents to improve cash flow. However, neither of these two management techniques tell him much about how to do his job. His priorities are to deliver newspapers as efficiently and as quickly as possible. He tries to keep costs down by using the most fuel-efficient vans, planning delivery routes to keep distances travelled to a minimum and watching his staff overtime bill very carefully. He also knows that if

he does his job well, the business should be profitable.

When Alex is doing these things, he is working to the budget for his department. Budgets are financial plans given to each manager in a large business to let them know how much they can spend on various items in the area under their control. Alex, for example, will know how much he can spend each month on items such as:

- Fuel.
- Maintenance of vehicles.
- Transport staff wages.

At the end of each month, he will receive information from the finance department telling him how much he has actually spent under each heading. He may have to take action if he is overspending.

What does a budget look like?

Desklamp is a business located near Birmingham. It produces a small range of lamps for use on office desks. Each lamp is produced by a separate department. One of the lamps is called Flexilight. This lamp uses a low voltage bulb which requires an electrical transformer. This allows the lamp to have a telescopic arm which means that it can be adjusted to operate in several positions.

The Flexilight department assembles the lamps from bought-in components. The manager of the department is called Lianne. Her monthly budget is shown in Figure 3.10.

Item	Planned monthly Expenditure £
Bulbs	2,000
Plastic bases	1,500
Telescopic arms	3,500
Switches	1,000
Transformers	5,000
Cables and plugs	1,800
Screws	500
Wages	5,000
Total	**20,300**

Figure 3.10 *Flexilight budget*

This information tells Lianne that she is allowed to spend the amounts of money shown for the different items. The budget was produced during a discussion with her line manager and it fits in with the overall financial plan for the business.

Producing a budget

In large organisations, budgets are produced once a year for each department. These departments are sometimes known as **cost centres**. The overall process is shown in Figure 3.11. Suppose that a business has its budget year from the start of April one year to the end of March the next year. Before the start of the first year, from January to March, managers make their financial plans for the budget year. They do this by making sales and expenditure forecasts. They could use break even analysis and cash flow forecasts to help them.

When the financial plan for the business as a whole has been agreed (A), it is broken down into sections, one for each department or cost centre (B). At the end of each month the items of expenditure for each department's budget are calculated and the results shown to the manager (C). If the figures produced are close to those

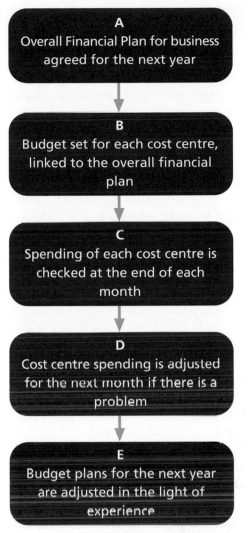

A
Overall Financial Plan for business agreed for the next year

B
Budget set for each cost centre, linked to the overall financial plan

C
Spending of each cost centre is checked at the end of each month

D
Cost centre spending is adjusted for the next month if there is a problem

E
Budget plans for the next year are adjusted in the light of experience

Figure 3.11 *The budget process*

forecast, there is not a problem. If there are one or more significant differences, particularly if more money has been spent on an item than was planned (D), the cost centre manager will be expected to take action. Towards the end of the budget year – in this case January to March again – the experience of operating the budget will be used to help plan the next year's forecast. In other words, the process is repeated on an annual cycle.

Budget planning

Budget planning is often a fraught time for budget holders and managers. Budget holders don't want budgets that are so low that they are constantly having problems trying to run their departments. Senior managers don't want budgets too high because this encourages wastage and reduces overall profits. The 'bidding' process for budgets often goes on several weeks, until the final figures have been agreed.

The process can be even more difficult if a cost centre is new or is going to undertake new work or different types of activities. These will involve new costs which must be calculated carefully against the target output. If these costs are set too low, the manager will struggle to meet targets and stay within budget and may ask for the figures to be reviewed as soon as possible. Senior managers are likely to want evidence that there really is a problem before they will agree to this.

Budgets and spreadsheets

Like cash flow forecasts, budgets are often produced using a spreadsheet. The benefits are similar. The figures can easily be entered and amended and, providing the formulas are correct, the calculations will be done accurately. Previous versions of budgets can be saved for reference. In particular, all the departmental budgets can be linked together as a master spreadsheet to link to the overall financial plan.

Budgets and cash flow forecasts

At a quick glance budget forecasts and cash flow forecasts appear to be very similar. The chart below highlights these similarities but also the differences. It should help you to understand the principles involved.

Business terms

Budget A financial plan for a department (cost centre) listing the amounts of money which should be spent on various items.
Budget holder The manager responsible for ensuring that expenditure stays within budget.
Budget process The whole process of setting budgets, monitoring performance and taking corrective action.
Variance The difference between planned and actual expenditure within a budget. This will be discussed further in a later section.
Cost centre A department in an organisation which has a budget.

Similarities	Differences
• Both forecast expenditure over a future period. • Both are normally broken down into monthly intervals. • Outcomes are checked against plans.	• Budgets are produced for individual departments but cash flow is for the business as a whole. • Budgets are the responsibility of several individual managers whereas cash flow is checked by the Finance department. • Cash flow is concerned with money entering and leaving a business's bank account. With budgets, the department concerned is only charged for materials when resources are used, whether they have actually been paid for or not.

Figure 3.12 *Similarities and differences between budgets and cash flow forecasts*

1 For each of the following statements write down whether they are true or false.

   a Budgets are concerned with the amount of cash in the businesses bank account.

   b In the case of both cash flow and budgets, outcomes are checked against plans.

   c Budget holders check the bank balance every month.

   d Budgets are only set for a month in advance.

   e Most managers in a large business have a budget to control.

   f Budgets and cash flow forecasts are both concerned with forecasting expenditure over a future period of time.

2 Write out the following statement and complete it correctly using the following words or phrases.

   budgets, variance, budget holder, budget process, senior managers.

   'Before the start of a year, _____ plan the financial performance of the business for that year. Each _____ is then given a list of items which they can spend money on, together with amounts they can spend. These lists are called _____. The difference between the amount planned to be spent in a budget and the actual amount spent is called a _____. The whole procedure is called the _____.'

3 Write down the amounts of money you expect to spend in the next week. Do this by first making a list of all the items you normally buy. Then write the amount you plan to spend on each type of item. During the week, keep a record of all the money you spend each day and what you spend it on. After a week, make a list of all your expenditure and compare it with the list you made at the beginning.

   Did you keep to your plan? Are there any large differences between the two lists – if so, why?

Talking point

View 1: *Budgets are a waste of time and effort. It should be obvious what needs to be spent to get the job done.*

View 2: *Nothing, not even a box of paper clips, should be bought without formal approval.*

With which viewpoint do you approve – and why?

Monitoring monthly expenditure

The aim of producing a budget is to give each manager a maximum target figure of expenditure on each item. Continual checks are made to find out how actual spending compares with target expenditure on each item.

By cost centre

The financial manager or controller will usually be responsible for checking that each cost centre's spending is on target. This is where computerised systems are particularly valuable, as the controller can see at a glance how much each cost centre has spent and enter this figure into a master budget.

Senior managers will study the master budget and expect budget holders to account for major differences. You will find out more about this on pages 240 and 245.

Against budgets

The cost centre manager will be responsible for checking his or her actual expenditure against the planned expenditure in the budget. If there is a difference between the two, this is known as a variance. The action the manager is expected to take will depend upon two factors:

- Whether the variance is favourable or unfavourable.
- The size of the variance.

Calculating favourable and unfavourable variances

In the case of Desklamp you saw the planned budget expenditure for the Flexilight department on page 237. Now look at the budget for March below. You will notice that two columns have been added, 'actual' and 'variance'. It is the end of the month and the money Lianne has spent on each item has been entered into the 'actual' column. The final variance column shows the difference between the two sets of figures. This is the information in which Lianne, the budget holder, is most interested. This type of document is known as a **budget report**.

Item	Planned £	Actual £	Variance £
Bulbs	2,000	1,900	100
Plastic bases	1,500	1,500	0
Telescopic arms	3,500	5,000	–1,500
Switches	1,000	1,070	–70
Transformers	5,000	3,000	2,000
Cables and plugs	1,800	1,750	50
Screws	500	500	0
Wages	5,000	4,500	500
Total	20,300	19,220	1,080

Figure 3.13 *Flexilight budget report – March*

Favourable variances

In the Flexilight budget report, some of the figures in the variance column are positive, or favourable – bulbs, transformers, cables and plugs and wages. This means that less money has been spent than was planned. You may think that the budget holder would be pleased with positive variances since the business is saving money. To an extent this is true, but any large variances would need an explanation. In this instance the £2,000 less spent on transformers could be due to a discount achieved by purchasing for buying in bulk. The smaller variances, such as the £100 for bulbs and £50 for screws would probably not cause too much concern.

Unfavourable variances

Negative figures will always be of more concern than positive figures. This is because these show an unfavourable variance. In this instance, £5,000 has been spent on telescopic arms. This is £1,500 more than was planned – a large negative variance. One of the concerns is that, if this pattern continued for a year, the overspend would be £18,000 (1,500 × 12). The budget holder would be expected to investigate the problem, take action to correct it, and report this situation to senior managers. For example, if we assume that the problem with the telescopic arms was that these had been damaged in storage and several were then unusable, this is unacceptable wastage. Lianne would have to take action to make sure that the problem would not happen again.

The £1,500 overspend on the telescopic arms was the only major negative variance in the report. Switches showed a negative variance of £70. This is a relatively small amount and would not cause too much concern.

The final figure of interest in the budget is the total variance figure at the bottom right of the report. In the case of a budget, this is the 'bottom line' figure of most interest to all managers. It shows that, overall, the department has spent £1,080 less than planned. This would please Lianne and her senior managers because, if this continued, the business as a whole would make a higher profit than had been forecast.

Business matters

A special type of budget is used for specific projects. In this situation, something unique is to be built and the budget is designed to cover all the resource requirements. Whether this successfully keeps costs under control is another matter – as you will see below!

Holyrood is the name of the new Scottish parliament building. It was planned to have revolutionary features including an oval debating chamber, water gardens, a roof garden and even a bicycle shed! Design work began in June 1998. The total cost was estimated to be about £40m and the building was due to open in 2001. Work fell behind schedule and the forecast price kept rising – from £109m in June 1999 to £195m in April 2000 then £325m in December 2002 and £400m in October 2003. On that date, the building was not expected to be completed until 2004.

The Government, responsible for paying the final bill, was not pleased. The final cost was about ten times more than the original estimate and building work was taking twice as long. What had gone wrong? Few details were available. The forecast price of the assembly hall lights had been £250,000 but the actual cost was £1.9m. The cost of woodwork in the chamber rose from £5m to £12m. Only a few costs were below estimate, such as security systems at £1.28m instead of £1.7m. An enquiry was set up to investigate the problem, with its own budget of £1.2m. Hopefully the enquiry team will be better at keeping within budget than the builders!

Some projects, however, do come in on time and within budget. One example is the new Wembley Stadium – the traditional national home of football in England. The project to replace the out-of-date stadium started in 1995 and some of the funding was obtained from the Lottery Council. The design work began in 1997.

The total cost was forecast to be £757m, including £120m for the design process, £103m to purchase the old stadium, £99m to demolish the old stadium and £325m to build the new one. The contract is managed by Multiplex Construction UK who will have to stay within budget or pay for any extra expense themselves.

You can find out about progress and take a virtual tour of the stadium at the Wembley Stadium website – a link is available at www.heinemann.co.uk/hotlinks (express code 1386P).

This is what the new Wembly stadium will look like

Business brief

Double checking in a spreadsheet

Very often there is a special cell in a spreadsheet where the answer to a calculation can easily be double checked. In Flexilight's budget report this is the final variance total – £1,080 (see Figure 3.13).

This is because you can arrive at this total *either* by deducting the actual total from the budget total *or* by adding up all the variances.

If you are sensible, you will double-check this total. Do this by finding the total using your preferred method from the options above. Then move to a nearby blank cell and enter the formula to obtain the total using the second method. Both your cells should show the same amount – otherwise you have gone wrong.

If they are identical, then delete the second total in the blank cell before you print out your spreadsheet.

Over to you!

1 Practice using a spreadsheet to produce a budget and carry out some basic calculations.

a Lianne has asked you to draw up her Flexilight budget for April using a spreadsheet. It is the start of the new budget year and the amount she is allowed to spend on some items has been changed. Create a spreadsheet using the headings and layout shown below. Then enter the budget amounts for each item and total these using a sum formula. Check with your tutor that your answer is correct.

Item	Planned £	Actual £	Variance £
Bulbs	2,200		
Plastic bases	1,500		
Telescopic arms	3,000		
Switches	1,200		
Transformers	5,000		
Cables and plugs	1,800		
Screws	500		
Wages	5,250		
Total			

Flexilight April budget

b At the end of the month, Lianne gives you her expenditure figures. Enter these in the 'actual column' and total them. Remember that you can replicate the sum formula for your Budget total to do this.

Item	Actual £
Bulbs	2,100
Plastic bases	1,500
Telescopic arms	2,800
Switches	1,250
Transformers	4,800
Cables and plugs	1,700
Screws	500
Wages	5,000

Lianne's actual expenditure for April

c Enter a formula for your first variance to give you the difference between the Budget and the Actual amount spent. Check that this figure is correct and then replicate the formula for the rest of the items. You can continue to do this for the final total as well, if you wish.

d Check that your final variance total is correct by double checking the total in a blank cell. If you have forgotten how to do this, reread the Business Brief on page 241. Then amend your heading to read 'Flexilight budget report – April' and print out your budget for your tutor to check.

2 Lianne's budget has changed slightly since the start of the new budget year. The amounts she can spend on some items have increased, although one has decreased.

Working in small groups, compare the amounts she can spend now with last year (shown in her March budget on page 240). List all the differences you can find and then think of one reason why these figures may have been changed since last year. Compare your ideas with those of other groups.

3 Plasprods is a business that makes various types of moulded plastic containers such as storage boxes, desk trays and waste bins. One department specialises in making waste bins that can be hung on lamp posts and other supports. They are bought by local authorities, colleges and other large organisations. The bins are often made to order for customers who want particular colours and logos. The main process is a moulding machine which produces the bins themselves. This machine uses a lot of electricity to heat and soften the raw plastic. After this metal brackets are fitted so that the bins can be attached to lamp posts or other supports.

a The monthly budget for June is shown opposite. Create a spreadsheet to record this information. Insert a formula to total the planned expenditure column.

b During June the following events occur in the department. The settings on the moulding machine are found to be faulty which results in more plastic being used than necessary. The repairs to the machine result in lost production and the staff have to work overtime to catch up. On the brighter side, a member of staff makes a suggestion which means that a

Item	Planned expenditure £
Raw plastic	25,000
Power	6,000
Metal brackets	3,000
Nuts and bolts	1,500
Machine maintenance	2,500
Wages	10,000
Total	

Waste bin budget – June

Item	Actual expenditure £
Raw plastic	28,000
Power	5,700
Metal brackets	2,000
Nuts and bolts	1,600
Machine maintenance	4,000
Wages	12,000
Total	

Waste bin actual expenditure – June

cheaper version of the metal bracket can be used.

At the end of June, the manager of Plasprods waste bin department receives his actual expenditure report which is shown above.

Insert this information into the spreadsheet which you have just produced and add a variance column. Enter the formulas needed to produce the total actual expenditure, the

variances for each item and the total variance – and then double check this figure.

c Examine the figures you have produced and make a note of the areas which you think the budget holder would examine. Suggest reasons for any major variances and what the budget holder should do about them, in preparation for the next section. Use the information in section **b** to help you.

Talking point

View 1: *Budgets are a waste of time for major projects because there are so many unknown factors.*

View 2: *Budgets are essential for major projects but they have to be carefully thought through and monitored at every stage.*

With which viewpoint do you agree – and why?

Budgets and flexibility

In the Plasprods example, the manager of the department has to produce a certain number of bins each month. To achieve this, he knows the amount of materials he will need and how much these cost. He can therefore calculate how much he should spend on each item each month and

these are likely to be the amounts entered into his budget as planned expenditure.

In some types of cost centre, the budget has to be more flexible. For example, a marketing manager may have a budget of £50,000 but be given some flexibility as to *how* this money is spent. He or she could decide to concentrate on advertising in magazines and newspapers or put most of the money into a television campaign. The manager can also make decisions about *when* to spend the money. This is important when a business's market is cyclical and sales rise and fall depending on the time of year. Your college, for example, will promote many of its courses mainly in late August and early September for the start of the new academic year. In contrast, many retail businesses spend most of their advertising budget as Christmas approaches.

Budget holders are often allowed to switch expenditure from one item to another, as long as they keep within their overall budget limits. The correct term for this is to vire the amount. So a marketing manager could **vire** some of his planned spending on press advertising to a radio or cinema campaign if this would be more effective. You will see how this works in the exercise below.

Over to you!

Modelshop is a business which produces plastic models for a specialist market. Its models are sold in sets which, after painting, are used in board games. The market is seasonal. Sales are fairly quiet in the summer but build up in the autumn to a peak just before Christmas.

The marketing department is responsible for promoting the products so as to achieve maximum sales. The marketing manager, Feroz, is told that his budget from July to Christmas is £130,000. After discussions with his team, he decides to spend the money as shown below.

Television advertising is a new development for the business. Until now the main emphasis has been on specialist magazines and promotions through posters in model shops. The commercials will take place on specialised satellite channels. In addition, the business produces its own magazine which is sold in the shops and sent by mail to known customers. Modelshop also has a website which generates a small but increasing amount of business. Finally, the company has its own representatives who visit retailers to discuss promotions with the shop managers. The reps also visit shops which do not currently sell their products to see if they can be persuaded to do so.

You work for Feroz, who has asked you to complete the following tasks.

1 Feroz has asked you to let him have the following information:
   a The total amount he has planned to spend on promotional activities, each month, between July and December.
   b Confirmation that his overall planned spending total matches the allowed budget figure of £130,000.

Do this by entering all the information in the budget illustration, below, into a spreadsheet. Then create a 'total' column at the right hand side. Enter formulas to find the sum for each method of promotion and total these figures to check his overall planned total. Don't forget to double check this figure!

2 Feroz wants to be able to check that he is on target at the end of each month. He therefore asks you to add a row below the monthly total and label this 'cumulative total'. He wants this row to show cumulative amounts. Therefore at the end of August, it will show the combined July and August totals – and so on.
   a Enter a formula to obtain this total for each cell on the row. If you are unsure how to do this, talk to your tutor.
   b Look carefully at the last total on this row under December. What do you notice about this figure? Check your ideas with other members of your group.

Item	July £	August £	Sept £	Oct £	Nov £	Dec £
TV advertising	0	0	10,000	5,000	5,000	5,000
Sales representatives	5,000	5,000	5,000	5,000	5,000	5,000
Posters	2,000	4,000	4,000	0	0	0
Own magazine	5,000	0	5,000	0	5,000	0
Magazine advertising	0	4,000	6,000	6,000	6,000	4,000
Website	1,000	1,000	1,000	1,000	1,000	1,000
Marketing administration	3,000	3,000	3,000	3,000	3,000	3,000
Monthly total	16,000	17,000	34,000	20,000	25,000	18,000

Modelshop marketing budget – July to December

3 At the end of September, Feroz checks his sales figures. The figures are lower than expected and he decides that the television advertising has not been effective. He decides to cancel the rest of the TV advertising and to use this money to carry out a special poster campaign in October and November, spending the available money equally in each of these months.

   a How much money will Feroz have available to spend on his poster campaign?

   b How much will he spend in October and then in November?

   c Make these changes on your spreadsheet. Has Feroz stayed within his overall budget? Give a reason for your answer.

4 At the end of October, Feroz is asked to carry out a special promotion for Wonderworld, a game based on a film which is expected to be a Christmas blockbuster. His manager tells him to double his budget for magazine advertising for November and December. Adjust your spreadsheet again to include these changes.

   a Why do you think the manager agreed to a budget increase?

   b What are the new amounts Feroz can spend on magazine advertising in November and December?

   c What is the new final budget overall total?

Talking point

This is a variation on the other talking points you have seen. As a group, decide how you would answer each of the following comments by Feroz's boss in January, assuming that you are Feroz and you don't want your budget cut!

View 1: *I see Christmas sales were excellent. We obviously didn't need to spend so much on marketing so we can reduce your budget next year.*

View 2: *Christmas sales were poor so marketing obviously doesn't work. I think we should reduce your budget next year and use the money to improve customer service and our packaging design instead*

Reporting budget variances and taking action

All managers study budget reports very carefully – and very frequently! Budget holders check them to ensure that they are within budget. Senior managers check them to ensure *all* budget holders are keeping to their budgets.

When managers look at budget reports, they concentrate on major differences between planned and actual performance. Small differences are accepted since no forecast can be completely accurate. The process used to analyse a budget report such as those for Flexilight or Plasprods can be summarised as follows:

- Look for all major variances, both favourable and unfavourable.
- Large favourable variances are usually good news as this means that the business should be more profitable. However, a reason should be found as to why the difference between estimated and planned spending was so high. Otherwise it would be too easy for all managers to put a very high 'planned' figure against each item and then obtain a favourable variance every time!
- Large negative variances are worrying since they mean the business may be spending more than it can afford. These situations need to be investigated and corrected where possible.

A report needs to be given to senior management by the budget holder.

- The total variance figure also needs to be examined. A positive figure or a small negative figure should not be too much of a problem. A large negative figure would be a serious concern to senior managers since this means that the business as a whole is likely to be less profitable than forecast. They would expect the budget holder to investigate and report back on the causes and proposed solutions.

Monitoring budget variances

In most organisations, a financial controller or manager is responsible for monitoring all cost centre budgets. He or she will also have the task of notifying both budget holders and senior managers about variances. There may be a monthly meeting between this controller and each budget holder when the figures are studied and the reasons for variances are noted and recorded. The controller can also give advice to budget holders on how, perhaps, to vire future spending to keep within the overall limit.

If a variance is both unfavourable and large, both the controller and senior managers will expect to have been notified in advance by the budget holder. It is not normally expected for a budget holder to have no knowledge of an overspend – as it would then appear that he or she is not keeping check on what is happening in the department.

Management action to adjust actual to planned expenditure

Budget holders are expected to take action if they are overspending. Sometimes this is relatively easy, such as reducing spending on advertising for a month. On other occasions it is more difficult – or the effects would be detrimental. For example, if there has been overspending on extra temporary staff because of illness, there is little that can be done. Equally, if essential raw material prices have risen, and there are no suitable alternative suppliers, then the only way to reduce spending would be to buy less. In this case, fewer products could be made, which is not normally a good idea.

If budget holders have a particularly difficult problem, they are likely to discuss this with a more senior manager who may be responsible for several cost centres or departments, each with its own budget. In this situation, the senior manager's tasks are to:

- Negotiate and agree budgets with each cost centre manager for the coming financial year.
- Make sure that the combined individual budgets fall within the overall financial plan for the year.
- Examine the budget reports showing actual expenditure and variances on a regular basis.
- Deal with any major problems, such as a department which overspends month after month.
- Take money from a department which underspends and maybe use it somewhere else – sometimes known as **clawback**. This can be used to solve difficult overspend problems, e.g. on temporary staff or more expensive raw materials, without the overall budget being overspent.

Managers often resist clawback

- Set budgets for the following year taking into account any lessons learned from operating the current budget.

In other words, a senior manager looks at a broad picture, using this information to try to make sure that the business as a whole is profitable.

Revision of future budgets in the light of experience

As you saw on page 245, when you completed Feroz's spreadsheets, some senior managers try to use almost any event as a good reason to reduce budgets for the next year! Although this may seem ridiculous, managers actually want to avoid a situation where every item, on every budget is automatically increased, year after year. It is actually good practice to challenge some of the amounts being spent, to see if the money can be used more wisely given modern technology, changing methods of production and marketing and other developments.

Discussions about future budgets should therefore take account of:

- Current spending levels.
- Unavoidable increases (e.g. on staff wages because of a pay rise).
- Problems encountered during the current year.
- New ideas for saving money or doing business in a different, more cost-effective way.

Actually increasing the amount of money in the budget is often the last resort – as you will see from the chart in Figure 3.14, which summarises the types of managerial action which are likely to be taken if there is a budget problem.

Business terms

Clawback To take money from the budget of an underspending cost centre and use it to solve a problem in another area.

Vire To use the money within a budget on different items of expenditure than were first planned.

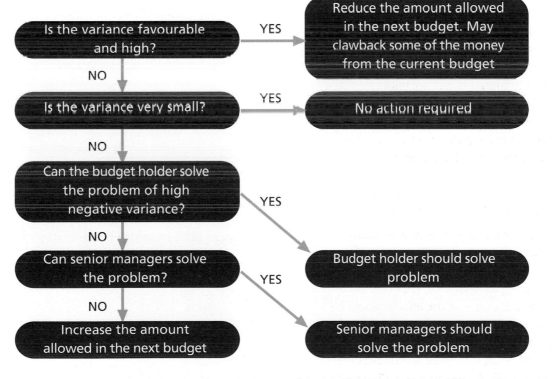

Figure 3.14 *Types of managerial action taken to solve a budget problem*

Over to you!

1 Work through the chart in Figure 3.14 with your tutor and check that you understand each option. Then, working in a small group, use the chart to decide which of the actions should be taken in the case of each of the following problems.

   a A production line has to stop at regular intervals because an outside supplier will not deliver components on time. The managing director tells the purchasing department to find a reliable supplier.

   b The marketing department is underspent because sales are high and not much promotion is needed. At the same time, there are problems because one of the main file servers is old and keeps crashing.

   c The staff restaurant is over budget because there is too much wastage. Staff are rejecting traditional choices such as chips and sausages because they have become more health conscious and want less fattening food.

   d Over a six-month period, the distribution department is budgeted to spend £1,500 on diesel fuel. It actually spends £1,497.60.

   e The production department of a chocolate factory is overspent by £5,000. The reason is that the price of cocoa on the world market has risen considerably and is unlikely to fall.

2 A colleague is in your office when your boss bursts through the door in a rage after a budget meeting with senior managers. He says 'I don't believe it. They said I could vire the money allowed for travel – which we don't need – to buy more laptops, which we most certainly do. Now, because I haven't bought them yet, they're threatening clawback because Jim wants new loading equipment in the warehouse.'

   Your colleague is mystified. How would you 'translate' your boss's statements into plain English?

3 a In a group, list as many benefits as you can for having a budgetary control system. When you do this, assume you are thinking about this from a Managing Director's point of view and that the business has several departments or cost centres, each with a budget.

   b Now consider the disadvantages. To help, try to think what it would be like to manage a budget yourself and have to argue about the money you needed and the problems you were having. Compare your ideas with those of other groups.

Talking point

View 1: *So long as the monthly sales figures are healthy, the Managing Director has nothing to worry about.*

View 2: *The Managing Director should insist on weekly budget reports and go through each one in great detail. He/she needs to do this to be sure that no disasters can happen.*

With which viewpoint do you agree – and why?

Now that you have completed this section, you should understand what is meant by the terms budgets and variances. You should also understand the action managers take if there is a problem with expenditure.

Check your understanding of this section by answering the following questions. Check your answers with your tutor before you continue.

1 a Explain what is meant by 'planned expenditure' on a budget.
 b Suggest **two** reasons why budgets are used by business organisations.
 c What is meant by the term 'variance'?
 d Explain the difference between a 'favourable' and an 'unfavourable' variance.
 e Explain why managers are more concerned about unfavourable variances than favourable ones.
 f What is meant by the term 'budget holder'?
 g What is a flexible budget?
 h A cost centre has a large, favourable budget variance for a number of months. Suggest **one** way in which senior managers are likely to respond.
 i A budget holder knows that he has considerably overspent on an item for reasons outside his control. Explain what action he should take and why.
 j Identify two issues that would be considered at a meeting to revise future budgets.

2 Jim owns a garage and has just completed his six-month budget forecast. This is shown below, scribbled in Jim's handwriting! Unfortunately,

Budget for next six months						
Item	Jan £	Feb £	March £	April £	May £	June £
Wages	5,800	5,800	5,800	5,800	5,800	5,800
Heating	1,000	1,000	1,000	1,000	1,000	1,000
Telephone	200	200	200	200	200	200
Electricity	1,000	1,000	1,000	1,000	1,000	1,000
Equipment maintenance	2,500	2,500	2,500	2,500	2,500	2,500
Building maintenance	500	500	500	500	500	500

Jim's notes

Jim doesn't understand spreadsheets or budgets very much and has asked for your help. Assist him by completing the following tasks.

a Prepare a spreadsheet to show Jim's six-month budget. You can use the headings Jim has used but will need to add rows for monthly totals, cumulative totals and the six-monthly totals.
b Insert Jim's data and then add formulas to complete the calculations.
c Jim forgets about his budget until the end of June! He thinks that everything has gone quite well. He then works out his total expenditure over six months for each item and gives you the following note.

Expenditure, Jan to June	
Wages	£50,000
Heating	£5,900
Telephone	£2,000
Electricity	£4,000
Equipment maintenance	£16,000
Building maintenance	£6,000
Jim	

Jim's expenditure

Add a column to your spreadsheet and enter the actual expenditure figures. Then add a final column and calculate the variance for each item and the total variance.

d Jim has asked you to meet him to talk about these variances. In each case decide what he should do. At the same time, list the benefits for Jim of reviewing his actual budget results regularly – rather than every six months!

This section covers

Manual and automated recording of transactions

Petty cash and day books

Fraud/theft and methods of combating it

What are transactions?

A transaction occurs when a person buys a product or service from a business and pays for it. When you buy a drink or a magazine from a shop, for example, this is a transaction. You receive the drink or magazine and hand over the money. Transactions also occur when businesses deal with other businesses. Other examples of transactions are:

- Your school or college could pay a landscape gardening business to maintain its hedges and flower beds.
- A customer buys groceries from a local superstore.
- A man pays a monthly subscription to a fitness centre.
- A car manufacturer buys windscreen wiper blades from a specialist producer.
- A shop that sells electrical goods offers to deliver and install a new washing machine and includes this service in the purchase price.

Transactions take place more often than you might think

As you can see, there are many different types of transaction but the common feature of all of them is that whatever types of goods or services are received, they have to be paid for. Some are paid for at the time of purchase and some are paid for later, for example, when a business is allowed credit by a supplier (see page 229).

No matter how payment is made, or when it is made, all transactions are recorded by businesses. In this section you will learn about different methods of recording these, including the use of day books. Day books are lists of transactions, recorded as they happen.

Unfortunately, all businesses have to protect themselves against fraud. Fraud takes place when money or goods are stolen from a business – or when services are not paid for. Fraud may take place when transactions are being recorded. You will find out why fraud is of concern to managers, and what they can do to try to prevent it.

Different types of transactions

Millions of transactions take place and are recorded every day. The way in which payment is made often varies, depending upon the type and size of transaction. This often affects the way in which the transaction is handled and recorded.

Transactions with individuals

- The owner of a takeaway kebab shop or a newsagent would be likely to receive most payments in cash from individual customers. The shop will therefore have a basic cash register to record the transaction and hold the money safely.

- In a large superstore, customers may pay by cash, credit or debit card or by cheque, mainly because higher sums of money are often involved. Normally more sophisticated cash registers are installed, linked to the main computer system.
- Many other businesses, however, rarely see cash payments. Householders who pay electricity bills, council tax, credit card bills and household insurance are more likely to pay by other methods, e.g. by cheque, direct debit (where regular payments are automatically made by the bank) or electronically. This option is becoming popular as more individuals bank online. In all these cases the transaction will be recorded direct on the main computer system.

Many organisations are trying to persuade their customers to pay electronically because this saves them money. A business that receives thousands of payments every day, such as a large credit card company, doesn't have to open an envelope, extract a cheque and record the amount received. Instead it can print out a daily statement of its bank account to see the list of payments received electronically and then log these against each customer account. This reduces the number of staff needed to process and record transactions.

Business-to-business (B2B) transactions

When businesses deal with other businesses, the method of processing the transaction will normally depend upon the size of business and the size of the transaction.

- Local tradesmen, such as electricians or plumbers, will buy their supplies and pay in cash, by cheque or card – just like private individuals.
- Businesses that continually buy large quantities of supplies – such as Tesco, Marks and Spencer and Office World will often use BACS (Banks Automated Clearing System) to pay regular or repeat customers by direct credit. This enables regular automated payments to be made and reduces the risk of loss late payment and theft. BACS can also be linked to an e-commerce B2B purchasing system so that accounts can automatically be settled electronically. This also provides a permanent record of all transactions on the computer system.
- Businesses that buy from overseas suppliers will also pay electronically for ease of transfer. This is one reason why Richer Sounds uses this method – as you will see on the StudentZone at www.richerstudentzone.co.uk

Remember that in a business to business transaction, both the supplier *and* the customer must keep records – and these should match!

Business brief

When going slow increases profits!

Many businesses are concerned about the time it takes for banks to process payments. If a business transfers money to another business electronically on Monday, it can take until the end of the week before this money arrives in the supplier's account. This can cause problems, especially for small firms, as it can affect their cash flow. The Federation of Small Businesses (FSB) is lobbying the government to introduce a Payment Systems Bill to make banks transfer money more quickly. In Canada, for example, it only takes 24 hours.

Why do banks operate so slowly? Quite simply, because they can make more money. Banks lend

the money they hold – and charge interest on it. If you think of the value of all the business transactions in a week, you can see that just keeping this money for an extra day or two can be very profitable indeed.

So banks aren't too interested in working more quickly!

If you pay any bills electronically you need to bear this in mind. If the date the bill must be paid is the 20th of the month, you may have to transfer the money as early as the 14th or 15th to ensure that it is paid on time. Unless, of course, the FSB wins its campaign. You can find out more about FSB on its website – a link is available at www.heinemann.co.uk/hotlinks (express code 1386P).

Over to you!

1 a Write one or two sentences explaining what the word 'transaction' means.

  b Oliver runs a hairdressing salon. Write down **eight** different business transactions with which he could be involved when he is running his business, for example paying the window cleaner. Bear in mind that he will be both a customer and a supplier. Compare your ideas with the rest of your group.

2 a Check that you understand the main methods by which payments are made by reading the summary table in Figure 3.15.

  b Working in small groups, and in agreement with your tutor, investigate **one** of the following websites each – links to them are available at www.heinemann.co.uk/hotlinks (express code 1386P). Write a brief description to explain how the information you find would help a retailer who has to process sales transactions and make payments to suppliers. In some cases this will mean searching specifically under the 'retail' section of the site. Then present your information to the rest of your class.

  i UK Credit Cards.
  ii Barclays Merchant Services.
  iii Switch UK.
  iv Fastpay.
  v Direct Debit UK.
  vi Direct Credit UK.

Payment method	Advantages	Disadvantages
Cash	Money is received immediately and can be paid into the bank straight away.	Security problems associated with storing and transporting large amounts of cash. Cash is untraceable if stolen.
Debit card	Money is transferred automatically from the customer's bank account into the supplier's account. Can be used for telephone and online purchases.	Supplier has to have agreement with a merchant service to accept cards and possess a swipe machine. There is a small fee charged for each transaction processed.
Credit card	Payment is guaranteed if the transaction is authorised and the card holder is present. Can also be used for telephone, mail order and online transactions.	The merchant service levies a charge for each transaction. Payment from the credit card company takes a few days. There is a risk of fraud with card not present (CNP) transactions.
Direct credit/ Direct debit	Automatic transfer of money from one bank account to another. Safe, cheap and efficient way particularly for regular payments.	Few, if any, as once the arrangements are set up payments continue automatically.
Electronic transfer	Account holder gives instructions online for money to be transferred. Ideal for large payments and business to business transactions.	Transfers can take 3–5 days which can inconvenience many small businesses.
Cheque	Useful for one-off transactions and payments by post. Payments up to fixed limit guaranteed when backed up by guarantee card.	Payment not guaranteed if the amount is over the card's stated limit.

Figure 3.15 *A summary of payment methods*

Two government departments keen to encourage more online transactions are the Inland Revenue, which collects tax payments from businesses and HM Customs and Excise, the government department that collects VAT. The Inland Revenue offers several online services. Anyone who is self-employed and has to complete self-assessment tax forms can do this online and take advantage of tax calculation software to see how much they owe – and then make a payment. Employers can file PAYE returns and forms and make payments. Businesses can file corporation tax forms and individuals and families can apply for tax credits or child benefit.

You can find out more about this on the Inland Revenue website – a link is available at www.heinemann.co.uk/hotlinks (express code 1386P).

Businesses can also complete and submit their VAT returns online and pay electronically. For some reason this has been less popular. In 2003 only 0.02 per cent of businesses were filing their VAT forms online and 89 per cent were still paying by cheque. This may change when the two tax departments merge into one super department in the near future.

Talking point

View 1: *Banks need to make profits to provide other services and facilities for their customers. It should therefore be acceptable for them to take their time over money transfers, so they can make a profit on this service.*

View 2: *It is ludicrous that in an electronic age it can take banks between 3 and 5 days to move money online. The FSB is right to insist that such banks should been fined and small businesses should be compensated for these delays.*

With which viewpoint do you agree – and why?

Records of transactions

Why are records necessary?

Can you remember how much money you spent yesterday, where you spent each amount and what you bought? If you have a good memory, the answer might be yes but then could you prove all of this? If you were asked these questions about items that you bought two months ago, could you remember? It is very doubtful! As you will see later, businesses *must* be able to account for every transaction for several reasons. It is therefore essential that they are all recorded as it would be useless to rely on people's memories.

Suppliers need to keep records of all transactions but it is often important for private customers to have a record as well. From an individual customer's point of view, a record takes the form of a receipt which is given to them by the supplier when the goods are purchased. Customers need to receive and keep receipts for one or more of the following reasons.

- They cannot be accused of stealing the goods if challenged by a security guard when they are leaving a shop.
- The receipt is proof of purchase if the goods need to be returned because they are faulty.
- If the goods are an unwanted present, the supplier will probably offer an exchange, refund or voucher provided that a receipt is presented and they are returned in good condition.
- Conscientious customers can check credit card, debit card and cheque payments against their account statements since errors can occur.

Suppliers also need to have a record of each transaction. There are different ways of doing this, as will be explained shortly. The reasons why records are necessary are as follows.

- Small businesses (i.e. sole traders and partnerships) have to provide income and expenditure information for income tax purposes.

- Businesses registered for VAT have to supply similar information, and must possess a VAT invoice for every item purchased.
- Limited companies have to produce detailed accounts that summarise all transactions. These accounts provide a basis for calculating corporation tax as well as VAT. Large companies must also have their accounts audited, or checked, and the auditor will want to refer to the documentary evidence if there are any queries. The accounts of the public limited company are published and scrutinised by investors, such as shareholders who want to know how wisely the money they have invested is being spent, and by the financial press.
- Businesses also need to keep records for similar reasons to customers, for example, in case there is a fault with an item purchased and a claim is made under warranty.

Information needed about transactions

The type and amount of information recorded about transactions will depend upon whether the business is VAT registered or not. However, some essential information is required for legal purposes and for the calculation of the accounts. This is because businesses pay tax on their profits and therefore the company accountant has to ensure that the correct records are kept.

Many businesses also choose to record additional information, such as the name of the salesperson, for their own purposes. The *minimum* information which is normally needed is listed below.

- Name and address of supplier.
- Name of customer – and/or some other form of identification, such as credit card number. This is not normally needed for small cash purchases.
- The amount of money paid.
- Details of the item purchased or service provided.
- The date of the transaction.

Manual sales recording

Most routine sales to customers are recorded automatically by cash registers and a receipt is produced at the same time. However, there are occasions when the information needs to be recorded manually. This can happen when a small business hasn't the resources to buy a cash register or it is just not worth the expense. For example, an estate agent could act as an agent for renting property until it is sold. Because only a few rents are collected each month, it is not worth buying a cash register which would also take up valuable office space.

Manual recording can also take place when business transactions occur away from the business's premises. Taxi drivers will issue a manual receipt for a business person who needs to claim back the money from their firm.

Traditionally, service engineers issued manual receipts in people's homes although today many have laptop computers on which they can produce an electronic receipt that is automatically logged into their accounts system.

KBH Plumbers
61 High Street
HIGHTOWN
HG1 SB2

Telephone: 01213 456789   Receipt number: 77

Received from *Peter Wilson, 23 Garden Street, Hightown*

the sum of *Fifty one pounds*

£*51.00*

in payment for *repairs to leak on heating boiler*

Received by *A Bretherton*   Date *31 Oct 2000*

Figure 3.16 *A hand written receipt*

Above is an example of a hand written receipt. This contains all of the information listed above. In this case, the receipt is pre-printed so that the information specific to the sale can be added. Although some businesses may have their receipt specially printed, many use specially printed receipt books in which the receipts are numbered sequentially and are produced in duplicate. The customer is given a tear-out copy and the duplicate copy is kept in the book. The book containing the duplicate copies is kept by the supplying business as evidence of the transaction. In addition, the information is transferred to other documents to help to compile the business's accounts.

Cash register recording

Cash registers vary from very basic machines to those which are designed to link to the computer systems of large retail businesses.

In a small shop, many of the items you buy will have a price sticker attached. When you take an item to the counter, the sales assistant will read the amount from the label and key this into the cash register. At the press of another button the cash drawer is released. The assistant then takes your money, puts it in the drawer and selects your change. At the same time, the machine records the amount of money spent and can often also produce a receipt.

On slightly more sophisticated machines, the assistant will key in the amount owed, the amount of money you offer and the cash register will display the change owed to you. This saves both you and the assistant from having to work this out. Another variation is often found in businesses which sell a limited amount of products such as a bar or fast-food restaurant. These machines have buttons with labels on them. These labels each have a short description of each product. When a button is pressed, the price of the product automatically appears on the screen. This saves the assistant having to remember prices.

EPOS systems

When cash registers are linked to computers, there is an opportunity for many other processes to take place. In large stores several machines are linked to a central computer. This system is known as EPOS – Electronic Point of Sale. This allows some or all of the following functions to be performed and is particularly valuable for retail businesses with many separate branches, because the information from each branch is available for senior managers at head office.

- Bar code readers can identify each product and find the price from the computer. The total spent by each customer is also calculated.
- Stock records can be updated as soon as a product is sold. This also allows low/high turnover stocks to be identified. Stock types which need re-ordering can also be identified.
- Some systems also update delivery requirements and send these automatically to a central distribution centre.
- The identity of the sales assistant dealing with every transaction can be recorded. Each assistant who is trained to use the till has a unique PIN number or swipe card and must 'log on' and 'log off' when they operate the machine.
- Credit/debit card payments can be processed through a 'swipe' terminal linked to the cash register.

- Detailed receipts can be printed which include each item purchased, together with the price, and information about the business including the VAT number. Payment card details are also printed and promotional messages can also be included.
- Details about the customer can be captured, such as their name and address, and then used for marketing purposes. Businesses can also use this data to draw up customer profiles and to track and compare sales trends by store and by region. They can use this to refine stock levels and the type of stock held at different times of the year and in different outlets.

Cashing up

Regardless of the system used, at regular intervals the money received is counted and compared with the information recorded on the cash register. For security reasons, even small businesses should keep the number of banknotes in a till to a minimum throughout the day, even if they only 'cash up' at the end of trading. Large stores have a separate security drawer in which the operator can 'post' notes at regular intervals. In addition, the cash drawer itself is protected by perspex, to prevent a thief snatching the money when the drawer is open.

When the money is counted and recorded it is balanced against the information recorded for that cashpoint or against each operator's ID. The two amounts should be the same. If they are not then this must be investigated. The reason could be because of a simple mistake – or because there is fraud taking place, as you will see later.

Direct computer input

Many EPOS or POS systems are basically computers with special software installed which stores the prices of all goods in the stock database and records all transactions on a central computer. This is the type of system used at Richer Sounds and you can see what it looks like and check out how it works on the StudentZone at www.richerstudentzone.co.uk. It

Both credit and debit cards are a convenient way of making and receiving payments. However they have their problems because they are open to particular types of fraud. The main types are:

- **Stolen cards**. Thieves use stolen cards for face-to-face transactions in shops or for buying goods over the telephone or online before the owner has noticed the loss or has had time to report the card missing.
- **Skimming**. The data on the card's magnetic strip is electronically copied onto another card, without the cardholder's knowledge. The data is used to produce a counterfeit card which can then be used by a thief.
- **Identity theft**. This is a more complex type of fraud. Criminals obtain personal details of an individual and use this information to apply for cards.

The fastest growing fraud is when goods are bought by telephone, mail order and over the Internet. In these situations, only the card details are provided. This is known as 'card not present' (CNP) fraud and was estimated to amount to £300,000 a day in 2003. The problem is that businesses normally have to stand the cost of any fraudulent transaction if the card has passed basic checks, i.e. it has not been reported stolen and there are sufficient funds in the account.

Several new services have been introduced to try to solve the problem and to offer more protection to retailers, such as Verified by Visa and MasterCard SecureCode. These both check credit cards more thoroughly. Another service, CV2AVS, ensures the customer is actually holding the card by asking for the security number on the reverse to be read. It also checks the address. Finally, the EPDQ service also checks identity. The problem is that there are extra charges or fees to pay for these services, which can deter many small retailers from signing up to them.

Banks are also introducing new 'chip and pin' cards that contain a microchip holding unique information about the cardholder. Instead of providing a signature, the cardholder will key in a PIN when making payment. This will help to prevent skimming as there will be no magnetic stripe to copy. In addition, there will be no need for the cardholder to hand over the card at any point in the transaction. Customers are also advised to protect themselves against identity theft by shredding any document that contains their card number and personal details after use. You can find out more at the Cardwatch and Chip and PIN websites – links are available at www.heinemann.co.uk/hotlinks (express code 1386P).

enables the managers at Richer Sounds to have an up-to-date analysis of all sales at any time.

Many non-retail businesses record payments received direct on to their computer system. Examples include:

- **The Inland Revenue**, when it receives tax payments from self-employed people.
- **Credit card companies**, when they receive payments from card holders every month.
- **Utility companies**, which receive payments for gas and electricity supplies.
- **Your college**, when students enrol on courses on which a tuition fee is payable.
- **Your bank**, when you pay money into your account.

At your college, the person receiving the payment will normally key in the amount received and any other details which must be recorded. Businesses that process large amounts of transactions normally use an automated system. Both payment slips and cheques are marked with machine

Figure 3.17 *A machine readable payment slip*

readable codes so that they can be scanned into the system. This saves time and minimises operator errors as the amount is automatically listed in the correct account. An example of a payment slip with these type of codes is shown above.

Businesses also record outgoing payments on their computer system. Your college will do this when it pays its suppliers. It will also record all the salary payments it makes to staff.

Business brief

Business accounting software

Even small businesses can benefit from a computer package which links sales transactions and payments made and received to accounting records. This is because, once the transaction has been entered, the software records this in the correct account. It will also produce any related reports or accounts that are required. For example, it will:

- Keep customer records and customer accounts that show invoices sent, money received and any payments that are overdue.
- Keep supplier records and supplier accounts that show invoices received, payment terms, payments made and any payments still outstanding.
- Work out bank balances and cash flow

- Check bank statements against the business's own records.
- Create invoices and statements.
- Store budget forecasts and produce budget reports.
- Store product records and prices.
- Produce accounts and reports, such as the profit and loss account and the balance sheet.
- Calculate VAT accounts and produce a VAT summary.

One of the most well-known and most commonly used software accounting packages is called Sage. There are several versions available, tailored mainly for different sizes of organisations. To find out more look on the Sage website – a link to the site is available at www.heinemann.co.uk/hotlinks (express code 1386P).

1 a Each of the following items of information was included on the hand-written receipt on page 255. Explain why you think each item is needed.
   i Name and address of supplier.
   ii Receipt number.
   iii Customer's name and address.
   iv Amount of money paid.
   v Reason for payment.
   vi Signature of staff member receiving payment.
   vii Date of payment.

b Why do you think that the amount of money is written in words and then in figures on a hand-written receipt?

c Suggest **two** items of information which are found even on the most basic receipts.

2 a Give **three** reasons why a customer needs to have a record of a transaction.

b Give **three** reasons why a supplier needs to have a record of a transaction.

3 When you withdraw money from a cash machine you normally have a choice whether to accept a receipt or not.
   a Identify **two** benefits of opting to accept one.
   b Explain why you shouldn't throw it away immediately afterwards.
   c Your card is stuck in the machine and someone offers to help. They suggest you re-enter your PIN carefully. What would you do?

d A cash machine gives you more money than you asked for! What would you do – and why? Discuss your ideas as a group.

4 It is likely that, within your group, there are several students who have worked in retail businesses and received payments. Divide into small groups and try to ensure that each group includes at least one person with experience of working in a retail store and/or taking payments. Then decide your answers to the following questions and discuss your findings with suggestions from other groups in your class.
   a Why do many retail businesses refuse to let new employees handle cash?
   b What features are commonly found on cash registers?
   c Why do most businesses insist that only one operator uses a cash register at a time?
   d Why are cash registers normally left empty overnight with the drawers open?
   e Who normally cashes up in an organisation – and why?
   f A mistake is made giving change and the customer is still owed £5. Can the cashier just open the till and take out this money? If not, what must the cashier do?
   g A petrol station manager insists that any cash discrepancies are paid for by staff out of their wages. Can he do this? (Keep your response to this question safe, as you will find the answer later in this section!)

Petty cash recording

On page 257 you saw that when businesses deal with suppliers they prefer to pay them by cheque or, increasingly, electronically. The main reason for this is that most business-to-business purchases are carried out on a credit basis. The goods are delivered and are paid for later. Often the sums involved are very large indeed.

However, there are a few situations when businesses have to buy much smaller items and have to pay cash at the time of purchase. Some examples are:

- A manager needs to pay for a taxi to the railway station to catch a train to London at 6am.

- The same manager buys breakfast on the train and pays cash.
- The window cleaner calls once a month and likes to be paid in cash.
- An important visitor is due and a member of staff is sent to a local store to buy a bunch of flowers for the reception area.
- A senior administrator wants to buy some postage stamps for the office. These are kept so that any urgent letters which are only ready after the mailroom has closed, can still be stamped and posted that day.

In all these transactions the amount of money involved is quite small. Indeed, 'petty' means 'small'. In addition, the transactions do not normally occur very often – perhaps a few times a week.

Petty cash procedures

Petty cash in a business is normally the responsibility of one person, called the petty cashier. The cash is kept in a lockable metal cash box or a small safe. The cashier also has petty cash vouchers for each time someone needs to be paid and an accounts book for recording all petty cash transactions. Alternatively, the transactions may be recorded on computer using a spreadsheet package such as Excel.

When any member of staff makes a purchase on behalf of their employer they must normally obtain a receipt. They then complete a petty cash voucher, like the one below, and take this to the petty cashier with the receipt. The member of staff claiming repayment must sign the voucher, to confirm the expenditure, and the cashier also signs it to confirm that the transaction has been authorised. The cashier then makes the repayment and records the transaction in the petty cash book or on the spreadsheet.

Received £	Date	Details	Voucher no.	Total Payments £	VAT	Item (net)
400.00	1 Feb	Balance				
	1 Feb	Petrol	132	15.00	2.23	12.77
	3 Feb	Coffee	133	3.50	-	3.50
	5 Feb	Petrol	134	45.00	6.70	38.30
	8 Feb	Buffet lunch	135	52.25	-	52.25
	8 Feb	Train ticket	136	85.30	-	85.30
	15 Feb	Tea	137	1.75		1.75
	17 Feb	Stationery	138	31.05	4.62	26.43
	19 Feb	Art materials	139	20.93	3.12	17.81
	23 Feb	Sandwiches	140	14.75	-	14.75
		Total		269.53	16.67	252.86
		Balance		130.47		
400.00				400.00		

Figure 3.19 *Example of petty cash book page*

If you study the sample page from a petty cash book (Figure 3.19), you should notice the following.

- The first amount of money entered is £400.00. This is the amount of cash which was put into the fund at the start of the month. It is known as the **float** or, occasionally, the imprest.
- Entries are made each time petty cash is paid out. These are cross-referenced to each petty cash voucher by quoting the voucher numbers.
- If the business is VAT registered, then the amount of VAT paid is always written separately, in its own column, so that it can be reclaimed at a later date.
- At the end of the month, the total amount that has been paid out is added up. The petty cashier can double check the calculations because the amount of VAT and the 'net' column totals, when added together, equal the total amount spent.
- The amount spent is deducted from the float figure. This is the amount which has not yet been spent and is therefore the balance remaining.
- The balance of money remaining in the petty cash box is counted. This amount must agree with the written balance. In the example this is £130.47.
- If everything is in order, the fund is topped up again, ready for the next month. If the two amounts do not agree, the petty cashier has to track through all the transactions to try to find out where the mistake has been made.

PETTY CASH VOUCHER	No: 601	Date: 21/7/2004		
Name: PAUL HAWARTH		Dept: Sales		
Purpose (attach all receipts & invoices)		TOTAL (inc. VAT)	VAT (A)	Net (A) (excl.VAT)
Taxi to station		3.50	✓	✓
Taxi from station		3.50	✓	✓
Breakfast on train		12.75	✓	✓
The sum of (in words as far to the left as possible) Nineteen pounds – 75p		£19.75	£	£

Approved by: L Whitehead	date: 22/7	Allocation	
Received by: P Hawarth	date: 23/7	Amount	Account

Figure 3.18 *A completed petty cash voucher*

Date (200–)	Customer	Invoice No.	Amount (£)
1 Oct	T Ahmed	27384	550.00
10 Oct	L Hyson	27385	270.00
14 Oct	D Knight	27386	1250.00
21 Oct	L Hyson	27387	330.00
25 Oct	L Langhorn	27388	120.00
30 Oct	T Ahmed	27389	1500.00
31 Oct	Y Bhatti	27390	750.00

Figure 3.20 *Example of Sales Day Book*

- The first column shows the date when the invoice was issued.
- The second column is the name of the customer and/or customer account reference.
- The third column contains the number of the invoice which is sent to the customer.
- The final column shows the amount involved in the transaction.

Day Books are used to capture the initial information on a transaction. This information can then be analysed and transferred to all the other separate accounts later, such as the customer accounts and the sales accounts.

Today most businesses use computer packages to compile Day Books. So for the Sales Day Book, the details from the invoice are entered into the computer. If a business accounting package is used, such as Sage, then this information may automatically be posted to all the other relevant accounts. For that reason, the use of the word 'book' is really just a reminder of the way the accounts used to be prepared.

The Sales Returns Day Book records all occasions where goods are returned from customers – for example, because they are faulty or damaged. In this case, the customer has to be refunded (or another item given in exchange). The returns therefore reduce the overall value of sales made by a business so, to obtain an accurate picture of sales for a month, a manager would look at the total sales in the Sales Day Book and subtract the value of any returns.

In a similar manner, the Purchases Day Book records all items which have been bought by the business and the Purchase Returns Day Book records any returns. The difference between the two is the value of all the purchases which have been made by the business.

Day Books

The accounting systems used by businesses to record transactions are designed to ensure that every penny is accounted for. You have already seen that each customer will have his or her own account, and so will each supplier. Then there is an account to show how much money is in the bank and how much money is held in cash on the premises. To track transactions using the main accounts may be quite complex and involve several different accounts. For that reason, many businesses also use Day Books.

The most common types of Day Books are:

- **Sales Day Book** – which records all sales made by date.
- **Sales Returns Day Book** – which records any goods returned from customers, again by date.
- **Purchases Day Book** – which records all purchases by date.
- **Purchase Returns Day Book** – which records any goods returned to a supplier (e.g. because of a fault), again by date.

Opposite is a sample page from a Sales Day Book. Try to identify the following features.

- Each line gives information on a particular sales transaction.

Petty cash A system that allows small purchases to be made in cash. It includes methods of recording and checking the amounts paid.

Float The amount of cash put into a cash register or the petty cash box at the start of a period. The money is topped up at regular intervals.

Day Books A method of recording different types of transaction as they happen. The normal books are sales, sales returns, purchases and purchases returns.

Over to you!

1 Suggest the most likely method each business would use to record the following transactions. In each case give a reason for your answer.
   a The sale of a coat at River Island.
   b The payment of a fee to your dentist for doing a filling.
   c The payment of a year's season ticket at a major football club.
   d The purchase of a scarf at the same club.
   e A packet of large envelopes bought by a member of staff who now wants her money back.
   f All the purchases made by an organisation in a week.

2 Samira is in charge of petty cash and is approached by people asking her to refund them for the items listed. Working in twos or threes decide which requests Samira should grant, and which she should not, with reasons. Then compare your answers to those of other groups.
   a £750 for a garage to fit a new gearbox to the delivery van. The delivery driver says that the garage have asked for cash before he can have his van back.
   b £50 for a glazier to replace a window broken in a storm. He can produce a handwritten receipt immediately.
   c The Administration Manager forgets his wife's birthday. At the last minute, he sends his assistant round to the local florist to arrange for a bunch of flowers to be delivered. She uses her own money to pay for the flowers and comes back with a receipt for £35.
   d The office stationery supplier forgot to include envelopes in the latest delivery. Jan was asked to buy some from the local newsagents shop. The envelopes cost £5 but while she was in the shop she bought a packet of crisps and a can of diet Coke. All three items are on the receipt and Jan says that, since she went to the shop in her

lunch break the firm should pay for her snack.
   e The dairyman, Tom, delivers milk to the canteen every day. He insists on being paid in cash once a week. The bill normally comes to about £15–£20 and he is happy to produce a receipt on the spot. The business prefers to pay suppliers monthly by cheque or electronic transfer.
   f Gail spills toner on her skirt when she was changing the cartridges on the photocopier. Normally these are sealed units but there was a crack in the new one she was handling, which was faulty. The dry cleaners charge her £10 to remove the stain.
   g Patrick has bought a new mouse for the computer he uses at work because the one that he was supplied with broke and Computer Services had no replacements in stock. He has lost the receipt but wants Samira to refund his money.

3 a This week Samira has paid out against the following vouchers: coffee £6.30, papers £3.50, taxi fare £14.50, train fare £48, reference book £25, sandwiches £15. If she started the week with £200 in her petty cash tin, how much should she have left?
   b Samira notices that some of her blank petty cash vouchers have gone missing. Does this matter? Give a reason for your answer.

4 Say whether you think that the following statements are true or false:
   a A Day Book is a record of one particular type of transaction in the order in which they happen.
   b Each Day Book only records information about transactions on a single day.
   c Day Books can easily be used to find the total amount of goods bought or sold.
   d All Day Books have to be completed manually.
   e The Purchase Day Book is completed when goods are bought.

With which viewpoint do you agree – and why?

Business brief

Fraud or theft?

These two words mean similar things. Technically, fraud is anything which a person does to obtain unfair advantage over another person or business. So, for example, this could include someone who gives false references in a job application.

Theft is defined by law (the Theft Act 1968) as dishonestly taking property from another person or business. So an employee who takes £50 from the cash register would be guilty of theft because he or she is depriving their employer of money.

In simple terms, the word fraud covers a broader range of offences than theft. Almost everything described in this section would fall into the category of theft. However, to cover all eventualities, the term fraud will be used.

Shrinkage, fraud and theft

Shrinkage is a term used in the retail trade. It is the difference between the stock bought by a store for resale and the amount actually sold. In the UK this figure is thought to be about 1.7 per cent. In other words, for every £1,000 of goods held by a store, goods worth £17 cannot be sold.

Some of this loss is due to factors such as breakages, damage and food not sold before its sell-by-date. However, these types of factors only account for about 20 per cent of the total shrinkage, i.e. £3.40 out of every £1,000. The remaining £13.60 (80 per cent) is lost because of fraud or theft. If you think that this isn't much, work it out for a business which buys £10 million worth of stock for sale every year!

Fraud can mean taking goods without paying or not paying the full price. It can also refer to stealing money.

Business brief

Who does the stealing?

The most obvious type of fraud from stores is shoplifting – where customers take goods from a store without paying. It is thought that about half of all fraud from retail stores happens this way.

The other 50 per cent is through staff stealing goods or money. This also includes **collusion**. This happens when a member of staff helps a customer (such as a friend or family member) to steal goods. One example of this is called **sweethearting** – which means giving illegal discounts or not charging for all the goods taken to the checkout. False refunds or false markdowns also come into this category.

Methods of stealing

All businesses want to prevent theft and fraud by both customers and staff. They are well aware of the more common methods of stealing which include the following.

- Staff or customers simply walking out of the store with goods which have not been paid for. This is particularly common in clothes shops where stolen goods can be worn.
- Goods placed in outside rubbish bins – to be collected later.
- Staff putting goods in a parcel and posting it to themselves.

Not all theft is this easy to spot!

- Goods signed for on delivery but not actually received. The delivery driver takes them away again. This requires collusion between the driver and the member of staff checking in the goods.
- Staff passing goods to friends through doors/windows.
- Eating food/sweets intended for sale to the customers. This is known as **grazing**.

Fraud by staff associated with sales transactions includes:

- Cash stolen from the cash register.
- Receiving cash and not recording it.
- Recording a smaller amount on the till than the price of the product (which the customer has paid) and pocketing the difference.
- Undercharging friends or relatives.
- Over-ringing a refund and pocketing the difference.
- Recording a non-existent refund.
- Marking down goods to a discounted price when they should not be – then the staff member pays the lower price.
- Keeping a receipt which should have been given to a customer. The staff member then produces the receipt as evidence that they have bought the goods.

- Using own store card instead of the customer's to 'steal' bonus points.

Why are managers concerned about fraud?

The most important reason why managers are concerned about fraud is that the amount of money lost comes *straight out of profit*. If the business is a small one where the profit is the owner's income then any fraud is taking money directly out of the owner's pocket. Lower profits mean that there is less money to re-invest in the business. This in turn means that the business could be less profitable in the future. If staff are paid a bonus based on the profits, then fraud is taking money from everyone who works for the organisation!

Another way of looking at this is to work out how much more a business has to sell to compensate for money lost because of fraud. If a business has an average markup of 5 per cent, this means that for every £1 that is stolen, another £20 worth of goods must be sold to compensate.

The same argument applies to security measures, such as CCTV cameras, and employing security guards. These can reduce fraud but have to be paid for out of profit since they do not contribute to sales. It will still worthwhile if the expenditure on security pays for itself. For example, if a business invests £3,000 a year on security but fraud is reduced by £6,000, the money has been well spent.

A third aspect of fraud which concerns managers is the disruption caused when fraud is suspected and being investigated. Most staff are honest and will be upset when they are interviewed about suspected fraud. In some instances, where fraud can be narrowed down to a small group of people, all of the group, including the innocent may have to be dismissed. This is legal as long as no one person is victimised.

Taking stock!

Cash is a valuable item in a business, and has to be protected. So, too, is stock – especially in a business which deals in goods that are small, valuable or easy to carry. If you worked for a diamond merchant, you would find that more emphasis is placed on the security of stock than on the takings in the till!

All businesses check their stock regularly by carrying out stocktaking. This means manually counting how many of each product item they have in stock. You may think that if they simply keep records of how many items are bought and sold, they would automatically know this figure. However, this would not include any goods that are damaged or have been stolen. In the case of food, items may have to be scrapped because they have passed their sell-by-date, although most retailers will try to sell it off cheaply or will have a policy of giving it to charity. Then it must be 'written off' the stock figures.

The total number of items held is always compared to the number of recorded items. If there is an unknown discrepancy then this is apt to point to theft and will be investigated.

Measures taken to reduce fraud

All managers want to reduce the risk of fraud taking place during sales transactions. They can take measures:

- To try to prevent theft by employees.
- To keep any fraud or theft to a minimum.
- To improve the chances of catching staff who attempt to steal money or goods.

Prevention measures

Many experts consider it is better to take a positive view of people's behaviour and to treat staff well, so they have fewer reasons to want to 'cheat' their employer. Businesses which take this view will therefore do the following.

- Pay good wages so that staff are not short of money. If people are poorly paid, they tend to see fraud as a way of making up for money that they are not being paid. Also, if people are well paid, they will not want to risk losing their job by being caught stealing.
- Have generous staff discount schemes to reduce the temptation to steal goods.
- Have other staff benefits such as a subsidised canteen to help people feel that their employer is looking after them.
- Offer a counselling service for staff who have personal problems – such as staff who get into financial difficulties.
- Have a hardship fund, so that staff can ask for loans if they have a short term financial crisis.
- Look after staff well so that they feel they are valued and appreciated. This was covered in unit 1, on page 69. If people enjoy their jobs and feel their employer is fair then they are far less likely to steal – or tolerate stealing by anyone else.

Measures to keep fraud or theft to a minimum

- Have a thorough staff selection procedure which includes obtaining character references on all applicants from previous employers.
- Have a clear policy on dealing with fraud. Fraud or theft is normally considered to be gross misconduct which means the person concerned can be dismissed instantly as part of the disciplinary procedure. You will learn more about this if you study specialist unit 5.
- Ensure that all new employees attend an induction programme which includes a thorough explanation of the procedures for handling transactions as well as the support and counselling available to them if they have a problem. In addition, the disciplinary procedure should be carefully explained.
- Limit the number of staff who can use the tills. Many businesses employ one cashier to handle cash transactions, particularly in restaurants and clothes shops. Other staff are employed to assist customers.
- Ensure staff log on and off the till(s) using a PIN, a personal key or swipe card. Some businesses remove all cash from the till when staff change over and start again with a new float.

- Ensure tills are positioned so that money cannot be snatched, or drawers are protected by a perspex shield and emptied regularly. All till drawers should to be closed immediately after any transaction.
- Do not allow any staff to serve relatives or friends.
- Ensure all staff purchases are authorised by a supervisor or manager.
- Insist that all customers are given a receipt. If receipts are left behind for any reason, they should be torn up immediately or handed to the manager.
- Have a policy, which is written into the contract of employment, where any shortfalls in the amount of cash in the till can be deducted from staff wages. The law states that the maximum which can be deducted is 10 per cent of a wage payment. It must also be the case that the business can clearly identify who was using the till when the shortfall occurred.
- Use bar code readers because these prevent 'under-ringing'. Under-ringing is a term used when staff enter a price less than the true cost which means that staff can steal the difference in cash.
- Position all tills so that the amount entered is clearly visible to the customer. This also helps to prevent under-ringing.
- Have strict procedures for marking down the price of goods, giving refunds and 'voiding' a sale. This is another way in which staff could avoid paying the correct price for goods or could obtain access to the till.
- Have a separate staff area where outer coats and bags must be left. If necessary install lockers in which bags, purses and wallets can be stored. Staff uniforms may be issued which do not include pockets.

Measures to improve the chances of catching staff who steal

- Install CCTV cameras at each sales point to monitor staff actions.
- Reward staff who report fraud. The procedure should ensure that information is treated in confidence. This makes it even more risky for individuals to steal because they cannot depend on their colleagues 'covering up' for them.
- Install cash registers that enable management checks to be made if theft is suspected. This is simple on computerised systems. On older tills a balance can be obtained by a supervisor through taking an 'x' reading, so that tills can be cashed up, if necessary, during the day. This may be necessary if a customer says that he or she has been short-changed by a large amount or if there is suspicion that theft has taken place. Alternatively a 'z' reading can be taken which clears the till balance to zero. This is normally only done at the end of a day.
- Include the right to stop and search employees before they leave for the day if there is a valid reason to suspect theft. This must be stated in the Contract of Employment so that all employees are aware that the employer can do this.
- Tag valuable items so that an alarm sounds if these are removed with the tag still attached. Only allow authorised supervisors or managers to remove the tags.

Business terms

Shrinkage The difference between goods received and goods able to be sold by a retail business.

'X' reading A reading by a supervisor of the amount of cash recorded on a till at points during a day.

Cashing up Counting the amount of money in a till drawer and comparing this figure with the amount recorded on the till.

Welfare Extra benefits available to staff, such as a subsidised canteen, a staff football team and a free meal at Christmas. The term also includes counselling, medical insurance and hardship funds. (See also Unit 2, page 151).

Grazing Staff eating consumable items, such as biscuits and sweets, without paying for them.

Staff discount Allowing staff to buy goods at prices less than those charged to members of the public. It is argued that, the larger the discount, the less likelihood of staff theft.

Business matters

In the future, shoplifters – and 'stock' lifters – may be in for a shock because goods will be invisibly tagged to track any items after they have been taken.

At the moment barcodes are used to identify goods and clumsy security tags are attached to stock to prevent unauthorised removal. These must be taken off at the point of sale or an alarm is triggered. By about 2005, you can expect goods to contain chips which will emit radio signals instead. These will be so small that they cannot be seen. They enable stolen goods to be tracked, stocks in the store room to be constantly monitored and stocks on shelves to be checked. Any item that is moved can be detected instantly.

The system is known as RFID – short for Radio Frequency Identification. In Britain, Tesco has already tested the system. In America, Wal-Mart has insisted that all its suppliers include chips on their products by 2005. Retail businesses are very enthusiastic but others are less sure. They argue that retailers can use the technology to find out who is buying their goods and insist there must be methods introduced to disable the technology if customers have bought items legally.

Over to you!

1 The list below shows the types of items which are most commonly stolen. In a group, identify the main factors which make it likely that something will be stolen.

Goods most likely to be stolen

CDs
Phone cards
Chocolate
Cosmetics
Duracell batteries
DVDs
Bosch power tools
Gillette Mach 3 razors
Kodak film
Leather garments
Major designer brand clothing
Mobile phones
Sony Playstations
Spirits - vodka, whisky etc.
Trainers
Video tapes
Watches

2 Say whether you think that the following statements are true or false. For those which you think are false, write a statement which is the true version.
   a If a sprinkler goes off in a clothes shop and some clothes are smaller when they dry out, this is called shrinkage.
   b 95 per cent of fraud is carried out by customers.
   c When a shop assistant helps a friend to steal, this is called collusion.
   d Fraud and theft are two words which mean similar things.
   e Apart from fraud, shrinkage is normally caused by mis-counting stock.
   f The term used when customers steal goods from shops is shoplifting.

3 a Identify **four** ways in which staff can commit fraud when they are processing sales transactions.
   b Identify **two** actions an employer can take in each case:
      i to promote good working conditions and minimise theft by employees
      ii to make theft difficult for employees
      iii to catch employees who steal.

Talking point

View 1: People will always steal no matter how well they are treated.

View 2: If businesses look after their employees well, then all staff will be far less inclined to steal.

With which viewpoint do you agree – and why?

3.4 Section review

Now that you have completed this section, you should understand what is meant by a transaction and be able to explain the importance of recording information about them. You should also be able to describe various methods of recording this information. In addition you should be aware of the problems businesses have due to fraud, the more common types of fraud and ways in which it can be minimised. Test your skills now by doing the following activities.

Check your understanding of this section by answering the following questions. Check all your answers with your tutor before moving on.

1
  a Explain briefly why petty cash is used.
  b Identify **two** items you would find on most receipts.
  c Explain what is meant by 'manual' sales recording.
  d Identify **two** benefits for a business of using an EPOS system.
  e Identify the main purpose of a Sales Day Book.
  f Give **two** reasons why businesses must record all their sales and purchase transactions.
  g Identify **two** ways in which fraud can occur when sales transactions are being processed.
  h Suggest **two** ways in which a small business could protect itself against theft by its employees.
  i What is meant by the term 'float'?
  j Suggest **two** reasons why fraud is of concern to managers.

2 Divide into small groups for this activity. Each group should prepare notes to advise one of the businesses listed below on:

  a A suitable method of recording transactions.
  b **Five** fraud prevention measures which would be effective in reducing staff fraud.

When you have made your choice, discuss your results with other groups to see if there are similarities and differences.

- A college bookshop where several of the staff are students working part time.
- A newsagent which does not accept debit or credit cards. Price labels are stuck onto all goods for sale.
- A clothes shop which frequently has discounts and sales. All clothes carry a bar code.
- A hotel where receptionists receive payment by guests at the end of their stays and also receive payments for small items, like towel hire or the use of safety deposit boxes.
- A doctor's practice which charges patients for travel vaccinations.
- A designer jeweller's shop which sells very valuable items.

3 Use the Richer Sounds StudentZone at www.richerstudentzone.co.uk to find out the type of precautions that are taken by that organisation to reduce fraud.
  a Suggest **three** that relate to the conditions of employment and the way in which staff are treated.
  b Suggest **two** that relate to precautions that the business takes to make fraud difficult.
  c Suggest **one** that relates to the measures that are taken if a member of staff was found to have committed fraud.

  Compare your answers as a group.

Unit 5 Employee contribution to working conditions

This specialist unit covers key aspects of your employment in an organisation. You will learn about employment contracts, important related aspects of employment law, and how staff are recruited and trained in business. You will find out how conflict can occur and be resolved.

You will also learn about changes in the workplace that mean workers must adapt to be able to respond positively.

This unit builds on many aspects of employment that you first met in Units 1 and 2, helps you to prepare for your first job, and to be a more effective employee.

5.1 Terms of employment contracts

This section covers

The terms of a written contract of employment
Types of employment and people's preferences
Observing the written job description and contract
Key elements of employment legislation
Key employer responsibilities

The terms of a written contract of employment

A contract of employment is a legal document that sets out the details of a person's employment. It defines the legal relationship between the employer and the employee. When both parties have signed it, it is then binding. This means that both employer and employee have to obey and observe its terms. If they do not, then they are in breach of the contract and there are legal repercussions. An employee who breaches the contract can be disciplined and may be dismissed. If an employer breaches the contract the law is on the side of the employee, who may decide to take legal action. You will read more about this in Section 5.3.

If you work part-time, you should have already received a contract or written particulars of the Main Terms of Employment for your current job. Because your contract of employment is so significant, it is important that you understand the items any contract is likely to contain and how these will affect you at work. This is because the contract document defines the actions that you

and your employer can take – and those which you cannot.

Business brief

Legal rights

All employees have two types of legal rights at work.

Statutory rights are the legal rights of everyone in the country, defined in law, such as the right to be paid at or above the minimum wage rate. No employer can reduce these rights. These are not normally included in a contract of employment because it is not your employer's job to tell you what they are. Some of your key statutory rights are given on pages 278–80.

Contractual rights are the additional rights which are contained in a contract of employment. As an obvious example, many people are paid above the minimum wage rate and their starting salary will be shown in their contract.

The Contract of Employment

All employees must receive details of their terms and conditions of employment within two months of starting work for an organisation. This applies to full-time, part-time, permanent and temporary employees. You may receive a letter with these details or a more formal document, entitled Contract of Employment or Main Terms of Employment.

You will be instructed to read the document, sign one copy and return it as proof that you accept and agree to the conditions. It is therefore important to check that you understand it!

Key items in a contract of employment

Your letter, contract or statement of main terms must contain certain, specific items. Other items of information must also be provided but can be in a separate document or you must be told where you can find them.

Within the contract must be the following information:

- Your job title.
- Your hours of work.
- Your place of work.
- The main terms and conditions of your employment.
- Your pay and other benefits, e.g. sick pay and holiday pay.
- The date on which your employment commenced.
- The name of your employer.
- Your own name.

Additional information that can be given in a separate document is as follows:

- In some cases, if the job is temporary, the date on which the job will end.

- Details of any trade union agreements which relate to you.
- Details of your employer's grievance and appeals procedure (see page 271).

Further information to which you must have access is:

- Details about sickness benefits and sickness entitlement if you are ill.
- Pension scheme details.

Statement of Main Terms of Employment

This statement, together with the Employee Handbook, forms part of your Contract of Employment and sets out the main terms of your employment with Perivale Services Ltd.

Name: Chloe Bell

Job title: Marketing Assistant

Place of work: Perivale Services Ltd, High Street, Brankston BR3 2RE

Date of commencement of employment: 24 October 2004

Salary: £12,000 per annum plus employee bonus scheme

Date paid: 28th day of each month by BACS credit transfer

Hours of work: 37.5 hours each week over 5 days, Monday to Friday

Holidays: Annual holiday entitlement and holiday pay is calculated on the basis of 20 days for each full calendar year of employment plus 8 statutory public/bank holidays. The annual entitlement increases with length of service, details of which are provided separately. The holiday year runs from 1 April to 31 March and unused holiday entitlement may not be carried forward from one year to the next.

Holiday pay: Normal rate for all holidays including statutory public/bank holidays.

Sick pay entitlement: You will be entitled to paid absence due to sickness or injury under the company's sick pay scheme on the following basis: Up to 8 weeks' service: Nil; After 8 weeks service: Up to 2 weeks at full pay and 3 weeks at 50% pay in any 12 month period. You may also qualify for statutory sick pay.

Absence from work: Your supervisor's permission must always be obtained in advance for planned absence. In the case of an unexpected absence you must notify your supervisor by 10am on the first day whenever possible. To qualify for statutory sick pay and payment from the company's sick pay scheme, you must complete a self-certificate when your absence lasts from 0.5 to 7 days, including Saturday or Sunday. A doctor's or hospital certificate must be produced for all absences exceeding 7 days.

Health and safety at work: All employees must comply with the company's health and safety policy and with all the rules laid down by the Health and Safety at Work Act and all other relevant regulations. A copy of the health and safety policy and the relevant requirements will be issued during your induction period.

Notice: This contract can be terminated by notice by either party as follows: Notice by employer: Under 1 month's service – Nil; Over 1 month but less than 5 years' service – 1 month; 5 year's service or more – 1 week for each completed year of service up to a maximum of 12 weeks. Notice by employee: Under 1 month's service – Nil; Over 1 month – 1 month.

Disciplinary rules and disciplinary procedures: The disciplinary rules and procedures are fully explained in the employee handbook.

Grievances and grievance procedure: If you have a grievance relating to your employment, you have the right to express this in accordance with the company's grievance procedure. This procedure is described fully in the employee handbook.

Date of issue of this document: 30 October 2004

I acknowledge receipt of my Statement of Main Terms and the Employee Handbook and confirm that I have read and understand these documents. I understand that any amendments to this statement will be agreed with me and confirmed in writing within one month.

Signed .... (Employee)

Signed .... (Employer)

This contract is subject to the information submitted on your application form being correct. The company reserves the right to withdraw any offer of employment or to terminate your employment without notice if any information provided by you is found to be false or misleading.

Figure 5.1 *Main terms of employment*

- How much notice you must give if you want to leave the job.
- Details of your employer's disciplinary rules and procedures (see below).

An example of a Statement of the Main Terms of Employment is shown in Figure 5.1. It is called this because a full contract would contain all the above information. Instead, like many organisations, Perivale Services Ltd prefers to summarise the main terms and refer the employee to other documents for further details.

Terms and conditions within a contract

If you compare your contract with a friend, or with a more senior member of staff in a workplace, you are likely to find certain differences. This is because the exact terms and conditions of your jobs are unlikely to be the same. As long as the employer doesn't include anything which is against the law, this is quite permissible. For example:

- **The responsibilities** that apply to all employees will be stated in the contract, such as compliance with the company's policies and rules on issues such as health and safety, the use of IT equipment, non-smoking and security. In some cases the seniority of staff or type of job may mean that additional responsibilities affect the terms and conditions. Some senior staff, for example, may be allowed a benefit such as a company car, but they may also be expected to work flexible hours without additional payment. Other staff may work shifts, be paid overtime for additional hours or have specific starting and finishing hours. Some staff may be expected to conform to a company dress code. These differences would be reflected in the wording of the contract.
- **The accountability** of employees relates to the way in which they must explain or 'account for' their actions. For example, there will be procedures employees must follow if they are ill, and cannot come to work, or if they want to book annual leave. The contract will state exactly what employees must do in these and other relevant situations.
- **Payment terms**. Your contract will state your salary, how often you will be paid and the

method of payment. Most businesses now pay by BACS transfer, in which the money is transferred directly into the employee's bank account. Details of any bonus or commission schemes will also be included, in addition to information on sick pay. There is no legal entitlement for your employer to pay you sick pay but many employers pay for a maximum number of days at the employee's normal rate. The number of days will vary between organisations.

- **Payment and leave arrangements**. All full-time employees have the legal right to a minimum of 20 days' paid holidays – often referred to as 'annual leave'. (See page 273 for information about part-time and temporary employees). Some employers may be more generous and this would be stated in your contract, together with any restrictions on holidays. For example, if your employer is very busy at a certain time of the year, holidays may not be allowed at this time except by special agreement with a senior manager. You may be interested to note that in the UK, there is no automatic legal right to having time off on a Bank Holiday, unless this is stated in your contract!
- **Notice and termination of contract**. There is a minimum amount of notice that you, or your employer, must provide if the contract is terminated. This is to allow you to find another job, or your employer to replace you. Some employers extend this, particularly for senior staff. For example, a manager might have to give longer notice than a more junior employee.
- **Grievance and disciplinary procedures** The Employment Act 2002, made these a legal requirement for all organisations and the Dismissal and Discipline Regulations 2004 lay down standard procedures employers must follow if they are contemplating dismissing or taking disciplinary action against an employee. Basic information must be included in the written statement of employment and this must also state where the employee can find full details of the employer's procedures. These are discussed in more detail on page 294.
- **Time off work**. By law, employers must allow employees to be absent from work in certain circumstances. Apart from pregnant women,

who must be allowed to take time off for any specific medical appointments, employers only have to allow 'reasonable' time off. This must be **with pay** if the employee is:

- Carrying out duties as a safety representative or receiving training.
- Carrying out duties as a trade union official.
- Being made **redundant** and looking for another job or receiving training.
- Acting as an official employee representative and discussing important staff concerns, e.g. proposed redundancies.
- A young person studying for a relevant qualification.

In the following cases, leave can be **without pay**, but some employers are more generous and offer more than the legal minimum requirements. In this case the conditions stated in the contract will apply.

- Emergency leave for a problem involving a dependant. This includes issues such as illness and compassionate leave.
- Taking part in certain trade union activities, e.g. attending a meeting.
- Carrying out a public duty, such as being a member of a jury.

- **Additional leave arrangements**:
  - **Maternity leave**. Pregnant women automatically qualify for maternity leave for a minimum of 26 weeks. Many have the right to receive a minimum level of pay during this time and those who have worked for longer with an employer can take additional unpaid leave. During this time the woman's terms and conditions must remain the same and she must be allowed to return to her old job afterwards. If changes have been made so that the job is redundant she must be offered suitable alternative work. If she is sacked or made redundant then this would automatically be classed as unfair dismissal (see page 295).
  - **Paternity leave**. Most working fathers can take up to two weeks' paid leave following the birth of their partner's baby.
  - **Adoptive leave**. This gives similar rights to a couple who are adopting a child as to those who are expecting a baby.
  - **Parental leave**. All parents are entitled to 13 weeks' unpaid parental leave after one year's continuous service with an employer. They can take this normally until the child's fifth birthday unless the child is disabled, when up to 18 weeks' unpaid leave can be taken until the child's 18th birthday.

- **Right to trade union membership**. If a trade union is recognised by the employer, then all employees have the right to join – or the right to refuse. This is a statutory right, so, as such, will not be stated in a contract. However, you must be told about any union agreements that relate to you. Employers do not have to recognise a trade union, but many are prepared to do so if the majority of employees would prefer this.

Business brief

What is redundancy?

Redundancy occurs when there is no work for a person to do. If workers have to be made redundant, then the organisation must follow an agreed procedure to make sure it is fair, which involves consultation with the trade unions and employees. Staff being made redundant must be told about the payments they will receive and their legal rights. Free counselling or retraining may be offered and redundant staff must be allowed time off to attend training or interviews for new jobs.

Types of employment and people's preferences

Some jobs can only be done at certain times of the year

Many businesses offer different types of employment. This normally suits everyone. Employers benefit because there is increased flexibility, and employees can find work which suits their family commitments.

- **Full-time employees** are contracted to work for the standard operating hours of the company. These may vary from 37 to 42 hours per week, but can be more.
- **Part-time employees** work for less than the standard operating hours but each individual contract may be different. One employee may be contracted to work 15 hours per week and another only 5 hours.
- **Permanent employees** work for a set number of hours per week from a specified start date. They will continue to work until the contract is terminated because the employee leaves, retires or is dismissed. Note that permanent employees can work either on a full-time or part-time basis.
- **Temporary employees** are employed for a fixed term. Examples include seasonal workers, employees covering for a member of staff absent on maternity leave, those who are employed on a short-term basis because the firm is very busy, or those employed to do a specific task. The final date of the contract may be stated if this is appropriate. A variation are **casual** workers, who have flexible hours which are normally specified by the employer. Casual workers are only offered work when they are needed, which may not be on a regular basis.

Employment preferences

People's preferences for employment often depend upon their personal circumstances. When you are young, single and want to build a career, you will normally prefer to work full-time to widen your job opportunities and earn more money.

You may also prefer a permanent job for security. However, if you are planning a 'gap year' travelling the world, or struggling to find the right job, then you may look for temporary work which will help you to improve your skills and experience – but will be easier to leave.

Families, of course, have greater problems, particularly single parents. Many prefer part-time employment which they can fit around their childcare commitments – but may not want to change their place of employment after having a family. From April 2003, the Flexible Working Regulations 2002 gave parents with children under 6, or disabled children under 18, the right to ask their employer to consider giving them more flexible working patterns, including part-time work, if they have worked continuously for that employer for more than 26 weeks. This enables new mothers, for example, to adjust their working hours after starting a family. Their employer must consider the request seriously.

Business brief

Equal rights

The law states that part-time employees and employees on a fixed term contract must not receive less favourable treatment than permanent, full-time employees. This means that their overall package of terms, conditions and benefits must normally be comparable on a pro rata basis. For example, if all full-time employees receive 20 days' paid holiday a year, then part-time or temporary employees working 50 per cent of hours must receive 10 days' paid holiday.

The same protection does not apply to students on work placements or work experience. It does, however, cover students employed during the holidays!

Over to you!

1 If you work part-time then study your contract of employment carefully and check you understand what it means. Compare information with other members of your class on your terms and conditions – and then decide whose are the best!

Alternatively, check the example contract and the terms and conditions that apply on the Richer Sounds StudentZone at www.richerstudentzone.co.uk

2 As a group, decide two advantages and two disadvantages for an employee of:
   a Having a full-time permanent job.
   b Having a part-time permanent job.
   c Having a temporary job.
   d Being able to work flexible hours (although a basic minimum must always be worked).
   e Having the opportunity to work paid overtime.

Observing the written job description and contract

What is a job description?

A job description summarises all the basic facts about a particular job and the role of the job holder. It is often prepared or revised when a vacancy is created and before it is advertised. You may receive a copy when you apply for a job to enable you to understand exactly what type of work you will be asked to do.

The job description is important because it explains the type of work you will be asked to do. If you claimed to be able to do this work at interview, and then could not, then your employer may have grounds to dismiss you. (See page 255). An example of a job description to link with the Main Terms of Employment on page 270 is shown below.

Advantages and disadvantages of job descriptions

Job descriptions are helpful for the following reasons:

- Thinking about the tasks undertaken can help the employer to recruit the best person.
- Job applicants and job holders can see exactly what they are supposed to be doing.
- The type of tasks and job levels in the organisation can be compared to ensure that salaries are fair.
- If job descriptions are automatically updated when a job holder leaves, this enables the organisation to change duties and responsibilities when necessary (see also Section 5.4).

They are not, however, without some problems:

- It is virtually impossible to list every task or activity a job holder may be asked to do. For that reason a 'catch all' phrase is normally included at the end.
- Most job descriptions only cover broad tasks and don't go into detail – otherwise they would be several pages long. For that reason, you can expect to do several tasks that aren't specifically listed in any job.
- Job descriptions can be misleading as it is tempting to think that the most time will be taken on the longest items on the list. In reality, the reverse can occur.
- Job descriptions don't indicate the amount of variety in the job. Some tasks may be done every day, but others only occasionally.
- Some job holders may try to stick grimly to their existing job description even if conditions change. Most contracts of employment prevent this but there can still

Perivale Services Ltd		Job Description
Department:	Marketing	
Job title:	Marketing Assistant	
Hours of work:	37.5 per week, normally 9am–5.30pm Monday to Friday with one hour lunch, but some flexibility required	
Salary scale:	£12,000–£14,000	
Responsible to:	Marketing Manager	
Responsible for:	Not applicable	
Job purpose:	To provide general support for the marketing team, to prepare marketing materials, to keep the website up-to-date and monitor online responses.	

Duties and responsibilities
1. Receive telephone calls, deal with general enquiries and take messages for other team members as necessary.
2. Assist in the monthly update of the product brochure by writing basic product descriptions and obtaining artwork as necessary.
3. Keep the customer database up-to-date.
4. Assist in the preparation and distribution of mailshots to customers.
5. Update the marketing section of the company website with new product details or special offers as requested.
6. Monitor website activity and produce a monthly report for the Marketing Manager.
7. Ensure all customer email enquiries receive prompt responses, if necessary referring these to a more senior member of staff for resolution.
8. Attend any training course or team events that may be considered appropriate by the Marketing Manager.
9. Maintain staff confidentiality at all times and be aware that breach of this could lead to instant dismissal.
10. Undertake any other relevant duties which may be identified.

This job description is not intended to be fully prescriptive and will be the subject of regular review and possible amendment. The post holder may be required to undertake related tasks which are not specifically mentioned above.

August 2004

Figure 5.2 *A job description*

be a dispute over changing tasks and whether new tasks are 'reasonable' or not.

Line of reporting

Your job description will normally include the name of your supervisor or line manager. This is the person directly above you and to whom you are accountable. Your contract and/or staff handbook will also give details of other senior members of staff, for example the Human Resources supervisor or Wages clerk who can answer any specific questions you may have about your working conditions or pay.

If there is an organisation chart included you are wise to study it as you can then identify the seniority of other members of staff and different managers. You should also check to whom you should report if you are ill, or if your own manager is absent for any reason.

Key employee responsibilities

Some of these will be fairly obvious, because they will be stated in your contract of employment or in the job description. These are called **express terms**. Others are not included because they are considered so obvious! These are known as **implied terms** and a list of the main ones is given in the table below.

In practice, these responsibilities mean that you should be aware of the following important areas:

- **Standard of work**. An employer can take action if an employee is incapable of doing the work to the required standard, either because he or she has made false claims about qualifications or is incompetent and keeps making serious mistakes. If the situation continues even after the employee has received adequate training then the employer can legally dismiss (sack) the employee.

- **Working hours**. Your total hours of work will be expressly stated in your contract. If these are variable, then there are unlikely to be stated starting and finishing times. Any specific terms and conditions that apply will be stated in the contract or in the employee handbook. Your working hours do not normally include any rest breaks you are allowed, nor the time it takes you to travel to and from work. You may be paid overtime for additional hours you work or expected to help out without being paid. Generally this should only be on special occasions, not on a regular basis. The Working Time Regulations restricts working hours for the majority of employees (see page 280).

  You must turn up, in person, for the hours you are contracted to work unless you are sick or have been allowed leave.

- **Annual leave and sickness leave**. Your contract will state the number of annual days' leave you are allowed with pay and whether you will also be allowed Bank Holidays. You are not normally allowed to carry forward any unused holidays from one year to another – as you will see if you read the contract on page 270. There may also be rules about booking annual leave to prevent too many people being absent simultaneously or to prevent anyone being away at very busy times.

All employees have the following responsibilities, whether or not they are expressly stated in their contract or their job description.
- Meet the terms of the contract, i.e.
  - Work the hours stated.
  - Turn up for work or comply with absence procedures.
  - Do the work they are asked to do as part of their job.
  - Comply with any other conditions stated in the contract.
- Follow health and safety regulations.
- Comply with other laws related to their work, e.g. not drinking and driving.

In addition, the employer can expect that the employee:
- Is reasonably competent and possesses the skills claimed at the interview.
- Is 'ready and willing' to do the work and will do what any 'reasonable' employee would do in a situation.
- Will take reasonable care of the employer's property (e.g. equipment and furniture).
- Will work towards the objectives of the organisation.
- Is prepared to carry out reasonable instructions and requests.
- Will be honest.
- Will not disclose confidential information.
- Will behave responsibly towards other people at work.
- Will be prepared to change when the job changes, e.g. when new technology is introduced into the workplace.

Figure 5.3 *Implied terms of employment*

Your contract or handbook will also include the exact procedure to follow if you are absent because of sickness. An example is shown in the contract on page 270. You must also notify your employer if you are absent for any other reason, such as a family emergency. Unless it is a crisis, you would normally be expected to negotiate any additional leave with your line manager. Any employee who was absent, for any reason, without notice is liable to be disciplined and would probably be dismissed if this happened regularly.

- **Period of notice**. The minimum periods of notice allowable by law are shown in the contract on page 270. In many contracts these may be longer, although there are two main situations when notice periods may be waived.

  – If you wanted to leave immediately and your employer agreed. For example, if you were offered another job and wanted to start there very quickly. However, your employer has the right to refuse your request if this would cause problems.

  – If your employer would prefer to pay you instead of expecting you to work through your notice period. This basically means you are paid to stay at home. Employers often prefer this if there has been a dispute and/or if the employee regularly deals with confidential information.

- **Standards of dress and relationships**. An employer is normally within his or her rights to have a dress policy, or dress code, providing this does not discriminate against any group of employees, for example on grounds of sex or race (see page 278). Specific dress codes are unusual for white collar workers – although there may be a requirement to dress smartly. They are more often found for catering staff or those where hygiene standards are very important. In addition, an employer can also insist that all employees wear protective equipment, such as hard hats or safety boots,

In food outlets, strict hygiene standards are a legal requirement

and discipline any employees who refuse to comply.

It is an implied responsibility of all employees that they will act in a sensible and professional way – without the employer having to state this in a contract. This relates to their relationships with other staff, at all levels, and all other people with whom they come into contact in the course of their work.

- **Confidentiality**. This is another implied responsibility, but some employers specifically include a confidentiality clause in their contracts. An employee who breaches confidentiality can be disciplined. The outcome would depend largely upon the sensitivity of the information and to whom it was disclosed.

- **Use of IT facilities**. Most organisations today have IT policies which cover the use of IT equipment, the sending of emails and attachments and use of the Internet. This is because they must inform employees if they are monitoring computer use. If you use a computer at work then you need to read the policy carefully. Most employers allow staff to use the Internet occasionally for personal use and to send emails to friends, providing that the content and material which is sent or exchanged is not offensive or does not breach company rules. Some organisations are more strict – so it is sensible to check.

- **Data protection requirements**. The Data Protection Act restricts the use of personal information stored on computer and in structured paper files. It requires your employer to ensure that all personal data is processed fairly and lawfully, kept up to date and not retained longer than necessary. In reality, this usually relates to information held on customers and staff. Your employer will have a policy to ensure that it complies with the Act and will expect you to abide by it. Under the Act, however, you should note that you have the right to ask to see any information held about you – although your employer can make a small administrative charge for providing this. You can find out more at the Information Commissioner's Office website, a link is available at www.heinemann.co.uk/hotlinks (express code 1386P).

Business brief

Company policies, rules and regulations

These are often set out in a separate document. They include rules that employees must follow but also company policies that identify the codes of behaviour expected by everyone at all levels. These usually include:

- **Equal opportunities** – to ensure all staff are treated fairly and equally and no one is bullied, victimised or harassed.
- **Maternity, paternity and parental leave policies** – which must be at least the minimum allowed by law, but which may be more generous.
- **Policies on breaks from work** and emergency leave.
- **Welfare policies** for staff, such as assistance if someone is ill for a long time.

The rules and regulations will often depend upon the type of business undertaken. For example, companies which deal with highly confidential information or valuable items may have specific policies and rules and include express clauses in the contract of employment to cover these areas.

Business matters

Jobcentre Plus employee Matthew Thompson objected when he was disciplined for not wearing a tie to work. He claimed it was sexual discrimination that he had to wear a collar and tie when his female colleagues could wear T-shirts. In April 2003 he won an employment tribunal case against his employer, the Department of Work and Pensions (DWP). Since his victory, 8,000 male employees of the Jobcentre Plus network have lodged similar applications. However, the DWP have now been allowed to appeal against the decision on a point of law. The outcome of the appeal, which has not yet been heard, will determine the success of the other applications and whether this case marks the end of the traditional white collar and tie male dress code.

Interestingly, during the case, the employment panel considered how they would interpret the DWP's 'smart casual' dress code. The result showed that whereas society's ideas on dress codes for women have changed radically, they have remained more constant for men.

Both dress and personal appearance can cause difficulties at work. In 1996 the supermarket chain Safeway dismissed a male worker for having long hair, which he wore in a ponytail. He claimed it was discriminatory for men to have conventional hairstyles not below shirt collar length. He lost his case because he worked in a delicatessen where hygiene requirements were considered vital. In a similar case, a Sikh employee of British Rail complained that it was discriminatory that he must wear a hard hat because he could not put it on over his turban. Although the tribunal agreed this was discriminatory it felt the need for safety was paramount so the difference was justified.

Key elements of employment legislation

On page 269, you saw that all employees also have statutory legal rights because of Acts or Regulations passed by Parliament. Understanding the main laws not only helps you to understand your own rights and responsibilities better, but also to see the reason for many company policies on equal opportunities, parental leave, health and safety and other related areas.

Equal opportunities and the law on discrimination

Discrimination was first covered in section 2.3, on page 152. It basically means treating someone differently and unfairly because of a reason unrelated to their job. It can occur at any stage of the employment process, such as during an interview or when offering opportunities for training or access to staff benefits. It also includes **harassment** and **victimisation**. Turn back to page 152 now if you have completely forgotten what these terms mean!

To prevent discrimination, many companies have **equal opportunities policies**. There are several benefits:

- These state the firm's commitment to equal opportunities and to operating a workplace free from discrimination.
- They promote good workplace relations.
- They specify the standards all managers and staff must uphold.
- They help to protect the employer against claims of discrimination or bullying, harassment or victimisation in the workplace.
- Employment tribunals look more favourably on organisations which have such a policy – and keep to it – than those who don't.

There are five specific laws to protect against discrimination and a further law to protect employees from harassment. From 2006, discrimination on the grounds of age will also be unlawful.

The law and equal pay

For many years, it has been a government aim that men and women who do the same or equivalent

---

Laws on discrimination

The Sex Discrimination Act 1975 (as amended)

This Act makes it illegal for anyone to be discriminated against on grounds of gender (or gender reassignment) - either directly or indirectly. In employment, this applies to recruitment and selection for jobs and promotion, training, the way you are treated in a job, dismissal and redundancy. Discrimination can occur in two ways:
- Direct discrimination is where one gender is obviously excluded, e.g. 'only men need apply.'
- Indirect discrimination is where a condition would make it more difficult for one sex to comply, e.g. 'only those over 6'6' need apply'. Even if this is unintentional, the employer is still guilty of discrimination.
There are some exceptions, such as acting and live-in jobs, if the employer can show that a Genuine Occupational Qualification (GOQ) applies to that job.

The Race Relations Act 1976 (as amended by the Race Relations Act 2000 and the Race Regulations 2003)
This Act makes it unlawful for anyone to be discriminated against or harassed on grounds of colour, race, nationality or ethnic origin. Again, both direct and indirect discrimination apply, although the definition of indirect discrimination is broader. It also covers other areas in addition to employment including education and vocational training, access to goods and services and social protection. Anyone advertising 'only white people need apply' would be guilty of direct discrimination - from an employer to a housing association. Similarly, anyone advertising 'only those with English as a first language need apply' would be guilty of indirect discrimination.

Again, there are certain special circumstances under which discrimination may be justified, such as restaurants, for authenticity, but these are relatively rare.

The Disability Discrimination Act 1995 (as amended)
This Act is concerned with discrimination against people with disabilities in employment, when obtaining goods and services, buying/renting land or property and in relation to access to business premises. The disability may be physical, sensory or mental, must be relatively long term and includes long term progressive conditions, such as MS and cancer. Public bodies must have clear policies and action plans to tackle discrimination and no employer must treat a disabled person less favourably than able-bodied persons unless this can be justified. Employers must also be prepared to make reasonable adjustments to the workplace to enable a disabled person to do the job. In this case, discrimination is not divided into 'direct' or 'indirect' but is 'less favourable treatment that cannot be justified'.

The Employment Equality (Sexual Orientation) Regulations 2003
These Regulations make it unlawful to discriminate against workers because of their sexual orientation, whether they are bisexual, lesbian, gay or heterosexual. This includes employees, agency workers, anyone undertaking vocational training or otherwise working for the organisation. They protect people from discrimination (both direct and indirect), harassment or victimisation both about their own orientation and those of their friends or family.

The Employment Equality (Religion or Belief) Regulations 2003
These Regulations make it illegal to discriminate, harass or victimise anyone on the grounds of their religion or belief. This does not, however, include political beliefs. The Regulations relate to issues such as the provision of a 'quiet room' for prayer, time off for special religious events, choice of menu in worker canteens, social events (at which non-alcoholic drinks must be available) and dress codes.

Anyone who suffers discrimination can complain to an employment tribunal.

Men and women doing the same job must be equally paid

work are paid the same wage. **The Equal Pay Act 1970** was introduced to make it illegal to offer different pay and conditions just because one person is male and another is female. However, it is necessary to ensure that the jobs are 'equal' especially when the duties of each person may be different.

- A woman is doing 'like work' to a man if she is employed to do the same type of job. For example, if a woman and a man are both production workers and she packs apples while he packs onions they must both receive the same rate of pay.
- A woman must be paid the same as a man if the jobs have been rated as the same under a job grading study.
- If there has been no official job grading study, a woman can claim her job is of 'equal value' to a man's. In this case, an independent specialist may be appointed to decide on the value of

each job. At the time of writing the trade union UNISON is currently claiming that all teaching assistants do work of 'equal value' in Lancashire to male technicians employed by the council and therefore should receive the same hourly rate. You may want to check the outcome on the UNISON website, a link to this site is available at www.heinemann.co.uk/hotlinks (express code 1386P).

If men and women are paid at different rates, an employer can defend this on two grounds:

- There is an important difference between the two workers which has nothing to do with their gender. For example, the man might have worked for the company much longer or be better qualified.
- There is an important difference between the two jobs. For example, a man is expected to do heavy cleaning jobs and therefore cannot be compared to a woman who does light cleaning duties.

Your other statutory employment rights

There are a large number of employment laws that give you rights at work. Three of these were identified and described briefly in Unit 2 on page 192. They are:

- The Employment Rights Act 1996.
- The Employment Relations Act 1999.
- The Employment Act 2002.

Turn back to that page now, to remind yourself of the key aspects of those laws. Other statutory rights of which you should be aware, for your own protection, are given in the table on page 280. Note that these do not include every single right that you may have – there are far too many to list in this book!

💬 Talking point

> **View 1:** *Comprehensive legislation is important because it protects everyone's rights. It is up to all employers to learn what is involved and follow it – or pay the penalty in law.*

> **View 2:** *Comprehensive legislation is fine for large employers that can afford to employ human resource specialists. It is a nightmare – and costly – for small businesses who, in many cases, should be exempt from many of the regulations.*

With which viewpoint do you agree – and why?

Business matters

The Equal Opportunities Commission (EOC) is the official agency which was established in 1975 to help to eliminate sexual discrimination. It works to promote and monitor equal opportunities, provides advice and information and helps to bring cases for employees who suffer from sex discrimination. Its equivalent bodies are the Commission for Racial Equality (CRE) and the Disability Rights Commission (DRC).

According to EOC research, despite the Equal Pay Act, women still earn an average of 18 per cent less per year than men – even when qualifications are identical. It wants all employers to carry out equal pay reviews and audits to check pay rates in their own organisation. In the meantime, women can check whether they are being paid fairly by using a salary calculator on the commission's website.

Women have the legal right to know how much their male colleagues are being paid to do the same job. A woman first needs to select someone who she thinks is being treated more favourably and doing an equivalent job in her organisation. She can then submit a questionnaire about his pay to her employer. A man can do the same thing, if he feels a woman is being treated more favourably than him, but claims cannot be made about someone of the same sex.

In 2006, a new Commission for Equality and Human Rights will take the place of the EOC, CRE and DRC. In the meantime, you can find out more about their work on the EOC, CRE and DRC websites. Links are available at www.heinemann.co.uk/hotlinks (express code 1386P).

Other statutory employment rights

- The right to be paid a salary at or above the minimum wage rate if you are over 18. You can find out the current rate on the DTI website – a link is available at www.heinemann.co.uk/hotlinks (express code 1386P). From October 2004 it is likely that a minimum wage rate will also apply to 16 and 17 year olds.
- The right not to be forced to work more than 48 hours per week, averaged over a 17 week period or to be asked to work more than 40 hours per week or do night work if you are aged 16–18.
- The right to choose whether or not to work on a Sunday.
- The right to receive maternity, paternity and parental leave in accordance with the law and the right to take time off in a family emergency.
- The right to receive redundancy pay if you are dismissed because there is no work for you to do, after having been continuously employed for at least two years.
- The right to apply to work flexibly if you have a child under 6 (or a disabled child under 18), providing you have been working for at least 26 weeks. The employer can refuse your request but only for certain specific reasons.
- The right to see computer records about you or paper files which contain your personal details. Your employer can make a small charge for providing this information.
- The right to be given reasonable time off to study or train for a qualification up to NVQ2 if you are 16 or 17 and working or the right to complete training you have already begun if you are 18 when you first start work.

The law and health and safety

It is a requirement of the Health and Safety at Work etc. Act 1974 that all employers with more than five staff must have a safety policy and safety procedures and keep staff up to date with any new procedures. They must also monitor risks in the workplace and take action to eliminate or minimise these wherever possible. Legally they are responsible for the safety of employees, visitors, contractors and customers visiting the premises. This includes providing suitable first aid facilities and regularly checking and maintaining all working equipment.

The Health and Safety at Work etc. Act was first outlined on page 153 of this book and you can turn back to that page to see its main provisions. You should also note that this is an 'umbrella' Act under which many other Regulations have

Health and Safety Regulations

Those which apply to most employees in a business environment:

Workplace (Health, Safety and Welfare) Regulations. These cover four specific areas: **a** the work environment (ventilation, temperature, lighting, space); **b** safety (in respect of traffic routes, floors, windows, escalators, stairs etc); **c** facilities (toilets, water, seating, rest areas); **d** housekeeping (maintenance and cleanliness).

Fire Precautions Act and Regulations. All businesses must be able to demonstrate that they undertake fire risk assessments and have controls in place - such as fire-resistant doors, fire extinguishers, break-glass alarms and a fire alarm system.

Employers' Liability (Compulsory Insurance) Regulations. All employers must take out insurance so employees who are injured at work can claim compensation.

Health and Safety (First Aid) Regulations. All organisations must provide adequate and appropriate first-aid equipment and facilities as well as trained first-aiders. The number of first-aiders must be appropriate to the risks in the workplace.

Health and Safety (Safety Signs and Signals) Regulations. Safety signs must be displayed to identify risks and hazards and written instructions on how to use fire-fighting equipment.

Reporting of Injuries, Diseases and Dangerous Occurrences Regulations (RIDDOR). All organisations must notify the Health and Safety Executive (HSE) of any serious or fatal injuries and keep records of certain specific injuries, dangerous occurrences and diseases.

The Display Screen Equipment Regulations. All employers must assess the risks to staff using VDUs and workstations, pay for eye tests and spectacles/lenses if these are prescribed for VDU work and plan work activities to incorporate rest breaks.

The Control of Substances Hazardous to Health Regulations (COSHH). All hazardous substances (such as toxic cleaning fluids) must be clearly labelled and stored in a special environment and users provided with protective clothing.

The Electricity at Work Regulations. These govern the design, construction, use and maintenance of electrical systems.

The Noise at Work Regulations. These require employers to check noise hazards and reduce these where possible and provide ear protectors if necessary.

The Provision and Use of Work Equipment Regulations (PUWER). These relate to the maintenance and safety of all work equipment. Employers must make regular checks and inspections and provide appropriate training and instructions for users.

The Manual Handling Operations Regulations. These govern the way items should be lifted and handled. Preferably a mechanised process is used but if items are moved manually employees must be trained properly to minimise injury.

Personal Protective Equipment at Work Regulations. Protective clothing and equipment must be provided when risks cannot be eliminated. They must be free of charge, fit properly and be kept in good condition.

been – and can be – passed to keep health and safety laws up-to-date. These include rules to provide basic hygiene facilities, such as working toilets, hot and cold water, clean working areas with regular waste removal, sufficient space, ventilation and comfortable working temperatures.

The aim of many of the regulations is to minimise the risk of accidents happening. A summary of the main ones is given above.

Key employer responsibilities

Employers have many legal responsibilities. They must comply with all statutory laws and regulations, such as the ones you read about in the last section. They must obey the terms of their own contracts and they also have implied responsibilities.

Statutory responsibilities

All employers must obey all the laws of the land – just like everyone else. This includes all employment laws and health and safety law. It is also their responsibility to keep up to date with any new laws or amendments and to change their procedures to include these.

- They must have clear disciplinary and grievance procedures, ensure all staff are informed about these and that the procedures are followed if there is a dispute or problem.
- They must have up-to-date policies to cover equal opportunities and discrimination
- They must take prompt action if any employee complains about discrimination, harassment or victimisation and investigate these thoroughly and fairly. If the complaint is upheld, then action must be taken to minimise any chance of a recurrence.
- They must fulfil their responsibilities in relation to health and safety. These include:
  - Providing a safe working environment.
  - Drawing up a safety policy and procedures for employees to follow if there is an emergency or if an accident occurs.
  - Regularly carrying out risk assessments.
  - Providing first aid facilities in accordance with the level of risk.
  - Putting in place preventative measures including erecting safety signs, providing protective clothing and storing hazardous substances safely.
  - Providing training for all employees on health and safety.
  - Providing information on health and safety to employees, visitors and anyone else working on the premises, and ensuring all information is regularly updated.
  - Investigating accidents and keeping an accident book.
- They must take out Employers' liability insurance to cover any claims from employees who are hurt or ill as a result of their work. The minimum legal cover is £5 million.
- If they employ 5 people or more, they must offer their employees access to a stakeholder pension scheme.
- If they recruit a new employee, they must check that person is eligible to work in the United Kingdom.

Contractual responsibilities

All employers must also abide by the terms of the contract of employment and statutory laws relating to the contract. This means, for example, that they must:

- Issue contracts of employment or a statement of the main terms of employment within two months of each employee starting work.
- Pay employees according to the contract.
- Issue an itemised payslip showing gross and net pay and any deductions.
- Provide any benefits or additional payments that are identified.
- Allow employees to have their rightful holiday entitlement.
- Allow employees to have additional leave as stated in the organisation's policies.
- Allow all employees to join a recognised trade union or a staff association.
- Allow employees access to confidential records kept on them as employees.
- Discuss and agree any proposed changes to the contract with the unions, staff association or the employees; then inform employees in writing within a month of any resulting changes being made to the written statement.
- Not discipline employees for failing to conform with a specific requirement that is not clearly stated in the contract.
- Provide clarification over any issues relating to the terms and conditions of employment if these are unclear or causing problems.

Implied responsibilities

In addition, employers also have implied responsibilities. This means that, regardless of anything you receive in writing, you can expect every employer:

- To treat you reasonably.
- To give you the opportunity to participate in and be consulted on company matters which would directly affect you.
- Never to ask you to do anything which is illegal.

Over to you!

1 Your friend Charlie has received the Statement of Main Terms document from Perivale Services shown on page 270. Read this carefully and use it to answer the following questions.

a Charlie can't remember whether he will work fixed hours every day (e.g. 9am to 5pm) or more flexible hours. According to the contract, which is more likely to be correct?

b Charlie aims to visit relatives in Australia next year and would like to take extra paid holidays. He thinks one way to do this would be to 'save up' holiday from this year. Can he do this?

c Charlie finds that his supervisor, who has worked there for several years, has more holidays than him. He thinks this is unfair and wonders if he can complain. What would you tell him?

d What must Charlie do if he wakes up one morning with flu?

e Why do you think Charlie won't qualify for sick pay from his first day at work?

f Why is it important that both the employer and the employee must give notice if the contract is being terminated?

2 a For either your own or any other contract of employment suggest:

i **Three** express or explicit terms you are likely to find.

ii **Three** implied terms which are not included because they are considered obvious.

b Identify **three** responsibilities of your employer, after you have signed your contract of employment.

5.1 Section review

1 The following terms have been used in this section. Define each one.

a Discrimination.
b Maternity leave.
c Paternity leave.
d Contract of employment.
e Annual leave.
f Statutory employment rights.
g Contractual employment rights.
h Equal opportunities policy.
i Harassment.
j Parental leave.

2 If you work part-time as a student and want to check your rights, then download the booklet on student rights at work from the TUC website, a link is available at www.heinemann.co.uk/hotlinks (express code 1386P). This tells you what you can expect now, as a student and part-time employee.

3 WorkSMART is the TUC website which aims to answer all your questions about your rights at work. Divide into six small groups. Each should research **one** of the following topics and report back to the rest of the class. You can find the information you need on the WorkSMART website, but you might also like to find out more on employment law from the DTI website as well as in your college library. Links to the two websites mentioned above are available at www.heinemann.co.uk/hotlinks (express code 1386P).

a Employer and employee responsibilities in relation to health and safety law.
b Working life and family policies.
c Discrimination and harassment.
d Discipline, rules, regulations and policies.
e Pay and contracts of employment.
f Working hours, holiday, breaks and leave.

This section covers

Professional recruitment procedures

Appraisal procedures and documentation

Training needs and opportunities for personal development

Professional recruitment procedures

Both interviewer and interviewee should be well prepared

Many people can recount horror stories about interviews. Nobody enjoys the experience but it is less overwhelming and far easier to do your best if you are dealing with a professional organisation and a well-trained interviewer. Thankfully, because of the increasing emphasis on equality of opportunity, more and more businesses have recruitment procedures that all staff must follow. This has several benefits.

- The recruitment process is expensive – unless it is done well both time and money can be wasted.
- There is a greater likelihood that the best candidate will be hired at the first attempt.
- Poorly treated candidates talk about their experiences and this does little for the firm's reputation in the locality.
- If unsuitable staff are hired they may struggle to do the job properly, upset existing staff or customers or leave quickly – which means the process has to start all over again.

- It helps to ensure equality of opportunity, i.e. that all applicants will be treated fairly.
- It helps to protect the company against allegations of discrimination by a candidate.

The policy will cover all stages of the recruitment process – from placing the advertisement to confirming the appointment.

Stages in the recruitment process

There are normally nine specific stages in the recruitment process. These are explained below.

- **Agree the vacancy**. Staff are expensive and in most organisations managers need to obtain permission to recruit a new member of staff. If the business is struggling, they may also need agreement to replace someone who is leaving. Normally, therefore, there is a specific procedure managers must follow before the recruitment process can be started.
- **Agree the job description**. The job being advertised may be new, in which case a job description needs to be devised. Even if someone is being replaced, it is useful to update the job description in case any tasks or duties have changed. An example of a job description was shown on page 274.
- **Draw up a person specification**. This identifies the essential and desirable qualifications required and the skills and attributes of the person required. This helps to ensure that the advertisement covers all the important aspects and also makes it easier to compare applications when these are received. An example of a person specification to match the job description shown on page 274 is illustrated in Figure 5.4.

Perivale Services Ltd　　　　　　　　　　**Person Specification**

Department:	Marketing
Job title:	Marketing Assistant
Vacancy Number:	509

Personal attributes	Essential	Desirable
Qualifications	4 GCSEs grade C or above, including English or equivalent business qualification	CLAIT or e-skills qualification
Experience	One year's previous experience working in business	Previous experience of working in marketing
Skills and abilities	Verbal communication skills Webpage updating Neat handwriting	Use of Microsoft Office
Personal attributes	Keen interest in working in Marketing Willing to undertake further study Neat and tidy appearance	Friendly and outgoing personality Creative abilities

Figure 5.4 *A person specification*

- **Advertise the vacancy**. The method of advertising will depend upon the vacancy – a senior post may be advertised in the national press or a trade magazine, an administrative vacancy in the local paper or placed with a job agency and a driver's job handed to the Jobcentre. The best choice must be made in relation to the type of job and the cost of the advert.

  The advertisement must then be drafted from the information in the job description and person specification. The essential requirements are usually made crystal clear because without these a candidate will not normally be offered an interview. The conditions of employment should also be included and applicants told how to apply or find out further information. This might include writing a letter and attaching a CV (curriculum vitae) or completing an official application form. There is likely to be a closing date after which no more applications will be considered.
- **Processing applications**. All applications are normally logged on receipt, often by allocating each one a reference number. They will normally be kept safely until the closing date by the human resources department.
- **Shortlisting applicants**. Many vacancies attract far more applicants than can be interviewed. In this case the applications are 'pruned' to select the most suitable candidates. This must be done systematically and according to specific procedures and agreed criteria. Normally:
  - Any candidates without the essential requirements are rejected.
  - Those with the essential requirements and all (or most) of the desirable requirements are put in a priority pile.
  - If this is still too many the applications are assessed again on other aspects, such as neatness and style.
- **Interviewing applicants**. The type of interview will often depend upon the job. A basic, one-stage interview is usual for manual or junior vacancies in a large company and for most vacancies in a small one. A two-stage interview, which may even involve a panel of interviewees, may be used for senior or highly skilled vacancies. Some interviews may include basic tests of aptitude or specific skills, such as keyboarding or numeracy.

  All interviewers should be trained so that they know how to question candidates skilfully and fairly. They should know how to spot 'gaps' on application forms, understand how to 'follow up' inadequate answers and have the skills to encourage shy or reserved candidates to do their best. They must also be clear about the laws on discrimination and how these relate to the interview process. This normally means asking all candidates the same questions, for fairness, even though the discussions that follow may be different, depending upon the response. It also means avoiding any questions which can be considered discriminatory – such as asking a woman if she has any plans to have a family!
- **Assessing applicants**. A lot of businesses use a process of awarding candidates a numerical score against specific criteria. Many of these scoresheets include points for the initial application, their performance in any tests, and at the interview. When the interviews are completed the scores are totalled and

compared, after which the highest scoring candidate will normally be offered the job.

This system is fairer and more objective than relying on impressions, which may be misleading. It also enables any interviewer to give more precise information if a candidate asks for feedback and can be vital, as proof of fair play, if anyone claims that an interview was biased.

- **Making an offer.** Once a person has been selected, the organisation makes a formal job offer. The other candidates are normally not contacted at this stage, in case the first-choice candidate refuses, because then an offer can be made to the second choice – and so on. Only after the offer has been accepted are the other candidates told they are unsuccessful.

Because most organisations realise that 'waiting for news' is agonising for candidates, it is normal to try to reach a decision quickly and notify candidates promptly. Sometimes, to speed things up, the successful candidate is contacted by phone so that the remaining letters can be sent out quickly.

Business brief

The law and references

Most organisations ask for two references and expect one to come from a 'current' source. However, many people applying for a job don't want their current employer to know that they are job hunting. For this reason, applicants are within their rights to ask that their current boss is not contacted unless they are offered the job and organisations must abide by this. They may then make the offer 'subject to satisfactory references'.

Employers have a legal obligation to ensure that any reference they provide is accurate and fair. To prevent problems and claims of inaccuracy, some firms refuse to provide one. Others simply stick to basic facts, such as starting and leaving dates, position held and reasons for leaving.

Over to you!

1 As a group, collect several examples of job advertisements related to business, both from your local newspaper and/or from the Internet at sites like fish4jobs. A link to the fish4jobs website is available at www.heinemann.co.uk/hotlinks (express code 1386P). Analyse the job advertisements to check if you can identify the essential and desirable requirements in each case. Then select a job that appeals to you and, with guidance from your tutor, write a letter of application and prepare your CV as if you were applying for the job.

2 Working in a small group, and using one of the job advertisements collected for 1 above, carry out the following tasks.

   a Prepare a list of interview questions that you would ask all applicants. Compare your list with those of other groups and decide which questions, out of all the suggestions, are the most appropriate.

   b As a potential candidate, consider how you would answer each of the questions. Compare your suggestions with those of other members of your group.

   c Assume that your group is an interview panel. Draw up a scorecard you could use to assess candidates for the job. Then suggest what you would do if:

      i Two candidates obtained exactly the same score.

      ii Two of you disagreed about the final choice.

Appraisal procedures and documentation

In many interviews candidates ask about their opportunities for career development and promotion. Good organisations normally have a policy which includes:

- An appraisal scheme, which links to
- Staff development and training opportunities.

In this way, members of staff benefit by improving their own skills and abilities and the organisation benefits through motivated employees who are more capable of helping the business to achieve its objectives.

Appraisal schemes and performance reviews

An **appraisal interview** is a confidential interview between a member of staff and, usually, his or her immediate manager. These discussions normally take place once or twice a year and cover:

- The work the employee has done well since the last appraisal – including areas the employee wishes to highlight. This will include targets that were identified on the last **action plan**, or **personal development plan (PDP)**, and have been achieved.
- Any areas where the employee feels less confident or has performed less well (including targets not achieved), with suggestions for how these problems can be overcome.
- The type of work (or jobs) the employee would like to do in the future.
- Any other areas of personal and professional development the employee would like to discuss.

In some companies these are called **performance reviews** because the employee's performance since the last review is discussed.

The aims of appraisals

The aims of the appraisal are:

- To enable an employee and manager to discuss current and future performance in confidence. If this is done well, it can encourage and motivate employees.
- To identify the employee's future ambitions and link these to the business objectives (see Unit 1, page 47).
- To assist the employee to create a personal development plan for the next period and set key targets for achievement.
- To identify training and development requirements for that employee.
- To assess future potential or suitability for promotion.
- To help the employee to plan his or her career.

The appraisal process

Appraisals aren't left to chance. There is normally a formal process which must be followed by both managers and staff. Although this may vary slightly between organisations, the main steps are identified below.

- Advance notification is given to the employee that the review, or appraisal, is due. A mutually convenient time and date for the interview is then agreed between the manager and member of staff.
- The appraisal documents are given to the employee. These explain the process. Normally, employees can choose a different person to do the review if, for any reason, they feel it would be unfair if it was done by their line manager.
- The employee prepares for the interview by completing an appraisal form which identifies key points for discussion, e.g. achievements and targets met since the last appraisal, current strengths and weaknesses, future ambitions, areas for development. Unless they are new employees, the previous personal development plan (PDP) is also updated.
- A copy of the documents is given to the manager a few days before the interview, so that consideration can be given to the points raised.
- The interview takes place. Normally only managers who have been trained to do so can carry out appraisals, as it can take considerable skill to identify problem areas or discuss someone's weaknesses without demoralising them. A successful appraisal should result in an employee feeling more motivated and in control of his/her future. It should also result in a list of new targets which benefits both the business and the employee.
- The result of the discussions are recorded on the appraisal form and a new PDP is completed which lists the development areas agreed and target dates for achievement. Both manager and employee have a copy.
- The manager must then take steps to ensure that any agreed training or development activities are arranged and take place.

Training needs and opportunities for personal development

Training is important in all jobs

Most employers expect their staff to take an active interest in their own training and self-development – which is why it is a key topic discussed at appraisal interviews. Under normal circumstances, a reputation for being keen and eager to improve and learn new skills, plus a track record of doing so, is an important factor in deciding internal promotions.

Identifying training needs

Training needs are identified on both formal and informal occasions, for example:

- At the interview, immediate training needs may be discussed and agreed. For example, a potentially ideal candidate may need training to learn one aspect of the job.
- All new employees normally undertake **induction training**, to learn about the business and how it operates. This helps them to settle in and become productive more quickly.
- Ongoing training needs are formally identified during an appraisal interview or performance review. These usually focus on higher level qualifications or skills and training events organised in the company.
- Retraining may be needed – sometimes by all employees – if there is a change in technology or working practices (see section 5.4).

Types of training

The word **training** usually refers to specific opportunities to develop job related skills and abilities. Examples would be learning a new software package or attending a first aid course. In addition, today employees are expected to focus on their own **personal development**. This refers to any activities that increase knowledge, skills or experience – whether job related or not. It could include working in another department or learning a foreign language.

'Learning while you work' is often called **on the job training**. This is appropriate to learn how equipment functions or how to do a certain task. **Off the job training** means that the employee learns away from the desk. This could be within the organisation – in a training room, for example – or outside at an FE college or specialist centre.

Many young employees make the mistake of thinking that all training should be free, organised by the employer and only take place during working hours! Essential training will be provided in this way, but departmental budgets are normally fixed each year, so 'free' training will be limited to the amount of money available. Equally, some external courses are very expensive and can cost thousands of pounds, particularly if they also involve accommodation and travel. Therefore it is inevitable that there is never enough money to suit everyone and every manager will have to prioritise the training needs for staff.

This should not prevent bright, creative and ambitious young employees from finding ways to learn which do not involve their employer's time and money. Many attend evening classes, some go on weekend courses, others learn online at home. Whichever way they choose, in every case they are increasing their own skills and making themselves more eligible for promotion either in their own organisation or elsewhere.

Internal vacancies and promotion opportunities

Some organisations have a policy whereby only junior positions are filled from outside. This is the case at Richer Sounds – because they believe that all promotion opportunities should be offered to existing staff who have proved their loyalty and ability. The only exception would be if existing

staff did not possess the specialist skills required for a job.

Other organisations have a policy of advertising vacancies both internally and externally. In this case all candidates apply in the same way, regardless of whether they are internal or external. The benefit of this is that 'new blood' can be brought in when necessary to revitalise an area. The danger is that if many jobs are given to external applicants, existing staff may become demotivated and demoralised. They may feel that they can only get on by leaving the company. This may be the case anyway, in a very small firm, where there are rarely promotion opportunities and not much scope for career advancement.

The procedure that is followed also varies between organisations. In some small private companies you may simply be called into the boss's office and told you have been promoted! In the public sector, and larger organisations, there is far more likely to be a formal process – very similar to the recruitment process on pages 284–5. This is to prevent allegations of favouritism by other staff and any problems relating to discrimination.

Equal opportunities and promotion

The law is very clear that discrimination can occur at any point in the employment process – and this includes promotion. Therefore any system relating to promotion must be seen to provide equal opportunities to all staff. This means ensuring that:

- All staff are informed of promotion opportunities in good time to apply. This often means advertising internal vacancies in several ways, e.g. on noticeboards, in a staff magazine and by email.
- The criteria for interviewing candidates does not disadvantage one group of candidates in any way.
- Interviews of internal candidates are carried out as carefully and sensitively as those of external candidates – and the scoring is equally fair.

Personal aptitudes and career options

If you are reading this book then it is likely that – at the moment, anyway – you are thinking of working in business. The marvellous thing about business is that there are literally dozens of different types of jobs to choose from, depending upon your particular aptitudes.

Personal aptitudes

There are a variety of aptitude tests that you can take, but all have the aim of identifying the areas of work you would like, and those you would not. Anyone on a business course, for example, is unlikely to opt for 'must work outside every day' or 'must have lots of physical activity' as key aspects of their job!

You may have taken an aptitude test before you started your current course. If not, then talk to the careers advisors in your college or contact Connexions to obtain more information.

Your personal aptitudes can also help to guide you towards the area of business you would prefer. For example:

- Creative extroverts are often attracted to areas like marketing, advertising and public relations.
- Careful methodical workers, with specific numeracy or literacy skills are more likely to be involved in finance, administration or legal matters.
- If you love IT, then you could look at website development and maintenance or a computer services role.
- Those who like dealing with people are often attracted to human resources or customer services.
- If you like wheeling and dealing, then you are more likely to be attracted to sales or purchasing.

But there are always exceptions! So if you are interested in a particular area then it is important to investigate it further – as you will see.

Career options

Within business, you have several alternatives.

- You can work in different types of organisations – retail, IT, manufacturing, finance, legal – the choice is almost endless!
- You could work for the government or for your local council, police authority or hospital.
- You could specialise in different types of work, e.g. human resources, finance, marketing, sales or IT.
- You can work at different levels – and train for management if you are ambitious.

At this stage, you probably know you like the idea of business but may have less idea of any area in which you would like to specialise. This is both normal and sensible. Until you have more experience, and learn more about the different alternatives, it is often wise to keep an open mind.

When you start work, then you will be in a better position to evaluate different alternatives. If you work for a medium or large company, then you may be able to work towards your eventual career goals within the firm – even if this means changing direction once or twice. If you work for a

Higher level and professional qualifications

- Many people at work study for NVQ awards. There are literally dozens available, linked to specific careers. NVQs are offered at five levels and most people start at level 2. Levels 4 and 5 are high level and only available in certain topics. For a business career, look under Providing Business Services to find NVQs in accounting, administration, customer service, IT, purchasing and management.
- There are a wide range of IT qualifications and awards – from general awards (such as CLAIT) to those concentrating on
  e-skills or on competence with a particular package, such as spreadsheets or graphics.
- Business studies can be studied to degree level, both full and part-time. It is then possible to progress to do an MBA – a Master's degree in Business Administration.
- Anyone wanting to learn management skills can take specific part-time qualifications, such as NEBSM (for supervisors), CIM (Certificate in Management) and DMS (Diploma in Management Studies).
- Specialist, professional qualifications include those offered by many professional bodies, for example:
  -- The Chartered Institute of Marketing.
  -- The Chartered Institute of Purchasing.
  -- The Chartered Institute of Personnel and Development.
- Trainee finance staff and accountants can start with AAT awards (the Association of Accounting Technicians) then progress to either ACCA (for chartered accounting) or CIMA (for management accounting).

Figure 5.5 *Business related qualifications*

small firm, then you may have to map out your own career plan and incorporate a few 'moves' along the way.

In most cases, if you want to move 'upwards and onwards', you have to think about obtaining additional, high level qualifications. The ones that are best will depend upon your own career plan. Some options are shown in Figure 5.5.

Talking point

View 1: *Many firms only communicate with shortlisted candidates. They do not write to applicants who didn't make the shortlist because they say it is too expensive. This is sensible as some jobs receive hundreds of applications.*

View 2: *It is only good manners to respond to job applications – no matter how many there are. Businesses that don't do this are irresponsible and create a bad impression.*

With which viewpoint do you agree – and why?

Over to you!

1 Some appraisals are very successful – others can be a disaster. If you work part-time then you may have already been involved in an appraisal interview and have your own views. If so, then share your experience with the rest of your group – and listen to theirs.

As a group, suggest at least four factors that would contribute to successful appraisals which achieve their purpose. If nobody in the group has ever been involved in an appraisal, ask your tutor to recount some of his or her (non-confidential!) experiences.

2 Some golden rules for drawing up targets for a personal development plan (PDP) are given below. Bearing these in mind, and your current strengths and weaknesses, draw up a PDP for yourself and identify some relevant targets with achievement dates. Then discuss your ideas with your tutor. Suggested headings are:
- Area of development
- Learning method
- Target achievement date

> **Check that all your plans and targets for your own career development equate to SMARTY**
>
> - **Specific** – state exactly what you want to achieve.
> - **Measurable** – state how you will measure your progress.
> - **Achieveable** – identify the next logical step from where you are now. If you are too ambitious, you'll only be disappointed.
> - **Realistic** – setting too many is silly and overwhelming.
> - **Time-focused** – set a date for achievement.
> - **Yours** – so you can't shift the blame if anything goes wrong!

5.2 Section review

1 The following terms have been used in this section. Define each one.

   a Job description.
   b Person specification.
   c Shortlisting.
   d Appraisal interview.

2 **a** Draft an advertisement for the Marketing Assistant's job shown in the job description on page 274 and the person specification on page 285. Use examples of job advertisements in your local paper to help you. Remember that you must include all the essential requirements. Invent any other details you need to inform candidates how to apply for the job and make sure you include a final date for applications to be received by.

   b Briefly describe the recruitment procedure you would recommend to ensure that all applicants were treated fairly.

3 Either on your own, or in a small group, decide on a business-related occupation or profession you would like to investigate further.

   a Visit your local careers or Connexions service to find out how people can enter this type of job.

   b Either in a newspaper, at a Jobcentre or online, try to find at least two examples of vacancies. Then note down the job requirements and salaries offered.

   c Find out what qualifications can be taken by people doing this job. You can find out about NVQs on the QCA website – a link is available at www.heinemann.co.uk/hotlinks (express code 1386P). Student or customer services at your college should be able to tell you more about professional qualifications.

   d Summarise your information for the rest of your class.

This section covers

The scope for conflict in business
The role of trade unions
Understanding the key principles of negotiation
Ways of seeking redress for an employment grievance

The scope for conflict in business

Every so often a dispute between employees and management hits the headlines. In 2003, for example, there were three well-publicised disputes.

- The year began with a continuation of the firefighter's dispute – concerned with pay and plans to modernise the fire service and change working practices. The Fire Brigades Union (FBU) thought employers were using modernisation as a way of cutting jobs. The initial pay offer in August 2002 was 4 per cent but the FBU demanded 40 per cent.
  The eventual settlement was 16 per cent over three years and future pay will be linked to modernisation.
- In July, British Airways check-in staff at Heathrow went on strike, stranding thousands of passengers. This row was about a new electronic clocking-on system at the airport, incorporating the use of swipe cards. Staff thought this would be used to force through changes in pay and conditions. Unions took action when BA tried to impose the new system without any discussions.
  The eventual agreement was that swipe cards could be used providing the new system would not be used to calculate or affect staff pay.
- In October, wildcat strikes by Royal Mail workers in several areas led to letterboxes in London being sealed. The disagreement focused on working practices and a three-year plan to introduce efficiencies which would include scrapping second deliveries and cutting up to 30,000 jobs.

In December agreement was reached after the Communication Workers' Union (CWU) and management met at ACAS – the Advisory, Conciliation and Arbitration Service (see page 299).

Scope for conflict

Conflict occurs when two (or more) people fundamentally disagree. At times, disagreement can be healthy if it leads to lively debates and creative ideas. This is **constructive conflict**. In contrast, destructive conflict is when two parties disagree and what may start as a fairly small difference of opinion or a minor dispute can escalate into something more serious.

Collective disputes

A collective dispute relates to the whole workforce or one section of the workforce. All the examples above were collective disputes and, typically, they had three common elements:

- **Pay**. This can relate to pay increases, the way pay is calculated or possible loss of pay because of a change in the basis of payment, e.g. if performance-related pay was introduced.
- **Conditions of service**. Arguments can relate to changes in working hours, overtime or shift patterns, time off or holidays.
- **The changing nature of work**. Examples include changes in job content, the transfer of employees from one type of job to another, new methods of working (e.g. from manual to mechanised or computerised systems).

Individual disputes

In this case only one employee is involved in a dispute. In this case, the reasons for the dispute can be the same as above but may also involve other issues:

- **Pay**. If this was not in accordance with the contract, had been calculated wrongly or if a case for discrimination could be made (e.g. a female employee has identified that a male colleague doing the same work is paid more) or if a person thinks they are not paid enough for the work they are doing.
- **Discriminatory or unfair treatment** involving harassment, victimisation, bullying or any other discriminatory issue.
- **Contested disciplinary action** where the employee alleges that disciplinary action is unfair or the correct procedures have not been followed.

- **An imposed change to the terms and conditions of employment** stated in the contract which disadvantages the employee.
- **An imposed change to the tasks and duties** defined in the job description.

All businesses should have grievance and disciplinary procedures to help resolve any disputes between individuals and managers. This is now a legal requirement under the Employment Act 2002 and the Dismissal and Discipline Regulations 2004.

The role of trade unions

In many cases, it is easier for employees if there is a recognised trade union in the workplace. This is because union reps will give advice on individual rights and support and advise employees involved in grievance or disciplinary

---

Business brief

Disciplinary and grievance procedures

Disciplinary procedures state what action the employer will take if there is a problem with an employee. They are invoked if the employee breaches the contract, fails to follow an instruction or comply with disciplinary or organisational rules, or does not fulfil his or her responsibilities. There are several stages and normally only senior managers can issue written or final warnings.

- **A verbal warning** is given for a first or minor offence.
- **A written warning** is given for subsequent minor offences or a more serious offence.
- **A final warning** is issued for repeated offences or a very serious offence.
- **Dismissal** can follow a final warning or be the first step if an employee commits **gross misconduct**.

Grievance procedures tell the employees what action to take if a dispute cannot be resolved informally and if the employee feels there is a legitimate complaint. Most grievances are individual but a collective grievance can be

pursued by a group of employees. Again there are several stages:

- The first stage is to investigate the complaint within the department.
- If the complaint is still not resolved, it is investigated by a more senior manager.
- Finally, the complaint may be pursued outside the organisation, such as with ACAS (see page 299).

The information given to employees must include other relevant details, e.g. any disciplinary or organisational rules that the employee must abide by, the procedure to follow if an employee has a grievance, those people who are eligible to accompany the employee to a grievance or disciplinary interview (normally a union representative or colleague), the length of time a 'warning' would stay on an employee's record, the type of offences which could lead to instant dismissal, how to appeal against a decision and so on.

hearings. They will also take action to address collective grievances relating to pay or conditions of employment.

Legal advice on employment terms

Trade union representatives are normally involved in helping to resolve disagreements at an early stage. This is because they encourage their members to ask them for help and advice if they have a problem. The union rep can then:

- Discuss the problem with the employee and employer to try to resolve it quickly and informally.
- Advise the employee about his or her legal rights and whether there is a valid complaint (by employer or employee). The union rep can refer any complex legal queries to the branch or head office for clarification. All unions have access to employment law and health and safety experts to help and advise their members.
- As a witness, attend grievance or disciplinary meetings with the employee.
- Support and advise the employee if a problem goes before an employment tribunal. This may be the case if the employee has been dismissed and wants to claim that this was unfair.

Trade unions and collective bargaining

Trade union representatives also represent groups of employees who have a common grievance.

- The first step will be discussions and negotiations between the management and trade union representatives.
- Proposals, suggestions and offers by management must be discussed with the members at each stage.

Business brief

Types of dismissal

There are four types of dismissal:

- **Fair dismissal** is when an employee is sacked for a valid reason and this is 'reasonable' in the circumstances, for example:
  - He or she has breached the terms of the contract of employment or indulged in unacceptable conduct, e.g. persistent lateness or theft.
  - The job is being made redundant.
  - The employee is incapable of doing the work despite training.
  - The employee has been involved in illegal activities, e.g. taking unlawful strike action or a lorry driver losing his driving licence.
  - There is some other substantial reason, e.g. continually refusing to carry out reasonable requests.
- **Unfair dismissal** occurs when an employee is dismissed for no good reason. Certain reasons are automatically considered unfair, including being a trade union member or taking part in trade union activities, acting as an employee

representative, being pregnant, taking maternity or paternity leave, insisting on statutory employment rights.
- **Wrongful dismissal** occurs if an employer ignores the statutory notice period or breaches a longer period of notice stated in the contract. This can be waived only if the employee commits gross misconduct. Otherwise a dismissed employee must be able to 'work out' their notice or receive pay in lieu.
- **Constructive dismissal** occurs if an employee leaves under protest, e.g. because of unfair treatment or worsening terms and conditions which management refuse to amend such as a reduced salary or unsafe working environment.

Anyone who has been dismissed unlawfully can take their case to an employment tribunal (see page 298). In many cases (but not all) the employee needs to have been continuously employed for 12 months before this is allowed and the complaint must be made within three months of the original problem or date of dismissal.

- In the majority of cases, agreement is reached before any industrial action is required.
- If not, the union may call for a 'non-strike' protest such as:
  - **Work to rule** – when employees only do the duties defined in their job description and nothing else.
  - **Overtime ban** – when no additional hours are worked.
- As a last resort, the union may call for strike action. Employees normally have to feel strongly to take this action, as they do not receive any pay when they are out on strike.

Before any type of industrial action is taken, members of the union must be balloted. There are strict rules relating to how ballots are operated and how the votes are counted. If these are not observed, then any subsequent action is unlawful. These are often called **wildcat** strikes. Because these are unlawful the employer can sack those involved quite fairly. This was the case when the BA check-in staff went on strike. Although BA could have sacked them all, this would not have been sensible because all the check-in staff were involved!

Union involvement is not, of course, only to resolve conflict. In most organisations there are continual talks between unions and management over working conditions and pay, and the unions must be consulted by law if management want to make changes which would directly affect employees. Such negotiations are often called **collective bargaining** because the union is negotiating on behalf of all its members.

Union recognition

In many organisations there is no recognised union. In this case a staff association or works committee may undertake a similar role. If the majority of staff want the business to recognise a union then they can vote on this issue. They will also receive help and guidance from the TUC. However, in many companies, like Richer Sounds, employees are quite happy with the arrangements that are in place. The two points to note are:

- Businesses that care about their employees, treat them well, employ specialist staff to deal with employee concerns and have good communication systems rarely experience serious problems or disputes.
- In cases where disputes do occur, organisations that have properly trained union representatives resolve problems and grievances more easily because the issues involved and the legal rights of each party can be fully discussed at the outset. This is often the case because trained union reps can be skilful negotiators. And this can help when either individual or collective issues are being raised.

Over to you!

1 Your college will have disciplinary and grievance procedures for students. Find out *exactly* how these would apply if you:
   a Breached the regulations at college relating to the use of IT equipment.
   b Had a serious complaint about the college.

2 All of the reasons given below are legally classed as 'fair' reasons for dismissal. As a group, decide which offences would normally result in instant dismissal and those in which the employee would normally receive a warning first. In each case assume that the culprit has not been disciplined before.
   a Stealing, either from the employer or another employee.
   b Being drunk or taking illegal drugs at work.
   c Hacking into computer files.
   d Being late for work.
   e Being absent for work for no good reason.
   f Ignoring health and safety regulations.
   g Fighting at work.
   h Taking a day's holiday without permission.
   i Wearing unsuitable clothes or being scruffy.
   j Sending an abusive email.

3 As a group, suggest four additional offences which could lead to dismissal at work. (If you work part-time, check out your employee handbook for ideas!)

Understanding the key principles of negotiation

Negotiating on behalf of hundreds of union members is a skill that takes many years to learn. Union representatives attend training courses and then start to practise their skills by helping to resolve issues and disputes raised by their members. Union leaders like Sir Bill Morris of the T & G Union, who was involved in the BA dispute, have many years' experience of dealing with senior management and know how to handle the situation. In particular, they aim for a 'win-win' resolution where there are benefits for everyone. So when the dispute with BA ended, he announced 'It's a good day for the employees, a good day for the company and an even better day for the passengers.' There was no gloating that BA had backed down. Instead Sir Bill focused on the fact that pay would no longer be linked to the clocking-on issue. In other words, he had focused on the problem – but been generous with the people.

These principles can be applied whenever you are negotiating – such as for a pay increase for yourself, or over an issue about which your group feels strongly.

Golden rules when negotiating

Negotiating is never easy, particularly if you are faced with someone who holds very different views to you. Key points to remember are:

- Negotiating is *not* the same as arguing! When you negotiate you are discussing how to solve a problem or difficulty, either for yourself or other people. Ideally, in a conflict, both parties should be focused on finding a workable solution.
- Preparation is important. This means:
  - Knowing what you would ideally like to achieve, but also knowing what you (or other people) can live with. The two should be rather different!
  - Identifying the key issues involved and the points you can raise in support of your request.
  - Thinking about the situation from the point of view of the other party, so that you can prepare a response to the points they will raise.
  - Identifying benefits that can be achieved by the other party (so that they 'win' too).
- The meeting to discuss the issues should be held:
  - In private, to avoid anyone 'losing face' in public.
  - By arrangement, so both parties are prepared.
  - At a convenient time. Never when a manager is distracted or busy with something else.
- During the meeting:
  - Try to get the other person to outline their position first, then you know the degree of difference between you. It may be less than you thought.
  - After you have stated your case, be prepared to listen to counter-arguments.
  - Keep calm and be professional. This means no giggling or fidgeting.
  - Concentrate on key issues and facts.
  - Make suggestions and sound out possibilities.
  - Float ideas which will result in joint benefits.
  - Be prepared to change your position if this will help. Never 'paint yourself

into a corner' from which you can't back down, or make silly threats.

- Invite trading 'if you will do this, I/we will do that'.
- Ask for time to think if you are stuck or not certain how to respond.

- Success often depends upon:
  - Good timing (e.g. asking for a pay rise when you've just won a large order!).
  - Making realistic requests.
  - Keeping your emotions in check.
  - Having a positive attitude and using appropriate body language. This includes making eye contact when you are talking and sitting up straight.
  - Being prepared to give the other party 'thinking time' if this will help by having a short break.

Ways of seeking redress for an employment grievance

In some cases negotiations within the workplace are unsuccessful. Or an employee may have been dismissed and feel this is unfair. In either case the employee may have the right to take further action by taking the case to an employment tribunal.

Employment tribunals

An employment tribunal is like an informal court set up to deal with employment disputes. Although it is 'informal' in that nobody wears a wig or gown, it is still a court. A legally qualified chairperson is in charge and usually sits with two non-legal (lay) people. One of these will be chosen to identify with the employer's view (such as a business person) and the other to identify with the employee's situation (such as a trade union representative). Normally a claim must be made to a tribunal within 3 months of the original problem or complaint.

The panel listens to both sides of the argument and may ask witnesses questions. The person making the complaint may be represented by a trade union official, a solicitor or present his or her own case. The tribunal panel considers the employee's previous behaviour and work history and the actions taken to solve the problem by the employer. This will include checking the disciplinary or grievance procedures that operate in the company and whether or not these have been followed. The panel then comes to a decision. If the employee wins the case the tribunal can order that he or she is:

- **Reinstated** (gets his/her old job back), is given a similar job or
- **Financially compensated**. This can comprise:
  - A basic award up to a maximum amount, usually based on the amount of redundancy pay a sacked worker would have received.
  - A 'compensatory' award, up to a maximum amount, to compensate the employee for any other economic loss, such as loss of job prospects or any period of unemployment. This amount may be reduced if the tribunal feels the employee contributed to the problem or could have obtained another job sooner.

However, there is no maximum amount for financial awards on the grounds of discrimination if these claims are found to be justified.

It is often unrealistic to expect an employee to return to work for an employer in these cases and therefore by far the most usual outcome is a compensation award.

Tribunals can also award costs of up to £10,000 against anyone who brings a case which has little, if any, chance of success. This prevents people using the tribunals to 'get even' if they have no legal case.

You can find out more on the Employment Tribunals website, a link is available at www.heinemann.co.uk/hotlinks (express code 1386P).

In 2002, Employment Tribunals awarded compensation totalling £6.41 million in cases of unlawful discrimination. Just over half were awarded for sex discrimination, involving 259 cases. There were 89 cases of race discrimination and 70 cases of disability discrimination. Two record awards were £1.37 million for sex discrimination and £761,867 for race discrimination. These, however, are exceptional. The average amount awarded for race discrimination was just over £20,000.

In one notable case in 2003, a 22-year-old former trainee car sales executive won nearly £180,000 for sexual harassment after working for just one week in a new job. Her near-record award covered injury to feelings, injury to health, costs of care, loss of earnings and aggravated damages because of the serious nature of the harassment. Her ex-employers had no written policy on sex discrimination or harassment nor equal opportunities in general. Neither did it provide training or advice to its employees about sexual harassment or take any steps to prevent managers or supervisors harassing junior employees.

ACAS – the advisory, conciliation and arbitration service

An 'arbitrator' is someone who hears both sides in a dispute and then decides how the dispute must be solved. ACAS, the Advisory, Conciliation and Arbitration Service, was originally set up to assist in industrial disputes and disagreements. It still operates an arbitration scheme but today its main focus is on producing guidebooks on employment rights, answering calls on its employment hotlines and helping to stop small disputes escalating to become tribunal cases.

ACAS also publishes **codes of practice** which give guidance to employers on how to handle disciplinary and grievance situations. Because of the introduction of the Dismissal and Discipline Regulations in 2004, ACAS produced a new draft code giving guidance to employers to ensure that they followed the correct procedures. Otherwise any dismissal would automatically be classed as unfair by an employment tribunal. Equally, however, an employee who ignored the procedures set down in the Regulations can also have any subsequent award for unfair dismissal reduced.

The ACAS arbitration scheme operates as an alternative to going to an employment tribunal. Whenever a claim is sent to a tribunal, an ACAS official is notified and must be consulted. This official has to try to find out whether both sides are interested in solving the dispute and reaching an agreement out of court. If they are willing to do so, then the matter is settled and the complaint never reaches the tribunal. From October 2004 fixed periods for conciliation will be specified, the aim being to resolve claims more speedily and to reduce the number being heard by the Employment Tribunal Service.

The ACAS procedure is less formal than a tribunal. The arbitrator asks questions and assesses the situation bearing in mind general principles of fairness and good practice. The arbitrator then gives his or her decision. If the employee's complaint is upheld the same remedies – reinstatement, re-engagement or compensation – are available as at a tribunal. However, in this situation the award is confidential and will not be publicised.

You can find out more on the ACAS website, a link is available at www.heinemann.co.uk/hotlinks (express code 1386P).

Business brief

A question of appeal

If there is an argument about a point of law, employees or employers can appeal against the decision of a tribunal. In this situation the case is then referred to a higher level. The first step is to the Employment Appeals Tribunal. Beyond that, the case can be taken to the European Court of Justice.

Sometimes this can lead to changes which aren't very popular. One case which reached the European Court involved a woman who worked for south West Hampshire Area Health Authority. She was told she had to retire at 60 but objected that this was discriminatory as her male colleagues could work until they were 65.

When she won her case, the British government was told to review retirement ages. It concluded that it could not afford to pay the state pension to men at 60 so therefore the retirement age for women must increase. From 2020, all women will have to work until they are 65 before they can claim their state pension.

Talking point

View 1: Unions and their members are just troublemakers. They always make unrealistic demands which firms can't afford, hate change of any kind and will strike at the drop of a hat.

View 2: Unions are invaluable as they prevent businesses from exploiting their employees by ignoring their rights and paying them as little as possible.

With which viewpoint do you agree – and why?

Over to you!

1 A trade union representative is approached by each of the following workers with a grievance. In each case decide whether the worker is likely to have a case or not and what the representative would advise.

   a An employee's elderly father is seriously ill in hospital. She asked for time off work to be with him but was refused.

   b A young man is struggling to do his job using a database and updating web pages, and was told he must go on a training course. He refused and was then told that unless he did, he would lose his job. He says this is unfair and that he is experienced in IT although he has no certificates to prove this.

   c A sales representative is convicted for drink driving and loses his licence. He has just been told that he is being dismissed.

   d A new employee says that his supervisor is making his life a misery. He has been forced to work late for the last two weeks and yesterday was told that he could not join the others on Friday for a team meeting at lunchtime. When he complained the supervisor said he would be disciplined if he reported the matter.

   e A member of staff who was recently given promotion to supervisor has been told that she will have to be demoted now that she is pregnant as it will be inconvenient for her to keep having time off.

2 Try your hand at negotiating! Divide into teams to negotiate the following cases either against each other or against your tutor.

   a You have been informed that, because of work pressures, no staff will be able to take holidays this year between September and December. Several of your colleagues are married and are under pressure from their partners to take off-peak holidays. Others are less bothered but want compensation for agreeing to the change.

   b Your employers have offered a pay award of 6 per cent over two years. They say that this is very generous and far higher than the rate of inflation. Your colleagues argue that the company made record profits last year and still pays less than its major competitors.

1 The following terms have been used in this section. Define each one.

   a Collective bargaining.

   b Employment tribunals.

   c ACAS.

   d Gross misconduct.

   e Constructive dismissal.

   f Wildcat strike.

2 As a group, you are setting up in business and need to devise rules for your employees. For each of the following headings, decide what you would specify. Remember that none of your rules must discriminate against any particular group of workers.

   a Timekeeping.

   b Absence.

   c Holidays.

   d Health and safety.

   e Standards of work.

   f Personal appearance.

   g Use of IT equipment.

   h Smoking.

   i Discrimination and professional working relationships.

3 Each of the following cases actually happened. As a group, decide whether you think the employment tribunal considered the decision was fair or unfair in each case.

   a A prison officer told his colleague a joke about Osama Bin Laden and was instantly dismissed, despite the fact that he had an exemplary employment record for 21 years and immediately apologised.

   b An RSPCA inspector was dismissed because he was found guilty of mistreating his own pet dog at home.

   c A male applicant was told that he would not get the teaching job because there were already two male teachers at the school and more women were needed.

   d A car production worker was dismissed after reacting violently when his supervisor told him to stop singing Elvis songs.

   e An office worker was sacked for sending emails in which he made derogatory remarks about his colleagues and divulging confidential information to someone who worked for a competitor.

   f A trade union activist was demoted from his supervisory job for alleged misconduct on picket lines during a pay dispute.

   g A woman was passed over for promotion and a less experienced and unqualified man was promoted above her.

This section covers

Understanding the potential for technological and structural change
Identifying information sources
Identifying the potential implications of change

Fewer craftsmen exist today

Businesses operate in a rapidly changing world and continually need to change, modify or adapt their operations to remain competitive. This means that jobs are continually changing, too. Some jobs disappear and new ones emerge, often requiring new types of skills. Existing jobs, and job locations, change and adapt.

A good example is your local or college library. Traditionally, libraries held books and were run by librarians whose main expertise was in the range and content of books available on different subjects. Today libraries have books. They also have computers, CDs, Internet access and photocopiers. Your college library is also likely to

have access to networked or online databases of information for research purposes. Librarians need to know the range of materials available both online and in traditional formats. Indeed you may find that your library is linked to, or part of, a learning centre with online access for all students. The skills needed by staff who work there would be unrecognisable to a librarian twenty years ago.

Understanding the potential for technological and structural change

Change occurs in all organisations but some are more susceptible to continuous change than others because they operate in a more dynamic environment. You first met this idea in unit 2. Whereas farmers, funeral directors and solicitors may only be marginally affected by new technology or other developments, many other businesses – such as banks, retailers, advertisers, software houses – and educational establishments have seen more rapid change. The two main reasons for this relate to:

- Changes in technology.
- Changes in structure.

Technological change

Technological developments have changed the way in which people do their jobs and the way in which businesses operate. PCs, laptops and printers are commonplace, emails are a standard method of communication and virtually all businesses today have a website, although some may be little more than a passive advertisement. Many jobs previously done manually are now automated or mechanised – such as calculating the accounts and sending out mailshots. Many businesses now have an e-business strategy to ensure they remain competitive.

Business brief

E-business strategies

An e-business strategy is a future plan to make the most of e-business opportunities, for example:

- Selling goods over the Internet.
- Receiving payments online.
- Improving customer information by regularly reviewing online search facilities.
- Obtaining and analysing customer use of online facility.
- Providing customer support or customer service online.
- Increasing the amount of information/services available online for employees and other stakeholders.
- Increasing the number of items bought online.
- Increasing marketing online.

To be successful, any e-business strategy has to be an integral part of the organisation's plans for the future. Unless all, or part, of this is outsourced, staff in every department are likely to find that their jobs are changed because the organisation is now doing business in a different way. You will learn more about e-business if you study specialist Unit 8.

Structural change

In this case the change is created by a reorganisation or a different method of operating. This may, or may not, be triggered by new technology.

- **Outsourcing**. This means paying a specialist to do a certain job (see page 60). In your college, security is probably outsourced to a specialist company that provides qualified security guards. Outsourcing is appropriate if a service is not part of the core business operation. Your college is in the business of educating students, so outsourcing security is sensible. Other operations which are often

outsourced by businesses include payroll, debt collection, computer maintenance and online marketing.

New technology has enabled some operations to be outsourced abroad, such as call centres, to save money (see page 212). Outsourcing will often be attractive if savings can be made. If an existing area is outsourced then staff doing these jobs may be made redundant, although most businesses try to offer alternative employment and appropriate retraining.

- **Mergers/takeovers**. This occurs when two businesses join together or one business buys another (see page 19). This can have several effects.
  - There may be duplicate jobs, so a reorganisation of different departments is required.
  - Some offices or branches may be closed and existing staff may have to relocate (see below) or lose their jobs.
  - The methods of working and the paperwork at each business may be different and will have to be clarified.
  - There are likely to be new bosses with their own preferences and dislikes. In many cases, after a short time in the job, many new bosses prefer to reorganise or restructure the business which can mean radical changes in the type or number of departments and the roles of staff within each one.
- **Relocation**. Businesses relocate for several reasons. They may be expanding or contracting and need more (or less) space; they may want to move to a better location (e.g. nearer their customers) or they may want to save money. This can often mean moving out of a city centre and towards the suburbs – or even to a different area of the country if rents and labour are cheaper.

Moving to new premises in the same locality is not normally too much of a problem for staff. Travelling a much longer distance to work might be. Staff may be offered the opportunity to keep their jobs if they are prepared to relocate, their decision is likely to depend upon pay, seniority and family commitments. A senior manager is far more likely to do this than an assistant who earns less and can obtain another job in the area without any difficulty.

Business matters

When Richard Baker took over as Chief Executive of Boots he made a series of sweeping changes to try to improve competitiveness. These included opening 100 more of its larger stores on Sundays, changing store-opening hours to coincide with those of local surgeries, and making price cuts. He felt these were essential to compete with superstores who also offered over-the-counter medicines, pharmacy services, toiletries and cosmetics seven days per week.

To finance the changes cost savings were essential. In 2003/4, 1,400 jobs were cut at Boots headquarters over a period of seven months – almost half of the head office workforce. The job losses were estimated to cost the company £47 million in redundancy payments but, overall, savings will be made. The cuts were part of Boots' 'Getting into Shape' programme which aims to save a total of £100 million by 2007. £5 million of the savings were used to create 290 new roles in Boots stores and more power was given to store managers. Boots has about 60,000 staff employed in its stores and, as far as Richard Baker is concerned, these are the key staff because they are involved in dealing with customers on a day-to-day basis.

Identifying information sources

Employee reactions to change usually vary, depending upon the type of change, their own personality and the way in which they have been informed. It is quite natural for people to worry if they think a major change could seriously affect them, and to feel resentful if they are never consulted.

An amendment to the 1999 Employment Relations Act has made it a legal entitlement for workers to be consulted about significant changes that affect them (see page 192). Most responsible business managers would do this anyway, knowing full well that they are more likely to receive cooperation if workers understand the reasons for change and, wherever possible, can make suggestions relating to their own job or working area.

Employees may be the first to be consulted about potential change, but other stakeholders will also need to be told. The type of method will vary, depending upon the type of change and the group of stakeholders involved.

- **Internal company communications**, such as staff meetings, emails, notices, newsletters and memos will be used to consult employees and keep them informed about proposed changes. The exact method will depend upon the situation – and its sensitivity. Mass communication methods should only be used for general information of interest to everyone. Changes relating to individual staff or staff teams are normally not announced until agreement has been reached in more focused discussions with the people involved.
- **External company communications**. When a change has been agreed and external stakeholders need to be informed this may be done by letter, telephone call or visit by a representative. Business customers and suppliers may also be informed about basic changes, such as new contact details, by means of small notices included in other business mailings. Information on relevant changes can also be posted on the business website.
- **Newspapers** can be used to inform stakeholders locally, regionally or nationally. It will depend upon the scale and scope of the business. The organisation can pay for advertisements summarising changes relating to the business name, contact details or other information following a merger, takeover or relocation. Press coverage may be given if the change would have some interest value for the readers. Local newspapers may be prepared to write a short article if the business is a regular advertiser. Major changes by a national organisation are more likely to be covered in the business pages of the national press.

Normally the mass media is mainly interested in contentious or alarming issues. Closures and mass redundancies, strikes and ongoing disputes are the ones most likely to gain headlines in the papers and on the television news channels!

- **Trade journals** are a standard method of notifying business stakeholders of changes. Again, the business can place an advertisement or ask for an article to be written about the event.

Finally, if you are looking for information about future changes two useful sources may be the 'grapevine' – where gossip and rumours abound – and present trends. Try to match grapevine rumours with hard evidence from internal communication and, if you are trying to work out future changes from present trends, remember that there is a limit to any one type of change. Richard Baker, for example, could hardly make all the staff at Boots headquarters redundant because some key operations will always take place there. He will therefore need to look for other areas to improve if further changes are necessary in the future.

Identifying the potential implications of change

If you look back at the implied terms of employment on page 275, you will see that two of these relate to change. One condition is that employees will work towards the objectives of the organisation. Another is that employees will be prepared to change when the job changes.

These are important because flexibility is essential for businesses to be able to operate effectively. Managers and supervisors must be able to take action to deal with temporary problems and crises, such as short-staffing through illness, a backlog of orders or an important deadline. This is why many contracts today include express terms to cover flexible working.

Despite this, employers cannot simply vary the terms and conditions of employment without consultation, particularly if this would result in detrimental changes, such as shorter holidays, more travelling or longer/more unsocial hours. In this case the employer will normally try to negotiate agreement with the employees, usually through a trade union or staff association.

If no agreement is reached, the employer can still go ahead, but still cannot make sweeping changes that would severely worsen anyone's terms and conditions of employment. In this case, the employee has legal rights and could refer the matter to the Employment Tribunal.

In some cases, of course, changes can improve working conditions and bring more variety to a job. For this reason, when any change is being discussed, it is important to assess these carefully and to identify all the positive points and opportunities, as well as any negatives. The main areas to consider include the following.

- **Working conditions**. Changes may relate to:
  - The physical environment, such as a relocation to more modern premises where there is more space, noise levels are lower, heating and ventilation are improved and so on.
  - Job content, such as a change of duties or greater responsibility.
  - Team changes, such as working with a different group of people.
- **Personal skills and future employability**. Today most people are expected to be **multiskilled**. This means they can do several tasks. Most people prefer this because it adds variety to their job. Employers benefit because people can work more flexibly.

  Changes are likely to increase the need for new skills to be learned and also for existing skills to be developed to a higher level – often called **upskilling**. For example, you may be an experienced IT user but you would have to improve your existing skills and learn new ones if you wanted to become involved in website design. This is likely to increase your future employability, and enhance your promotion prospects, because you are broadening your experience and increasing your skills.
- **Identifying opportunities for personal development**. This means taking note of

potential future changes and identifying how you can use these to further your own skills and future career. It may be possible to discuss this at an appraisal interview or at a performance review so that your manager is aware that you are looking for opportunities. In addition, a positive approach to change and a willingness to become personally involved is always considered an asset. In this case both the business and the employee reap the benefits as times change and the organisation moves forward.

Talking point

View 1: *Change is essential for businesses to stay up-to-date and provides opportunities for staff to move on and develop their skills. It should be welcomed by employees.*

View 2: *Many changes are unnecessary and just a way of saving money. They normally result in poorer working conditions and should be resisted by employees.*

With which viewpoint do you agree – and why?

Over to you!

1 a Suggest **two** types of technological change and **two** types of structural change that can take place in an organisation.
b Identify **three** reasons why changes may be needed.
c Suggest **two** reasons why good communications are important when change is taking place in the short or medium term future.
d Identify **two** ways in which information about change may be communicated:
  i To staff.
  ii To external stakeholders.

2 As a group, suggest how an employee might be affected by each of the following changes, both in terms of positive and negative outcomes. When you are considering these it may help if you think about aspects such as: status or prestige; job security; social ties and working relationship; personal ambitions or anxieties; existing skill levels.
a Increasing the responsibilities of a job.
b Changing working hours to an earlier or later start/finish.
c Restructuring an organisation so people work in different departments or with different teams.
d Introducing new technology.
e Outsourcing an operation previously done within the business.

5.4 Section review

1 The following terms have been used in this section. Define each one.
  a Structural change.
  b Merger.
  c Takeover.
  d E-business strategy.
  e Outsourcing.
  f Multiskilling.
  g Upskilling.

2 Divide into four groups. As a group, and in agreement with your tutor, select **one** of the following types of organisations. Investigate

and identify the main changes that it has experienced over the last four or five years, suggest how these have affected the jobs of the people who work there and forecast two future changes you think may take place. Finally, compare your ideas with those of other groups who have investigated different businesses.

  a Banks.
  b Schools or colleges.
  c Large retailers.
  d National newspapers.

Unit 7 Sales and customer service

This specialist unit focuses on sales and customer service activities. You will learn how to contribute to sales promotions and the main legal and regulatory guidelines which apply to these. You will also learn about the customer service skills required to make effective retail sales and the types of after-sales service which are provided to promote repeat sales.

Note that sections 7.2–7.4 are supported by detailed information on the Richer Sounds StudentZone at www.richerstudentzone.co.uk

7.1 Explore sales promotion techniques

This section covers

Designing a sales promotion
Organising a sales promotion

Sales promotions are a key feature of the retail trade

A sales promotion is one aspect of marketing goods or services. Whereas advertising is normally undertaken over a period of time to give customers information or persuade them to take action, a sales promotion is a specific activity undertaken to tempt customers to buy.

Most sales promotions have a time limit. They may relate to a one-off event, such as an open day, demonstration or in store promotion. Or they may involve a short-term deal, such as a free gift, price reduction, competition or special offer. There are many different alternatives and the best combination will depend upon the occasion, the product or service, the main purpose of the promotion and its intended outcome.

Sales promotions can be aimed at both private customers and at trade customers, such as wholesalers and retailers.

- Those aimed at private customers tempt us to try a new product, buy more or reward loyalty. A full list of possible outcomes is given on page 310.
- Those aimed at trade customers offer incentives to increase the amount of stock held and give rewards for higher levels of sales.

Designing a sales promotion

There are many different types of promotions and the methods used will depend upon several factors:

- The type of product or service.
- The aim of the promotion.
- The budget for spending on promotional materials.
- The resources and materials you already have – and those you need to buy.

- The time scale for preparing the materials.
- The talent and creativity of your team.

It is silly planning an elaborate and costly promotion if you have no money and little time. Sometimes, too, the simplest ideas are the best if they are done well. This means that the promotion is coordinated in terms of its theme and the materials that are used.

Promotions are normally more successful if they are combined with other marketing techniques, such as advertising or free publicity (see page 312). Advertising builds brand and product awareness and a sales promotion can sharply increase sales through focusing customers on the product. This is why famous brands like Dairy Milk, Persil, Coca-Cola and PG Tips advertise constantly on television and in the press. The manufacturers then reinforce these adverts and boost sales with special promotions, such as competitions or discounted offers in stores. As another example, your college may advertise or obtain publicity for its activities throughout the year but only hold promotional events at times when potential students want information on specific courses, services and facilities.

Deciding upon the format of the promotion

The format relates to the type of promotional methods you wish to use, how these will link together and the overall design of your materials. These normally include corporate colours and logos so that the range of materials is coordinated. In many cases, the name and address of the promoter is a legal requirement on any printed materials – as is the name of the printer.

The format for an event will vary depending upon the **target customer** and the desired outcome. This will also influence the style of the event and any materials.

Deciding the style

This must link with the format of the promotion and be compatible with its aims.

- A product promotion should be linked to the target customer (see page 309) and the brand image. For example, any free gifts being given as a reward for purchase should link to the age/gender/lifestyle of the typical customer.
- The style of any event should be reflected in the promotional materials. For example, an informal event (like a fun day) will have informal materials – jazzy notices in bright primary colours, balloons, informal food – hotdogs, candy floss etc. Conversely, a formal event, such as the opening of a new building to which business customers are invited would have formal invitations, finger food, a choice of soft drinks or wine, printed leaflets and so on.

The main point is consistency between all the different aspects of the promotion and clarity of your materials.

Use of materials

There are many different types of materials you can use. The range for a specific promotion will depend upon its purpose and your budget.

In-house materials

These are materials you create yourself or which are designed and printed by a company's own marketing department. They can include notices, posters, leaflets, catalogues and point of sale materials – as you will see from the materials produced by the Richer Sounds marketing team.

Most marketing departments have access to IT equipment, graphics packages, a scanner and colour printers and employ creative/artistic staff. If you are asked to produce materials yourself, without the same resources, then a good rule of thumb is to keep things simple. Clear, simple materials are far better than over-ambitious attempts that haven't worked. For example, if you have a choice of design then you should aim for:

- **Good colour contrast** on any notices or posters, e.g. black/yellow, blue/yellow, green/white.
- **Block letters** on any signs, preferably in a plain font (often known as sans serif).
- **Appropriately sized letters** – so that on a notice or poster they are clear and readable from a distance.

Purchased materials

These include any special 'give-aways', e.g. carrier or goodie bags, pens, calendars, key fobs, badges, T-shirts, stickers and so on. In addition, you may want professional posters and specialist promotional materials – such as cardboard stands, hanging signs or coloured leaflets or brochures with photographs.

Key messages

The key message will depend upon the type of organisation, the intended outcome of the promotion and the target customer, for example:

- The purpose of an industrial promotion may be to sell more goods or to provide information

---

Business brief

Display materials

Many types of promotions are supported by a special display. These include:

- **Point of sale (POS)** materials and displays – to encourage impulse buys at the checkout.
- **Point of purchase (POP)** materials such as posters and shelf displays – to encourage customers to select a particular product.
- **Themed or seasonal displays** – to promote a range of similar products (e.g. Indian food or Hallowe'en items).
- **Life-style displays** such as holiday posters and beachwear.
- **Co-ordinated displays**, e.g. dining table with cutlery, table linen and crockery; luggage locks, travel alarms and beach towels with suitcases and flight bags.
- **Mass displays** – boxes of apples in supermarkets, large display of the same book (e.g. the latest Harry Potter) in bookshops.

Mass displays often have more impact

---

about products.

- A retail store may have a promotion to sell more of certain types of goods, to promote its other services (e.g. credit facilities), to inform the public about new facilities or product ranges, special offers or a special event (e.g. a discount shopping evening).
- A charity may have a promotion to attract support and raise more money, to attract

volunteers, to provide information linked to its cause or to sell goods by catalogue or through its charity shop.

- A pressure group may have a sales promotion to win support for a topical cause or to attract donations.
- Educational establishments will have promotions to give specific information about courses, to attract potential new students and their parents, and to give information about the institution itself.
- Central government departments have promotions and to give information on new laws, to promote health and safety and to discourage antisocial or unlawful behaviour.

Key messages are often summarised in a good slogan, such as the NSPCC's Full Stop campaign, an appropriate name for an event such as Summer Fun Day or a banner headline on a poster, e.g. Sales Clearance. This makes the message obvious! Customers should never have to 'guess' the meaning of the key message or have any doubt

Business brief

The importance of AIDA

The main rules of promotional messages are often abbreviated to the acronym **AIDA**. The message must:

- Attract **attention** (through colour, good layout, good headline or slogan).
- Gain **interest** (through special offer, eye-catching pictures or tempting text).
- Create **desire** (by persuading customers of benefits of ownership/participation).
- Tell the customer how to take **action** (when an event takes place, how to participate in the promotion etc.).

about what is meant.

Intended outcome

The intended outcome of the promotion may be one, or more, of the following.

- To increase sales – especially at seasonally important times of the year (e.g. Back to School

campaigns).
- To encourage impulse buying.
- To tempt customers to try a new product.
- To tempt potential customers to visit the premises.
- To stimulate interest in the product or service.
- To build customer loyalty by repeat purchasing.
- To obtain/reward long-term customer loyalty.
- To sell or clear high levels of unsold stocks.
- To publicise a new location, the opening of a new department, to introduce staff to customers.
- To link to a national promotion and a well known brand name.
- To attract new customers.
- To differentiate the product or service from those offered by competitors.
- To encourage brand switching away from a competitor's product.
- To make/keep the public familiar with the brand or business name.

This will affect the promotional methods used, the materials produced, the format, style and message.

Reference to product unique selling points

You first learned about unique selling points (USPs) in Unit 2. These are the aspects of a product (or service) that distinguish it from those offered by competitors. They may relate to aspects such as quality, availability, range, price, after-sales service, technical expertise, friendly service, free delivery, extended credit or other unique customer benefits.

Any promotional activity must include reference to the business or product USPs. If possible, these should also be reflected in the promotional materials. For example, a business that sold expensive goods and stressed USPs of high quality and staff expertise would need to produce high quality promotional materials and ensure that information and advice provided by staff reflected these values. Mercedes focuses upon car build quality as a USP, and it produces hardback brochures to reflect this. Equally, a business stressing fun and approachability as its USP would have a different approach, such as more jazzy materials and friendly staff 'greeters' dressed informally.

Sale locations

These may relate to specific locations in a store, or different stores at different addresses. All promotional materials should make it clear where and when any promotional events are being held, such as sales or special demonstrations.

Further product information

Specific product information is often included on the front and back of special packs. If the product is linked to a specific promotion then additional details must be included, for example:

- **The terms and conditions of any special offers**, including eligibility (e.g. whether a purchase is necessary) or competitions – including the closing date.
- **Detailed information on any specific products** or services being promoted.

- **Where customers can obtain** additional advice or information.

Organising a sales promotion

Sales promotions take time, effort and money to prepare. It is therefore important that they fulfil their aims or main purpose. Careful planning and preparation is therefore essential. This will include consideration of:

- **The various methods of advertising and promotion** – often known as 'above the line' and 'below the line'.
- **Deciding on more detailed aspects of the promotion** bearing in mind the competition, market sensitivity, promotional appeal and relevant codes of practice and legislation.
- **Agreeing how to monitor the effectiveness** of the promotion.
- **Deciding how to handle possible complaints**.

Over to you!

1 For each of the following promotions decide **three** intended outcomes from the list on page 310.
  a A women's clothes store sends invitations to all its customers for a pre-showing of next season's fashions. Those who attend have the opportunity to win a free outfit and a spa day.
  b A chocolate manufacturer has special wrappers printed containing jackpot numbers with the chance to win £10,000.
  c A new recruitment agency offers free cups of coffee to all callers.
  d A publisher arranges for an extract from a new recipe book to be printed and attached to the front cover of a best selling women's magazine.
  e An upmarket garage invites customers on its database to bring a friend for a test drive in a new sports car followed by a cheese and wine evening and talk by a racing driver.
  f A cornflake manufacturer includes collectable figures in its boxes.
  g A newspaper prints tokens for cheap flights to the USA.

  h Your college holds a 'Saturday fun day' for visitors with a balloon race, bouncy castle, kiddie rides, farmer's market and craft stalls, free refreshments and tours of the building/facilities.
  i A large store has a multi-buy promotion of pens, pencils and writing paper in late August.

2 Most colleges produce leaflets to promote their courses. Obtain a leaflet for your own course or one that interests you and identify the following information:
  a The key message.
  b A reference to the product's USP.
  c Further product information.
  d The intended outcome of the leaflet.

3 a Investigate the Richer Sounds main website (www.richersounds.com) and identify **three** USPs of the business. Compare your ideas with other members of your class.
  b Suggest how these USPs will influence the style of promotions undertaken by Richer Sounds.

Above the line, below the line – or through the line!

Traditionally, every type of advertising or promotion was classed as 'above the line' or 'below the line'. These terms were originally used to differentiate the methods that paid commission to agencies – called 'above the line' – and print-based methods that did not. Today these are separated more by marketing definitions. 'Above the line' refers to different methods of advertising or brand marketing. 'Below the line' refers to direct or promotional marketing. Today many agencies do both – hence the term 'through the line'. Figure 7.1 gives the traditional separation but a more up-to-date and comprehensive explanation can be found on the Student Forum at the Ad-Mad website, a link is available at www.heinemann.co.uk/hotlinks (express code 1386P). Quite simply, TV, press and the Internet can be used for direct messages today – as well as for adverts. It all depends on what you are saying!

The range of methods and materials selected for a particular sales promotion is known as the **promotional package**. The best package will depend upon the type of product, the target market, the actions of competitors and the budget available. If advertising is being used, this must be chosen carefully bearing in mind the main advantages and disadvantages of the different methods.

Above the line (advertising or brand marketing)	Below the line (direct and promotional marketing)
Television Press, e.g. local/regional/national newspapers, magazines, trade and professional journals Commercial radio Outdoor, e.g. billboards and posters, bus, railway and tube adverts, New media, e.g. on the Internet, in emails, by text message, on electronic kiosks or billboards etc. Cinema	Sales literature, e.g. leaflets, brochures, booklets, catalogues, diaries, guarantee cards, competition entry forms POS material, e.g. mobiles, posters, dummy packs, dump pins, dispenser boxes for leaflets, trade figures, models/working models, display stands, coasters, tickets, public address systems/LED displays, samples, mouse mats Aerial advertising, projected adverts, skywriting, air balloons Calendars CDs, DVDs or videos/audio tapes Carrier bags Clothing, e.g. T-shirts, sweatshirts, caps, headbands, visors, scarves, towels, bar towels, bags etc Company flags Give-aways, e.g. pens, key fobs, calculators Badges and stickers

Figure 7.1 *The traditional split*

Media	Advantages	Disadvantages
Television	Vast audiences, persuasive, easily repeated, can be targeted by area/programme/time.	Very expensive, only suitable for mass consumption products.
Press (newspapers and magazines)	Can target by type of paper/magazine, can include quite detailed information, can include coupons/forms for readers responses.	Short life – today's papers thrown away tomorrow. Needs to be effective to attract attention. Only suitable if target audience are readers.
Commercial radio	Cheaper than television, audience can be targeted by programme, good for fast, immediate messages	Can be expensive for popular 'spots' (e.g. 8.30am but not 9.10am!), not appropriate for all target markets.
Outdoor advertising/ transport advertising	Excellent for attracting attention at key times. Not expensive.	Message must be brief so easily readable. Choice of sites important for effect.
New media	Ideal for attracting people to a website, can be targeted to those searching on a related topic. Easy to measure effectiveness.	Must be clear and appealing to attract 'click through'. May be ignored or irritate users if too intrusive.
Cinema	Captive audience, can target selected towns, longer films possible than on television.	Mainly suitable for younger market – most cinema audiences under 25.

Figure 7.2 *Strengths and weaknesses of above the line promotional methods*

Business matters

Good ideas can often save money when sales promotions are being devised. Local businesses can gain valuable free publicity from local newspapers and on local radio if they can think of an 'angle' to the promotion which would interest the press. The angle, or story, can link to a person, product or event. Papers normally like human interest stories, features relating to local history, or those with topical interest – the more dramatic the better. For ideas, check your own local newspaper to see the type of stories they like to cover.

An alternative is to devise a linked promotion which benefits more than one business. Your student ID, for example, may allow you discounts in some local shops which are advertised in your college diary. The official term for this is **cross-promotional marketing** and it occurs when two businesses can cooperate because they share the same target market but do not directly compete with each other. As another example, you could run a competition and talk your local cinema into offering free tickets as a prize. The cinema benefits because it obtains free publicity on your materials. You benefit because you increase the number of prizes on offer without any cost.

Competitor analysis

A competitor analysis is an investigation and analysis of key competitors who also advertise and promote the same products and services. Businesses normally want to stay ahead in the promotional race and will carefully watch the behaviour of their closest competitors. This is why, when one national newspaper offers free flight tokens, another may start a competition and a third may give away a CD with every purchase!

There are three main steps in undertaking a competitor analysis:

- Identify and list your main competitors.
- Summarise the key points about them, e.g. their location, types of products, quality, customer service features, advertising and promotional methods used.

- Imagine you are a customer and list your competitor's strengths and weaknesses.

To do this you need to obtain information about your competitors. Sources include their website, visiting the premises, talking to their customers (if possible), analysing their advertisements, looking at their displays at exhibitions and reading press reports on their activities.

There are several benefits of carrying out this analysis before starting to devise the promotional package:

- You can ensure that you don't just copy them but differentiate your own product or service in some way, such as by emphasising the USPs.
- You can look for good ideas and adapt them.
- You can identify their target customers and see if these match your own. If not, then you may be able to appeal to a broader range of customer with your own promotion or to some customers whose needs are not being met by the competition.

Business brief

Market segmentation and customer attributes

Market segments give more information about the target market for a product or service:

- **Demography** covers age, marital status, size of family, income and occupation.
- **Lifestyle** covers about interests, leisure activities, shopping habits, amount of time available.
- **Usage** includes how often people buy and how they use the product.
- **Benefits** explain why people buy, e.g. to treat themselves, to make an impression, to save money, to relax, because the product is ethically sound, to feel fashionable, because they like/dislike something new.

Understanding the attributes most likely to be possessed by the target customer helps an organisation to target its promotions more successfully. (See also Unit 2, pages 109 and 110.)

Market sensitivity

By using Thierry Henry in their latest campaign, how do you think Renault are targetting their market?

The market comprises all the different customers who may be tempted or persuaded to buy a particular product or service. You first learned about markets in Unit 2, about how they were segmented and how businesses aim to appeal to their target market. If you have forgotten about this, turn back to page 109.

Each market is often unique in some way with specific features that do not apply to other markets, for example:

- Customers mainly belong to a certain age group or gender.
- They have certain, common expectations.
- They display similar buyer behaviour.

This means that a market is often sensitive to certain issues or events that may not affect other markets. For example, the clothing market for young people is very sensitive to changes in fashion and new trends – and so is the music market. Programmes like Pop Idol use this information to their advantage. The travel market is sensitive to safety and security scares – hence the fall in demand for travel after 9/11. Health scares can affect food sales – from red meat to eggs or farmed salmon. Political events can also affect demand in some markets, although, as you will see below, this can sometimes create opportunities for other suppliers.

Market sensitivity, and the type of issues which concern customers, should be reflected in the words and imagery used in the promotion – such as freshness for food, safety for cars – and excellent student results for your college! Equally, promotional materials should avoid associations that would provoke negative sensitivity, such as giving away fast-food vouchers in a health farm!

Business matters

At the start of 2002 US exports to Saudi Arabia fell by more than 40 per cent as a result of customer boycotts against many well-known American names, such as Coca-Cola, Pepsi and McDonalds. The reason was anger about US economic links and support for Israel. As a result, two Muslim entrepreneurs have stepped into the breach.

First the Iranian Al-Majarah Soft Drinks Co won exclusive rights to distribute Zamzam Cola, named after Mecca's Zamzam holy spring water. The drink immediately went on sale in Saudi Arabia and Bahrain.

A year later a French entrepreneur, Tawfik Mathlouthi launched Mecca Cola, initially in Muslim neighbourhoods in France. As demand has increased he started to export the drink to several countries in Europe, including Britain. Mr Mathlouthi has promised that 10 per cent of the profits will go to charities such as Unicef to provide aid in Palestine. You can find out more on the Mecca Cola website, a link is available at www.heinemann.co.uk/hotlinks (express code 1386P).

Although the aims of these suppliers may be different from the makers of 'the real thing' – their packaging is almost identical, with swirly logos and red and white colour schemes.

Types of promotional appeal

What type of promotions appeal to you? The answer is likely to depend upon your age, gender and personality as well as the novelty value of the promotion itself.

Despite this, surveys show that some promotions generally have more impact than others

Position	Type	Score
1	Buy 1 get one free	4.2 out of 5
2	3 for the price of 2	3.7 out of 5
3	Coupons	3.3 out of 5
4	Loyalty cards	3.1 out of 5
5	Reusable containers	2.9 out of 5

Figure 7.3 *Promotional impact*

regardless of the product – as you can see from the chart below.

If your promotion is more concerned with information then you need to attract attention. Various methods are used. Some aim for the 'wow' or the 'ahh' factor. Others try for humour. Some go for a novel approach – but do think about your target customer before you decide to hand out large lollipops or free doughnuts! For example:

- Badges and balloons are only likely to appeal to young children.
- Informative leaflets may be appropriate for older age groups but would need to contain lots of illustrations/colour to appeal to young people.
- 'Give-aways' must be linked to the main product and/or complementary interests of potential customers.

The ASA and the CAP code of practice

In Britain, most advertising and promotion is self-regulating. This means that the industry itself acts as monitor and policeman. This is done through issuing Codes of Practice, drawn up by industry members.

- The British Code of Advertising, Sales Promotion and Direct Marketing – known as **the CAP code**, regulates all **marketing communications**. This is the term used for most types of print or online advertising and promotions, e.g. advertisements, sales promotions, mailshots, cinema advertisements, banner ads and Internet pop ups, text messages and outdoor posters. Compliance with the code is monitored by the ASA – the Advertising Standards Authority.
- Different codes exist for broadcast media. The ITC (Independent Television Commission) code regulates television advertising and the RA (Radio Authority) code covers advertising on commercial radio. Compliance with this code is monitored by Ofcom, the Office of Communications which regulates the media and telecommunications industries. Ofcom replaced the ITC and the RA in 2003.

Anyone in Britain who objects to an advertisement or promotion can complain to the relevant body, i.e. the ASA or Ofcom. Complaints about point of sale promotion materials should be made to the local environmental health office (the number is in the Phone Book) and complaints about a company's website content direct to the firm.

Business brief

EPIC promotions!

Promotional materials can give information or aim to persuade us to do something. For example:

- A leaflet on a bank savings account and a holiday brochure both provide **factual** information. They may use tempting language but also contain important details that potential customers need.
- Some adverts and promotions use slogans, images and offers to appeal to our **emotions** and tempt us into to buying something, go somewhere or do something.

Some promotions include both aspects. A travel agent will have posters *and* brochures, and possibly even free tastings of foreign food or drink; a bank will have leaflets and offer free gifts to new account holders.

Experts say that to stand out, a promotion must have **EPIC**:

- **Empathy** so that customers identify with it.
- **Persuasion** so that they are tempted to become involved.
- **Impact** so it is striking.
- **Communication** so that it sends the correct message.

The CAP code

This states that all marketing communications:

- Should be legal, decent, honest and truthful.
- Should be prepared with a sense of responsibility to consumers and society.
- Should respect the principles of fair competition generally accepted in business.

It also states that no marketing communication should bring advertising into disrepute. You can find further details on the CAP website – a link is available at www.heinemann.co.uk/hotlinks (express code 1386P).

The ASA

The Advertising Standards Authority is an independent organisation which investigates complaints from the public about the content of any marketing communications. It provides information for consumers and advertisers – and for students. You can find full details of its work on the ASA website – a link is available at www.heinemann.co.uk/hotlinks (express code 1386P).

Other relevant organisations

Businesses and their staff undertaking regular sales promotions can also become members of the ISP – the Institute of Sales Promotion. This provides legal advice and assistance on producing sales promotions. Members can submit draft promotions to the legal advisory service team for comments. The ISP also offers training and qualifications, awards and advice on best practice. You can find out more on the ISP website – a link is available at www.heinemann.co.uk/hotlinks (express code 1386P).

The Advertising Association is responsible for promoting and protecting the rights, responsibilities and role of advertising in the UK. It comprises 25 trade bodies which represent the advertising and promotional marketing industries. You can find out more on the Advertising Association website – a link is available at www.heinemann.co.uk/hotlinks (express code 1386P).

Consumer law

Consumer legislation applies to anyone in the business of advertising or promotion – as well as to all organisations involved in selling or supplying goods and services. These give rights to customers and protect them against unfair or inaccurate descriptions, shoddy goods and services, unsafe items, being misled over prices, and other malpractices. They also give rights to retailers or sellers of goods who act in accordance with their legal responsibilities and this helps to protect them against false allegations and claims from unscrupulous customers.

Figure 7.4 on the next page highlights the main Acts and the areas they cover.

Business brief

Updating the Consumer Credit Act 1974

This Act is being brought up to date to allow for the various methods of obtaining credit today and more sophisticated advertising by lenders. The government and consumer groups are concerned that some financial products are very complex and many lenders are irresponsible. They do not check if consumers can afford to borrow when the slightest change in circumstances – or even a rise in interest rates – can cause problems.

The new legislation is likely to include aspects like:

- Scrapping early settlement charges, which penalise customers who pay off their loan early.
- Ensuring that key information about the credit is in large clear 'honesty' boxes.
- Strengthening credit licences to prevent loan sharks and rogue money lenders.
- Give extra powers to the Office of Fair Trading to enforce the law.

The new law is likely to be introduced in stages, starting in October 2004 and then April 2005. You can find out more on the Office of Fair Trading website, a link is available at www.heinemann.co.uk/hotlinks (express code 1386P).

Consumer protection legislation

Sale of Goods Act 1979 as amended by the Sale of Goods (Amendment) Act 1994, Sale and Supply of Goods Act 1994 and Sale of Goods (Amendment) Act 1995 and Supply of Goods to Consumers Regulations 2002.

This states that all goods sold, whether new or second-hand, must be:

- **As described** – e.g. waterproof boots must not leak.
- **Of satisfactory quality** – in relation to the price paid, description and age of the item.
- **Fit for the purpose for which they are intended** – e.g. walking boots would be expected to be sturdy.

In addition, the goods must be fit for any specific purpose the buyer has made clear (such as boots for hiking or climbing).

If these conditions are not met the seller must refund the buyer or, if reasonable, allow the buyer to opt instead for a repair or replacement. A free repair can be offered but if this is not satisfactory the buyer still has the right to a refund. If defects appear within six months of purchase, the seller is assumed to be liable. This does not cover faults caused through general wear and tear because of heavy usage and in the case of second–hand goods the buyer's rights will depend upon the age of the item, amount paid and description. Sale goods are also covered, unless the fault was clearly obvious or pointed out at the time of sale and the reason for the reduction.

Faulty goods can be returned by post if this is more convenient, or the customer can ask the shop to collect at its own expense. All faulty goods posted by a customer are returned at the seller's risk.

Supply of Goods and Services Act 1982

These cover buyers against services such as garage repairs and building work. The Act states that all services should be carried out:

- For a reasonable charge.
- Within a reasonable time.
- With reasonable care and skill.
- Using satisfactory materials.

Consumer Protection Act 1987

This Act relates to price and safety. Under this Act it is an offence to:

- Mislead customers as to the price of any item.
- Mislead consumers over sale prices and exaggerate price reductions.
- Supply goods which are not reasonably safe. In 1994, this aspect of the Act was strengthened by the General Product Safety Regulations.

Consumer Credit Act 1974

This Act controls consumer credit and requires most businesses which offer loans to customers to be licensed. Retailers who arrange for customers to obtain credit through a separate finance company need a different licence.

The Act also:

- Requires lenders to give details of the true cost of borrowing the money including the total charge for credit, the Annual Percentage Rate (APR) and the cash price for the goods.
- Protects borrowers against unfair deals and extortionate interest rates.
- Enables borrowers to claim compensation from the finance company as well as the supplier if the goods are faulty and cost over £100. This applies to goods bought by credit card as well as by credit agreement and can be very useful if the seller has ceased trading or the goods were bought overseas.

Continued on next page

Continued

- Gives a 'cooling off' period of up to 7 days to borrowers who sign a credit agreement in their own home and also provides specific cancellation and withdrawal rights, especially for loans secured against the borrower's home.
- Prevents creditors demanding early repayment or trying to change the terms of an agreement without notice.
- Enables customers to find out the information held on them by a credit reference agency for a small fee and for retailers to provide details of the name of any CRA used to ascertain their credit rating.

Under the Act the wording of any advertisements promoting credit must be truthful and accurate with appropriate warnings especially if the loan is to be secured on the borrower's property.

Trade Descriptions Act 1968

This Act makes it a criminal offence to give a false or misleading description of goods or services, for example:

- Selling goods which are wrongly described by the manufacturer.
- Wrongly describing goods.
- Making false claims for services, accommodation and facilities.

Usually the spoken word of the seller overrides the written description of the goods, as the buyer can rely on the expertise of the salesperson. However, this can be difficult to prove if there is a dispute.

In this situation, the case should be reported to Trading Standards Officers who could prosecute the firm concerned. Private individuals cannot do this.

Consumer Protection (Distance Selling) Regulations 2000

These regulations protect customers who buy goods sold over the Internet, by mail order, by digital television, phone or fax. They include:

- Providing clear information to consumers on all aspects of the goods or service and the transaction process.
- Sending written confirmation after the purchase has been made.
- Giving customers a cooling–off period of seven working days.
- Giving a refund if the goods are not provided by the agreed date or within 30 days from the order.

These rights do not apply to online auction sites such as eBay or the purchase of insurance online.

Monitoring promotional effectiveness

One advertiser claimed that he always knew he wasted half his budget. He just didn't know which half! This is the reason why promotions are monitored – to check that the money spent and all the effort has been worthwhile. If a promotion is very successful then the format can be repeated in the future. If not, then the lesson must be learned and different methods used next time. Unless monitoring takes place, the same mistakes could be made again and again. Methods of monitoring include:

- For events, count the numbers of visitors or people you attract. The technical term for this is **footfall**. Retailers are constantly interested in footfall and often refer to the FootFall National UK Index, produced by FootFall Ltd, which provides monthly and weekly averages of visitors to retail outlets compared with a national average.
- For special offers, competitions, coupons and vouchers – count the **take-up**. You can find this out by counting competition entries, the number of free gifts issued or coupons/vouchers received or redeemed.

- Check the effect of the promotion on sales. You can do this by comparing sales at the time of the promotion with previous sales levels.
- Online promotions can be assessed by tracking either the rate of 'click-throughs' (the number of people who click on an advertisement) or the number of **unique impressions**. These are individual users of the website and this is more accurate than 'hits' which count every page on which one user clicks.
- Ask the customer! Many organisations routinely ask new customers where they found out about the business.

Business matters

Some promotions can be too successful! In November 2003, Thorntons launched its Early Bird promotion to encourage early Christmas shopping. It promised to reward customers spending £15 or more with a free box of chocolates. It planned to give away about 500,000 boxes of chocolates.

The promotion was so successful the company ended up giving 700,000 – far more than budgeted. As a result the overall profits for the year were lower than forecast!

I got these free when I bought my mum some chocolates

Dealing with complaints

Complaints are likely to occur only if any customers or visitors feel they have been misled or let down.

- People will complain if a promotion does not live up to its expectations, e.g. free offers, gifts or leaflets run out too soon, an event is badly organised or poorly staffed.
- People will be offended if they take exception to any promotional materials on the grounds that it is discriminatory or tasteless. Do be aware that it is unlawful to discriminate in promotional materials.
- People may also claim that the law has been broken if regulations are not heeded relating to the way competitions, lotteries or prize draws are held or judged and prizes are awarded. Promoters can check the correct course of action on the ISP website, a link is available at www.heinemann.co.uk/hotlinks (express code 1386P).
- Promoters must also, obviously, observe all other consumer laws that apply.

Minor complaints ought to be solved quickly by staff on duty who should apologise for the problem, provide the help or assistance required and check that the customer is now satisfied.

If the problem is more serious then the matter should be referred to someone more senior immediately. If there is a delay, then full details should be taken and the customer assured that action will be taken as soon as possible.

You should note that enlightened businesses see complaints as an opportunity to impress a customer. They argue that if the customer is very impressed with the way a problem is handled, they will not only return again but will also recommend the business to their friends!

Talking point

View 1: *Most sales promotions are a waste of time and money. Suppliers would be far better off reducing the price of a product.*

View 2: *Sales promotions enable suppliers to use interesting and varied ways to sell both products and services and are a valuable type of marketing.*

With which viewpoint to you agree – and why?

Sales and special offers are one type of sales promotion

Over to you!

1 a Retail sales promotions include many types of special offers, including multipacks, linked products and reduced prices. Match the offers below against the products you think they would be most appropriate for, using each offer once only.

Product	Offer
Aftershave or perfume	Multipack at discount price
Organic spaghetti	Buy one get one free
Packs of carrots	Free toothbrush
Tabloid Sunday newspaper	Free CD of popular music
Computer magazine	Free pasta sauce
Toothpaste	Half price luxury shower gel
Blank video tapes	Free games CD

b Divide into **two** groups. Each group identifies **six** everyday products to be promoted, then the other group presents its ideas for each one. Discuss the ideas raised at the end of each presentation.

2 Working in small groups, each choose **one** of the following organisations and find out the types of materials, advice or information it provides by visiting its website. Links to the websites for the companies listed below are available at www.heinemann.co.uk/hotlinks (express code 1386P). Then prepare a short presentation for the rest of your class explaining your findings.

a ADS Visual.
b Ofcom.
c Institute for Sales Promotion.
d The Office of Fair Trading.
e Advertising Standards Authority.
f FootFall.
g Marley Media.

3 Look in your local supermarket and retail stores and check magazines and newspapers to find **six** examples of current sales promotions.

Compare your findings with those of other members of your class and vote to find the top **four** you think are the most effective – with reasons.

1   The following terms have been used in this section. Define each one.

  a   POS displays.
  b   POP displays.
  c   Promotional package.
  d   Cross-promotional marketing.
  e   Above the line.
  f   Below the line.

2   Figure 7.4 shows a summary of the steps involved in planning and preparing a sales promotion. Divide into small groups and choose **one** of the promotions listed below, or, in agreement with your tutor, work on your own idea.

  Follow the summary to produce a promotional plan which includes your suggestions for a successful and effective promotion. Sketch out at least **one** promotional item to illustrate your ideas. Finally, discuss all the promotional plans as a group and decide the strengths and weaknesses of each one, with reasons.

  a   A local kennels has just opened an extension and wants to boost trade.
  b   A shop which sells cut-price fashions wants to sell off its unsold stock before the next season.
  c   A new milk delivery service wants to promote sales of associated products in an area, e.g. orange juice, yoghurt, soya milk etc.
  d   A computer store wants to promote its new, changed location.
  e   A department store wants to increase sales of its bathroom ranges.
  f   A card shop wants to boost sales of Valentine's cards and other associated items
  g   Your college is holding a charity fashion show.

Decide on the aim and purpose of the promotion

↓

Check available materials and resources, including skills of team, and agree budget

↓

Identify the target market and its key features

↓

Decide on the format of the promotion, e.g. the types/combinations of media and promotional methods to use

↓

Decide a central theme and choose a logo, colour, design that will link all aspects of the promotion

↓

Decide a short and simple key message to appeal to customers to support your theme

↓

Identify the key selling points and USPs to include in your promotional materials

↓

Decide how to measure the effectiveness of the promotion

↓

Create the promotional materials, using appropriate graphics techniques, colour, print and type styles

Figure 7.4 *Steps involved in a successful sales promotion*

This section covers

Preparing to sell

Customer service training

Preparing the physical sales
  environment

Note: this section should be read in conjunction with the related pages on the Richer Sounds StudentZone at www.richerstudentzone.co.uk, which give comprehensive information on all these aspects of selling at Richer Sounds.

Most organisations ensure that their sales staff receive appropriate training before they are allowed to start selling, although the content of the training will vary, depending upon the types of product being sold and the customer. Selling technical equipment to a business buyer is obviously a far different matter than selling a packet of envelopes in a local newsagent! Despite this, there are certain aspects of selling that all sales people need to know. In this unit, you will find that the practical information relates mainly to selling consumer durables – where customers expect staff to have a sound product knowledge and to be able to give them advice and assistance on which products would best meet their needs. If you visit a store which hasn't ensured that staff have this basic knowledge then you are likely to notice it quite quickly – and may find the whole experience of trying to make a purchase both irritating and frustrating.

Preparing to sell

You will see from the StudentZone (www.richerstudentzone.co.uk) that until new colleagues at Richer Sounds have attended the three day Virgin Seminar they wear a 'Trainee' name badge and must be shadowed when they are serving a customer. After they have successfully completed the seminar they are upgraded. They can then wear a Junior Sales Assistant badge and serve customers on their own. Richer Sounds colleagues only become fully fledged Sales Assistants after they have received 25 'excellent' customer feedback questionnaires.

In other words, at Richer Sounds, sales assistants are trained how to sell and then must prove they can do this consistently well over a period of time. The types of training they receive, both in store, on the Virgin Seminar and other training courses, cover all the following aspects of selling:

- Company procedures – including health, safety and security in stores.
- The basics about consumer law.
- How to deliver excellent customer service.
- How to handle problems or questions from customers.
- Technical aspects of the equipment they sell.
- How to process sales and use the EPOS system.
- Other relevant aspects of their jobs – from carrying out stock checks to updates on product developments.

Customer protection legislation

The main laws relating to customer protection were summarised on pages 317–8. It is essential that all sales staff understand the legal rights of customers and their legal responsibilities as sellers. These include the following aspects:

- **Faulty goods**. Customers who return a faulty product have the right to a full refund. Many retailers have a returns policy which is more generous than this and will also allow exchanges and refunds if a customer has simply changed his or her mind about the purchase (see page 331). Staff must know the policy which applies in their own store and who to ask for help if they have a problem.

- **Descriptions**. All goods must be described accurately and benefits, features or performance must not be exaggerated.
- **Safety**. All goods sold must be safe to use. Sales staff must remove from sale any goods which are damaged and may be hazardous to use.
- **Price**. Customers must not be misled over the price being charged or the way in which the price is calculated. All quotations must be accurate and include all the separate items, including VAT and delivery charges. It is therefore sensible for written estimates and quotations to be double checked by another member of staff before they are given to a customer.
- **Sale prices**. Goods in a sale must have previously been offered at a higher price for a

Business brief

The terms of a contract of sale

When you buy something you enter into a contract of sale with the seller. This does not need to be in writing. If you offer to buy an item (e.g. by picking it up and offering money) and the seller accepts your offer (e.g. by wrapping it up and taking your money) then this is a contract – just the same as if you had made a written offer (e.g. by completing an order form) and received confirmation in writing.

The contract is ended in three ways:

- **By performance** – you accept the goods, pay for them and are now the legal owner.
- **By agreement** – you return the goods and obtain a refund.
- **By breach** – when the terms of the contract have not been met, e.g. failure to pay by the buyer or faulty goods supplied by the seller.

Some contract terms are in writing, such as an order confirmation which describes the goods to be supplied. At your request it may also include a specific delivery date. These are known as **express terms**. If these are not kept, for example the goods received are different, then you can legally reject them. If you specified that 'time is of the essence' then you can also refuse the goods after the agreed delivery date. This is useful if you need goods for a specific date, e.g. for a leaving present, after which time they would not be any use.

Not all terms are written down. Other terms are **implied**, e.g. that you will pay for the goods and that they will be in working order. It is assumed that these are so obvious they don't have to be specified in the contract.

Terms are also divided into **conditions** and **warranties**. A condition is a vital term. If this is breached the contract can be rejected. For example, if you bought a mobile phone you would expect it to work so that you could make calls. Otherwise you could reject the contract. However, if the phone had been advertised with a carrying case, but when you bought it they told you none were left, this would be classed as a warranty. This is not a vital term. Therefore you could not reject the phone on this basis but could offer a lower price because the contract had not been met in full.

The **Unfair Contract Terms Act 1977** prevents retailers from limiting or taking away a customer's statutory rights under the Sale of Goods Acts (see page 317). A retailer who tries to do this is guilty of a criminal offence. For example, a dry cleaner may have terms and conditions to try to escape responsibility for clothes which are lost or damaged. However, it could only do that if it showed that any clause it inserted in the contract was reasonable. If an outfit was damaged because of sheer carelessness by an employee then the clause would become void and the customer could claim compensation. Similarly, any notices which restrict the length of time by which a customer must complain about a faulty item are also unlawful and so, too, are any attempts to escape negligence which contributes towards death or personal injury – such as from a dangerous fitment or item of equipment.

stated period, in accordance with the terms of the Consumer Protection Act 1987.

- **Selling on credit**. Sales staff who complete credit agreements must understand all the relevant terms and conditions of the Consumer Credit Act (see pages 316 and 317).

Differences between business sales and retail sales

Some organisations specifically produce and sell goods to business organisations – such as specialist software, equipment and machinery. Others sell goods both to businesses and to private customers – such as office equipment firms Office World and Staples and computer suppliers like Dell and PC World. Others only sell goods to retail customers, such as Tesco, Next and Superdrug.

Business buyers were first covered in Unit 2, pages 102–6. Business buyers are different from ordinary retail buyers as they are usually professionals who have an in-depth knowledge of the type of goods they are responsible for purchasing. Organisations that sell to business buyers are very aware of this and have different systems in place to meet their needs.

Sales to business

- **Specialist buyers** buy goods on behalf of the whole organisation. They will know their own needs and requirements. In any debate about product suitability the buyer and seller discuss the best products to meet the buyer's needs in relation to specification, quality, price and delivery. Information about the buyer's future needs would be passed on to product developers in the business who have the responsibility of planning future lines.
- **Possible supply constraints** must be taken into account when delivery dates are negotiated. This is particularly important for customised goods that are produced by a supplier/manufacturer after the order had been received. Sales staff must consult production staff before agreeing delivery dates. Most sales staff are trained that it is far better to '**under promise and over deliver**' – in other words,

to delight the customer by doing better than expected – rather than promise something that they can't do, leaving the customer disappointed.

- **In depth product knowledge** is vital. Many businesses employ specialist sales representatives with in-depth product knowledge to visit customers as a routine part of their job to keep them up-to-date on product improvements and developments. In the case of specialist items then product developers, such as engineers or software developers, may make sales visits. Businesses like Office World and PC World will often have different staff to sell to business buyers who may want customised systems to suit their own needs.

The sales and/or customer service department also employ trained staff to deal with orders and enquiries relating to products in the catalogues, orders in progress, delivery dates, refunds of returned goods and so on.

- **Business customer sales histories**. These are updated regularly from sales transactions and representative's reports to include details of contact names, previous order history and buyer preferences. Customers on the mailing list routinely receive updates of brochures, catalogues and price lists as well as promotional mailshots on new and existing products.

Sales history information may also include details of financial history. This will include the customer's credit rating and any credit limit set (see Unit 3, page 233). Sales staff will follow specific procedures if new orders are received when a customer is approaching this limit. This helps the business to avoid bad debts by supplying goods to a customer who has financial difficulties.

- **Clarifying pricing policies**. Pricing policies may be more complex for business customers. Most businesses that sell to trade customers offer discounts for large orders. This may be at a fixed rate, known by all sales staff. Alternatively there may be a range of 'packages' available to business customers relating to the basic sale and then maintenance or other benefits. For example, business software suppliers will normally include free staff training to secure a sale. For large, customised and valuable industrial orders the final price may be negotiated by senior managers – particularly if they are bidding for the business against their competitors.

Business brief

Pricing policies

Supermarkets traditionally had 'pile it high and sell it cheap' pricing policies, and everyone has heard of 'loss leaders' which were used to attract people into the store. Now only Netto and Aldi are known for this. Today the 'big four' – Tesco, ASDA, Morrisons and Sainsbury's – prefer to focus more on value or 'everyday low price' (EDLP) campaigns – emphasising continual low prices that shoppers can trust.

At the opposite end of the scale a small shop selling specialist or designer items may deliberately sell at a high price to gain a reputation for exclusivity and to attract a certain type of customer.

Other pricing strategies include promoting new products with a low introductory price or special offer or offering money-back guarantees if the same goods can be found on sale at a cheaper price in a local store within a certain period of time. Richer Sounds does this. You can read about their price promise on the StudentZone (www.richerstudentzone.co.uk) and what they do if a competitor is undercutting them.

Business matters

Blunders on Internet sites can cause problems for suppliers. Travel agent First Choice mistakenly priced its flights to Florida for £15 on its website, but agreed to honour its commitment.

Amazon was less generous when it offered hand-held computers on its site for as little as £7 and was inundated in orders. It refused to meet the orders – just as Argos did when it advertised TVs for £3 in error.

This is quite legal because a sales contract only exists when there is both an offer and an acceptance. Although customers offered to buy Amazon's computers their offers weren't accepted, so no contract existed. In addition, the law recognises that when a mistake is obvious customers aren't entitled to take advantage of it.

So whether you are online or walking around your local shops, if you see a bargain that seems too good to be true, it probably is, and the shopkeeper can very nicely turn down your offer to buy!

Over to you!

1 Your friends and family have heard that you have been studying consumer protection and asked for your help. How would you advise them in each of the following cases – and why?
   a Your aunt bought an umbrella because it was labelled 'New, windproof design. Never blows inside out.' She tells you this is rubbish because last week, when it was very windy, that's exactly what it did.
   b Your friend and his wife have just moved into a new flat. They ordered a leather sofa which was delivered last week. When they removed the protective packaging they noticed a scratch down the back. The firm says it isn't liable because they signed the delivery note to say it was 'received OK.'
   c Your sister receives two identical CDs for her birthday and doesn't know what to do.
   d Your mother's new toaster gets so hot around the sides that you think it is positively dangerous. The shop that sold it says this is the fault of the manufacturer, not them.
   e Your brother left his watch to be repaired at a jeweller's. When he returned to collect it he was told it was stolen when the sales assistant left it on the counter. The notice behind the counter says that all goods for repair are left at the owner's risk.

f Your friend pays £250 by credit card to buy a mountain bike from a website supplier. The mountain bike never arrives and when he tries to contact the firm he gets no response.

g Your friend is upset because she has saved to pay off a loan early but has been told there is an extra fee if she does this.

2 Tim worked part-time in a high street computer store when he was a student. At first he mainly sold software and consumables like floppy disks, CDs and printer cartridges but, after a few months, he was allowed to demonstrate PCs and laptops to customers.

Tim has now seen a full-time job working as a sales representative for a firm which specialises in supplying and installing specialist IT equipment and software to large business organisations. He thinks his previous experience will stand him in good stead.

a Suggest **three** attributes Tim can claim as a result of his experience.

b Identify **four** differences between selling to retail customers in the high street store and selling to business organisations.

3 a If you bought this textbook from a retail store, or from the Heinemann website, then you are a private buyer . If your tutor bought it a class set – or bought a set of books to sell to your group – then he or she is classed as a business buyer.

As a group, suggest **three** ways that publishers like Heinemann will try to promote textbooks to business buyers like your tutor.

b Richer Sounds mainly sells goods to private individuals, but also sells goods to business buyers. Check the main website under Corporate Sales and find **two** differences in the services offered to businesses.

Customer service training

As you will see on the StudentZone at www.richerstudentzone.co.uk, customer service training is very extensive at Richer Sounds. The reason for this is simple. Richer Sounds firmly believes that customers judge the business by the service they receive. It prides itself on exceptional customer service so that every single customer feels special and important. To achieve this all sales colleagues are trained how to respond from the moment customers walk into the store until they have left – whether or not they buy.

If you contrast this to the service you receive in stores that are less fussy about customer service training, then it isn't hard to see why some customers would rather travel several miles to visit a Richer Sounds store than go anywhere else.

The variety of clientele

Customers and clients come in all shapes and sizes. Even if the goods you sell are aimed at a specific market then you still have to deal with customers buying on behalf of other people. Some customers may be regulars, whereas others are first-time buyers. Some are meek, others may be assertive or even quite aggressive. Some have carefully checked out different products and features first, and know what they want. Some are in a rush, others want to make a day of it! And, on top of all that, each customer has individual wants and needs. So, given this diversity, how do you cope?

For the sales person there are three fundamental rules.

1 Never pre-judge a customer on the basis of age, gender or appearance. The young woman looking at second-hand cars may be a qualified automotive engineer – and the older man in gardening clothes may be a millionaire! If you treat everyone in a friendly, courteous and professional way then these types of differences don't matter.

2 There is no 'one size fits all' solution for dealing with different customers. Treat each person as an individual and learn how to listen. Then you can find out what the customer already knows and wants. This helps you to recommend the most appropriate product to meet the customer's individual needs and requirements.

3 Your job is to form a professional relationship with the customer, not a personal one. This means that you must still be pleasant and courteous even if a customer is boring, annoying, sarcastic or uncommunicative. If you have serious problems dealing with someone because they are abusive or personally insulting then get help. Otherwise, count to ten under your breath and keep smiling!

Business matters

There are many studies which group customers in different ways according to their behaviour. This can make it easier for sales staff to learn how to identify and deal with them. Some examples are given below from a customer animal farm!

Roosters strut into the store and want to be treated as special and important. They are impatient – keep them waiting and they'll walk out. The rooster often acts on impulse, likes questions to be answered quickly and has scant regard for the staff who serve them.

Foxes are crafty. They have probably researched the product well and know comparative prices. Unlike roosters they won't crow about what they know, but will keep quiet to see if they can get a better deal by outwitting the sales person. They may time their visit to take advantage of special offers. They only respect sales staff who have excellent product knowledge.

Dogs love personal service. They like sales staff to welcome them warmly, smile and use their name. For this reason they prefer small shops to large stores. They will be influenced by the views of other people who enthuse about a product.

Sheep only have one reason for buying – because everyone else is doing so. Logical arguments for purchase are a waste of time – the key point is that it's the most fashionable item available.

Jackdaws like to collect brochures and leaflets about a product, study them carefully, and then return to buy at a later date. They also keep receipts and external wrappings so that if there is a problem everything can be returned as it was sold.

Bulls are aggressive. They expect immediate service and assume they are always right. They will not be worried about having an argument to get their own way and can frighten inexperienced staff.

Mr and Mrs Farmer always shop together. In the trade they are sometimes called the 'two-headed' customer. This is because they may not agree on what they want! One may be impulsive, the other cautious. One may be factual and logical; the other may be more emotional. The sales person has to try to keep them both happy – at the same time!

The range of customer requirements

Different customers have different priorities – not just in the way they are served but also in the type of product they want and additional service features. Their main considerations are listed below.

- **Price**. Most customers have a budget. Finding out how much a customer is thinking of spending is a useful starting point and saves recommending products which are too expensive.
- **Availability**. Many customers want to make an immediate purchase and are not interested in waiting longer for new stock to arrive or for out of stock items to be delivered. This is particularly the case if they can easily obtain the item elsewhere.
- **Features**. Some customers may have specific brand preferences that they associate with quality and reliability. Acknowledge their right to this opinion even if you are recommending other brands which are now considered better. The range of features or type of performance of a product often affects the price and many buying decisions are a compromise between the ideal and what can be afforded.
- **Appearance**. This varies in importance depending upon the product and the customer. Many sales people claim that women are more concerned about 'form' (appearance) while men focus more on 'function'. Whilst this is a generalisation you may find it interesting to see how this affects many advertisements – such as car adverts which stress engine performance more in men's magazines than in women's!
- **Personal circumstances/specific requirements**. This will affect the buying decision in terms of size of item, colour, usage, whether to wait or purchase immediately. For example, customers may be buying a product to match or fit with others they already own – or to go in a specific space. Richer Sounds gives away tape measures to customers who cannot make a decision because they forgot to measure the space available first!
- **Additional benefits**. Aspects such as

immediate availability, prompt or free delivery, product guarantee and competitive or free credit terms can help to persuade a buyer to make an immediate decision.

Business matters

It has taken several years for many companies to realise they were losing business because of inflexible or unreliable delivery dates.

The importance of a good delivery service cannot be overemphasised, particularly for companies that sell online or by mail order – or for stores that sell large household items that customers cannot transport themselves. Customers, many of whom work full-time, must be able to rely on the goods being delivered as promised.

Strategies to improve delivery services by retailers have included:

- **Allowing the customer to specify a date** for mail deliveries (and 'am' or 'pm' for store deliveries or service calls).
- **Enabling customers to have goods delivered to a work address**; to a neighbour's house or to specify where goods can be left if they are out.
- **Delivering goods free of charge** – or free above a certain minimum charge.
- **Using private couriers** who can deliver in an evening and collect items for return.

Customers who buy goods regularly online or by mail order also have two other choices. They can use the Royal Mail's Local Collect service for parcels that are sent by post by nominating the local post office to which the package should be redelivered. There is a 50p charge on collection. Alternatively they can invest in a Hippo Box or ParcelEater. Both are locked boxes for outside the front door. They will hold parcels securely until the householder comes home and empties them. You can find out more on the Giraffe Marketing and ParcelEater websites, links are available at www.heinemann.co.uk/hotlinks (express code 1386P).

The degree of attention for different products

Products can be sub-divided into two main categories for selling to private individuals or businesses.

Consumer goods are bought by individuals for their own use. There are two types:

- **FMCGs – fast moving consumer goods**. These are the low priced items you buy every day, such as sweets, soap, newspapers, cereal, frozen food, bread and milk. After purchase they have no value. In the retail trade they are often known as 'low ticket, high volume items'. Most carry 'sell by' dates and are branded products made by large firms, e.g. Mars, Cadbury, Heinz, Birds Eye and Kellogg.

  These goods largely sell themselves and are found in self-service supermarkets, local convenience stores, motorway service area shops and petrol station retail outlets. The main role for staff is to know the range stocked, where they are located and how to process sales.

- **Consumer durables** are goods bought for longer-term use such as furniture, cars and carpets. This category includes **white goods** (washing machines, refrigerators, and other kitchen items) and **brown goods** (TVs, radios, DVD players etc – so called because they were originally made in brown bakelite!) All these have a second-hand value after purchase. An alternative term is **SMCGs – slow moving consumer goods** – because they are bought less often so stock turnover is less than for FMCGs.

  Customers usually take longer to decide on these purchases because they are spending more and they often have to choose between alternatives with a range of different features and prices. Expert product knowledge by sales staff is usually essential to advise customers.

Industrial goods are sold to industry and business organisations.

- **Capital goods** are expensive items which are bought to last and to be used over time, e.g. equipment, machinery, vehicles, computers. These are sold by sales representatives or other specialists and the purchase may be the subject of negotiations for several weeks.

- **Consumables** are those items that are constantly used and replaced by businesses, such as stationery, cleaning materials and lubricants. These are advertised in business catalogues and staff will receive orders by phone, fax, mail and online. Rapid processing of orders, prompt delivery and discounts for bulk purchases are usually essential aspects of the service.

Business brief

The importance of product knowledge

It is reasonable for any customer to expect sales staff to understand the products they are selling. In fact, there is nothing more irritating for the customer than staff who don't seem to know or care what is in stock, where it is kept or how it works!

To sell effectively, staff should know:
- The range of stock items normally carried by the store.
- The seasonal lines that are stocked – and over what period.
- Where particular goods are to be found in the store.
- The prices of individual items and the price ranges of different types of products.
- The variations that are available, e.g. colour, sizes, models, additional options or extras.
- The key selling features of each product.
- The different uses of each product.
- How to demonstrate a product.
- The delivery time for products currently out of stock.
- How to advise on use, care and maintenance.
- The after-sales service available.

Customers are always impressed if they receive a positive response when they ask about a product that is not stocked. It may be possible to offer a substitute item. If not, staff should be helpful and recommend an alternative supplier. Richer Sounds is often asked about items like furniture for audio equipment. It doesn't sell these but keeps a copy of Argos and Ikea catalogues behind the counter so that it can give information about these items to customers who enquire.

Training in negotiation skills

Sales representatives and other specialists who sell to professional business buyers must be trained negotiators. This is because a business buyer will always want to get the best possible outcome or 'deal' for his or her organisation. This means haggling over the different factors relating to the purchase to see if terms can be improved, such as price, discount terms, specification, size, consumable items, maintenance agreement terms, product training, breakdown service and payment terms. The buyer will compare the total package on offer from each supplier and will constantly challenge competing suppliers to improve their individual offers. To successfully cope with this and make a sale normally means that the product is competitively priced and good value. It also indicates that the seller has very good negotiation skills.

Fortunately, selling to most private customers is normally rather easier! You are unlikely to be challenged about the price of chocolate or sweets! If you are selling consumer durables then you will normally find that your role as a negotiator is limited by organisational policies. Therefore, no matter how tempted you are, you wouldn't be allowed to offer a 25 per cent discount to a customer just because he was very insistent! There are two reasons for this:

- To prevent staff selling goods too cheaply or offering a 'package' which is so expensive the business will lose money providing it.
- To reduce the risk of losing loyal customers who find out that other people have had better 'deals'. Having an agreed policy means everyone is treated fairly.

This doesn't mean to say that you will never be challenged by a customer who wants a better deal

Negotiating with a customer

Negotiating occurs when the customer is trying to get you to do something which isn't normally a part of the deal, e.g. deliver earlier/later than normal, allow a discount etc.

- Know your company policies - what you can and cannot do and who can help you if you have a problem.
- Negotiation normally starts after you have shown the customer all the options and he/she has stated specific interest in buying a certain item.
- Listen to what the customer wants without interrupting. This may be something you can easily agree to. In this case do so to get the sale.
- If the demands are far too excessive then simply say 'No, I'm afraid not'. That is far better than giving the customer false hope e.g. by saying 'I'll have to ask' or 'I'll find out'.
- Ideally, try to meet the customer part-way. Many customers are quite happy if they win some concession, no matter how small. One strategy is the creative compromise. At Richer Sounds staff are taught to focus on value rather than price. They may therefore throw in one or two extra cables or connectors, but cannot lower the price - which implies it was too high in the first place!
- It can be easier (or harder) to negotiate if you are dealing with two or more people. A tip is to focus your persuasive skills on the person who obviously wants the product the most or who is in the greatest hurry!
- If the buyer keeps asking for more extras, summarise the value of everything agreed so far. Stress aspects such as product quality and reliability, after-sales service and other benefits. Stay confident. If you are selling a good product that is competitively priced then if your customer rejects your office he/she has to start shopping around all over again. Instead, repeat the concession you have already agreed and ask for an agreement to buy in return.
- If this doesn't work, let your customer walk away. If you've stayed pleasant and professional throughout the discussion then you may find that the customer returns to take you up on your original offer at a later date!

Figure 7.5 *Negotiation skills*

– and this is when basic negotiation skills are invaluable. In this case the hints and tips in Figure 7.5 may help you.

The significance of lapses in courtesy and efficiency

What annoys you most as a customer? Try some of the following:

- Being ignored by a sales assistant who is talking to a colleague, tidying up or doing paperwork.

- Being served by a sales assistant who is talking to a colleague at the same time, or another customer, so is obviously distracted.
- Being hassled by someone who won't let you look around in peace.
- Not being able to find anyone to help you when you want help or advice.
- Having to wait for ages in a queue because – out of seven possible cash points – only two are staffed.
- Asking to buy an item on display to be told there are none in stock and display stock cannot be sold.
- Sales staff who cannot answer basic queries – such as what they stock and/or where to find it – let alone explain the features of a product.
- Sales staff who treat you like an idiot or a nuisance.
- Sales staff who cannot seem to carry out the most basic procedure without asking for advice from a colleague.

No doubt you have had most of these experiences! Do you still shop at these stores? The answer may be 'yes' if you have few alternatives in your area. The answer will definitely be 'no' if there are lots of competing suppliers and the others give a far better service. This is main significance of such lapses. Customers will choose to go elsewhere in future – where they receive better service and are treated as important individuals.

Interestingly, unless customers are in a frantic hurry, they are often very tolerant about minor problems or with new or rather inept staff providing the assistant is polite, trying his or her best and prepared to acknowledge and apologise for the problem. Sales assistants who pretend nothing is wrong, who sigh heavily to gain sympathy or – even worse – complain about being overworked or underpaid are another matter entirely, and clearly in the wrong job. Customers visit a shop to make a purchase, not to listen to staff moans!

Referral procedures to match customers with experienced staff

There are many situations when a sales assistant may need to refer an enquiry to someone else, such as technical queries, unusual problems or serious complaints. It is important that all staff should know the type of situations they should not try to handle themselves – and that they should *never* try to 'bluff' or guess an answer they don't know. They also need to know how to contact someone else who can help them in this type of situation.

- In small shops or stores, a junior assistant can ask a senior assistant, supervisor or the manager for help and information.
- In larger stores, there is often a separate customer service desk for handling queries and complaints.
- In many large stores, specific staff may be called to sales floor by internal phone or by tannoy if they are needed to assist a customer.
- Organisation charts and internal telephone lists identify the various departments within an organisation and the job titles of the staff who work there. This enables assistants to identify the best person to contact over a particular query. At Richer Sounds, the structure of the organisation is discussed with new colleagues during the Virgin Seminar so that they know the type of issues to refer to their store manager and who to contact over other matters, such as repairs or stock.

Clarification of return/exchange policies

Most retailers have specific returns policies which should be known by all their staff. The benefits are that:

- All customers are treated in the same way.
- The policies comply with the law on consumer rights.
- Sales assistants can deal with most queries and problems themselves, without having to constantly ask a supervisor.

Legally all businesses must replace faulty goods or give a full refund. However, no business is obliged to accept returned goods simply because buyers have changed their minds. Many do, however, because having a 'no quibble' returns policy can give a store an edge over its competitors. This is because customers are more tempted to make impulse purchases if they know they can return or exchange them if necessary.

Some stores will only allow customers a limited time to return unwanted goods, such as a month from purchase. Many insist that all returns are accompanied by a receipt. Legally, however, any proof of purchase should be allowed (such as a credit card voucher or bank statement) and must be acceptable in the case of faulty goods that are returned.

All sales staff must be aware of the legal rights of a customer returning faulty goods:

- The responsibility to put matters right rests with the seller, not the manufacturer of the goods.
- The buyer has the right to a refund and does not have to accept a credit note or voucher.
- A buyer who agrees to a free repair does not lose the right to a refund if the repair is unsatisfactory.
- The recipient of a gift can return a faulty item, not just the person who made the actual purchase.

In addition, the policies should also guide staff who have to deal with returned items that are less straightforward, for example:

- Unwanted goods that have had all the price tickets removed or look as if they might have been used.
- Pre-recorded DVDs, CDs and videos which are reported as faulty but have had their seals removed – and which could have been copied before being returned.
- Goods that are faulty but have obviously been used for some time. In this case the decision will depend upon the type of item, type of use and period of use. This is because the law stresses 'satisfactory quality' and 'fit for the purpose for which it was intended.' For that reason, if your new jacket fell apart the second time it was washed, it doesn't matter that you have worn it and washed it, the jacket fails on both these points of law and you can claim a refund. The situation would be very different, however, if you had owned it for six months and worn it nearly every day!

- Goods that may have been damaged by the owner after purchase but are being returned as faulty.

Unless the returns policy gives clear guidance, staff should know which member(s) of staff to contact if they have a difficult problem to resolve.

Training for security personnel

Security guards are trained to be friendly and helpful to genuine shoppers

Retail crime, including shoplifting, costs stores nearly £2,000 million a year. For that reason, as you saw in unit 3 (pages 263–7), all retailers are keen to implement security measures to keep theft and fraud to a minimum.

- The staff in a small shop or store should be trained to be vigilant and to know the specific security procedures to follow related to the opening and locking of the shop, handling cash or valuable stock and using security equipment. They should know the action to take if they suspect someone is shoplifting – and also know what to do in an emergency such as a raid, without putting their own safety at risk.
- In some stores, specially trained plain clothes security staff, known as store detectives, are employed to mingle with normal shoppers and to watch for shoplifters. They may be employed by the store or, more often, by a security agency.
- In other cases, uniformed security guards patrol the premises. Whilst they act as an

1 a Find out about the referral system used in your college if a student calls in to ask for details of a full-time course and wants to talk to a tutor.

   b Compare this to the system used in most retail shops and stores. Find out about this by investigating what happens if there is a complex problem which an assistant cannot handle alone. You can do this by comparing experiences from students in your group who have worked in the retail trade, checking on the StudentZone at www.richerstudentzone.co.uk to see what happens at Richer Sounds or asking what would happen when you visit a store you know well.

2 Working as a member of a small group, decide the best way to handle each of the customers described in the 'customer animal farm' on page 327. Then compare your ideas as a class.

3 From your own experience as a customer, identify **two** occasions when you felt that the courtesy and efficiency you experienced in a store was unacceptable. Then compare your suggestions with others made by members of your group.

Add your own suggestions to the list on page 331 and, as a group, decide which **three** failures are the most serious and the most annoying to customers.

4 Your sister has recently bought a small shop and will mainly be selling silver jewellery. You are concerned that she has thought little about security. Either on your own, or working in a small group, investigate the following websites and prepare a list of key points she should consider. Links are available at www.heinemann.co.uk/hotlinks (express code 1386P).

   a Guidance by the Home Office on reducing retail crime.

   b The security directory at the British Retail Consortium website, then follow links to security companies you think would be useful.

obvious deterrent to thieves many businesses are concerned that they are offputting to customers. One way of alleviating this problem is to train security guards to be 'customer friendly' so that they are friendly and helpful to customers with genuine enquiries and can give specific help if necessary. These guards are normally employed by specialist agencies and the store has a contract with the agency to supply the guards. This is the same system used to guard many types of industrial premises.

Preparing the physical sales environment

The physical sales environment is extremely important. An attractive, welcoming entrance which leads to a retail area with goods clearly displayed and easily accessible has many advantages:

- **It encourages shoppers** to enter.
- **It helps shoppers** to find what they want quickly.
- **It tempts shoppers** to browse and look around – which encourages impulse buying.

Today large chain stores have a specific image and 'look' which sets them apart. This helps to make them distinctive and easily recognisable in any town in Britain. The factors which help to define this are the subject of this section.

Accessibility

From October 2004, the requirements of the Disability Discrimination Act (see page 278) include the access and layout of all business premises, including small shops and service providers – from restaurants and pubs to swimming pools and hospitals. This means that even your local hairdresser or newsagent must reassess their premises and make 'reasonable adjustments' to any physical features which act as a barrier to access for disabled customers. The term 'reasonable' means that the adjustment should be sensible bearing in mind the type of business, its size and the cost and practicalities of carrying out the adjustment.

According to the Disability Rights Commission this is plain business sense. Over 8.6 million people in the UK have some form of disability and, collectively, they are estimated to spend over £50 billion a year. In addition, the type of measures taken to meet their needs also make shopping easier for many other groups of customers, such as parents with children in pushchairs and the elderly.

Ideally, the features which should be assessed include:

- **Signs** – which should be clear, easy to read and placed so none are hazardous for the visually impaired.
- **Access steps** which would ideally be replaced with ramps.
- **The colour and width of access doors** and their ease of opening.
- **Lighting** to ensure there are no dark areas in the shop.
- **Width between aisles** for wheelchair use.
- **Height of shelves, clothing rails and hooks** – to be within reach of wheelchair users.
- **Ease of access to checkout or cash points** and counter heights.
- **Layout and design of other customer areas**, e.g. changing rooms and toilets.
- **The availability and access to exits**, particularly in an emergency.

Layout, furnishings and decor

Most retailers have a corporate image that relates to every aspect of their business, their logo, the fascia above the shop, colour scheme and décor, the design and layout of the stores, the appearance of their staff, the product displays and signage. In addition to helping you to recognise the store instantly this also distinguishes it from its competitors.

The image of the business and the type of products sold will influence the decisions that are made about layout, furnishings and overall decor.

- Self-service and convenience stores favour a 'grid' layout where the customer enters at a fixed point, often by a wall, and walks around between vertical and horizontal display units. This layout is very economical in terms of space and good for security – as all customers must exit past the checkout. The overall appearance is very clean and functional with basic shop fitments, usually fixed to a tiled or wooden floor. There is usually bright lighting so customers can clearly see the goods. Some areas may have different lighting for effect, such as pink for an in-store fresh meat area. Examples of these stores include all large supermarkets, Superdrug, B&Q, Boots, Toys R Us, Office World, PC World, most greetings card shops.

Clear signage is vital in large stores

- Other shops want to encourage customers to browse and take their time. They are therefore likely to use a different layout, which creates a more relaxed atmosphere. Goods are grouped together in displays and customers can circulate between them. Cash points are sited at strategic intervals among the displays.

Examples include Next, River Island, Claire's Accessories.

The store can be made more distinctive and luxurious by using carpeting, mirrors, chairs and soft lighting. Natural light will be a consideration if clothes or furnishings are being sold and particular displays are often illuminated for effect such as spotlights on jewellery counters to intensify the brilliance of precious stones. In changing rooms lighting is usually more subtle – and mirrors angled, to make the wearer look good. Coloured lights may be used in stores popular with young people. Examples include Marks & Spencer, Jaeger, Oasis, or any independent high quality shop in your town selling clothing, jewellery or expensive gifts.

Allowing people to browse and handle goods increases sales

- A third type of layout divides up the selling area to focus on different types of products. This system is used in large bookshops where you will find different sections for fiction, non-fiction, children's books, travel, cookery etc. This works well, too, in large music stores which sell a mixture of CDs, DVDs and videos on different subjects and on the ground floor of department stores where you can buy a range of products from cosmetics to handbags or hosiery.

In this case, each area may have a slightly different atmosphere. For example, in a bookshop the children's area can be brightly coloured and furnished with small tables and chairs. Examples include Hamleys, Virgin Megastores, large HMV stores, Blockbusters, Waterstones, or the ground floor of any large department store such as John Lewis or Selfridges.

Use of music

Many sales assistant grumble that the thing they dislike most about Christmas is not that they are so busy but that they have to listen to Christmas music all day, every day from early November! The aim, of course, is to get customers in the mood for Christmas shopping as soon as possible.

Background music is used in a variety of different businesses. In restaurants, pubs, hotels and many stores, piped music is used to help customers relax, to avoid silence and to mask unacceptable background noises, such as the clatter of plates in the kitchen. Music is likely to be more muted in general outlets and livelier in shops or store areas targeting young buyers, such as Miss Selfridge. Some stores play more upbeat music at weekends than during weekdays. Some studies have shown that customers shop more quickly when music is lively and dawdle when it is slow; and the University of Leicester has proved that playing French or Italian classical music influences the type of food people choose!

Record stores often play tracks from newly released CDs to tempt customers – just like Blockbuster stores play newly released films – to promote them to people browsing.

Health and safety

Health and safety is a legal requirement for all businesses, including retail stores. All selling environments must be assessed for risks so that any hazards are minimised. Sales staff must also be trained to act correctly in an emergency, such as an evacuation when the fire alarm sounds.

This is particularly important in large stores where dozens of customers will not be familiar with emergency exit routes. Staff must also know what to do if an accident occurs. In many large stores there are trained first-aiders who can be summoned. If not, sales staff need basic training so that they know not to move anyone who has had a serious accident and they also know how to obtain assistance.

The key areas of health and safety which relate to selling environments are summarised below.

- **The building itself and the store layout**. Architects, designers and professional shopfitters are fully aware of all the building and other regulations which apply to retail premises. These include safety glass in doors, handrails on steps and non-slip flooring. Staff should be trained to identify and report any problems they notice through wear and tear, such as a floor tile becoming dislodged.
- **The delivery and storage of goods**. Ideally goods will be delivered through a separate entrance which leads directly to the stockroom. Heavy goods should only be moved using trucks or trolleys and all staff should be trained how to lift boxes safely. Loads must be stacked safely and in accordance with any specific labels (e.g. This Way Up or Fragile) and perishable goods must be stored in appropriate conditions. Goods unloaded from refrigerated lorries must be stored immediately in chilled or frozen food storage areas and potentially hazardous items, such as knives or glasses, must be stored safely preferably in protective packaging.
- **Store fixtures and fittings**. Shelves must be stable and preferably have raised front edges to prevent items falling forwards. Staff must never overload shelves above the safe maximum weight. Fixtures must not have sharp edges and floor level plinths should not protrude so that customers can trip over them. All stock must be stocked safely. Ideally, all heavy items should be stored lower down and only light items placed on high shelves. Wall hooks in changing rooms must not be positioned where they could be hazardous.

- **Displays of merchandise**. These should be created during quiet times and placed where they cannot be knocked over. Displays of heavy items should be constructed so that they cannot topple over and hurt someone, even if an item at the base is removed. Dangerous items should never form part of a display.
- **Equipment and appliances**. Staff must be trained to use any potentially hazardous equipment and must observe all relevant safety precautions. Only specialists should carry out routine maintenance or repairs to equipment such as freezers and chilled cabinets. Electrical devices should be installed to attract and kill pests such as flies and midges. Food stores or catering outlets have to comply with many additional legal regulations and staff who handle food may need to obtain special food handling qualifications. These staff will wear protective clothing and be trained how to guard against a wider range of hazards, such as boiling water and hot pans.
- **Cleanliness and tidiness**. The store should be cleaned after customers have left or, in the case of 24/7 stores, at the quietest times. This includes routine shelf cleaning and filling, and the cleaning of chilled cabinets and freezers. Aisles should be kept clear and empty boxes removed as soon as restocking has taken place. Items on display must be kept clean and bottles of liquid checked to ensure they are securely fastened.
- **Working practices**. Wherever possible maintenance work should take place when the store is closed. Any areas under repair during opening hours should be cordoned off and merchandise re-sited. Stock repositioning should also take place out-of-hours or at the quietest times.

All staff should be trained to be vigilant and to act immediately if they spot a problem. Spillages and breakages must be cleaned up immediately. The area must be cordoned off until the floor is dry and/or safe to walk on. Faults and hazards should be reported immediately so that action can be taken.

Implications of market competition

Retailers normally aim to differentiate themselves from the competition. There are various ways in which they can do this:

- Locate in a distinctive type of building which reflects the company image – from a purpose-built out-of-town superstore to a high street shop.
- By a shop front and fascia (i.e. the board above the window) which is instantly recognisable.
- By the furniture, fixtures and fittings, colour scheme and materials used in the store, such as wood, tiles or carpet on the floor. Alternatively, there may be a mixture of these to denote different areas.
- By the size of the interior, its layout and the amount of space. Generally, the more cluttered the shop, the more 'down market' it will appear.
- By the type and style of the displays, the slogans and the lettering used.
- By the number of staff available to give personal service and the way that they are dressed.

Market competition also means that any store wants to stay ahead of its competitors. It may do this by:

- Reducing its prices and/or having sales promotions.
- Constantly re-evaluating stock lines so that these reflect current customer demand and trends.
- Increasing the range of facilities to customers, such as a coffee shop, car parking, toilet areas, cash machines.
- Offering additional services, e.g. help with packing and carrying goods, rapid checkouts, a gift wrap service, free alterations for regular customers, free delivery, a 'no quibble' returns policy.
- Changing its opening hours.

Occasionally a retail outlet will re-evaluate the whole design of the store and decide to change it. It may argue it is outdated and needs modernising. The result of a refitting exercise is that new customers may be attracted out of curiosity – and the store will aim to impress them so that they will return again and again. This is essential if an expensive refitting exercise is to be cost effective.

Buyer behaviour

Dawn French learned about buyer behaviour the hard way when she discovered that very few shoppers liked to be seen entering her Sixteen47 clothes shops for larger women. She and her partner have solved the problem by closing the shop and selling over the Internet instead.

Buyer behaviour was first mentioned in Unit 2 (page 110). It relates to the way we behave when we go shopping – where we go, what we buy and how often, how much we spend, how we use the things we buy and so on. It proves, if you ever had any doubt, that few people shop with the idea of buying what they need, as cheaply as possible, and going home again! Instead, our lifestyle, the views of our friends, current fashions, what else catches our eye, the mood we are in – and a dozen other things besides – all influence your buying behaviour. And the big stores know it!

When any store is designed the merchandisers prepare a map, called a **planogram**, which identifies where every product should be situated – shelf by shelf and aisle by aisle. The aim is to maximise selling space – and therefore profits. **Power aisles** are identified. These are aisles which lead customers to all parts of the store and which will contain major displays of merchandise. At the end of power aisles will be situated **power displays**, where goods sell very quickly indeed.

Store planograms are based on thousands of interviews with customers and hours of monitoring customer behaviour in stores. Researchers know, for example, that customers usually bear right as they enter a store; they know how they act when they are in a hurry and when they are not. They know they walk faster on wooden floors and more slowly on carpet. They know that the smell of newly baked bread or freshly brewed coffee makes them hungry.

Experts claim that planograms have enabled them to predict almost 95 per cent of purchasing behaviour – which is why stores all over the world look the same. One aim is always to maximise cross-selling and up-selling opportunities. **Cross-selling** is when we buy related goods because they are placed together (e.g. spaghetti, pasta sauce and pesto;) **up-selling** is when we are tempted to buy a more expensive product than we first intended because it catches our eye nearby or in a display.

Another aim of many superstores today is to stock more non-food items to persuade us they can satisfy all our needs – from clothing to medicines and DVDs to insurance. This saves us time – and helps them to increase their profits. Some of the other strategies they use to tempt us to spend more of our money under their roof are listed below.

- Differential pricing strategies to cover all needs and all pockets, e.g. Tesco Value, Tesco ordinary goods and Tesco Finest.
- Using a wide range of sales promotions all the time, with an emphasis on value for money, give-aways and 'not to be missed' special offers.
- Operating Loyalty schemes to reward returning customers.
- Offering a 'one-stop' shop where customers can buy anything from petrol, CDs and clothes to food, electrical equipment and toys.
- Making a feature out of new trends – from organic food to healthy options.
- Siting confectionery, tobacco and newspaper areas near the door (often on the right) so customers can call in just for these items. Sandwiches are often found in the same area.

Business matters

Sainsbury's store of the future

Sainsbury's at Hazel Grove is a 'futures' store in the retail world with an almost unique physical environment, such as no proper ceiling! At the entrance is a 24-hour vending machine selling 150 products and a separate Quick Shop, followed by a Welcome Wall with a huge plasma screen. At the left the normal aisle format has been changed for a more random design interrupted by fresh food counters. Vegetables are displayed in wooden baskets on rough straw and grouped together to give shoppers ideas of which vegetables complement each other. At the right hand side of the store there is a horizontal power aisle lined with weekly offers.

The store employs Ambassadors who act as greeters, trouble-shooters and general helpmates. For £5 they will take a customer's shopping list and do it. They are supervised by the customer experience manager who deals with customer complaints and is also responsible for seeing the Mystery Shopper score increase, and for adding the 'Wow' factor in customer service by always finding a solution that impresses the customer.

Managers constantly walk the aisles, judging displays to be red, amber or green. Red means a messy display with several gaps; amber is one that needs attention. On the next walkabout, these displays must have turned to 'green'.

You can find out more on the Sainsbury's website – a link is available at www.heinemann.co.uk/hotlinks (express code 1386P). See how Sainsbury's features its products and its displays. You can also find out more about mystery shoppers on the StudentZone at www.richerstudentzone.co.uk

- Putting fresh fruit and vegetables near the entrance and using natural materials (e.g. baskets) and natural lighting. This gets shoppers in a better mood at the start than seeing rows of tins!
- Putting popular lines just below eye level (often 'own brand' items!) and displaying popular lines in a block, vertically, on a shelf.
- Placing high demand items at the back of the store to tempt customers past higher-price impulse lines, such as cosmetics and toiletries.
- Widening the aisles where high profit items are to be found, to make browsing easier, and narrowing the aisles where low profit items are situated to keep people moving.
- Placing popular items near the door (to start customers buying early) and large/heavy goods near the exit (so that customers don't fill their baskets or trolleys too quickly).
- Having changing seasonal displays and moving these around to encourage impulse buying, e.g. barbecue fuel near the entrance in summer.
- Changing stock and merchandise displays to suit regional buying habits and ethnic diversity.

💬 Talking point

View 1: *Some very successful stores, such as IKEA, are constantly criticised for their customer service. This proves that customers will put up with anything if the price is right.*

View 2: *Stores that offer poor customer service only get away with it because there are no alternatives. Richer Sounds has proved that in a competitive market excellent customer services pays.*

With which viewpoint do you agree – and why?

Over to you!

1 Many local shops may now need to make any reasonable improvements that can improve access for disabled customers.

   a Investigate the Disability Rights Commission website – a link is available at www.heinemann.co.uk/hotlinks (express code 1386P). Take part in the shopping game 'The Little Shop of Horrors' – which helps you to understand the issues involved.

   b Download the leaflet 'Bringing the DDA to life for small shops' and note the key points.

   c As a group, discuss the local shops in your area and suggest reasonable improvements you think they should make.

2 Divide into four groups. Group A is planning to help design and plan a local convenience store. Group B is helping to do the same for a specialist card and gift shop in the local village. Group C is planning a cut-price clothing outlet for young

teens. Group D is planning and designing a man's fashion shop selling designer clothes.

Visit shops in your own area, check out websites such as Rapeed Design, Duram, Concept Display Systems and SDEA (follow the links on this site), and the websites of shopfitters in your own area for ideas. Present your ideas to the rest of the group and compare your results.

Links to the websites mentioned above are available at www.heinemann.co.uk/hotlinks (express code 1386P).

3 Divide into small groups. Each group should critically assess **one** of the superstores in your area to check how its layout, displays and offers are focused on influencing buyer behaviour.

Then check out **one** of your local convenience stores to see if it has copied these ideas or could do more to increase its own sales. Compare your findings as a group.

1. The following terms have been used in this section. Define each one.

   a. Pricing policy.
   b. Supply constraints.
   c. FMCGs.
   d. Consumer durables (SMCGs).
   e. Buyer behaviour.
   f. Power aisles.

2. You have been asked to suggest topics to include on a training course for new staff who will be working in a high street store selling computer game machines and computer games.

   Working in small groups, suggest **ten** items you would include with reasons.

   Then compare your ideas with other groups in your class and identify the best **ten** from the whole group.

This section covers

Effective sales practice

Note: it should be read in conjunction with information on the Richer Sounds StudentZone (www.richerstudentzone.co.uk) about selling to customers.

Learning how to sell effectively can take some time to master. It helps if you have had some experience of retailing in general, and at least realise the importance of a smart appearance and a friendly face! The next step is to gain some product knowledge, so that you feel confident about giving customers advice and information.

You are then ready to develop your selling techniques so that you learn how to find out about an individual customer's needs, preferences and concerns and match these to product availability. This way, you not only improve your chances of pleasing the customer with the exceptional service you are providing, but should actually find the whole experience far more enjoyable and satisfying yourself.

Each of the main steps in the selling process is explained below. The final stage is to gain practice in developing your own style and selling skills.

Meeting and greeting customers

Knowing how to approach and greet a customer is very important. Most customers dislike being pounced on as soon as they walk through the door. Equally, no-one likes being ignored when they want information or attention. A good compromise is to acknowledge customers on arrival – a smile is fine – and then leave them to look around. This gives them chance to look at your product lines and to check the range of goods you have on display. If you watch their body language you will be able to spot when they are interested in something they see, when they are not and when they need assistance, as they will normally look up to try to attract attention.

If you do approach a customer who is still browsing, don't creep up on them and make

them jump! Approach them from the front or side with a friendly enquiry, e.g. 'Hello – if there's anything you want to know, please ask.' If they refuse your help don't take it personally. Just move away, give them more space, but watch to see if they attract your attention later. If you look friendly, personable and positive then people will be more willing to approach you than if you appear over-eager or pushy.

Some customers may have special needs or requirements. Fundamentally, this should not change your basic approach, although additional sensitivity to obvious areas is advisable. Some useful guidelines are given overleaf.

Asking questions and listening to answers

Handling customer questions is the next stage of the selling process. This means knowing about your products and the features and benefits of different brands or versions you stock. It also means asking questions to find out what the customer wants and needs.

- **Price range**. A useful first step is to find out how much the customer is expecting to spend. This helps you to decide the range of goods in which they are most likely to be interested. *Never* ask 'How much can you afford?' The tactful version is 'What price range were you thinking of?'
- **Preferences**. Next find out if the customer has any preferences in terms of make or model. Some customers are particularly loyal to certain brand names – others have no specific preference.
- **Specific requirements**. The discussion should then focus on the customer's specific requirements in terms of features, product use,

size, colour or other details. Never ask questions one after the other, so that the customer ends up being interrogated! Instead, encourage the customer to talk to you about his or her needs – and link the information you are given to the range of products you have in stock.

Business brief

Customers with special needs

If you are treating all customers professionally and as individuals, then you will not find it difficult to offer appropriate attention to anyone with special needs.

- **Foreign visitors who can't speak English very well**. Don't expect them to understand signs and forms without explanation. Speak quite slowly using common English words. Don't use jargon or local expressions. Use short sentences. Listen carefully and repeat what they say to clarify you have understood them correctly. Ask for help if you are still struggling.
- **Customers who are deaf or hard of hearing.** Most people with a hearing impediment wear a hearing aid or lip-read. Help them by looking at them when you speak and *don't* shout. If someone is profoundly deaf then they will probably gesture this fact to you and may signal you to write down what you want to say. Give leaflets to explain the products they are interested in.
- **Customers who are blind or visually impaired**. Not all blind people carry white sticks or arrive with a guide dog. You may not be able to tell until you are close to someone that they have a visual problem. Remember that people with a visually impairment usually

rely more on their other senses – such as sound and touch. If you are explaining a product to someone who is visually impaired, expect them to want to touch it to check that it has clear buttons or knobs which they would be able to operate. Offer to complete a form for them and show them where to sign. Ideally the business will provide customer information in large print as an option – if not then suggest it.
- **Customers with mobility problems**. Customers may need to use a stick, crutches, or a wheelchair, because they have a long-term or temporary mobility problem. They will obviously find it easier if there is good access to the building. Make sure aisles remain clear and are wide enough, otherwise, under the Disability Discrimination Act, your employer could be breaking the law. Some organisations, such as Tesco, provide powered wheelchairs to customers. Remember the 'reach' of anyone in a wheelchair will be restricted, so help them to access and examine products and move out from behind any high counter or desk that would be a barrier. Be ready to open doors and offer anyone using a stick or on crutches the chance to sit down if they are struggling to walk or stand for any length of time.

Effective sales presentations and demonstrations

Business representatives frequently make a presentation about their products to interested buyers. Ideally this should be well-prepared, cover all the key points simply and clearly and be supported by informative sales materials such as leaflets and brochures. The sales person should be quite capable of answering related questions both during and at the end of the presentation.

In the retail trade an effective presentation – or demonstration – can be invaluable to show a customer how a product works and to highlight its different features. At Richer Sounds there are special demonstration rooms for hi-fi and audio/visual systems. These are considered essential because they are the only way in which customers can judge aspects like sound or picture quality for themselves. Similarly, garages expect customers to test drive a car they are interested in and furniture sellers are quite used to customers sitting down on their sofas and lying on their beds!

Listening skills

Most people are terrible listeners. They can't wait for the other person to finish speaking and often interrupt! Tips to improve your skills include the following:

- **Focus on the person** who is speaking.
- **'Switch back on'** if you feel your mind wandering.
- **Concentrate on the topic** – imagine you will be tested on what was said afterwards.
- **Make notes** if the information is complex or important.
- **Don't interrupt** – wait for a natural break in the conversation.
- **Repeat key facts back** in your own words to check your understanding.

If you are giving a presentation or demonstrating a product to a customer, especially if it is quite technical, then there are several golden rules.

- **Have a clear beginning, middle and end.** In other words, say what you are going to do, do it and then summarise what you've just done.
- **Speak clearly and at a reasonable pace.** Point out or demonstrate one feature at a time, preferably in a logical order.
- **Demonstrate one feature at a time** and explain it as you do it. Don't make anything look too complicated or the customer is likely to lose interest.
- **Avoid technical terms or jargon** that the customer won't understand.
- **Let the customer touch the product** and try out the operation for him/herself.
- **Summarise the main selling features** of the product at the end.
- **Answer any questions** the customer raises honestly. If you do not know the answer then say so – and refer the query to a more experienced colleague.

Supplying additional information

At this point some customers may want to complete a sale but others will still hesitate. This is normally because there is something worrying them. Sales experts call this 'a barrier to the sale'. It may be the price, size, colour, type of material, reputation of the manufacturer, a bad report from a friend or simply a question of timing, e.g. 'We won't be able to take delivery for two weeks because we're going on holiday.'

Some customers will voice any doubts or objections without prompting. Others will not. There are several strategies sales staff can use at this point.

- **Supply appropriate product information** that may overcome specific objections or hesitation, e.g. 'It's extremely economical to use' or 'It's fully weatherproof so you don't have to bring it inside when it rains.'
- **Check possible alternatives**, such as whether the customer would prefer to see different makes or models. Sometimes customers initially state they want to pay a low price but are then disappointed as these models do not include some of the features they wanted. Experienced sales staff see this as an opportunity to 'sell up', i.e. suggest a higher priced model which would meet their needs better.
- **Offer to prepare quotations or estimates** so that the customer can compare the prices/benefits of different makes and models. Put these in writing, so that the customer can take it home to study it later. Make sure, too, that the customer has all the relevant literature relating to each model *and* your business card and contact number.
- **Repeat delivery and cost information** that may help to clinch the sale. This is particularly important if the product is on special offer or if there are only a few in stock. The customer may prefer to make a decision rather than risk non-availability or a higher price at a later date.

The pace of interaction

Some customers prefer a brisk, no nonsense approach. They may arrive well-prepared and be rapid decision makers. Others may have less background knowledge, need technical information explaining more slowly or want 'thinking time' before they make a decision. In addition, some customers may have special needs you must consider, as you saw on page 342.

Some inexperienced sales staff feel that if they stop talking for one second or – worse – let the customer out of their sight then they will lose a sale. This is not only untrue but can actually have the opposite effect. Customers often hate feeling pressurised – and a couple may want to discuss their individual preferences in private, especially if they are close to making a decision. Experienced sales staff know when to talk, when to shut up and also know when to leave the customer alone. At Richer Sounds, sales staff are specifically trained to encourage customers to go away and

Business brief

Non-verbal communications

'Body language' refers to the way we communicate without speaking. It includes your facial expressions, posture, gestures and the way you use your eyes. If you are communicating with a customer it is useless 'talking the talk' if your non-verbal signals are saying that you are fed up, bored or completely uninterested.

Appropriate body language when you are selling includes:

- **Making eye contact** – otherwise you look shifty.
- **Standing tall** so that you look confident.
- **Smiling at people** so you look friendly and approachable.
- **Leaning forwards** towards the customer, to show you are interested and listening to people.
- **Using 'reflective gestures'** such as nodding or shaking your head, to show you are in agreement with the customer.
- **Turning your body** and feet towards the person you are talking to, not just your head.

think about it if they cannot make their minds up. More often than not, the customers return later! Therefore, when you are selling:

- Only talk to the customer when you have something useful to say and don't feel you must fill 'natural silences' when the customer is thinking.
- Never try to rush a customer into making a decision before he or she is ready.
- Be prepared to leave couples on their own to talk and agree their preferences.
- Be aware that many sales aren't agreed at the first attempt. Although some customers may not return, others will – and are more likely to do this if they were impressed with the service and professionalism they encountered the first time. Therefore, if you have done all you can, don't keep offering different alternatives. Instead suggest that the customer goes away and thinks about it.

Working towards closure

The time taken before a customer makes a decision often varies, but experienced staff recognise when this stage is reached – often when the customer starts asking questions about delivery, guarantees, after-sales service or credit facilities. This shows that the customer has stopped assessing the product and has started to weigh up other aspects of the purchase.

At this point, as the seller, you are involved with finalising the sale effectively. This may include:

- **Completing the sales administration**. Depending upon the transaction there may be forms to complete in relation to credit arrangements or product guarantee or warranties. Assuring the customer that this will not take long and is a simple process will help to remove any barriers relating to the paperwork.
- **Liaising with warehousing/distribution departments** about product availability or delivery and agreeing a convenient date and time with the customer. This will be the case if, for example:
  - The goods are too large to be taken by the customer (e.g. a freezer or three piece suite).

- The goods are being installed or fitted as part of the service (e.g. a dishwasher or carpet).
- The required model is out of stock but the customer is happy for it to be delivered at a later date.
- Your company offers a free delivery service as standard on all large items.

Closing the sale

The final stages of closing the sale include:

- **Processing the transaction** which may involve accepting credit cards, the use of the EPOS system, providing receipts, ensuring customers have relevant information on product use and future care/maintenance to facilitate any repeat purchases or after-sales service enquiries.
- **Checking you have obtained customer contact details**, such as name, address and telephone number. Depending upon the transaction, you may have obtained this information as part of the sales administration or delivery requirements. If not, it is still extremely useful as you can then send follow-up promotional literature. However, a word of warning! Some customers

Closing the sale includes accepting payment and taking customer contact details

actively dislike being constantly targeted by mailshots because they once visited a company. It is therefore both wise and courteous to *ask* a customer if you can add them to your mailing list – and point out the benefits, such as obtaining advance information on sale goods and special offers.

Business brief

Doing two things at once

It is difficult to concentrate on finalising a sale or explaining important product features to one customer if you have other customers waiting, unless you know how to cope in this situation.

- Acknowledge any waiting customers with a smile and a nod. This shows that you have noticed them and reassures them that they won't be ignored.
- If the customer you are serving hasn't yet made

a decision, use this as an opportunity to give them thinking time. Simply say 'Are you all right if I leave you for a moment to serve this customer?'
- If the second customer has a complex or lengthy query then you need help as you can't leave your first customer for very long. Ask the second customer to wait a moment whilst you get assistance from a colleague.
- Otherwise, serve the second customer and then go back to the first.

Over to you!

1 In Unit 2 you learned about ethical business (page 159). In retailing, ethical selling means selling fairly and honestly and genuinely trying to meet customer needs. That said, an experienced sales person will often make a sale where an inexperienced person would not. In each of the following examples decide whether you think that the sales technique is ethical or not and give reasons for your opinions.

   a A customer is undecided about which model to purchase because none seems to offer all the features she wants. The salesperson sees this as an opportunity to sell a higher priced item than the customer originally intended to buy.

   b A burglar alarm salesperson emphasises the importance of security by showing old people photographs of householders who have been seriously injured during robberies.

   c A salesperson is aware that a particular model is not stocked by his firm, even though it is the customer's first preference. He therefore explains the merits of alternative brands and models that are available.

   d A salesperson knows that a particular model is out of stock until next month, but the customer is insistent that this is the one he wants. The salesperson therefore finalises the sale agreeing delivery for next week.

   e A shoe salesperson is paid commission on all associated products sold. After selling a pair of expensive boots she recommends a range of cleaning products which will help to keep them in good condition.

   f A salesperson in a computer store closes a sale by explaining to a customer how he is hard up at the moment and desperately needs the commission.

   g A car salesman persuades a young couple to buy an expensive car on a credit agreement, even though he is aware they are short of money.

2 Problem customers include those who talk too much, those who won't talk at all and those who object to everything! Work in pairs to develop your skills by:

   a Identifying a product to sell, such as a particular mobile phone.

   b Each listing all the benefits and the objections to the purchase.

   c Trying to sell to each other.

The buyer can choose to be reticent or talkative and can raise objections.

The seller should practice using 'open questioning' to find out customer needs if he/she is reticent and listening skills if the customer is talkative. In addition the seller must try to overcome objections by converting negative responses to positive selling points.

Then reverse roles and choose a different product to sell.

3 Visit three retail stores in your area where customers ask sales staff for help, advice and information about products and observe sales staff in action. If you wish, you can ask for information about a product yourself.

Afterwards, award a maximum of five points for each of the following:

   a Appearance of staff.

   b Friendly manner.

   c Prompt (but not pushy) service.

   d Product knowledge.

   e Listening/questioning skills.

Compare your results with other members of your group and see which organisations score the best in your area.

Talking point

View 1: It's a good idea to rubbish the competition to make it clear to the customer that your store is the best around.

View 2: The worst thing you can do is to talk down your competitors – instead talk up your own product or service.

With which viewpoint do you agree – and why?

1 Explain the meaning of each of the following terms.
    a Non-verbal communications.
    b Pace of interaction with a customer.
    c Customer contact details.
    d Written quotations or estimates.

2 Select a small product of your own that you know well and like using. This could be your mobile phone, a camera, electric toothbrush, hair straighteners or similar device.
    a List the major features of the product that tempted you to buy it in the first place.
    b Prepare a brief presentation which highlights these features and includes a short demonstration of the product.

Work in pairs and make your presentation to a fellow student. Answer any questions that are raised and try to overcome any objections in a positive manner, bearing in mind all the main principles of selling that you have just read.

Then listen to your colleague's performance. Finally, assess each other and list strengths and weaknesses you have identified.

3 Access the Richer Sounds StudentZone at www.richerstudentzone.co.uk and find out more about the way sales staff are trained. Then list the **ten** most important aspects of their training which you think enable them to offer professional service to their customers.

This section covers

After-sales service

Note: it should be read in conjunction with relevant information on the Richer Sounds StudentZone at www.richerstudentzone.co.uk.

After-sales service relates to all the activities which take place after the sale has been finalised. It includes providing customer information, dealing with returned or faulty goods, handling complaints or other problems.

Retail businesses are frequently assessed on their after-sales service. Word rapidly gets round if customers find that sales staff have little interest in them once a sale has been completed. This is short-term thinking. If retailers want to make repeat sales then they need to meet their customers' needs not just when they are selling goods but on every occasion when the customer makes contact.

For this reason, all businesses need to consider:

- All the reasons why customers may want to contact them after a purchase has been made, for example:
  - To obtain information or advice.
  - To return an item.
  - To have something repaired.
  - To order a spare part.
  - To make a complaint.
  - To request information about other goods.
- How such contacts will be handled.
- What use can be made of the information which is obtained.

Information and advice

Customers may contact a seller after purchase for information or advice. This is particularly the case if they have bought something which is complicated to operate, which needs connecting to other items or must be assembled by the customer.

Any business should be able to answer basic enquiries relating to the products it sells without any hesitation. If the query is complex, relates to technical fault finding and repair or is otherwise outside the scope of the person receiving the enquiry then it should be referred promptly to someone who can provide specialist help, such as a member of the technical staff.

Business brief

Dealer networks

Many consumer durables, such as washing machines, cookers and fridges are sold with information booklets and leaflets relating to nationwide or even international dealer networks relating to that product. These give a list of regional addresses and telephone numbers for customers to contact.

Trained staff who receive the call can give advice on technical queries, supply spare parts or arrange for repairs to be undertaken. If the product is not under guarantee or warranty then they will provide a quotation for the repair.

An example of a large network is BSH Appliance Care, based in Milton Keynes, which services Bosch, Siemens, Gaggenau and Neff products throughout the UK. In 2003 it won an award for providing outstanding service. Check out its website to find out more about the service it offers and the feedback it obtained from customers to help it to win this award, a link is available at www.heinemann.co.uk/hotlinks (express code 1386P).

Preparation for returns

Customers return goods for many reasons.

- They may regret the purchase, even though there is nothing wrong with the item.
- They may have been given the item as a present and want to exchange it.

- The colour, size or another feature may be wrong.
- The goods may be faulty or not 'as described'.

Returns and exchange policies were first discussed on page 332. All staff working in sales, customer services and dealing with after-sales service enquiries must be familiar with the policy that applies in their organisation.

If an organisation provides goods that are installed in a customer's home then it is usual to arrange for someone to make a visit before discussing alternatives such as a repair or compensation.

Dealing with complaints

Virtually all organisations have procedures which all staff must follow when they are dealing with customer complaints. The aim of these is to ensure that:

- All complaints are taken seriously. This is important as a dissatisfied customer may shop elsewhere in future – and tell their friends to do the same!
- All staff know the correct way to deal with a customer complaint – whether this is over a minor matter or more serious.
- All customers who are making a complaint receive a prompt response.
- All complaints are handled fairly and in the same way.
- All complaints are treated confidentially.
- All serious complaints are investigated properly by the right person.
- All complaints, and the action taken, are logged so that recurring areas of concern can be remedied and the service improved.

Most organisations encourage their staff to deal with minor matters as they occur and, wherever possible, to use their own initiative to solve the

Dealing with customer complaints

Know the correct procedure to follow in your organisation. If there is no specified procedure, the following may help.

- Listen carefully. Don't 'second guess' what the customer is going to say and never interrupt someone who is making a complaint.
- Look interested and concerned. Focus on the customer and solving the problem.
- Listen carefully. Make notes if the matter is complicated.
- Never, ever, contradict a customer by saying 'you must be mistaken' or 'I think you're confused' as this will make the situation worse.
- Apologise – not because you are admitting blame personally but because of the inconvenience the customer has been caused.
- If there is a sensible explanation for a temporary problem then explain this to the customer.
- Don't make any judgements or admit your company (or a colleague) must have been at fault. Until you know all the details you can't tell who is right or wrong.
- Find out what action the customer wants you to take. Some people just feel better for talking about a problem! In this case, if you assure them you have taken their complaint seriously and will pass it on, this may be enough.
- Never commit yourself or a colleague to a specific course of action without checking with a supervisor or manager.
- If you can put the problem right immediately, without overstepping your authority, then do so.
- Record the complaint in the appropriate log or book so that it can be noted and monitored by managers.
- If a customer is very angry and you feel you can't cope then get help immediately. No matter what the problem is, no member of staff should be expected to tolerate insults or threats in any situation.

problem quickly. More serious matters should always be referred to someone in authority to prevent the situation becoming worse.

An example of a procedure for dealing with customer complaints is shown below.

Repairs and replacements parts

Requests for repairs and replacements parts may be handled by a dealer network (see page 348) or the supplier of the goods. In some cases the manufacturer will operate a repair service for products still under guarantee. The options available are told to the customer at the time of purchase.

- Repairs which are carried out in the customer's home, such as to a washing machine, cooker or burglar alarm are normally undertaken by qualified service engineers. The customer makes contact with the dealer network or supplier and agrees a time for the engineer to visit the premises and carry out the repair. Engineers normally carry spare parts with

Repairs of large or fixed household appliances are normally done in the customer's home

them so that routine problems can be rectified in one visit.

- Portable goods, such as a DVD player, computer games machine, digital camera or watch will normally be returned to the shop where they were bought, especially if they are still under guarantee or warranty. The shop will return the item to the manufacturer on behalf of the customer unless it operates a repair service itself. Richer Sounds has its own repairs and servicing department so that returned goods can be dealt with quickly and effectively without the customer having to wait too long.
- In some cases, customers can opt for a home repair service when they purchase a large item such as a computer. There is an extra charge for this but it is often worthwhile, especially when the goods have been bought online (so would need to be returned by post) or when an IT system is used in a small business where downtime could be disastrous.
- Today many smaller consumer durables, such as jug kettles and toasters are not repairable quite simply because the cost of the repair

would be greater than replacing the item. Many environmentalists criticise this policy, arguing that it contributes to our 'use and throw away' society. Retailers are unlikely to share this view, as they would prefer to make repeat sales than undertake repairs. This situation could change in the future, however, if suppliers and manufacturers become responsible for scrapping and disposing all defunct household goods!

- Customers can also obtain replacement parts from a dealer network or the manufacturer. If the goods are new then the only replacements the customer is allowed to fit, without

Business brief

Guarantees and warranties

Most electrical and household goods are sold with one- or two-year guarantees to cover the buyer against any repairs or replacement parts which are needed during this time. Many stores offer customers the opportunity to purchase an extended warranty, at the time of sale, to lengthen their cover for two or three years – or even longer.

The market for extended warranties is very valuable – and worth about £900 million a year to retailers. However, it has often been criticised. Discount offers are often conditional on the customer buying the retailer's own warranty. In addition, according to the Consumers' Association, most warranties are not worth the money that customers pay for them. With most goods it is cheaper to pay for repairs as and when they are needed.

In 2003 the Competition Commission investigated the market for warranties on behalf of the Office of Fair Trading. Many people thought that, as a result, retailers would be banned from selling extended warranties. Instead, however, the government wants greater consumer protection in this area, including the right for customers to cancel at any time and obtain a proportion of their money back. It has also advised customers to shop around for the best offers. The OFT has promised to review the market in 2005 to see if things have improved.

invalidating the guarantee, are external or detachable items such as knobs or plastic covers. If the goods are not under guarantee or warranty then, if a repair is required, a customer with the necessary technical knowledge could order any parts, such as a new motor or mechanism, to carry out the repair themselves.

Recognising opportunities for repeat purchases

In many organisations staff are trained to use all customer contact as an opportunity to make repeat purchases. For example:

- A customer deposits a large cheque into their current account at the bank – and the bank teller promptly recommends that the customer opens a savings investment account which would be more suitable.
- An engineer repairing a washing machine comments that it would be much cheaper to buy a new model than to keep paying warranty payments on the existing machine.
- The sales person dealing with a customer who has called in to collect a repaired DVD player talks about the features available as standard on later models.
- The sales person dealing with the customer who wants a new computer printer talks about the benefits of newer PCs with Bluetooth technology and paper-thin screens.

In some cases this is useful, particularly if the customer is considering a purchase anyway. But sales people have to be careful. At times it can be annoying and even unethical. British Gas engineers were criticised for their policy of recommending replacement boilers on service visits because this was seriously worrying some customers who were then concerned about the safety of their existing appliances.

Richer Sounds is also against the idea that all customer contact should be seen as a sales opportunity. A few days after purchase, sales staff make Customer Happy Calls to check that buyers are quite satisfied with the goods they have bought. On these occasions sales assistants are specifically trained *not* to use this as a sales opportunity because this is not the purpose of that particular contact.

Many businesses, therefore, prefer to have a strategy to try to ensure repeat purchases at the time of sale. Large stores often operate loyalty schemes, such as Boots, Bhs or Tesco. This is not just the preserve of large companies. One small independent shoe chain, Charles Clinkard, stamps a card when customers buy their first pair of shoes. Customers then receive a stamp for each subsequent purchase and, if they achieve six in a year, are allowed up to 50 per cent discount off the seventh pair.

To encourage repeat purchases, many retailers send regular mailshots to customers on their mailing list, providing them with updates of new products and sale previews. Businesses that sell online can send customers regular email updates, providing the customer has agreed to this.

Many businesses monitor purchasing activity by customers who have bought from them previously, including those who have registered online. If the customer fails to place an order for some time the retailer will send them a voucher or coupon which can be used to buy goods in store, by post or online to tempt them to place an order.

Recognising opportunities for positive or negative recommendations and publicity

There are various ways in which businesses can ask for recommendations. There are two main reasons for doing this. Positive recommendations can often be used as free publicity. Negative recommendations focus attention on areas of the service which should be improved.

- Customers can be offered a reward for recommending the business to a friend who then goes on to make a purchase. Rewards are often in the form of vouchers or a discount on future purchases.
- Customers can be sent (or given) a survey to complete that summarises their experience. This method is often used by service organisations, especially when branch or local staff are responsible for providing the service

but the head office wishes to obtain feedback, for example:

- – Holiday companies, who issue these to customers on the flight home.
- – Opticians, who send them out following a customer's eye examination and the subsequent purchase of glasses or contact lenses.
- – Funeral directors, who send them out following a funeral to check that the family was satisfied with all the arrangements made locally and the quality of service and support provided.
- Many organisations encourage customers to report problems and to make suggestions. Some stores, such as Tesco, also have suggestion boxes so that customers who want to suggest a good idea or think something could be improved can write down their views. All these suggestions are normally acknowledged unless the customer states than no reply is necessary.
- Many online sites encourage feedback by asking the customer to complete a short pop-up survey or encouraging email feedback. Virgin Wines emails registered customers who look at the site, but then leave it without making a purchase, with a 'where did we go wrong?' email.
- In some organisations, sales staff telephone customers who have cancelled a contract or agreement, or who have returned goods or haven't made a purchase for some time to check the reason. They will note areas of satisfaction/dissatisfaction and may offer the customer a financial incentive to stay with the company or make a purchase.
- Richer Sounds has quite a unique method of obtaining customer feedback, which you can check out on the StudentZone at www.richerstudentzone.co.uk

If you complete a survey form then you will normally read in the small print at the bottom that the business refers the right to reproduce any positive comments you give. This is so that they can be used for publicity as testimonials. If you check the Heinemann website, you will see that online feedback is requested on any books as this can then help other buyers. Amazon operates a similar system – as do many other shopping websites.

Customer recommendations can also be used in press advertising. Sometimes celebrities also endorse products but this isn't always because they use or like them. It is more likely to be because they are paid to do so!

Identifying particular sources of customer dissatisfaction

Specific areas of customer dissatisfaction can be identified from:

- Complaints logs and records.
- Survey results.
- Listening to staff feedback.

Another option is for the business to have a focus group or customer panel to give feedback on general issues (see page 117).

Identifying these sources does not always mean that action can be taken. As a student there may be several aspects of your course or college that you do not like, such as the location of the library, your timetable on a Monday morning and the food in the refectory. However, there is a limit to the number of things that can be changed to suit you – and much will also depend upon the opinions of everyone else. If all the students are complaining about refectory food it is far more likely that action will be taken than if you are on your own.

Complaints and comments from dissatisfied customers are divided into two groups – those which were preventable and those which were not. For example, busy traffic nearby and difficulty parking may be a source of customer dissatisfaction but is outside the control of the business. If Richer Sounds spent money buying car parking space for its customers in some areas then it would have to increase the price of its products to finance this – which would annoy other customers. So Richer Sounds classified parking as a 'non-preventable' problem.

This means that it can concentrate its efforts on any issues of customer dissatisfaction where action can be taken to make things better. Continually improving is one of Richer Sounds' main aims and this is only done through staff vigilance and suggestions and by taking note of continuous feedback from customers.

View 1: *Some people are just born moaners and don't deserve to have their complaints taken seriously.*

View 2: *Encouraging people to complain can be useful as it can give staff good ideas for making improvements.*

With which viewpoint do you agree – and why?

Over to you!

1 a A store wants to log all customer complaints to check if there are any common problems that should be addressed. What type of information do you think should be collected and how should it be analysed?

b Suggest **two** reasons why returned goods should always be logged in a record.

2 Appearing professional and efficient to a customer isn't always easy. Suggest how you would respond in each of the following situations to the customer and, where appropriate, the action you would take as a result.

a A customer who has called twice for an item which is being repaired. It was due back a week ago.

b A customer who wants to exchange an item because she has changed her mind. The item is in perfect condition and she bought it using her credit card. Your company policy is to credit her card in that situation but she says she hasn't got it with her and asks for a cash refund.

c A regular customer mentions to you that he doesn't like being served by Simon, one of your colleagues, because he's never very friendly. You don't like Simon very much and also think he's quite snooty to customers.

d A customer rings to complain that although she has twice asked for a catalogue to be sent to her home, nothing has arrived.

e A customer complains that he has called in especially because he was told that the product he wanted would be in stock today. When you check the list you find it hasn't been delivered.

7.4 Section review

1 Explain the meaning of each of the following terms:

a Dealer network.
b Complaints procedure.
c After-sales service.
d Extended warranty.

2 As a group, suggest the main features of the after-sales service you would expect to find in each of the following types of organisation

a A large garden centre.
b A furniture store.
c A computer supplier.
d A designer clothes shop.
e A mail order company.

Unit 8 Business online

This specialist unit looks at different types of online business activity. When businesses consider whether or not to have an online presence they need to decide the extent to which this would help it to achieve its aims and objectives.

In this unit you will learn about the advantages and disadvantages of doing business online, the different types of online presence that businesses can choose and the factors that influence their decisions.

8.1 Online business activity

This section covers

The range of online business activities

The sectors of business which operate online

The levels and types of online presence

Features of an online business operation

The range of online business activities

If you use the Internet regularly, then you may already have some idea of the vast number of organisations and individuals who have an online presence. According to Google, in 2004 it was monitoring data from over 4.8 billion websites. Some are run by private businesses, others by governments, pressure groups, charities and individuals. They range from the very basic – perhaps just a web page or two – to the extremely sophisticated.

The tendency for so many businesses to want to do business online today isn't surprising. According to Neilsen/NetRatings, the total number of people actively using the Internet in January 2004 was 294.5 million – out of an estimated 447.9 million global users. Predictions are that, before long, nearly 1 in 10 of the global population will be online.

This first section looks at some of the main activities that are carried out by online businesses and the key features of their operations.

Business matters

Traditionally, all access to the Internet was through a PC with browser software, such as Microsoft Internet Explorer. Many Internet users are now starting to acquire multiple methods of access – their PC at home and at work; a palmtop or laptop when they are travelling; their 3G/WAP phone: a PDA (personal organiser) or smart phone (a PDA and WAP phone combined). In the home, interactive digital televisions (iTV) and digital radios are becoming more popular.

All these methods are often termed **new media** – in contrast with the 'old media' of newspapers, magazines, posters and analogue television and radio.

They increase the range of opportunities for businesses to contact their customers over the Internet, particularly with customised information such as sports news, travel updates, special offers and sales promotions.

Online terminology (1)

Although this unit concentrates on the business aspects of being online, it is useful to understand some of the basic terms involved. To start, check you understand each of the following definitions:

- **Browser** – the software that allows you to use the Internet, e.g. Microsoft Explorer or Netscape. Each browser displays pages slightly differently so website designers must take this into account when they design a website.
- **HTTP** (HyperText Transfer Protocol) – this is the format of the web and shows at the start of every address when a browser is looking at a webpage, i.e. http://
- **URL** (Uniform Resource Locator) – another name for the website address, e.g. www.richerstudentzone.co.uk

- **IP address** (Internet Protocol address) – the unique numeric address assigned to every computer connected to the Internet, e.g. 108.390.223.4. Because people couldn't possibly remember these, domain names were born.
- **Domain name** – the registered website address which is assigned to a numerical IP address. The Domain Name Service system converts these into IP addresses. Businesses should have a simple, distinctive domain name so that customers can remember them easily (e.g. lastminute.com or Amazon.com) or use their company name (e.g. Tesco.com).
- **ISP** (Internet Service Provider) – a company that provides its customers with Internet access for a fee (e.g. AOL or Wanadoo).

Online auctions

Auctions are an historic way of buying and selling goods. The most common method is for a seller to describe the item being sold, buyers bid a price to buy it and the highest bidder obtains the goods. The seller can choose not to sell below a certain price by setting a reserve price. If all the bids are below the reserve price then the item is withdrawn from sale.

These type of auctions are held in sale rooms all over the world. Some are very famous, such as

Sotheby's and Christie's. The buyers either need to attend in person, bid over the telephone or leave their bid with the auction house. On the Internet the system is slightly different, because buyers can log on to the site any day and any time. There is therefore normally a time limit set over which bids are accepted, illustrated by a countdown timer for each item on the site.

The Californian auction site eBay is the most well-known, with a market share of over 85 per cent. It was formed by computer programmer Pierre Omidyar in 1995 and is estimated to have around 10 million items for sale at any one time and 42 million registered users worldwide with at least one million in the UK. The company makes its money by taking a cut of every transaction that takes place on the site and made over $250 million in profits in 2002–2003.

eBay's success has spawned many rivals – such as QXL and eBid, and associated businesses who make money through their links to auction sites. These include

Traditional auctions are now having to compete with online auctions, which are now becoming more and more popular

affiliated sites – who advertise the auction site and get a cut every time someone 'clicks through' from them – and e-booksellers advising users how to bid, how to buy and how to make a profit on auction sites.

eBay is used by both businesses and private individuals. Other auction sites are only used by businesses and are restricted to certain participants, such as registered or approved trade members. They may use a different system where the buyer asks suppliers to compete for a contract e.g. to supply 100,000 compost bins. Normally the lowest bid will be accepted, although other factors such as quality and delivery may be relevant. Alternatively, suppliers of perishable goods such as fruit or flowers may hold a Dutch auction. In this situation the price is lowered until someone bids, at which point the item is sold. Details of how different types of online auction work are shown in Figure 8.1. (See also e-procurement on page 360.) Specialist software is available for those who regularly buy and sell at auction, to monitor and track bids in real time.

Selling goods at online auction

- Access to customers worldwide.
- Disposal of overstocked items rapidly and cheaply.
- Sales completed quickly and efficiently.
- Price set by the market and linked to demand and desirability.
- Reduce marketing, advertising and selling costs.

Buying goods at online auction

- Access to suppliers worldwide.
- Materials and equipment can be bought from a wide range of sources.
- Saves time looking for and negotiating with suppliers.
- Can result in large cost savings.
- Can buy second-hand items cheaply.

Figure 8.2 *Advantages of auction sites to businesses*

If you know someone who has bought or sold something on eBay or another auction site they will tell you how easy it is to register. There are also clear help screens to aid new users. Individuals use these sites to sell things they don't want any more and to try and buy goods at bargain prices. For businesses there are several additional advantages which are shown in Figure 8.2.

Banking online

Virtually all the high street banks now offer both private and business customers the option to bank online. The customer first has to register for online banking and is allocated a unique ID and password which must be keyed in to gain access to a secure area on the bank's website. In this area the customer can:

- Access all bank accounts held to see balances and recent transactions.
- Print out statements and other records.
- Transfer money between accounts, pay bills and even apply for a loan.

Figure 8.1 *Different types of online auctions*

Customers can do this at any time of the day or night, 7 days a week, and from any Internet linked location in the world. Without going anywhere near the bank, an online customer can carry out almost every type of bank transaction apart from physically paying in or withdrawing money.

Many banks offer associated online services including:

- Online savings accounts with higher levels of interest than standard accounts, because these are cheaper for the bank to operate.
- Online share buying and selling through the bank's links with share dealers.
- FastPay where money can be transferred by SMS or email to another person or business or used to pay for goods bought on the net when the site shows a FastPay button. More details about this are available on the FastPay website, a link is available at www.heinemann.co.uk/hotlinks (express code 1386P).
- Advice on many different aspects of starting and running a business, completing a tax return, paying wages, compiling a business plan and so on.

Business matters

Since 2003 many of the main high street banks have been targeted by phishers. **Phishing** (the word comes from a hacker's derivation of fishing) is the name for Internet scams when fraudsters send customers an email that looks like it comes from an authentic bank, credit card company or auction site. It may even direct the customer to a 'spoof' site, set up to look identical to the real one (see also page 393). The email normally gives some reason for the customer to have to enter and confirm their account or credit card details. If the customer believes the message, clicks on the link and types in the details, the phishers have all the information they need to empty the bank account.

All online banks now feature warnings on their sites. Even more importantly, Internet users are recommended not to access a financial site through an email link or make a payment through a link, but instead type in the URL themselves into the address line in the web browser.

Business brief

Financial security online

A critical aspect of business online is protection from financial fraud regardless of whether you are buying, selling or banking. Businesses are very aware that a major problem could lead to a collapse in user confidence – and a reduction in trading. For that reason they are very keen to ensure there are good security systems in place.

When you access a secure part of a site there are two indications. Firstly, you will see a locked padlock at the bottom right of your browser window. Second, the first part of the address line will change from http:// to https://. This means that any data you now send is encrypted (put into code). You will also find extra safeguards. For example, the full number of a credit card does not appear on any printed documents. On banking sites, if there was unauthorised access to a customer's account online, then the bank would have to reimburse the customer.

All these precautions, of course, cannot protect someone who buys in an auction and, after paying the money, fails to receive the goods. To help to prevent this problem – particularly for expensive goods – many auction sites offer protection systems. eBay employs 800 people to fight fraud and features on the site include a feedback system, where buyers and sellers rate each other, and money often transfers via a **PayPal system** for a small fee. In this case, no financial details are revealed to either party. In addition, eBay offers a limited insurance fund and will mediate between buyer and seller if there is a problem. Some auction sites use the **escrow system**. In this case the buyer pays a third party who holds the money securely until the goods have been received, and then releases it to the seller. This protects both parties and is particularly important if the transaction involves an item of value.

Internet chatrooms

Chatrooms, as you probably know, are Internet areas where people can communicate with one another in real-time. Many chatrooms are run by major ISPs – although the one operated by MSN was withdrawn in September 2003 after worries about children being 'groomed' on the Internet by paedophiles.

Some chatrooms are safer than others because they require users to register by providing their email address and also include safety features, such as 'ignore' buttons. The best ones are moderated by the presence of an adult. On others software is installed which alerts a moderator to the use of inappropriate or abusive language. Any user who breaks the rules is warned and can be barred from the chatroom. All it takes, however, is a change of email address to obtain a new identity and access can be resumed again. This is one reason why many people are still very wary about youngsters using chatrooms.

Chatrooms are not the only way of communicating over the Internet, however. Other alternatives include:

- **Email**. Anyone with Internet access and email software installed is likely to be given their own email address as part of the Internet package provided by their ISP. Alternatively – or in addition – they can sign up for an address from Hotmail or one of its competitors, e.g. Google (Gmail) or Yahoo!, and can then access their mail from any computer.
- **Instant messaging (IM)**. There are several IM programs available, such as MSN Messenger. Users install the IM program on their computer and list the name and email address of the contacts they want to talk to. Each contact must then agree to this before being activated on the user's IM list. The user can check which contacts are online at the same time and can then decide whether to start up a conversation or respond to any instant messages received. The user can also change his or her status to 'away' or 'busy' to avoid interruptions.
- **Message boards or message groups**. Users can post messages on a message board for other

people to read. As an example, the BBC features message boards for different radio and television programmes. Listeners and viewers can read these and add their own comments. This can provide valuable feedback for programme makers. Both Amazon and Heinemann ask shoppers to comment on books they have bought and post these on their websites. These are a form of message board as they communicate one reader's views to others.

- **Forums** are online discussion groups who chat about topics in which they have a common interest – from football teams or gardening to solving IT problems. In a forum, users read messages and post replies. More than one topic may be discussed and these are identified by 'threads' on a summary board. Users can select which threads (or topics) they are interested in and click to read the discussion and contribute to it. In business many forums are set up for professional collaboration between people working at a distance. They can be used to provide help and support for users as well as guidance and comments on communal projects.
- **Chatbuttons** on websites. The user clicks on the button to ask a query or discuss a purchase with the seller. The advantage is that visitors to the site can resolve queries quickly, the disadvantage is that someone has to monitor the site all the time – and may struggle to end some chats quickly. For these reason, most sites prefer to have a 'phone me button' or 'email contact button' instead.

Gambling online

A bit of fun – or a serious problem? Whatever your views, the number of gambling sites on the Internet has increased considerably in the last few years. You can play Lotto online, bet on a racehorse, enter an online casino, try your hand at poker or blackjack – all from the comfort of your computer. This, of course, assumes that you are over 18 and can afford to pay for your potential losses!

From a business perspective, firms want a share of the £700 billion spent around the world on gambling every year – over £40 billion in the UK

Gamblers can lose money both online and offline

alone. This is why many household names such as Littlewoods advertise their betting shops and casinos on the Internet as well as more familiar names like William Hill the bookmaker. This increases their income streams by attracting a different type of customer. The other benefit, of course, is that local or national gambling regulations do not apply to Internet firms, who can set up in a country without strict laws and then market their sites on a worldwide basis.

According to KPMG Consulting, the Internet gambling market is estimated to be worth £5 billion by 2006. In addition, gambling by iTV and mobile phone will increase the market by a further £5 billion as it will enable people to gamble on sports events as they are watching or listening either at home or when they are travelling.

The growth of iTV and entertainment websites are creating new types of gambling opportunities, such as playing Who Wants to be a Millionaire online, and betting on reality shows such as 'Pop Idol' or 'I'm a Celebrity... get me out of here'.

In Britain, the law on gambling is currently under review and is likely to result in an increase in the number of 'bricks and mortar' casinos. Whether this will make life easier – or more difficult – for online gambling operators in the UK is not yet clear. What appears to be clear is that, given the popularity of Lotto, scratchcards and reality TV shows, the British public are likely to welcome new 'soft-edged' gambling opportunities providing

these are promoted responsibly to adult audiences. You can find out more about the government's plans on the Office of the Deputy Prime Minister's website, a link is available at www.heinemann.co.uk/hotlinks (express code 1386P).

Job searches

Traditionally if you wanted a new job – or a first job – you would buy a newspaper, visit the Jobcentre or a local employment agency. Today you can look online at some of the many websites featuring job vacancies. Some specialise in certain types of industries and careers – from the health service to catering such as NHS Careers and Caterer.com. Others are aimed at different levels, such as graduates at Milkround Online. There are also more general sites with a range of jobs in different fields, such as totaljobs.com and fish4jobs. Links to the job websites mentioned above are available at www.heinemann.co.uk/hotlinks (express code 1386P).

Job sites are run by agencies that advertise vacancies on behalf of employers. For an additional fee they will also undertake other tasks, such as checking applications and advising on a shortlist.

Job hunters can search for jobs in a variety of ways – e.g. by job title, by type (permanent/temporary or full/part time), by location or by salary. They can email their CV in response to online advertisements and can also register to receive email alerts when suitable jobs come up. This obviously has many benefits. It is quicker than searching through printed advertisements in newspapers and journals and the online sites cover a broader geographical area than local papers. Job hunters can register their interest immediately online which has advantages both for them and for potential employers.

Last minute services

The most well-known 'last minute' site is lastminute.com – formed by Brent Hoberman and Martha Lane Fox in October 1998 and floated as a public company in 2000. Its bumpy road into profits has been covered in detail in every newspaper, mainly because it was the first dotcom site to use the new 'last minute' business model.

The idea is simple. The site sells flights, holidays, weekend breaks, theatre tickets and gifts online. What is different is that the content is geared for people who want to do things at the last minute – either on impulse or because they have been too busy beforehand. It is also ideal for people who are looking for a bargain.

The clever part is that suppliers can use the site to sell-off surplus stocks at a discount at the last minute – which means that prices for buyers are competitive. For example, a London hotel with spare rooms next weekend can contact lastminute.com with its vacancies. These are offered cheaply because the hotel would prefer to receive some income rather than none. Someone wanting to make a last minute reservation in London can check out the site and make the booking online. Lastminute.com then receives a cut for its part in the process.

The last minute 'model' is also used successfully by many other operators, particularly in the field of travel, accommodation and holidays.

Business brief

Online terminology (2)

You will often see the following terms used to describe the type of business or the way it trades over the Internet:

B2B = business to business trading, e.g. Heinz to Tesco.

B2C = business to consumer trading, e.g. Tesco to you.

C2C = consumer to consumers, i.e. one individual dealing with another such as a private buyer and seller on eBay.

Bricks and mortar = a business which sells only from a traditional retail store, e.g. your corner shop.

Clicks and mortar = a business which sells from a traditional store *plus* a website, e.g. Debenhams, Next or Richer Sounds.

Dotcom company or virtual business = a business which only operates online, e.g. lastminute.com or eBay.

Procurement and sourcing

Businesses purchase their supplies in three stages, regardless of whether they are buying online or not.

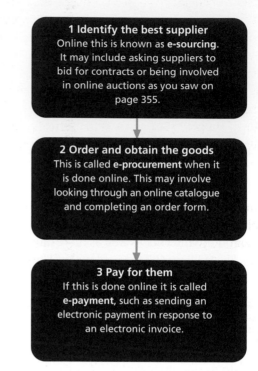

1 Identify the best supplier
Online this is known as **e-sourcing**. It may include asking suppliers to bid for contracts or being involved in online auctions as you saw on page 355.

2 Order and obtain the goods
This is called **e-procurement** when it is done online. This may involve looking through an online catalogue and completing an order form.

3 Pay for them
If this is done online it is called **e-payment**, such as sending an electronic payment in response to an electronic invoice.

Figure 8.3 *Stages in e-procurement*

A large organisation, buying thousands of items a week, will have specialist software installed which controls, records and monitors every transaction. A small business can buy online by means of email and online banking. Another alternative is for businesses to join a buying group or take part in an **electronic marketplace** where buyers and sellers come together online. As an example, Covisint links buyers and sellers of car supplies and was formed by a group of manufacturers including Ford, General Motors and Renault-Nissan – a link to the Covisint website is available at www.heinemann.co.uk/hotlinks (express code 1386P).

For a large company, such as Ford or British Aerospace, the amount of time and money saved by buying online can be huge, as you will see on page 381. Because of the savings that can be gained the Government has told all Local Authorities that they, too, must be capable of buying all their requirements online by 2005.

Product supply

In December 2003, British consumers spent over £2.5 billion Christmas shopping on the Internet – an increase of 70 per cent from the previous year. 16 million people bought a wide range of electrical consumer goods, including digital cameras, mobile phones and DVD players, as well as perfume, beer, wine and spirits online. IMRG, the leading UK online business industry association, put this growth down to people's increased confidence in buying online and their wish to escape from the hassle of shopping in crowded stores. Instead they preferred to shop online at quiet times of their own choosing and have their presents delivered to the door – often gift-wrapped.

Businesses who responded to the challenge, and supplied the products customers wanted, such as Amazon, Argos, John Lewis and Tesco, saw their sales soar. Those who were less prepared lost

For the buyer

- Shopping around usually results in cheaper prices.
- Goods can be sourced 24/7.
- Orders can be tracked online.
- Less paperwork.
- Only authorised staff (with appropriate ID/password) can use the system.
- Fewer errors when producing orders.
- Software can monitor orders against budgets.
- Goods can be sourced/obtained more quickly, therefore fewer stocks required.

For the seller

- Less sales paperwork.
- Faster processing of orders.
- Wider customer network.
- Can compete with larger suppliers.
- Improved payments so fewer cash flow problems.
- Orders can be received 24/7.
- Can adjust prices/notify buyers of change more quickly.
- Fewer staff needed to process sales so costs reduced.

Figure 8.4 *Advantages of e-procurement*

business. IMRG think the growth trend will tempt more stores online before Christmas 2004, when they estimate online sales will double – and continue to do so until they amount to 30 per cent of all shopping in the UK. By then it will be even more important for online businesses to provide features which give customers a positive buying experience. You can read more about this in Section 8.2, and a link to the IMRG website is available at www.heinemann.co.uk/hotlinks (express code 1386P).

It isn't only private consumers who buy online, of course. As you saw under e-procurement, above, businesses also buy from B2B product suppliers – from car parts to office stationery or hairdressing supplies. The advantages of B2B trading online for both buyers and sellers are summarised in Figure 8.4.

Research

The Internet is an excellent way of finding out information. In fact, it was originally invented because nuclear physicists wanted to share their research data. In some ways this tradition has continued because some high level research studies only appear on the Internet, such as those at Jitta, an online journal. If you want to find out more, a link to the Jitta website is available at www.heinemann.co.uk/hotlinks (express code 1386P). The Internet has certainly revolutionised the way in which research is carried out – in schools, colleges, universities and in business. So much so that some universities are installing software that routinely scans student assignments to check if any part of it has been copied in chunks from an online source!

The only difficulty with researching on the Internet can be finding what you need. Basic fact finding can normally be started through a good search engine, such as Google, Yahoo! or HotBot – and tips on how to use Google were given at the start of this book on page vi. If you want to know more about alternative search engines and how to use them, the Search Engine Watch website has more information. If you are doing any type of academic research on a particular subject, then a good place to start is the

NoodleTools website which includes several useful, free features for students. Links to Search Engine Watch and NoodleTools are available at www.heinemann.co.uk/hotlinks (express code 1386P).

If you are looking for business information then you can find current news on the sites for all daily newspapers – as well as the BBC and Ananova. If you are looking to find information on a particular website, Alexa can help. Alexa gives the popularity of different websites and alternative sites people visit. For example, if you checked out Richer Sounds on Alexa, it would tell you the ranking for that site and also list the other (similar) sites people visited as well as Richer Sounds. If you want to find out more, links to Ananova and Alexa are available at www.heinemann.co.uk/hotlinks (express code 1386P).

Let's assume, for example, that you work for a company that is considering starting to sell online. You didn't know about the IMRG report mentioned on page 361, yet you have been asked to research about the growth of the Internet and how much people are buying online now. What are your options?

- You could start in Google and search under 'UK retail spending online' or in news sites such as the BBC or *The Times* and search on the same criteria. Articles you read may include relevant links to other appropriate sites.
- As you continue searching you will find that some sites allow you free access to information whereas others do not. For example, you can obtain information from the IMRG website, including a list of their members and a copy of their latest reports that will include references to other related sites which may be worth investigating. However, some sites would charge you for information, such as Hitwise.
- Other specialist sites charge a fee for research information such as Jupiter Research, which carries out in-depth business and technology market research, particularly relating to new technology. Businesses who want to receive reports must subscribe – although you can read their press releases for free at the

Jupitermedia website. A company which needs continuous research undertaken on specialist topics would probably subscribe to the main suppliers of research reports and updates. Similarly, most colleges and universities subscribe to research information services on academic topics – such as the LexisNexis website for law reports and updates for legal students.

If you want to find out more, links to the IMRG, Hitwise, Jupitermedia and LexisNexis websites are available at www.heinemann.co.uk/hotlinks (express code 1386P). You will also learn more about researching online if you study specialist Unit 6.

Supply of games and music

If you are a computer gamer then you will already know the sites you prefer. Games sites are popular because they contain the very latest information, something that games magazines and other promotional methods cannot easily provide. Also, games websites often contain forums in which players can exchange information. These sites enable you to research games before you buy, read write-ups, try out new games, get help if you're stuck, and buy or trade games online. Examples include the IGN and Computer & Video Games websites.

Music sites such as the Launch Music and NME websites feature video and music clips as well as information and gossip about the charts and artists. All the major record companies have sites, such as Reprise Records, and you can register to watch and download music videos at the Music Brigade website.

The latest trend has been for many commercial sites to join the ranks of allowing music downloads for a fee, such as MyCokemusic, Apple iTunes and the Napster 2.0 site. Wal-Mart, Dell, Sony and several others are all due to offer the feature shortly. The Official Charts Company (OCC) now publishes monthly figures on downloads and will integrate them into its main charts during 2004. Many predict that this will result in the eventual death of the single, sales of which have been steadily falling for some time.

Business matters

Your tutors may remember Peter Gabriel more for being a founder member of Genesis than for being a business visionary. In fact, he is both. Together with co-founder Charles Grimsdale he owns OD2 – On Demand Distribution – the only European company selling music online. (Apple iTunes, Napster, Coke and Sony's Connect are all US companies.)

OD2 supplies digital downloads to the industry – so it operates a B2B business, not a B2C one. It links with Internet retailers to help them to place music on their websites, including databases of a variety of tracks, artist bios, videos, pictures and other information. It also sells a 'shop in a box' site builder so that any website or retailer can sell music quickly and easily, with OD2 looking after the catalogue, checkout and online payment. Examples include the Tower Records and Playlouder websites.

If you are dealing with a site that uses OD2 then you won't know it. This is because the role of OD2 is to source the music, promote it, arrange for distribution and collect royalty payments for the artists. If the future is online music, then Gabriel and Grimsdale are going to be very successful indeed.

Peter Gabriel – the co-founder of OD2

You can find out more on the OD2 website – a link is available at www.heinemann.co.uk/hotlinks (express code 1386P).

If you want to find out more, links to some of the websites mentioned above have been made available at www.heinemann.co.uk/hotlinks (express code 1386P).

Virtual property tours

You can take a virtual property tour of many places online – from 10 Downing Street to Club Med holiday accommodation. If you want to see how these types of graphics are created, then go to the Panormania website and find out!

Virtual property tours enable anyone thinking of moving or renting accommodation to see exactly what the inside of a property looks like. The easiest way to experience this is to click on some of the many sites that offer this facility. You can check out city apartments and country cottages for sale,

cottages and villas to rent, view the inside of a luxury cruise liner or a port on the Mediterranean! Sites with this feature include Homes Online, City Living and Country Holidays.

The idea of using graphical images or video recordings on web pages is not restricted to property, of course. It is ideal in any situation where text alone would not give enough impact or detail. For that reason you will find virtual tours for tourist destinations, e.g. the Eden Project and video clips on news sites, film sites, music sites and websites promoting 3D graphics, creative artists or film studios. Sites worth viewing – if you are on broadband – include Framestore (first mentioned in Unit 2, page 137), Disney, Universal Studios and the British film company Working Title Films.

Business matters

Website design is changing all the time, driven by technological developments such as faster download speeds on broadband connections. This enables website designers to include sophisticated graphics and video clips which would take too long to download on dial-up connections. The day of fast movie downloads is not far away.

Other graphical developments include a 3D system to create an avatar – or virtual representation – of every online shopper. Your avatar would look like you, move like you – and be the same size as you. This makes online clothes shopping easy – you just tell your avatar to try things on – and move around so you can see what they look like! This system is being developed by Toshiba in conjunction with Digital Fashion, an Osaka-based software company and is due to be released in 2006. After that date,

you can expect this to be a feature offered by many online shopping sites.

This isn't the first time that avatars will have been used to sell clothes online. The disastrous website boo.com, which crashed spectacularly in 2000 used Miss Boo to try on clothes, Flash graphics and 3-D images. Unfortunately, at that time with older technology (and no broadband), the site took an age to load and couldn't be seen at all by anyone with an Apple Mac computer. The techies at Boo were ahead of their time – too much so, as it happened. The 'Boo' name was bought by Fashionmall, and a link to the Fashionmall website is available at www.heinemann.co.uk/hotlinks (express code 1386P). You can also read more about Boo on page 372.

Links for the websites mentioned above are available at www.heinemann.co.uk/hotlinks (express code 1386P).

Suitability of digital information

In February 2004, Eidos, the British software company famous for Lara Croft computer games, released a new game called *Whiplash*. This featured two animals being abused in a laboratory. Players release them by destroying security cameras, wrecking the laboratory and fighting police officers to 'ruin the evil corporation' that carries out animal testing. The aim, according to Eidos, is for children to develop a positive awareness about the subject. MPs, the police, the RSPCA and the Research Defence Society all took a different view claiming the game is irresponsible and inaccurate. They argued that the scenarios, linked to make-up testing, were unrepresentative of ethical and humane testing for medical reasons and would give young children the wrong impression. They were concerned that using violence to free the animals in the game gives tacit approval to militant animal rights activism. In this case, Eidos, which made a £17.4 million profit in 2003, was called the 'evil corporation' by the press as it released the game regardless of the possible effects on young people.

The degree to which young people are affected by unsuitable digital content – whether games, music, videos, photographs or text – is a hotly debated topic. There will always be arguments about controversial games like *Whiplash*, racist or sexist rap lyrics, videos like *Death Race 2000* and access to explicit photographs or text over the Internet. What is more generally agreed, however, is that control is needed over some of the more unsavoury aspects of the digital revolution. These include:

- Spam emails which can clog up mailboxes with unwanted offers or offensive material.
- Hackers who try to gain unauthorised access to business or private computer systems or download viruses. This activity can result in a computer being 'hijacked' for the storage and distribution of pornographic material, without the knowledge of the owner.
- Pornographic, racist, violent or otherwise offensive material in any format.
- The dangers to young people of using chatrooms.

Some technology buffs have recommended that the whole structure of the web should be reviewed and an upgraded version launched with more controls. Realistically this is unlikely to happen. In China the state has responded by encircling the country with a firewall to keep out unacceptable content. In Britain we would complain about lack of freedom if the government did this. Instead, we prefer to put our trust in technological developments, security measures by software providers and ISPs, and the common sense of individual users for protection. This is becoming more urgent as the growth of broadband – where users are online continuously – makes home computers far more vulnerable to spam, hostile attack and other problems. Some developments are summarised below.

- **Spam**. Most email software, such as Hotmail, comes with filters that help to minimise spam. The user can set these to progressively higher levels – at the top level refusing all emails unless they are sent by known users. Whilst this is effective, it can obviously block important emails from new contacts. At a lower level of protection, spam filters spot words which signify the email is likely to be spam – but this means that a few are still likely to get through. Most ISPs now offer a screening service for possible spam emails as an integral part of their service. The biggest danger is when spam emails arrive with a virus attachment. Many countries, including Britain and the US have passed laws to try to prevent spam but these are unlikely to be very successful as most spammers operate from other countries. According to Bill Gates the answer lies in technology – and he has vowed to solve the problem by 2006. Time will tell if he keeps his promise!
- **Hackers** obtain illegal access to computers, often by sending email attachments which give them backdoor access to the host computer. The hacker can then download files, including pornography, without the owner's knowledge. Spy software planted by the hacker can record keystrokes to find out passwords and security codes. Microsoft has been criticised for security problems with its operating systems that have allowed hackers to exploit its software – and is now under

pressure to redesign some of its systems. In the meantime, users are reliant on security 'patches' which are downloaded from the Microsoft site. They should also ensure that they have essential software installed for their own protection, such as a firewall (which monitors and restricts traffic between a computer and the Internet) and antivirus software.

- **Sophisticated security systems** are routinely installed on workplace computer networks. These enable network administrators to block potentially dangerous or offensive content, block specific files and restrict the activities of computer users. This is essential to prevent the system being disabled by a hostile attack (see page 393), to fulfil corporate responsibility in relation to the use/misuse of the computer system and to prevent sensitive company information finding its way onto the Internet.

Some security systems work better than others

Parental control is a similar equivalent for a home system. This, too, restricts access to certain types of sites and/or material. This can be achieved in several ways. Many ISPs, such as AOL, NTL and BT offer parental control as an option. Filters can be set on

Microsoft Explorer by following the instructions on the Microsoft site. Special filter software programs can be purchased and installed to prevent access to certain sites, an example of this is Net Nanny. Spy software can also be installed to record and log every keystroke.

- **'Grooming'** children is now a criminal offence in England under The Sexual Offences Act 2003. This includes the activities of adults who stalk Internet chatrooms with the aim of befriending children for sex. Those convicted can be jailed for up to ten years.

Whilst this is a valuable deterrent even more important is educating children to use the Internet safely. This has a more powerful and positive effect and, on the basis that no monitoring system can ever be 100 per cent foolproof, it teaches children how to use a computer responsibly and sensibly on their own and when to get adult help.

Business matters

Heinemann hotlinks are a key feature of this book – and every other Heinemann publication which includes references to websites. This is to protect you, the buyer, from accessing websites which may have closed down, or where the content may have been changed since the book was written. In some cases changes may be quite innocent, but not always.

A few years ago a schools textbook was published which included references to a website that later changed hands and included pornographic content. As a result the books had to be withdrawn from sale and destroyed, which was costly for the publisher and inconvenient for students and tutors.

Websites and domain names are not always taken over legitimately. The BBC had problems in 2004 when parents reported that users of its CBBC children's pages were being diverted to a pornographic site when they keyed in the address line. At Heinemann, the hotlinks are constantly checked to ensure this cannot happen to you when you are using any of the links on the site.

Business brief

Basic protection measures

UK computer users are becoming more aware of the dangers of being online, particularly as they progress to broadband when they are online all the time, broadcasting their IP address to anyone who is interested. Basic protection systems are then essential, i.e.

- **Install a firewall** on the computer. This software acts as a protective barrier and regulates access to the computer.
- **Install reputable antivirus software** which is regularly updated by the software provider.
- **Install software which routinely checks the hard drive** to find and repair any security breaches.
- **Download any protective patches** or other recommended updates available on the Microsoft website.
- **Never open email attachments** from unknown senders – or reply to spam emails. Just delete them.
- **Never tell anyone your password**.
- **Check that any young children in the family are protected** by the installation of parental control software and know how to use the computer safely.

1 Extend your knowledge of technology terms by using the Internet to research the meaning of each of the following.

   a Home page.

   b Hypertext.

   c Portal.

   d EDI.

2 Discuss with your tutor whether you should carry out this activity on your own or in small groups.

   a For each of the types of online business operations which have been covered so far (e.g. auctions, banking and so on), access at least **one** site from two categories. Then identify **three** features of each online operation. For example, for a retail operation such as Tesco you could identify: products and prices advertised online; customers can order online; customers can pay for goods online.

   b Compare your findings with those of other members of your group to identify the type of features which are similar to particular categories and those which are not.

3 **a** Your brother has started work teaching at a local primary school and wants to prepare a poster for children – and a short leaflet for their parents – on using the Internet safely.

   Divide into two groups. Group one should research information relating to child safety and the use of computers. Group two should research information for parents including the different types of security and control systems available.

   Pool your information and prepare the poster and leaflet required.

   Sites that you might find helpful include SUSI, NSPCC, NCH, Parents Online, The BBC, Software4Parents, Childspy, Cybersitter, Clearview and Chatdanger. Links to these sites are available at www.heinemann.co.uk/hotlinks (express code 1386P).

   b A survey in February 2004 found that whilst some children are turning away from chatrooms, others are actively ignoring the warnings because they like the thrill of taking a chance. As a group, decide what would you do – and why – if you found your 11 year old sister doing this.

4 In January 2004, Neilsen/WetRatings calculated there were over 26 million Internet users in Britain. Find out the latest web usage trends and check the current users in various countries of the world at the Nielsen NetRatings website – a link is available at www.heinemann.co.uk/hotlinks (express code 1386P).

Sectors online

As you saw on page 354, in 2004 Google estimated that it analysed data from nearly 5 billion sites. The Alexa site estimates that it obtains information from over 3.5 billion separate Internet sites and this number is rapidly increasing all the time. Although many sites are created and run by private individuals, the vast majority relate to business organisations. These represent all the different sectors you first met in unit 1 of this scheme.

The public sector

This sector, as you know, includes the government, its departments and associated agencies (such as the Jobcentre or Benefits Agency); local authorities and public corporations such as the BBC, the Bank of England and British Nuclear Fuels plc.

The portal for accessing virtually every public sector site in the UK is the Government's homepage, a link is available at www.heinemann.co.uk/hotlinks (express code 1386P). The searches on this site are excellent and enable you to find any government department (A-Z); any local authority (A-Z); to use a QuickFinder; to look under different public services, such as health or education; to search for jobs, to browse by subject and do many other things as well.

This site does not contain links to public corporations like the Bank of England because these operate as separate and independent organisations.

The private sector

Most websites on the Internet belong to private organisations – from small hotels and retailers to large multinational enterprises. You can identify these immediately because unlike British public sector sites (which end in .gov.uk) the main suffix for British companies is .co.uk or .com. If you have forgotten how the suffix relates to the type of organisation and where it is located, look back at the Guidance notes about researching on the Internet on page vi.

Private sector companies, as you know, are in business to make a profit. They will therefore only be interested in having a presence on the web if it will help them to achieve this objective. You will learn more about this later in the unit.

The voluntary/not-for-profit sector

As you saw in Unit 1, this sector comprises a wide variety of organisations – from Network Rail to several agencies which provide services to the public such as The Prince's Trust and Citizen's Advice Bureau, and to all the voluntary and charitable organisations in the UK. Most of these are identifiable online by the suffix .org.uk.

You can find any registered British charity through the listing at the Charity Commission, a link is available at www.heinemann.co.uk/hotlinks (express code 1386P). However, until the new Charities Act is passed you may find some surprising omissions in this list – such as Amnesty International. This is because the current requirements for registering a charity in the UK only include those set up for certain specific purposes. This law is about to be changed but in the meantime you can check other sites such as BUBL UK which provides links to a wide range of not-for-profit organisations.

Levels and types of online presence

The type of online presence will depend on the main business activity of the organisation and the main purpose of the website. Note that a business may choose one or more of the following options and *in each case* the website may be simple or sophisticated, depending upon the size, scale, image and objectives of the organisation.

Passive brochureware

This type of site is used to promote the business online and to provide information which helps to build the business or brand name either locally, nationally or internationally.

The name derives from the original, minimalist website which consisted of just the firm's brochure replicated on the site. This idea was often criticised for two reasons. Firstly, the layout of a printed brochure and its style is rarely suitable for a webpage because users read information differently online. They are normally more impatient and expect less printed information – as you will see on pages 386–7. Second, they may be surprised if there is no way in which they can interact with the site – for example if they then have to pick up the telephone to communicate with the business. This is where the term 'passive'

Business matters

The UK government has been keen to promote the use of new technology both for itself and for UK businesses. In the late 1990s Tony Blair went on record as saying that he wanted to make Britain 'the best place for e-commerce'. In terms of the public sector he wanted more information provided online and for people to be able to undertake more routine tasks from their computer – from renewing a passport to buying a TV licence.

As part of the strategy, in 2000, the government launched UK Online for Business to encourage more individuals and businesses to go online. Over the next three years more than £25 million was spent promoting the project but in spring 2004 the project was disbanded and the site was transferred to the DTI. A link is available at www.heinemann.co.uk/hotlinks (express code 1386P).

Making money online

The main reason why private and voluntary sector organisations go online is usually to make more money. Private organisations aim to increase their profit, charities want to increase their donations (as well as to recruit more volunteers). They may do this by attracting new customers or members through their online presence, or by commercial activities online, for example:

- **By attracting more enquiries** for the services that are promoted online e.g. all colleges and universities, and businesses such as Moonfish – which undertakes a range of new media services.
- **By introducing buyers and sellers** and taking a commission, e.g. eBay and Priceline
- **By selling goods online**, e.g. Amazon, Tesco and charity shops such as those operated by the NSPCC and RSPB.
- **By accepting a subscription** and/or charging online, e.g. Friends Reunited, Apple iTunes or any gambling site.

- **By providing a free information service** which attracts visitors and allowing relevant paid advertising on the site. An obvious example is Google. If you search for flights you will soon see advertisements appear from online travel companies such as Travelocity, Expedia and Teletext Holidays. These companies have paid Google to have advertisements in prominent positions. Experts estimate that Google's revenue from paid advertising alone is expected to be in the region of $300 million in 2004.
- **By targeted advertising** linked to email content. Google's Gmail service will recognise topics being discussed in emails and will sell advertising space for adverts to appear alongside the text. So, if you are emailing about your favourite band, you can expect adverts for music downloads, CDs or tickets to appear within your email.

could be argued as inappropriate in relation to a website. In most cases it is better if the customer can interact electronically, such as by email, even if this is just to request further information.

However, if the site is well designed so that the information is clear and easy to read and graphics are used to illustrate important aspects of the business, then brochureware can be very useful for

Starting small

One method for many small organisations to go online quite quickly with a basic presence is to obtain a listing on a larger site. For example, on the Yell website a business can list its name and type of business. Or a listing can be included in a local search engine, e.g. 2cUK. Through associations with other websites like Multimap, listings of hotels, restaurants and rental cottages in the area can be found.

Voluntary and charitable organisations can also get free help to build their website – and free web hosting – from Contributions.org. This is a linked project between Project North East,

ZebraHosts and Domaincheck. The site hosts a wide variety of organisations including small, local sports associations, arts projects and voluntary services.

In other cases, community service projects are more ambitious – such as the website of The Buckland Community Centre in Portsmouth. This is a good example of a 'brochureware' site which simply and clearly covers all the services available and enables individuals to make online contact if they wish.

Links to some of the websites mentioned above are available at www.heinemann.co.uk/hotlinks (express code 1386P).

a small enterprise. The main aim of the site is to tell customers the name of the business, what it does, where it is and how to make contact. This purpose is the same whether or not the site is owned by a small business or large enterprise. Compare, for instance, the sites for Bourton Lodge with Visit Norway and those for Stump Cross Caverns and Alton Towers. Links are available at www.heinemann.co.uk/hotlinks (express code 1386P).

Complementing offline services

There is obviously some overlap between this category and the previous one in that every business with an offline presence is using its website to promote its activities. However, in this case the website may also be used to extend the range of services and methods of contact with the customer, for example:

- A service organisation can also offer online facilities, such as banks offering online banking, the Royal Mail site features parcel tracking and postcode searches online, the Passport Agency includes online applications for new or renewed passports, the WeightWatchers site enables people to join the programme online and Samaritans now encourages contact by email as well as by telephone.
- Manufacturers can promote their products and services online, often with information on where to find retail outlets. Some designer sites are very original and contain some very novel features. Those worth viewing include the Lamborghini.com, Hugo Boss and Versace websites. Another site worth looking at for its original approach is that of Graham Brown – the wallcoverings manufacturer.
- Retailers who do not sell online can provide additional information about the business, such as product information and customer service and support. Two good examples are Habitat and IKEA. Neither sell over the Internet – but both still find it useful to have a comprehensive website with a number of useful features.
- Producers of news or information can provide this online as well as offline, e.g. the BBC website complements television broadcasts and newspaper websites complement daily papers.
- Event websites, such as those for Glastonbury and Wimbledon, provide information on essential information such as tickets, operate shops and may include other features, such as webcasts, when the event is in progress.

Links to some of the websites mentioned above are available at www.heinemann.co.uk/hotlinks (express code 1386P).

Inviting online transactions

This can be done on a small or large scale. Many mail order companies have extended their operations to include a web-based catalogue, such as Lands' End Clothing and Lakeland Ltd. In other cases, a traditional bricks and mortar company has started an online operation with a web storefront, e.g. Thorntons Chocolates and Bettys and Taylors of Harrogate. In every case key features of the website must include an ordering system and the facility for receiving and processing payments securely.

- A basic site may just give a list of products and space for order details alongside, such as London Ticket Site.
- A simple online catalogue may be a virtual copy of a printed version.

The Wimbledon website complements its offline services

Searches may be very limited and ordering may only be done by entering a product code. This can become quite tedious for the customer. Surprisingly, this is the case for the Next website.

- An extensive catalogue offers flexible searching under a range of criteria and simply clicking on an item can transfer it to the shopping basket. For example, in addition to product headings you can also search under areas of interest, gender, price or ages for appropriate items. Sites which offer this facility include Boots and John Lewis.
- At the top end, the site interacts with the customer. Examples of these sites include eBay and Amazon – as you will see below.

Links to some of the websites mentioned above are available at www.heinemann.co.uk/hotlinks (express code 1386P).

Interactive customisation

Interactive customisation relates to sites which adjust their content according to the preferences of the user. In essence, the site is intelligent. This is achieved when users register their own preferences or purchase certain items. The site then uses this information to 'push' similar content of interest to that particular user. Examples of sites which customise their content based on the user include:

- Yahoo!, which creates 'My Profile' pages for each user. These are customised as the user enters information into the database. From then on, the user can opt to go to 'My Yahoo!' to view their personalised site.
- Amazon, which 'upsells' to registered customers by offering suggestions for new purchases based on their interests, previous purchases and purchases of people with similar buying habits. It also compiles a list of 'recently viewed' items so that visitors won't forget items they have browsed. The main areas of interest and buying habits create the customer's 'own store' area which is displayed when a returning customer re-enters the site from his or her usual computer.

The technology behind customised websites – for those who like to know!

How do large sites operate so that they can interact with the customer – and how are they constantly updated? Two important aspects are cookies and dynamic content.

- **A cookie** is a small data file which is placed on the user's computer when they first visit the site. It identifies when that computer returns to the website and recognises repeat visitors and registered users – so they don't have to log in again and again. The cookie can also provide information about the user's habits on the site. The aim is to turn the site into a virtual salesperson – who always promotes the right products, remembers those the customer was interested in before and tempts the customer to spend more than originally intended!

- **A dynamic site** is one where the content is constantly changing because the site is driven by a database. The database manages and displays the information. For example, the BBC website is automatically updated through news reports which are logged into the database and programmed to appear on the website. A large online retailer, such as Amazon, has both product databases and registered customer databases which are linked to the website. As new books, for example, are received in stock these are simply added to the product database. The system is programmed to promote these to customers with those interests when they access the site.

Main channel of business activity

For a virtual or dotcom business, the website is the only channel of activity. It may be possible, in a few cases, for customers to telephone the company if there is a query but the vast majority of communications will be online. Examples include:

- Dell – which manufactures and produces computers but only sells them online.
- Amazon, eBay, Friends Reunited, lastminute.com, Expedia – all of which have been mentioned earlier in this section.
- All search engines and most ISPs, e.g. Google, Yahoo!, AOL, Wanadoo.

In addition, the Internet has offered new opportunities for other businesses, such as no-frills airlines which prefer to accept all their reservations online. This reduces the cost of handling bookings and cuts out the middlemen, i.e. the travel agents. A new type of cooperative business venture is now emerging on the Internet. An example is Opodo. This is a purely online airline booking site, but is owned and financed by most of the major European airlines working together. Have a look yourself and find out which ones!

Today several virtual businesses are operating profitably – but this is a relatively recent phenomena. The dotcom story has gone from boom to bust in a very short period, as you will see below. Today's managers are far more inclined to consider carefully the advantages – and disadvantages – of doing business online before they make a decision, and will tailor the website to their own needs. Fundamentally this means ensuring that it meets the needs of the target audience. You will learn more about this in the next two sections.

Business matters

Many travel sites now advertise their use of **dynamic packaging**. This enables customers to visit the website and then select their destination, hotel flight, airport transfer, car hire, theatre tickets – and book everything in one go. This is possible because all the options are stored in a product database linked to the website. The top sites to offer this include lastminute.com, ebookers.com, Expedia and Travelocity. This saves customers time 'shopping around' and saves them money, too. Dynamic content gives these sites the competitive edge over other travel sites, such as those operated by no frills airlines, which only sell airline tickets and then leave the customer to obtain accommodation, car hire and other aspects of their holiday from a different supplier.

Business brief

Boo hoo dot com

During the dotcom boom of the 1990s, huge amounts of money were invested – much of it unwisely – in new virtual businesses. Many people thought that the Internet would be the new way of doing business and, not surprisingly, wanted to make money out of it. Unfortunately many online enterprises – such as Boo.com – were managed by inexperienced entrepreneurs who had a good idea but very little else! Business plans were poor and financial skills were almost non-existent – with the result that many businesses crashed and many investors lost all their money. Boo alone managed to spend over £100 million of investors' money without ever making a profit.

Many people thought the days of online business were over, but that has proved too pessimistic. The new wave of dotcom businesses has proved that, with good business and financial skills, it is possible to do online business profitably. In the early days, managers often saw online business as something different and gave the responsibility for handling it to the IT department, which had little appreciation about buying and selling in the company.

Today it is accepted that it normally makes more sense to integrate online business with other aspects of the business, such as marketing for promotions and finance for processing payments. If an organisation treats its website as an 'extra feature' that hasn't much to do with the rest of the business then it is unlikely to make the most out of doing business online.

Intranets and Extranets

Two important features of an online operation are Intranets and Extranets. In some cases these may provide even more benefits for an organisation than standard online Internet access or a business website.

- An **Intranet** is a private network which is only available to the company's employees. It can be used to share information, including project files, stock lists and drawings. Colleges and universities normally have extensive Intranets because of the potential for providing different types of information online to their own tutors and students.
- An **Extranet** is a website where access is restricted, either by password or by encryption. It is invaluable for large manufacturing businesses as trusted suppliers can be given access and involved in file sharing, collaboration on technical drawings and other types of data transfer.

The features of an online business

When businesses go online they must consider which aspects, or features, of their business to include in their online operations. As you have seen, this will depend upon:

- The type of business operation (retailing, gambling, banking etc.).
- The sector (public, private or not-for-profit).
- The type of online presence required – from a simple, static 'brochureware' site to a fully interactive site which allows payments online, customer service and so on.

This decision will usually depend upon the size and type of operation, the needs of the customers and the resources that the business is prepared to commit to an online presence. It is, of course, quite possible to start simply and then progress to meet changing or increasing customer demands, as you will see in Section 8.4.

If you look at the online business operation of your

No website or online presence.

Basic web presence, e.g. listing on Yell.com.

Basic brochureware site to promote the business. Includes information about organisation, products/services and offline contact details.

Basic interactive site to complement offline services. Customers can search site, make email queries.

Catalogue site which allows customers to buy and pay online and includes customer service features, e.g. order tracking.

Interactive, dynamic site linked to product and customer databases. Recognises returning customers and customises page content accordingly.

Figure 8.5 *Types of online presence*

own college, for example, you can identify the features it offers. These may include:

- Details of courses and programmes and the cost of these (including the ability to search for what you want).
- Details about the college facilities.
- Information for prospective students (e.g. about finance, travel etc.).
- The ability to request a prospectus.
- The ability to request an application form online *or* to complete an application form online.
- The ability to enrol online for part-time courses.
- A student email facility (to each other or to their tutors).
- A staff email facility.
- Online student learning resources (normally only available via the Intranet).
- Forthcoming events.

- Job vacancies.
- College news.

In addition, tutors will also be able to access a wide variety of information on the college Intranet. Therefore, the features that are included are those that will provide students (or employees) with the facilities and information they need and complement the offline business of attracting and educating new students.

Successful online businesses are those that put the customer first when they are considering the main features to include in their online operations. They think about what customers want, ensure their website is attractive and easy to use, and are absolutely certain that they can fulfil all the promises they make – such as rapid order processing or delivery. The features should also complement offline activities. However, these businesses also realise that launching a website is merely the first stage in establishing an online presence and that they will need to refine the site and make adjustments to better achieve their online goals over time (see also Section 8.4).

Talking point

View 1: *Shopping online is OK for predictable goods, like DVDs, books and groceries, but is hopeless for things like shoes and clothes. It'll never replace 'proper' shopping where you can enjoy trying things on and looking around.*

View 2: *In 100 years most retail stores will have shut down. Everyone will be able to buy anything in minutes on the Internet using avatars, holograms and 3D imagery. The choice will be huge and prices very competitive.*

With which viewpoint do you agree – and why?

A key feature of the Richer Sounds website is its special deals

Business matters

In October 2003 Forrester Research evaluated the online operations of 51 leading European retailers. It found that the best and most successful features were often the simplest – such as 'one click' shopping invented by Amazon. Argos came top for several reasons including enabling customers to have their order delivered or collect it in their local store, allowing in store returns of online purchases and including home collection of returned goods at no extra cost. It can allow in-store returns because sales clerks can use the Internet kiosks in its stores to check the customer and product information. Customers can also use the Internet kiosks in store. So the features of its offline and online activities complement each other.

Tesco ranked less well because shoppers have one basket and checkout process for groceries, but need another basket to buy other types of goods, such as electrical equipment. It was also criticised because customers must register before they can look for product information (which puts off people browsing on price). However, it ranked highly because special promotions that operate offline are also a feature of its online activities.

A German catalogue retailer, Otto, was highlighted for good practice. Its features include allowing users to decide the best time within a 12-hour window for delivery, receiving SMS alerts from the nearest delivery drop-off point and 24-hour customer service.

Over to you!

1 From the following options, suggest the most appropriate type of online presence for each of the businesses listed below. In each case give a reason for your choice.

Businesses:
a Local estate agent.
b Private language college specialising in intensive business courses.
c Virtual company specialising in tailor-made holidays.
d Central London hotel.
e National toy retailer.
f Small retail company selling specialist food products.

Options:
i Passive brochureware with contact number.
ii Basic online transaction (e.g. booking or reservation).
iii Catalogue online and online shopping facility.
iv Interactive customisation.

2 Many businesses have a jazzy website to promote their products. Examples include Giorgio Armani, Harvey Nichols and the other designer businesses mentioned on page 370 as well as many car producers, such as Lexus. Some people would argue this is a waste of time and money. Others would say it is good business sense. As a group, suggest **two** reasons to support *both* arguments.

3 Hertz and Avis are both car hire companies that operate on a national basis. Intack Car Hire is a much smaller, Lancashire-based operation. Website links for all three are available at www.heinemann.co.uk/hotlinks (express code 1386P).

a Investigate the website of **one** national car hire company of your choice and identify the main features of its online operation.
b Check out the website of Intack Car Hire or a small car/van hire business in your own area. Identify the main features of that online operation.
c Identify the main differences between both types of online operation and suggest reasons for your findings.

4 Tim and Aysha run a successful music exchange in your town called The Record Exchange (see page 401). They sell new CDs but specialise in the exchange of rare and deleted vinyl records, CDs and also sell pop memorabilia. They are considering going online in the near future.

a As a group, suggest the key aspects of the business they should incorporate as features of an online presence and any other features they may need to develop.
b Decide whether you think going online is a simple matter with few problems or more complex, with a wider range of issues to consider. Give reasons for your views.

1 Divide into groups and investigate the following sites – links are available at www.heinemann.co.uk/hotlinks (express code 1386P). In each case decide:

    a The sector in which the business operates.
    b **Four** key features of the online operation.

       Site 1: NHS Direct.
       Site 2: Richer Sounds.
       Site 3: Your own college website.
       Site 4: Guide Dogs for the Blind.
       Site 5: Thorntons Chocolates.
       Site 6: The Samaritans.

2 Many organisations promote their businesses online, often through passive brochureware. These are likely to be small businesses that provide a particular service. Examples include local hotels, driving schools such as BSM, DJs, and many small firms in your own local area.

Use the Internet to find **two or three** online operations relating to service organisations in your own area. For each one you find decide:

    a The main purpose of the online operation.
    b The features of the operation that help the business to achieve this.

Compare your ideas with other members of your group.

3 You have been asked to describe the key features of an online operation to a member of your family who has little idea about the Internet and how it operates. Choose a simple business operation that you know and understand, then outline the 'story' of its online business presence by identifying and explaining the main features it decided to offer consumers online. Finally, mention how these link to the features that are offered offline.

This section covers

The general benefits of online trading

The supply chain and related benefits

Reduced stockholding and other benefits

Broadband and other developments

The benefits which businesses gain by going online obviously depend upon the size and type of business activity carried out. A small manufacturing company, for example, may want to reduce its costs by buying its supplies online and getting them delivered rapidly, reducing its storage space; whereas a retail store will want to attract new customers and increase sales by selling online. In both these cases, the goals of going online should link to the overall aims and objectives of the business – which you first learned about in Unit 1.

As you work through this section you will learn about the variety of possible benefits of having an online presence. However, note that there will always be some types of business that do not benefit because the nature of their main activity would not make an online presence worthwhile. This is mainly true of local businesses that provide an immediate, personal service – such as your dentist or hairdresser. In neither of these cases would an online presence significantly help them to achieve their main aims and objectives. Your dentist may have more patients than he or she can cope with and be more concerned with the quality of oral hygiene and treatments than extending the practice. Your hairdresser will probably benefit more by building a reputation through word-of-mouth promotions and local advertising.

The general benefits of online trading

The general benefits of online trading are quite straightforward.

- **Global 'round the clock' visibility**. Websites never close and are available to customers 24/7 from any online location in the world. This can vastly increase promotional and trading opportunities for the business.

- **Opportunities for expansion, particularly within the European market**. A web presence increases access to a wider range of customers, especially from abroad. Opportunities are maximised if the business offers competitively priced products and an excellent service. However, customs regulations and other barriers to trade may prevent growth to some countries. This is less of a problem in the European Community because goods can be freely traded between member states and the legislation is broadly the same throughout the area.

- **Equality of presence regardless of size of business**. The customer judges the business on the appearance and usability of its website, not on the size of the business or the scale of its operation. Therefore a small business with a well designed site and excellent service can compete, in theory, with much larger businesses. However, the business must be able to supply the anticipated extra demand and this may not be possible unless careful thought has been given to the production, distribution and selling operations.

- **Rapidity of response to customer interest**. A web presence provides the opportunity to respond quickly to customers – but not all firms take advantage of this. A website can provide several opportunities for customer contact, such as 'call me' buttons and email messages, but speed of response is vital. Research has shown that Internet users expect a faster response than customers who enquire by telephone or letter. If the company responds very late or, even worse, fails to respond altogether, then not only is a potential sale lost, but the image of the business is tarnished. To prevent this, nominated staff must be given the task of responding to website enquiries promptly. Alternatively, this can be handled through an automated system.

- **Opportunities to analyse online competition**. It is quicker and easier to understand and compare competitor activities online than by visiting their stores or obtaining information on their products and services offline. Even before a business goes online it should analyse the web presence of each of its main competitors. This can show the size of the electronic marketplace and the style and content of competitor's websites. They should aim to be at least as good – and preferably better. The Internet also enables businesses to track new competitors and check their market share. If this is falling action must be taken – as you learned in unit 2. Businesses should also realise, though, that once they are online competitors can also keep an eagle eye on their operations!

- **Opportunity to keep up with competitors** The aim here is to prevent competitors getting the online 'edge'. This may be by improving on the products or services offered, the speed of delivery, the cost of delivery and/or constantly reviewing the style and design of the website itself to utilise new technological developments as much as possible. The Internet has made it much easier for businesses to find out about competitor's products and services but this applies to customers, too! Customers can quickly 'shop around' online and, for consumer goods, comparative sites will do this for them – such as Kelkoo, Pricerunner, easyValue, and many others. This puts greater pressure on online retailers to be competitive. Links to Kelkoo, Pricerunner and easyValue are available at www.heinemann.co.uk/hotlinks (express code 1386P).

The supply chain and related benefits

A supply chain comprises every single business that is involved in the eventual supply of a product or service. As a basic example, let's assume that you buy a bottle of water from your local shopkeeper who visits a cash and carry twice a week to stock up on essential items. In this case the supply chain may be shown as in Figure 8.6 (below).

This supply chain is quite long – but would be even longer if we started looking at who supplied the plastic for the bottles, and the paper for labels! For our purposes it is long enough, because it helps to show the problems that are associated with traditional supply chains:

- The water bottling plant is reliant on plastic bottles and labels to be delivered on time for production to continue. Fortunately, if they extract their own water, they are not dependent upon a supplier for any other key raw material. The point to note is that if any major supplier fails to deliver on time, production is delayed.
- Every business involved in distributing the product wants a 'cut' or a share in the profit, to make it worth their while. So the final selling

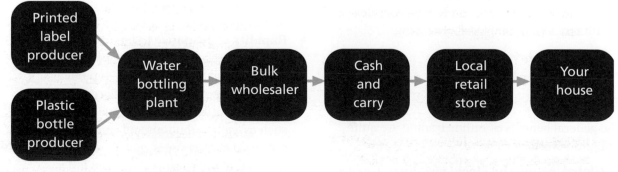

Figure 8.6 *A traditional supply chain*

price to the consumer may be high, and considerably different from that charged by the manufacturer.

- It takes time to move goods through the chain from start to finish. If the bottling plant closed down over Christmas and supplies ran out, there may be a week or two before your local shop could restock.
- The chain is usually slow to respond to rapid changes, such as if demand for water increased because of a sudden heatwave. This is the main reason why, virtually every Christmas, there is panic buying by parents to get the 'must-have' toy of the year before stocks run out! Quite simply, the supply chain cannot operate quickly enough to cope with the surge in demand.

Achieving a responsive integrated supply chain

To solve these problems many businesses have tried to change the supply chain in various ways.

- **Shorten it**. This is done by cutting out or by-passing as many intermediaries (middlemen) as possible. For example, Dell manufactures computers and sells them online direct to the buyers. This means there are no wholesalers and no need for retail shops. This speeds things up and reduces the final price for consumers.

- **Integrate it**. The aim here is to speed things up by changing the traditional 'line' where information passes from one stage to the other. Instead, the online system is used to make continuous communication between different parts of the chain possible. For example, suppliers are given access to the stock or spares databases and can then supply their own goods when required. This can be done quickly and easily using automated systems.

Benefits that follow

If the business achieves its aims of improving the supply chain then several benefits normally follow.

- **Offering punctual delivery as a sales feature**. If the supply chain is short and integrated, then normally the seller will have more control over delivery. This is fairly

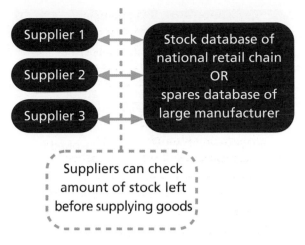

Figure 8.7 *An integrated supply chain*

obvious. If you were making a product yourself, or were in constant contact with the producer, then you would know exactly what promises you could and could not make.

- **Access from a wide range of devices**. People who are part of an electronic supply chain can liaise to improve product delivery and reduce the times between order and supply – known as 'lead time'. They can also check stocks at any time, using a range of devices.
  - Sales representatives, technicians, repair workers and other staff working away from the office can access live stock information 'on the go' using PDAs (personal digital assistants), palmtops or laptops.
  - Staff working within the business can check stock levels on their computer at any time. This prevents mistakes being made and promises being made to customers that can't possibly be kept.
  - Customers can check stocks online providing these are updated automatically on the webstore. Many online businesses put a note on the site when an item is currently out of stock and offer to email customers when stocks are replenished.
  - Customers can place orders on the website (from home, by laptop or from a 3G mobile), by email, by phone, by fax or by post.
  - As orders are processed by the system, stock levels are automatically updated with the information. This triggers automated electronic orders to relevant suppliers when stocks fall to a pre-set level.

The growth of c-commerce

Most people have heard of e-commerce, which means selling online, but what about c-commerce? This is the term used for **online collaboration** between different groups or organisations – including those involved in a supply chain.

Our supply chains on pages 378–9 were fairly simple. If you tried to draw one for a car or airplane you would need rather more paper! Now think about the cooperation and communication that is needed for specialist parts to be produced to the right specification and on time, especially when new products are being developed. Quite simply, this is normally far more successful if everyone involved works together and shares information – even if they work for different businesses. This can mean, for example, suppliers having access to production plans or stock lists so that they know what raw materials will be required and when.

Once a business is online, there are various ways for staff within and outside the business to communicate.

- Staff can communicate over a computer network. Computers linked in one location by cable are known as a **LAN** (local area network). Those which transfer data by radio waves are wireless LANs or Wi-Fi's (see unit 2, page 191). A network which links different sites is a **WAN** (wide area network). A **VPN** (virtual private network) is a secure network which links remote offices. This may include different businesses, e.g. manufacturers and suppliers.
- Communications can take place over Intranets and Extranets – which you first met on page 373.
- Staff can also use email, instant messaging and video conferencing to communicate and collaborate. Project teams can liaise in online newsgroups or post information to shared discussion areas. They can work together on a problem regardless of where they are situated.

- **Opportunities for e-procurement/ sourcing**. This was first covered on page 360. Now let's look at it again from the point of view of the supply chain. In this case our water bottling plant can shop around to buy its plastic bottles and printed labels more cheaply. If its needs are fairly small, it can join a buying group online which will purchase on behalf of the whole group and therefore gain higher discounts. It could take part in online auctions to buy more cheaply (see page 355).

Ideally, our bottling plant will find the best supplier in terms of price, quality and flexible ordering/delivery systems. This reduces the quantity of empty bottles which must be held in stock, and the amount of space required for these. Eventually it can develop its online buying operations so that it integrates its purchasing systems with those of its suppliers.

- **Online order tracking**. This enables customers to check every stage of their order from a section of the supplier's website. With B2C transactions, this is often integrated into the automated response system which is triggered when a customer's order has been received and payment authorised. At this stage, the system automatically sends a confirmatory email to the customer. This email informs the customer about tracking the order and includes a link to the website. On more sophisticated systems, the customer can check the progress of the order at any time and find out whether it is still in the warehouse or on the road. On all systems, a further email should be sent to automatically notify the customer when the items have been dispatched. Critically, the customer's credit card must *never* be charged until the item has either been shipped or delivered.

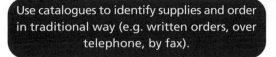

Use catalogues to identify supplies and order in traditional way (e.g. written orders, over telephone, by fax).

↓

Use Internet to compare suppliers and prices but order in traditional way.

↓

Some business supplies bought online by a few members of staff.

↓

Many orders placed electronically by staff. Ordering system linked to company acounts system.

↓

Orders placed and paid for electronically through integrated system between organisation and its suppliers

↓

Orders placed electronically using fully integrated e-produced system where suppliers are aware of current plans and sales figures.

Figure 8.8 *Stages in purchasing – offline to online*

Business matters

The Worldwide Retail Exchange was set up in March 2000 by 17 international retailers. Their aim was to simplify and automate the supply chain and to get rid of inefficiencies. By 2004 there were 64 members – all household names. These included Boots, Marks & Spencer, Tesco, Toys R Us, Woolworths and many more. It is now estimated that members of the WWRE have saved over $1 billion.

Tesco is also renowned for its own Trading Information Exchange (TIE). This is an electronic link with suppliers which enables them to respond immediately to Tesco's needs as a buyer. This system is hosted using Global eXchange Services (GXS), which is a method by which retailers can communicate and link online.

You can find out more on the WorldWide Retail Exchange and Global Exchange Services websites or by searching for Tesco + 'trading information exchange' on any good search engine. Links to the WorldWide Retail Exchange and Global Exchange Services websites are available at www.heinemann.co.uk/hotlinks (express code 1386P).

• **Reduced overheads and labour costs**. A shorter and more integrated supply chain means that all orders are processed and fulfilled more cheaply. This is because there is likely to be:
  – Fewer middlemen or intermediaries required – all of whom would have to be paid for their services.
  – Less warehouse space required, because supplies are sourced more on a 'just-in-time' basis and because demand peak and troughs can be forecast based on previous order history.
  – Fewer (or no) shops required if the business also sells online or deals direct with customers.
  – Fewer staff required to process paperwork relating to buying supplies or customer orders.
  – Fewer staff needed to deal with customer enquiries or telephone/fax orders.
  – A better organised transport system which should result in fewer journeys.

1 Julie Brennan makes designer jewellery. Her workshop is on the outskirts of a small village in Norfolk. Suggest **two** aims of her business and **six** benefits she could gain by having an online presence.

2 **a** Explain the meaning of the term 'supply chain'.

   b Explain what is meant by an 'integrated supply chain'.

   c Suggest **three** benefits a shoe manufacturer could gain through an online presence. At least **one** of these should relate the supply chain.

3 Dell sells computers online and does not have any stores. PC World sells computers in its stores and also has an online presence.

   a Access both websites, links are available at www.heinemann.co.uk/hotlinks (express code 1386P). Identify **three** differences between these sites that reflect the different online operations of these firms.

   b Suggest **four** ways in which Dell saves money by operating as a dotcom computer supplier.

   c The leading online technology supplier in the UK is Dabs – a link to the website is available at www.heinemann.co.uk/hotlinks (express code 1386P). It processes over 5,000 customer orders every day. Access its site and compare its operations to those of Dell and PC World and identify the key differences. If you were buying a computer, which supplier would attract you the most – and why?

4 Find out more about PDAs and handheld computers by researching these on the Internet at sites like PC World and Dabs. Assume you have £250 to spend. Which one would you buy – and why?

Reduced stockholding and other benefits

You have just seen that a business can save money in several ways by shortening its supply chain, making this more responsive or integrating it. It can also save or make money by taking other actions relating to operating as an online business.

- **Reduced stock holding**. Flexible and responsive electronic ordering systems means that the quantity of stock which must be held at any one time is reduced. This creates savings in terms of the amount of money tied up in stock, the space required, the number of staff needed to handle or maintain the stock and even the security precautions that are required.

- **Improved cash flow and fewer bad debts**. Cash flow improves if customers are paying as they make a purchase. This is the case with B2C transactions online because all customers pay by credit or debit card. The card payment is always checked and authorised before the goods are dispatched, so there is less chance of sending goods which are never paid for. However, do note that – legally – an online business cannot charge for goods before they are dispatched or delivered! In B2B transactions, electronic ordering and payment systems speed up the whole process and reduce the need for lengthy credit terms. Buyers cannot make the excuses that you read in Unit 3, e.g. that 'the cheque is in the post' or 'the invoice hasn't been received'! This means fewer bad debts overall for the business.

- **Low cost locations**. A virtual business or dotcom company which trades purely over the Internet has far more freedom in choosing its location than other types of businesses. If it sells goods over the Internet then it must ensure that it can obtain and dispatch these without problem, so a distribution channel is still important. Other than that, it can choose where to locate. If the business provides a service, such as website design or writing technical manuals, then it can locate absolutely anywhere, as it can deal with all its customers or clients online. Friends Reunited started from an ordinary semi-detached house in the suburbs of London and only moved when it outgrew the space available. In other villages and towns in England, online businesses operate providing a variety of goods and services – sometimes from the most unexpected places!

Business brief

Types of ISPs

ISPs can be divided into different groups. Those which provide mass market content services/information pages to their customers and those which provide specialist ISP services.

- **The largest mass market provider** is AOL. AOL is unique because it uses its own browser. This must be installed by AOL users to gain access via that ISP. This has enabled AOL to control its own content to a greater degree than other ISPs – and offer, for example, higher security and greater levels of parental control.
- **Mainstream ISPs** include Wanadoo, Tiscali, NTL and BT Openworld. These all offer content sites for their customers in addition to ISP services.
- **'No frills' ISPs** simply offer a connection service and technical assistance for a fee e.g. Hostway or Netscalibur. These are frequently used by business organisations (and private individuals) who are not interested in other services.

- **Affiliations with ISPs and portals**. An 'affiliation' simply means a link between two sites for mutual advantage.
  - A business would only be likely to form an affiliation with an ISP which operated a content site. For example, BT Openworld offers a wide range of information services on its website. Most of the pages and services it will operate itself – but not all of them. It offers UK route planning, but if you click on this service you will see the address line changes to Multimap – even though you are still in the BT site. This is an affiliation. Effectively, BT has outsourced route planning to Multimap, because this is

more cost effective than providing this service itself. Now check all the other services on the site, such as horoscopes, and look for other companies that may be helping them to offer these services.
  - A portal is a site, often featuring a variety of services, which is used as a hub or gateway either to the Internet or to a specialist topic. A good example of a large UK portal is Lycos. This site is aimed at UK net users aged between 18–30 and its content reflects this. However, it also has affiliations with other sites. For example, if you click on the links relating to job hunting then the page says 'in partnership with Fish4jobs'. Similarly for cars (Fish4cars) and houses (Fish4homes). This shows a fairly strong affiliation between Lycos and 'Fish4'!
- **Accessibility to different users**. The Internet has been a godsend to many people who, for one reason or another, never before had easy access to a wide range of information or competitively priced products. Whilst many busy working couples may be delighted to shop online for their weekly groceries at Tesco, so, too, is anyone who is disabled or housebound. People who live in remote or rural areas no longer need to worry about making arrangements for special shopping trips to buy items they can't obtain locally.
- **Popularity of additional access points**. Internet kiosks and cybercafés are a common feature in all large towns and cities. They enable anyone without a PC, or anyone away from home, to access the Internet easily. Web access points are also found in some outlets such as Starbucks and stores such as Argos, which have both offline and online operations (see page 374). The growth of Wi-Fi (see page 191) is likely to mean that, given the technology, most people will be able to access the Internet from almost anywhere before too long. For example, in 2003 GNER – which operates trains between London and Scotland – announced the start of an onboard broadband service. This means that train passengers can use Wi-Fi enabled laptops and handheld or pocket PCs to access the Internet or check their

emails on their journey. Tunnels, apparently, will be a minor inconvenience but will not cause a disconnection! Wireless hotspots are the almost inevitable way ahead, which will mean that anyone with the right portable technology won't need to use an Internet café. Instead they will use public access points in restaurants, airports, hotels and coffee shops all over the country. This will increase the number of people who are constantly online at any one time.

Links to some of the websites mentioned above are available at www.heinemann.co.uk/hotlinks (express code 1386P).

Broadband and other developments

Originally, Internet users were connected by means of a computer with a modem and a narrowband connection which transferred data at a fairly slow rate. Individual users had a 'dial-up' service through their ISP which meant that they used the telephone to gain access to the Internet. Unless they had more than one phone line, this meant their telephone line was engaged whenever they were surfing. In addition, it could take a long time to download some web pages and files – particularly those with elaborate graphics. Video content was virtually impossible to access.

Broadband connections enable data to be transferred much faster than narrowband. In addition, there is a permanent connection that does not tie up a normal phone line. The user can choose get online by an ADSL connection (which uses the phone lines but allows simultaneous telephone calls), a cable line, wireless or via a satellite dish – providing it is facing south with a clear and unobstructed view.

Business matters

Silver surfers is the name given to Internet users over 50 who are, according to research, taking up 'surfing' in droves to 'shop around', compare prices and services and buy online. Apparently, they now spend more time online than any other group, because they have more free time, and have a huge amount of buying power.

Portals which have been devised to focus on the interests of this group include 50connect, Seniority and CenNet, which is also concerned about the user-friendliness of websites for older people. It carried out a survey asking users to assess websites according to the following criteria: accessibility; layout; general usability;

colour; information; links and resources.

Although most silver surfers are hale and hearty, disabled surfers of any age often have special website needs but more through ignorance than design, few website developers think about these. The worse case was the original site for the 2000 Australian Olympics which was actually deemed unlawful by the Australian Human Rights and Equal Opportunity Commission because it couldn't be accessed by the disabled and had to be redesigned in time for the Olympics.

In Britain the Royal National Institute for the Blind (RNIB) is leading a campaign for good web design and awards a See It Right logo to those sites it approves. It is initially targeting online banking and shopping, the UK Government, ISPs and web designers. In many cases simple changes can assist visually challenged surfers – such as careful choice of background and text colours and the use of large text with clear fonts. You can read more about the campaign on the RNIB website and check some of the 'approved' sites, a link is available at www.heinemann.co.uk/hotlinks (express code 1386).

A Freeview study in 2003 showed that users who access the Internet through a broadband connection not only go online more often but they also spend more time online per session. This has obvious implications for online businesses as broadband take-up increases.

Broadband was slow to take-off in the UK but, by the end of 2003, Oftel – the telecommunications watchdog – was claiming that it was available in more than 3 million homes. There were two problems:

- Oftel's figures included users with minimum connection speeds of 128 and 150kbps (kilobits per second). 'True' broadband is really considered to start at 512kbps.
- Whilst 80 per cent of the UK can get broadband by ADSL and cable, this access is largely restricted to urban areas. Rural communities are left with a problem. To overcome this several rural communities are taking action themselves with the help, needless to say, of a website. The Community Broadband Network (CBN) website helps to link rural communities who want to get together to get connected. The initiative is being backed by the government which wants Britain to have more broadband users than comparative countries by 2005 and BT is aiming for 6 million users by 2006.

Government support

As you saw on page 368, the UK government originally championed the cause of online business through the website UK Online which was closed in spring 2004. Information and advice to small businesses is, however, still available from the Department of Trade and Industry and from Business Links advice centres. As you have seen above, the government is also keen to promote greater broadband take-up across the country, although critics argue that it should do more to promote faster connection speed availability and lower prices.

At the start of 2004, BT was investigating methods to allow its broadband users to increase their connection speed to up to 2mbps (million bits per second) at the click of a mouse, and also launched a cheaper 'no-frills' service. To find out more about broadband services and take-up in the UK versus other countries, go to the Point Topic website, a link is available at www.heinemann.co.uk/hotlinks (express code 1386P).

Secure payment arrangements

Customer confidence is absolutely vital for online payments. Newspaper headlines about fraud, hackers and phishing quite obviously put people off. To be secure, all online payments need to be:

- **Private and confidential** between the buyer and the seller.
- **Authentic** because both people are who they claim to be.
- **Conveyed intact** and without any changes or alterations during transmission.
- **Erased** from the system after the process has been completed.

This is achieved by specific security standards.

SSL (Secure Sockets Layer) allows a standard browser, such as Microsoft Explorer, to transmit and receive information securely. This is because the data is encrypted – or scrambled – using encryption keys that change every time the browser is used. Customers know when this is happening because they are warned that they are 'about to view information over a secure connection' and then see the locked padlock symbol and 'https' on the address line. They can then double click the locked padlock symbol to read the authentication/security certificate that confirms the site is legitimate and the 'seller' is who they claim to be. However, with this system there is no check that the buyer is genuine and, for example, is the true owner of the credit card being used to purchase goods.

SET (Secure Electronic Transfer) is a more sophisticated system for credit card transactions. When the cardholder buys online the credit card company authenticates the card via a digital signature. This proves that the cardholder is genuine. It will then only pay the seller when it has checked the seller's identity – against a digital certificate. Again, critical information, e.g. the card number, is encrypted and decrypted but is never actually made known to the seller – only to the card's issuing bank.

Businesses can basically arrange to receive payments in three ways:

- **Include an order form on the website** that customers can complete with their credit or debit card details. When this is received by the seller the card details are processed in the same way as telephone orders. This method is rarely used because most customers are reluctant to email credit or debit card details, despite the fact that their Internet browser will have SSL encryption as standard.
- **Pay a Merchant Service or Payment Service Provider (PSP)** to collect and process payments on its behalf. This is very useful for small businesses. In this case, when the customer makes a payment it is captured on the secure site belonging to the PSP – not that belonging to the business. PSPs charge a fee for this service. They also hold on to the money for between 30 and 60 days as a precaution against fraud. Only then will they pass it on to the supplier. Examples include WorldPay and NetBanx – links to these sites are available at www.heinemann.co.uk/hotlinks (express code 1386P).
- **Arrange with their bank to operate their own merchant service** and process their own payments on a secure website. Banks will only agree to this if they are convinced of the financial status of the business, the security arrangements in place and are satisfied with the terms and conditions of online trading.

Web authoring tools

There are a number of web authoring tools, from entry level packages to more sophisticated software. The most well-known entry level package is Microsoft FrontPage, which has wizards to help non-experts to create a simple website without any specialist knowledge. You can find out about other alternatives by looking on the shelves in your local PC World or other suppliers – or checking out the type of packages available online at the PC World website.

Macromedia, a specialist web development software company, produces packages such as Dreamweaver, Fireworks and Flash technology which enable professional developers to produce a range of different effects and designs. You can

Business brief

Design, usability, navigation – and Jakob Neilsen . . .

Hundreds of website design agencies in the UK boast that their main USP is how well they can design websites. Design and usability are the key aspects of a website and include navigation, i.e. the way in which you move around a site by means of menus and options at the top, left, right or bottom of the screen.

Design, usability and how the user is guided through a site has evolved hugely since the early days of the Internet, when a few talented amateurs started to design websites. But there is still a fair way to go. According to Jakob Nielsen, one of the world's leading authorities on website usability, companies today should be spending at least 10 per cent of their online budgets on analysing usability – and the other 90 per cent putting that into action.

Jakob Nielsen is the Jeremy Clarkson of online operations. He checks websites, assesses them and criticises them. He identifies ways in which businesses can save money and increase business by improving their online operations. For example, he claims that a badly designed Intranet can cost a 10,000 employee company $15 million a year in lost productivity as they search in vain for what they need. If you think your College Intranet could be improved, perhaps you should look at Nielsen's site before you make any suggestions! A link is available at www.heinemann.co.uk/hotlinks (express code 1386P).

find out more about these on the Macromedia website.

A very small business can obtain help and advice through many free services and local agencies, such as the Chamber of Commerce. Others will prefer to obtain the assistance of many professional development agencies – both small and large – depending upon their individual needs and budget.

Links to some of the websites mentioned above are available at www.heinemann.co.uk/hotlinks (express code 1386P).

'Sticky' websites

It is said that customers decide whether they like a website within two clicks. A website is known as 'sticky' when people stay with it for some time, going from page to page. This is what businesses want – it is pointless designing a website that turns off customers almost as soon as they arrive.

The problem is that amateur websites can do this by accident because the designers had no idea of some of the most important issues. For example:

- Site does not appear properly on all platforms (e.g. Apple Mac, Netscape, Internet Explorer).
- Sites that are slow to load.
- Pages which hold too much information.
- Requests for personal information before people can access the site.
- Links that don't work.
- Errors on the site.
- Out of date information.
- Poor navigation – customers cannot find their way around.
- Incomprehensible instructions on the site.
- Loads of pop-up adverts.
- Lack of contact information.
- No search facility/irrelevant search results.

In this case the business can do itself more harm than good by having the site, because it is giving

Sticky websites keep you there a long time

out negative signals to potential customers. This is why many businesses are better obtaining professional advice and assistance on the design and navigation aspects and how to present the content in the best way.

Brave sites include a note asking visitors to comment on the site – and use this to improve the design!

Business matters

A major benefit of an effective website which is often overlooked is the promotional value. Most online stores – Tesco, John Lewis, Boots, Debenhams, Amazon – try to ensure that visitors register on the site and provide their contact details, especially their email address. If they give their permission, the store can then legally target the customer with promotional emails which advertise special offers and other bargains, often linked to special occasions such as Christmas, Valentine's Day, Mother's Day and so on. (See also the Privacy and Electronic Communications Regulations, Unit 2, page 191).

Many online businesses use this information as part of their CRM strategy. CRM stands for **Customer Relationship Marketing** (see also page 111). Basically, customer information is captured from customers who register or use the website and is then analysed to profile customers more accurately. This enables future customisation of the site – or dynamic elements to be introduced – to more accurately reflect the needs of individual customers.

The Internet can also be used to help promote and launch new products, often through the creation of a microsite (see page 396) or through the main website. The fastest growing category is cars, with more and more manufacturers choosing to launch new models online. BMW was the first, in 2001. It set up its BMW Films initiative and hired top directors to shoot short films specifically for the web. In the first year alone over 40,000 people registered to receive further promotional information. Since then other manufacturers, including Volvo and Mazda have produced Internet films and Mazda launched its Mazda 6 range online. Mitsubishi joined them with a European launch campaign for its 'Evo' car in 2004 which included a games website on which visitors could take part in driver simulation and racing games.

Marketing experts think other brands can learn much from online car advertisers and their innovative approach to website promotions. Instead of simply seeing the web as another way to display car brochures, car companies use film to stir the customer's emotions by demonstrating each car's personality in a unique type of lifestyle.

Talking point

View 1: The most important factors about a website are its design and usability.

View 2: The most important factor about a website is that it meets the customer's requirements.

With which viewpoint do you agree – and why?

Over to you!

Links to some of the websites mentioned below are available at www.heinemann.co.uk/hotlinks (express code 1386P).

1 To see how websites have developed over the past ten years, go to Archive.org. Select a well known website (e.g. BBC news) and then see how it looked on at least **two** occasions in the past. Take a print-out of each example for your site and then compare your findings with those of other members in your group who have investigated other websites.

2 Suggest the main benefits to each of the following businesses of having an online presence, linked to their overall aims and objectives.
   a The National Union of Students.
   b A small, specialist manufacturer like firms like K C Mobility, which adapts cars for disabled drivers.
   c A large store, such as Boots.

3 Your neighbour is considering setting up a website. She specialises in creating dried flower displays, particularly those made out of flowers from special occasions, such as wedding bouquets.
   a Identify **two** likely aims or objectives of her business.
   b Suggest **three** benefits she would gain by going online.
   c Recommend the most appropriate type of online presence for her, with reasons.
   d She has heard that she could earn money for her site by becoming involved in some affiliate programs. Find out more about these on the UK Affiliates website and suggest **two** that would be appropriate, with reasons.

4 An online presence is only any use if customers know about the site and, when they find it, can use it easily. Websites can be promoted through offline marketing materials, such as press and poster advertisements, on business stationery and on company vehicles as well as through online advertising and search engines (see also page 396).
   a List the domain names of **five or six** sites you know and use regularly, and identify how you found out about each one.
   b For **two** of these sites, identify the aspects that you like most about them and the features of the online operation that most appeal to you. In particular, assess the sites under the following headings:
      i Ease of use and navigation.
      ii Download time.
      iii Quality of content.
      iv Layout and design.
      v Search facility.
      vi Graphics.
      vii Logical organisation of content.
      viii Access to customer service/help, if appropriate.
      ix Up-to date content.
      x The appropriateness of the site to the type and style of online business operation.
   c Suggest any improvements that you think could be made to improve the usability of the sites. If you are stuck, then glance back to the Business Brief on page 387, to see if this gives you some ideas.
   Compare your ideas with other members of your group.

5 If you are interested in some of the special effects that can be included on websites, and want to know more, go to the Macromedia website. Macromedia produces a wide range of web authoring tools, such as Flash, Dreamweaver and Fireworks, which are used to create these effects. Then suggest **three** factors a business should take into consideration when deciding whether its online operations would benefit from these type of effects or not.

Links to some of the websites mentioned below are available at www.heinemann.co.uk/hotlinks (express code 1386P).

1 As a group, for each of the aims and objectives linked to going online that are listed below, suggest **one** way in which an online operation may help their achievement.

> To make a profit.
> To increase or maximise profits.
> To provide goods or services to the local community.
> To expand operations.
> To increase or maximise sales.
> To improve quality.
> To be more competitive.
> To attract new customers.
> To reduce costs.
> To enhance the brand image and increase brand awareness.
> To find out more about the customers.
> To provide a charitable or voluntary service.
> To raise funds for a charitable or voluntary service.
> To increase customer awareness of activities.
> To complement the offline business.

2 The benefits of an online presence should link to the overall aims and objectives of the business. For each of the following examples, suggest **two** likely aims of the business and **three** related benefits that are likely to be gained from an online presence:

   a A holiday complex, e.g. CenterParcs.
   b A school uniform manufacturer, e.g. Trutex.

   c A mobile phone retailer such as Carphone Warehouse.
   d A small business supplying wedding cars, e.g. Whitton Cars.
   e a charity such as Help the Aged.

3 Richer Sounds was concerned about selling hi-fi and related equipment online because it feels strongly that it is better if customers can see these type of goods before purchase and talk to expert staff about the different models and options available. Despite these reservations it still chose to have an online presence.

Suggest **four** reasons why it decided to do this.

4 Ten years ago many organisations only operated offline but now operate online as well. Examples include your local council, your college, Dabs.com (which used to be Dabs Direct, a mail order company) – even your local football club.

   a For **two** of the organisations named above, suggest **three** benefits of operating both offline and online.
   b A friend argues that whilst a Premiership team like Manchester United should have a website, it is pointless for smaller clubs in the lower divisions to have one – such as Bristol Rovers or York City. Do you agree or disagree? Give a reason for your answer and compare your views with other members of your class.
   c Suggest **three** other examples of businesses which now operate both online and offline and, in each case, identify the benefits the organisation has gained. Then compare your ideas and suggestions with other members of your class.

This section covers

Problems relating to exposure

Vulnerability to hostile attack

Potential unpopularity with staff

Financial uncertainties

As you saw in the first section, the British Government has been keen to promote online business in the UK. It was therefore quite a surprise when a study by consultants Booz Allen Hamilton in 2003 found that *fewer* small and medium-sized firms were using the Internet than in 2001. It appears several had closed down their websites and decided against any online presence.

The main reason put forward was not just the cost of creating or developing a website presence, but a failure to obtain any real benefits. According to the experts, one of the problems is that some small businesses think that it is enough just to create a site and put it up on the Internet whereas there are other factors to consider if a business wants to maximise the possible benefits – as you will see in this section and the next. In some cases businesses hadn't fully considered the potential problems and worked out how to overcome these at the planning stage.

This is important. Earlier you saw how dotcom businesses like Boo failed in the late 1990s, often through over-optimism. Before any business should consider the feasibility of an online presence it is important to identify the potential problems as well as the benefits. This is the subject of this section.

Problems relating to exposure

Going online immediately exposes a business to the wider world. Some of this exposure is good, as it attracts potential customers or suppliers. On other occasions this exposure can be more problematic, for a variety of reasons.

- **Hostile chatrooms and negative publicity**. There are numerous ways in which an organisation can annoy or irritate its customers – poor service, late deliveries and uncompetitive prices are three examples. In the past, customers with a problem had to contact the business to complain. If they still felt they had been poorly treated there was little they could do. Today they can. Dissatisfied customers not only spread the word through chatrooms they also, in some cases, set up their own websites to challenge the organisation concerned.

BT Openwoe is one example. This is a user forum for customers who are dissatisfied with the service and, quite obviously, may put off potential customers from using the BT Openworld service. A more general site for customer woes is Blagger – which can be checked by anyone before they do business with a new supplier. Several independent shopping sites, like Ciao, have review sections as well as more specialist sites such as DVD Reviewer, and Fodors provides feedback on travel companies.

Quite simply, an online business that gives poor service may suddenly find itself under attack in several chatrooms and on several sites simply because the public can communicate and express themselves far more easily online – and to a far wider audience. Unfortunately, it may also find the same thing if just one customer has a grudge and starts an online campaign against the company. Links to some of the websites mentioned above are available at www.heinemann.co.uk/hotlinks (express code 1386P).

- **Customer fears over payment security/ unfamiliar trading conditions**. The main reason why online trading was relatively slow to take off was because of customer worries about giving credit card details online. In the early days of shopping online, there were many scare stories about the activities of fraudsters. Interestingly, it has now been proved that there is far more likelihood of fraud through 'skimming' (see page 257) or when giving card details over the telephone than by paying online. In some cases, security procedures are so robust that online stores like Amazon are quite happy to give written guarantees to underpin any transactions made online by their customers.

  Initially, too, customers were worried that they wouldn't know exactly what to do to buy online. Magazines, newspapers and television programmes have helped by giving customers information and advice on how to buy online and recommended that they use well-known brands or stores for security. Normally, once a new customer has successfully placed an order, received confirmation and then obtained the goods without any problem they become an immediate convert to online shopping. Basically, it is a question of consumer confidence and, as trading at Christmas 2003 proved (see page 361), this is steadily increasing as security improves and many virtual companies continue to build a relationship with their customers.

- **Potential problems of defamation.** Most people are aware that if they say or write something untrue about someone they may be breaking the law. They may, however, be less aware that this also applies if they publish something on the Internet or print off from it. This applies to material on websites, to the subjects debated by discussion groups and to emails sent within and outside a company. The law of defamation is quite clear. Spoken untrue statements are slanderous, written statements are libellous. The only real defence is to prove that what has been said or written is true and was said without malice; otherwise the injured party can sue for compensation.

- **Inability to cope with massively increased market interest.** All businesses go online in the hope of generating additional business. The problem occurs if there is a huge surge of interest which the company cannot handle. On one level this can result in the site crashing, because too many people are trying to use it simultaneously. On another level it can mean enquiries cannot be answered quickly or orders cannot be filled because there is insufficient stock or too few staff to process them. In this case, the company has not only failed to take advantage of the new business but will have actually done itself a disservice as the dissatisfied customers are unlikely to contact it again in the future.

Business matters

In Britain, ISPs and other website publishers are not held to be responsible for defamatory material on their site if they can satisfy two criteria. First, they must prove they took reasonable care to ensure the material was not published. Second, if they are alerted to a problem they must take immediate steps to resolve it.

In 2002, Friends Reunited took immediate action when a retired teacher complained that an ex-pupil had made defamatory comments about him on the site. It immediately removed the offending material. The teacher later sued the ex-pupil and was awarded £1250 in damages, but he did not sue the website operators who could have claimed they had taken reasonable care.

In March 2000 Demon Internet, an ISP, was less fortunate because it failed to take note of a fax which alerted it to defamatory material posted by a newsgroup it hosted. The complainant, Laurence Godfrey, was awarded £15,000 plus legal costs which Demon had to pay.

In 2001, defamatory comments about the Internet service provider Totalise plc were posted on two financial websites – The Motley Fool and Interactive Investor International – by an anonymous user who called himself Zeddust. When the company took legal action both websites were forced to reveal the user's identity – traceable through the IP address.

Cybercrime terminology

You came across the term phishing in the last section. Some other terms relating to e-crime or cybercrime are given below.

- **A hacker** is a person who gains unauthorised access to a computer for the purpose of stealing or corrupting the data.
- **A virus** is a rogue program which attaches itself to a genuine program. When the program runs, the virus program runs first. It can make copies of itself (which uses up all the memory) or destroy the host program. It is spread when an infected file is sent from one computer to another.
- **A worm** is similar to a virus but does not attach itself to other programs. It can replicate itself and use memory. Instead of infecting files they infect whole disks or computer systems. Most are spread by email. A famous example was the Anna Kournikova virus which infected Windows systems when the user opened an email attachment.
- **A Trojan horse** is another type of malicious code which, when downloaded onto the computer, carries out destructive actions of which the computer user is unaware. For example, a Trojan horse can open a backdoor into a computer system and allow hackers to connect to the computer without the knowledge of the user.
- **A spoof website** is one which, to all intents and purposes, looks exactly the same as the original but which has been set up by a hacker. Spoofing is normally used in connection with phishing as users are directed to the spoof website (e.g. a retail store or a bank) and told to enter personal details or credit card information. Microsoft has been criticised for the fact that spoofers can create website addresses which replicate the original in the browser window. Customers should check a site is secure by first noting that the padlock at the bottom right of the screen is locked, then double-clicking on this to check that the security certificate was issued to the correct registered domain name.

Vulnerability to hostile attack

According to the National Hi-Tech Crime Unit (NHTCU), cybercrime is costing British businesses billions of pounds a year. Large businesses are threatened by phishing, spoof websites or denial of service attacks; small businesses are more vulnerable to staff misuse of company websites and lack of care in relation to security, such as forgetting or sharing user IDs and passwords. All computer users are threatened by major viruses such as MyDoom which caused a denial of service (DOS) attack at The SCO Group – an American software company.

- **DOS attacks and other cybercrimes**. A DOS attack occurs when a website is overwhelmed with data, such as email messages, in a very short time. In the case of SCO, the MyDoom virus first infected hundreds of thousands of computers which were then instructed to start contacting the SCO website at the same time. The onslaught brought down the site for several days.

In a new twist, in February 2004, websites were reporting on a new breed of hacker called **hackmailers** who threaten a site with a DOS attack unless they are paid. They target sites at their most vulnerable times (such as Wimbledon in June). In early 2004 several bookmakers had been targeted – in the run up to major sporting events such as Euro 2004. Quite obviously a DOS attack at that time would lose the firms millions of pounds.

- **ISP collapses**. All computer users are totally dependent upon their ISP to stay online. If the system develops a technical fault, then Internet access is lost until the fault is repaired. With a business this can create huge problems, particularly if a website is 'down' for any length of time. ISP reliability, therefore, is important for all users but critically important for businesses.

ISP service can be affected not just because of its own actions but through those of its own suppliers. All ISPs need access to phone lines and in 2002, America's second largest telephone company, WorldCom, filed for bankruptcy after admitting to a £2.5 billion accounting fraud (see page 195). Many ISPs relied on WorldCom, because it routed 28 per cent of global Internet traffic. According to Jupiter Research, more than 20 million business customers relied upon it for their websites, even if they didn't know it.

Fortunately most ISPs use multiple telecoms providers and had also seen what happened when the US company Excite@Home went bankrupt in 2001. Users were quickly switched to an alternative network but this meant issuing them with a new email address. Anyone sending an email to the old address simply received a 'message undeliverable' response. Many small businesses were concerned about losing customers who were responding to advertisements showing the old address.

Potential unpopularity with staff

Developing an online presence may create worry and anxiety for staff. It depends upon the type of operation, its size and the way any changes are managed. Staff may be concerned that their jobs will change – or disappear altogether.

- It is likely that new staff will be needed with specific skills – such as a Webmaster whose job is to manage the website and keep it up-to-date. In a small business this may be done very informally by someone as an additional part of their job role. In a large business there is likely to be a specialist web team comprising developers, designers and online marketing experts.
- The jobs of existing staff will change to take account of new methods of working, such as buying supplies online and dealing with customer queries online. Staff will need to learn new skills and ways of working to cope with the change.
- In some cases, certain jobs may be outsourced to external specialists. This is possible because customers accessing online facilities have no idea of the person who answers their enquiry or responds to their email.
- Successful online operations may result in redundancies for other staff (see page 399).

Business matters

According to a joint survey by Evalueserve/NASSCOM, between 2003 and 2010 about 272,000 jobs will move offshore from Britain in a range of different occupations from help desks to software development. They argue this will be a good thing, because Britain will have a labour shortage by 2010. It is therefore in everyone's interest if these jobs are outsourced.

Many company bosses would agree. Between 2002 and 2004 over 30 firms, including Abbey National, Norwich Union, HSBC, Prudential and Lloyds TSB outsourced more than 55,000 jobs to India alone and the number of call centres rose from 50 to over 800. The reason was simple. Average call centre salaries there are about £1,200 a year, compared to £12,500 in Britain. This vastly reduces operating costs for British companies.

Financial uncertainties

The final group of potential disadvantages relates to money. It is possible to set up a simple website quite cheaply. However, this is only one component of having an online presence, and the most basic type of website may not be appropriate for the business.

In addition, calculating the potential benefits in monetary terms is not easy. A major pitfall to avoid is having an expensive online presence which brings few, if any, financial benefits. Often a more cautious start can bring considerable benefits. The first stage involves careful and realistic financial planning.

- **Initial investment costs**. The specific set up costs will depend upon whether the developments are being managed by a specialist agency or being done in house and the scale of the operation. For example, whereas a small business will pay an ISP to host the website a large company will host its own site, but this will require extensive hardware and qualified staff. Generally, the most typical categories of expenditure are likely to include the following:
  - **Additional hardware requirements**, e.g. computers, servers, printers, scanners etc. **Software requirements** – including operating system, applications programs (e.g. Microsoft Office), web authoring software, graphics packages etc.
  - **Additional set-up costs**, e.g. registering domain name, charge made by ISP for

hosting site (if appropriate).
  - **Agency costs**, if specialists are employed to design the site and handle any changes.
  - **Staff training** costs/cost of hiring new specialist staff.
  - **Marketing and promotional costs** – so that potential customers know the site exists!

These should be fairly easy to quantify. At one extreme there is the small enterprise that decides to create its own site or to pay someone to launch a simple, brochureware site consisting of a few pages of text and some straightforward graphics. At the other is the large organisation that pays a professional agency to create a sophisticated, dynamic site. In both cases there should be a realistic budget agreed which takes into account the aims and projected benefits of the online presence.

What may be less easy to predict are the future running costs or the costs of any additional development work that is required once the site is operational.

- **Set-up expenses versus uncertain future revenue streams**. If the cost of setting up a website can be quantified, the potential income is more difficult to assess. This will depend upon the extent to which the site achieves its objectives and the speed at which it does this. Normally, **benchmarks** are set which identify specific targets and when they should be achieved – as you will see on page 400.

Talking point

> **View 1:** *Security issues and the Internet are exaggerated by the media. There is no need for staff to worry too much about hackers or viruses so long as basic security measures are in place.*

> **View 2:** *Staff complacency about security is a huge danger for online businesses. Thoughtless actions, such as opening spam emails or replying to them, can cause huge problems.*

With which viewpoint do you agree – and why?

Business brief

Links to some of the websites mentioned below are available at www.heinemann.co.uk/hotlinks (express code 1386P).

The importance of e-marketing

Originally, many people believed that all they had to do was launch a site and people would flock to it in their thousands. There are two problems with this theory. Firstly, out of 4.8 billion sites, what is the chance of someone finding your site? Even more important, what is the chance of a potential customer finding your site?

People need to know a site exists to be able to use it so website promotion is very important – but this needs to be targeted at potential customers and not the world in general. The key methods used are therefore by taking advantage of the ways in which customers find sites – that is, by *searching* for them.

- **SEO (search engine optimisation)**. This means ensuring that major search engines, such as Google, Yahoo!, Altavista etc will include the site high in their listings. This is done by tailoring the content of the website so that 'webcrawlers' – used by search engines to find sites – will recognise it.
- **Pay per click advertising**. As an alternative a business can pay to be included in search results on different search engines. A major site that coordinates this is Overture. Websites bid to be included in a search engine's lists and the highest bidder takes the top slot.

  The advertiser is only charged when a user clicks on their link. Google also accepts this type of advertising which it includes as coloured entries at the top and blocked adverts down the side of the page. All these

advertisers pay Google every time a user clicks to their site. The chances of this are quite high because the adverts are generated to link to the type of search being made so that they will be of interest to the user.

- **Affiliate marketing**. This is when an advertiser works with a website on a long-term basis to attract new visitors to the advertiser's site. In this case, every 'click through' normally earns income for the host site.

  When you were investigating the PC World site earlier, you may have seen that the site included details of its affiliate programme. If not, go back and check this out through the link on the home page. You will often see these programmes highlighted on websites and can click to find the details. To see a more comprehensive range, go to the UK Affiliates website and look at all the businesses looking for affiliates and see what they are offering.

Other online promotional methods include:

- **Viral marketing**. This is a campaign that spreads itself from customer to customer such as when you forward an email advert or SMS to a friend. You can find the ten most popular viral campaigns each week by visiting a part of the Lycos website.
- **Microsites**. These are special 'mini' websites created for a special campaign. This may be part of a larger site or a separate site which is created for a special reason and taken down when the campaign is over.
- **Online advertising, e.g. banner and pop-ups**. These invite people to click on them to go to the advertiser's website. Although some may be static adverts, others incorporate Flash technology, video and other interactive elements to capture the attention of the surfer.

Over to you!

Links to some of the websites mentioned below are available at www.heinemann.co.uk/hotlinks (express code 1386P).

1 a Find out more about cybercrime and the National Hi-Tech Crime Unit by visiting the NHTCU website. Then find out more about current cybercrimes in the news by visiting the Silicon website. You will also find other useful updates relating to online business on this site.

b As a group, identify the measures that have been taken by your college to protect against hacking, viruses or other problems. If possible, find out if a member of your technical staff can talk to you about the problems of monitoring a large online presence and how this is carried out.

2 Your local butcher has read about the success of Jack Scaife – whose business takings rocketed from £70,000 a year to £700,000 a year through his website, which won an e-commerce award in 2000. He says it will be a simple matter to copy the idea. You are not so sure. To your knowledge the shop is always a bit disorganised and the staff don't seem very efficient.

As a group, investigate Jack Scaife's website and find out more about the company.

Then identify the main ways in which your disorganised butcher would have to alter his ways to benefit from an online presence.

3 Jack Scaife is just one business that has won an e-commerce award for their website and online operations. Find out about other businesses that have done the same – including some very small start-up firms which have been particularly successful – on the E-commerce Awards website. Select the one that appeals to you the most and then, as a group, decide what makes them special.

8.3 Section review

Links to some of the websites mentioned below are available at www.heinemann.co.uk/hotlinks (express code 1386P).

1 Advice to potential online businesses, to help them to identify potential pitfalls, is given on several sites including most commercial banks, and is also on the Microsoft and Scottish Enterprise websites. As a group, investigate these sites and suggest **six** ways in which this type of advice can assist potential online businesses.

2 Suggest **three** advantages of using a professional agency to create a website. Then suggest **three** occasions when this wouldn't be necessary or needed. For further information research sites such as OnlineBizBuilder, 123Live, x2cms, Moonfish, and any other sites offering website services.

3 In a survey carried out by Forrester Research in 2003 the following were listed as the main challenges of operating an online retail website.

> ### Challenges of operating a retail website
>
> Keeping promises to customer.
> Offering superb customer service.
> Operating an effective and reliable IT system.
> Converting 'browsers' into 'buyers'.
> Attracting new customers.
> Seeing competitors copy all our ideas.
> Keeping stocks at the right level.
> Promoting the site but within budgeted levels.

a Add **five** further problems some other businesses may face, as a result of the issues you have read about in this section.

b As a group, suggest any other reasons that you can think of, which you didn't list under **a** above.

c As a group, suggest ways in which all the problems you have listed may be minimised or overcome.

This section covers

Implementation issues of going online

The desired speed of change and other aspects

A SWOT analysis and deciding the way ahead

You have already seen that, apart from local businesses who provide a personal service, most organisations can obtain a considerable number of benefits if they have an online presence. They may be able to increase their sales, reduce costs or provide information to customers more effectively. They may be able to achieve other business aims and objectives more effectively and efficiently. However, they must also think about the potential problems associated with an online presence and plan carefully to ensure they are prepared for these and can overcome them. This final section looks at the major points businesses must consider as they do this.

Implementation issues

Some small businesses – such as Jack Scaife – slowly develop their IT solutions and only go online after they have been trading successfully offline for some time. They may start with a very basic website and then improve this as time goes by and they increase their expertise from experience.

In other cases a new business may want to go online immediately or an SME (small/medium sized business) may want to rapidly extend its online presence from – say – a basic informational website to one that is more comprehensive to keep pace with its competitors.

You have already seen that there is a great danger in going online without sufficient resources in place to meet new customer demand and to cope with other issues. There is also no point in going online if the website cannot help the business to meet its main aims and objectives. However, if the major competitors of a business are online then an online presence is essential to remain competitive.

Assuming the business has decided it needs an online operation, then good planning is vital because going online can mean quite substantial changes to the way a business operates. This can create problems with staff inside the company and with customers. There may also be additional difficulties if people are so involved in the changes and in learning new ways of working that they neglect their current jobs. In addition, final costs can be greater than envisaged. Important issues to consider, and decisions to make, are listed below.

Business brief

Key issues of online operations

Experts argue that the key issues about the feasibility and implementation of online operations include the following points.

- **Identifying how to promote the brand** so that online operations support and enhance offline operations. A good example are the promotions by car manufacturers mentioned on page 388.
- **Being reactive to customer demand and feedback**. Online operations are different because they are interactive and give power to the user to influence developments.
- **Setting benchmarks to measure success**. These are covered on page 400.

- **Potential requirement for customisation**. A basic website, as you already know, can be created from an 'off-the-shelf' web authoring package such as Microsoft FrontPage. More adept website designers can create more sophisticated websites by using other packages

– such as Dreamweaver, Flash and Fireworks. However, the greater the need for customisation, i.e. creating a one-off 'specialist' site, the greater the need for specialist skills. This means that the design costs will be higher.

- **Desired extent of online operations**. On page 368, you learned that some websites contain purely passive brochureware, others are partially interactive (customers can communicate or order online) and some – such as Amazon – are fully interactive. The extent of the operations affects the specialist skills required and the cost of implementing the proposed strategy.

If the business intends to sell online then considerations must include which stock to feature, whether additional stock will be required, where it will be stored, how payments will be accepted, how the goods will be distributed and the legal issues of selling online. (For details see specialist Unit 7, page 318.)

In addition, the ability of the website to cope with the projected number of visitors is important. Otherwise it will 'fall over' or perform so slowly as to be useless. This means carefully considering site capacity and the projected amount of 'traffic' to the site during the planning stage. Famous examples of website 'crashes' include the BBC site on September 11th 2001, the Government's Census site on its launch date and MyCokemusic on its first day.

- **Changing user specifications**. All websites must be kept up-to-date, accurate and relevant to the customer. In some cases, the needs and demands of the customer may change over time, so that the website has to be revised to incorporate increased service levels, such as automated confirmation of orders, online order tracking and online communication with staff.

For this reason, from the outset, the updating and review of the website content must be planned to take place at regular intervals to ensure that it always meets the needs of its users.

Desired speed of change and other aspects

There is obviously more pressure on staff if the desired speed of change is rapid – and less opportunity to consider and prepare for all the potential effects. The pace of change is likely to be influenced by the following factors.

- **Pace set by competitors**. The pressure to change quickly will be greater if the business is currently losing out to competitors. The situation is different if the business is at the leading edge in its field and is ahead of its competitors.

- **Adaptability of key staff**. Most job descriptions today include a requirement for reasonable flexibility to help the business to take advantage of new technology. However, staff still need to be consulted about the proposed changes and are far more likely to be cooperative if they are involved at the outset. Proper training is essential for any staff whose jobs will significantly change.

- **Potential redundancies and industrial relations problems**. This is mainly likely to occur if a large business would radically change its operations as a result of an online presence and there would be no work for many existing employees. In 2004 Ebookers, the online travel group, closed 10 shops in the UK and mainland Europe and made 270 staff redundant. It no longer needed these stores because its online service was now profitable and less costly to operate. The law on redundancy means that if more than 20 people are involved there must be consultation with the trade unions or any staff association. Redundant staff with over two years' service will be eligible for redundancy pay and have other rights, such as the right to take time off to look for alternative work. If you want to find out more, a link to the ACAS website is available at www.heinemann.co.uk/hotlinks (express code 1386P).

- **Timescale for effective online operation**. The time taken to achieve this will depend upon several factors such as: the size of the business, the complexity of the change, the number of operations affected, the amount of staff training required, whether certain tasks will be carried out both manually and online for a short time. Ideally all timescales should include time for testing and also have 'slack' built-in so that unexpected problems can be remedied promptly without jeopardising other related schedules – such as marketing plans to promote the site launch.

- **Difficulties in transition**. In many cases a 'pilot run' is undertaken so that any problems can be identified and solved before the whole system 'goes live'. This is particularly important for key operations involving staff or customers – such as paying wages electronically or handling customer enquiries online. In this case, a sample number would be handled by the new system and the success of this assessed before the entire system changes over.

A small scale website can be tested offline by members of staff, who can report back on usability issues and give suggestions for improvements. However, a better method is to use a company which employs an independent panel to assess and report on the website before it is launched.

- **Increased sales or service supply**. The whole aim of online business should be to improve the business, e.g. by greater efficiency, better customer service, higher level of overall sales, opportunities to sell new products or services. Areas to examine closely include the speed of operation, the quality of service, the overall sales performance and decisions made by staff and management that affect sales or service supply.

- **Anticipated timescale of benefits**. The most important benefits should be given top priority so that these are gained first. If the main aim is to improve sales and customer service then these targets should be set first. The sales of new products, additional product features or the development of other services may be achieved over a longer timescale.

The normal method is to set **benchmarks**. These are SMART objectives (see page 47) to be achieved

It is important to check if your company has reached its benchmarks by checking your website's activity

by a specific date and normally include:

- The number of visitors to the site.
- The action you want visitors to take (e.g. ordering a brochure, buying goods).
- The number of visitors who take this action (called the 'conversion rate').
- The average order value per visitor (for retail sites).

- **Anticipated competitive disadvantage of not going online**. This will depend upon the type of products or services being sold and whether these are suited to online trading, whether competitors are online, whether customers or suppliers trade online, whether online business would help to achieve the main aims and objectives and whether there would be direct benefits such as increased sales, reduced costs or improved efficiency.

SWOT analyses and implementation plans

An e-business SWOT analysis helps to identify the internal strengths and weaknesses of the business plus external opportunities and threats. This helps to take account of factors such as competitors, the market, future opportunities for growth and current customer relationships.

Internal factors	
Strengths Good product knowledge Specialist stocks held Good sources of supply Strong commitment to online operation	**Weaknesses** Only known regionally to date No knowledge of global market Lack of specialist IT knowledge Problems of fulfilment if demand high
External factors	
Opportunities Access to new customers Ability to offer new products/services, e.g. auctions for rare records, music downloads etc. Ability to build brand name	**Threats** Strong competition from established sites May see downturn in offline business Competitors may offer better/faster customer service

Figure 8.9 *SWOT analysis for The Record Exchange*

SWOT analyses were first covered on page 133. If you have forgotten all about them, turn back to Unit 2 and refresh your memory. (If you have studied specialist Unit 9, you will also know about them in relation to small businesses.) An example of a SWOT analysis for Tim and Aysha's online business operation for their music exchange (see page 375) is given in Figure 8.9.

If the SWOT analysis identifies that there are significant benefits and opportunities to be gained, then the next stage is to prepare an **implementation plan**. This should identify how the business can maximise the benefits but also overcome some of the main problems associated with an online presence. The main factors to consider are illustrated in Figure 8.10.

Figure 8.10 *Planning an online presence – factors to consider*

The implementation plan should include the following aspects:

- The agreed level of online presence.
- The goals of the online operation and expected benefits.
- The key aspects of the website and features of the online operation.
- A realistic timescale for design, testing and implementation.
- Identified risks and problems and ways in which these can be overcome.
- The proposed effect on the organisation and staff.
- The agreed budget for the online operation (both set-up costs and operational costs).
- Benchmarks/SMART objectives to check success.
- Staff training requirements.
- How the site will be tested to ensure it is user-friendly.
- How the site will be promoted (offline and online).
- Launching the site.
- Monitoring usage, customer reactions and benefits (including financial benefits).

- Identifying a 'webmaster' or person responsible for ensuring the website is constantly secure, up-to-date and is fulfilling customer expectations.

Business brief

Measuring success

A business that sells goods online can obviously measure success by calculating the value of sales and the rate at which these are increasing. The popularity of informational sites, however, is less easy to assess.

For that reason, many organisations provide software solutions to help businesses measure the popularity of their websites. An example is Webtrends which tracks visitors to the website. Webtrends can identify the search engines that visitors used to reach the site, the most popular pages, the length of time spent on the site and various other essential aspects – such as the number of repeat or returning visitors. A link to the Webtrends website is available at www.heinemann.co.uk/hotlinks (express code 1386P).

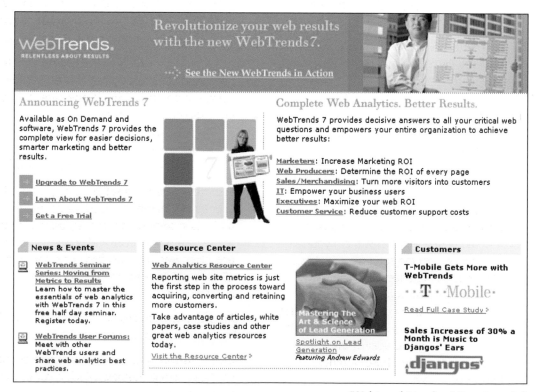

'Webtrends' tracks visitors to certain websites

Business matters

DMC Internet is an Internet services provider. What might interest you more, if you look at its website, is that its director Carl Churchill is only 19 years of age. Apart from other things, his claim to fame was being placed top of the prospective 2020 Rich List, commissioned by the Royal Bank of Scotland. His company is forecast to be worth over £100 million by then.

You can find out more about the company by visiting the DMC website. You can find out more about Carl Churchill, people like him and Internet developments in general on the Internet Works website. This is the online version of the Internet Works magazine which includes articles for anyone interested in online business.

Links to the two websites mentioned above are available at www.heinemann.co.uk/hotlinks (express code 1386P).

Talking point

View 1: *Businesses must go online quickly if their competitors are online. They can learn from their mistakes as they go.*

View 2: *Businesses should take their time and plan carefully before they go online. The main point is not to make any mistakes.*

With which viewpoint do you agree — and why?

Over to you!

Links to some of the websites mentioned below are available at www.heinemann.co.uk/hotlinks (express code 1386P).

1 A survey of 46 travel websites by research company Shelley Taylor & Associates identified that the bottom five places belonged to British sites: Flybe, Ryanair, Bridge the World, Holiday Autos and Travel Bag. The top five sites were all American: Expedia, Travelocity, Hilton, Orbitz and American Airlines.

The sites were scored on elements such as site entry, navigation, the home page, pre-sale information and ease of booking.
  a Select **one** site which scored well and **one** which scored poorly and access them yourself. See if you agree with the survey by identifying at least **two** key differences between them.
  b Suggest **four** problems that you think could affect the operation of an online travel business and say what preventative steps you think will have been taken to guard against these. Compare your ideas with those of other members of your class.

2 Technology Means Business provides ICT advice to SMEs, i.e. small and medium sized businesses both online and through a national network of advisers. You can find out more on the TMB website.

Access the case studies on the site which describe how small businesses have been encouraged and helped to go online. Select **one** case study that interests you and identify:
  a The main advantages to the business of an online presence.
  b Any problems or pitfalls it had to overcome.

3 eBusinessClubs were set up at various locations by The British Chamber of Commerce to offer advice to SMEs in setting up websites, using the Internet to improve productivity and achieving other aims and objectives. You can find out more on the eBusinessClubs website or at your local Chamber of Commerce.

Read the case studies on the web and find the nearest club to your own area.

Identify **three** ways in which this type of operation will help a small business which is considering an online presence.

1 Mark Butler and Matthew Kenton are garden designers. They also specialise in decking and water features. They have a good reputation in their local area but would like to expand the business. As part of this strategy they are thinking of having a passive online presence. Mark is particularly keen on this as two of their major competitors have recently launched websites.

They are currently carrying out a SWOT analysis to decide whether an online presence is feasible.

a From their statements below, identify which are internal strengths and weaknesses and which are external opportunities and threats. Then, using the same format as the table on page 401, enter each comment in the appropriate section.

- We don't have the IT skills to build our own site, we'll have to pay someone to do it.
- Customers will be able to contact us through the website.
- We can include 'before' and 'after' pictures to illustrate our work.
- Our two main competitors have better sites than we could afford.
- We are renowned for high quality work.
- We can buy specialist supplies cheaper online.

b As a group, suggest **one** additional comment for each section.
c Suggest **three** potential benefits of having an online presence.
d Suggest **two** pitfalls they should be aware of.

2 Your friend Kerry has just been reading about Hard to Find Foods which delivers gourmet food nationwide. Kerry did a catering course last year but, beyond that, has very little business experience. Nevertheless she is very excited about this opportunity and thinks you could go into business together as quickly as possible.

You can find out more about this idea on the Hard to Find Foods website. Links are available at heinemann.co.uk/hotlinks (express code 1386P). Working in a small group, answer the questions below.

a Bearing in mind your own local area – and Kerry's skills – draw up a simple SWOT analysis for Kerry's proposal which will help her when she prepares an implementation plan.
b Identify **three** pitfalls that Kerry will need to try to avoid when she implements her e-business plan.

3 Find out more about planning an online presence and asking the right questions online. The Website Creation site is full of useful hints and tips and gives you five good reasons to build a website, 10 bad reasons for doing so (including wanting to be a dotcom millionaire!) and includes a checklist which incorporates taking account of business aims and objectives.

Alternatively, look at the Government's DTI Best Practice website – which replaced the UK Online for Business service. The site contains an e-planner to guide you through the process. Then working in small groups, complete this checklist for any small business idea of your choice. Assume the business currently employs about 10 members of staff but only has an offline presence. Finally, draw up a short proposal which includes:
a The benefits of having an online presence.
b **Five** common problems or pitfalls that are often associated with implementing an online presence.
c Your ideas for the ways in which these problems could be overcome.

Index

above the line advertising 312
accountants 68
accounts 63, 64, 232
action planning 118, 138
adaptability to change 302
administration department 56
adoptive leave 272
Advertising Standards Authority
    (ASA) 315
Advisory, Conciliation and
    Arbitration Service (ACAS)
    299
affiliate marketing 396
affiliated sites 356
after-sales service 348
aims of business 5, 45
    and resources 50
Amnesty International
    functional areas of 55
anti-virus software 71, 366
appraisal procedures 286, 287
arms trade 162
Arthur Anderson 195
assets 43, 147

B2B marketing 104
B2B trading 360
B2B transactions 74, 251
B2C trading 360
bad debts 63, 64, 230, 234
bank loan 147, 223
banking online 356
bankruptcy 16, 196
bar code readers 273
barriers to entry 129
batch production 72
below the line advertising 312
benchmarks 133, 136, 400
best value 52, 107
black economy 162, 165
board of directors 63, 81
body language 344
bottleneck 72
brand image 133, 156, 308
brand name 43, 51, 133
break even 46, 200, 202, 213–218
broadband 384
browsers 355
budget planning 238
budget, the 179
budgets 64, 89, 236–247
bunker, the 66
business
    accounting software 258
    activities 2
    aims/goals 5, 45
    buyer 104, 324
    cycle 175

objectives 50
online 354
performance 9
rates 179
responses 119, 120, 195
scale 20, 21
sectors 11
size 17, 18, 19
strategy 81
buyer behaviour 110, 111, 338

C2C trading 360
calculating
    costs 205, 207, 208
    revenue 203
    variances 240
call centres 212, 303, 394
CAP code of advertising practice
    315
capital 43, 146, 147
    goods 329
        intellectual 43
        investment 64
cartel 125
cascade of management direction
    83
cash
    float 262
    flow 63, 64, 145, 147,
        221–234
    registers 255, 258
cashing up 266
e-commerce 380
centralisation 56
chain of production 25
change – and potential implications
    305
changing legislation 191
changing technology 135, 189
charities 8, 9, 15, 16, 106
chatrooms 358, 391
classification of business activities
    26
clawback 246, 247
cold calling 76
collective bargaining 295, 296
Commission for Equality and
    Human Rights 280
Commission for Racial Equality
    (CRE) 280
communications 190, 304
    online 358
companies 12, 13
company accounts 232
competition act 123
competition
    and the internet 125
    direct and indirect 123

competitive
    advantage 124, 125
    market 123, 124, 128
    pressures 123, 135
competitor analysis 313
complaints – dealing with 319, 349
complementing offline services 370
Computer Aided Design (CAD) 80,
    190
Computer Integrated
    Manufacturing (CIM) 72, 190
computer network 69
Confederation of British Industry
    (CBI) 37
confidence – and the economy 177
conflict in business 293
consumables 64
Consumer Credit Act 316, 317
consumer
    demand 27, 175
    durables 329
    law 316–318, 322–324
    market 102
Consumer Protection Act 317, 324
Consumer Protection (Distance
    Selling) Regulations 318
contract of employment 69,
    269–272
contracts of sale 105, 323
cookies 191, 196, 371
coordination 82
corporate scandals 194
corporation tax 179
corrective action 87
cost centre 237, 238
cost price 8
costs 5, 6, 202
credit
    cards 257
    control 232
    controller 63, 233
    reference agencies 232, 234
    sales 229, 234
creditors 196, 234
crisis management 169, 171, 192
customer
    attributes 108, 313
    expectations 94
    key 113, 308
    relationship marketing (CRM)
        111, 388
    requirements 328
    service 133
    service department 57
    service training 326
customers
    as stakeholders 144
    dissatisfaction 352

greeting 341
    with special needs 342
cybercrime 393

Data Protection Act 277
day books 261, 262
dealer networks 348
debit cards 257
debtors 234
decentralisation 56
decision making unit (DMU) 104, 107
decline – types of 36
defamation 392
demand and supply 148
denial of service (DOS) attacks 393
deregulation 131, 132
design 75
digital
    information – suitability of 364
    interconnectivity 191
direct computer input 256
direct mail 68
Disability Discrimination Act 279, 333
Disability Rights Commission (DRC) 280, 333
disciplinary procedures 76, 271, 294
discrimination 278
Dismissal and Discipline Regulations 271
dismissal – types of 295
display materials 309
disposable income 109, 113, 175, 181
disputes
    collective 294, 295
    Individual 295
distribution 33
distribution department 59
diversification 3
dividends 12, 147
domain name 355
donations 9
dot.com company 360, 372, 373
downtime 64
dynamic websites 371, 372

e-business strategies 303
economic
    boom 175, 181
    depression 176, 181
    growth 175, 181
    recovery 176, 181
    slump 176, 181
    variables 174
economies of scale 129
efficiency targets 48, 51
elections 172

Electronic Point of Sale (EPOS) 65, 256, 258
e-marketing 67, 73, 396
employment 38
    and grievances 298
    and preferences 272, 273
    by sector 35, 37
Employment Act 192
Employment, Contract of 269 –272
Employment Equality (Sexual Orientation) Regulations 279
Employment Equality (Religion or Belief) Regulations 279
employment law 69, 192
Employment Relations Act 192
Employment Rights Act 192
employment tribunals 298
endorsement 68
engineering 31
entrepreneur 18
Enron 194
environment
    and damage 159
    and issues 185
    concerns of local communities 157
e-procurement 191, 360, 380
equal opportunities 152, 154, 278, 279, 290
Equal Opportunities Commission (EOC) 280
Equal Pay Act 279
equal rights 273
exchange rates 181
expenditure 89, 175, 202
exploitation of labour 159, 161
exposure online 391
express terms
    of contract of sale 323
    of employment 275
extranet 373

facilities management department 60
factoring 233
fat cats 185
feasibility of going online 398
finance department 63
financial accountants 63
financial stakeholders 146
firewall 64, 366
fixed costs 205, 206, 207
    reducing 210
flexibility and budgets 243
Flexible Working Regulations 273
flow production 72
Fast Moving Consumer Goods (FMCGs) 76, 329
footfall 318
formulas
    and break even 217

and spreadsheets 225
franchises 12, 19
fraud 257, 263–267
freight 33
functional departments 54, 55
    and links 79
future trends 130

gambling online 358
games and music online 362
global markets 98, 100
GM crops 183
greeting customers 341
grievance procedures 271, 294
Gross Domestic Product (GDP) 37
goals, business 5, 45
    and business performance 8
    and supplying service 8
government
    buyers 105
    departments 13, 105
    spending 180
    support for online business 368, 385
growth and decline of sectors 35
guarantees and warranties 350

hackers 65, 66, 365, 393
harassment 152
health and safety
    and dangerous conditions 160
    and retail stores 335
Health and Safety at Work etc. Act 153, 281
Health and Safety Regulations 281
health trusts 14, 100
hierarchies 80, 83
housing market 178
human resources 43, 55
HyperText Transfer Protocol (HTTP) 355

implementation issues of going online 398
implementation plan 400, 401
implied terms
    of contract of sale 323
    of employment 275
income 202, 204, 209
income tax 179
induction programme 68
industrial market 102
industrial relations problems 399
industries 27
inflation 176, 181
information sources – identifying 304
inputs 86
interactive customer communications 371
interest payments 147

interest rates 177, 179, 181
internal markets 99, 100
international relations 172
Internet Protocol (IP) address 355
Internet Service Provider (ISP) 355,
    383, 392, 393
Intranet 64, 373
investment 37, 64
investors 146, 196
Investors in People (IIP) 288
inviting online transactions 370
invoices 229, 234
IT department 64

job descriptions 274, 284
job development 151
job production 72
job searches online 359
job security 152
job titles 81
Just-in-time (JIT) 72

Key business failures 194
key customer 113, 308
key stakeholders 142, 165
kidults 113

last minute services 359
layout of stores 334
leave arrangements 271, 272
legal rights of employees 269
lifestyle 109, 110
limited companies 12
limited liability 13
links between functional activities
    and departments 79
listening skills 343
lobbying 165
local authorities, 13, 14
local communities and
    environmental concerns 157
local markets 98, 100
location of businesses 44, 51, 110
logistics 60
loss 200, 202

macroeconomic variables 174
management
    accountants 63
    action 218, 245, 246
manual sales recording 254
manufacturing 30, 36
margin of safety 215
market
    analysis 112
    and competition 123, 128,
        337
    concentration 132
    consumer 102
    leaders 127, 132
    position 133, 136

potential 115
presence 43, 51
research 67, 112, 116, 117
segments 99, 100, 108, 313
sensitivity 314
size 98
share 46, 127, 132
target 113, 156
trends – monitoring 116
marketing
    department 66
    mix 66, 88, 112
maximising
    income 209
    profits 45, 49
    sales 6
mass
    market 98, 100
    production 72
maternity leave 272
media 68
merchandisers 76, 107
mergers and takeovers 19, 303
microsite 67, 396
mission statements 10, 65
monitoring
    expenditure 225, 238
    performance 86
monopoly 125
moonlighting 162, 165
motivation 69
multinational organisations 18, 161
multi-skilling 305

national
    income 175
    markets 98, 100
negotiating 297, 330
network (computer) 64
new media 68, 354
niche markets 99, 100
nuclear waste 187

objectives – of business 47
    SMART 47, 48, 93
oligopoly 125
online
    auctions 355
    banking 356
    benefits of 377
    business 354
    communications 190, 358
    disadvantages of 391
    feasibility of 398
    features of 373
    investment costs 395
    range of activities 354
    security 357, 364–366
    speed of change 399
online payments – security of 257,
    385, 392

operational plans 81, 82
organisational markets 111
output 35, 36, 37, 86, 175
outsourcing 60, 303, 394
overdraft 147, 223, 226
overheads 206

parental leave 272
Parmalat 195
partnership 12
passive brochureware 368
patent 43
paternity leave 272
payment methods 252
payments and cashflow 229
penalty clause 105, 107
performance indicators (pis) 82, 86
performance
    monitoring 86
    reviews 287
person specification 284, 285
personal aptitudes and career
    options 290
personal development 288, 289
personnel department 68
PESTEL analysis 169, 170
petty cash 259, 262
planning process 81, 85
Point of purchase (POP) materials
    309
Point of sale (POS) materials 309
Point of sale systems 64, 256, 309
political issues and effects 172
portals 383
powdered baby milk 162
press release 68
pressure groups and ethical
    concerns 159
price differentiation 112, 113
pricing policies 324, 325
primary sector 25, 28
private sector 12, 32
product
    adaptation 115
    design 75
    differentiation 130, 132
    features 102
    flops 96
    knowledge 329
    life cycle 130
    quality 133, 184
    safety 184
    supply online 360
production
    department 72
    developments 190
    targets and monitoring 88
    line 72
productivity 6
profit 5, 6, 146, 200, 202
    and loss account 202

margin 215
    maximisation 45, 49
promotion opportunities 289
promotional
    appeal 314
    materials 309
    methods 308
public corporations 14, 15
public sector 13, 32
publicity campaign 68
purchasing department 73

qualifications – professional 291
quality assurance 72

Race Relations Act 279
receipts 255
recession 37, 176, 181
recognising sales opportunities 351
records of transactions 253
recruitment procedures 284
redeployment 51, 52
redundancy 152, 272, 399
references and the law 286
regional markets 98, 100
relocation 303
repairs and replacement parts 349
repeat purchases 351
reputation 134
Research and development (R & D)
    department 74
research online 361
reserves 63, 64
resources 41, 50
responses
        to customer feedback 119
        to external events 195
        to new trends 120
retail buyers 103
return and exchange policies 331,
    349
revenue 5, 202, 203, 209
risk assessment 60, 61

Sale of Goods Acts 317
sales
        and customer service 307
        and maximising 6
        contract 105
        department 76
        environment 333
        lead 76
        opportunities 351
        practice 341
        presentations 343
        promotions 307, 311
        targets and monitoring 88
        turnover 5, 19, 202
scale of organisations 20, 21
Search engine optimisation (SEO)
    68, 396

secondary sector 25, 29
sectors of production 27
    growth and decline of 35
sectors online 367
security personnel 332
servers 64
service payments 147
Sex Discrimination Act 279
Shareholders 146
share prices 194
shrinkage 263, 266
size of organisations 17, 18, 19
small and medium sized enterprises
    (SMEs) 18
SMART objectives 48, 49, 87, 292
SMS marketing 68
social injustice 184
social issues 182
socially harmful products 162, 164
socio-economic groups 109
sole trader 12
spam email 191, 196, 365
span of control 80
specialisation 3, 54
specification 107
sponsors as stakeholders 156
sponsorship 68
spreadsheets 225, 238, 241
staff
        associations 70, 149, 150
        benefits 150, 155
        discounts 266
        expectations 150
        training and development 154
        turnover 69, 153
        welfare 266
stakeholders
        and expectations 142
        and concerns 165
statements 234
statistics 38
statutory accounts 63, 64, 232
stock 258, 382
stock control 258
stock market variations 193
strapline 112, 113
strategic plan 81, 82
substitute products128, 132
supplier funding 147
suppliers as stakeholders 144
supply and demand 148
supply chain 43, 378
Supply of Goods and Services Act
    317
supplying information to customers
    343
sweatshops 161
SWOT analysis 133, 170
    for e-business 400

takeovers 19

takings 258
target market 113, 156
targets 48, 82, 86, 292
tax 9, 179
        avoidance and evasion 161
technological change 302
technological developments 135,
    189
telesales 76
tenders 106, 107
tertiary sector 25, 32
theft 263 - 267
time lags and the economy 176
tobacco industry 163
total cost 205
Trade Descriptions Act 318
trade unions 69, 149, 150, 272,
    294, 296
    and collective bargaining 295,
    296
training needs 69, 288, 289
transactions 250
    and VAT 254, 255
transnational businesses 161, 165
turnover 5, 19, 202

unfair contract terms act 323
unique impressions 319
unique selling points (usps) 134,
    136, 310
unlimited liability 13
unsold stocks 116
upskilling 305

validity 116
value added tax (VAT)179, 253,
    254
variable costs 205, 206, 208
    and reducing 211
variances 238, 240, 245, 246
victimisation 152
viral marketing 68, 396
vire – and budgets 247
virtual business 360, 372, 373
virtual property tours 363
viruses – computer 65, 66, 393
voluntary organisations 8, 9, 106
voluntary sector 15, 32
voluntary sectors buyers 106

weather and business 170
web authoring tools 386
website design 364, 386, 387
wholesalers 33
Wi-Fi 191, 383
workers' cooperatives 12
working conditions 151, 305
    and dangers 160
WorldCom 195, 394